Introduction

Village London was first published in 1883 under the title 'Greater London'. Written by Edward Walford, a noted Victorian historian and antiquarian who was concerned to record the history and appearance of the hamlets, villages and market towns that made up the metropolitan area before they were overtaken by the urban sprawl that was then beginning to take place.

There was then a great deal of interest in London's history, but now, when there is little or nothing to differentiate between one district and another except the names on the railway stations, it has become even stronger.

Each village has its own history, in some cases stretching back to Roman or Saxon times and beyond. This is the story of these one-time villages and towns which grew up around coaching inns or river fords, or even Royal palaces — now long since demolished and ancient manors that are now tree lined suburban avenues. Every part of London has its own history and historical characters, ranging from Hampton Court's Cardinal Wolsey and Tooting's Daniel Defoe, to Enfield's Mother Wells. This book tells the fascinating story of Greater London's past, as distinct from its inner city; the battlefields — Epping, Barnet, and Brentford and many more; its palaces — Nonsuch, Croydon, Enfield and Hampton Court. But more importantly it recreates the atmosphere of the old villages, the inns and churches, the pastimes and pleasures of ordinary people as well as the rich and famous.

Edward Walford had the gift of writing history so that it would be of interest to the casual reader as well as the serious student and he brings the long lost days of rural London vividly to life.

VILLAGE LONDON

THE STORY OF GREATER LONDON

by

EDWARD WALFORD, M.A.

PART 1 – West and North

THE ALDERMAN PRESS

First published 1883/4 by Cassell & Co. Ltd.
under the title *Greater London*

Published in hardback by The Alderman Press
under the title *Village London Vol. 1* 1983

British Library Cataloguing in Publication Data.
Walford, Edward
    [Greater London]. Village London: The Story
    of Greater London.
    1. London (England) — History
    I. [Greater London] II. Title
    942.1   DA677

    ISBN 0-946619-11-5 (Pt.1)
    ISBN 0-946619-12-3 (Pt.2)
    ISBN 0-946619-13-1 (Pt.3)
    ISBN 0-946619-14-X (Pt.4)

This edition published 1985
The Alderman Press 1/7, Church Street,
Edmonton, London, N9 9DR.

Printed in Great Britain by
BAS Printers Limited, Over Wallop, Hampshire

CONTENTS.

—◦—

CHAPTER I.

CHISWICK, TURNHAM GREEN, ACTON, STRAND-ON-THE-GREEN.

CHAPTER II.

GUNNERSBURY, EALING, AND HANWELL.

CHAPTER III.

BRENTFORD.

CHAPTER IV.

HESTON, ISLEWORTH, AND SION HOUSE.

CHAPTER V.

HOUNSLOW AND HANWORTH.

CHAPTER VI.

TWICKENHAM.

CHAPTER VII.

TWICKENHAM (continued).

CHAPTER VIII.

TWICKENHAM (continued)—POPE'S VILLA.

CHAPTER IX.

TWICKENHAM (continued)—STRAWBERRY HILL.

CHAPTER X.

TEDDINGTON AND BUSHEY PARK.

CONTENTS.

CONTENTS.

CHAPTER XXIII.

ICKENHAM, RUISLIP, AND HAREFIELD.

CHAPTER XXIV.

PINNER AND HARROW.

CHAPTER XXV.

HARROW (continued)—THE SCHOOL, ETC.

CHAPTER XXVI.

HARROW WEALD, KINGSBURY, ETC.

CHAPTER XXVII.

HENDON.

CHAPTER XXVIII.

EDGWARE AND LITTLE STANMORE.

LIST OF ILLUSTRATIONS.

LIST OF ILLUSTRATIONS.

CORONATION STONE KINGSTON

MANOR HOUSE HIGHBEECH

HARROW CHURCH

GREATER LONDON.

INTRODUCTORY.

"GREATER LONDON!" What a vague and ill-defined term! We all know London proper, comprising the City and Westminster, and making up one metropolis. But "Greater London!" What can the words mean? What and where are its limits? and how far afield will it carry us? Do you mean the area ruled over by the Metropolitan Board of Works, or by the authorities of the Census Department, or by the Metropolitan Police, or that which the Postmaster-General takes as the limits of his suburban deliveries of letters?

The question is not very easily answered off-hand, for we are free to own that there are several "Greater Londons," and that these are far from being coincident. The district ruled over by our Board of Works, though large, covers very little ground that has not been already travelled by us in "Old and New London," except in a single direction—that of the estuary of the Thames, the very district in which we have stopped the shortest. Again, the postal suburban limits are subject to frequent changes; and the Census authorities have fixed on somewhat ill-defined and arbitrary bounds, as to which it is impossible to say on what principle they have been settled. It remains, therefore, that we select, as open to the fewest objections, the circle of the Metropolitan Police jurisdiction, which extends, in every direction, about fifteen miles on an average from the centre of modern London, namely, Charing Cross. This embraces the whole of Middlesex and a part of Surrey, together with most of the suburban districts of Essex and Kent, reaching from Dagenham in the east to Uxbridge in the west, and from Colney and Cheshunt in the north to Epsom and Warlingham in the south—an almost perfect circle, some twenty-eight miles in diameter.

Greater London! "The spread of material London," it has been observed—"the London of bricks and mortar and stucco—is becoming a gigantic—one might almost say an appalling—factor in our national existence. Every day it becomes more difficult to say where the limits of the capital have been reached, and at what point the cockney may fairly be said to begin his long-sought 'day in the country.' Every week new building speculations absorb the green fields and hedgerows, and the quiet little village station becomes a suburban junction. To introduce some guiding principle into this labyrinth, Sir Brydges Henniker, our Registrar-General, has, in his returns, divided London into two portions—an inner and an outer zone. The inner zone comprises the fixed and permanent city, spreading in a continuous mass from Hampstead on the north to Norwood on the south, and from Bromley on the east to Hammersmith on the west. This area comprises, in round figures, about 78,000 acres, and, with the exception of parks and open spaces which have been saved by Parliament from the ruthless grasp of the builder, is already fully utilised for building purposes. . . . . It must not be forgotten that whilst there has been very considerable growth in districts within the central area, but approaching the outer zone, a process has been constantly at work in all the most central parts of London tending to drive further outwards the resident population. We may instance the construction of the new terminus of the Great Eastern Railway in Liverpool Street, and the lines of railway converging at that point; the construction of new thoroughfares by the various public bodies, all of which have passed through densely-populated districts; and the vast number of dwelling-houses which

have been swept away from the heart of London, upon the site of which now stand tall piles of warehouses and offices."

But in truth, when we speak of "London," we do not mean so much a city as a collection or gathering together of cities. Not only is our metropolis many-handed, like Briareus, and many-headed, like Cerberus: it is manifold. It is no longer singular, but plural; it consists no longer of one city, but of many. It has engulfed gradually many cities, towns, villages, and separate jurisdictions. Its present surface, as already intimated, includes large portions of four commonwealths, or kingdoms, those of the Middle Saxons, of the East Saxons, of the "South Rie" (Surrey) folk, and of the men of Kent. Taken in its widest acceptation, as above shown, London—or rather, the district which is under the rule of the Metropolitan Police—now embraces, not only the entire cities of London and Westminster, but the entire county of Middlesex, all the boroughs of Southwark and Greenwich, the towns of Woolwich and Wandsworth, the watering-places of Hampstead, Highgate, Islington, Acton, and Kilburn, the fishing-town of Barking, the once secluded and ancient villages of Hanwell, Cheshunt, Harrow, Croydon, Finchley, Twickenham, Teddington, Chigwell, Sutton, Addington, and many others. It will be seen, therefore, that there is some truth in the witty definition which has been given of London, namely—"That world of stucco which is bounded by Barnet on the north and Croydon on the south; which touches Woolwich in the far east, and Richmond and Twickenham in the far west."

"The growth of a great city," observes John Timbs, "must be an interesting study to a larger number of persons than we may at first imagine; its claims upon their attention are world-wide when that city is London. It may seem like national partiality when we speak thus; but it is only philosophic reasoning when we remember that no city of equal size and importance exists in the world, or ever did exist. Babylon 'the Great' was not so large, and imperial Rome was smaller in its palmiest days; even when mistress of the world it by no means rivalled modern London."

Of late years, the removal of dwellings in "London proper" for commercial purposes, and the consequent erection of others in the suburbs and outlying villages, has been rapid in the extreme. Streets, terraces, and villas, of all shapes and sizes, are springing up in all directions, and quite altering the hitherto rural aspect of the spots encroached upon. That this growth of London has not been one of a sudden and impulsive nature, consequent on some great panic or mania for building that may have seized on the commercial world—after the fashion of the " railway mania " of forty years ago —may be inferred when we state that Horace Walpole thus writes to his friend Sir Horace Mann, under date 1791 :—" There will soon be one street from London to Brentford ; aye, and from London to every village ten miles round !"   The era of which he prophesied has long since arrived ; and not only Brentford, but Hounslow, is now connected with the metropolis by an almost unbroken row of bricks and mortar, in the shape of cottages, shops, and villas.

The elder D'Israeli, in " The Curiosities of Literature," mentions some remarkable features of the dread which our countrymen entertained of an overgrown metropolis :—" Proclamations warned and exhorted ; but the very interference of a royal prohibition seemed to render the metropolis more charming ;" though for all this, from Elizabeth to Charles II., proclamations continually issued against new erections.   James I. notices " those swarms of gentry who, through the instigation of their wives, did neglect their country hospitality, and cumber the city : a general nuisance to the kingdom."   He once said—" Gentlemen resident on their estates are like ships in port, their value and magnitude are felt and acknowledged ; but when at a distance, as their size seemed insignificant, so their worth and importance were not duly estimated."   The England even of the present century is changed out of all possible knowledge ; indeed, those are yet living who can look back with a smile at the solemn county balls, which were almost as difficult of access, and as jealously guarded, as a Court presentation of these days.

Nor were good reasons wanted for eschewing London.   Only two centuries ago a Sussex squire, Mr. Palmer, was fined in the sum of £1,000 for residing in London rather than on his own estate in the country, and that even in face of the fact that his country mansion had been burned within the two years before his trial took place !   We are told that this sentence struck terror into the London sojourners ; and it was followed by a proclamation for them to leave the city, with their " wives and families, and also widows."   And now we have no difficulty in understanding why there are so many large mansions in small country towns.   The habit of making the best of a hard lot influenced the gentry even long after it would have been safe to have followed Mr. Palmer's example ; and so we find, up to the Hanoverian period, large old-fashioned houses in some small country towns, that look, as Dickens says, as if they had lost

their way in infancy, and grown to their present proportions.   The tendency of families to migrate to the county town instead of London in the " season," was partly owing to the difficulty of the roads (for nothing now in England can give an idea of the undertaking of a journey of 200 miles to London), but partly, also, to a singular law, which forbade, as far as possible, any country gentleman who was not in Parliament from residing in London.   Railways, of course, have rapidly and completely changed the scene.   The old moralist in Thackeray laments the change of times, when a man of quality used to enter London, or return to his country-house, in a coach and pair, with outriders, and now his son " slinks " from the station in a brougham.

Whether or not the architectural aspect of the streets of London is being improved by the wholesale demolition of its ancient buildings, and the erection on their sites of huge warehouses and commercial edifices, is not for us to say ; but a great advance has certainly been made of late years in the architectural appearance of the better class of suburban residences.   It is true that there are many excellent specimens of house architecture even of Queen Anne's reign in remote villages within twenty miles of London.   Many of these houses are now turned into boarding-schools or village tenements, having been shouldered out of the way as ugly and old-fashioned.   But a reaction has at last set in against the massive and tasteless style so long characteristic of town and suburban buildings, and houses of the Queen Anne type are being erected in the suburbs on every side of London.

With all this, there are happily many places round London still unbuilt upon, within the limits of our present work, to which the cockney holiday-maker may take a day's excursion, where he will find the fields still green, the hedgerows fresh, and the forest-trees in summer-time in full leaf, and waving bravely in the breeze.   That portion of the county of Surrey which will fall within the scope of our peregrinations has, to a very large extent, up to the present time, kept clear of the man of bricks and mortar.   Indeed, it is not a little remarkable that a county so near to the metropolis should still contain so large an amount of waste lands.   At the beginning of the present century it was reckoned that a sixth of its whole acreage was in a wild and uncultivated state ; but this condition of things has been greatly altered by enclosures.   Still, however, near London there are Wimbledon Common and Putney Heath, Wandsworth and Clapham Commons, Streatham, Tooting, and Kennington Commons—in all, nearly 2,000 acres. Farther afield are Bagshot Heath, Epsom, Leatherhead, Ashtead, Weybridge, Epping Forest, and other open spots, of many of which we shall have occasion to speak.

This area, almost every nook and corner of which—thanks to our railway system—may be visited on the Saturday afternoon holidays in summer, and most of them even in winter, contains, as we need hardly add, much that may interest the ordinary visitor, should he care for quiet and peaceful rural scenery, or the artist who may be in search of choice "bits." It does not include in its sphere a single cathedral, or castle, or abbey, at all events with extensive buildings above ground; but there are breezy heights commanding extensive views, mansions, and other buildings possessing historical associations; and we have only to mention a few names of places and persons who have been connected with it as residents, or by the accident of birth or death, in order to satisfy the reader that these five hundred and odd square miles are not devoid of interest. There are, for instance, Waltham Cross and Abbey, the latter traditionally the grave of the unhappy Harold; there is Chislehurst, with its memories of the antiquary Camden and the emperor Louis Napoleon; there are Hayes and Keston, the favourite haunts of Pitt and Wilberforce; there is Isleworth, with its monastery of Sion; Harrow, with its school and its memories of Byron's youth. At Hounslow we shall find camps and footpads; the latter also at Finchley; at Merton we shall come upon Lord Nelson and Lady Hamilton; at Stanmore we shall visit the grave of Lord Aberdeen; at Mortlake we shall find Dr. Dee; at Elstree we shall rub shoulders with Thurtell and Hare; at "princely" Canons we shall be introduced to George Handel, and to his patron, the Duke of Chandos; at Wanstead we shall see the magnificent mansion of the Tylneys, brought to ruin, alas! by a Wellesley; at Gunnersbury, at Kew, at Brentford, at Kingsbury, at Nonsuch, at Enfield, and in Hainault Forest, royal memories will meet us; and we shall be overwhelmed by them when we come to Richmond and Sheen; Pope and Horace Walpole, Kitty Clive, Gay, Thomson, and a host of children of the Muses, will surround us at Twickenham; at Barnet we shall view the battle-field which crushed the hopes of the house of Lancaster; at Bexley we shall encounter the cavalcade of Chaucer's "Canterbury Pilgrims," whom we left at the *Tabard* in Southwark; at Barking we shall walk over the site of perhaps the earliest convent for ladies in England, full of sacred memories; at Theobalds we shall find King James, with all his wit and pedantry; at Edmonton we shall shake hands with Charles Lamb; at Croydon we shall have much to talk about in the long roll of primates who occupied the palace there till Addington became their home; at Epsom we shall see "the quality" drinking the waters, and Lord Derby and his friends inaugurating those races whose name is not only national, but world-wide; at Beddington we shall find the Carews and Sir Walter Raleigh; at Kew and Brentford we shall run up against "Farmer George" taking his morning rides; and at Kingston-on-Thames and at Hampton Court we shall reconnoitre the spots on which our Saxon kings were crowned, and our Tudor sovereigns and their courtiers walked and talked. In each and all of these places, and a score of others, we shall try to bring our readers face to face with the great men and women who have added a light to the pages of English history, and, we doubt not, greatly to the advantage of the former, without doing harm to the latter, or calling them up from their silent graves. In this way we shall hope to render the history of our land more full of enjoyment than heretofore, investing its heroes and heroines with the interest which attaches to personages who live and move amongst us, and have been animated by like passions with ourselves. Our notices of them, as a rule, cannot be more than brief, but that is the necessary result of our plan, which may, indeed, be thought open to the charge of being desultory, though we hope that it will be acquitted of dulness and of malice.

With these few remarks by way of introduction or preface, we once more beg the reader to take in hand his pilgrim's staff, and to accompany us on our pleasant pilgrimage.

We ended our sketches of "Old and New London" near Chiswick Church and Turnham Green, and therefore it would seem but natural to begin again where we left off. Accordingly, while the Scotchman—if we may believe Dr. Johnson—always travels south, and never looks behind him, we shall trudge along in a westerly direction for some days, and pursue our way leisurely up the valley of the Thames, which, at all events, will have much more to detain us now than it had in those unreckoned ages when it was an estuary of the silent sea.

CHAPTER I.

CHISWICK, TURNHAM GREEN, ACTON, STRAND-ON-THE-GREEN.

"Rus in urbe, urbs in rure."

Gradual Extension of London—Horticultural Fêtes at Chiswick—Eminent Residents at Chiswick—Royal Visits—Corney House—Fairfax House —Grove Park—Sutton Court—Turnham Green—Bedford Park—Acton Green—Professor Lindley—Acton—Its Early History—Berrymead Priory—Lady Dudley's Bequest—Acton a Stronghold of the Puritan Party—The Rev. Philip Nye—Richard Baxter and Sir Matthew Hale— Other Distinguished Residents—An Anecdote of Sir Walter Raleigh—Ancient Manors and Houses—Lord Ferrers' Coach—Clergy Orphan Schools—The Village of Acton—The Parish Church—The Registers—Charitable Bequests—A Centenarian—The Steyne—Skippon, the Parliamentary General—South Acton—Acton Wells—Acton Races—Friar's Place Farm—The Goldsmiths' Almshouses—Strand-on-the-Green.

THE gradual extension of London is sweeping away, bit by bit, much of the rural aspect of its surroundings. We have already seen in various chapters of "Old and New London" how it has affected Paddington and Bayswater, Stoke Newington and Hackney, Clapham and Camberwell. Although Chiswick still retains many of its suburban charms, still, the handiwork of the builder of recent times has already made a perceptible difference in the look of the smiling village which stood here half a century ago, before a part of the gardens of Chiswick House first became the head-quarters of the Horticultural Society, and the place began to wear a fashionable appearance during the London "season." Up to that time—for it must be remembered that there was no such a thing as railway conveyance in those days, and steamboats to Chiswick and Kew had scarcely come into existence—very few of the ordinary inhabitants of London even thought of visiting the place; but when the horticultural fêtes* were held here Chiswick achieved great popularity with the "upper ten thousand," and soon rose to be a place of popular resort.

The village, it is true, even as far back as the last century, contained many good houses, and could then, as now, boast of its "Mall" overlooking the river; and it has numbered among its residents many men whose names have become famous, such as Sir Stephen Fox, the friend of Evelyn, who occupied the Manor House; Pope, who lived for a time in Mawson's Buildings; Lord Heathfield, the defender of Gibraltar; Hogarth, Zoffany, and Loutherbourg, the painters; and Barbara, Duchess of Cleveland, who spent the last few years of her life here. The open-air entertainments given in the grounds of Chiswick House by the Duke of Devonshire formed a great attraction for the upper circles during the London "season" in days gone by. The place, too, has

even had the advantage of visits from royalty, for in 1814 the Emperor Alexander I. of Russia, and the other allied sovereigns, honoured the Duke of Devonshire with their presence here, and in 1842 Her Majesty and the late Prince Consort visited His Grace at Chiswick. Two years later the duke gave here a magnificent entertainment to the Emperor (Nicholas) of Russia, the King of Saxony, and a large number of the nobility. Several of the finest trees in the grounds of Chiswick House were planted by royal hands, to commemorate the visits of the Emperor Nicholas, Queen Victoria, and other illustrious personages. More recently, the house has been tenanted by the Prince of Wales, as a nursery for his children; and, later, by Lord Bute.

As stated in the foregoing remarks, we now set out on our perambulation from the point where we parted company in our narrative of Chiswick in "Old and New London," namely, the grounds of Chiswick House and Corney House, leaving on our left the steam launch and torpedo manufactory of Messrs. Thorneycroft, which covers part of what once formed the grounds of Corney House, the residence of Lord Macartney, and where several scores of busy hands now find daily employment. At Chiswick Church we turn sharp to the right, past an old mansion, called Fairfax House, because at one time it was tenanted by that general. Here are preserved the kitchen clock and one or two other relics of Hogarth, removed from his house. On our right is the lofty stone wall which shuts out from view the duke's villa; on our left are broad and level meadows, reaching down to the silver Thames, which here makes a southward sweep. The meadows are as green as ever; no history attaches to them, and as yet they are not built upon. Of late years the sewage of Chiswick has been precipitated here, and utilised for the neighbouring market-gardens. Chiswick, evidently, is in advance of the rest of the metropolis. A little further to the north-west stands Grove House, a mansion once inhabited by titled families; it still

---

* The Horticultural Gardens here were first opened in 1818–19, for the purpose of advancing the science of gardening in this country.

BEDFORD PARK.

1. Houses in South Parade.	3. The Church.	5. Gable of the School of Art.
2. A Porch.	4. The "Tabard."	6. Houses in Bath Road.

has a fine portico, but has been docked of a storey in height, the late Duke of Devonshire not wishing to have any "grand" neighbour.   The estate belongs to the duke, who has laid out Grove Park for villa residences.   A church, St. Paul's, has

SIR MATTHEW HALE.

been built, and a district formed out of Grove Park and Strand-on-the-Green, of which latter place we shall have more to say presently.   The edifice consists of chancel, nave, and aisles, and is in the Early Decorated style of architecture ; it was erected chiefly at the expense of the ducal owner of the estate, and at a cost of about £5,000.   The Grove Park estate adjoins the Chiswick station of the South-Western Railway.   A road from Grove Park, called Sutton Lane, to Turnham Green, passes Sutton Court, once the residence of the lord of the manor, but now a school.   Its grounds adjoin those of the Duke of Devonshire.   Sutton Court was at one time the seat of the Earl of Fauconberg ; the grounds attached to it had in them, two centuries ago, a very pretty maze or wilderness, somewhat after the fashion of that at Hampton Court.

A few minutes' walk brings us on to Turnham Green, which is here separated by a branch of the Metropolitan District Railway from another grassy plot to the west, called Acton Green, which leads on towards Gunnersbury.

According to Stukeley—whose word, however, must always be taken with some little reserve—the road from London to Regnum—possibly Ringwood, or Chichester—went through Turnham Green and Brentford.   Of Turnham Green, and of the skirmish

of the Royalists with the Parliamentary army at the "Battle of Brentford," we have already spoken at some length ;* but we may be pardoned for adding, on the authority of Whitlocke's "Memoirs," that when the Parliamentary army was here, such was the popular enthusiasm that the ladies of London sent them all sorts of supplies in the way of wine and good cheer, and even helped in throwing up the trenches.   John Evelyn tells us in his "Diary" that he "came in with his horse and armes just at the retreate," but adds no further details.

Sir John Chardine's gardens, at Turnham Green, are mentioned more than once by John Evelyn as being very fine, and full of exquisite fruit.   Sir John Chardine was a learned man and a great traveller, and having returned from the East with a good fortune, was made Paymaster of the Forces under Charles II.

A few years ago Turnham Green was a lonely and unlovely common, flat and dreary, and earlier still a favourite resort for footpads and highwaymen ; but now it has grown more civilised, and the entire neighbourhood is putting on a more artistic look.   On the west of Stamford Brook Green there has lately sprung into existence a veritable village, or rather, a little town, of "Queen Anne's" houses.   These are built in small groups, or isolated, and stand in tiny patches of ground, with gardens attached, in which sun-flowers, holly-

RICHARD BAXTER.

hocks, and other old-fashioned flowers predominate.   The land all around is level, and the houses

---

* See "Old and New London," Vol. VI., pp. 560-61.

suit the surroundings. The resident ladies, and even the very nursemaids and children as they stroll about, seem to have an old-fashioned cut about their dress which equally suits the houses. The church—dedicated to St. Michael, though it does not stand on an eminence—is also "pure Queen Anne," and externally, therefore, most ugly, for that style of architecture is secular, and not ecclesiastical. There are "Queen Anne" stores opposite, and a "Queen Anne" post-office, and the inn at the corner of the Common, in exactly the same style, rejoices in the sign of the *Tabard*. Why, however, it is impossible to say, as the place has no connection whatever with Chaucer or his pilgrims, and "tabards," as articles of clothing, are certainly of an older date than our last Stuart queen. Two minutes' walk from the "Tabard" is the "Club," where dramatic entertainments, balls, debates, &c., constantly take place. The architect is Mr. Norman Shaw, R.A., who also designed the church and several of the houses on the estate. The district is called Bedford Park, as having formed part of the estate of the Earls of Bedford.*

Acton Green, or Acton Back, adjoining Turnham Green and Bedford Park to the west and north-west, is said to have been the scene of the skirmish between the Royal and Parliamentarian armies (the latter under the Earl of Essex) in November, 1642. Here, in 1865, died Professor Lindley, F.R.S., the eminent botanist, for many years editor of the *Gardener's Chronicle*. Dr. Lindley was a native of Catton, in Norfolk, and was born at the end of the last century. After leaving school, he devoted himself to botanical science, and at the age of twenty published a translation of Richards's "Analyse du Fruit," which was followed closely after by another work, entitled, "Monographia Rosarum," in which he described several new species of roses. About the same time he contributed to the "Transactions of the Linnæan Society" various papers on botanical subjects. Some time afterwards he was appointed Assistant Secretary to the Horticultural Society, and was engaged by Mr. Loudoun to write the descriptive portion of his "Encyclopædia of Plants." In 1829 he was appointed Professor of Botany at the London University. Shortly after was published his "Introduction to Systematic and Physiological Botany, and a Synopsis of the British Flora," which was followed by "The Natural System of Botany" and "The Vegetable Kingdom." Dr. Lindley was most diligently employed as a practical botanist in describing new species, on which he wrote a large number of papers, contributed to botanical publica-

tions. In 1841 he became editor of the *Gardener's Chronicle*, which he conducted with great ability. In 1860 he was appointed examiner in his favourite studies in the University of London. He received the medal of the Royal Society as a reward for his services to botanical science.

Passing a little to the north-east, we arrive at Acton, a large parish, which is bounded by Hammersmith and Chiswick on the south and south-east, by Shepherd's Bush on the east, by Ealing on the west, and by Willesden on the north. As we learn from Kelly's "Post Office Directory," it is in the Kensington division of Ossulston Hundred; it is five miles from London on the road to Uxbridge, and it has a population of about 12,000 souls. In 1871 it numbered 8,360 residents, which was nearly double of what it had contained ten years previously. In the beginning of the century we are told (in the "Beauties of England and Wales") that the parish comprised about 2,000 acres of land, "chiefly used for farming purposes." The soil is a stiff clay to the north, and towards the south a rich loam.

The name of Acton is but slightly altered from "Oak-town," though it would seem now rather to have deserved the name of "Elm-town," for the trees which formed part of the Weald have mostly disappeared, except at Old-Oak Common, the name of which itself suggests such a change, and tells its own tale. In other parts the oak takes its turn in the hedgerows with the ash and elm. The name, however, is still appropriate enough to its northern parts, as will be seen by a walk across the fields towards Twyford Abbey, of which we shall have more to say hereafter. There is no doubt that in the Saxon times Acton was part of a large oak forest, a portion of the "weald" which stretched across Middlesex, north of London. One of the first notices of the parish is to the effect that the Bishop of London, who lived at Fulham, regarded it as pannage, or feeding for his pigs, which doubtless throve on its acorns. The Briton, the original tenant of the soil, had been driven out by the sword of the Saxon invader, and had carried with him into the far west not only his Druid worship, but such Christianity and civilisation as he had learnt from the Romans. One thing, at all events, remains to prove the reality of the Roman occupation in this part, and that is the great road which led this way to the West of England.

The Saxons were worshippers of Thor and of Woden, and their worship was chiefly carried on in the forests. Consequently, it is easy to imagine Ac-ton, the Oak Town, with its open-air temple, surrounded by low wooden huts, occupied by the priests and their attendants. Hither, perhaps, day by day came from the then distant Londinium many worshippers to offer their sacrifices in the village of the oak groves, to receive at the hands of the priests the sprinkling of the victim's blood, to feast on the pans of simmering horse-flesh, and to drink from twisted horn-cups draughts of mead or ale.

Scarcely, however, had the Saxons been weaned from this heathen worship by the great St. Augustine, when, as they had driven out the Britons, they were themselves attacked by the Danish sea rovers, and possibly the little Christian church had to witness a revival of Pagan rites. Be this as it may, the annals of Acton are a blank till after the Norman conquest, when, possibly, a Norman castle was built on its rising ground, to keep the Saxon serfs in awe and subjection. The district now known as Acton, along with Ealing, became part of the great manor of Fulham, and was granted, or probably re-granted, to the see of London. In the parish were several lesser manors. "Peter, the son of Aluph," runs the old chronicle, "in the year 1220, gave to Geoffrey de Lucy, Dean of St. Paul's, in the City of London, his manor of twenty acres at Acton. Moreover, the dean bought three acres more from Walter de Acton, and then with the whole twenty-three acres founded a chantry in the said church of St. Paul's, for the good of his soul," the rent being, doubtless, applied to the payment of a priest to sing or say mass for him daily. The Almoner of St. Paul's has still a claim on some lands at Acton, and probably the claim has its origin in this bequest.

We next find that Henry III. (A.D. 1216-72) had here a mansion or palace, to which he often retired from the strife of tongues and from the Court, and from his turbulent nobles arrayed against him under Simon de Montfort. From this date Acton is without a history until the first inscription on a brass in the church—"Here lyeth Henry Gosse, and Alice, his wyff, 1485."

That the Reformation did not at once take full effect at Acton is clear from an inscription in the church in 1542, in which John Boid, priest, parson of Acton, begs the prayers of the faithful for the repose of his soul. Two years later a large part of Acton changed its owners, for Henry VIII. seized on one of its manors, and gave it to John, Lord Russell. It is probable that this manor consisted of the lands which had belonged to Berrymead Priory, and to another religious house which must have existed at Friar's Place. From Lord Russell these lands passed, probably by purchase, into the hands of Herbert, Earl of Worcester.

From the rolls of the reign of Edward VI., it appears that Acton contained 158 "houselyng folk," i.e., heads of families who communicated at Easter, a number which does not appear to have increased very rapidly, for in 1670 there were only 88 houses "assessed tow^{ds} the relief of maimed soldiers." In the Record Office is a return, dated August, 1552, of the church plate and other treasures, including pyxes, censers, bells, chrismatories, paxes, and painted cloths for the (Easter) sepulchre.

After the break-up of the existing state of things by Henry VIII., the village of Acton, being a pleasant suburb, became the residence of many families of the upper class. Thus we read that Lord Conway, afterwards Secretary of State to James I., had a mansion here : his widow's benefaction to the education of the poor still remains to perpetuate the name.

Berrymead Priory, on the south side of the high road at the entrance of Acton from London, was formerly the seat of the Marquis of Halifax (who died here in 1700), and afterwards of the Duke of Kingston, in whose time George II. was a frequent visitor at the house. The Priory, which is still standing, is a picturesque Gothic edifice of the Strawberry Hill type, and occupies the centre of several acres of ground, which are planted with fine trees and evergreens.

In 1640 Lady Dudley gave a carpet and some communion plate to the church of Acton ; this is still in use, and the flagon is of fine workmanship, but scarcely of ecclesiastical design. The bills for expenses incurred in bringing the plate from Lady Dudley's house are to be seen in the parish accounts. The carpet has long disappeared.

In the reign of Charles I. Acton became a busy place. It appears to have been a great stronghold of the Puritan party, and was made one of the head-quarters of Lords Essex and Warwick, at the head of the Roundhead Parliamentarian army. Accordingly, their cropped hair, high-crowned hats, and broad collars, appeared in every street and almost every house in the village. They turned out the rector, Dr. Featley, in order to accommodate Colonel Urry, one of the colleagues of Hampden and Holles, who encountered the king's troops near Brentford. Hearing that the Doctor was a "malignant," that is, a supporter of the king and of the Book of Common Prayer (styled by them "pottage"), they forced their way into the church, and tore up and burnt the rails of the communion table in order to prove their piety ; they also set fire to the rector's barn and stables. The Doctor escaped to Lambeth, but he died before the Restoration. In the register there are several entries of the burials of poor soldiers and troopers killed in various skirmishes between Acton, Brentford, and Turnham Green.

The Rev. Philip Nye, the next rector appointed by the Puritans, was a man of quite a different stamp from Dr. Featley. He was a rigid and austere Puritan, and was sent as a commissioner to the king when a prisoner in Carisbrooke Castle. He was very haughty and imperious, and wore a long beard, of which he was very proud. Hence the oft-quoted allusion in Butler's "Hudibras"—

"With greater art and cunning reared
Than Philip Nye's thanksgiving beard."

Nye did not vouchsafe to live among his own

Hampton Court. The Recorder also addressed him in terms of high compliment, and he was conducted with great pomp along the road to London. Nye had his reward, for in 1653 he was appointed one of the committee of "Triers," *i.e.*, those who tested every clergyman on his appointment as to whether he was for Calvinism, the Parliament, &c., and would follow the new "Directory" of public worship. In this post he seems to have behaved

ACTON CHURCH AND ACTON TOWN AT THE END OF LAST CENTURY.
(*From old Prints in possession of the Rector of Acton.*)

people, but kept a house in town. If we may trust a pamphlet entitled, "The Levites' Scourge," "he rode to London every Lord's day in triumph, in a coach drawn by four horses, to exercise them." It is clear, therefore, that he had no mean opinion of himself, and had not adopted the modern Sabbatarian notions.

This Nye was rector when Cromwell, after his "crowning mercy" at Worcester, was met at Acton on his way back to London, by the Mayor and Aldermen of London and a host of his Puritan admirers, and a train of more than 300 coaches. Nye doubtless delivered an address of welcome to the Lord Protector before he turned aside to

neither better nor worse than many of his colleagues.

At the Restoration in 1660 the intruder had to give place to a Royalist and loyalist. Nye was, naturally enough, ejected, and exempted from the general pardon. He spent his latter days in obscurity and retirement, nursing and displaying the beard of which he was so proud. His successor was Dr. Bruno Ryves, chaplain to the king, and Dean of Chichester. In his loyalty he erased from the registers and other parish books the titles, such as "right honourable," bestowed on Cromwell's lords and their "ladies," under-scoring their names with the words "traytor" and "knave." The tomb and monument of Philippa, wife of Rous, Provost of Eton College, and one of Cromwell's lords, may be seen thus defaced on the wall of the church; and in the register the same is done to the entry of a marriage, in April, 1655, between a Mr. Richard Meredith and Susannah, daughter of the "Right Honourable" Major-General Skippon, which was performed by a layman—"Sir" John Thorogood—Mr. Nye enlivening the occasion by a discourse, to which it is to be hoped the young people paid due attention.

But Puritanism still lived on at Acton in spirit. The snake was only "scotched," not killed. Hence, apparently, Richard Baxter came to live here on refusing to subscribe to the Act of Uniformity in 1664. His first house was opposite the old church door. Here he wrote his "Saint's Rest." Here, whilst preaching in his house, he narrowly escaped being shot by a stray Cavalier's bullet, and being denounced by a female spy, who had found her way into his conventicle as a "godly" person. During the Great Plague he left Acton, and went down into Buckinghamshire, but found his family all safe on his return. Baxter tells us that the Fire of London was a very grand and terrific sight as seen at Acton, and that the east wind carried large flakes of burning books as far afield, and farther.

We get some pleasant reminiscences of Sir Matthew Hale and Richard Baxter, as neighbours at Acton, in the Rev. R. B. Hone's "Life" of the former. He writes:—"In the year 1667 Sir Matthew Hale took up his residence at Acton, near London, and there commenced an acquaintance with Mr. Baxter, who resided in the same place, which proved agreeable to both parties, and ripened into warm friendship." Baxter himself, writing to another friend, gives us a few details of the origin of the acquaintance between the neighbours :—"We sat next each other at church many weeks, but neither did he ever speak to me, nor I to him. At last my extraordinary friend (to whom I was more beholden than I must here express), Serjeant Fountain, asked me why I did not visit the Lord Chief Baron? I told him, because I had no reason for it, being a stranger to him, and some against it, viz., that a judge, whose reputation was necessary to the ends of his office, should not be brought under Court suspicion or disgrace by his familiarity with a person whom the interest and diligence of some prelates had rendered so odious (as I knew myself to be with such), I durst not be so injurious to him. The serjeant answered—'It is not meet for him to come first to you ; I know why I speak it ; let me intreat you to go first to

him.' In obedience to which request, I did it, and we entered into neighbourly familiarity. I lived then in a small house, but it had a pleasant garden and back side, which the honest landlord had a desire to sell. The judge had a mind to the house, but he would not meddle with it till he got a stranger to me to come and inquire of me whether I was willing to leave it. I told him I was not only willing, but desirous ; not for my own ends, but for my landlord's sake, who must needs sell it ; and so he bought it, and lived in that poor house till his mortal sickness sent him to the place of his interment."

Baxter says elsewhere that "the house was well situated, but very small, and so far below the ordinary dwellings of men of his rank, as that divers farmers thereabouts had better; but it pleased him." The purchase was made in 1670.

Baxter did not leave Acton, but removed to another house, the Chief Baron maintaining much friendly intercourse with him, and finding his taste for metaphysical subjects of study and conversation in accordance with his own. "I will tell you" (writes Baxter to Sir Matthew's friend, a Mr. Stephens) "the matter and manner of our converse. We were oft together ; and almost all our discourse was philosophical, and especially about the nature of spirits and superior regions, and the nature, operations, and immortality of man's soul. And our dispositions and courses of thought were, in such things, so like, that I did not much cross the bent of his conference."

Baxter tells us what books Sir Matthew chiefly read :—"All new or old books on philosophy," to which he gave himself up "as eagerly as if he had been a boy at the university ;" and he defends him at needless length from the charge of being guilty of "idle speculations." The judge was slow of speech, and an excellent listener to Baxter's remarks. They talked but little on controversies, or on the then all-prevailing question of Conformity. "Once," writes Mr. Hone, "when Baxter advanced objections to the wealth and distinction assigned to the bishops, he gave no answer. He seems to have thought silence the wisest course in those heated times, and so to have trimmed his sails as not to fall out with either the king or the Parliament. He used, however, to express his regret at the spiritual neglect into which the country parishes were allowed to fall, and his wish that both Baxter and Calamy would accept bishoprics, or some high positions in the Establishment, if ever an altered state of things should come about. So far from being a High Churchman of the school of Laud, it is remarked by Baxter as singular that Sir Matthew did not bow in church at the name of Jesus, and that he would stand during the reading of the lessons. It appears, however, from Baxter's own testimony, that in essentials the two friends and neighbours were one at heart, though the former, for a time, sus-

attended the church both morning and evening. Sir Matthew Hale, it appears, approved of this proceeding. "The judge told me," says Baxter, "that he thought my course did the church much service, and would carry it so respectfully at my door that all the people might perceive his approbation."

But it is not to be wondered at that the rector regarded the plan as tending rather to schism than love; and perhaps, as he had been persecuted and plundered by the Presbyterians, he may on that account have looked with

1. HIGH STREET, ACTON.
2. THE CHURCH, FROM THE RECTORY.

pected Hale of being too much given to philosophy and doctrine, neglecting the more practical parts of Christianity. In the end, however, Baxter was fully satisfied that 'he plied practicals and contemplations in their season.'"

The house into which Baxter moved when he quitted that which Sir Matthew Hale had purchased was commodious in size, and, like the former, near to the parish church. Here he commenced a practice of assembling in it on Sundays some of the inhabitants of Acton, and of preaching to them between the services, always taking care, however, that they

a less favourable eye on Baxter's doings. Be that as it may, he procured the issuing of a warrant for Baxter's apprehension, and the judge gave him no "counsel," though he showed his sorrow by tears— "the only time," adds Baxter, "that I saw him weep." Baxter was committed to prison for six months; but, by the advice of his friend Serjeant Fountain, he moved for his release, and then "I found," he says, "that the character which Judge

Hale had given of me stood me in some stead, and every one of the four judges did not only acquit me, but said more for me than my counsel." But this imprisonment, he afterwards relates, " brought me the great loss of converse with Judge Hale, for the Parliament in the next Act against conventicles put into it divers clauses suited to my case, by which I was obliged to go dwell in another county, and to forsake both London and my former habitation, and yet the justices of another county were partly enabled to pursue me." With this ends the

physician to Charles II.; and Charles Fox, who gave a house and ground on the Steyne, on the north of the church, as a site for the almshouses still existing there.

Besides those already noticed, Acton can show a good list of names of people more or less celebrated in their day. Philip Thicknesse, the eccentric author of "Memoirs and Anecdotes," "The New Prose Bath Guide," &c. who died in 1792, lived here. The Countess of Derwentwater was living in the large house

BERRYMEAD PRIORY. (*See p. 9.*)

connection of Baxter with Acton and Sir Matthew Hale.

From this time the local history of Acton is little more than a list of distinguished persons who have been resident within its bounds. Notably, Lord Chief-Justice Vaughan, who died here in 1673 ; and, soon afterwards, Lloyd, Bishop of St. Asaph, one of the seven bishops who were tried in Westminster Hall for refusing to accept King James's "Indulgence in Matters of Religion " ; Sir Charles Scarborough,

opposite the church at the time of her husband's execution for his share in the abortive Scottish rising in 1715. It is said that the iron gates at the end of the garden have never been opened since the day when her lord last passed through them on his way to the Tower. Alderman and Lord Mayor Gascoigne lived at Acton ; so did Mrs. Barry, an actress under Sir William Davenant at the theatre in Lincoln's Inn Fields, who gained some celebrity in her day as excelling in the part of *Roxana*. Her last appearance was in " Love for Love," performed for Betterton's benefit, when she spoke the epilogue (1709). She died in 1713. In 1700 William, Marquis of Halifax, died at the Priory, which then passed into the hands of the Duke of Kingston, whose crest is still to be seen in one of the rooms. He was often visited here by George II. and his Court. Quite in our own day, the Priory was tenanted by Sir Edward Bulwer Lytton, who wrote within it one at least of his many works. Whether the notorious Judge Jeffreys ever lived at Acton is not quite certain ; but at all events, Pennant tells us that he saw at Acton House an original portrait of that Judge, taken in 1690, when he was 82 years of age.

Acton may be said to have been in some way connected with Sir Walter Raleigh and tobacco. Aubrey implies that on its first introduction tobacco was regarded as a forbidden thing. He writes :—"Sir Walter Raleigh, standing in a stand at Sir R. Poyntz's park at Acton, took a pipe of tobacco, which made the ladies quit it till he had done." "Within these few years," he adds, "it was scandalous for a divine to take tobacco."

It is stated in the MS. additions to Norden's "Speculum Britanniæ" that King Henry III. had a mansion-house, and lay often at Acton. But no traces of its site are known, and the tradition is not confirmed. Still, Acton in its time has possessed a good many old mansions, though these are gradually passing away. Mr. Brewer tells us, in the "Beauties of England and Wales," that at the beginning of the present century there were "vestiges of several moated houses" here ; but some have disappeared. Lysons writes in 1795 :—"About half a mile to the north, in a field still called the 'Moated Meadow,' is a deep trench, enclosing a parallelogram about 100 yards in length and 40 in breadth, supposed by some to have been a Roman camp, but the name of the meadow seems to imply no greater antiquity than that of a moated farm-house or grange."

Near the Great Western Railway Station is an old moated house, with part of the moat remaining, called Friar's Place Farm. Another house, hard by, is said to have once had Oliver Cromwell for its occupant for a time, but the tradition cannot be verified.

In the parish of Acton there are two manors, one of which has belonged from time immemorial (as already stated) to the see of London, the other once belonged to the Dean and Chapter of St. Paul's, but was seized upon by Henry VIII., who alienated it. It has passed through various families : the Russells, Somersets, Lethuelliers, Fetherstonhaughs, &c.

One day in 1760 Acton was astonished by the arrival of a coach and six—it was the same in which Lord Ferrers had driven to be executed at Tyburn, and he had ordered it to be sent onward. The carriage was kept in a shed at Acton till it literally fell to pieces.

In 1749 the new Clergy Orphan Schools, since removed to St. John's Wood, were erected here.

The High Street, nearly half a mile in length, is quaint and irregular, large and small houses being strangely intermixed. Many of the old red tiles remain on the roofs. New streets have sprung up between the railway station and the town ; these are irregularly built, and in many of them trees are planted. Altogether, from the quiet, out-of-the-way village of half a century ago, Acton has now become a very populous place, owing to the building of villas, consequent on the opening of the railways. It now possesses two or three churches ; it has Congregational, Baptist, Wesleyan, and other chapels, a lecture hall, and also its Local Board of Health, public library, and reading-room.

"At the entrance of the village from London," writes Mr. Brewer in 1815, "is a public conduit, built by Thomas Thorney in 1612, and maintained by a small endowment left by him for repairs. Its use having been perverted, the right to its use was recovered in the last century by a lawsuit, and it has been superseded by a modern pump, erected by a Mr. Antrobus in 1819." The pump is now chained up and walled in, a notice being added that "the water is not fit for drinking purposes," probably in consequence of the opening of a new cemetery in its rear. Why does no charitable person revive the Acton pump, in the shape of a metropolitan drinking fountain, obtaining a supply from a fresh source ?

The parish church, dedicated to St. Mary, as usual marks the centre of the original village, for cottages always sprang up round the manor-house and the house of prayer which was its adjunct. Brewer describes it in his day as of little interest—rebuilt of brick in a homely manner. The present edifice is built of red brick, with stone dressings. In 1766 the church tower was re-cased with brick ; the oldest of the bells has the date 1583, the last was hung in 1810. In 1837 the church was enlarged, and became, in the opinion of Bishop Blomfield, the ugliest in the diocese. In 1865 the nave, chancel, &c., were pulled down, and a handsome Decorated building erected in its place, the old tower, which had been "new cased with brick" in 1766, being suffered to remain. This, however, was pulled down in 1877, and an elegant new tower erected in its place, as a memorial to two members of the Ouvry family. The bells were re-cast at the same time. It will be seen, therefore, that there have been three churches in succession since Her Majesty's accession ; for the very plain structure of the last century was pulled down in 1838, and rebuilt in a still more hideous style, and that was pulled down in 1865, when the present handsome structure was built. It consists of a nave, chancel, and aisles, and many of its windows are already filled with stained glass.

The registers commence in 1539. Skippon's titles have been scratched out in the register, and over the name of Sir John Thorogood, who officiated at the marriage of Skippon's daughter, is written the word "knave," the word "traytor" being also twice written over the Major-General's name. Cromwell created Skippon a peer, but it is only fair to add that he refused to sit as one of the king's judges. The Protectorate titles, too, have been obliterated from the registers of "Lord" and "Lady" Rous. The former was buried at Eton College. In spite of being an author, Rous is mentioned by Lord Clarendon as "a person of very mean understanding"; and A'Wood tells us, in his "Athenæ Oxoniensis," that he was called "the illiterate Jew of Eton." His foundation of three fellowships at Pembroke College, Oxford, is perhaps his best memorial. Rous's house was styled in 1795 "The Bank House."

Bruno Ryves, who was appointed vicar by Charles II., was a contributor to our national history. He deserves to be remembered as the author of the "Mercurius Rusticus," a narrative of the sufferings of the Royalists in different parts of England.

Lady Dudley, whom we have mentioned in our account of St. Giles's-in-the-Fields* was a great benefactor to the parish and church, to which she gave (as stated above) a carpet and the communion plate.

The ancient font is now all that remains of the original church. All the ancient monuments have been carefully preserved, though those in the interior of the building have been mostly removed to the west end and to the entrance under the tower. Among them is one to Anne, Lady Southwell. On each side of this monument hangs a wooden tablet inscribed with panegyric verses, in the quaint and conceited style of the period (1636) :—

" The *South* wind blew upon a springing *well*,
  Whose waters flowed, and the sweet stream did swell
  To such a height of goodness, that," &c.

There are also monuments to Catharine, Lady Conway, who was a great benefactor to the parish ; to Mrs. Elizabeth Barry, the actress already mentioned in connection with Betterton and Lincoln's Inn Theatre ; and to Mr. Robert Adair, inspector-general of hospitals, and his wife, Lady Caroline Adair, daughter of the Earl of Albemarle. Inside the communion rails was a

small brass commemorating John Byrde, who died in 1542, having been fifty-three years vicar of Acton.

Among the charitable bequests is that of a Mr. Edward Dickinson, who left a third part of the interest of £5,000 to be distributed annually among three poor and industrious couples who had been married at Acton in the preceding year. It is satisfactory to the statistician to learn that this charity has never lapsed for want of claimants.

Lady Conway's dole of bread, and loaves left by other charitable persons, are still disbursed on Sundays after service, at the west end of the nave, where they are set out in a row, between two gilt figures of wheatsheaves.

It is to be presumed that Acton is a healthy parish ; at all events, it can boast it had at least one "veritable centenarian" among its residents. In the churchyard is buried William Aldridge, wheelwright, who died in 1698, in the 115th year of his age. A portrait of him when aged 112 may be seen in Lysons' "Environs," and a copy of it hangs in the vestry. Other centenarians' names appear in the register.

The living is a good one in point of emolument, and is still in the gift of the Bishop of London. The rectory house, a solid and substantial building north of the church, was built about 1725. The then rector, Mr. Hall, died soon after, and his successor, the witty Dr. Cobden, recorded the fact in some Latin lines, which he scratched with a diamond on a window-pane.

To the north of the church is a nearly square piece of ground, about two or three acres, called the Steyne. It appears as if it had been a village green, and to have been dug out for gravel, or, if that is not so, then terraces have been raised round two sides of it. It is covered with modern cottages, and fringed with some almshouses and schools.

Near the churchyard stood a house built by Sir Henry Garway in 1638, and which was, for a time, the residence of Skippon, the Parliamentary general mentioned above. It was afterwards used as a convent by the ladies of a religious order, who fled from the Continent during the first French Revolution. It was pulled down early in the present century. Its successor is now called Derwentwater House ; it is probable that Sir Matthew Hale was tenant here.

South Acton has been cut off, and formed into a new ecclesiastical district, and a new church, of florid Gothic style, and built of red brick, was consecrated in 1872. It is dedicated to All Saints, and consists of chancel, nave, aisles, tower, and a lofty spire. One part of South Acton, having been largely occupied by artisans' dwellings, is now

---

* See "Old and New London," Vol. III., p. 198.

known as Mill Hill, after a windmill which once stood on it; it has its own church, chapel, and schools, and bids fair ere long to become a separate ecclesiastical district.

We must now make a slight detour of a mile eastwards to visit Acton Wells, before we take up our pilgrim's staff *en route* for Ealing. We are, however, rudely woke up from any dreams of the beauty and fashion of the reign of the Georges by finding ourselves within a "measurable distance" of the new military prison erected on Wormwood Scrubs, and soon after reach the line of the Great Western Railway. A "spa" which was discovered here in the early part of the last century became very fashionable as a place of resort about the year 1750, and its waters are mentioned along with those of Hampstead, Cheltenham, Bath, &c., as "on sale at Mr. Owen's original mineral water warehouse in Fleet Street." There were, in fact, three wells of mineral water here, which once possessed a fashionable name, and attracted to the neighbourhood many of the sick and gay. In Lysons' "Environs" we find a minute description of the waters, which were saline, and "supposed to be more strongly cathartic than any other in the kingdom of the same quality, except those of Cheltenham."

We have already seen at Hampstead * the transitory nature of the celebrity obtained by medicinal springs. "Acton," writes Mr. Brewer, "had its share in the day of fashion. An assembly-room was built, and for a few years East Acton and Friar's Place, a small adjacent hamlet, were thronged with valetudinarian and idle inmates, allured by the hope of remedy or tempted by the love of dissipation. Both classes have long" (he writes in 1815) "abandoned the spot; and the assembly-room has for many years been converted into a private dwelling." Dr. Macpherson says that these wells were popular from the year 1750 down to about 1790, and that races were run for the amusement of the company. The discovery of these medicinal waters, and the consequent resort of people to drink them, caused many pleasant houses with gardens to spring up around Friar's, or Prior's, Place, so called from having once belonged to the Prior of St. Bartholomew at Smithfield. The "season" here was in the summer. The wells went to decay before the end of the last century, but their site is still to be made out in the kitchen garden of a farmhouse near the Great Western Railway, and close to "Old Oak Common." How few of those who travel by the Great Western Railway at this point are aware that they are passing

over one of the fashionable resorts of the reign of George III. No print of the wells here is known to exist, and the place seems to have escaped notice in the comedies and satires of the day. Here is now a stud-farm, close to the old place where fashionable dames disported themselves. Not far off here, the "People's Garden," a place of Sunday amusement for the middle classes, was opened under German auspices in 1870. It is said to have the largest dancing platform in the country, but it never attracted any of the upper classes.

Between West and East Acton, on the north side of the London Road, are the Goldsmiths' Almshouses for ten poor men and ten poor women, who receive each a pension and an allowance for coals. They were founded in 1656–7 by John Perryn, of East Acton, and the houses were rebuilt in 1811 or 1812, at the cost of £12,000. They form three sides of a quadrangle. In 1878 a church and parsonage-house were built by the Goldsmiths' Company on their estate in the rear of their almshouses.

In spite of its chalybeate attractions, East Acton is described in the "Beauties of England and Wales" (1815) simply as "a small hamlet or assemblage of houses to the north of the London road."

Leaving Acton, and retracing our steps for a mile southwards across Acton Green to Grove Park, already mentioned, we find ourselves at a quaint little old-fashioned waterside settlement, known as Strand-on-the-Green. It is almost wholly inhabited by fishermen, but partly occupied by malt-houses and hostelries. The place is as little changed as any spot within ten miles of London. Its low small mansions and red-bricked river-side cottages form a picturesque scene.

Down to the early part of the last century the hamlet of Strand-on-the-Green was inhabited almost wholly by fishermen, or by men whose daily avocations were carried on by the river-side. On the springing up of some better class of houses, however, the place for a time became more popular, and numbered among its residents one or two individuals whose names have become famous. Here, for instance, dwelt David Mallet, the poet; his first wife, who died in 1742, is buried in the churchyard of Chiswick. Here, too, lived for many years the facetious Joe Miller, whose tombstone is in King's College Hospital. He died here in August, 1738. Zoffany, the painter, lived at Strand-on-the-Green, and several of his fishermen neighbours sat as models for his pictures; he died here on the 11th of November, 1810, and his remains were interred in the neighbouring churchyard of Kew, on the

* See "Old and New London,' Vol. V., p. 468.

other side of the Thames. The house which Zoffany inhabited is still shown. It faced the river, in about the middle of the little terrace. We shall hear of him again at Brentford.

Some almshouses were built at Strand-on-the-Green in 1725, but they have been demolished.

The Kensington branch of the South-Western Railway here crosses the Thames by a handsome latticed iron bridge, which was built in 1869.

Opposite Strand-on-the-Green is an ait, or eyot, used by the Thames Conservancy Board for manufacturing and repairing purposes, and this forms a pleasing foreground to the river-side view of Kew Bridge from the east.

CHAPTER II.

GUNNERSBURY, EALING, AND HANWELL.

"Regumque palatia villis
Interfusa nitent."

Gunnersbury—Descent of the Manor—The Princess Amelia a Resident here—Horace Walpole a frequent Guest—The Property bought by the Rothschilds—The Gardens and Grounds—Gunnersbury House—Ealing—Extent and Nature of the Soil—The Manor—The Parish Church—Sir John Maynard—John Horne Tooke—John Oldmixon—Christ Church—St. John's Church—Seats and Mansions—Dr. John Owen—Dr. William King and other Eminent Residents—Ford Hall—Castle Bar Hill—Princess Helena College—The Old Cross House—The Town Hall—Ealing Great School—Ealing Common—Mrs. Lawrence's Gardens—Fordhook House, and Henry Fielding the Novelist—The "Old Hat" Tavern—Hanwell—The Grand Junction Canal—The Parish Church—Jonas Hanway—The Town of Hanwell—The Central London District Schools—Charitable Institutions—Hanwell Lunatic Asylum—The Cemeteries—Electric Telegraphy in its Infancy.

HAVING arrived at the foot of Kew Bridge, where the loop-line of the South Western Railway converges with that of the North London, we will step aside from our westward path, and retracing our way for a few yards towards West Acton, we will pass up a lane to the left, which takes us to Gunnersbury Park, in the parish of Ealing, though on the borders of Turnham Green. A century ago it was the residence of the Princess Amelia, daughter of George II., and aunt to George III. Here, while the young king lived at Kew, she gave fashionable parties to the be-wigged gentlemen and be-hooped ladies of "quality," and, indeed, kept up a sort of rival Court. She seems to have entertained very generously and hospitably, and to have been very popular with her friends, and at one time to have exercised some personal influence with members of the Cabinet. But sometimes her good-nature led her to do foolish things. For instance, Lord Brougham tells us, in his "Lives of Statesmen," that when Lord Bute had fallen from the favour of the king, the princess invited him and her nephew, the king, on the same afternoon, and caused them—quite accidentally, of course—to meet in one of the shady walks of her garden. Her stratagem, however, did not succeed; and the king was so offended and angry at the liberty which she had taken, that he desired such a trick might never be played on him again. "His word was law," even with his aunt; and the ruse was never repeated. It is dangerous to trifle with kings.

Gunnersbury stands on ground which may be called high in comparison with the flat market gardens which lie between it and the Bath road. The name of Gunnersbury is probably derived from Gunilda, or Gunylda, the niece of King Canute, who resided here. It was a manor in the parish of Ealing, but its manorial rights have largely fallen into neglect and disuse. Little is known of its descent; but in the fifteenth century it belonged to Sir Thomas Frowick, an Alderman of London, and father of Sir Thomas Frowick, Lord Chief Justice of the Common Pleas. The property was afterwards held by the knightly family of the Spelmans, and in the middle of the seventeenth century it passed by purchase into the hands of Sir John Maynard, who was an eminent lawyer under the Stuart kings, and who died here in 1690. Gunnersbury remained for many years in the occupation of his widow, who married Henry, Earl of Suffolk. On the death of the Countess Dowager, in 1721, the estate became the property of Sir John (afterwards Lord) Hobart, by whom it was ultimately sold to a Mr. Furnese. The place figures constantly in Bubb Dodington's "Diary," 1749-50.

On the accession of George III., in 1760, the estate was purchased for the Princess Amelia. Horace Walpole was one of the most frequent guests at her parties. He writes to his friend, Sir Horace Mann, in 1761, saying that he has been there once or twice a week ever since the late king's death; and a month later again he writes to Mr. Conway:—

"I was sent for again to dine at Gunnersbury on Friday, and was forced to send to town for a dress coat and a sword. There were the Prince

GUNNERSBURY HOUSE.
(From a Water-colour Drawing by Chatelain).

of Wales, the Prince of Mecklenburgh, the Duke of Portland, Lord Clanbrassill, Lord and Lady Clermont, Lord and Lady Southampton, Lord Pelham, and Mrs. Howe. The Prince of Mecklenburgh went back to Windsor after coffee, and the Prince and Lord and Lady Clermont to town after tea, to hear some new French plays at Lady William Gordon's. The Princess, Lady Barrymore, and the rest of us, played three posts at commerce till ten. I am afraid that I was tired, and gaped. While we were at the Dairy, the Princess insisted on my making some verses on Gunnersbury. I pleaded being superannuated, but she would not excuse me. I promised she should have an ode on her next birthday, which diverted the Prince; but all would not do."

The verses here referred to are printed in H. Walpole's "Letters," Vol. IX., p. 55, but they are scarcely worth repeating here.

In the last century Gunnersbury was a sort of rival of Strawberry Hill, as may be inferred from the song—

"Some cry up Gunnersbury,
For Syon some declare;
Some say with Chiswick's Villa
None other can compare,"

The Princess Amelia died in 1786, and soon after that the mansion was pulled down, and the land sold. A Mr. Copland, who bought the lion's share, built a new house on the higher part of the grounds, and this still stands as a puny rival of the present mansion, which is in the Italian style.

It was bought about the middle of the present century by the Rothschilds, and is now owned by Sir Nathaniel Rothschild. It contains several fine paintings and statues, and a fine collection of china. The pictures in the principal rooms are chiefly portraits of the family and their friends. In the billiard-room there is one painting of historic interest—the introduction of the late Baron Lionel Rothschild into the House of Commons, on his first being allowed to take his seat for London, in 1858. He is walking up the centre of the House between his sponsors, Lord John Russell and Captain Bernal Osborne; and among the occupants of the front benches on either side are Lord Palmerston, Mr. Disraeli, Mr. Gladstone, Sir G. Cornewall Lewis, Lord Stanley, and other celebrities of the time.

The gardens and grounds are laid out with great taste; the latter extend to nearly a hundred acres,

EALING CHURCHES.

1. ST. JOHN S.   2. ST. MARY'S (THE PARISH CHURCH).   3. CHRIST CHURCH.

But the house is scarcely visible from any spot outside, owing to a lofty stone wall which surrounds the estate.

Of the house, as it was when occupied by the Princess Amelia, there is a scarce print by Evans, published in 1787. It was built by Webb, a son-in-law of Inigo Jones, and would seem to have been a plain, square, solid edifice, in the Classical or Italian style, of three storeys, and without wings. It is represented as embosomed in trees, and having a small lake or pond in front.

The windows in the centre of the first floor are different in shape, but the house is substantially the same as it was a century ago. The straight piece of water or canal is now altered into a serpentine form, and is called the Horseshoe Pond. There are other pieces of water in the grounds, which are made to curve in such a manner as to give an idea of greater extent than they possess. The cedars and other evergreens are very fine. Some of the summer-houses in the grounds, especially one called the Temple, bear the marks of Inigo Jones's design.

The vineries, hothouses, &c., are very extensive and most productive, and admirably arranged ; and in the fernery are two gigantic trees of the fern kind, which were brought from Tasmania by Sir Charles Du Cane, and sent hither as a present.

Ealing—or, as it was sometimes written, Zealing, Yealing, and Yeling—lies on the high road to Uxbridge, and is about six and a half miles from the Marble Arch by road, and five and a half from Paddington by railway. It has two stations on the Great Western Railway, one in the " Broad-way," and the other at Ealing Dean—known as Castle Hill. Ealing is also the terminus of the Metropolitan District Extension Railway, and the parish will soon be connected with other parts of London by a branch of the South Western line. The parish is bounded by New Brentford, Acton, and Chiswick on the south and east, by Greenford, Perivale, and Twyford on the north, and by Han-well on the west. It extends from the river Brent in the valley north of Castlebar Hill almost to the Thames. Old Brentford is part of the ancient parish of Ealing ; but now, with New Brentford (originally part of Hanwell), it forms a distinct township, and will accordingly be more conveniently dealt with hereafter.

The name of Ealing does not occur in the Domesday Book, so that apparently it had not become strictly parochial at that date. According to Lysons, it contains about 3,100 acres, about half of which in his time were grass lands, and about 1,220 arable, the rest being occupied by market gardens or left waste. The manor of Ealing has belonged to the see of London from the earliest times, and its history before the six-teenth century is a blank.

At the end of the reign of Henry VIII., or at the beginning of that of Edward VI., Bishop Bonner leased the Manor of Ealing-Bury to the Protector Duke of Somerset, after whose attainder, how-ever, the lands passed to the Crown. The Manor, having passed through several intermediate hands, came into the hands of the Penruddockes, and in the eighteenth century to the Longs. In a sur-vey taken about the time of the Restoration, it is described as "ruinated and lying open since the plundering thereof in the beginning of the last troubles," but the precise date and the extent of this "ruination" are unknown.

The chief manor still belongs to the see of London. It contains three subordinate manors, those of Gunnersbury, Coldhawe, and Pitshanger, the descents of which, though recorded by Lysons, have nothing of interest for our readers.

The parish church is dedicated to St. Mary. Robert, Bishop of London in the reign of Henry I., gave the tithes of Ealing to augment the salary of an officer of the church of St. Paul's, called the " Master of the Schools," and a part of them was subsequently settled on the Chancellor of St. Paul's, and on the Dean and Chapter, for the repairs of the cathedral. The living is now in the gift of the Bishop of London.

Robert Cooper, vicar in the reign of Charles I., was ejected by the Puritans during their ascendency, but reinstated at the Restoration, which, however, he survived only a few months. His successor was the learned Dr. William Beveridge, afterwards Bishop of St. Asaph. His portrait is in the vestry room.

The old church having begun to sink in 1729, a new one was built under an Act of Parlia-ment, aided by a "brief," but it was not completed for ten years. It was almost entirely rebuilt, and considerably enlarged, between the years 1866 and 1872. The building is constructed of brick, and consists of a nave and chancel, organ chamber, ambulatories, and a square tower. The style of architecture is Romanesque, and the reredos is a striking feature of the interior.

The church is basilican in appearance, both out-side and within ; and its fine roof and handsome, new-painted windows are much admired. A bap-tistery stands where one would naturally look for a south transept. The monuments from the walls of the former structure are mostly collected in re-cesses at the west end.

At the entrance to the chancel is a mural tablet to " John Bowman, Batchelour of Divinitie and Chancellour of St. Pawle's, parson of this parish," with the date 1629. Another tablet in the chancel of " Jacobean " workmanship, and adorned with a grim death's head and cross-bones over an hour-glass, records a Mr. Richard Taverner, who died in 1638. On the north wall of the chancel, near the vestry door, is a rather fine brass to the memory of Richard Agmondesham (who is described as " Merchant of the Stapel of Calais "), his wife and children, of the date of Henry VII.

Here, too, lies buried Sir John Maynard, the eminent lawyer, who took the leading part in the prosecution of Strafford and Laud. He died at Gunnersbury not long after the Restoration of 1690. King William, noticing his great age when he came to court, observed that he must have out-lived nearly all the men of the law who had been his contemporaries; he wittily replied, " Yes, sir ; and if your highness had not come over here, I should have survived even the law itself."

Here, in 1812, was buried John Horne Tooke, who died at Wimbledon, and desired to be in-terred there, but his wish was not carried out. Sir Francis Burdett and other politicians of the " advanced " school followed him to the grave. His tomb is a railed slab just in front of the south porch. It bears simply his name and the dates of his birth and death, 1736—1812, with the brief addition, "con-tented and grateful." There are many monuments to persons connected with the parish : one of them commemorates the wife of Mr. Serjeant Maynard, mentioned above.

In the old churchyard is buried John Oldmixon, the political writer of the last century, and the author of a " History of England " and of " The British Empire in America." He died in the year 1742. He is thus satirised by Pope in the "Dunciad," Book ii. :—

" In naked majesty Oldmixon stands,
  And, Milo-like, surveys his arms and hands."

The old churchyard has long been closed for interments, and a parish burial-ground between Ealing and Brentford has been in use for many years. Sir William Lawrence, the eminent surgeon, who died in 1867, is also interred here.

Whereas half a century ago there was one church in Ealing, there are now four permanent churches, besides two iron chapels, which here-after will doubtless blossom into churches.

Christ Church, which is situated in the Broad-way, on the Uxbridge Road, was built in the year 1852, at a cost of about £10,000. It is in the " Geometrical Decorated " style of architecture, and was erected from the designs of the late Sir Gilbert Scott. Some of the windows are filled with stained glass.

St. John's Church, in Ealing Dean, was built in 1876. It is a brick structure, relieved with stone and terra-cotta dressings, and in the Early English style of architecture. St. Stephen's Church, near Castle Hill, is a stone building of Gothic archi-tecture, and was erected in 1875.

There is a Wesleyan chapel at Ealing, with a somewhat striking pointed spire ; and there are also chapels for the Congregationalists, Baptists, and Primitive Methodists. There is also a Pres-byterian church.

The parish of Ealing in former days contained some fine gentlemen's seats, some of which are still standing. Among them may be mentioned Ealing House, once the abode of Sir James Mon-tagu, Baron of the Exchequer, and afterwards of Nathaniel Oldham, the *virtuoso* and collector of paintings, of William Melmoth, the author of " A Religious Life " and the translator of Cicero and Pliny, and of Alderman Slingsby Bethell, Lord Mayor of London ; and Ealing Grove, the seat successively of the Earl of Rochford and the Dukes of Marlborough and Argyll. At Place House, in Little Ealing, lived Sir Francis Dashwood, Sir Richard Littleton, Lord Brooke, and Lord Robert Manners. General Dumouriez also lived at Little Ealing, an outlying cluster of houses between Great Ealing and Brentford.

Amongst other residents of Ealing was Dr. John Owen, whom Lysons styles " the most voluminous and temperate among the Dissenters of the seven-teenth century." Though a divine, he was returned as M.P. by the University of Oxford, and was both Dean of Christ Church and Vice Chancellor during Cromwell's usurpation. He died at Ealing in 1683. Wood mentions him in his " Athenæ Oxonienses " as affecting the layman, in spite of his high position at Oxford. " Instead of being a grave example, he scorned all formality, undervalued his office by going in *querpo* like a young scholar, with powdered hair, snake-bone band-strings with very large tassels, lawn band, a large set of ribands pointed at his knees, and Spanish leather boots with lawn tops, and his hat mostly cocked."

Another resident of Ealing was Dr. William King, author of " Recollections," and editor of South's Sermons.

Zachary Pearce, Bishop of Rochester, was brought up at Ealing. Charles Dibdin wrote many of his best sea songs at his house in Hanger Lane.

Ford Hall, in this parish, was formerly the seat

of Sir Alexander Denton, a judge of the Common Pleas.

At his residence at Hanger Vale, in this parish, died at an advanced age, in October, 1863, Mr. John Bowyer Nichols, F.S.A., well known as an antiquary and a printer, and as the editor and proprietor of *The Gentleman's Magazine.* Mr. Nichols was the last surviving son of Mr. John Nichols, F.S.A., the historian of Leicestershire, and literary biographer of the eighteenth century, the disciple and successor of William Bowyer, the learned printer, and one of the friends of Samuel Johnson in his last days. The Duke of Kent lived many years at Castle Bar Park. The House was pulled down shortly after his death, which took place in 1820.

The great Lord Heathfield, the hero of Gibraltar, lived on Castle Bar Hill as General Eliott. At Castle Bar Hill is the College of the Society for Training Teachers of the Deaf, and for the diffusion of the "German" system in the United Kingdom. The students of the institution here are taught the art of teaching the deaf.

The Princess Helena College at Ealing was originally located near the Regent's Park, but in 1881–2 the new building here was erected and opened. It was founded for the purpose of a training school for governesses, and for educating the orphan daughters of officers of the Army and Navy, and of members of the Civil Service and clergymen. The work of this institution, which was formerly known as the Adult Orphan Institution, has been carried on in a quiet and unostentatious way; but the good results which it has achieved have been extensive and lasting. It has throughout its history been specially patronised by the royal family. It was founded in memory of Princess Charlotte, was warmly encouraged by Queen Charlotte, and for many years Princess Augusta was its president. Since about 1876 her Royal Highness the Princess Helena (Princess Christian), whose name the institution now bears, has held the office of president and has taken a strong personal interest in its welfare. It has been the aim of this institution not only to impart to the pupils at the college a sound education, but also to develop the mental and moral character which is so essential in a teacher; and to this laudable object the comparatively small size to which the institution has been confined has materially contributed. The college provides instruction for about thirty foundationers or scholars, with about the same number of paying boarders; and the college is so designed that the class-rooms, &c., can be enlarged as the demand for greater accommodation may arise. In connection with it is a high school for girls.

The oldest part of the village is grouped quaintly and pleasingly round the church, in a most irregular fashion. On the north side the street opens out very broad, and here probably once stood a village cross. At all events, a tablet at the entrance of the churchyard informs us that the vestry hall (since re-constructed) was "built in 1840 out of the proceeds of the sale of the old Cross House."

This Cross House stood on the west side of the street, facing the tower of the parish church, adjoining the old workhouse and other parochial tenements. The house may have taken its name from a village cross in the street adjoining, or from standing near the place where four cross-roads met; and it may possibly once have been the residence of the parson.

There was no Town Hall when Lysons wrote his History in 1790, but a large building was erected in 1877 for the use of the Local Board for Ealing, and comprises the requisite offices for such a body.

In the main street, on the west side, is a large private school, often called Ealing Great School, which enjoyed in the last generation a high reputation under Dr. Nicholas. It is now modernised into a large and lofty Italian villa. Not many private educational establishments can show a longer or more worthy roll of scholars than could its former master, Dr. Nicholas, who here educated as boys Sir Henry Lawrence and his brother Lord Lawrence, Bishop Selwyn, Charles Knight, Sir Henry Rawlinson, William Makepeace Thackeray (before he was sent to the Charterhouse), and last, not least, Cardinal Newman, who mentions it in his "Apologia." Charles Knight, in the first chapter of his "Passages of a Working Life," speaks tenderly and lovingly of this school:—
"My school-life was a real happiness. My nature bourgeoned under kindness, and I received unusual favours from one of the masters, Mr. Joseph Heath, of St. John's College, Oxford." He gratefully records the fact that this gentleman introduced him to Mr. (afterwards Sir) Henry Ellis, of the British Museum, from whom he derived his earliest antiquarian and historical tastes. It is stated that Dr. Nicholas's school was the largest private school in England; if so, it probably owed some of its numbers to the attack made by Cowper on our public schools in his "Tirocinium." The unfortunate Dr. Dodd also kept a school at the Manor House, since called Goodenough House. He was taken prisoner here, and carried off hence to Newgate to be tried for forgery. Here, too, a

school was established by the late Lady Byron in 1833.

Ealing is well off, if not for parks, at all events for open spaces. Besides the green and the commons, there are what are called the "Lammas lands," part of which were bought in 1881 to be devoted to the purposes of recreation for the inhabitants of the village.

Ealing Common lies to the east of the village, between Ealing and Acton. It is now being planted round the edges and made level, in order to fit it for a recreation-ground. The house with walled grounds at the south-west corner of the Common, formerly the residence of the Right Hon. Spencer Perceval, is now a Lunatic Asylum for Indian soldiers. It was at one time called Hickes-on-the-Heath, and afterwards Elm Grove, and was successively inhabited by Sir William Trumbull, the friend of Pope, and by Dr. Egerton, Bishop of Durham.

Some meadow land in the vicinity of the village has also been, since 1865, occasionally used as a race-course; but the races which have taken place here have never achieved the celebrity of those at Hampton or Sandown, and other suburban spots where such sports and pastimes have become popular; indeed, they have been generally voted more of a nuisance than otherwise by the inhabitants of this parish.

Near this part of the village was a small nursery of the Horticultural Society of London, before they obtained a lease of the grounds at Chiswick, as already described by us.*

Much of the land in the neighbourhood of Ealing is cultivated as market gardens. Mrs. Lawrence's gardens at Ealing Park have in past times enjoyed such a world-wide reputation, that we must not omit to make mention of them here. They were constantly frequented during the summer season by all the rank and fashion of the metropolis, and formed a counter attraction to Chiswick.

One of the most interesting houses in the parish of Ealing is a building in the Uxbridge Road, standing in its own grounds, and embowered in trees; it is called Fordhook House, and is now the residence of Captain Tyrrell. It was once the residence of Henry Fielding, the novelist, who here wrote "Tom Jones" and "Amelia;" but has largely grown in size since it was the small cottage inhabited by Fielding, who has told us with what regret he left it when he went abroad—to die at Lisbon. The opening passage in the journal of his journey has often been quoted, but it is too pathetic not to bear repetition. Under date of

Wednesday, June 26, 1754, he writes :—"On this day, the most melancholy sun I had ever beheld arose, and found me awake at my house at Ford-hook. By the light of this sun I was, in my own opinion, last to behold and take leave of some of those creatures on whom I doated with a mother-like fondness, guided by nature and passion, and uncured and unhardened by all the doctrine of that philosophical school where I had learned to bear pains and to despise death. In this situation, as I could not conquer nature, I submitted entirely to her, and she made as great a fool of me as she had ever done of any woman whatsoever; under pretence of giving me leave to enjoy, she drew me in to suffer the company of my little ones during eight hours; and I doubt not whether, in that time, I did not undergo more than in all my distemper. At twelve precisely my coach was at the door, which was no sooner told me than I kiss'd my children round, and went into it with some little resolution. My wife—who behaved more like a heroine and philosopher, though at the same time the tenderest mother in the world—and my eldest daughter followed me; some friends went with us, and others here took their leave; and I heard my behaviour applauded, with many murmurs and praises, to which I knew I had no title: as all other such philosophers may, if they have any modesty, confess on like occasions." Fielding died on the 8th of October following.

Fordhook was afterwards tenanted by Lady Byron; and in 1835 the poet's daughter, "Ada, sole daughter of my house and heart," was married in its drawing-room, by special licence, to Lord King, now Earl of Lovelace.

On the road towards Hanwell is a wayside inn, "The Old Hat," the sign-board of which claims for it three centuries of existence as a house of call and entertainment. If this assertion be true—and there is no reason for doubting it—what tales could its bar and snug parlour not tell! If neat and modernised in its outside, "The Old Hat" is old-fashioned enough in its interior arrangements. This ancient tavern is apparently not mentioned in Larwood's "History of Sign-boards," the author of which work suggests that "The Hat" "was the usual hatter's sign, although it may also be found before taverns and public-houses; in which case, however, it is probable that it was the previous sign of the house, which the publican on entering left unaltered; or it may have been used to suggest a 'house of call' to the trade."

The parish of Hanwell adjoins Ealing on the west, and is bounded on the south by Norwood and Heston, on the west by Southall, and on the

---

* See ante, p. 5.

north by Greenford. Although it figures in the Domesday Survey of William the Conqueror, under the name of Hanewelle, where it is stated that the manor " answers for two hides," and that "there was a mill of two shillings and twopence, pannage for fifty hogs," &c. ; and although it is on record that the manse was given at a very early period to Westminster Abbey, Hanwell seems to be one of those fortunate places whose history is a blank ; indeed, there is no allusion to it in any of

Catholics, the Congregationalists, Baptists, Wesleyans, &c., while the Established Church is represented by two edifices.

The parish church stands far away from the village, in the fields towards Greenford, on a knoll almost surrounded by the Brent, which here winds its way, almost choked with water-lilies, rushes, and reeds, its banks being lined with alders, the grass lands sloping pleasantly down to the banks of the stream. The present church is a poor

EALING GREEN.

Horace Walpole's " Letters," nor in any of the other gossiping chronicles of bygone days, so far as we can trace.

Hanwell lies on the Uxbridge Road, and partly occupies a broad valley through which the Brent river winds its course. The neighbourhood consists mostly of pasture land, pleasantly undulated, and affords much diversified and picturesque scenery. Near the centre of the parish the valley of the Brent is crossed by a lofty viaduct, nearly 700 feet in length, over which passes the Great Western Railway, which has a station here. The Grand Junction Canal also passes the village on its western side, on its way to join the Thames at Brentford. In the town there are churches and chapels, of more or less merit, for the Roman

specimen of modern Gothic, with large galleries and no chancel. It is a modern erection, having been built in 1841, in the place of an older structure, which had become too small for the increasing population. It was designed by Messrs. Scott and Moffatt, and is in the Early English style of architecture. It is constructed of dark flint and brick, with stone dressings, and consists of nave, aisles, and transept, with a tower and spire at the western end. Its predecessor was a mean and uninteresting brick building, dating from 1782, when it was erected on the site of a much more ancient edifice. Its form or plan was an oblong square, and its western end was adorned with a turret and cupola. The old church was devoid of monuments, with the exception, perhaps, of a single flat stone recording the decease of Sir John Clerke, Bart., in 1727, and his mother, Dame Catherine Clerke, who died in 1741. Its church-yard covers part of the slope to the bank of the river on the north, but it contains no tombs or memorials of interest. In the old graveyard was buried Jonas Hanway, whose name was almost as widely known as that of Captain Coram in the middle of the last century as the joint-founder of the Magdalen Hospital, and on account of many

the style of the period, and his face is strongly marked with benevolence and good sense. The early agenda books of the institution are religiously kept, and in them are to be seen the autographs of Hanway, of Mr. Benjamin D'Israeli (Lord Beacons-field's grandfather), and other celebrities of the reign of George II.'s day. The latter part of Hanway's life was employed in supporting, by his pen and personal exertions, a variety of charitable and philanthropic schemes; and he gained so high

The Old Hat in the Uxbridge Road.

other schemes of benevolence, and to whom we are mainly indebted for that very useful article of daily need, in our variable climate at least—the umbrella.* Hanway was also a social reformer, for it was mainly through his intercession that a Bill was introduced into Parliament for the regu-lation of the infant poor of several parishes in the metropolis. In the office of the Marine Society in Bishopsgate Street may be seen a very fine full-length portrait of this worthy philanthropist; the painter was no mean limner, but his name is not recorded. Hanway is represented as seated at a table, dressed in a blue suit, with ruffles, &c., in

and honourable a name, that a deputation of the chief merchants of London made it their request to Government that some substantial mark of public favour should be conferred on him. He was in consequence made a commissioner of the navy. Hanway was one of the great promoters of schools for the poor.

An account of this good man and philanthropist will be found in Dr. Smiles's "Self-Help." The son of a storekeeper in the dockyard at Portsmouth, he was brought up to a mercantile career, and made a fortune by trading in Russia. That fortune he spent in works of public utility and benevolence. He improved the highways of the metropolis; he organised a volunteer body of marines; he founded

* See "Old and New London," Vol. IV., p. 471.

the Marine Society (which is still one of the largest and most important of London charities) ; he largely re-modelled the Foundling Hospital ; he was one of the founders of the Magdalen ; like Howard, he explored the fever-dens of the poorer classes of London, and forced on the parochial authorities a system of registration, in order to protect infant life ; he got an Act passed for the protection of climbing boys employed by chimney-sweeps ; and, strange to say, was rewarded by the Government for his philanthropic efforts by being made a member of the Victualling Board. " His moral courage," writes Dr. Smiles, " was of the first order. It may be regarded as a trivial matter to mention that he was the first who ventured to walk the streets of London with an umbrella over his head. But let any modern London merchant venture to walk along Cornhill in a peaked Chinese hat, and he will find that it takes some moral courage to persevere in it. After carrying an umbrella for some thirty years, Mr. Hanway saw the article at length come into general use." Jonas Hanway died childless, and he left his fortune to those whom he had befriended in his lifetime.

Hanway was buried here, pursuant to his own request, in the month of September, 1786. Lysons, in his " Environs of London," thus writes of him : —" This valuable man, whose whole life was a continued scene of active benevolence, was the first promoter of various schemes of public utility, which he lived to see realised and established as permanent institutions. That useful charity the Marine Society, in particular, may be said to have owed its existence to him. His writings were very numerous, and all bore the marks of the most benevolent intentions, whether his object was to secure the health, or improve the morals and religion of his fellow-creatures, to abolish evil customs, or recommend the most deserving objects of charity. Besides the numerous treatises on these subjects, he published an account of a journey from Kingston to Portsmouth, and his travels through Russia, Persia, &c." Mr. Hanway was a commissioner in the Victualling Office from 1762 till 1783, and he frequently visited his friend and relation, Dr. Henry Glasse, at the rectory here. Dr. Glasse translated Mason's " Caractacus " and Milton's " Samson Agonistes " into Greek, and was also the author of " Contemplations from Sacred History." There is no monument in the church to the memory of Hanway, but one was erected in Westminster Abbey.

The village of Hanwell mainly consists of a long and wide High Street, which carries on the line of houses from Ealing, and ends at a bridge at the west end of the village, beyond which is the County Lunatic Asylum. The houses and shops are most irregularly built, and yet they are far from being tasty or elegant. In fact, a duller and plainer street is not to be found, even in Middlesex.

The Central London District Schools are an extensive range of buildings on Cuckoo Farm, about a mile northward of the railway station.

Among the charitable institutions of Hanwell is one founded by William Hobbayne, or Hobbyns, in 1484, for the benefit of the poor, and for twenty-four boys of the parish to be educated and provided with a suit of clothes free of charge, in the parochial school of Greenford Magna. There is also a Catholic Convalescent Home for women and children.

Standing on an eminence opposite to the church, but actually within the parish of Norwood, is the Hanwell Lunatic Asylum—one of the two lunatic asylums for the county of Middlesex. This asylum, since its first erection in 1829-31, has been repeatedly enlarged and greatly improved, and now affords accommodation for nearly 2,000 inmates. It is a conspicuous object for a long distance round, covering as it does a large space of ground, and occupying an elevated site. The general plan of the building is that of the letter E, or, in other words, a centre, in which is the principal entrance, with projecting wings at either end, the wards set apart for male patients being on the left of the entrance, and those for females on the right. Architecturally, the building is a model of simple plainness. There are extensive airing-grounds and gardens in the front and rear of the premises, laid out with shrubberies, gravel-walks, &c. ; and besides the wards of the asylum, there are kitchens, sculleries, larder, dairy, wash-houses, and laundries, bakehouse, brewhouse, and general store-room. The wards are provided with day-rooms, in which the patients take their meals, and where they spend the greater part of their time. The wards have not less than two attendants in each, in some there are three ; and on an average about fifty convalescent patients are under the care of two attendants, but in the refractory wards two attendants have the charge of about twenty-five patients. The attendants have to pay strict attention to the directions of the medical officers as regards the treatment, employment, amusement, and exercise of the patients, and in every instance they are required to treat them with the greatest kindness.

This institution owes its origin to an Act of

Parliament passed in the reign of George III., enabling the justices of the several counties to erect asylums for the reception and maintenance of the insane and lunatic poor, and to improve and ameliorate the condition of lunatics, by rescuing them from the neglect and inattention of the workhouse, or the cupidity, ignorance, and cruelty too often practised by those who farmed them in private asylums.

Nothing can more strongly mark the progress which society has made since the latter end of the last century than the different aspect under which the insane have been viewed, and the different way in which they have been treated. Formerly there was but little difference in the treatment of the criminal and the insane. In 1792, an intelligent and noble-hearted Frenchman, named Pinel, in the midst of surrounding horrors, brought commiseration and kindness within the walls of a lunatic asylum, and it is to his courage and humanity that we owe the many beneficial changes which have been brought about in this country in the treatment of the insane. The change of treatment, however, in this country was of slow growth; for long after the example which Pinel had set, though there were isolated attempts to introduce a humane system of management into the asylums, they were the exceptions only. Cruelties of the most revolting kind continued to be practised by sordid, unprincipled men. Mr. John Weale, in his "London Exhibited in 1851," observes that "almost the first, and certainly the greatest, benefit conferred upon the insane pauper was the Act of the 9th George IV., cap. 40, which was intended to facilitate the erection of county lunatic asylums for the poor, and to improve the condition of lunatics. Thenceforth, in those counties that wisely took advantage of the Act, the friends of the insane pauper could be assured of that which the laws of society are bound to afford —protection against cruelty and security against neglect."

On the completion of Hanwell Asylum, the committee appointed Dr. William Ellis and Mrs. Ellis to be the superintendent and matron, and from their united efforts the institution derived great benefit. Among the useful suggestions for which the asylum was indebted to Dr. and Mrs. Ellis was the extensive employment of the patients. In his very first report, Dr. Ellis mentions that considerable amelioration had taken place in the condition of the insane poor of the country, and adds :—" But with even the greatest solicitude for their comfort, the want of sufficient air and exercise, which can only be obtained in a large building

with ample grounds, presents the most formidable obstacle to their cure." In December, 1832, Dr. Ellis writes that the system of employing the patients has been pursued most perseveringly in every variety of work adapted to their respective qualifications; and concludes by stating that "not a single accident had occurred from the patients having been trusted with the tools used in their different occupations." These, among other less formidable weapons, were spades, bill-hooks, and scythes. The same earnest endeavours to employ the patients in useful handicraft labour continued to engage the mind of Dr. Ellis during the remainder of his career as superintendent at Hanwell. During all this time the non-restraint system was gradually making its way, by the exertions of intelligent men, in two or three other public establishments in the kingdom, and was to some extent adopted in a few amongst the best conducted private establishments. Long experience had taught Dr. Ellis that the sufferings of the insane were often frightfully augmented by undue coercion, needless restraint, and the want of employment, and that their malady by these means was increased rather than alleviated. Well he knew that the cries of poverty and sickness can make themselves heard, while the voice of the mentally diseased does not reach the ear. Thus was he stimulated to try gentleness, employment, liberty (as far as was prudent), and social intercourse. His perfect success induced him to labour for the establishment of such a system for the wealthy classes of the insane, calling public attention to the subject by a work which he published on "Insanity," and taking every opportunity of influencing in private those who might assist in furthering his scheme. Dr. Ellis was knighted by William IV. soon after his nomination to the governorship of Hanwell Asylum. He resigned his appointment here in 1838, and died two years afterwards.

In their choice of a successor to Dr. Ellis, the committee of visiting justices, with whom the government of the asylum was placed, were not fortunate, for in less than a twelvemonth it became necessary to appoint another physician in his place. The choice fell upon Dr. John Conolly, the author of numerous works on insanity, and on the "Construction and Government of Lunatic Asylums," &c. To this gentleman the asylum is mainly indebted for the full establishment of the humane and rational system of non-restraint which had been introduced by Dr. Ellis. In one of his reports to the visiting justices, Dr. Conolly observes : "The great and only real substitute for restraint is invariable kindness. This feeling must animate every person employed in every duty to be per-formed. Constant superintendence and care, con-stant forbearance and command of temper, and a never-failing attention to the comfort of the patients, to their clothing, their food, their personal cleanli-ness, their occupations, their recreations—these are but so many different ways in which kindness shows itself, and these will be found to produce results beyond the general expectation of those who persevere in their application." Caroline Fox in her "Journals," June 22, 1842, writes: "Met Colonel Gurney at Paddington, and reached Han-well in a few minutes. Were most kindly received by Dr. Conolly; he has had the superintendence for two years, and at once introduced the system of non-coercion in its fullest sense, though feeling that it was a very bold experiment, and required intense watching; but he dared it all for the sake of a deeply suffering portion of humanity, with the most blessed result. All the assistants seem in-fluenced by his spirit, and it is a most delightful and heartcheering spectacle to see madness for once not treated as a crime."

The average number of patients at Hanwell Asylum is close upon 2,000, of whom by far the larger portion are females. The management of the patients, as regards their classification, employ-ment, and treatment, is under the direction of two resident medical officers, one for the male, and the other for the female department. There is a bazaar upon the premises, for the sale of fancy and other needlework, &c., the produce of the female patients during the daytime who are desirous of amusing themselves by the production of such articles. The bazaar is under the care of a superintendent; and the profit arising from the sale of such work to visitors is expended in little extra indulgences for the patients. There is a school for the male patients, and the schoolmaster occasionally gives lectures in the evening on some amusing subject. The amusements for the patients, in fact, are varied.

In the wards a good supply of books, bagatelle-boards, cards, &c., is kept up; and in some of the wards there are also pianofortes, which have been presented by visitors for the use of those patients who are musically inclined. The male patients, and such of the female patients as may be fit for manual labour, may be seen from time to time labouring in the gardens and fields which lie round the asylum, and so contributing to the good of the institution, whilst harmlessly and healthfully employed.

The previous chapels having proved insufficient, a new chapel, in the Early English Gothic style, was added to the asylum in 1880. The architect was Mr. H. Martin, and it will seat about a thousand worshippers. It is of brick, and has a lofty tower and spire. Standing in front of the main entrance, it forms a conspicuous and central object in the general view of the place.

There are at Hanwell two cemeteries, one be-longing to the parish of St. Mary Abbots, Ken-sington, and the other to St. George's, Hanover Square.

In these days of electric telegraphy, when a message can be sent from London to the uttermost corner of the globe in almost less time than it would take to be carried by hand from one end of the metropolis to the other, it is somewhat interesting to read such a scrap of intelligence as the following, which we cull from *The Mirror* of December, 1839:—

"ELECTRO-MAGNETIC TELEGRAPH OF THE GREAT WESTERN RAILWAY.—This telegraph, which is the invention of Mr. Cook and Prof. Wheatstone, of King's College, has been, during two months, con-stantly worked at the passing of every train between Drayton, Hanwell, and Paddington. At the former station it, for the present, terminates. As soon as the whole line is completed, the telegraph will ex-tend from the Paddington terminus to Bristol; and it is contemplated that then information of any nature may be conveyed to Bristol, and an answer received in twenty minutes."

CHAPTER III.

BRENTFORD.

"We will turn our course
To Brainford, westward, if thou says't the word."—*Ben Jonson.*

Traffic through Brentford in the old Coaching Days—Government of the Parish—Old Bridge of the Brent—The Priory of the Holy Angels
Inundations—Fondness of George III. for Brentford—The Dangers of the Road—Early History of Brentford—The Soil and the Pleistocene
Deposits—Murder of King Edmund—The Battle of Brentford—Visit of the Grand Duke of Tuscany—The "Two Kings of Brentford"—The
Dirt and Squalor of Brentford—How the Duke of Wellington nearly came to grief here—Ancient Hostelries—Old (East) Brentford Church—
New (West) Brentford Church—St. Paul's Church—The Town-hall and Market-house—Manufactories and Grand Junction Waterworks—
Grand Junction Canal—Drinking Fountain—Bear Baitings—The Old Market-place—The Elections for Middlesex—"Wilkes and Liberty!"
—A Brentford Elector—The Manor of Bordeston—Boston House—Sion House Academy—Wyke Farm—"Old Gang Aboot"—The Pitt
Diamond—Mrs. Trimmer—Extracts from the Parish Register.

WE now make our way in a south-westerly direction, skirting the hamlet of Little Ealing, and shortly find ourselves at Brentford, a long straggling village or town on the Hammersmith and Hounslow road, and extending about a mile and a quarter west from Kew Bridge, almost parallel with the Thames. The chief road to the west and south-west of England passed through Brentford in the days of coaching and posting. Some idea of the traffic along this road from London at the end of the reign of William IV. may be formed from the fact that the tolls of the Hammersmith Turnpike Trust were let in 1836 for £19,000 per annum, and that 247 coaches and public conveyances, and seven mails, passed through and returned to town on this road daily. Nearly all this traffic must have gone through Brentford. The road, at one time bordered by hedgerows, and passing through cultivated fields and market gardens, has been within the last half-century considerably altered in its appearance by the "demon of bricks and mortar;" indeed, Sir Horace Mann, writing under date of 1791, observes that "there will soon be one street from London to Brentford," and the era of which he prophesied, as we have already remarked in our opening chapter,* has long since arrived. Brentford is not included in any parliamentary borough, nor is it a corporate town ; but it is governed by a Local Board of Health. It is really a township in the parishes of Hanwell and Ealing : West, or New Brentford, being in the former parish, and East, or Old Brentford, being in the latter. The west, however, is really the older part of the town.

At the west end is a bridge of one arch over the Brent, superseding that mentioned by Leland in his "Itinerary." In his time it had three arches, and close to it stood a hospital of brick ; but we are not informed as to its character.

In the *Gentleman's Magazine* for 1802 is an engraving of the seal of "The Priory of the Holy Angels in the Marshlands, near Brentford." This is called by Bishop Tanner in his "Notitia Monastica," after Weever and Newcourt, a friary, hospital, or fraternity of the nine holy orders of angels, consisting of a master and several brethren in a chapel at the west end of Brentford, or, according to Stow, "by the bridge." Lysons mentions it, and places it "in Isleworth, at Brentford End." All Christian passengers were free of toll on passing this bridge, but Jews and Jewesses were forced to pay a halfpenny if on foot, or a penny if on horseback. Many centuries later, if we may trust Spence's "Anecdotes," the Jews offered to Lord Godolphin to purchase the town, with all its rights and privileges of trade, but that statesman declined the offer.

Its name explains itself*—the ford over the Brent, a small tributary of the Thames, which rises in Hendon, between the Hampstead and Stanmore hills, and, flowing in a south-westerly course for about eighteen miles, falls into the Thames at this point. Its situation on the banks of the Thames and the Brent being low and flat has been at times one of great inconvenience, owing to inundations. In 1682 we read of a great flood here, when "boats rowed up and down the streets, and the water got into the pews of the church."

In January, 1841, great damage was occasioned here by the rise of the waters of the Brent and the Grand Junction Canal, owing to an unusually rapid thaw and the bursting of a reservoir at Hendon. Numbers of boats, barges, and lighters were torn from their moorings and driven through the bridge towards the Thames, several barges being sunk, and many of the houses inundated.

"All the land to the south of the road passing from Brentford through Hounslow to Staines is so nearly level as to have no more than a proper drainage ; and much the greater part is less than ten feet above the surface of the river at Staines Bridge, and not more than from three to five feet above the level of the rivulets flowing through this district. From Staines, through Ashford and

* See *ante*, p. 3.

* See however, below, p. 31.

BRENTFORD, FROM THE RIVER.

Hanworth Common, to Twickenham, a distance of seven miles and a half, it is a perfect level, generally from ten to twenty feet above the surface of the Thames."*

King George II.—like his successor—it is well known, preferred Kew to Windsor, and loved the dead level of the neighbourhood. On the same principle he was very fond of Brentford, because its long low street reminded him of some of the towns in his kingdom of Hanover. For this reason he always ordered his coach to be driven slowly through it, in order that he might enjoy the scene.

The road connecting this town with the metropolis was, in the last century, much on a par with the other great thoroughfares radiating from London, so far as the dangers from highwaymen and footpads were concerned. We read in the *Gentleman's Magazine* for 1776, that in the September of that year the then Lord Mayor of London was stopped at Turnham Green, a mile east of Brentford, in his chaise and four, in the sight of all his retinue, and robbed by a single highwayman, who swore that he would shoot the first person that offered any resistance.

Cyrus Redding, in his "Fifty Years' Recollections," tells a strange story in connection with this place :—

"I had a relative, who, not long before railways were established, on stating his intention to come up to town, was solicited to accept as a fellow-traveller a man of property, a neighbour, who had

never been thirty miles from home in his life. They travelled by coach. All went on well until they reached Brentford. The countryman supposed he was nearly come to his journey's end. On seeing the lamps mile after mile, he expressed more and more impatience. 'Are we not yet in London, and so many miles of lamps?' At length, on reaching Hyde Park Corner, he was told they had arrived. His impatience increased from thence to Lad Lane. He became overwhelmed with astonishment. They entered the inn; and my relative bade his companion remain in the coffee-room until he returned, having gone to a bed-room for ablution. On returning, he found the bird flown; and for six long weeks there were no tidings of him. At length it was discovered he was in the custody of the constables at Sherborne, in Dorsetshire, his mind alienated. He was conveyed home, came partially to his reason for a short time, and died. It was gathered from him that he had become confused more and more at the lights, and long distances he was carried among them; it seemed as if they could have no end. The idea that he could never be extricated from such a labyrinth superseded every other. He could not bear the thought. He went into the street, inquired his way to the westward, and seemed, from his statement, to have got into Hyde Park, and then out again into the Great Western Road, walking until he could walk no longer. He could relate nothing more that occurred until he was secured. Neither his watch nor money had been taken from him."

It is time now for us to speak of Brentford itself.

---

* Middleton, "View of the Agriculture of Middlesex," p. 23.

In spite of the general opinion that Julius Cæsar, in his second invasion of England, crossed the Thames, at the Coway Stakes, near Shepperton (as we shall presently see), there are not wanting those who consider that it is more probable that the scene of that passage was much nearer to London, and the Rev. Henry Jenkins, in the "Journal of the British Archæological Association" for June, 1860, maintains at some length his belief that it was at Old Brentford that the emperor crossed his army. We learn from Gibson's edition of Camden's

since it allowed the Britons more space to fortify them with stakes, and, at the same time, afforded the Romans a fairer opportunity of plying their engines over the heads of their own men as they entered the river, and of striking the enemy posted on the topmost verge of the opposite side. Thus, whilst the cavalry, sent in advance to cross higher up the stream, were threatening the flank, the main body of the legions pressing forward in front, and sheltered, as it were, by the military engines, made good the passage of the river. Cæsar's words are

THE STABLES OF THE "THREE PIGEONS," BRENTFORD. (*See p.* 34.)
(*From an Etching by W. N. Wilkins*, 1848.)

"Britannia," that at Old Brentford the Thames was annually fordable with great ease, and was so still in Bishop Gibson's time, as now, there being at low ebb not above three feet of water in the bed of the river. "Here," writes Mr. Jenkins, "on many accounts, I am inclined to place the passage of Cæsar. Its British name, Brentford—*i.e.*, Breninford—the king's road or way,* favours this supposition; for the name, even if it should not apply personally to Cæsar, establishes the fact that this part of the Thames was known to, and used by, the Britons as a ford. The height of the banks also at this place is an important consideration,

præmisso equitatu. By this I understand that the cavalry were sent in advance to attempt passage higher up the stream, at Kingston, Walton, or elsewhere, in order to distract the enemy's attention, and to draw off a part of his forces, whilst the infantry pressed forward to the ford directly in their front. The cavalry and infantry did not cross the stream together and at the same place. Such a plan would have caused inextricable confusion."

So far Mr. Jenkins, who considers that as soon as the emperor had brought together all his forces on the north side of the river at Old Brentford, he marched straight east. "His first and chief object, after he had crossed the Thames, must have been to have led his army into Essex, and form a junction with the Trinobantes;" and this he did, keeping between the river on his right and the forest on his

---

* This derivation entirely sets aside the derivation given above, which makes Brentford to have been so called from the ford across the Brent. It is not usual for towns, which, of course, are after-growths, to give names to rivers; the converse is almost always the case.

left. In this case he would have passed across what is now the north of London, passed the Lea at Old Ford, and so on to Ilford and Barking, on his way to head-quarters at Cæsaromagus, which Mr. Jenkins fixes at Billericay, near Brentwood.

A long, narrow strip of waste land, some two acres in extent, forming an island in the Thames, and known as " Brentford Eyot," adds not a little to the beauty of the river scenery at this point. It is overgrown with trees, and a suggestion has been raised by the Commissioners of Woods and Forests to sell it for the sake of the timber ; but the idea has been strongly resented by the inhabitants.

The soil of Brentford is, or has been, very rich in remains of extinct species of animals ; and in digging out brick-earth and excavating for other works, many of their bones have been found. In 1740 the skeleton of a "large beast of the bull kind" was found here. Professor Phillips, in his " Geology of Oxford and the Valley of the Thames," says—" At Brentford the pleistocene deposits above the London clay have been successfully examined, long since by Mr. Trimmer, and subsequently by Morris. The paper of Mr. Trimmer, referred to by Professor Phillips, was printed in the *Philosophical Transactions for the Year* 1813. In it an account is given of many interesting discoveries of bones of animals about ten feet below the present surface of the ground. There were found teeth and bones of both the African and Asiatic elephant, of the hippopotamus, and of several species of deer. The remains of hippopotami were so abundant that, in turning over an area of 120 yards, parts of six tusks of that animal were found, besides a tooth and part of the horn of a deer, parts of a tusk and a grinder of an elephant, and the horns, with a small portion of the skull of an ox." Many of these fossils are now in the possession of Thomas Layton, F.S.A.

" Since the period referred to by Professor Phillips and Mr. Trimmer," observes the Rev. T. E. Platten in his " Memorials of Old Brentford," "various excavations have been made for railway purposes at Kew Bridge and near the present Gunnersbury station. At Kew Bridge were found bones of several species of deer, horns of reindeer and red-deer, tusks of hippopotami, and remains of bisons." At Gunnersbury, where the London clay was reached, were discovered the remains of sharks, a fossil crab and fossil resin (amber), fine specimens of nautili, and other marine shells.

" If we could have looked on the place in those days," continues Mr. Platten, "a strange scene would have been presented to our eyes. The Thames then probably spread its waters from the

Richmond hills on the south to the Harrow heights on the north. In its shallow pools, and amid the high thick rushes which lined its banks, the hippopotamus made his lair and bathed his unwieldy limbs. Here the elephant slaked his thirst at night, and the huge Irish elk, the largest of the deer species and now long extinct, took refuge from his ferocious enemies, and stood at bay in the waters of the friendly stream. It was a wilderness of waters —an arm of the sea rather than a river. The beasts held the land for their own, and reigned with undisputed sway, revelling in the warmth and rich luxurious vegetation of a tropical clime. Such is the scene of the distant past which these discoveries suggest.

" The next period, the records of which have been preserved by the river, is the stone age, carrying us back to a time when men did yet not know how to work the metals. In many parts of the Thames between Sion House and Strand-on-the-Green during dredging operations interesting discoveries have been made of various stone implements, known as celts—*i.e.*, chisels and hammers of stone, some of which have been found let into bone or wooden handles. The stones are in many instances carefully shaped to suit the purposes for which they were required, but at the best they could not be very efficient implements to work with. To the stone succeeded the bronze age, and that again was followed by the iron. Of the bronze and iron ages, also, many relics have been found. There have come to light a great many specimens of bronze weapons, such as swords, spear-heads, wedges, axes, and part of the boss of a shield. Britons, Romans, and Saxons, from time to time, must have fought many battles in this neighbourhood, and these relics were probably the arms of soldiers who perished in trying to cross the Thames for attack or in flight. It seems probable," Mr. Platten adds, " that for a considerable time the river formed a boundary separating Britons from Romans, for as a rule ancient British remains are found along the left bank, while the Roman are mostly confined to the south side of the Thames."

Brentford has figured in history on at least two occasions : in the Saxon times, and again under the Stuarts. It was here that Edmund Ironside defeated the Danes in 1016, when many of the English were drowned in the Thames. A few days later King Edmund was himself treacherously slain at Brentford. Local tradition fixes the Red Lion Inn yard as the scene of the murder. Here, in 1642, Prince Rupert routed two regiments of the army of the Parliament, under Colonel Hollis, driving them out with considerable loss. The importance of this engagement, and the number of the slain, both in the encounter and in the skirmishing of the following day about Turnham Green, are probably much exaggerated. We are told in Clarendon's "History of England," that the common soldiers taken prisoners by the king's "army at Brentford were discharged on their simple promise not to take up arms again ; but that the Puritan camp chaplains declared that they were not bound by such an oath, and absolved them from the necessity of keeping it !" We learn also that after the battle great damage was done in the neighbourhood by the Royalist soldiers, and liberal collections in aid of the sufferers were made. The Puritan John Lilburne was one of the prisoners taken in the encounter; and Charles I. rewarded the Scottish Earl of Forth for his share in the engagement by creating him Earl of Brentford. The earldom was renewed by William III. as the second title of his favourite officer, the Duke of Schomberg ; but it became extinct a second time in 1719. On the news of this repulse, the Parliament at once ordered fortifications to be thrown up, in order to prevent the king from pressing on to London, and next day they sent out the Trainbands, under the Earl of Essex, who encamped on Turnham Green ; and after a day of irresolution the king drew back to Kingston-on-Thames. On this occasion, as we learn from Whitelock's "Memoirs," "the good wives and others, mindful of their husbands and friends, sent many cart-loads of provisions, and wines, and good things to Turnham Green, with which the soldiers were refreshed and made merry, and the more when they heard that the king's army was retreated." Brentford must have seen Oliver Cromwell pass in a sort of triumphal procession through the town.

Samuel Pepys would seem to have been a frequent visitor here ; at all events, several notices of the place occur in his Diary between the years 1665 and 1669. A Mr. Povy, who resided here at that time, was one of his friends. He was evidently a rich man, inasmuch as his stud of horses was, according to Pepys' notion, "the best confessedly in England, the king having none such." In August, 1665, Mr. Pepys found that "the plague was very bad round about here ;" and in the following month, one of his watermen (he seems generally to have gone by water between London and Brentford) "fell sick as soon as he landed me in London, when I had been all night upon the water, and I believe he did get his infection that day at Brentford, and is now dead of the plague." A spot now known as "Dead Men's Graves," near the north end of Green Dragon Lane, is said to be the place of interment of those who died of the plague. In

no suburb of the metropolis were the deaths from this cause heavier than here.

Charles II. stayed a night here at an old house which was taken to form the approach to St. Paul's church, from the High Street. Nell Gwynne lived for a time at Brent House, in the Butts.

Brentford figures also in the blacker pages of English history, six persons having been burnt here in 1558 for advocating the "new" opinions.

Cosmo III., Grand Duke of Tuscany, who was travelling in England in 1669, passed through Brentford on his way to London. In the account of his travels which he afterwards wrote, he calls the place "a very large village," and adds that he "dined there in company with all the gentlemen who had been to wait upon him." His visit no doubt caused a general commotion in the neighbourhood, for he further remarks that "a very great number of people—men, women, and whoever were curious enough to come—were allowed to enter the dining-room."

Brentford was the capital of the kingdom of the "Middle Saxons," whose name survives in Middlesex. The "two kings of Brentford" have passed into a proverb. As to the precise date when they reigned history is silent, but it must have been, if ever, in the Saxon times. The Duke of Buckingham's Play, "The Rehearsal," was written as a satire upon Dryden and the playwrights of his time, who often made reference to two kings fighting for a throne. "The Rehearsal" contains no regular plot, but some of the scenes are amusing. The scene of the play is Brentford. There are "two kings" and "two usurpers," and the two kings are represented as being very fond of each other. They come on the stage hand-in-hand, and are generally seen smelling at one rose or nosegay. Hearing the bystanders whisper, they imagine that they are being plotted against, and one says to the other :—

"Then, spite of Fate, we'll thus combinèd stand,
    And, like true brothers, still walk hand-in-hand."

They are driven from the throne by the usurpers; but towards the end of the play "the two right kings of Brentford descend in the clouds, singing, in white garments ; and three fiddlers sitting before them in green ;" upon which one of the usurpers says to the other :—

"Then, brother Phys, 'tis time we should be gone."

The usurpers having disappeared, the first right king thus expresses his sentiments :—

"So firmly resolved is a true Brentford king
    To save the distressed and help to 'em bring,
    That ere a full-pot of good ale you can swallow.
    He's here with a whoop, and gone with a holla."

A dance is then performed before them, which is said to be "an ancient dance of right belonging to the kings of Brentford, but since derived, with a little alteration, to the Inns of Court."

Cowper, in his "Task" (Book 1), alludes to this dual sovereignty, comparing it to a "settee," or "sofa."

"United, yet divided, twain at once:
So sit two kings of Brentford on one throne."

There is also an old ballad by an anonymous writer, commencing :—

"The noble king of Brentford
Was old and very sick ;
He summoned his physicians
To wait upon him quick.
They stepped into their coaches,
And brought their best physic."

Again, in Prior's "Alma," we read :—

"So Brentford kings, discreet and wise,
After long thought and grave advice,
Into Lardella's coffin peeping,
Saw nought to cause their mirth or weeping."

The reference here would be obscure and unintelligible were it not for the light thrown upon it by the play of "The Rehearsal," above.

Brentford, however, has gained notoriety in other ways than through its "two kings." In the "Merry Wives of Windsor," Falstaff is disguised as "the fat woman of Brentford;" and the town is referred to by Thomson, Gay, Goldsmith, and others, chiefly on account of its dirt. "With its long, narrow High Street, back slums, factories, and rough river-side and labouring population," writes Mr. J. Thorne, "Brentford has always borne an unenviable reputation for dirt and ill odours." He also quotes the following story from Boswell :— "When Dr. Adam Smith was expatiating on the beauty of Glasgow, Johnson cut him short by saying, Pray, sir, have you ever seen Brentford?' This, Boswell took the liberty of telling him, was shocking. 'Why then, sir,' he replied, ' You have never seen Brentford." No doubt he meant that dirty as parts of Glasgow may be, Brentford is worse.

Gay speaks of

"—— Brentford, tedious town,
For dirty streets and white-legged chickens known."

Thomson, who lived at Richmond, as our readers will remember, was a keen observer of nature, and thus alludes to Brentford at the end of his "Castle of Indolence" :—

"Ee'n so through Brentford town, a town of mud,
A herd of bristly swine is preeked along ;
The filthy beasts, that never chew the cud,
Still grunt and squeak, and sing their troublous song.
And oft they plunge themselves the mire among,
But aye the ruthless driver goads them on."

The readers of Oliver Goldsmith will not forget the mention of this place in the "Citizen of the World," where he describes a race "run on the road from London to a village called Brentford, between a turnip-cart, a dust-cart, and a dung-cart." It was through Brentford, too, as readers of Charles Dickens will remember, that little Oliver Twist was made to tramp by Bill Sikes on his way to the burglary at Shepperton, which had such an effect on his subsequent career.

The long dreary High Street of Brentford is not only dirty, but dull and monotonous, and quite devoid of interest. Almost the only incident connected with it worth narrating respecting it is that the Duke of Wellington, returning to London from Windsor Castle late at night in 1814, met with an accident to his carriage, which might have proved fatal to the future conqueror of Waterloo. Lord William Lennox, who was with him as his aide-de-camp, tells us that the townspeople, on hearing who was the occupier of the chariot, wanted to fasten ropes to it, and to drag it on to town.

The inhabitants of this place seem to have been regarded as vulgar, for Shenstone writes :—" There are no persons more solicitous about the preservation of rank than those who have no rank at all. Observe the humours of a country christening ; and you will find no court in Christendom so ceremonious as ' the quality' of Brentford."

Lying on the direct road to the west of England, Brentford has long been famous for its hostelries. Near to the old market house was an ancient timbered inn, "The Three Pigeons," mentioned by Ben Jonson—" We'll tickle it at the Pigeons"—and the scene of some of the "Merry Jests" of George Poole, the early dramatist. It is known that many of Shakespeare's friends were visitors here ; and it is probable that the immortal poet himself may have been within its walls. The house was taken down several years ago, and its low carved and panelled chambers disappeared. Mr. Thorne says that "at the *Lion* Inn, Henry VI., in 1445, assembled a large party, and after supper created Alonzo D'Almada Duke of Avranches, and next morning held a Chapter of the Garter (the only instance of a Chapter being held at an inn), at which he created two knights." He gives, however, no authority for the statement.

The "Wagon and Horses," near Kew Bridge, probably occupies the site of a certain "inn that goes down by the water-side," where the genial old gossiper Samuel Pepys tells us that he was entertained, and returned by water to London, having attended service at Brentford Church, "where a dull sermon and many Londoners."— (Aug. 20, 1665.)

Another noted hostelry here was the "Tumble-down Dick," a sign, by the way, which has given rise to some little speculation as to its meaning. "Tumble-down Dick," says the *Advertiser*, No. 9, 1752, "is a fine moral on the instability of great-ness and the consequences of ambition." As such, it was set up in derision of Richard Cromwell, the allusion to his fall from power, or "tumble down," being very common in the satires published after the Restoration; and amongst others, *Hudibras*, thus, Part III., canto ii., 231 :—

> " Next him, his son and heir apparent
> Succeeded, though a lame vicegerent,
> Who first laid by the Parliament,
> The only crutch on which he leant,
> And then sunk underneath the State
> That rode him above horseman's weight."

The same idea, and almost the identical words, occur again in his "Remains," in the tale of the Cobbler and the Vicar of Bray :—

> "What's worse, old Noll is marching off,
>   And Dick, his heir apparent,
> Succeeds him in the Government,
>   A very lame vice-regent.
>
> He'll reign but little time, poor tool,
>   But sinks beneath the State,
> That will not fail to ride the fool
>   'Bove common horseman's weight."

We meet with it also in the ballad, " Old England is now a brave Barbary "—*i.e.*, horse—from a " Col-lection of Loyal Songs " reprinted in 1731, Vol. II., p. 321 :—

> " But *Noll*, a rank rider, gets first in the saddle,
>   And made her show tricks, and curvate, and rebound ;
> She quickly perceived he rode widdle-waddle,
>   And like his coach-horses,* threw his highness to ground.
>
> " Then Dick, being lame, rode holding the pummel,
>   Not having the wit to get hold of the rein ;
> But the jade did so snort at the sight of a Cromwell,
>   That poor *Dick* and his kindred turned footmen again."

"Tumble-down Dick " furnished the theme of many an old song, and it was also the name given to a dance in the last century.

In 1718, as we learn by a report in the *Original Weekly Journal*, a most brutal murder was com-mitted at the above inn.

Old (East) Brentford Church, dedicated to St. George, is perhaps the ugliest of all the ugly churches which were built in the darkest period of architectural science, the first decade of George III. It is literally a square box of bricks pierced with apertures for windows, and nothing more. It is be-pewed and be-galleried to the utmost possible extent. Its only redeeming feature is a painting over the communion-table, representing the Last Supper. It was painted for this church by Zoffany, who lived (as we have already stated) at Strand on-the-Green. It is said that the faces of the apostles were all taken from local fisher-men, except that of St. Peter, which is a portrait of Zoffany himself ; his own black slave is also introduced. Zoffany, it may be added, was a native of Frankfort-on-the-Maine, and was born in 1735. Early in life he went to Italy, where he studied painting for some years. After his return to Germany, he practised for a few years as an historical and portrait painter at Coblentz on the Rhine, from which place he came to England a few years before the foundation of the Royal Academy, as he was elected one of its first members in 1768. In England Sir Joshua Reynolds and Garrick be-came valuable patrons to him, and he painted the latter in several of his characters. He also painted portraits of George III. and other mem-bers of the royal family. About 1781 Zoffany went to India, and lived for some time at Luck-now, where he met with the greatest success, and painted many large pictures of Indian life. He returned to London about the year 1796 with a large fortune, and afterwards settled at Strand-on-the-Green.

New (West) Brentford Church, at the other end of the town, is not quite so monstrous a building, though its body dates from about the same period. The old tower still stands. It is dedicated to St. Lawrence, whose festival was the day of Brentford Fair. This church was built originally on account of the springing up of a large river-side population, who could not go two miles to "hear masse" at their own parish church. The edifice was rebuilt in 1762. John Horne Tooke was minister * here before he threw up his orders and entered Parlia-ment.

In the tower of this church is an ancient bell, supposed to be one of the earliest cast in England. The register, which dates from 1570, contains the names of two centenarians, one of them a surgeon in practice in the town. Apparently he took good care of his own health. In the year of the Great Plague the burials here were 103, the annual aver-age being about 36.

This church contains some fine monuments in

---

* In allusion to Cromwell's accident in Hyde Park in October, 1654, when his coach-horses ran away, and his highness, who was driving, fell from the box between the traces, and was dragged along a considerable distance.—See "Old and New London," Vol. IV., p. 382.

* " Brentford, the Bishopric of Parson Horne."—*Mason.*

stone and alabaster, including one in the chancel to Noy, the Attorney-General of Charles I., whose name figures in history in connection with the question of "ship-money." Noy's house, with its quaint barge-board roof, still stands close by the vicarage.

Among other persons buried here were Luke Sparks, a comedian of Covent Garden, and a friend of Quin—he spent his last years here, and died in 1768; Henry Giffard, and his wife Anna Mascella, who died in 1772 and 1777. He

1867–8, and is in the Early Decorated style of architecture, consisting of chancel, nave, aisles, tower, and a lofty spire.

The town-hall and market-house is a commodious building, and was erected in 1850.

Brentford is well stocked with works of various kinds, giving employment to a large number of hands. Here, for instance, are the gas-works, some extensive breweries and malt works, a large soap manufactory, a pottery, the Great Western Railway docks, spacious timber-yards and saw-mills.

BOSTON HOUSE. (See page 39.)
(From an old Print of 1799.)

was proprietor of the theatre in Goodman's Fields when Garrick first appeared as one of his company.

Weever, in his "Funeral Monuments," mentions here the tombs of William Clavet, who died in 1496; Christopher Caril, Norry king-at-arms (1510); Richard Parker, "servant in the butlery to Henry VIII.," and his wife Margaret, "servant to the Lady Mary's Grace." There are also monuments to the Clitherows and Spencers.

Maurice de Berkeley was a great benefactor to this parish, and the arms of Berkeley are preserved in stone on the walls of the church. Brentford, in fact, is well endowed with charities, schools, &c.

St. Paul's Church, in Old Brentford, was built in

At the entrance to the town from Ealing is a tall chimney, erected for the Grand Junction Waterworks; its height is nearly 200 feet, and it forms a conspicuous object from whichever side it is seen. There are six engines, by whose united power 12,000,000 gallons of water are propelled daily thence to the main reservoir at Paddington. Both the town and the neighbourhood are supplied from these works. The Grand Junction Canal is here brought into contact with the Thames; it passes the grounds of Osterley Park, and runs through a rich corn district near Hanwell, Norwood, Harlington, West Drayton, Cowley, and Uxbridge, to Harefield, not far from Rickmansworth, where it leaves the county. Its rise of level from Brentford to

Harefield is a little over a hundred feet. This canal was established by Act of Parliament, passed in 1793; it incorporates the Brent, rendering it navigable for upwards of a miie before it joins the Thames. The canal connects the metropolis with Warwickshire, Staffordshire, and Lancashire.

Opposite Kew Bridge is a handsome drinking-fountain, opened by the Duchess of Teck in 1879.

Brentford in former times was among the places celebrated for its "bear-baitings." It is to this knight relates the chapter of accidents which there befel him :—

> "And though you overcame the bear,
>   The dogs beat you at Brentford fair,
>   Where sturdy butchers broke your noddle."

In the second part of the same poem is told, in doggrel verse, the story of Hudibras and a French mountebank at "Brentford Fair."

Down to little more than a quarter of a century ago Brentford had a quaint old wooden market-

MRS. TRIMMER. (*See page* 40.)
(*From a Portrait in the possession of the Family.*)

place, probably, that Butler alludes in his "Hudibras," Part I., cant. 1, 677 :—

> "In western clime there is a town,
>   To those that dwell therein well known.
>
>   *   *   *   *   *
>
>   To this town people did repair
>   On days of market or of fair,
>   And to crackt fiddle and hoarse tabor
>   In merriment did trudge and labour.
>   But now a sport more formidable
>   Had raked together village rabble :
>   'Twas an odd way of recreating,
>   Which learned butchers call bear-baiting."

At all events it is probable that Brentford, to the "west" of London, is meant, especially when we remember the lines in Part II., cant. 3, where the place, with a clock-tower and a roof of high pitch, like those with which we meet in the West of England. Edward I. granted a weekly market and an annual fair on St. Lawrence's Day. After the Reformation, the profits of the market and fair were held under the Crown, but they subsequently passed into private hands. The market-place stood in the Butts, which was also the scene of the elections for Middlesex. The market-day is now on Tuesday, and fairs are held three days in May, and also three in September. The elections for Middlesex were held on Hampstead Heath till the year 1701, when they were transferred hither. They appear generally to have been conducted in a very riotous fashion, one of the most disorderly being that of 1768, when Mr. John Glynn and Sir W. B. Proctor were the candidates. "The remembrance of the famous contests of 1768 and 1769, when party feeling ran so high in favour of the popular candidate, is still kept up," writes Lysons, "by the sign of Wilkes's Head and No. 45."

Brentford is still conventionally regarded as the chief town of Middlesex for election purposes, a fact which strongly attests our innate conservatism. The nominations of the county members have taken place here "from time immemorial," and all sorts of good stories and jokes are extant respecting these elections.

Bubb Dodington writes, under date March 8th, 1749 :—"The election for the county of Middlesex. Sir Francis Dashwood, Messrs. Furnese, Breton, and I, went in Sir Francis's coach at eight o'clock to Mr. Cooke's in Lincoln's Inn Fields. A great meeting there. We set out with him about nine —my coach following—and went through Knightsbridge, Kensington, by the Gravel Pits, to Acton, and from thence to Stanwell Heath, which was the general rendezvous. From thence to Brentford Butts, which was the place of poll. It began about one. I polled early, and got to my coach, which was so wedged in that, after much delay, I found it impossible to make use of it, so that Mr. Breton and I were forced to take two of my servants' horses, with livery housings, and ride without boots ten miles to Lord Middlesex's at Walton, to meet their Royal Highnesses at dinner. . . . My coach did not arrive till nine. . . . Poll for Mr. Cooke, 1617 ; for Mr. Honywood, 1201. We carried it by 416."

Paul Whitehead thus refers to the election at Brentford :—

> "Now, nearer town, and all agog,
> They know dear London by its fog ;
> Bridges they cross, through lanes they wind,
> Leave Hounslow's dangerous heath behind ;
> Through Brentford win a passage free
> By shouting 'Wilkes and Liberty !'"

The cry of "Wilkes and Liberty!" held its ground for many a long day. Was it in order to furnish an example of the meaning of this cry that, in the election riots of 1769, when Wilkes was a candidate, the mob destroyed the poll-books, and killed one person at the hustings?

Colonel Luttrell and Wilkes were standing together on the hustings at Brentford, when Wilkes asked his adversary, privately, "whether he thought there were more fools or knaves among the large crowds of Wilkites below?" "I'll tell them what you say, and so put an end to you at once," said the colonel. Wilkes was unmoved ; and on Luttrell asking him why he felt no fear at such a threat, he replied quietly, "Because I should tell them that it was a fabrication, and they would put an end to *you*, and not to me."

Mr. J. T. Smith, in his "Book for a Rainy Day," prints the following letter from Lord North to Sir Eardley Wilmot, under date of 1st April, 1769, having reference to the candidature of Colonel Luttrell and Wilkes :—

"My friend Colonel Luttrell having informed me that many persons depending upon the Court of Common Pleas are freeholders of Middlesex, &c., not having the honour of being acquainted with you himself, desires me to apply to you for your interest with your friends in his behalf. It is manifest how much it is for the honour of Parliament, and the quiet of this country in future times, that Mr. Wilkes should have an antagonist at the next Brentford election, and that his antagonist should meet with a respectable support. The state of the country has been examined, and there is the greatest reason to believe that the Colonel will have a very considerable show of legal votes, nay, even a majority, if his friends are not deterred from appearing at the poll. It is the game of Mr. Wilkes and his friends to increase those alarms, but they cannot frighten the *candidate* from his purpose ; and I am very confident that the voters will run no risk. I hope, therefore, you will excuse this application. There is nothing, I imagine, that every true friend of this country must wish more than to see Mr. Wilkes disappointed in his projects ; and nothing, I am convinced, will defeat them more effectually than to fill up the vacant seat for Middlesex, especially if it can be done for a fair majority of legal votes. I am, Sir, with the greatest truth and respect, your most faithful, humble servant,

　　　　　　　　　　　　　　　　　　"NORTH."

The judge, in his answer, dated on the following day, observed, "It would be highly improper for me to interfere in any shape in that election."*

The author of the work above quoted mentions several humorous ballads on this subject, particularly "The Renowned History and Rare Achievements of John Wilkes." The chorus ran thus :—

> "John Wilkes he was for Middlesex,
> They chose him knight of the shire ;
> And he made a fool of Alderman Bull,
> And called Parson Horne a liar." †

The popularity of Wilkes was carried to so great an extent, that his friends in all classes displayed some article on which his effigy was portrayed, such as salad or punch bowls, ale or milk jugs, plates, dishes, and even heads of canes. The squib engravings of him, published from the commencement of his notoriety to his silent state when Chamberlain of London, would extend to several volumes. Hogarth's portrait of him, which by the collectors was considered a caricature, is recom-

---

* See the Wilmot Letters, in the British Museum.
† "Parson Horne," of course, is Mr. Horne Tooke

mended as the best likeness by those who knew him personally.

In his personal appearance Wilkes was exceedingly ill-favoured, as a glance at his portrait will show ;* and the peculiar squint which he unfortunately possessed gave rise to the epigram in "Wine and Walnuts," beginning—

"The d——l at Lincoln climbed upon the steeple,
As Wilkes did at Brentford to squint at the people."

Macfarlane, the author of the "History of George III.," was killed by the pole of a coach during one of the election processions of Sir Francis Burdett, at the entrance of the town. In fact, as the *Annual Register* of 1802 informs us, to such a state of turbulence had the inhabitants of Brentford arrived on these occasions that "it is impossible for any but those who have witnessed a Middlesex election to conceive the picture it exhibited : it was a continued scene of riot, disorder, and tumult."

A good story is told of one of the inhabitants of Brentford in the last century. Happening to be travelling in Germany, where "Electors" are, or were, not uncommon, he was called on, as he entered the gates of a town, to describe himself, after the usual manner of strangers. "I am an elector of Middlesex," he replied. The German officials, knowing that an Elector was inferior only to a king or a prince, but knowing nothing of the meaning of the term in England, immediately ordered the guards to be called out, and received him with military honours.

The only manor in this parish, according to Lysons, is that of Bordeston, or Burston, commonly called Boston, which formed part of the possessions of the convent of St. Helen's, Bishopsgate. Edward VI. granted it to the Duke of Somerset, on whose attainder it reverted to the Crown. Queen Elizabeth granted it to Robert, Earl of Leicester, who sold it in the same year to Sir Thomas Gresham. Having passed through several intermediate hands, it was bought in 1670 by James Clitherow, Esq., a merchant of London, of which he was Lord Mayor and a representative in Parliament, and in whose family it still remains. Boston House stands on gently rising ground, a little less than a mile north-west of the town. It was built partly by Lady Reade, and partly by Mr. Clitherow. About half a mile to the north a large oak-tree, called Gospel Oak, divides Brentford from Hanwell.

Sion House Academy, near Brentford, was the first school to which the poet Shelley was sent as preparatory for Eton. Even here he showed that

he was something of a philosopher, and that he had his own views on most subjects upon which boys are generally disposed to accept the opinions of others.

Wyke Farm, between Brentford and Osterley Park, was the residence of John Robinson, who rose by the favour of Lord Lonsdale from the position of a foot-boy at Lowther Castle to be M.P. for Appleby and for other places, and ultimately Secretary to the Treasury under Lord North's administration. A good story about this place is told by Mr. Serjeant Atkinson:—"King George III., in returning from the chase to Kew Palace, was obliged to ride across Wyke Farm. One day, on riding up to one of the gates, he found it locked. The king hailed a man who happened to be close by to open the gate, but the fellow was too lazy or too stupid to go out of his way to oblige a stranger. 'Come, come,' said the king, 'open the gate, my man !' 'Nae, ye maun gang aboot,' was the reply. 'Gang aboot, indeed !' said His Majesty. 'Open the gate at once ; I'm the king !' 'Why, may be,' said the chap, 'ye may be the king, but ye maun gang aboot for all that.' And sure enough His Majesty was obliged to ride round nearly the whole enclosure of Osterley Park. In the afternoon Mr. Robinson, who had been away in London, returned home, and heard of the king's disappointment. He at once ordered his carriage, and drove over post haste to Kew to offer his apologies. He was admitted without ceremony, as usual, and the king, in answer to his apologies, merely replied, 'Ah ! I wish I had such fine honest fellows in my pay as your old "gang aboot." Tell him from me that I like his honesty, and shall be glad to see him here some day.' Mr. Robinson was at once put at his ease ; and as for the man, he soon found out a more direct way than all round Osterley Park to Kew, where he was kindly received by the good-natured king. It is said that His Majesty never saw Robinson afterwards without making tender inquiries after 'Old Gang Aboot.'"

Among the former residents of Brentford was Mr. Pitt, the grandfather of the first Earl of Chatham. He is said to have been the son of a tradesman in a small way here, and his son's name is handed down to us by Pope in connection with what was known as the "Pitt diamond."

Pope is supposed to allude, in a well-known passage in the third epistle on his "Moral Essays," to this diamond, a gem brought to this country by Thomas Pitt, Governor of Madras, about 1700. Mr. Pitt purchased this celebrated diamond, which goes by his name, for £20,400, and sold it to the King of France for more than five times that sum.

---

* See "Old and New London," Vol. I., p. 420.

It was then reckoned the largest jewel in Europe, and weighed 127 carats. When polished it was as big as a pullet's egg; the cuttings amounted in value to eight or ten thousand pounds. It was placed among the crown jewels of France, and afterwards adorned the sword of state of Napoleon. The report that Mr. Pitt had obtained this diamond by dishonourable means was very general; and he was at last induced to publish a narrative of the circumstances connected with its purchase. The affair of the Pitt diamond may have suggested the incident of the stolen gem to Pope; but the whole episode appears fanciful, and the history of Sir Balaam and his family is highly improbable.

At Brentford lived for many years Mrs. Trimmer, so well known by her writings for young persons in the time of our parents and grandparents. She helped largely the thread of education here. This lady was the daughter of a Mr. Joshua Kirby, of Ipswich, and was born in 1741. Her father was a clever draughtsman, and held for some time the appointment of "tutor in perspective" to the Prince of Wales, afterwards George III. Miss Kirby was married at the age of twenty-one to Mr. Trimmer. Her literary labours commenced about the year 1780, the first of her published works being a small volume entitled "An Easy Introduction to the Knowledge of Nature." She died in 1810, very suddenly, in the arm-chair which she used generally to occupy in her study in the house in Windmill Lane, where she had resided for many years.

The parish rates of Brentford, it is said, in former times, were mainly supported by the profits of public sports and diversions, especially at Whitsuntide. If this story be true, the good people of Brentford, in spite of the dull situation of their town, must have been a jolly set of good fellows. Among the sports here referred to were such amusements as "hocking" and "pigeon-holes." These are constantly mentioned among the entries in the "chapel-wardens'" account books of the seventeenth century. At a vestry meeting held here in 1621, several articles were agreed upon with regard to the management of the "parish stock" by the chapel-wardens. The preamble, which is quoted by Lysons, states that "the inhabitants had for many years been accustomed to have meetings at Whitsuntide, in their churchhouse and other places there, in friendly manner, to eat and drink together, and liberally to spend their monies, to the end neighbourly society might be maintained; and also a common stock raised for the repairs of the church, ...intaining of orphans, placing poor children in ser .;e, and

defraying other charges;" which stock not having been properly applied, it was ordered that a particular account should be given from year to year of their gains at those times, and the manner of the expenditure. In the "accoumpts for the Whitsontide ale, 1624," the "gains" are thus set forth :—

		£	s	d
Imprimis, cleared by the pigeon-holes	.	£4	19	0
,, ,, by hocking	. . .	7	3	7
,, ,, by riffeling	. . .	2	0	0
,, ,, by victualling	. .	8	0	2
		£22	2	9

The "riffeling" here mentioned is synonymous with "raffling." The hocking occurs almost every year till 1640, when it appears to have dropped. It was collected at Whitsuntide.

	£	s	d
1618 Gained with hocking at Whitsuntide	£16	12	3

Other curious entries in the account books, evidently bearing upon the public sports and pastimes of Brentford, are as follows :—

	£	s	d
1620 Paid for 6 boules	£0	0	8
,, for 6 tynn tokens . . .	0	0	6
,, for a pair of pigeon-holes .	0	1	6
1621 Paid to her that was Lady at Whitsontide by consent	0	5	0
,, to Goodwife Ansell for the pigeon-holes	0	1	6
,, for the games	1	1	0
1623 Received for the maypole . . .	1	4	0
1628 Paid for a drumbe, stickes, and case .	0	16	0
,, for 2 heads for the drumbe . .	0	2	8
1629 Received of Robert Bicklye for the use of our games	0	2	0
,, of the said R. B. for a silver bar which was lost at Elyng . . .	0	3	6
1634 Paid for the silver games . . .	0	11	8
1643 Paid to Thomas Powell for pigeon–holes	0	2	0

Among other articles of church furniture in the hands of the chapel-wardens in 1653 was "one little collar, a bell, one little bowl, and a pin of silver."

There are other singular entries in the account-books, as follows :—

	£	s	d
1621 Paid for a beast for the parish use . .	£2	6	8
,, Given to the French chapel by consent .	1	0	0
1625 For a coffin to draw the infected corpses .	0	8	8
1633 Given to a Knts. son in Devonshire, being out of meanes	0	0	6
,, Paid for a book of sporting allowed on Sundaies	0	0	6
1634 Paid Robt. Warden, the constable, which he disbursed for conveying away the witches	0	11	0
1688 Paid for a "Declaration of Liberty of Conscience"	0	1	0
,, For a form of prayer for the Dutch not landing	0	1	0
,, For a thanksgiving for deliverance from Popery	0	1	0

The two last entries immediately follow each other.

CHAPTER IV.

HESTON, ISLEWORTH, AND SION HOUSE.

Osterley Park—Sir Thomas Gresham visited by Queen Elizabeth—Lord Desmond—The Manor of Heston—Heston Church—The Soil—Sir Joseph Banks and Anthony Collins residents here—Isleworth—Its Etymology—The River Cran—Sion House—Vicissitudes of the Nuns of St. Bridget—The Rule of the Order of St. Bridget—Early History of the Monastery—The Wardrobes of the Nuns—The Duties of the Abbess, Cellaress, &c.—Dissolution of the Monastery—Touching History of the Sisterhood—Remains of the Monastery—Katherine Howard a Prisoner here—Funeral of Henry VIII.—Building of Sion House—The Family of Percy, Dukes of Northumberland—The Princess of Denmark at Sion House—Description of the Building—The Gardens and Grounds—The Parish of Isleworth—Descent of the Manor—The Parish Church—Charitable Institutions—Church of St. John the Baptist—Brentford Union—Gumley House—Kendal House—Lacy House—Royal Naval Female School—Silver Hall—Gordon House—Sir Clipesby Crewe—Worton Hall—Syon Hill—Honnor's Home—London International College—Spring Grove.

A LITTLE to the north-west of Brentford, in the parish of Heston, lies Osterley Park. The estate, which now belongs to the Earl of Jersey, was formerly the property of Sir Thomas Gresham, the great merchant of Elizabeth's reign, and founder of the Royal Exchange. He began to re-build the manor-house about the year 1570, when the estate was granted to him by the Crown. Norden, who published his "Survey of Middlesex" in 1596, says, in the quaint language of the period :—"Osterley, the house nowe of the Lady Gresham, a faire and stately building of bricke, erected by Sir Thomas Gresham, knight, citizen, and marchant adventurer of London, and finished about anno 1577. It standeth in a parke by him also impaled, well wooded, and garnished with manie faire ponds, which affordeth not only fish and fowle, as swanes and other water-fowle, but also a great rise for milles, as paper milles, oyle milles, and corn milles, all which are now decayed, a corn mille only excepted. In the same parke was a faire heronrie, for the increase and preservation whereof sundry allurements were devised and set up, fallen all to ruin."

Gresham had no fewer than four or five stately mansions in Norfolk ; but of these his favourite and chief residence was Intwood House, or, as he always called it, his "poor house at Intwood." Besides these, he had in his latter years this estate of Osterley, a magnificent old place (Mayfield) in Sussex, and apparently one or two houses in other parts of the kingdom, in which he occasionally resided.

In 1578 Queen Elizabeth visited Sir Thomas Gresham at Osterley Park, and was there entertained in a very sumptuous manner. "The Devises of Warre, and a Play at Awsterley, her Highness being at Sir Thomas Gresham's," is the title of a pamphlet mentioned by Lysons as having been published by Churchyard ; Lysons adding that it is "not known to be now (1795) extant." Fuller tells the following story of Queen Elizabeth's visit to Osterley :—"Her Majesty having given it as her opinion that the court before the house would look better divided with a wall, Sir Thomas Gresham in the night sent for workmen to London, who so speedily and so silently performed their task, that before morning the wall was finished, to the great surprise of the queen and her courtiers, one of whom, however, observed that it was no wonder that he who could build a Change should so soon change a building ; whilst others (reflecting on some known differences in this knight's family) affirmed that any house is easier divided than united."

From certain minutes in the Privy Council books of the period, it appears that some of Gresham's park-paling at Osterley was burned while the queen was there ; that Her Majesty being very much offended, commanded that the offenders should be searched out and punished ; and that shortly after four individuals were committed to the Marshalsea prison, charged with the offence. The same industrious investigator has further discovered that Gresham's great enclosure at Osterley was very unpopular, and that complaints were laid against him by sundry poor men for having enclosed certain common ground, to the prejudice of the poor.

The author of the "Life of Sir Thomas Gresham," in Knight's "Weekly Volumes for all Readers," observes that "it is not wealth that always makes the best temple for the household gods, and neither wealth nor caution could keep sorrow and sickness and fears out of this splendid mansion. In the year 1570 one of Gresham's servants fell sick of the plague in Osterley House, upon which the knight and his family fled in great dismay into Sussex."

In most of his places Gresham would seem to have sought, with more success than most persons, how to unite his profit and his pleasure. At Osterley he had within the circuit of his park both oil-mills and corn-mills, and also a paper-mill—the latter, it is said, being his own device of the first mill of that kind set up in this country. And besides this, he made himself useful to his royal mistress in a variety of ways, acting occasionally as one of Her Majesty's gaolers, or keepers of State prisoners ; for as money was saved by such an arrangement, it became a common practice with

Elizabeth thus to quarter her State prisoners, or those whom she wished to keep under her own control, upon her nobles and the richer gentry, making them personally answerable in case of their cage-birds escaping. Thus it appears that the Lady Mary Grey, the sister of Lady Jane, was for some time an inmate of Osterley Park. Upon one occasion, the knight and his wife would fain know what they are to do with my Lady Mary, "trusting that now Her Majesty would be so good as to remove her"—that is, send her to some other gentleman. But all was in vain; the queen seems to have thought that her captive could not be in safer or better keeping, and—sometimes in the London

herself in her captivity and grief with reading. As some of her books were French, and one or two Italian, it may be presumed that she knew those languages, and that, like her eldest sister, the Lady Jane Grey, she was an accomplished person.

Sir Thomas Gresham died in the following year (1579), and on the decease of his wife, to whom it had been left, the property was inherited by Sir William Read, her son by a former marriage. Soon after Lady Gresham's death, Lord Chief Justice Coke (then Attorney-General) appears to have been a resident at Osterley. One of his children was christened in the chapel there on the 3rd of January, 1597. George, Earl of Desmond, and his Countess

OSTERLEY PARK.

house, and sometimes at Osterley Park—the Lady Mary continued to reside with the Greshams from the month of June, 1569, to the end of 1572.

It should be explained that, alarmed at her sister's sufferings for having contracted a match with one of the highest nobles in the land, the Lady Mary had privately married a plebeian youth, named Keys; and that for this offence, and for this only, the unfortunate lady was detained in custody by the jealous queen, who apparently would allow of no marriages, whether high or low, among her kinsfolk and acquaintance. The poor woman died in 1578, in the parish of St. Botolph, Aldersgate, having outlived her husband only seven years. In Osterley she enjoyed a splendid residence, at once a palace and a prison; but she finished her days in poverty, leaving little behind her, except a few trinkets and a score or two of books. She appears to have been very fond of her books, and to have solaced

(who was one of the co-heirs to the estate) resided at Osterley for several years. Lysons, in his "Environs of London," tells a very remarkable story of this couple, on the authority of the "Strafford Letters:"—"Young Desmond (says Mr. Garrard, writing to Lord Wentworth), who married one of the co-heirs of Sir Michael Stanhope, came one morning to York House, where his wife had long lived with the duchess during his two years' absence beyond the seas, and hurried her away, half-undressed, much against her will, into a coach, and so carried her away into Leicestershire. At Brickhill he lodged, where she, in the night, put herself into milkmaid's clothes, and had likely to make her escape, but was discovered. Madam Christian, whom your lordship knows, said that my Lord of Desmond was the first that ever she heard of that ran away with his own wife. Modern times, however, have furnished a parallel. Lady Desmond's adventure was in 1635. It was about four years afterwards that she and the earl came to Osterley, where she bore him a numerous family."

After a few more changes of ownership, the manor was sold about the year 1655 to the famous Parliamentary General, Sir William Waller, who was resident at Osterley in the year 1657, and who died in 1668. Later on, the property belonged to Mr. Francis Child, the banker of Fleet Street, who rebuilt Osterley House, with the exception of the old turrets, and from whom it passed to his

The staircase of the house, as left by Mr. Child, was ornamented with a fine painting, by Rubens, of the Apotheosis of William III., Prince of Orange, brought from Holland by Sir Francis Child. The picture-gallery is forty yards in length, and contains some choice works. The mansion formerly contained a large and valuable collection of books, Mr. Child having purchased the whole library of Mr. Brian Fairfax, and a printed catalogue of the same was drawn up by Dr. Morell in 1771. In 1879 the

HESTON.

brother Robert, who completed the work, and fitted up the interior with great taste and magnificence. Mr. Robert Child's granddaughter, Lady Sarah Sophia Fane, daughter of the tenth Earl of Westmoreland, conveyed the estate in marriage to the fifth Earl of Jersey, grandfather of the present earl, who does not, however, reside here.

Osterley House is a large, square, red-brick building, and stands in an extensive park, in which is a lake covering several acres. Lady Ducie, a former occupant of the mansion, established in the garden a menagerie, containing a large collection of rare birds, which was, however, dispersed on the death of her ladyship. At the end of the last century an artist at Southall published in monthly numbers a series of coloured prints of the rare and curious birds from this menagerie.

building was greatly damaged by an outbreak of fire.

The village of Heston, about half a mile westward from Osterley Park, is situated on the cross-road between the main roads leading from London to Uxbridge and Staines. It was in ancient times annexed to the manor of Isleworth; and it appears by an inquisition taken after the death of Edmund, Earl of Cornwall, in the year 1300, that he died seised of that manor. The parish church, dedicated to St. Leonard, is a modern edifice, having been built in 1866. It is a stone structure, consisting of nave, aisles, and chancel, and was erected in the place of an ancient edifice, the tower of which alone was left standing, and which, although very old, is in a fair state of preservation. The old church, which was built principally of flints, comprised a nave and two aisles, and a double chancel. There were in it a few ancient monuments, but none of any public interest.

The church of Heston was given at a very early period to the monks of St. Valerie, in Picardy, to whom it was confirmed by Henry II. In 1391 the Prior of St. Valerie granted the rectory and advowson to the Warden and Fellows of Winchester College, whose successors surrendered it to the Crown in 1544. Queen Elizabeth, however, granted them to Bishop Grindall and his successors in the see of London. The parish registers date back to 1560, but during the last century they were very imperfectly kept up. From the entries of burials in 1665, it appears that the effects of the Great Plague of London were felt as far westward as Heston, for no less than thirteen persons are said to have died of the plague in this parish during that year.

The soil of this parish is, in general, a strong loam, and is noted for producing wheat of a very fine quality—the finest, at all events, in Middlesex. Camden speaks of it as having, long before his time, furnished the royal table with bread ; and Norden, who bears the same testimony to its superior quality, says it was reported that Queen Elizabeth had " the manchets for her highness's own diet " from Heston.

Among the persons of eminence who have lived at Heston may be mentioned the learned and accomplished philosopher, and founder of the Linnæan Society, Sir Joseph Banks, of whom a biographical sketch will be found in the pages of OLD AND NEW LONDON.* He lived for some time at Smallbury Green, in this parish, probably in order to be near Kew, Chiswick, and Ealing. Anthony Collins, a deistical writer of some note in the seventeenth century, was born at Heston in 1676.

Isleworth adjoins Heston on the south; the boundary line between the two parishes, however, has not always been clearly defined, possibly from the bounds not having been beaten as regularly as they might have been ; at all events, Lysons, in his " Environs," gives an account of a fray and dispute, which arose between the parishioners of Isleworth and of Heston in " beating the bounds " on a Rogation Day. Heston and Isleworth now, for educational and drainage purposes, together form a Local Board district, which includes the town of Hounslow. Isleworth is a large parish on the banks of the Thames, immediately westward of Brentford. It is a place of great antiquity, being mentioned in Domesday Book as " Ghistelworde." The name was afterwards spelt in various ways, as

Yhistelworth, Istelworth, and Thistelworth, the last-mentioned spelling being in vogue in Queen Elizabeth's time, and even used by Pope ; but for the last two centuries it has been usually spelt Isleworth.

Lysons suggests that Skinner's derivation of the etymology of Islington, from *Gisel*, a hostage, and *tun*, a town, might more justly, with the alteration of *tun* for *worth*, a village, be applied to this place ; for it does not appear that Islington in any ancient record is called Giselton, or Gistelton, but Isendune. " The most general idea of its derivation," he adds, " has been suggested by the modern name *Isleworth*; but I think that the constant usage of Istelworth for so many centuries leads one to seek for some other etymology, though perhaps it might be difficult to find one which would be entirely satisfactory." Might not its derivation be found in *Ise*, or *Isis*, which was a common Celtic name for a river, and *worth*, which in Anglo-Saxon is said to denote a nook of land between two rivers ? Gibson, however, regards *worth* as signifying a farmhouse. When scholars disagree, who is to decide ?

It was by Saxon husbandry and labour that Isleworth, Twickenham, &c., were reclaimed, enclosed, and improved. Before the reign of Henry III., the site now covered by Isleworth and its adjacent towns was part of the forest, or warren, of Staines. It extended from the river Brent to Staines, and even to the banks of the Coln, a little further west. It was disafforested in 1227. Very slight mention of this village is made in English history. It is, however, recorded that in 1263 Simon de Montfort and the other refractory barons pitched their tents in Isleworth Park ; and that four centuries later— namely, in August, 1647—General Fairfax fixed his head-quarters here at the head of the Parliamentary army.

The river Cran, or Crane, which rises in the neighbourhood of Harrow, falls into the Thames at this place, having been augmented by an artificial cut from the Colne, made in bygone times by the abbess and convent of the monastery of Sion, for the convenience of their water-mills.

Sion, or Syon House, the seat of the Duke of Northumberland, occupies the site of the above-mentioned monastery, and is situated at the south-eastern angle of the parish. The monastery—the original site of which appears to have been in the adjoining parish of Twickenham—was founded by King Henry V. in 1415, for the accommodation of sixty sisters and twenty-five brothers belonging to the order of St. Bridget, a modified branch of the order of St. Augustine. This religious house, together with its twin monastery at Sheen—for such

---

* See Vol. III., p. 191.

it really was—is the subject of an allusion by Shakespeare in his play of *Henry V.*, where the king says:—

> "Five hundred poor have I in yearly pay,
> Who twice a day their withered hands hold up
> Towards heaven to pardon blood; and I have built
> Two chantries, where the sad and solemn priests
> Sing still for Richard's soul."

The dedication stone was laid by the king in February, 1416. The dimensions of the premises on which the convent stood are thus stated in an ancient record, quoted by Lysons:—The length, towards the river, 2,820 feet; towards Twickenham Field, 1,938 feet; the breadth on one side was 980 feet, and on the other 960 feet. The building itself would appear to have been very small, and insufficient for the accommodation of the inmates; for within eighteen years of the foundation of the monastery—namely, in 1431—permission was granted to the abbess and the holy community to remove to a more spacious edifice, which they had built upon their demesnes within the parish of Isleworth.

The Rev. J. H. Blunt, in his Introduction to "The Myroure of oure Ladye," formerly belonging to the ladies of this convent, and written specially for its use, states that Sion was the most important monastery founded in England during the 180 years preceding the Reformation. Be this, however, as it may, there can be no doubt that it stood at the head of convents for females, both in respect of its wealth, its learning, and its piety, and that for at all events a century and a quarter it enjoyed an "exceedingly prosperous" existence. When it was suppressed by Henry VIII. its net annual income was assessed at a sum equivalent to about £20,000 of our money, an income exceeded by only Westminster, Glastonbury, Clerkenwell, St. Alban's, Gloucester, Croyland, and Pershore, and larger than that of the great Benedictine monasteries of Canterbury, Durham, or Winchester. Cobbett, in his "History of the Reformation," gives the value of this house, at the Dissolution, as £1,944, and reckons that in the middle of the present century it would have been worth £38,891.

It was the custom with our sovereigns, soon after their accession, to found one or more religious houses for the benefit of the souls of their predecessors—and their own at the same time. In pursuance of this custom, Henry V. gave up part of his manors of Sheen (Richmond) and Isleworth for the foundation of a house of Carthusian monks at the former place, and of a house of nuns of the order of St. Bridget at the latter. The order of St. Bridget, according to Mr. Blunt, was founded

by that Swedish princess and saint at Watstein, in the diocese of Lincopen, about the year 1344, and it owed its introduction into England to the marriage of Eric XIII. of Sweden with Philippa, daughter of our Henry IV., some of the Swedish sisters having been sent over for that purpose in 1415. In the March of the following year a charter in their favour was signed by the king, defining their duties: "to celebrate Divine service for ever, for our healthful estate while we live, and for our soul when we shall have departed this life, and for the souls of our most dear lord and father, Henry, late King of England, and Mary, his late wife, our most dear mother; also for the souls of John, late Duke of Lancaster, our grandfather, and Blanche, his late wife, our grandmother, and of other our progenitors, and of all the faithful departed." It was also decreed that the house should be called "the Monastery of St. Saviour and St. Bridget of Syon," but the name of St. Mary was commonly inserted subsequently between those of the Saviour and St. Bridget. "The buildings there and then commenced," we are told, "were situate near Twickenham, occupying a site which stretched for about half a mile along the river's bank, and about a third of that distance into the meadows."

The "Monastery," as stated above, was to consist of eighty-five persons: sixty sisters—of whom one was to preside as abbess—and twenty-five professed brothers. Of the latter, thirteen were to be priests, four deacons, and eight lay brothers, employed as sextons, gardeners, &c. The priests were to say and sing mass daily in the chapel for the nuns, and were to take turns with them also in saying the "offices," each seven times daily, so that the voice of praise and prayer was hardly ever silent within its walls. The choirs of the chapel were double, the two aisles being screened off from each other by a thick screen, or parclose, and there was no access from the one to the other, except only for the priests on their way to say mass at the altars. The monks and the sisters each also occupied a separate court.

"This double community," writes Mr. Blunt, "was in reality a combination, for purposes of Divine service, of two separate bodies, each of which had its own conventual buildings separately enclosed. Their two chapels were under the same roof, being, in fact, a double chancel, each with its separate stalls, and opening into each other by a 'grate,' or 'grille,' the gate of which was unlocked only for the entrance and departure of the clergy when they said mass at the altar of the sisters' chapel. The only other door of communication was one used at the profession of novices, which was in the sisters' cloister. To this there were two keys, differing from each other, one kept in a chest on the brothers' side, and the other in a similar chest on the sisters' side. To each of these chests there were three keys, none of the keys being alike, and these were kept by the abbess and two 'sistres that have drede of God on the one side, and by the Confessor-general and two brothers on the other, th at so al occasion of sclaunder be vtterly take away both outwarde and inwarde' by means of such precaution."

The rule of St. Bridget was, as above stated, a modified form of the Augustinian rule, to which that saint gave the name of the Saviour, in the belief that it had been communicated to her by our Lord Himself. We have fortunately this rule in existence, a translation of it into English by Richard Whitford, who styles himself in all humility "The Witch of Syon," having been printed by Wynkyn de Worde in 1525. It will be found *in extenso* in Aungier's "History of Isleworth." It is the most valuable record of monasticism that has come down to us, and it shows us the inner working of cloistered life. Additions to the rules of the monastery of Sion are preserved in the library of St. Paul's Cathedral. They were found some few years ago by the Rev. R. H. Barham, the well-known author of the "Ingoldsby Legends." The copy in the British Museum is imperfect.

We find an interesting sketch of Sion in Professor Burrows's "Worthies of All Souls." From this book we learn that it was founded by Henry V., by the advice of Archbishop Chicheley, afterwards the founder of All Souls College at Oxford. At its opening Chicheley officiated, as archbishop. The convent was endowed, like All Souls, by the Crown, out of the estates of suppressed alien priories, and as it was one of the latest mediæval foundations, so also it was one of the most aristocratic. Its monastic life under the rule of St. Austin (as then lately reformed by St. Bridget, Queen of Spain), its royal patronage, its great wealth, its beautiful position on the Thames at Isleworth, as well as its vast staff of eighty-five " religious," in honour of the thirteen apostles and the seventy-two disciples, made it a natural ally of the favoured college at Oxford so munificently dedicated by Chicheley to the memory of the princes of the House of Lancaster. "No doubt scholars of the one became chaplains of the other, and no doubt many a nun of Sion was to be found as a pilgrim making her offerings at the glittering shrine of All Souls. . . . But now, under Henry VIII., the crash came. While the college was spared, the nunnery of Sion found its way into

the hands of the Dukes of Northumberland, with whom it has ever since remained, and the nuns set forth on their toilsome wanderings abroad. The stout English spirit in their gentle blood forbade them to give way without a struggle, and their struggle was one of the most gallant and prolonged on record. It lasted three hundred years. After the failure of their fond attempts to settle near their own land in the Low Countries and in France, they eventually found a home at Lisbon, still keeping their English nationality through all vicissitudes. In the seventeenth century their convent was destroyed by fire, but that did not daunt them. They diligently begged for alms, and re-built their nest. Again their new abode was levelled to the ground in the famous earthquake of the seventeenth century, and again it was re-built. But what fire and earthquake had failed to effect was brought about by the Peninsular War. When Lisbon became the head-quarters of our army, the convent became the English hospital, and the forlorn relic of the sisterhood, consisting of nine English ladies, made their way back to their own land once more in 1810." We learn from Bandinel's edition of Dugdale that in 1825 two or three of them were still alive in the vicinity of the Staffordshire Potteries.

But to return to the early history of the house. The royal charter having been supplanted by a papal bull from Martin V. in A.D. 1418, the first profession of novices took place in the new building before Archbishop Chicheley, on April 21st, 1420. It would seem that some of the first sisters, and also of the brethren, were very naturally Swedes. Shortly before his death, in 1422, their royal founder conveyed to his favourite convent the whole of his manor of Isleworth, which had previously belonged to the Duchy of Cornwall; and his successor enriched them with broad lands in half the counties of England, chiefly from the spoils of the alien priories. Thus enriched, the community began to find their original quarters too narrow, and therefore obtained from the Crown a licence to erect new buildings a little further to the east on their demesne, the site, as already shown, being that of the present palace of the Duke of Northumberland. Here their new chapel was begun in 1426, the first stone being laid by the Regent John, Duke of Bedford, who gave a "cramp-ring" to each sister, and a handsome set of office-books for the use of the new chapel.

Five years later, in 1431, the sisters received from Henry VI. letters patent, giving them full licence to remove to their new abode without hindrance to their original rights and privileges.

They made their removal on November 11th, the feast of St. Martin, when their new chapel was consecrated, in the presence of Humphrey, Duke of Gloucester.

"From this time forward," writes Mr. Blunt, "the 'Daughters of Syon' appear to have remained in tranquil possession of their beautiful river-side home and of their lands, which were distributed over the country, from St. Michael's Mount to Windermere." He adds that if their income reached a sum representing the present value of £20,000 a year, this would give £250 for each member of the community. "How this large income was expended there is no evidence to show," he continues; "but the character of the Sion community suggests that it would neither be wasted nor spent in self-indulgence; but one longs for the discovery of their account-books."

The abbess, as the superioress was styled, was a dignified female ecclesiastic, and was called in her house the "Reverend Mother." She was elected by the sisters alone; and if they were unanimous, the election was said to be by the Holy Ghost. The choice was, however—whether divinely sanctioned or not—subject to the confirmation of the Bishop of London. The title of "sovereign," given to the abbess in the formal rule of the house, shows that, although elective, her power was somewhat absolute; and it is on record that she administered a variety of punishments to her novices and to the professed sisters, in case of rebellion or wilful contempt of the regulations of the house. A list of the abbesses from the foundation of the convent down to its dissolution and its final dispersion will be seen in Mr. Blunt's book. Agnes Jordan, who was the last but one, is commemorated on a brass in Denham Church, near Uxbridge, where she lies buried. Catherine Palmer, the last, who held the office under Mary, lived till 1576. Figures of these brasses are given in Aungier's "History," already quoted.

Next to the abbess was the prioress, and under her, again, the treasuress and under-treasuress, who had charge of the "temporal goods." On this subject a writer observes:—"They had a great chest, with two different locks and keys, each one keeping a key, so that nothing could be put into the chest or taken therefrom without the knowledge and consent of both. This was 'to put away all affection of covetousness and all occasion of suspicion of evil.' Another of their duties, in the absence of the abbess, was to attend to all such business as involved interviews with strangers, farmers, and others. We can well imagine what important personages these two sisters would become in the estimation of the rest of the community. Separated from the outer world, but not without some interest in it—for had they not fathers and brothers?—the treasuress would be the means of communication between them and what was passing in England during the stormy years of Henry VI., Edward IV., and onward to the end. The estates of the monastery were scattered over the country, from St. Michael's Mount to Windermere. Its annual income amounted to over twenty thousand pounds of our money, so that the 'farmers and other persons' who had business to transact with the recluses of Isleworth would come from all parts, and would bring details of the sanguinary encounters at Barnet or Towton, or Wakefield or Bosworth; while others, nearer home, would no doubt convey whispers of dark deeds said to have been committed in the Tower and elsewhere during the terrible War of the Roses. And then, when Henry VIII. began to be worried by 'domestic troubles,' we can easily understand how these good sisters, in their hours of recreation, would sit round and chat about Queen Catherine, Queen Anne, and the rest of the queens of that generation, and how some would sympathise with one, and some with another. Happy sisters! they were spared all the active sorrows of that troublous time, but were, no doubt, vexed with other, if minor, cares."

The chamberess had duties peculiarly of a feminine nature, having charge of the "clothes, lynin, laces, poyntes, nedelles, threde, and the sewing and repairing of them, and keeping of them from wormes."

From an ancient record, quoted by Mr. Blunt we obtain a curious insight into the wardrobes of the "Daughters of Syon." It is confirmed by another document, preserved in the Record Office, namely, the "Account of Dame Bridget Belgrave," who was chamberess in 1536-7, and who appears not only to have provided all articles of apparel for the sisters, but to have bought no less than twenty-three pairs of spectacles—doubtless for the use of those whose eyesight was not as perfect as it once was—besides large supplies of "pynnes of dyuerse sortes" and "tagging of poyntes," and to have paid for the grinding of razors for the brethren. Among the articles mentioned in her account are "russettes, kerseys, soope (soap), holand and other lynen cloth, bristelles, nedilles, thymbilles, cappes, shethes, coverlettes," &c. Another important personage in the monastic community was the cellaress, whose duty it was to provide the sisters with such inward comforts as they might require, "the meat and drink for sick and whole, and for the servants who lived in the house, as well as for those who lived outside, and for the strangers who not unfrequently stayed as guests at the monastery." It is pleasant to note that in all their arrangements, both of kitchen, cellar, and treasury, there was a desire to live sensibly and soberly, neither despising the good things of this life nor yet abusing them; and in all these were the care and refinement suitable to those who

list of the live-stock belonging to the sisterhood. The list includes the following " catall "—2 bulles, 20 keen (kine), 6 oxen, 4 heyfers, 5 wayners, 122 shepe, wedders (wethers), ewes, 5 lambes. The swyne were as follows—6 boores, 12 sowes, 25 hogges, and 21 wayners. The cellaress, it appears, was authorised to charge for " expences at London," " rewardes to the servantes at Cristemas with their aprons," " sede " for the garden.

THE OLD STABLES AT SION HOUSE. (See p. 50.)
(From Aungier's " History of Isleworth.")

did not cease to be English ladies when they became "Daughters of Syon," as they were usually designated.

The duties of the cellaress, however, would appear not to have been limited to the cellar of the house. She acted as purveyor-general, and not only bought and purveyed very many of the stores necessary for her fifty-nine sisters, but sold much of the produce of the estate. In the " accompte " of Dame Agnes Merett, cellaress in the year before the Dissolution, occur entries of " calve - skynnes " and " felles solde," besides " woode "—which seems to have fetched a good price. This account, which may still be seen in the Public Record Office, is interesting as giving a

" cover-lettes," sack-cloth, " cord," and " candill rushes."

The general superintendence of the sisters was in the hands of the prioress and four assistants, called " serchers," who are ordered to " have a good eye about" the house, and to see that order and silence are kept. The sisters of Syon, like those of most other religious orders, used to administer the discipline, not only to offenders against the rules of the house, but to each other at stated times, for their spiritual good. " Such exercises of those who live a cloistered life," remarks Mr. Blunt, " must not be criticised too closely by those whose life moves in a less narrow circle."

" The arrangement of the sisters' meals was that

SION HOUSE, FROM THE SOUTH.

of a high table and side tables, such as were then and long after common in the halls of bishops and great houses in the country, and such as may still be observed in colleges and public schools and inns of court. They were waited on by lay-sisters, or servitors, and there was a care and refinement about the arrangement of meals, such as befitted those who had not ceased to be ladies when they became nuns." The viands consisted of soups or "potages," sundry "metes, of flesche and of fysche, one fresche, another powdred boyled, or rosted, or otherwise dyghte after her discrecion, and after the day, tyme and nede requyreth, as the market and purse wyll stretche." Their drink was on some days water, on others ale, and the dinner was garnished with "two maner of froytes (fruits) at leste, yf it may be, that is to say, apples, peres, or nuttes, plummes, chiryes, benes, peson, or any such other." Some few trifling luxuries were allowed to those in weak health; and the Rules of the Saviour and of St. Austin were read aloud during meals by one of the sisters who acted as legister. It was the practice of the house—though its inmates were women—to keep silence, except at specified times, in every part of it.

A munificent endowment was provided for the monastery of Sion, the king, its founder, granting for its sustentation a thousand marks out of the revenues of the Exchequer, until other revenues should be provided; and at the dissolution the income of Sion amounted to the then considerable sum of £1,731 per annum.

Thomas Stanley, the second Earl of Derby, was buried within its precincts in 1521, a few years before its dissolution, which happened in 1532. Sion was one of the first of the larger monasteries that was suppressed, the convent having been accused of harbouring the king's enemies, and of being in collusion with Elizabeth Barton, the "Holy Maid of Kent." Henry VIII., indeed, is said to have selected this convent as an object of especial vengeance, as it was accused of affording an asylum to his "enemies." It was through the confessor of the convent at Sion that the monks of the Charterhouse in London were led to subscribe to the supremacy of Henry VIII., many of them having for a time refused to subscribe to the King's supremacy. Be this as it may, however, one of the monks of Sion, and also the Vicar of Isleworth, suffered at Tyburn along with Houghton, the prior of the Charterhouse.

After the dissolution the lands of the Sion sisterhood were sold or granted away by the Crown, but the house and its immediate domain were retained as the property of the sovereign.

The subsequent history of the sisterhood is touching and sad. They retired at first to a Bridgetine convent at Dermond, in Flanders. For two short years, at the end of Queen Mary's reign, they returned to their ancient home; but on the accession of Elizabeth, their sufferings recommenced. They again had to fly for refuge abroad, and found again a home with their Flemish sisters. After many changes of residence, and after undergoing great poverty, they were at last established in a new Sion, on the banks of the Tagus, at Lisbon, in the year 1594. Here they still remain after the lapse of nearly three centuries, restricting their membership entirely to English sisters, and still retaining the keys of their old home in the hope, never yet abandoned by them, of eventually returning to it. It is said that some half century or more ago, when they were visited at Lisbon by the then Duke of Northumberland, they told his Grace the story of having carried their keys with them through all their changes of fortune and abode, and that they were still in hopes of seeing their English home again. "But," quietly remarked his Grace, "the locks have been altered since those keys were in use." A full account of the wanderings of the sisters from Flanders to Rouen, and from thence to Lisbon, and their subsequent history, will be found in Aungier's "History and Antiquities of Isleworth."

It may be said, however, that though several ineffectual attempts have been made to revive the life of the Bridgetines in England—as at Peckham, in Surrey; at Newcastle, in Staffordshire; and at Spettisbury, in Dorsetshire—the "Sion" of Lisbon remains the real and legitimate representation of the "Sion" of Isleworth.

The nuns reckoned among their most remarkable treasures the original Martyrologium of Sion; the Deed of Restoration, signed by Queen Mary in 1557, and endorsed by Cardinal Pole; some curious seals and a silver bell; and a manuscript account of their wanderings in Flanders and Portugal.

No general view and but very few details of the original monastic buildings of "Sion" have been handed down to us; nor has its successor—the immediate predecessor of the present Sion House —fared much better. That it was a large and imposing structure there can be no doubt, considering the date of its erection. A doorway, of the Perpendicular period, highly ornamented, figures on the title-page of Aungier's work above quoted. The old stables, probably as old as the early Tudors, were mostly taken down about 1790. There is a view of them in Aungier's book (p. 136); where will be also seen a map of the domain.

The convent was probably renowned not only for its buildings, but for its furniture and fittings, and even for the vestments of its priests. In 1861 there was exhibited, under the auspices of the Archæological Institute, a magnificent cope from Sion, probably of the second half of the thirteenth century, which had been carried abroad by the sisters at the dissolution, and was presented by their successors to the Earl of Shrewsbury, who had given them a home in Staffordshire. It is described as "quite a storied vestment." On the higher part of the back is the Assumption and Crowning of the Virgin Mary; beneath is the Crucifixion; lower down is the Archangel Michael overcoming the dragon; high up on the right are the death of the Virgin, the doubting of St. Thomas, St. James the Less holding a club, another apostle with book and spear, St. Paul, St. James the Greater, the burial of the Virgin Mary, St. Mary Magdalen and our Lord, St. Philip, St. Bartholomew, St. Andrew, ten cherubim winged, and figures of religious persons holding scrolls. The hood, which was hung by three loops, is lost; the orphreys are two broad bands, bearing shields charged with the armorial bearings of several noble English houses; and the whole is surrounded by a narrower rim or fringe of shields, of somewhat later date than the rest. The dimensions of the cope are ten feet by four feet eight inches. The heraldic portions, about sixty in number, are probably woven, but the figures are all worked by the needle.

Another article of great value exhibited was a Mariola, or wax image of the Virgin Mary with the Saviour in her arms, probably the work of an English artist towards the close of the thirteenth century. This, too, was one of the Lares and Penates which the sisters carried with them abroad, and was also presented to John, Earl of Shrewsbury. Both of these in all probability were gifts to the convent at its first foundation. Another article exhibited at the rooms of the Archæological Institute in 1862 was a fine pectoral cross of solid gold of the sixteenth century, very probably a gift to the convent on its re-establishment by Queen Mary; and also a manuscript "Processionale ad usum Ecclesiæ de Syon," differing considerably from that in use at Salisbury. This was inscribed with the name of a sister named Slight, one of the inmates scattered by King Henry VIII., and brought back again by Queen Mary.

From the following extract from a letter of Thomas Bedyll, one of the "visitors" of the monasteries at the time of the dissolution, to Secretary Cromwell, under date of July 28th, 1534, it will be seen how the nuns of Sion were forced to acknowledge the king's supremacy. Bedyll writes:—"I have also been at Syon sith your departing with my lord of London, where we have found the lady abbas and susters as conformable in everything as myght be devised. And as towching the father confessor and father Cursone (whiche be the saddest men ther and best learned), they shewed thaimselfes like honest men; and I think the confessor wol now on Sonday next in his sermon make due mension of the kinges title of supreme hed, acording as he is commaunded. What towardnes or intowardnes we have seen in som other of the brethern there, I wol informe you at youre retorne to Londone, and omitte it now bicause I have som hope that by the wisdome of the father confessor and father Cursone the residue shal shortly be brought to good conformite. And if not, there be two of the brethern must be weded out, whiche be somewhat sediciose, and have labored busily to infect thair felowes with obstinacy against the kinges said title."

Later on, under date of 17th December, Bedyll thus writes to Cromwell, touching a visitation to Sion:—"As for the brethern, they stand stif in thair obstinacy as you left thaim. Here wer on Tuesday Doctor Buttes and the quenys amner to convert Wytford and Litell; and on Wensday here wer Doctor Aldrigge, Doctour Curven, Doctor Bawghe, and Doctor Morgan, sent by the kinges grace for that purpose, but they nothing proficted. I handled Whitford after that in the garden, bothe with faire wordes and with foule, and shewed him that throughe his obstinacy he shuld be brought to the greate shame of the world for his irreligious life, and for his using of badd wordes to diverse ladys at the tymes of thair confession, whereby (I seyed) he myght be the occasion that shrift shalbe layed downe throughe England. But he hath a brasyn forehed, whiche shameth at nothing. One Mathew, a lay brother, upon hope of liberte, is reformed. We wolde fanye know your advise what we shal do with Whitford and Litell, and a lay brother, one Turnyngton, whiche is very sturdy against the kinges title. We have sequesterd Whitford and Litell from hering of the ladys confessions, and we think it best that the place wher thes frires have been wont to hire uttward confessions of al commers at certen tymes of the yere be walled up, and that use to be fordoen for ever, ffor that hering of utward confessions hath been the cause of muche evyl, and of muche treson whiche hath been sowed abrode in this mater of the kinges title, and also in the kinges graces mater of his succession and mariage. On Wensday my Lord Wyndesore came hither, sent for by Maister Leighton and me, and labored muche that day for the converting of his suster and som other of his kynneswomen here ; and yesterday we had my Lord of London here in the chapiter house of women, and the confessor also, whiche bothe toke it upon thair consciences and upon the perill of thair soulys that the ladys owght by Gode's law to consent to the kinges title, wherewith they wer muche comforted ; and when we wylled al suche as consented to the kinges title to syt styll, and al suche as wold not consent therunto to depart out of the chapter house, there was found none emong thaim whiche departed. Albeit I was informed this nyght that one Agnes Smyth, a sturdy dame and a wylful, hath labored diverse of her susters to stop that we shuld not have thair convent seal ; but we trust we shal have it this mornyng, with the subscription of thabbes for her self and al her susters, whiche is the best fassion that we can bring it to. The persone whiche ye spak with at the grate, covyteth very muche to speke with you, seyng she hath suche thinges whiche she wold utter to no man but to you, and what they be I cannot conject. We purpose this after none, or els to-morow mornyng, to awaite on the king grace, to know his pleasir in everything, and specially towching the muring up of the howses of utter-ward confessions. Maister Leyghton hath wreten certen compertes unto you, and therefor I forber to speke anything therof. The ladys of Sion besecheth you to be good maister unto thaim, and to thair house, as thair special trust is in you, and that they all run not into obloquy and slander for the mysbehavor of one person. A greate number of the ladys desired me to speke unto you that Bisshope and Parkere myght be discharged from the house of Sion, and Bisshope and Parker desire the same. I mervaile that they desire not like-wise to be discharged of the person with whom ye talked at the grate, seing Bisshope's caus and that is one." *

After the suppression of this religious house the conventual buildings were retained in the posses-sion of the Crown during the remainder of the reign of Henry VIII., and in 1541 its gloomy walls were selected as the prison-house of the ill-fated Katharine Howard, while the sentence was being prepared which was to consign her to the

scaffold. Seven years later the body of the king himself rested here for a night on its way towards Windsor Castle. The story was long current that the swollen corpse burst and bled profusely, and that the dogs licked up the blood of the wicked monarch here, as other dogs in their day had licked up the blood of Ahab in Samaria.

In the first year of the reign of Edward VI., the monastery of Sion was granted to the Lord Pro-tector, Edward Seymour, Duke of Somerset, who had already rented some premises at Isleworth under the Abbess and convent ; and it was this nobleman who founded, on the ruins of the monastic building, the magnificent edifice which ultimately became the seat of the Northumberland family, and the shell of which, though in part considerably altered, still remains. The works carried out here by the Duke of Somerset were very extensive, and executed at great cost, and the grounds appear to have been laid out in a manner rather superior to the fashion which then usually prevailed. Here he had a botanical garden, formed under the superintendence of Dr. Turner, who has been often spoken of as "the father of British botany ;" and here were planted some of the earliest, if not the very earliest, mulberry trees introduced into England, many of which are still green and flourishing. Here the Duke of Somerset was living when Allen, the conjuror and astro-loger, was brought before him, charged with prac-tising his art to the injury of the king, and was committed to the Tower.

On the attainder of the Duke of Somerset for high treason, the mansion reverted to the Crown, and was shortly afterwards granted to John Dudley, Duke of Northumberland, but became the residence of Lord Guilford Dudley, the son of that nobleman, who married Lady Jane Grey. It was from this house that Lady Jane went forth on her way to the Tower, to claim the throne of England, on the death of Edward VI.

The estate was again forfeited to the Crown by the attainder of the Duke of Northumberland, and Queen Mary retained it in her possession till 1557, when, as stated above, she was prevailed upon to restore the convent of Sion. She endowed it with the manor and demesnes of Isleworth, and with sundry other lands ; but its restoration was but short-lived, for on the accession of Elizabeth this monastery was again dissolved, and the queen held the estate of Sion House in her own hands until 1604, when it was granted, together with the manor of Isleworth, to Henry Percy, ninth Earl of North-umberland. This nobleman expended large sums in the repairs and improvement of the mansion, the

---

* "Letters Relating to the Suppression of Monasteries." Edited by T. Wright, Esq., for the Camden Society.

occupation of which he enjoyed but for a short time; for, having been convicted by the Star Chamber of complicity in the gunpowder plot, he was stripped of all his offices, sentenced to pay a fine of £30,000, and to be imprisoned for life in the Tower of London. To liquidate the fine he petitioned the king to accept of Sion House, as being the only property that he could part with, the rest being entailed.

"The great house of Percy," observes a writer in *The Quarterly Review*, "was strikingly unfortunate during the reign of the Tudors, and indeed long before. Their ancestor, Josceline de Lovaine, a younger son of the ancient princes of Brabant, and brother of Adelicia, second consort of our Henry I., married in 1122 Agnes de Percy, the heiress of a great northern baron seated at Topcliffe and Spofford, county of York, on condition that the male posterity should bear the name of Percy. Their son Henry was great-grandfather of Henry Lord Percy, summoned to Parliament in 1299, whose great-grandson Henry, fourth Lord Percy, was created Earl of Northumberland in 1377, at the coronation of Richard II. He was slain at Bramham Moor in 1408. His son Henry Lord Percy (Hotspur) had already fallen at Shrewsbury in 1403. Henry, second Earl, the son of Hotspur, was slain at the battle of St. Albans in 1455. His son, Henry, third Earl, was slain at the battle of Towton in 1461. His son, Henry, fourth Earl, was murdered by an insurrectionary mob at Thirske, in Yorkshire, in 1480. Henry, fifth Earl, died a natural death in 1527, but his second son, Sir Thomas Percy, was executed in 1537, for his concern in Ask's rebellion. Henry, sixth Earl, the first lover of Queen Anne Boleyn, died in 1537, issueless, and the honours were suspended for twenty years by the attainder of his brother, Sir Thomas Percy, in 1537, during which time the family had the mortification to see the dukedom of Northumberland conferred on John Dudley, Earl of Warwick. But this nobleman being attainted in 1553, the Earldom was restored to Thomas Percy, the son of the attainted Sir Thomas, who became seventh Earl of Northumberland. He was eventually beheaded in August, 1572. His brother, Henry Percy, was allowed, in right of the new entail, to succeed as eighth Earl of Northumberland. In 1585 this Earl, still blind to his family sufferings, entered into the intrigues in favour of Mary Queen of Scots, and, being committed to the Tower, committed suicide 21st June." His son, Henry, ninth Earl, is the nobleman to whom we have just referred as being charged with complicity in the gunpowder plot.

By Algernon Percy, son of the above nobleman, and tenth Earl of Northumberland, the buildings of Sion were thoroughly repaired, under the direction, it is believed, of Inigo Jones himself. In 1646 the House of Commons deputed to this earl the care of the offspring of Charles I.—so soon to pass on to the scaffold; and it was from Sion House that the young children were conveyed to St. James's Palace, to take a last farewell of their unhappy father—an affecting scene, which has often been seized upon for pictorial representation. From that time to the present the lords of Sion House have continued to be the chiefs of the illustrious house of Percy.

During the fatal year of the plague of London, the business of the State appears to have been at times transacted here; at all events, we read in John Evelyn's Diary, under date of July 7, 1665, the following entry:—

"To London, and so to Sion, where his Majesty sat at Council during the contagion (Great Plague). When business was over, I viewed that seate, belonging to the Earle of Northumberland, built out of an old Nunnerie, of stone, and faire enough, but more celebrated for its garden than it deserves; yet there is excellent wall fruite, and a pretty fountaine; nothing else extraordinary."

In 1692 the mansion became the temporary residence of the Princess of Denmark (afterwards Queen Anne), during the misunderstanding which existed between her Highness and the Queen, occasioned by the influence of the Duchess of Marlborough. And Sion House has since, at various times, been graced by the presence of royalty. William IV. paid a visit to it on July 31, 1832, and again he and Queen Adelaide were entertained here in June, 1833.

We will say a few words concerning the building itself, the general outline of which appears to remain much the same as it was left by the Protector Somerset. The house, it is stated, stands on the spot where the church belonging to the monastery formerly stood, and is a very large, sombre, and majestic edifice. It is faced with Bath stone, and built in a quadrangular form, the centre being occupied by a flower-garden about eighty feet square. The house is three storeys high; and although each of the four fronts is without ornament, the general character of the edifice is rendered impressive by the dignity of its proportions and the massive solidity of its several parts. The parapets are embattled, and at each angle of the building is a square embattled turret. The entrance to the house, from the principal fronts, is by flights of stone steps. The house is fronted by a lawn of some extent, terminated by two stone lodges embattled in the same manner as the house. Towards the Thames the lawn is bounded by a lake, and a meadow which is cut down into a gentle slope, so that the surface of the water may be seen from all the principal apartments of the mansion, which are situated on the ground floor.

The entrance to the mansion from the great western road is through an elegant gateway built after a design by Robert Adam. It consists of a central arch, surmounted by the lion passant, the crest of the ducal House of Northumberland, and

representing the "Raising of Lazarus," is especially curious.

In 1874 the famous lion which had for many years surmounted the front of Northumberland House was removed hither on the demolition of that building, and now occupies a conspicuous place on the top of the mansion facing the river. "The head of the lion is placed towards London, and the animal has been raised on a pedestal of masonry sufficiently high to be seen from the roadway through the park at the back of the house, as well as from the river." As already stated by us in OLD AND NEW LONDON, there is an apocryphal

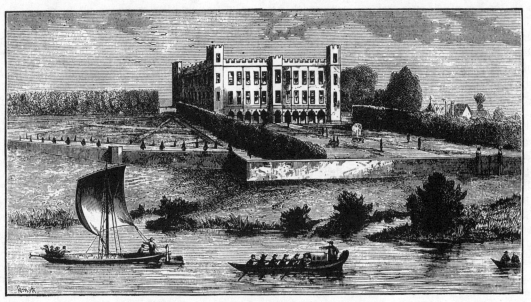

SION ABBEY, FROM THE SOUTH-WEST. (*See p. 50.*)
(*From a Print by H. Buck, 1737.*)

is connected by colonnades with two lodges. The principal doorway of the house is protected by a *porte-cochère*, from which a flight of steps leads to the great hall.

The great hall is paved with black and white marble, and the ceiling richly ornamented with stucco; and it contains some antique statues, &c. Adjoining the hall is the vestibule leading to the dining-room and other state apartments, some of which are of large dimensions, and fitted up in a most luxurious and costly manner. Among other objects of interest in the vestibule is a large vase, which was brought from Northumberland House, at Charing Cross. In original pictures Sion House is anything but rich; but there are some good historical portraits by Vandyke, Lely, and Kneller; and there are also a number of Dutch and Flemish paintings by Van Eyck and others: one of these,

legend in connection with this noble brute, that when he was at first deposited on Northumberland House, his head was placed looking in the direction of Carlton House and St. James's Palace, but that afterwards, on the occasion of some slight received by one of the Dukes of Northumberland, the animal was turned round with its face towards the Corporation of London, —a position, therefore, which he has been allowed to retain in his new quarters.

In Dugdale's "Monasticon" (edit. 1830), it is stated that only a few scanty fragments in some walls are remaining of the old conventual buildings here. Some very ancient mulberry trees on the lawn, their branches braced with irons, are believed not only to have been planted, but to have been in bearing growth, before the dissolution of the monastery. One of them has upon it the date 1546.

Beyond are the out-offices, with their remains of the monastic house, already mentioned. In Aungier's "History of Isleworth and Sion" it is stated that "during some recent improvements in the hall, two very rich and elaborate doorways of Gothic workmanship were discovered; they remain in a very perfect condition, having been preserved by a covering of plaster."

"The grounds of Syon," observes a writer in the *Illustrated London News* of about twenty years ago, worth Ferry, with the once notable gardens, had received little attention since the early days of Capability Brown, when the late Duke of Northumberland caused designs to be prepared for remodelling the whole of the grounds, seventy-five acres in extent. All the most interesting botanical introductions since Brown completed the gardens were then added to the collections of hardy trees and shrubs; whilst the most valuable ancient trees were preserved prominently in the new plan.

ISLEWORTH CHURCH. (*See p.* 57.)

"are beautifully diversified with rare shrubby and half-shrubby plants, and a double avenue of limes. Near the side of the water are admirable groups of deciduous cypress; and in other parts of the park, the old thorns have become trees. Picturesque groups of the common acacia exist on the westerly side of the park; and there are some extremely beautiful low-spreading horse-chestnuts and noble hop-hornbeams between the bridge and the entrance lodge. In going towards the mansion is a majestic cedar, one of the most venerable tenants of this truly fine old place. The extensive pleasure grounds skirting the Thames, from the middle of Brentford to Isle-

"Passing over the artificial rockery constructed for alpine plants, the grand feature of the improvements is the range of plant-houses, with the substitution of metallic framework for the wood-framed roofs and sides of the old school of hothouse manufactures.

"The range of plant-houses, four hundred feet in length, designed by Mr. Richard Forrest, consists of nine divisions, so contrived that each can be kept at its own independent temperature, suitable to the health and beauty of its plants; yet the doors can, upon any special occasion, be thrown open, giving the various climates of the world with their various inhabitants. These plant-houses take the form of a crescent; the centre rising into a dome sixty-five feet high; the two end houses being broader and higher than the intermediate part. The framework of the entire roof is formed of light iron bars; and the ends and centre have stone pillars and cornices. The whole range is filled with plate-glass. The metallic roofing was manufactured by Messrs. Jones and Co., of Birmingham; it has stood some twenty years without shrinking, and was the first metallic horticultural structure of any importance. The steam warming apparatus was fitted by Tredgold, the eminent engineer; the cast-iron pipes being laid beneath the pathways, and provided with valves for the admission, when required, of vapour, so conducive to the health of tropical plants; the whole being heated by one fire, three hundred feet from the building. The contractors for the heating apparatus were Messrs. Bailey of Holborn. Several things have, we believe, fruited here which have not borne fruit anywhere else in Britain; and many plants, which here fruit profusely, are scarcely ever to be seen in general collections. The houses stand upon a raised stone basement, adorned with elegant stone vases, sculptured with fruit and foliage, attributed to Gibbons. The end portions of the building are used as conservatories for orange-trees, camellias, &c., with a few showy flowers.

" In front of this range of plant-houses is a flower-garden, with a basin and fountain; and lines of standard roses by the side of the walks. The entire garden establishment is supplied with water from an artesian well four hundred and sixty-five feet deep.

" The kitchen-garden covers between three and four acres; and the forcing-houses have the roofs, fronts, and ends mainly of iron, the bars of the sashes being of copper. These, also, are the work of Messrs. Jones. The principal range, for early fruits, is four hundred feet long."

The late Dowager Duchess of Northumberland, who resided at Sion, was a distinguished botanist, and sometime *gouvernante* to our gracious Queen, who, during her minority, occasionally occupied, with the Duchess of Kent, the state apartments at Sion. The Queen's observation of the horticultural improvements here doubtless led to their originator, Mr. Forrest, being subsequently employed in the improvements at Frogmore, where he completed one of the most extensive ranges of metal-framed forcing-houses in the world, designed after that at Sion.

It may be added that the gardens and grounds of Sion have long occupied a foremost place in the horticultural world; and for private gardens may be said to be no mean rival to Kew.

Isleworth lies on the road from London to Sunbury and Shepperton, as we know from Charles Dickens, who makes Bill Sykes and little Oliver Twist travel through it in a market-cart, on their way to commit the burglary which ended so happily for the fortunes of the latter. The parish extends for about three miles along the north bank of the Thames, between Brentford and Twickenham, about a mile at the eastern end being taken up by the grounds of Sion House. The village itself almost surrounds the grounds of Sion, and with its red-brick houses, its sheds for boat-building, and its ivy-clad church tower, forms a pleasing break in the landscape, as seen from the opposite bank of the river at Kew. A considerable portion of land in the parish, which extends back from the river-side for about two miles, is cultivated as market-gardens and nurseries. There are also extensive brick-fields and cement-works here. Norden, writing at the commencement of the seventeenth century, mentions some copper and brass mills at Isleworth, where "workmen make plates both of copper and brasse of all syces, both little and great, thick and thyn, for all purposes; they make also kyttles." Lysons, in his "Environs" (1795), says that "these copper-mills still exist;" they have, however, long since been done away with, as also has another branch of industry, of more recent introduction, the manufacture of pottery and porcelain.

Isleworth, it may be here remarked, must have been a more important place than it is now in the days when the Thames was the great "silent highway." In a "Voyage up the Thames," published in 1738, for instance, there is an account of a public-house at Isleworth which was kept open all night for the express accommodation of parties travelling by the Thames, and the parties who frequented it were often of a most diverting character. A few years later we learn casually from Griffith's "Essay on the Jurisdiction of the Thames," that the fare from London hither was 3s. 6d., for a wherry that contained eight passengers. From the same source we learn that the Windsor carriers called here twice a week in the course of their voyage up the river from Queenhithe. At that time, too, doubtless, nearly all the produce of the market gardens about this locality was sent by water to the London market.

In the reign of Henry III., the manor of Isleworth, being vested in the Crown, was granted to the king's brother, Richard, Earl of Cornwall, and King of the Romans. The site of the ancient palace, or manor-house, is uncertain. Lysons says it seems probable that it was "a spot of ground behind the Phœnix Yard, called in old writings the 'Moted Place.'" Mr. Aungier, in his "History and Antiquities of Syon," places it near Isleworth House. It is on record that in 1264 Sir Hugh Spencer, "with a great multitude of the citizens of London, went to Isleworth, where they spoiled the manor-place of the King of the Romans, and destroyed his water-mylnes and other commodities that he there had." From the description of this manor in "Domesday Book," it will be seen that it includes Heston and Twickenham; and these two latter places are mentioned in an inquisition taken after the Earl of Cornwall's death as hamlets within the manor of Isleworth. Lysons states that in the parish chest at Twickenham is a small illuminated deed of the abbey and convent of Sion, with their seal annexed, and bearing date 22 Henry VI., whereby they discharge their tenants in the manor of Isleworth of a certain annual tribute, or payment of £20. In 1656 certain articles relating to the customs and privileges of the manor of Isleworth were agreed on between Algernon, Earl of Northumberland, and the principal copyholders. They were printed in the following year in the form of a pamphlet, entitled "Isleworth—Sion's Peace." Lands in this manor, observes Lysons, descend according to the strict custom of "Borough-English."

The parish church of Isleworth, dedicated to All Saints, is an attractive object from the river-side. It consists of a chancel, with nave and aisles, and the tower at its western end is profusely covered with ivy. Here, as is so often the case along the valley of the Thames between London and Windsor, the tower is the only old part of the church that is standing.

The body of the church, which was rebuilt in 1705, partly from the designs of Sir Christopher Wren—whose plans were first of all laid aside as too expensive to be carried out, but are said to have been at last brought out and used, subject to such modification and "improvement" as the churchwardens thought fit to make—is a poor structure, but since 1865 it has been considerably improved by the alterations of windows, &c. The materials of the old church were used in erecting at the west end of the churchyard a substantial mansion, the rent of which belongs to the poor.

A new chancel, of a correct ecclesiastical type, laid down with encaustic tiles, was added in 1866. The reredos represents the "Last Supper." The windows have been filled with painted glass, the roof heightened, and the old-fashioned pews made to give place to open benches.

Here are several monuments of more than ordinary interest; among them, one to Sir Orlando Gee, Registrar of the Admiralty, who died in 1705, in which the knight is represented by a marble bust to the waist, with peruke and long flowing cravat; another to Helena Magdalen, Countess de Randwick, a refugee from Holland, who died in 1797; another (a mural tablet) to Sir Richard Downton, Colonel of the Middlesex Militia under Charles II., who died in 1711; another to a poor woman who suddenly became enriched by a freak of fortune, and died equally suddenly. The person here commemorated was a Mrs. Anne Dash, better known by the name of Tolson. She was a great benefactress to the parish; and her history, as recorded in her epitaph, is very singular. She was the daughter of Mr. George Newton, of Duffield, Derbyshire, and having been twice married, first to one Henry Sisson, and afterwards to a Mr. John Tolson, was in her second widowhood reduced to very narrow circumstances, and obliged to set up a boarding-school as a means of procuring a livelihood; but blindness having rendered her unfit for that employment, she became an object of charity. In the meantime, Dr. Caleb Cotesworth, a physician, who had married a relation of Mrs. Tolson, died in 1741, having amassed in the course of his practice the sum of £150,000, the greater part of which—namely, upwards of £120,000—he left to his wife, who, surviving him only a few hours, died intestate, and her large fortune was divided between Mrs. Tolson and two others, as the nearest of kin. With a due sense of this signal deliverance, and unexpected change from a state of want to riches and affluence, she appropriated by a deed of gift the sum of £5,000, to be expended after her decease in building and endowing an almshouse at Isleworth for six poor men and six women. This lady died in the year 1750, aged 89, having married, subsequent to this deed of gift, a third husband, Mr. Joseph Dash, merchant.

In this church is a brass to Margaret Dely, one of the sisters of Sion in Mary's time; and a palimpsest brass, with a Flemish inscription, was to be seen some years since in the vestry.

The parish register, which dates from the middle of the sixteenth century, contains a few interesting entries. Among others there is recorded the baptism, in October, 1617, of Waller's "Sacharissa"—Dorothy, daughter of Sir Robert and Lady Dorothy Sidney. It appears by this entry that she was born at Sion House whilst her grandfather was a prisoner in the Tower. From the following extract from the parish accounts, it is clear that she resided at Isleworth in her widowhood:—"1655. Received of the Countess of Sunderland, for her rate for the poor for half a year, 15s." " Dorothy, the Lady and Countess of Northumberland, buried Aug. 14, 1619." She was " Sacharissa's " grandmother, wife of Henry, Earl of Northumberland, and daughter of Walter Devereux, Earl of Essex. By this date of her burial, it appears that she did not live to see her husband released from his confinement. The register also records the marriage, on the 27th March, 1679, of Henry Cavendish, Earl of Ogle, son and heir of Henry, Duke of Newcastle, to Lady Elizabeth Percy, daughter and heiress of Josceline, eleventh and last Earl of Northumberland. It also records the marriage of Lord Algernon Percy, afterwards second Lord Lovaine, with Isabella Susannah, sister of Peter, first Lord Gwydir ; the ceremony was performed at Sion House by Dr. Thomas Percy, afterwards Bishop of Dromore.

Among the minutes of the vestry is entered a licence, bearing date April 28, 1661, given by William Grant, Vicar of Isleworth, to Richard Downton, Esq., and Thomasine, his wife, to eat flesh in Lent " for the recovery of their health, they being enforced by age, notorious sickness, and weakness to abstain from fish." These licences were by no means uncommon at an earlier date. After the Restoration, the keeping of Lent, which had been neglected by the Puritans, who entirely set aside the observing of seasons, was enforced by a proclamation from the king, and an office for granting licences to eat flesh in any part of England was set up in St. Paul's Churchyard, and advertised in the public papers, in 1663.

Nicholas Byfield, Vicar of Isleworth, 1615—20, was a laborious or " painful " preacher of the Puritan school ; he was the father of Adoniram Byfield, one of the few persons stigmatised by name by Butler in his " Hudibras," and grandfather of Dr. Byfield, the " salvolatile " doctor, who is said in his epitaph to be " Diu volatilis, tandem fixus."

Dr. Cave, the learned author of the " Lives of the Fathers," " Primitive Christianity," &c., was Vicar of Isleworth from 1690 till his death in 1713. He is buried at Islington.

Aungier records the singular fact that Dr. Turner, the herbalist and physician to Edward, Duke of Somerset and Lord Protector, held the Deanery of Wells, though only a layman, and had a licence to preach at Isleworth against the errors of Pelagius. He is mentioned in Wood's "Athenæ Oxonienses." His lecture on this subject was answered in print, and his reply, dedicated to Bishop Latimer in 1551, was also published. The churchyard is spacious and well laid out. In the centre of it are three yew trees curiously linked together by a lych-gate, which forms a rustic arbour.

Isleworth was not neglected by the charitably-disposed in bygone times. Sir Thomas Ingram, in 1664, founded an almshouse here for six poor women, housekeepers of the parish ; and the late Mr. John Farnell built and endowed a range of almshouses for six poor men and six women. In 1750 came the foundation of Mrs. Anne Tolson's almshouses, already mentioned ; these houses have lately been rebuilt. Other almshouses have also been founded here by Mrs. Mary Bell and Mrs. Sermon.

The church of St. John the Baptist, in St. John's Road, was built in 1857, on a site given by the late Duke of Northumberland. It consists of chancel, nave, and aisles, and is in the Early English style of architecture. The are several meeting-houses and chapels for the various religious denominations in the village, besides schools and other public buildings. The Brentford Union is situated on the Twickenham Road, in the parish of Isleworth.

Among the residents of Isleworth, in the days of Queen Anne, was a large glass manufacturer named Gumley, whose only child and heiress carried his wealth into the Pulteney family by marrying the Earl of Bath. She is mentioned by Pope in his " Miscellanies," with a compliment at the expense of her husband—

" But charming Gumley 's lost in Pulteney's wife."

Gumley House was built towards the end of the seventeenth century ; and after the death of Mr. Gumley it became the residence of the Earl of Bath. The mansion subsequently became the property of General Lord Lake. It is now a Roman Catholic convent school for young ladies.

Shrewsbury Place—so named from having been formerly the residence of Charles Talbot, Duke of Shrewsbury, Secretary of State to William III. and Queen Mary—shared a similar fate to Gumley House, and became devoted to religious purposes. It is now a Roman Catholic school.

Not far from Gumley House, on the side of the road from Twickenham to London, stood another noted mansion, Kendal House, so called from the Duchess of Kendal, the favourite mistress of King George I., who resided there. The following story is related of her in the " Good Fellow's Calendar:"—" This gracious sovereign once, while *doing the tender* with the Duchess of Kendal, promised her that if she survived him, and if departed souls were so permitted, he would pay her a visit. The superstitious Duchess on his death so much expected the fulfilment of that engagement, that a large raven, or some black fowl, flying into one of the windows of her villa at Isleworth,

she was fully persuaded it was the soul of her departed monarch so accoutred, and received and
treated it with all the respect and tenderness of
duty, till the royal bird or herself took *the last
flight.*"

After the death of the Duchess (or the "May-
pole," as she was irreverently called by the people)
the mansion was sold, and opened as a place of
public entertainment, and was frequently advertised
as such in the years 1750 and 1751.

The *Daily Advertiser* of April the 4th, 1750, contains the following announcement :—" For certain,
Kendal House, Isleworth, near Brentford, Middlesex, eight miles from London, will open for break-
fasting on Monday, the 16th inst.   The long room
for dancing is upwards of sixty feet long, and wide
in proportion ; all the other rooms are elegantly
fitted up.   The orchestra on the water is allowed,
by all that have seen it, to be in the genteelest
taste, being built an octagon in the Corinthian
order, above fifty feet diameter, having an upper
and lower gallery, where gentlemen and ladies may
divert themselves with fishing, the canal being well
stocked with tench, carp, and all sorts of fish in
great plenty ; near which are two wildernesses,
with delightful rural walks; and through the garden
runs a rapid river, shaded with a pleasant grove of
trees, with various walks, so designed by nature,
that in the hottest day of summer you are screened
from the heat of the sun.   The small but just
account of the place falls greatly short of its real
beauties.   Great care will be taken to keep out all
disorderly people.   There is a man cook, and a
good larder ; all things as cheap or cheaper than
at any place of the kind."

The Princesses Amelia and Caroline, daughters
of George II., who, in 1733, brought the well at
Islington Spa, then called the New Tunbridge
Wells, into fashion, by going thither to drink the
waters, were, doubtless, occasional visitors here.
At all events, this place appears to have enjoyed
an equal share of popularity with its Islington rival,
for, in a song called " Modern Diversions," published in the *Universal Magazine* in 1753, the
following lines occur :—

> " To operas, assemblies,
>   Or else to masquerade,
> New Tunbridge, or to Kendal House ;
>   And this shall be the trade.
> We'll sally out to breakfast,
>   And hear the fiddlers play ;
> And there we'll revel, feast, and dance,
>   And make a merry day.
>   For a roving we will go, will go,
>   For a roving we will go."

When the taste for amusements of this kind

died out, Kendal House was pulled down, and
its site devoted to building purposes.

In the British Museum may be seen a perspective view of Kendal House, drawn by Chatelain
in 1756 ; it represents probably one of the grand
breakfast days for which the place was so celebrated.   A large orchestra, filled with musicians,
is " discoursing sweet music," while a number of
ladies, and gentlemen, the former dressed in hoops
of monstrous size, are walking about, and some
are amusing themselves by fishing.

The rivulet which runs through the grounds of
Kendal House, rises on Norwood Common, and
at Osterley it is formed into a canal of fish-ponds.
Next it passes to Hounslow, whence it crosses
the road and finds its way hither.

Kendal House, however, was not the earliest place
of amusement in Isleworth ; for the *General Evening
Post* of May, 1734, contains an advertisement of
the " Isleworth Assembly" held in that and the
previous year at " Dunton House "—a house which
it is now impossible to identify.

A large house, formerly standing near the river-
side, and known as Lacy House, was built by
Mr. James Lacy, one of the patentees of Drury
Lane Theatre.   It was at one time the residence
of Sir Robert Walpole, and of his daughter,
Mrs. Keppel, widow of Dr. Keppel, Bishop of
Exeter ; it was also some time in the occupation
of the Earl of Warwick, and of Richard Brinsley
Sheridan.

At St. Margaret's, towards the south-west end of
the village, is the Royal Naval Female School, an
institution founded " for the maintenance and
education of the daughters of naval and marine
officers."   The house was built for the Earl of
Kilmorey, but never occupied by him; it was
purchased in 1856, and converted to its present
uses.   The Marquis of Ailsa had a seat in this
part of Isleworth many years back, but that mansion has long been demolished and the park built
over.   George Calvert, Lord Baltimore, one of
Horace Walpole's "Noble Authors," likewise had
a country seat here.   His lordship was Secretary of
State to James I., and the original grantee and
founder, in 1729, of the city of Baltimore, the commercial metropolis of Maryland, in the United
States.

Silver Hall, which formerly stood on the south
side of the Twickenham Road, was built in the
seventeenth century by John Smith, Esq., who was
created a baronet in 1694, and whose arms were
over the piers of the gate.   The old building, which
was ultimately used as a school, was pulled down
some time ago, and a new mansion, called Silver

Hall, now the residence of Mr. Francis H. N. Glossop, erected on a different site.

Gordon House, in the Richmond Road, the seat of the Earl of Kilmorey, is a modern mansion. Isleworth House, close by, the residence of Mrs. McAndrew, is a fine building, and is celebrated for the beauty of its grounds and the views it affords of the river and surrounding scenery. The house was once the residence of Lady Cooper, who was here visited by William IV., by whose command, as Mr. Thorne tells us, in his " Environs of London," " the Syon vista in Kew Gardens was cut in order to open a view of pagoda and observatory to the front of the house."

Sir Clipesby Crewe was a resident of Isleworth in the seventeenth century, as we learn from the following entry in " Evelyn's Diary," under date of February, 1648 :—" I went with my noble friend, Sir William Ducy (afterwards Lord Downe), to Thistleworth, where we dined with Sir Clipesby Crewe, and afterwards to see the rare miniatures of Peter Oliver, and rounds of plaster, and then the curious flowers of Mr. Barill's gardens, who has some good medails and pictures. Sir Clipesby has fine Indian hangings, and a very good chimney-piece of water-colours by Breugel, which I bought for him."

Here, too, at one time, lived in a small house, retired from business, George Field, a metaphysician of the German school, and the author of some practical works on Chromatics, having made his money by preparing colours for painters. The exact site of his residence is now unknown.

Worton Hall, in Worton Road, midway between Isleworth and Hounslow, is a modern mansion, and perpetuates the manor of Worton, once a royal manor, which was granted by Henry VI. to the Monastery of Sion. In some records it is called the " Manor of Eystons "—thus perpetuating the name of a family which for three generations in the fourteenth century resided here, before they inherited Hendred, in Berkshire, where they are still located. The property now belongs to the Duke of Northumberland.

Syon Hill, a little to the south-east, a mansion built by the Earl of Holdernesse, who died in 1778, was at the close of the last century the residence of the Duke of Marlborough. The duke had a small observatory in the grounds, and, as Lysons observes, he "cultivated with much success the science of astronomy." The house has been taken down, and the park in part built upon.

At Spring Grove, in the north-eastern part of the parish, are some almshouses, recently erected, called " Honnor's Home." They were founded by a Mr. Honnor, a member of the Saddlers' Company, who are the patrons of the charity, and are for the benefit of decayed freemen, freewomen, and widows of freemen.

The London International College, founded under the auspices of the late Mr. Richard Cobden, is situated at Spring Grove. The institution was inaugurated by the Prince of Wales in 1867, and the college was established for the teaching of English, French, and German, side by side with mathematics, classics, and natural science.

Spring Grove was formed into a separate ecclesiastical district in 1856, out of the parishes of Heston and Isleworth. The church, dedicated to St. Mary, is a handsome building, consisting of a chancel, nave, aisles, and tower with a lofty spire, and stands on rising ground between the western high road and Osterley Park.

Before continuing our journey westward along the valley of the Thames, it will be as well to make a short *détour* to the north, in order to explore the classic regions of Hounslow, a portion of which lies really within the parish of Isleworth.

CHAPTER V.

HOUNSLOW AND HANWORTH.

" Formidare malos fures."—*Horace*. I., Sat. i. 77.

Situation of Hounslow—A Priory founded here—Martyrdom of Archbishop Scrope—Markets and Fairs—Remains of the Conventual Buildings—Holy Trinity Church—The Manor House—Hounslow in the Old Coaching Days—Present Condition of the Town—The Churches of St. Stephen and St. Paul—Salvation Army Barracks—Hounslow Heath—Military Encampments—Knights of the Road—Site of the Gibbets—A Bishop Counterfeiting the Highwayman—The Gallant Highwayman—The Highwayman Outwitted—Horse-racing, &c.--Gunpowder Mills—Cavalry Barracks—Whitton Park—Hanworth Park—Hanworth House—The Parish Church.

THE district which will form the subject of this chapter lies to the west of Isleworth, and is one which, considering its size and present condition, is perhaps better known than any other in England for the scenes of historical interest which it has witnessed, and for the notoriety which it gained at the hands of those "knights of the road" by whom it was infested during the seventeenth and eighteenth centuries.

The village, or town, of Hounslow, as stated in the preceding chapter, is situated partly in the parish of Isleworth; it is also partly in that of Heston. The place was called in "Domesday

came a certain man of his household to the house of the Holy Trinity at Hundeslaw for refreshment, who confessed that he was "one of three men who threw the corpse [of the king] into the river between Barking and Gravesend," whilst it was being conveyed from Westminster towards Canterbury for interment; and adds, "but the chest, covered with cloth of gold, in which the body had lain, we carried with great honour into Canterbury, and buried it." Nevertheless, in 1832, the royal tomb was opened in the presence of the Bishop of Oxford and others, and the remains of the

THE POWDER-MILLS, HOUNSLOW. (See p. 68.)

Book" Honeslowe, and later on it was spelt Hundeslawe and Hundeslowe. In the thirteenth century a priory, dedicated to the Holy Trinity, was founded here, the peculiar office of the brethren being to solicit alms for the redemption of captives. It is spoken of by Cobbett, in his "History of the Reformation," as "a friary."

One Clement Maydestone, a friar of this house, wrote a history of the martyrdom of Richard Scrope, Archbishop of York, to whom he had been a retainer, in which it is stated that within thirty days after the death of Henry IV., there

king were found in his coffin. This at once, of course, disposed of the story told by Maydestone.

In 1296 a weekly market was granted to the brethren of this priory, to be held on Wednesday, and an annual fair on the eve and feast of the Holy Trinity, and to last a week. The market has long been discontinued, but fairs are still held on Trinity Monday, and on the Monday after Michaelmas Day. At the dissolution the revenues of this priory were valued at £78 8s. 6d. In Cooke's "Topography of Middlesex," published early in the present century, it is stated that "the only remaining part of the conventual buildings is the chapel, which exhibits evident traces of the architecture of the thirteenth century. In the south wall of the chancel are three ancient stone stalls, and a double piscina, with narrow pointed arches, divided by a column. The chapel consists of a chancel, nave, and south aisle. In the nave is a small monument, with the effigies of a man in armour and his wife, kneeling; on the floor is a brass plate to the memory of Thomas Lupton, who died in 1512, and his wife Alice. In the windows of the south aisle there is some painted glass, representing the figure of St. Katharine and some other subjects." Mr. Brewer, in the " Beauties of England " (1816), says that " on one face of the exterior is a mutilated escutcheon, with the arms and quarterings of the Windsor family, who have been supposed, but, as it would appear, erroneously, to have been the founders of the priory."

This ancient chapel has now entirely disappeared, and in its place—although perhaps not quite on the same site—has arisen another church, dedicated to the Holy Trinity. This was built in the upper part of the main street about the year 1834; it is constructed of white brick, and is a plain and ugly edifice in the Italian style, of little or no architec- tural interest. It consists of a chancel, nave, aisles, porch, and bell-turret, and is surmounted with stone cupolas twelve in number. The build- ing was enlarged by the addition of a chancel in 1856.

In the " Beauties of England " it is stated that the manor and the site of the priory were an- nexed by Henry VIII. to the honour of Hampton Court, but were both leased in 1539 to Richard Awnsham, Esq. The property was for some time vested in the Windsor family, long seated in the neighbouring parish of Stanwell. In 1705 it was purchased by Whitlocke Bulstrode, Esq., the author of a "Treatise on Transmigration" and of other publications, who enlarged the manor-house, an ancient brick structure facing the heath, at the western extremity of Hounslow, and also repaired the chapel which contains his monument.

The town consists mainly of a long, uninterest- ing, and monotonous street, with scarcely one picturesque or redeeming object on either side. As far back as about 1650 it was noted for its numerous inns and ale-houses, and later on it became a great place for posting-houses. In the " Beauties of England," it is stated that " the chief dependence of the place is on the immense tide of road traffic, which rolls to and from the metropolis with surprising vehemence and bustle. As this hamlet is only one short stage from London, the principal business of the inns consists in providing relays of post-horses, and exchanges of horses for the numerous coaches travelling the road. All here wears the face of impatience and expedition. The whole population seems on the wing of re- moval; and assuredly the main street of Hounslow is a place from which the examiner would wish to remove with all the celerity familiar to the spot." At the accession of Queen Victoria there were as many as five hundred stage-coaches and one thousand five hundred horses daily employed in transit through the town. The " George Inn " was particularly noted as a great posting-house. Its several posting-houses were, in fact, very busy and prosperous till the traffic was diverted by the opening of the railways to Southampton and Bath.

For a long time after the coaching traffic of the high road had ceased, Hounslow remained in a very depressed condition; but business in the locality has, to a certain extent, revived, and the place has of late years acquired a fair local trade, whilst many of the new shops, public buildings, and new schools, all attest the progress which the town is now making.

In 1857 a Town Hall was erected. Here the ordinary public business of the town is transacted, and there is also a well-furnished reading-room within its walls, with a library containing upwards of a thousand volumes, for the use of the in- habitants.

St. Stephen's Church, situate in Hanworth Road, close to the London and South Western Railway Station, was built in 1875-6, and is in the Early English style of architecture. The ecclesiastical dis- trict to which it belongs was formed out of the parishes of Isleworth and Heston by an Order in Council, passed in 1877.

St. Paul's Church, which is in the Bath Road, near the heath, was built in 1873-4, the ecclesiastical district to which it is attached having been formed out of the parish of Heston. The build- ing, like the one just mentioned, is in the Early English style, and its spire, standing one hundred and thirty feet high, is conspicuous for some distance round.

Among the latest additions to the town has been the extension of the Metropolitan District Railway hither, and the erection of a Salvation Army barracks, bearing the strange and ominous superscription—" Blood and Fire."

The celebrated Hounslow Heath adjoins the town on the west, and extends into the parishes and hamlets of Hounslow, Heston, Isleworth,

Brentford, Twickenham, Feltham, Harlington, Cranford, Harmondsworth, Stanwell, Bedfont, Hampton, and Teddington. According to a survey made in 1546, it contained at that time four thousand two hundred and ninety-two acres; but other accounts made its area much greater, Rocque's map setting it down as six thousand six hundred and fifty-eight acres. It was estimated by Messrs. Britton and Brayley, in 1810, to comprise about five thousand acres. The soil was then thought "very improvable," and accordingly, since then,

once it has been the rendezvous of the principal military force of this kingdom.

In 1267 the Earl of Gloucester, leading the Londoners against King Henry III., assembled them on Hounslow Heath in order to give battle to the king. The army of Charles I. is said to have been entrenched here the day after the battle of Brentford, in 1642; and in November of the same year the army under the command of the Earl of Essex was mustered here. Five years later the heath witnessed a general rendezvous of the

HIGH STREET, HOUNSLOW.

much of it has been brought into profitable cultivation under several Acts of Parliament, which have been passed for enclosing different parts, but it still remains one of the most unproductive parts of the county of Middlesex.

Cobbett, in his "Rural Rides," writes as follows with regard to the general aspect of the land in this locality:—"A much more ugly county than that between Egham and Kensington would with difficulty be found in England. Flat as a pancake, until you come to Hammersmith, the soil is a nasty, stony dirt upon a bed of gravel. Hounslow Heath, which is only a little worse than the general run, is a sample of all that is bad in soil and villanous in look. Yet all this is now enclosed, and what they call 'cultivated.'"

As above stated, Hounslow has long enjoyed a celebrity, in its way, in the annals of England. Vestiges of camps—either British or Roman—were visible on its surface down to a comparatively recent date. It has been the scene of military and other assemblies at different periods, and more than

Parliamentary forces under General Sir Thomas Fairfax, when there appeared 20,000 foot and horse, with a great train of artillery. The *Perfect Diurnal*, August, 1647, gives the following account of this rendezvous:—"There were present the Earls of Northumberland, Salisbury, and Kent, Lord Grey of Wark, Lords Howard of Escrick, Wharton, Say and Sele, Mulgrave, and others, the Speaker of the House of Commons, and above 100 of the members. The whole army was drawn up in battalions, near a mile and a half in length. The general, accompanied with the said lords and commons, rode along the army from regiment to regiment, and were received with great acclamation. Having viewed the army, they took leave of the general, and some went to the Earl of Northumberland's at Sion, and others to the Lord Say and Sele's at Stanwell. Soon after the Palgrave came into the field, who, with the general and many gentlemen, viewed the army." The encampment was attended by Algernon Sidney and several other members, and the leader was everywhere hailed with great enthusiasm.

In 1678 the army of Charles II. was encamped on the Heath, a fact which is thus duly recorded by John Evelyn, in his "Diary," under date June 29th of that year:—"Returned with my son by

Hounslow Heath, where we saw the newly-rais'd army encamp'd, design'd against France, in pretence at least, but which gave umbrage to the Parliament. His Majesty and a world of company were in the field, and the whole army in battalia: a very glorious sight. Now were brought into service a new sort of soldiers called Granadiers, who were dextrous in flinging hand granados, every one having a pouch-full; they had furr'd caps with coped crowns, like Janizanis, which made them look very fierce, and some had long hoods hanging down behind, as we picture fools: their clothing being likewise pybald yellow and red."

In 1686 James II., resolving not to yield in his struggle with his subjects, formed a camp of some thirteen thousand men on Hounslow Heath. The Londoners looked on it with terror, which, however, was soon diminished by familiarity. The camp was visited, as was only natural, by the beaux and belles of the West End, who flocked to it in such overwhelming crowds that, to use Macaulay's words, "a visit to Hounslow became their favourite amusement on holydays, and the camp presented the appearance of a vast fair. In truth," he adds, "the place was merely a gay suburb of the capital." The king had hoped that his army—or rather, the sight of it—would overawe London; but the result was quite different, for the army instead took its cue from London. Various tracts and pamphlets sprang up out of the camp, and a hot controversy ensued, which helped to bring about the events of 1688.

Under date of June 2, 1686, Evelyn again mentions the camp being located at Hounslow, but being "forced to retire to quarters from sickness and other inconveniences of the weather." Four days later he writes:—"The camp was now againe pitch'd at Hounslow, the commanders profusely vying in the expence and magnificence of tents."

During the time of the encampment in 1687, there was in use here a curious tabernacle, or chapel on wheels, which had been built by command of King James, to accompany him in his royal "progresses," in order that mass might be celebrated in his presence by his chaplain. As soon as the abdication of the king was known to be a fact, this chapel was brought by road up to London, and placed upon the site long occupied by its successor, Trinity Chapel, on the south side of Conduit Street, Regent Street. At the request of Dr. Tenison—afterwards Archbishop of Canterbury, but at that time Rector of St. Martin's-in-the-

Fields—this wooden structure was subsequently used as a temporary chapel of ease, for the use of the outlying portion of the inhabitants of his then wide and scattered parish.

Every reader of English history, even Macaulay's "schoolboy," is aware that James II. was with his army here when the news of the acquittal of the seven bishops was signalled from London. "Nowhere," writes Macaulay, "had the acquittal been received with more clamorous delight than at Hounslow Heath. In truth, the great force which the king had assembled for the purpose of overawing his mutinous capital had become more mutinous than the capital itself, and was more dreaded by the Court than by the citizens. Early in August, therefore, the camp was broken up, and the troops were sent to quarters in different parts of the country."

In the library of the Corporation of London, at Guildhall, may be seen three different views of the camp of James II. One is a woodcut, entitled "An exact Prospect of the King's Forces encamped on Hounslow Heath, 1686;" another woodcut is of the same date, but has a letter-press inscription; the third is a copper-plate, engraved by Harris, of about the same date. In the first volume of "Poems on Affairs of State," about the same date, is a very severe attack on King James in connection with this camp and heath; but this is not mentioned by Mr. Wilkes in his poem above on "Hounslow Heath."

Three years later, namely, in 1690, Queen Mary reviewed her troops here in the presence of the Duke of Marlborough. On the alarm of a French invasion in aid of the Stuart cause, the whole nation was stirred with a martial spirit, and, according to Macaulay, "two and twenty troops of cavalry, furnished by Suffolk, Essex, Hertfordshire, and Buckinghamshire, were reviewed by Mary at Hounslow, and were complimented by Marlborough on their martial appearance."

King George III. more than once held reviews here, the troops inspected being furnished from the ranks of both the regulars and volunteers.

The camp here seems to have been conducted very much as our summer volunteer camp at Wimbledon, the crowds of visitors including many ladies of quality, and the hospitality of the officers being so profuse as to add very seriously to their expenses. It was constantly visited by royalty; and in 1740 the list of distinguished personages here included the "Butcher" Duke of Cumberland, the Duke of Marlborough, the Earl of Dunmore, and several other officers of the highest rank. The Duke of Cumberland stayed here a week on this occasion, and gave more than one grand entertainment under canvas.

The camp at Hounslow Heath was always popular with the Londoners; and, in 1744 (as we learn from the *Daily Advertiser* of March 13) it formed the subject of a popular exhibition, at the bottom of Hay Hill, Dover Street. It was patronised by the Prince and Princess of Wales, and the admission was a shilling. The following is a copy of the bill: "To be seen, the whole Prospect of the (late) Camp at Hounslow, representing in proper order, both Horse and Foot, every officer in his proper post, with the nicest distinction of both their liveries and colours; in proportion and magnitude representing life nearer than anything of the kind hitherto invented. The train of Artillery in its proper decorum."

Hounslow Heath is the chief rival to Finchley Common in the "Lives of the Highwaymen," and is one of the "happy hunting-grounds" of the "Newgate Calendar." It was in the seventeenth century that the locality acquired its celebrity as the haunt of highwaymen. The reason will be obvious to readers of Macaulay, who writes in his "History of England":—"The peace (1698) had all over Europe, and nowhere more than in England, turned soldiers into marauders. . . . . On Hounslow Heath a company of horsemen, with masks on their faces . . . succeeded in stopping thirty or forty coaches (of the nobility), and rode off with a great booty in guineas, watches, and jewellery."

Here General Fairfax was robbed by "Moll Cut-purse," the noted highway-woman, who was committed to Newgate for the offence, but managed to escape from the gallows.

Here, in 1774, on his way to Cranford, Lord Berkeley shot a footpad who wanted his money, and who would have shot his lordship if he had not been anticipated. An amusing, though possibly somewhat poetical, account of the affair will be found in Mr. Grantley Berkeley's "Life and Recollections," and in the seventieth chapter of Lord Mahon's (Stanhope's) "History of England." His lordship, in relating it, adds some remarks which tend to show the audacity of highwaymen, and the terror which they inspired as late as the reigns of our Hanoverian line. He writes in 1836:—"Much less than a century ago the great thoroughfares near London, and above all, the open heaths, as Bagshot and Hounslow, were infested by robbers on horseback, who bore the name of highwaymen. Booty these men were determined by some means or other to obtain. In the reign of George the First they stuck up hand-bills at the gates of many known rich men in London, forbidding any one of them, on pain of death, to travel from home without a watch, or with less than ten guineas of money.* Private carriages and public conveyances were alike the objects of attack. Thus, Mr. Nuthall, the solicitor and friend of Lord Chatham, returning from Bath in his carriage . . . . was stopped and fired at near Hounslow, and died of the fright. . . . These outrages appear to have increased in frequency towards the close of the American War. . . . It is strange," he adds, "that so highly civilised a people should have endured these highway robberies so long . . . but stranger still, perhaps, to find some of the best writers of the last century treat them as subjects of jest, and almost of praise. From such productions as the 'Tom Clinch' of Swift or the 'Beggar's Opera' of Gay we may collect that it was the tone in certain circles to depict the highwaymen as daring and generous spirits, who 'took to the road,' as it was termed, under some momentary difficulties: the gentlefolk, as it were, of the profession, and far above the common run of thieves."

Mr. John Mellish, M.P. for Great Grimsby, was shot by highwaymen on Hounslow Heath as he was returning from hunting with the king's hounds, in April, 1798. His daughter lived down to 1880.

Charles Knight, in the commencement of his "Passages of a Working Life,"† tells us that he well remembered as a child the murder of Mr. Mellish by a footpad near the "Magpies," and the hanging of these knights of the road on the common, the scene of their misdeeds. "Between the two roads, near a clump of firs, was a gibbet, on which two bodies hung in chains. The chains rattled; the iron plates scarcely held the gibbet together; the rags of the highwaymen displayed their horrible skeletons within."

Hounslow Heath was still a favourite haunt of highwaymen even so late as the present century. A Mr. Steele was murdered here in 1806. This murder is remembered from the fact that at the execution of the assassin thirty persons were crushed to death in the crowd before the gallows.

Cyrus Redding writes thus of this spot in the above-mentioned year:—"It was a cold night when I crossed Hounslow Heath, about midnight, after eighteen hours' travelling. All the coaches had guards, and our's prepared his pistols and blunderbuses soon after we left Reading: a paradoxical

---

* "Lettres d'un Français en Angleterre," 1745, Vol. III., p. 211.
† Vol. I., p. 40.

mark that we were approaching the more civilised part of the kingdom. An officer had been shot at in his carriage by a highwayman while crossing the heath a few days before."

The gibbets seem, from Rocque's map of Middlesex, to have stood on the point of land formed by the junction of the Bath and Staines roads. Not far from them was Albemarle House, an "Academy" for youths, who seem to have had this humanising spectacle constantly before their eyes.

removed on account of the constant passing and re-passing of the royal family along this road on their journeys between London and Windsor.

Crabb Robinson mentions in his "Diary" in 1819 crossing Hounslow Heath on a stage-coach, and being told by one of his fellow-passengers that forty years previously the road was "literally lined with gibbets, on which were in irons the carcases of malefactors blackening in the sun." He might safely have written "twenty" for "forty."

WHITTON PARK. (*See p.* 69.)
(*From a Print by W. Woollett, about* 1800.)

There is a print of this school in the British Museum; it shows the boys exercising as volunteers, doubtless in expectation of the invasion of the great Napoleon in 1804. In the "Asylum for Fugitive Pieces," 1785, are the following coarse and vulgar lines, addressed to the young gentlemen of the Hounslow Academy :—

> "Take notice, roguelings, I prohibit
> Your walking underneath this gibbet;
> Have you not heard, my little ones,
> Of Raw Head and of Bloody Bones?
> How do you know but that there fellow
> May step down quick and up you swallow?"

The gibbets could never have been a very agreeable or edifying sight; and accordingly they were

The dangers of the road, in fact, were not at an end till many years of the present century had passed away; and, indeed, lasted very nearly down to the introduction of railways, which gave the "knights of the road" their final *congé*.

That the life of the "dashing" highwayman was invested with a sort of sensational romance there can be little doubt. "In the last half of the seventeenth century," writes Mr. James Thorne, in his "Environs of London," "it was no uncommon thing for the gay young cavalier to take to the road as the readiest mode of mending his fortune by lightening the purses of the well-to-do round-head citizens he held in supreme contempt; but even a century later stories were credited of other than vulgar footpads resorting at times to Hounslow Heath. It is gravely related, for example, that Twysden, Bishop of Raphoe, playing the highwayman there in 1752, was shot through the body, and died from the wound at a friend's house, his death being announced as from inflammation of the bowels." This story is related on the authority of the Hon. Grantley Berkeley, who tells it in his "Life and Recollections."

The readers of the "Beggar's Opera" will learn

No less a writer than De Quincey has endeavoured not merely to whitewash, but to throw a *couleur de rose* over the ideal highwayman. He followed "a liberal profession, one which required more accomplishments than either the bar or the pulpit, since from the beginning it presumed a most bountiful endowment of qualifications—strength, health, agility, and excellent horsemanship, intrepidity of the first order, presence of mind, courtesy, and a general ambidexterity of powers for facing all accidents,

OLD HANWORTH CHURCH. (*See p.* 70.)
(*From a Print published* 1795.)

from Captain Macheath how rapidly the information was circulated as to the wealth of intending travellers along the great western road. That the highwayman could at times be the "very essence of politeness" is not to be wondered at if they were made of such gentlemanly stuff. Claud Duval, as Macaulay tells us, "took to the road, and became captain of a formidable gang;" he adds that "it is related how, at the head of his troop, he stopped a lady's coach, in which there was a booty of four hundred pounds; how he took only one hundred, and suffered the fair owner to ransom the rest by dancing a coranto with him on the heath." This celebrated exploit has been made the subject of a painting by Mr. Frith, and has been engraved.

and for turning to a good account all unlooked-for contingencies." He considers that, beyond a doubt, the finest men in England, physically speaking, throughout the last century, the very noblest specimens of man, considered as an animal, were the mounted robbers, who cultivated their profession on the great leading roads. For the forger, and such as he, De Quincey has no sympathy; but he maintains that the special talents which led to distinction on the road had often no other career open to them. When every traveller carried fire-arms, the mounted robber lived in an element of danger and adventurous gallantry, so that admiration for the thief sometimes was extorted from the person robbed. "If to courage, address, promptitude of decision (writes Dutton Cook) he added courtesy and a spirit of forbearing generosity, he seemed to be almost a man who merited public encouragement." For it might be urged plausibly that if his profession was sure to exist, and that if he were removed, a successor might arise who would carry on the business in a less liberal spirit. Indeed, De Quincey seems to think that a shade of disgrace had fallen upon England in a previous generation, inasmuch as the championship of the road had passed for a time into the hands of a Frenchman like Claud Duval.

Notwithstanding the bold front which the highwayman was in the habit of assuming, he was occasionally outwitted. "Stand and deliver!" were the words addressed to a tailor travelling on foot by a highwayman, whose brace of pistols looked rather dangerous than otherwise. "I'll do that with pleasure," was the reply, at the same time handing over to the outstretched hands of the robber a purse apparently pretty well stocked; "but," continued he, "suppose you do me a favour in return. My friends would laugh at me were I to go home and tell them I was robbed with as much patience as a lamb; s'pose you fire your two bull-dogs right through the crown of my hat : it will look something like a show of resistance." His request was acceded to; but hardly had the smoke from the discharge of the weapons passed away, when the tailor pulled out a rusty old horse-pistol, and in his turn politely requested the thunder-struck highwayman to give up everything about him of value, his pistols not omitted.

The locality of Hounslow and its Heath is at best anything but a haunt of the Muses; but still it has inspired at all events one poem, for the Rev. Wetenhall Wilkes, who was minister of the Chapelry in the reign of George the Second, dedicated to the Duke of Argyll a poetical epistle, in verse, after the style of Pope, entitled "Hounslow Heath." The lines are turgid and bombastical enough, but they give us some particulars which would else have escaped notice. And a modern reprint of the poem, by Mr. W. Pinkerton, F.S.A., contains some interesting notes, on which we have drawn considerably. For instance, we learn that a century and a half ago the Heath was a frequent meet for the royal stag-hounds and fox-hounds, and that the King, the Prince of Wales, and the Princess Amelia were frequently seen here pursuing the pleasures of the chase. In the early part of the last century, horse-racing of a more plebeian character was here indulged in; to use the bombastic phrase of Mr. Wilkes in his poem,

"Near to the town behold a spacious course,
The scene of trial for the sportive horse."

The site of Hounslow Racecourse is laid down on Rocque's Map (1754). It was on the left of the road to Staines, a short distance from the Bell public-house. Many notices of these races are to be found in the newspapers of the time; for instance, in the *Evening Post* of July 20 and 23, 1734, when seven horses started, and one broke its leg in the last heat. The names of the horses and of the owners are given; but they evidently were not of the same stamp as those of which we read as figuring at Newmarket.

"Houses and inhabitants," writes the Honourable Miss Amelia Murray, "now occupy that part of Hounslow Heath where the grim gallows once stood within my recollection;" and Mason thus celebrates the place—

"Hounslow, whose heath sublimer terror fills,
Shall with her gibbets lend her powder-mills."

Large gunpowder-mills stand on the banks of a small stream about two miles to the south of the village. The powder-mills here, like those at Faversham, in Kent, and at other places, have been subject to accidental explosions at different times. One of the most serious which has occurred here took place on the 6th of January, 1772, when damage to a very great extent was done, the effects of the explosion being felt for many miles round. In November, 1874, another explosion occurred here, when five lives were lost. Every precaution is now taken, by the separation of the buildings, &c., to localise the effects of such accidents as far as possible, should any occur. It is said that the first gunpowder manufactured in England was probably manufactured on Hounslow Heath; and at a very early date indeed; for we are told that one William of Staines was employed by Edward III. in 1346 to make the gunpowder which enabled him to gain the victory of Crecy, the first battle in which powder was used. We shall have more to say on the subject of gunpowder manufactories when we reach Waltham Abbey.

In 1793 extensive cavalry barracks, capable of accommodating above four hundred men, were erected by the Government on that part of the Heath which is in Heston parish. There is an exercising-ground, about three hundred acres in extent, which is used for reviewing troops. The 4th, or Royal South Middlesex Militia, has its head-quarters here, and there is also an arsenal.

Mr. Wilkes celebrates in his poem the song-birds of Hounslow, and also the game which was to be found in the neighbourhood. His "Philomele" may still be heard here in summer nights; but it is to be feared that his "Moorcocks," his

"Curlieus," his "Teal and Widgeon," his "Easter-lings," and "Snipes," if they had any existence beyond the poetical imagination of the writer, have long since "flown to another retreat" upon the Surrey Hills, further out of the way of Cockney sportsmen.

Mr. Wilkes writes in his poem already quoted:—

"Four large patrician elms behind the town,
True as a beacon to the traveller known,
Their lofty boughs with ancient pride display,
And to fair Whitton point the cheerful way."

According to Rocque's Map (1754), these elms stood a few yards down the Bell Lane, on the Whitton Road. Two of them still remain.

Whitton Park, on the edge of Hounslow Heath, the seat of Colonel Gostling-Murray, was, in the last century, the residence of the Duke of Argyll, formerly known as Lord Islay. The gardens were especially well laid out, planted and cultivated, and adorned with statuary. Among other ornaments was a celebrated group in marble by Gabriel Cibber: the figure of a Highland piper and his dog. It represents the piper described by De Foe in his "History of the Plague" as taken up for dead and carried off to his burial in the dead-cart, but awakening from his trance just as he was about to be thrown into the pit, sitting up in the cart, and playing on his pipes, after which it is said that he recovered. This is certainly wonderful; it would be more wonderful, however, to find that, being a Highland piper, and immortalised by the Duke of Argyll, he was anything but a Campbell. The group was afterwards to be seen in the flower-gardens at Stowe. The gardens of Whitton Park gave rise to the following epigram:—

"Old Islay, to show his fine delicate taste
In improving his gardens purloined from the waste,
One day bade his gardener to open his views
By cutting a couple of grand avenues;
No particular prospect his lordship intended,
But left it to chance how his walks should be ended.
With transport and joy he beheld his first view end
In a favourite prospect—a church that was ruined.
But, alas! what a sight did the next cut exhibit!
At the end of the walk hung a rogue on a gibbet!
He beheld it and wept, for it caused him to muse on
Full many a Campbell who died with his shoes on.
All amazed and aghast at the ominous scene,
He ordered it quick to be closed up again
With a lump of Scotch firs that would serve as a screen."

Again, Mr. Wilkes writes grandiloquently—

"To sing those scenes where peace and grandeur dwell,
Whitton demands her verse; the Nine conspire
To swell my numbers with poetic fire.
There nature's genial powers impregn the ground,
And all her fragrant sweets are spread around."

* "Walpole's Letters," Vol. I.

Although the Duke of Argyll was contemptuously called a "tree-monger" by Horace Walpole, the country is indebted to him for introducing many foreign trees and shrubs which, by the beauty of their forms and colours, have greatly contributed to the pleasing effect of the English landscape. Almost every tree at Whitton was raised from seed planted by the duke in 1724. The grounds were all laid out with careful precision, and included fish-ponds, a bowling-green, orange walk, a Gothic tower, a Chinese summer-house, aviary, &c. After the sale of the property to Mr. Gostling, shortly after the duke's death, the conservatory was converted into the elegant villa now known as Whitton House, upon the pediment of which is a bas-relief after the antique, representing the destruction of the Titans by Jupiter. There is a well-known print of the gardens at Whitton, as they appeared, filled with the "quality," in the time of the Duke of Argyll.

The southern portion of Hounslow, including the neighbourhood of Whitton Park, has lately been made into a separate parish under the name of Whitton, with a new church on a pleasant village green.

The mansion at one time occupied by Sir Godfrey Kneller stands near this, but in the parish of Twickenham, and consequently will be dealt with in a subsequent chapter.

Three miles south-west from Hounslow lies the village of Hanworth, the site of which was formerly a royal hunting seat. Hanworth Park was at one time a favourite resort of Henry VIII. One part of the gardens still remains just as it was laid out under the eye of Queen Elizabeth.

This was one of the jointure houses of the Queen Dowager, Katharine Parr, widow of Henry VIII., and here Elizabeth resided, both before and after the union of that lady with Lord Seymour of Sudley, whose loose conduct towards the young princess—apparently encouraged, or at least connived at, by his wife—was scandalous enough to deserve being mentioned in the histories of the time. If the "Burleigh Papers" are to be trusted, "on one occasion the queen held the hands of the young princess whilst the Lord Admiral amused himself with cutting her gown into shreds; and on another she introduced him into the chamber of Elizabeth before she had left her bed, when a violent romping scene took place (writes Lucy Aikin), which was afterwards repeated in the presence of the queen." It is clear, then, that whatever merits Catharine Parr may have possessed, the morals of this widow did not render her a fit duenna to the future queen of England. Happily, however, her stay at Hanworth did not last long after this, for a violent scene took place between the royal stepmother and stepdaughter, which ended, fortunately for the peace and honour of Elizabeth, in an immediate and final separation.

About the middle of the sixteenth century the manor of Hanworth was granted to Anne, Duchess of Somerset, the widow of the Protector, and mother of the Earl of Hertford. In 1578 Queen Elizabeth was here on a visit to the duchess; the queen was here again in 1600, when she "hunted in the park." The mansion was at that time leased to William Killigrew, whose son, of the same name, the friend and servant of Charles I. and II., and a dramatic author of some note, was born here in 1605.

In 1627 Hanworth became the property of Sir Francis Cottington, who in the following year was created Baron Cottington of Hanworth. His lordship in 1635 here entertained Queen Henrietta Maria and her Court. On the fall of Charles I. Hanworth was confiscated, and given to President Bradshaw. Hanworth was, however, recovered by Lord Cottington's cousin and heir at the Restoration; but in 1670 it was sold to Sir Thomas Chamber, whose granddaughter conveyed it in marriage to Lord Vere Beauclerk, who in 1750 was created Baron Vere of Hanworth—a title now absorbed in the ducal house of St. Albans.

Gossiping Horace Walpole thus writes to his friend, Sir Horace Mann, under date 1791:—"The Duke of St. Albans has cut down all the brave old trees at Hanworth, and consequently reduced his park to what it issued from—Hounslow Heath; nay, he has hired a meadow next to mine for the benefit of embarkation, and there lie all the good old corpses of oaks, ashes, and chestnuts, directly before *your* windows, and blocking up one of my views of the river! But, so impetuous is the rage for building, that His Grace's timber will, I trust, not annoy us long."

Old Hanworth House was destroyed by fire in March, 1797, but the moat and a few vestiges of the house may still be seen close by the western end of Hanworth Church. The grounds known as Queen Elizabeth's Gardens have retained to this day much of their old-fashioned character, being studded with fine specimens of pine and old yews, and other trees.

The present Hanworth House stands on higher ground than its predecessor, and is a well-built mansion of the ordinary type. It was long the property of Mr. Perkins, whose fine library, which was extremely rich in MSS., was dispersed under the hammer of Messrs. Gadsden, Ellis, and Co., in the year 1873. The collector of these treasures was Mr. Henry Perkins (of the firm of Messrs. Barclay and Perkins, of Southwark), who bequeathed them to his son, the late Mr. Algernon Perkins, who died in 1873. Under the tuition of the celebrated Dr. Parr, Mr. Henry Perkins acquired his love for books, and the bulk of the library was obtained between the years 1820 and 1830, from the great English and Continental sales. Among the treasures disposed of on that occasion were several curious MSS. of the thirteenth and fourteenth centuries; two copies of the noted Mazarine Bible, and a large number of ancient Bibles, Evangelaries, Missals, Books of Hours, Pontificals, &c.; there were also many very choice works of legend and romance, including Lydgate's "Siege of Troy," the "Romance of the Rose," &c. The house passed by sale into the hands of Mr. Lafone, a merchant of London.

Hanworth Church, dedicated to St. George, is a modern erection, having been built in 1865, on the site of the former parish church.

At Hatton, between this and Hounslow, Sir Frederick Pollock, many years Chief Baron of the Exchequer, spent the last twenty years of his life.

CHAPTER VI.
TWICKENHAM.

"Meadows trim, with daisies pied,
Shallow brooks, and rivers wide."—*Milton.*

Derivation of the Name of Twickenham—Situation and Extent of the Parish—Early History of the Manor—The Manor House—Arragon Tower—Eel-pie Island—The Parish Church—Holy Trinity Church—St. Stephen's Church—Charitable Institutions—Curious Easter Custom—The Metropolitan and City of London Police Orphanage—Fortescue House—Royal Naval Female School—The Town Hall—Perryn House—Economic Museum—"Bull Land"—Extracts from the Parish Register—An Amusing Anecdote of Sir James Delaval.

TWICKENHAM lies on the road between Isleworth and Teddington and Hampton Court, in a valley between the higher ground of Strawberry Hill on the north and Richmond Hill on the south, from which latter it is separated by the river Thames and some pleasant fertile meadows. It has long been a favourite locality for the residence of a large number of the aristocracy; indeed, in the last century it acquired much celebrity in the fashionable world as the favourite haunt of Horace Walpole, and in the literary world as the home of Alexander Pope. Many of its noted houses, it is true, have disappeared, but the halo shed over the spot by their former inhabitants still remains. Although the village and its surroundings have lost much of their rural seclusion of late years by the formation of a railway through its very centre, and the rapid increase of modern dwelling-houses in all directions, much of its sylvan beauties are still visible, and its river-side aspect is as attractive as of old. Indeed, the locality is a particularly favoured one by the followers of the "gentle craft" which Izaak Walton did so much to popularise. Hofman, in his "British Angler's Manual" (1848), writes thus of the place :—

"The neighbourhood of Twickenham is not only singularly beautiful and rich in its adornments of elegant villas and noble mansions, but it abounds in memorials interesting to the historian, the antiquarian, and the lover of literature and art. The manor-house was, for a long period, the jointure-house of the queens of England. Katharine of Arragon and Henrietta of France have here bewailed, in their day, a cruel and a martyred husband. Queen Anne was born here, in York House, and lost her promising son whilst inhabiting the mansion now, or lately, the property of Sir George Pocock, Bart., which was for some years inhabited by the present King of France, when Duke of Orleans. Strawberry Hill, the seat of the celebrated Horace Walpole (Lord Orford), the house where Lady Mary Wortley resided, that of Earl Howe, and several others of great interest, are all in view; and within a little distance is Marble Hill, immortalised by Swift and Gay; Ham House, the splendid seat of Lord Dysart; Twickenham Meadows House, once the property of the celebrated Richard Owen Cambridge : these met the admiring eye of the angler as he made his way to the *deep*, where he now rests, and from which he gazes, untired, on that spot of ground which presents the most remarkable objects and associations, endeared by time and taste. *Here,* Pope wrote 'The deathless satire, the immortal song,' which neither time, fashion, nor envy can obliterate; *here,* he entertained the most highly-gifted men of his own, or, perhaps, any other time, the most noble, influential, and amiable. The grotto which he formed, and where he loved to sit with his friends, is before us, as well as the garden he planted; but which was much enlarged in dimensions, as well as beauty, by his first successor, as an inscription informs us :—

" 'The humble roof, the garden's scanty line,
    Ill suit the genius of the bard divine ;
    But fancy now displays a fairer scope,
    And Stanhope's plans unfold the soul of Pope.' "

The name of the parish, formerly spelt Twicknam, is said to be derived from its situation between two brooks which run into the Thames, one at each end of the parish. An alms-dish in the parish church, however, has upon it an inscription which runs thus :—"For the parish of Twitnaham." This alms-dish bears no date, but on a paten, dated 1674, the name is spelt exactly after the modern fashion. Norden says that "in several very ancient records antecedent to the Conquest, the name is written Twitnam, or Twittanham, or Twicanham." Twittenham, or Twitnam, survived as the common pronunciation of the name down almost to the present generation; in the last century it was a customary form of pronunciation, even among the best educated. Horace Walpole, who did so much to make Twickenham classic ground, invariably wrote the name Twit'nam, at least in his earlier works. In some verses of his, called "The Parish Register of Twickenham," the name is constantly written in that form :—

" Where silver Thames round Twit'nam meads
    His winding current sweetly leads :
    Twit'nam, the Muses' fav'rite seat,
    Twit'nam, the Graces' lov'd retreat ;
    There polished Essex went to sport,
    The pride and victim of a court ;
    There Bacon tuned the grateful lyre
    To soothe Eliza's haughty ire."

Pope, whose name is as closely associated with the memories of the parish as that of Walpole, spells the name "Twitenham" in most of his writings; and many other poets and men of letters of the last century wrote it in a similar manner. Thus, in Dodsley's collection of poems by various hands, we read :—

" I saw the sable barge along his Thames,
    Beating in slow solemnity the tide,
    Convey his sacred dust. Its swans expired ;
    Withered in Twitnam bowers the laurel bough.
    Silent, the Muses broke their idle lyres,
    Th' attendant Graces checked the sprightly dance,
    Their arms unlocked, and caught the starting tear,
    And virtue for her lost defender mourned."

Thomson also, in his poem on "Richmond Hill," writes :—

" Here let us trace the matchless vale of Thames,
    Far winding up to where the Muses haunt,
    To Twitnam's bowers."

And again, the Rev. T. Maurice, in a poem on the same subject, dated 1807, writes:—

"Twitnam! so dearly loved, so often sung,
    Theme of each raptured heart and glowing tongue."

The town is situated along the northern bank of the Thames, and to the natural beauties and advantages with which it is surrounded it owes a great proportion of the renown which it has possessed for the last three centuries, during which period it has numbered among its residents those who have occupied positions of eminence and influence, owing either to their exalted station in life, or to their literary, artistic, or political abilities.

ing date 1301, "Twykenham is entered as a hamlet appendant to the manor of Isleworth." Another record, dated 1390, says that the manor and hundred of Isleworth had always been deemed of the same extent. Lysons observes that this did not imply any jurisdiction over the lands of religious houses, which exercised manorial rights upon their own estates. "The Brethren of the Holy Trinity at Hounslow," he continues, "had a small manor within the hundred, independent of that of Isleworth. The monks of Christ Church had another in this parish from very ancient times, as will appear by the following account. Offa, King of the Mercians, between the years 791 and 794, gave to

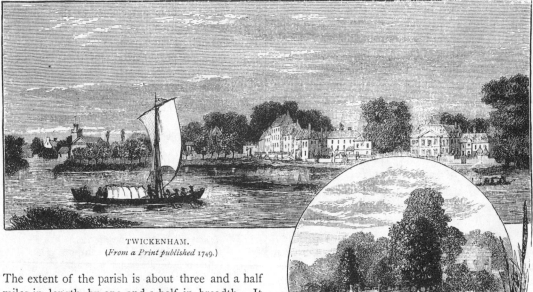

TWICKENHAM.
(*From a Print published* 1749.)

EEL-PIE ISLAND.

The extent of the parish is about three and a half miles in length, by one and a half in breadth. It contains, according to the Ordnance Survey, rather more than 2,415 acres; in the Isleworth Survey, taken in 1635, by order of Algernon, Duke of Northumberland, the number of acres is estimated at about 1,850.

The climate has always been celebrated for its pure and healthy influences, and in its vegetation it is the same as that of most parts of the course of the River Thames. Twickenham, in fact, with the country adjacent to it, has always been distinguished for the fertility of its gardens, which still send large supplies of vegetables and fruit, especially strawberries, to the London markets.

The parish is situated in the hundred of Isleworth, and for the most part within the ancient manor of Sion, of which the Duke of Northumberland is lord. The name of the place is not mentioned in "Domesday Book," for the simple reason, no doubt, that it was included in the parish of Isleworth. Lysons states that in a record, bear-

Athelard, Archbishop of Canterbury, among other benefactions, thirty tributaries of land on the north side of the river Thames, at a place called Twittanham, for the purpose of providing vestments for the priests who officiated in the church of St. Saviour in Canterbury. Warherdus, a priest, by his will, bearing date 830, gave to the church of Canterbury eight hides of land, with the manor of Twitnam, in Middlesex, which had been granted him by Ceolnothus, Dean of Canterbury (the same, it is probable, who was a few years afterwards Archbishop). In 941 Edmund the king, and Eldred his brother,

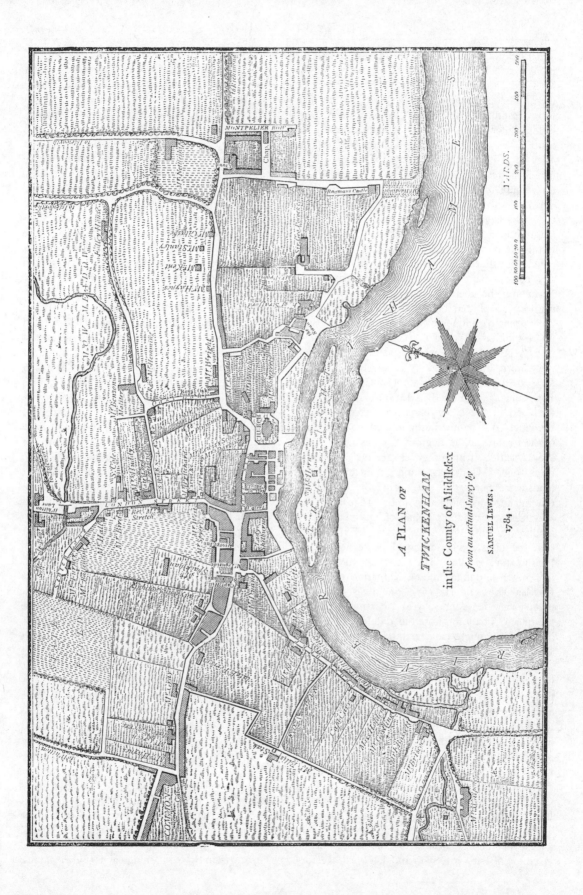

A PLAN OF
TWICKENHAM
in the County of Middlesex
from an actual survey by
SAMUEL LEWIS,
1784.

and Edmund, the son of Edmund, restored to the monks of Christ Church, in Canterbury, all the lands which they had unjustly taken away from them. Among these was the manor of Twittanham. This restitution seems not to have been very effectual, for it appears that King Eldred, by his charter, bearing date 948, gave to the said monks, as a small offering, for the love of God and the benefit of his soul, the manor of Twiccanham, in the county of Middlesex, situated upon the river Thames, with all its appurtenances, exempting it from all secular burdens, taxes, and tolls, excepting contributions towards the building of bridges and fortifications, and the king's expedition; his charter concludes with the following bitter anathema against any persons who should venture to infringe it— 'Whatever be their sex, order, or rank, may their memory be blotted out of the book of life, may their strength continually waste away, and be there no restorative to repair it.' I suppose this manor to have been the same which, being then vested in the Crown, was annexed by King Henry VIII. in 1539 to the honour of Hampton Court, between 1539 and 1541, granted to Edward, Earl of Hertford, and in the latter year surrendered by him to the king. It remained in the immediate occupation of the Crown till the reign of Charles I., by whom it was settled, with other estates, as a jointure, on his queen, Henrietta Maria. When the Crown lands were put up to sale during the usurpation, this manor was purchased (anno 1650) by John Hemsdell, merchant, on behalf of himself and other creditors of the State. . . After the Restoration the queen-mother resumed possession of her jointure, and held it till her death. In 1670 this manor was settled for life on Katharine, consort of Charles II.; and in 1675 the king granted a reversionary lease for 41 years, commencing after the queen's death, or from the date of such leases as the queen might have granted, to John, Earl of Rochester. William Genew, Esq., in 1688, had a lease of the manor for twelve years, to commence in 1707. Lord Rochester's lease, which commenced at the expiration of Genew's, becoming afterwards vested in Lord Bolingbroke, it was forfeited to the Crown upon his attainder in 1715." The lease of the manor subsequently passed by sale into the hands of different capitalists, whose names would be of no interest to the general reader. "The manor of Twickenham," as the Rev. R. S. Cobbett informs us, in his "Memorials of Twickenham," "extends through the parishes of Twickenham, Isleworth, and Heston. The customs are primogeniture, and fines arbitrary. The other manors are those of Isleworth Syon and Isleworth Rectory,

the former belonging to the Duke of Northumberland, and the latter now to the Ecclesiastical Commissioners, but formerly to the dean and canons of Windsor."

The Manor House, a large red-brick building, stood opposite the north side of the church. It was for some time called Arragon House, from a supposition that Katharine of Arragon retired hither after her divorce from Henry VIII. This, however, is but a doubtful tradition. Katharine of Braganza, queen of Charles II., is said to have inhabited the mansion for a time; and it is supposed also to have been part of the jointure of Queen Katharine Parr, who may have used it during her residence at Hanworth or Hampton Court. In the early part of the seventeenth century the house was in the occupation of Lady Walter, widow of Sir John Walter, Lord Chief Baron of the Exchequer, who, it is probable, had resided in it also, for at his death in 1630 he left a benefaction to the poor of Twickenham. In a survey of the house and park which was taken in 1650, mention is made of "two round rooms in a brick turret," and also "a fair hall wainscoted," in which was a screen of excellent workmanship. Mr. Samuel Scott, an artist who acquired some celebrity in his day as a painter of river scenery, occupied the house for some time prior to his death, in the year 1772, after which it became the residence of his pupil, Mr. William Marlow, F.S.A., who also became distinguished as an artist.

The greater part of the Manor House was taken down some few years ago, but a portion still remains, and is called Arragon Tower. Mr. Cobbett, in his work above quoted, states that the house was large, but possessed no features of peculiar interest. "It was evidently a Tudor structure (a mantelpiece in it indisputably belonged to that period), renovated in the time of William and Mary. In an apartment which was used as a cellar was a carved door of considerable antiquity, and several vacant niches with an ecclesiastical look about them, similar to those existing in the vicarage. A large garden adjoined the house, in which was a magnificent walnut-tree, which, when cut down, was sold for about £80. The royal arms of England were placed within, in the hall or over the entrance door."

Of the village—or, perhaps, more properly speaking, the town—of Twickenham there is but little to be said. At the western end, near the river-side, stands the parish church. In the river, nearly opposite the church, is an "ait," or eyot (island), containing about eight acres, chiefly laid out as pleasure-grounds, and known as Eel-pie Island. The Eel-pie House has been a noted place of resort for two centuries for fishermen and for pleasure parties. The old house was taken down in 1830. Church Street, a somewhat narrow, old-fashioned thoroughfare, runs westward from the church into King Street, the principal street of the town. Some of the river-side approaches here corresponded till quite lately to Pope's description in his own days :—

"In ev'ry town where Thamis rolls his tide,
  A narrow pass there is, with houses low ;
  Where ever and anon the stream is ey'd,
  And many a boat, soft sliding to and fro.
  There oft are heard the notes of infant woe,
  The short thick sob, loud scream, and shriller squall.
  How can ye, mothers, vex your children so ?

    *   *   *   *   *
    *   *   *   *   *

"And on the broken pavement, here and there,
  Doth many a stinking sprat and herring lie ;
  A brandy and tobacco shop is near,
  And hens, and dogs, and hogs are feeding by ;
  And here a sailor's jacket hangs to dry.
  At every door are sun-burnt matrons seen,
  Mending old nets to catch the scaly fry,
  Now singing shrill, and scolding oft between ;
  Scolds answer foul-mouthed scolds ; bad neighbourhood,
      I ween.

"Such place hath Deptford, navy-building town,
  Woolwich and Wapping, smelling strong of pitch ;
  Such Lambeth, envy of each band and gown,
  And Twick'nham such, which fairer scenes enrich,
  Grots, statues, urns, and J——n's dog and bitch.
  Ne village is without, on either side,
  All up the silver Thames, or all adown,
  Ne Richmond's self, from whose tall front are ey'd
  Vales, spires, meand'ring streams, and Windsor's tow'ry
      pride."

In 1882, however, the Thames front here was ornamentally embanked.

At the eastern end of the parish, where it joins on to Isleworth, a new district of villas has sprung up, known respectively as Cambridge and Twickenham Parks ; while westward, in the neighbourhood of the Common, the Heath, and Strawberry Vale, building has been going on largely of late years.

The parish church, as stated above, stands near the river-side, and is dedicated to St. Mary the Virgin. With the exception of the tower, it is a modern red-brick building, of the nondescript order of architecture, and of little or no interest, apart from the monuments which it contains. It stands on the site of the original edifice, the body of which fell to the ground on the night of the 9th of April, 1713. The church of Twickenham was of old appropriated to the Abbey of St. Valery (or Walerie), in Picardy. The date of its foundation

is unknown ; but "the style of the building, as exemplified by the tower," Mr. Cobbett observes, in his "Memorials of Twickenham," "must have belonged to the age of William of Wykeham ; and as the vicarages of Twickenham and Isleworth were given to the Crown by that prelate, we may conclude that the parish church was rebuilt under his superintendence. Its date, in that case, would be about the middle of the fourteenth century. The ground plan of the church comprised at that period a nave (with or without aisles), and the still existing western tower. As far as can be ascertained," Mr. Cobbett adds, "no old view or engraving of it exists ; the best notion of what it must have been like is supplied by the modern church of St. John's, Isleworth."

At the time of the fall of the church, Sir Godfrey Kneller was one of the churchwardens, and under his auspices the present building was erected. Mr. John James, who designed the church of St. George, Hanover Square, was the architect. "As a specimen of brick-work," writes Mr. Cobbett, "it is confessedly inimitable ; a repetition of the accident which had deprived Twickenham of one church was at least amply provided against for the future. The walls are of prodigious thickness ; every detail is carried out conscientiously and thoroughly, and in such respects it puts to shame many more pretentious modern structures." What historic interest the interior of the church may have possessed—from its association with the time of Walpole, Pope, and their friends—was wholly swept away between the years 1859 and 1871, during which period the old galleries were lowered and re-arranged, and the high cumbersome pews were made to give place to open benches. In lieu of a chancel, a *chorus cantorum* was formed at the east end ; a new vestry was erected on the south side of the church, and the restoration of the tower was effected. These alterations in the church provided additional sittings for about 400 adults, and a large increase of those for the school children. The wooden bell-turret which formerly crowned the tower, and is familiar to us in all old prints of the place, was taken down when the church was restored in 1859.

Apart from the parish registers, of which we shall speak presently, the monuments and their epitaphs are the only objects of interest to a casual visitor which Twickenham Church now possesses. Among these, the oldest is a stone slab placed upright against the south wall by the vestry door, and having upon it a brass plate in memory of Richard Burton, "chief cook to the king," and dated 1443. The monument erected by Bishop

Warburton to the memory of Pope is upon the north wall, and has upon it a medallion portrait of the poet, together with the line from the pen of Pope himself : " For one who would not be buried in Westminster Abbey," and the verse—

> " Heroes and kings, your distance keep ;
> In peace let one poor poet sleep,
> Who never flatter'd folks like you :
> Let Horace blush and Virgil too."

Why, however, Horace and Virgil should " blush " any more than the bard of Twickenham is not clear ; for were not all three courtier poets ?

On the east wall is a marble monument, erected by Pope to the memory of his parents and "to himself." In his " last will and testament" Pope gave the following instructions concerning his interment :—" As to my body, my will is that it be buried near the monument of my dear parents at Twickenham, with the addition, after the words *filius fecit*, of these only : ' *et sibi : Qui obiit anno* 17—*ætatis—;*' and that it be carried to the grave by six of the poorest men of the parish, to each of whom I order a suit of grey coarse cloth as mourning." The blanks left for the insertion of the date of the poet's death, and his age, have never been filled up, as they should have been.

Below the above-mentioned monument is a tablet inscribed to the memory of Mr. Richard Owen Cambridge, of whom we shall have more to say presently. Among the other monuments in the church are those to Sir William Humble and Sir Joseph Ashe ; to Lady Frances Whitmore, with an epitaph by Dryden ; to John, Lord Berkeley, of Stratton, who died in 1678 ; to Admiral Sir Chaloner Ogle, Sir Thomas Lawley, Sir Richard Perryn, and Louisa, Viscountess Clifden. Sir Godfrey Kneller lies buried here ; but, singularly enough, his monument is not here, but in Westminster Abbey, where his epitaph may be read. It is from the pen of Pope.

In the churchyard are a large number of tombs, of which may be mentioned those of Lieutenant-General William Tryon, sometime Governor of the Province of New York, who died in 1788, and Selina Countess Ferrers, who died in 1762. Admiral Byron, the author of the " Narrative of the Loss of the *Wager,*" who died in 1786, was buried here, but there is no monument to his memory ; and the searcher after quaint inscriptions may also look in vain for the following, which in most books on epitaphs is stated to be in Twickenham churchyard, but is probably apocryphal:—

> " Here lie I,
> Killed by a sky-
> Rocket in the eye."

There is, however, one epitaph on the chancel wall which will rivet attention ; it is that to the memory of Mrs. Catherine Clive—" Kitty Clive"— who died in 1758. It has a long poetical inscription, written by Miss Jane Pope, an actress, and commencing :—

> " Clive's blameless life this tablet shall proclaim,
> Her moral virtues, and her well-earn'd fame."

Dr. Charles Morton, F.R.S., sometime the principal librarian of the British Museum, who died in 1799, and Mr. Edward Ironside, the historian of Twickenham, who died in 1803, lie in the new burial-ground ; and in the graveyard in Royal Oak Lane are monuments to Field Marshal Sir Edward Blakeney, Governor of Chelsea Hospital, who died in 1868, to the Rev. Charles Proby, Vicar of Twickenham, who died in 1859, and many others of the principal inhabitants of the parish.

Dr. Terrick, afterwards Bishop of London, was Vicar of Twickenham in Horace Walpole's time. He was succeeded in the vicarage by the " learned " Rev. George Costard, who was also an astronomer of some note in his time. He died in 1782, and was buried in Twickenham churchyard, but no memorial marks the place of his interment.

Holy Trinity Church, on Twickenham Common, erected in 1840, is a poor specimen of architecture, built of brick with stone dressings; transepts and an apsidal chancel were added in 1863. Some of the windows are filled with stained glass, and there are tablets to the memory of Sir William Clay, M.P., and Lady Clay, late of Fulwell Lodge, on the road to Hanworth. Attached to this church are some schools, generally known as " Archdeacon Cambridge's Schools." They were built by subscription as a memorial of Archdeacon Cambridge, " and in grateful remembrance of his liberal contributions towards the erection and endowment of the church."

St. Stephen's Church, East Twickenham, was built in 1876, in place of Montpelier Episcopal Chapel, which, never having been consecrated, is now made to serve the purposes of a public hall. The old building had been used for the service of the Church of England for about 150 years. St. Stephen's Church is a Gothic building, and is constructed of Kentish rag and Bath stone.

Among the charities and institutions of Twickenham are almshouses founded in 1704 by a Mr. Mathew Harvie, and in 1721 the Hon. Sarah Greville bequeathed £200 towards the expense of erecting six additional almshouses. Bequests of land have been made at different times by the charitably disposed for the benefit of the poor, some of which are distributed in money and some in bread, and so forth.

It is said by Lysons that there was here "an ancient custom of dividing two great cakes in the church on Easter Day among the young people;" but that, being looked upon as a "superstitious relic," it was ordered by the Parliament in 1645 that the parishioners should "forbear that custom," and instead of it should " buy loaves of bread for the poor of the parish with the money that should have bought the cakes." It adds, "it appears that the sum of £1 per annum is still charged upon the vicarage for the purpose of buying penny loaves for poor children on the Thursday after Easter."

Wellesley House, a large mansion in the Hampton Road, is now the Metropolitan and City of London Police Orphanage, an institution founded in 1870 for the purpose of maintaining, clothing, and educating destitute orphan children of the police forces, and of "placing them out in situations where the prospect of an honest livelihood shall be secured." The orphanage is supported almost entirely by the members of the force, aided by occasional subscriptions from the outside world. The buildings will hold about 200 children.

Fortescue House, a somewhat heavy-looking mansion near the centre of the town, has been long devoted to charitable purposes. The house was at one time the residence of a former Lord Fortescue, who possessed in it a valuable collection of paintings by the old masters. It was for many years used as a ladies' boarding-school and for other educational purposes, and served for some time as the orphanage of the police before its transfer to Wellesley House. It is now a Home for destitute boys.

The Royal Naval Female School at St. Margaret's was founded in 1840, mainly through the bequest of Admiral Sir Thomas Williams, G.C.B., who gave £1,000 to be invested in trust as the basis of an endowment fund. In 1856 the present building was purchased, and the school removed hither from Richmond. The object of the institution is "to provide at the lowest possible cost a good education for the orphan and other daughters of officers of Her Majesty's Army and of the Royal Marines." The number of pupils is limited to ninety, of which number twenty-six are received at the annual payment of £50; fifty-six are boarded and educated at the entire cost to the parents or guardians of £12 per annum; and five, whose fathers died during the Crimean campaign, are nominees of the Patriotic Fund, the establishment defraying the larger amount of actual cost through the means of voluntary contributions.

Among the most recent additions to the public buildings of Twickenham is a Town Hall, erected at the expense of Sir Charles Freake. It is a handsome building of red brick, with stone dressings; it contains a large assembly-room, which is used for concerts, meetings, &c.

North of the railway station, at the junction of the roads leading to Whitton and Isleworth, stands Perryn House, so called from having been formerly the residence of Sir Richard Perryn, a Baron of the Exchequer, who died in 1803. About the year 1835 the property was sold to Mr. Thomas Twining, a resident of the neighbourhood: his son, of the same name, commenced in 1856 the formation of a permanent Educational Exhibition of things appertaining to domestic and sanitary economy, which, from its having been devoted to the furtherance of what may be called economic knowledge, took the name of the "Economic Museum." In a certain sense, however, the idea first took shape and form in one of the departments of the Universal Exposition at Paris in 1855. It was a collection of every possible description of household treasures : in short, of all material things needful to man. It included "marvels of cheapness," ingenious devices for the economy of space, and specimens of food and clothing. Visitors called it "the exhibition of cheapness," yet it was something more than that—it was an exhibition of prudence, of forethought, of cleanliness, and of sanitary arrangement, which together form the foundation of domestic economy. The building stood in the grounds of Perryn House. Its contents included models or specimens of building designs, intended as a guide to persons desirous of improving the dwellings of the working classes ; building materials, pictures, furniture, and household utensils ; textile materials, fabrics, and costumes ; food, fuel, and household stores ; sanitary appliances, &c. Attached to the museum was a valuable and comprehensive library of books, pamphlets, and documents, both British and foreign, selected and arranged for convenience of reference in matters of domestic, sanitary, educational, and social economy and practical benevolence. The usefulness of the museum, and of the lectures explanatory of the subjects of which it contained examples, compiled by Mr. Twining, and delivered by his agents in various parts of London and the suburbs, gradually became felt and acknowledged by many persons whose opinion was of great weight and value. The museum and all its valuable contents, including the library, however, were totally consumed by fire in 1871. It was calculated that £10,000 would not replace the loss.

Before proceeding to describe other houses in the parish, and to mention the many eminent inhabitants whose residence here has gone far towards making Twickenham one of the most popular suburbs of London, it will, perhaps, be best to close this chapter with a few extracts from the parish register, and to deal with one or two other matters which have affected the rise and progress of the town. The minutes of the vestry and the churchwardens' accounts are, for the most part, in good preservation, and date respectively from 1618 and 1606. In the latter, "Strawberry Hill" and the "Bull Lands" are mentioned for the first time. Of Strawberry Hill we shall have occasion to speak at some length presently. With regard to the entry concerning the " Bull Land," it may be stated that from a copy of the Court Roll of the Manor of Isleworth Sion, dated December 20th, 1675, it appears that one Thomas Cole surrendered four acres one rood of land, lying in several places in the fields of Twickenham, called the parish land, anciently belonging to the inhabitants of Twickenham, "in trust for the keeping and maintaining a sufficient bull for the common use of the said inhabitants."

Amongst the receipts for 1631, and other years, are sums, usually about six shillings and sixpence, paid by other parishes, among which Teddington and Cranford are named, " for the loan of the parish pewter," as the sacramental plate was described. In 1652 the churchwardens made an inventory of the parish goods, which they handed over to their successors in office. It is as follows :—" A greater silver and guilt cupp, with the cover, given by Mr. Hollingsworth. A lesser silver cupp with a cover. Two pewter flaggons. A greene velvett cushion for the pulpitt. Greene carpett for the comunion table. Blacke cloth for the ffuneralls. One joyned chest. Two joyned stooles. One little chest with two locks. One diaper table-cloth for the communion table." That the " free " and open seat movement was not thought of or dreamed about in the seventeenth century may be easily inferred from the following entry in the minutes of the vestry, under date of May 2, 1659 :—" That

SIR GODFREY KNELLER.   (See p. 75.)
(From the Painting by Himself).

the little seat, on the back side of the one where Gooddy Raynor sittes now in, and one on the south side of the seate where Gooddy Barker now sitteth in, shall be hereafter belonging to the house which Mr. Peirce now hath by the water-side, in lue of the seate which did formerly belong to the said house." And again, under date of May 9, 1667 :— " Ed. Gray having complained that yᵉ Erle of Clarendon's pew for his servants in the gallery had been taken away from him by the churchwardens," it was ordered " that noe person should sitt in yᵉ said pew but by leave of my Lord Clarendon or his servants." On September 20th, 1674, it was ordered that bells were not to be rung " but according to a declaration, under my Lord Chief Justice's hand, how he sayes they may be legally ringed."

On April 17th, 1676, a parish officer was appointed " to secure the town against vagabones, beggars, and other persons harbouring in barnes or out-houses, also to prevent ' theefing ' and robbing houses and grounds." That this precautionary measure did not have altogether the desired effect is pretty clear ; at all events, there were highwaymen busily plying their work here a century later, for Mrs. Kitty Clive writes to Garrick, under date June 10th, 1776 : —" Have you not heard of the adventures of your poor friend ? I have been rob'd (sic) and murder'd coming from Kingston. Jimey and I in a postchey (sic) at half past nine, just by Teddington Church, was stoppt. I only lost a little silver and my senses, for one of them come into the carriage with a great horse pistol to sarch (sic) me for my watch, but I had it not with me."

In 1686 the parish authorities were ordered by the deputy-lieutenancy of the county " to provide coats, hatts, and belts for sixteene maimed souldiers." A box was made to keep the articles so contributed.

Two curious entries occur in the accounts for 1688. The first is as follows :—" Item : Paid to the relief of a sick man brought naked out of the camp, and passing him away, 11s. 3d." James II., as we have already shown (see ante, page 64), had his camp at this time on Hounslow Heath. The other entry is as follows :—"Item : To Mr. Guisbey, for curing Doll Bannister's nose, 3s."

On May 11th, 1696, it was ordered that the beadle should have 20s. per annum and the Cross-house rent free, "for to ward within and about this parish, and to keep out all Beggars and Vagabonds that shall lye, abide, or lurk about the towne, and to give correction to such that shall anyways stand in Opposition contrary to the Statutes in that case made and provided." In the accounts of 1698 is this entry :—"Item : Paid old Tomlins for fetching home the Church-gates, being thrown into yᵉ Thames in the night by Drunkards, 2s. 6d."

In December, 1701, the parish allowed the Earl of Bedford, with the consent of His Grace the Duke

But Twickenham had not only its "rogues in grain," but its saints. At all events, at the end of the last century several of the leading inhabitants of the parish were staunch followers of the Wesleyan connection ; and it is recorded in the "Life of Wesley" that he dined with one of them here less than a fort-night before his death.

TWICKENHAM PARK HOUSE. (See p. 81.)

of Somerset, "to set up a pillar or column in the middle of Twickenham, as his lordship should see fit."

On December 5th, 1726, so many larcenies having been committed in the neighbourhood, and the sufferers being unwilling to prosecute, on account of expense, the vestry ordered that whenever any larceny, felony, or burglary was committed, Mr. James Taylor, of New Brentford, should be empowered to manage the prosecution of the same, and for his pains should be paid by a rate.

The churchwardens here, as in other country villages, were in the habit of paying for the destruction of vermin. In their accounts for the years 1773 and 1774, for instance, are these items : " Paid for 54 Hedgehogs, 18s. ;" and "Paid for 4 Pole-cats, 1s. 4d." Similar entries occur in large numbers down to quite recent times. On the 4th of October, 1790, it was ordered "that a whipping-post be put up at the workhouse *immediately.*"

in February, 1791. It was probably the last occasion of his leaving home.

Still there was nothing specially austere in the customs of the inhabitants. It is stated in the *Mirror* for 1840 that " at the recent petty sessions here the magistrates granted the request of some of the inhabitants to enjoy the ancient right of playing at football on Shrove Tuesday—a custom observed in the principal suburban parishes of Middlesex and Surrey from time immemorial."

Since the formation of a Local Board, the duties of the parishioners, "in vestry assembled," have been much lessened and curtailed. All the responsibilities attaching to the lighting of the parish, the care of its roads and highways, and especially the urgent question of drainage, devolve upon the Board, and are now no longer managed by special committees, elected for such purposes, as was the case previous to the year 1868.

The roads in Twickenham and its immediate neighbourhood were in former times mostly very narrow and ill-kept, which sometimes made travelling along them in coaches or other vehicles anything but easy or pleasant, and occasionally led to awkward blocks, from vehicles coming in opposite directions. An instance of this occurred on one occasion to the carriages containing Sir James Delaval and the Duke of Somerset. The latter, who is known to historians as the "proud" Duke of Somerset, was an inordinately arrogant nobleman, who seemed in his conduct as if vested with regal honours. His servants obeyed him by signs, and were not allowed to speak, and scarcely to appear, in his presence. His children obeyed his mandates with profound and servile respect. The story goes that the pleasant Sir James Delaval laid a wager of £1,000 that he would make the duke give him precedency; but that was judged impossible, as his Grace was all eyes and ears on such occasions. Delaval, however, having one day obtained information of the precise time when the duke was to pass a narrow part of the road on his way to town, stationed himself there in a coach, emblazoned for the day with the arms, and surrounded by many servants in the livery of the head of the house of Howard, who called out, when Somerset appeared, "The Duke of Norfolk!" The former, fearful of committing a breach of etiquette, hurried his postilion under a hedge, where he was no sooner safely fixed than Delaval passed, who, leaning out of the carriage, bowed with a familiar air, and wished his Grace a good morning. He indignantly exclaimed, "Is it you, Sir James? I thought it had been the Duke of Norfolk!" The wager thus won was paid, and the town made merry with the stratagem used by Sir James to gain it.

A map of Twickenham as it was in 1784, which we give on page 73, shows the distribution of property as it stood a century ago. At the extreme south-west is shown Strawberry Hill, marked simply "Mr. Walpole." Between it and the main street of the village are, on the river side of the road, the seats of Lord Sefton, Mr. Ellis (Pope's villa), Miss and Mr. Shirley, and Lord Poulett; on the other side, the grounds of Mr. Briscoe, Sir F. Bassett, Mr. Gostling, Miss Holden, and Mr. Blake. On the south side of the road leading to Twickenham Common stands the mansion of the late Lord Ferrers (the same who not long before had been executed at Tyburn). Fortescue House, at the north of the village, appears as "the late Lord Fortescue's." Around it lie the properties of several nobodies; and, curiously enough, the spot now occupied by the South Western Railway Station is marked "Staten" Field. To the east of the parish church we note the mansions of Mr. Shakerly, Mr. Whitchurch, and Mr. Condell, some of whom doubtless knew Alexander Pope in the flesh. Between the centre of the main street and the river stands the mansion of Lady Shelburne, enclosed apparently within walls, adjoining Water Street, which probably then was an important thoroughfare as leading down to "the silent highway" of the river. To the east of the map is Sir George Pococke's mansion, and beyond it Ragman's Castle and Montpelier Row and Chapel, with Mr. Hardinge's house by the river-side facing a small eyot. Between "Mow" Meadow, on the north, and the extreme north-east of the map are two bridle roads to Isleworth, on the one of which stands Mr. Nettleship's, and on the other "Folly House." Across the brook at the north, where Pope probably narrowly escaped drowning, as we shall see later, are the grounds of Mr. Cole, whose family was connected with Twickenham for some two or three generations.

CHAPTER VII.

TWICKENHAM (continued).

"To Twitnam's mead the muse repairs."

THERE are few, if any, places within "a measurable distance" of the metropolis where there have resided such a host of distinguished persons as Twickenham. Among its former inhabitants have

been statesmen, poets, philosophers, painters, authors, ecclesiastics, military and naval men, as well as many women of eminence in the worlds of society and of letters. Its classic bowers, in fact, gained for it from Horace Walpole the name of "The Baiæ of Great Britain." In the lapse of years it would be difficult, perhaps, in every instance, to point out exactly the residences and characteristics of all these Twickenham worthies; but still, enough remains upon record, or lives in local tradition, to identify a goodly list, with their respective homes. First and foremost stand the names of Pope and Horace Walpole; but of each of these there is sufficient to form a separate chapter.

In 1722, De Foe wrote, in his "Tour through England and Scotland":—"Twittenham, a village remarkable for abundance of curious seats, of which that of Boucher, the famous gamester, would pass in Italy for a delicate palace. The Earl of Marr, the Earl of Strafford, the Earl of Bradford, the Lord Brook, the Lord Sunderland, the Lady Falkland, have each their pretty villas in this parish; but I think that of Secretary Johnstone, for the elegancy and largeness of the gardens, his terrace on the river, and the situation of his house, makes much the brightest figure here." Horace Walpole, in his letter to Bentley, about thirty years later, writes of the place in much the same strain. He observes that "Nothing is equal to the fashion of this place: Mr. Muntz says we have more coaches here than there are in half France. Mrs. Pritchard has bought Ragman's Castle, for which my Lord Lichfield could not agree. We shall be as celebrated as Baiæ or Tivoli; and if we have not such sonorous names as they boast, we have very famous people: Clive and Pritchard, actresses; Scott and Hodson, painters; my Lady Suffolk, famous in her time; Mr. H——,* the impudent lawyer, that Tom Harvey wrote against; Whitehead, the poet; and Cambridge the everything." In dealing with the annals of this parish, we have, fortunately, the "Memorials of Twickenham," by the Rev. R. S. Cobbett, to draw upon, and from this work we shall have occasion to quote largely in this and one or two succeeding chapters.

Commencing our survey of the houses at the north-east corner of the parish, near the banks of the river, and at the junction of the parish with Isleworth, we shall commence with Twickenham Park, a spot which lays claim to being the oldest among the Twickenham demesnes. It was originally called Isleworth Park, and also the New Park of Richmond. Honest John Stow, in his "Annals," tells us that in 1263, during the disturbances in the reign of Henry III., "Simon de

Mountfort, with the barons, pitched their tents in Isleworth or Thistleworth Parke." The site of the encampment is in the parish of Twickenham. In this park there stood from 1414 to 1431, as stated in a previous chapter,* the ancient monastery of Sion. The Rev. Mr. Cobbett, in his "Memorials of Twickenham," says that in the parish chest of Twickenham are two deeds: one of them, dated 1444, is "a release from Matilda, abbess of the monastery, to their tenants of Istelworthe, of a certain yearly tallage of £20, which they were held to pay to the said abbess and convent;" and the other, bearing the same date, is a deed confirming the grant of sundry manors to the abbess and convent. One of these deeds had been lost sight of for many years, and came to light again only on the restoration of the parish church in 1859.

Robert Boucher was appointed keeper of Twickenham Park in 1547; but the park, as such, seems to have been soon after broken up; for Norden, in the manuscript additions to his "Speculum Britanniæ," made towards the end of the sixteenth century, remarks that "Twyckenham Parke is now disparked." In 1574 the estate was demised to Edward Bacon, third son of Sir Nicholas Bacon, the celebrated Lord Keeper. In 1581 it was leased to one Edward Fitzgarret. Sir Francis Bacon, whom Voltaire calls "the father of experimental philosophy," spent much of his time here during the earlier period of his studious life; and in 1592 he somewhat suddenly took refuge here with several friends, owing to "a pestilential distemper which broke out in London, and dispersed the members of Gray's Inn—a community to which Bacon then belonged." At the end of that year he was honoured by a visit from Queen Elizabeth, "at his lodging in Twickenham Park," when he presented her Majesty with a sonnet in praise of her favourite, the Earl of Essex. Among the MSS. in the British Museum is a paper entitled "Instructions from the Lord Chancellor Bacon to his servant, Thomas Bushell," in which is set forth a scheme which he entertained for the purpose of exploring abandoned mineral works. On the supposition that such a project would meet with due encouragement, he says, "Let Twitnam Park, which I sold in my younger days, be purchased, if possible, for a residence for such deserving persons to study in, since I experimentally found the situation of that place much convenient for the trial of my philosophical conclusions, expressed in a paper sealed to the trust, which I myself had just in practice, and settled the same by Act of Parlia-

---

* "This was Joseph Hickey, the 'most blunt honest creature' of Goldsmith's 'Retaliation,' whose 'one only fault,' in Oliver's estimation —though 'that was a thumper'—was that he was a special attorney."— Thorne's "Environs of London"

* See page 44, ante.

ment, if the vicissitudes of fortune had not intervened, and prevented me."

In the seventeenth century the ownership or lesseeship of Twickenham Park frequently changed hands. In 1608 it was held by Lucy, Countess of Bedford, whose memory has been preserved to posterity by the verses of Dr. Donne, Dean of St. Paul's, and by Ben Jonson, who wrote at her request an epigram or two. In 1618 the estate passed to Sir William Harrington, who, a few years later, sold it to Mary, Countess of Home. In 1668 it was alienated to John, Lord Berkeley of Stratton, who died here in 1678, and lies buried in Twickenham church. The estate was afterwards held by the Earl of Cardigan, who in 1698 sold it to the Earl of Albemarle; and about four years later we find it in the hands of Thomas Vernon, who had been secretary to the Duke of Monmouth. The property was purchased of his heirs in 1743 by Algernon, Earl of Mountrath, whose widow, Diana, daughter of the Earl of Bradford, bequeathed it by her will, dated 1766, in a somewhat curious manner, "to the Duchess of Montrose during the joint lives of the Duke and Duchess of Newcastle; but if the Duchess of Newcastle should survive the duke, the Duchess of Montrose to quit possession to her; and if she should survive her, to enjoy it again during *her* life. After the death of the Duchess of Montrose, to remain (revert) to Lord Frederick Cavendish and his issue; on failure of which, after his death, to Lord John Cavendish and his issue, with remainder to Sir William Abdy, Bart., and his heirs in fee." It is remarkable that, except in the instance of Lord John not surviving Lord Frederick Cavendish, everything happened for which the countess thus singularly provided. Lord Frederick Cavendish was owner of Twickenham Park House when Angus published his view of that place, in 1795. From this it appears to have been a large and roomy edifice of red brick with stone dressings, and to have consisted of three storeys above the ground floor, with eleven windows in each, the centre having a portico and pediment, and that and the wings slightly projecting. In Angus's work the building is described as "containing several handsome apartments, with a noble staircase, painted in a similar manner to that at Windsor Castle." Ironside, in his "History of Twickenham," gives the following minute particulars concerning this building:—"The house stands in the two parishes of Twickenham and Isleworth. In the hall, fronting to the south-west, is laid in the mosaic pavement of black and white marble a small iron cross, which divides the two parishes, and in their perambulation of the bounds,

the parishioners of Twickenham direct a man to enter a window at the north-west end of the house, who proceeds to the centre, comes down-stairs, and joins the company in the hall, where they sing the hundredth psalm. He then goes up-stairs, and proceeds to a south-west window, and comes down a ladder on the outside, joins the company again, and thus the ceremony ends."

Early in the present century the greater part of Twickenham Park was sold in lots for building purposes. In 1817 the old mansion was advertised for sale, and was eventually demolished; on its site sprang up a row of "neat villas," which has now culminated in almost a new town.

A large portion of the Twickenham Park estate was purchased by Mr. F. Gostling, whose seat in the parish of Isleworth adjoined it. The Earl of Cassillis (afterwards Marquis of Ailsa) subsequently built a house on part of the property. This, however, was taken down by Lord Kilmorey, when he lived in the large house which is now the Naval School.

Between Twickenham Park and Richmond Bridge, pleasantly situated in Twickenham Meadows, stands a house, called, after its most celebrated occupant, Cambridge House. It was built in the early part of the seventeenth century by Sir Humphry Lynd, whom Anthony à Wood describes as a "zealous Puritan." After his death it became the residence of Joyce, Countess of Totness, who died there in 1636. Later on the property was sold to Sir Joseph Ashe, whose son, Sir Windham Ashe, built the west front and greatly enlarged the mansion. In the middle of the last century it was bought by Richard Owen Cambridge, the well-known author of the mock-heroic poem of the "Scribleriad," and who may be said to have here realised the poetical delineation of Thomson, for in the society of a few choice spirits, he was here blessed with

"An elegant sufficiency, content,
　　Retirement, rural quiet, friendship, books,
　　Ease, and alternate labour."

Mr. Cambridge must be well known to the readers of Boswell's "Life of Johnson" as a man of high literary attainments. Besides the "Scribleriad" mentioned above, he was the author of some poems in the sixth volume of Dodsley's collection, and one of the ablest contributors to the periodical work called *The World*. He also wrote an "Account of the War in India between the English and French, on the Coast of Coromandel, from the Year 1750 to 1760," &c. Mr. Cambridge was born in London in 1717, and received his education at Eton and St. John's

College, Oxford. He was for some time a member of Lincoln's Inn, but ultimately determined to abandon the legal profession. He was living at Twickenham when Pope first went to reside in that neighbourhood, and he was on an intimate footing with him, as well as with the most distinguished characters in this country. Mr. Cambridge possessed great powers of conversation, and abounded in choice anecdotes, which he always told with peculiar neatness and point. His connection with *The World* gave rise to a *bon mot*, which is related by his son, Archdeacon Cambridge, who writes :—"A note from Mr. Moore requesting *an essay* was put into my father's hands on a Sunday morning as he was going to church. My mother, observing him rather inattentive during the sermon, whispered, 'What are you thinking of?' He replied, 'Of the *next world*, my dear.'" Mr. Cambridge wrote two epilogues, which were spoken by Miss Pope and by a daughter of Mrs. Pritchard at their respective "benefits." He died in September, 1802, at the age of eighty-five. In an obituary notice of him in *The Gentleman's Magazine*, it is remarked that he "enjoyed an advantage very rarely possessed by the poetical tribe, for he had the 'elegant sufficiency' which Thomson represents as a *desideratum* in human happiness, and was therefore enabled to follow the bent of his genius, and only obey the inspirations of the muse when she chose to be propitious. One of his last literary amusements was a very pleasant versification of the historian Gibbon's account of his own life, with which Mr. Cambridge used to entertain his friends in company, but would not commit to paper."

In the year after his death the literary works of Mr. Cambridge were collected and published in a quarto volume, with a memoir prefixed from the pen of his son, who speaks of him as "an elegant rather than a profound scholar. The liveliness of his parts," he continues, "was more adapted to quick discernment than deep thinking; he had, therefore, but little inclination for abstruse studies and those researches which demand laborious investigation. . . His fondness for books served to increase rather than diminish his study of human nature. His insight into men was correct, judicious, and acute ; he viewed with the eye of a philosopher the influence of the passions, not only in the great and leading points of human conduct, but in the trifling incident of human life. The follies of mankind excited his mirth rather than his spleen ; but his vein of comic humour was ever regulated by that native benevolence which would not allow him voluntarily to inflict the slightest pain. . .

In his political as well as all other opinions, he manifested that candour which arose from knowledge as well as temper. His life and principles were alike free from corruption ; his purity and independence equally untainted." Among his intimate and valued friends may be mentioned Lords Bathurst, Hardwicke, and Mendip, Sir Richard Lyttelton, Horace Walpole, Lord North, Garrick, Sir Joshua Reynolds, Dr. Johnson, Bishop Porteus, Lord Hyde, and Admiral Boscawen. His residence at Twickenham, in fact, became a favourite resort of the most distinguished among his contemporaries. Thus we find Boswell referring with unusual warmth to Mr. Cambridge's "extensive circle of friends and acquaintances, distinguished by rank, fashion, and genius."

After the death of Mr. Cambridge, his villa devolved on his son, the archdeacon, who, however, subsequently removed to a smaller house, which he built at a short distance southward. Cambridge House then became the residence of Lord Mount-Edgcumbe. About the year 1840 it became the seat of Mr. Henry Bevan, and afterwards of his daughter, Lady John Chichester.

Meadowbank, which is the name of the house mentioned above as being built for Archdeacon Cambridge, was for many years the residence of Mr. George Bishop, who had here fitted up an observatory, which has acquired a world-wide reputation from the observations and discoveries made in it under its distinguished superintendent, Mr. John Russell Hind, F.R.S., who resides close by, in Cambridge Park Gardens.

At a short distance westward from Meadowbank, and near the river-side, is Marble Hill—or, as it seems usually to have been called in former times, Marble Hall. The house was built at the expense of George II. for Mrs. Henrietta Howard, who was then a bed-chamber woman, but afterwards Countess of Suffolk, and Groom of the Stole to the queen. The building was designed by the Earl of Pembroke ; and, as Swift writes, " Mr. Pope was the contriver of the gardens . . . and the Dean of St. Patrick's (Swift himself) chief butler and keeper of the ice-house." " The intention of the architect," observes Mr. Cobbett, in his " Memorials of Twickenham," " was evidently to make the rooms on the first floor of most imposing proportions, and to effect this, the height of the lower and upper storeys has been somewhat unduly sacrificed. The staircase is made entirely of finely-carved mahogany, and some of the floors are of the same wood. . . The interior of the house is plain in the extreme." Mrs. Howard, in a letter to Gay, dated July, 1723, begs him not to mention the

MR. PITT'S HOUSE AT TWICKENHAM.
(*From a Print published by Boydell, 1753.*)

plan which he found in her room, as it was necessary to keep the affair secret, although, as she
ventures to tell him, " the house was almost entirely
furnished to her satisfaction." The reason of
secrecy thus enjoined on Gay was probably the
fact that the king had extensively contributed to
its cost.

Born a Hobart, the Countess of Suffolk—Pope's
"Chloe"—had for her first husband the Hon.
Charles Howard, and was appointed a Lady of the
Howard was looked upon as a very pattern of propriety." Lord Hervey tells us that Mrs. Howard had
£2,000 a year from the prince, and £3,200 a year
after he became king, besides several little 'dabs'
of money, both before and after. The final 'dab'
was £12,000 towards building Marble Hill. The
house was designed by Lords Burlington and Pembroke; the garden was laid out by Lord Bathurst
and Pope; whilst Gay, Swift, and Arbuthnot, constituted themselves superintendents of the house-

MARBLE HILL.   (See p. 83.)
(From a Drawing by P. De Wint, 1819.)

Bed-chamber to the Princess, afterwards Queen,
Caroline. She was noted for her sweetness of
temper and pleasant manners; and Pope writes of
her—

" Yet Chloe sure was formed without a spot."

Separated from her husband, she became mistress
to the prince, afterwards George II. All the wits
and poets of the day paid their court to her; poor
Gay, for instance, was always trusting to her influence for some appointment which would make
him happy, but it never came. " It is scarcely
possible," writes an annotator on Pope's works,
" to conceive anything more gross than the morals
of the English Court under the two first Georges,
as related by Walpole and Lord Hervey. Every
department was affected; and among the maids of
honour, just as among the wits and divines, Mrs.

hold at large. The lady's husband lived long
enough to become Earl of Suffolk, and dying
opportunely, left her, at the age of a little
over forty-five, in a position to marry the Hon.
George Berkeley. They lived together very happily
for eleven years. After Mr. Berkeley's decease, in
1746, she survived twenty-one years, gratifying her
neighbour, Horace Walpole, with Court anecdotes
long after all the actors in them had passed away."
" Lady Suffolk," says Walpole, " was of a just
height, well made, extremely fair, with the finest
light brown hair, was remarkably genteel, and
always well dressed with taste and simplicity.
Those were her personal charms, for her face was
regular and agreeable rather than beautiful; and
those charms she retained, with little diminution,
to her death."

It was from Lady Suffolk that Pope picked up much of the Court scandal of the day. Warton tells us that the poet being one day at dinner with her, heard her give an order to her footman to put her in mind to send to know how Mrs. Blount, who was ill, had passed the night. This incident, insignificant enough perhaps in its way, gave rise to the following couplet in Pope's "Moral Essays" :—

"Would Chloe know if you're alive or dead?
She bids her footman put it in her head."

Contemporary writers are unanimous in declaring that Lady Suffolk was gentle and engaging in her manners, and much beloved by all who knew her. Horace Walpole, who lived on terms of the greatest intimacy with her in her later years, and whose testimony to her personal charms we have already quoted, says that "her mental qualifications were by no means shining—her eyes and countenance showed her character, which was grave and mild. Her strict love of truth and her accurate memory were always in unison. She was discreet without being reserved, and having no bad qualities, and being constant in her connections, she preserved no common respect to the end of her life, and from the propriety and decency of her behaviour, was always treated as if her virtue had never been questioned." Her letters to and from her correspondents, which have been published, prove how much she was respected and beloved. Lady Suffolk died at Marble Hill in 1767, in her eightieth year. She was sister of John, first Earl of Buckinghamshire, who resided at Marble Hill for some time after the death of the countess. Later on, the house was occupied by Mrs. Fitzherbert, who had been privately married to the Prince of Wales, afterwards George IV., and subsequently it became the residence of Lady Bath.

Marble Hill afterwards was the residence of the Marquis Wellesley, brother of the Duke of Wellington; and on his quitting it, about the year 1824, it became the property and seat of the late General Peel, whose widow, Lady Alicia Peel, youngest daughter of the first Marquis of Ailsa, now resides there.

Readers of Swift will not forget his witty "Pastoral Dialogue between Marble Hill and Richmond Lodge," across the river, on hearing the news of the death of George I.

Marble Hill wittily complains that henceforth its lady owner, Lady Suffolk—

"—— will not have a shilling
To raise the stairs, or build the ceiling,
For all the courtly madams round
Now pay four shillings in the pound."

The poor mansion goes on to prophesy :—

"No more the Dean,* that grave divine,
Shall keep the key of my no—wine,
My ice-house rob as heretofore,
And steal my artichokes no more ;
Poor Patty Blount no more be seen
Bedaggled in my walks so green.
Plump Johnny Gay will now elope,
And here no more will dangle Pope.

*   *   *   *   *

Some South Sea broker from the City
Will purchase me, the more's the pity ;
Lay all my fine plantations waste
To get them to his vulgar taste.
Changed for the worse in every part,
My master, Pope, will break his heart."

In the upper part of Twickenham, towards Isleworth, lived the witty and poetical Dr. Corbett, Bishop of Norwich, whose house was a rendezvous for poets and men of letters. His house stood alone on a small common, and was a most secluded retreat from the noisy world. Here he was visited frequently by Daniel, the poet, and by Michael Drayton, author of the "Polyolbion," and by other choice spirits.

Another ancient house close by was in 1797 the residence of the Duke of Montrose.

In this parish, in 1742, died, in poverty and of a broken heart, Nicholas Amhurst, the author of the once-celebrated satire on Oxford, "Terræ Filius," and editor of the Craftsman, the most effective of all the publications aimed at Sir Robert Walpole.

Mr. H. G. Bohn, the publisher, has lived for many years at North End House, in the Richmond Road, where he formed a valuable collection of antiquities, rare books, china, and pictures.

Opposite the lane leading from Orleans Road down to the river formerly stood a small house, called "Ragman's Castle," at one time the residence of Mrs. Pritchard, the actress, who "enlarged and much improved the house, at a considerable expense." The house in the later stages of its existence was known as "Lawn Cottage." Its original appellation has been variously accounted for : some attribute it to the fact of its having been built by an individual who had amassed a fortune in the marine store, or "rag" and bone business, and others say that on its site formerly stood an alehouse, which was a favourite resort of bargemen, ragmen, beggars, &c. However this may be, on the death of Mrs. Pritchard, in 1758, the house became the residence of the Earl of Cholmondeley, and subsequently of Sir Charles Warwick Bampfylde. About 1783, Mr. George Hardinge, who had been

* Swift.

Attorney-General to Queen Charlotte, and afterwards a Welsh judge, took up his abode here. Judge Hardinge was "a man of learning, a good lawyer, and of infinite pleasantry and wit." He was the father of that brave Captain Hardinge who lost his life and his ship in fighting an American frigate of far superior force. Mr. Justice Hardinge died in 1816, and his speeches at the Bar and in the House of Commons, with his miscellaneous works, including a series of letters to Burke on the impeachment of Hastings, have been collected and published. "Ragman's Castle" was taken down by Lord Kilmorey during his occupation of Orleans House, near to which it stood.

Orleans House, so called from the late King of the French, Louis Philippe, having lived in it when Duke of Orleans, was built in the reign of Queen Anne by Mr. Secretary Johnstone, a man whom Pope satirised most bitterly. In one of these attacks, already quoted on page 75 *ante*, Pope refers with considerable spite to Johnson's "dog and bitch." No commentator on Pope's works," writes Mr. Edward Jesse, in *Once a Week* (Vol. III., p.110), "has ever been able to discover what was meant by a reference to these animals. I have, however, been the means of making the discovery. On each side of the lawn of Orleans House there are walls covered with ivy. In the centre of each wall the ivy appeared much raised above the rest. A friend residing near, at my request, examined these portions of the walls, and concealed in the raised ivy he discovered on one wall a dog carved in stone, and on the other a stone bitch."

Mr. Jesse narrates an anecdote of the poet concerning one of the old watermen who was employed for many years in rowing Pope on the Thames. Pope was in the habit of having his sedan-chair lifted into the punt. If the weather was fine, he let down the glasses; if cold, he pulled them up. He would sometimes say to the waterman (this is his own account), "John, I am going to repeat some verses to you; take care and remember them the next time I go out." When that time came, Pope would say, "John, where are the verses I told you of?" "I have forgotten them, sir." "John, you are a blockhead—I must write them down for you." John said that no one thought of saying, when speaking of him, "Mr. Pope," but that he was always called "Mr. Alexander." "It is certain," adds Mr. Jesse, "that when John punted the poet up and down the river he could readily see the anmals above referred to, and hence his satire."

Mr. Johnstone was very self-sufficient, and proud of his post as Scottish Secretary of State. He lived to a great age, in the enjoyment of a pension, to which Pope alludes :—

"Strike off his pension by the setting sun,
And Britain, if not Europe, is undone."

There was a house on this spot before Mr. Johnstone bought the property. In the Parliamentary Survey which was taken in 1650, it is described as a "pleasant and delightful tenement, about twenty poles from the river, built partly with brick and partly with timber, and Flemish walls, with comely chambers; the gardens not only rare for pleasure, but exceedingly profitable, being planted with cabbages, turnips, and carrots, and many other such-like creatures." In that ancient house the Princess of Denmark (afterwards Queen Anne) resided for some time before her accession to the throne, for the benefit of the air for her youthful son, Prince William Henry, Duke of Gloucester, who brought with him his regiment of boys, which he used to exercise on the ayot opposite the house.

The ancient structure was removed by Mr. Johnstone, who built the present house after the model of country seats in Lombardy. At one end of the house he constructed a large octagon room, especially for the reception and entertainment of Queen Caroline, consort of George II., who visited him here. The queen, during her residence at Hampton Court, was in the habit of coming down the river early in the morning to visit Lady Catherine Johnstone, and to breakfast in the beautiful gardens, in which Mackay (in his "Tour through England," which was published in 1720) says that "Secretary Johnstone had the best collection of most gentlemen in England; that he had slopes for his vines, from which he made some hogsheads of wine a year; and that Dr. Bradley, in his 'Treatise on Gardening,' ranked him among the first gardeners in the kingdom."

After the death of Mr. Johnstone, the property was purchased by Mr. George Morton Pitt.* It afterwards passed, through the marriage of that gentleman's daughter, to the Lord Brownlow Bertie, brother of the Duke of Ancaster. Shortly after the death of Lady Bertie, the estate was purchased by Sir George Pococke, K.B., who had married a granddaughter of Mr. Pitt.

The Duke of Orleans took up his residence here in 1800, on his arrival in England from New York, and it was whilst living here, in 1807, that he had the misfortune to lose his brother, the

---

* Ironside and other writers have stated that this gentleman was known as "Diamond Pitt," confusing him with Thomas Pitt, Governor of Madras, and grandfather of the Earl of Chatham.

Duke of Montpensier, whose epitaph on his tomb in Westminster Abbey was the joint composition of the Duke of Orleans and General Dumouriez. The following anecdote concerning Louis Philippe —when in after years, subsequent to his banishment from his kingdom, he was living again in England—is still remembered by some of the inhabitants of Twickenham. The ex-king was staying at the "Star and Garter" at Richmond, and walked one day by himself to Twickenham, for the purpose, as he said, of seeing some of the old tradesmen who had served him when he resided there. As he passed along that place, a man met him, pulled off his hat, and hoped his Royal Highness was well. "What's your name?" inquired the ex-king. He was told it. "I do not recollect it," said his Majesty. "What were you when I lived here?" "Please your Royal Highness," replied the man, "*I kept the 'Crown'*" (an alehouse close to the entrance of Orleans House). "Did you?" said Louis Philippe. "Why, my good fellow, you were lucky; you did what I was unable to do."

Among other good stories told here about Louis Philippe is the following:—His Highness was walking many years ago in a nursery-ground in the neighbourhood, and was directing the attention of a companion to a luxuriantly-loaded apricot-tree, when the head gardener came up, and offered the duke some remarkably fine Orleans plums. "I thank you, sir," replied the duke; "I have already had a taste of that bitter fruit, and no longer relish it."

In 1827 Orleans House was sold to Mr. Alexander Murray, of Broughton, M.P. for the county of Kirkcudbright; in 1846 it was purchased by Lord Kilmorey, from whom it was again bought by the Duc d'Aumale, who considerably altered and improved the building by the erection of a large picture-gallery and a commodious library. The Duc d'Aumale ceased to reside here when the fall of the French Empire rendered possible his return to France, and the house was subsequently for a short time occupied by another royal exile, Don Carlos. It was somewhat remarkable that the Orleanist should be succeeded by the Carlist. Don Carlos would, no doubt, have found more sympathy from the Comte de Chambord than he would receive from the Comte de Paris.

In 1876-7 Orleans House was offered for sale, and having been purchased by a company, has been converted into a club, called the Orleans Club, and as such, combines in itself all the advantages of a country house with the ordinary social intercourse and facilities of a club.

The house, a very fine one, overlooks the river, and the grounds, which are about forty acres in extent, come down to the water's edge. They are one of the prettiest sights on the river Thames during "the season." An ornamental wall has been built as a kind of embankment, which is crowned with vases, wherein the duke used to plant the loveliest flowers. A writer in the *Gentleman's Magazine*, in 1802, thus describes the house as it existed at the commencement of the present century:—"It is a handsome building of brick; but the front has been spoiled by removing the entrance, and throwing out a bow from the bottom to the upper storey. Before this alteration, there was a handsome door-case of Portland stone, with a window over it suitably ornamented. The present way into the house is in the centre of a wing added to it, or a passage to an elegant octagon room at the end, which was built on purpose for the reception and entertainment of her late Majesty Queen Caroline. These additional buildings make one very long wing, which has an awkward appearance, for want of somewhat to answer it on the other side for the sake of uniformity. This passage to the octagon is made use of as a music-room, in which is a handsome organ." A roadway intersects the lawn of the house from the river meadow, but there are tunnels, rustic bridges, and happily-contrived devices designed to obviate any objection which might be raised to this pretty place calling itself a river-side estate. The house was erected by a sensible architect, and the gardens laid out with a loving respect for nature. The deep shady recesses, the broad thick sashes dividing the panes, the deep wide fire-places, the marble halls, the conservatory corridors thickly planted with camellias, the cosy bed-rooms looking out over Richmond Hill, across the river, or back over the park to Twickenham, the libraries, the billiard-rooms, and the boudoirs, all are distinguished for their substantial comfort; whilst the gardens, lawns, and meadows, are so designed as to combine the ease of retirement with the sense of variety.

The Orleans Club is not a man's club alone, a mere dining place, a dim solemnity, an excuse for extravagance and play, but a social rendezvous, where ladies can adorn the lawn, preside over the drawing-room, and repose under umbrella tents, whilst the men play lawn tennis, or devote themselves to whatever form of violent exercise may please them. With this object the Orleans Club was started. There is a "bachelor wing," and also a "married wing," with luxuriously-appointed bed-rooms. There are card-rooms and billiard-rooms for the men; there are drawing-rooms, pianos, and boudoirs for the ladies; and, above all, there is that lovely garden, common to all. Here, under the beautiful trees or reclining on the indolent lawn, it will be possible to breathe the fresh air, and to forget the ball-room, the opera, and the perpetual park. It is not so much a question what to do at the Orleans Club as what cannot be done. There are lawn games in abundance; there are flower gardens and conservatories; there are boats and steam launches, ready at a moment's notice for a row to Moulsey or a long day to Windsor; there are stalls enough, too, in the stables to accommodate the Four-in-Hand and Coaching Clubs whenever they drive down from town; and every arrangement has been made for giving as capital a dinner as can be eaten at the close of the summer holiday.

Near Twickenham Church, and on the banks of the Thames, stands the building historically known as York House, the reputed residence of James II. when Duke of York, and for some time in the occupation of the Comte de Paris. The house was for many years the property of Sir Alexander Johnstone, and it is associated with the name of Lord Clarendon.

The mansion, with other valuable presents, appears to have been given by Charles II. to Lord Clarendon, on the public announcement of the marriage of his daughter with James II., then Duke of York. The Chancellor was accustomed to pass here the summer months; and when he attended the king at Hampton Court he was in the habit of coming home every night "to his own house at Twickenham." From the reply of Lord Clarendon (as given by his biographer) to the courtiers commissioned by King Charles II. to inform him of the clandestine marriage of his daughter Anne with the Duke of York (afterwards James II.), it has been concluded that his lordship was either a very unnatural father or a very great hypocrite. From his well-known affection for his accomplished child, it is highly improbable that he ever did officially advise her committal to the Tower; and from the tradition that "he actually presented his Royal Highness with his favourite villa, York House, observing that it was already named after him," it is probable he was aware of the duke's affection for his daughter, but feared to discover any knowledge or participation in an act which he knew would be displeasing to the king. Here the royal duke and his much-loved bride passed some years in uninterrupted happiness; here several of their children were born, and amongst them the Princesses Mary and Anne, successively Queens of England. The state-chamber,

which still bears the name of Queen Anne's Room, presents the same appearance which it wore when that monarch first saw the light, in February, 1665, saving those changes which time—merciless time—has inflicted on the perishable materials with which it was adorned. Tradition also says that the great Chancellor wrote some of his essays in the garden walks.

There is little difficulty in retracing the descent of this interesting property from the date of its original demise to T. Jermyn, in 1566, down to the present proprietor. In 1661, York Farm, a parcel of the manor, was granted to Lord Clarendon; at his lordship's death, in 1674, it passed to his second son, Lawrence Hyde, Earl of Rochester. In 1740 it was sold to J. Whitchurch, Esq., and by his representatives to Lieut.-Col. J. Webber, who disposed of the freehold to Prince Stahremberg, Envoy Extraordinary and Minister Plenipotentiary from the Court of Vienna. His Excellency retained possession of York Villa during the whole term of his ambassadorial attendance at St. James's, and the cheerfulness and hospitality of his disposition rendered it the scene of continued gaiety. Having fitted up one of the wings as a private theatre, dramatic representations were frequently exhibited there, when the prince and princess, their daughters, and several foreigners of distinction, displayed their talents in the histrionic art. The plays most frequently performed were the little French pieces which were then so popular in this country; and the lists of the *dramatis personæ*, published at the time, establish this fact, and disclose the titles of the eminent foreigners, who by their talents and accomplishments excited so much interest, and afforded so much intellectual amusement to the many families of distinction then residing in the vicinity.

York House subsequently became the residence of Dr. Cleaver, Archbishop of Dublin, who, from mental disease, was unable to discharge the duties of his see. In 1817 the house was purchased by the Hon. Mrs. Damer, of whom we shall have more to say when we reach Strawberry Hill. Mrs. Damer had acquired great reputation as a sculptress, and on taking up her residence here, she fitted up one wing of the house as a studio and gallery of art. It was here that many of those able performances which have conferred upon her an abiding celebrity were designed and executed. Mrs. Damer's attention was first called to this pursuit, so unusual amongst ladies, by that celebrated philosopher, David Hume, whilst he was private secretary to her father, Field-Marshal Conway. Having observed the precocious ability of the young sculptor, he exhorted her to cultivate it with her best energies; and it was by his advice, and at his pressing instance, that Mrs. Damer devoted her talents so entirely to the statuary art. Mrs. Damer towards the close of her life espoused the cause of the unfortunate Queen Caroline, whom she frequently entertained here. She lived to a great age, respected and admired by the most eminent of her contemporaries, and at her death in 1828 the estate of York House passed by bequest to her

two Brahmins standing on the terrace at York House, near the banks of the Thames, on the relative merits of the religion, customs, and manners of the Hindoos, and the religion, customs, and manners of the English. His design was to show how much superior the latter were to the former, by the wonderful progress which the English had made in a knowledge of government, arts, and sciences, while the Hindoos had remained stationary for ages; and to conclude by the pros-

PHILIP, DUKE OF WHARTON.
(See p. 91.)

LADY SUFFOLK.
(See p. 85.)

cousin, Lady Johnston, only daughter of Lord William Campbell, son of the fourth Duke of Argyle, on whose premature decease she had been placed under the guardianship of her uncle, the late Duke of Argyle. Afterwards, when she married, the estate became vested in her ladyship's husband, the Right Hon. Sir Alexander Johnston.

A frequent visitor to York House during its occupancy by Sir Alexander Johnston was the celebrated Brahmin and Oriental philosopher, Ramohun Roy, who drew up a sketch of a work while here, which, had he lived, he meant to have published, upon the plan of the "Tusculan Questions" by Cicero, and the "Minute Philosopher" by Berkeley,* professing to be a dialogue between

pects which are now held out, by the discovery of steam navigation, and the constant use of the route from England to India through Egypt, that the Hindoos (from being brought by these circumstances so much nearer to England than they were before) would soon become equal to the English in their knowledge of government, and in all the different arts and sciences which must raise their moral, intellectual, and political character.

Among the subsequent occupiers of York House were the Dowager Duchess of Roxburgh and Lord Lonsdale, the latter of whom died here in 1844. A few years afterwards the mansion was sold to the Duc d'Aumale for his nephew, the Comte de Paris, eldest son of the late Duc d'Orleans, and grandson of Louis Philippe, late King of the

* See the collected works of Berkley, Bishop of Cloyne, 1843.

French. The Comte de Paris vacated the house about 1871, and some two years later the house and grounds were submitted for sale by public auction.

The mansion, which occupies a pleasant position on an elevated plateau overlooking the river Thames, is built in what is now known as the "Queen Anne" style of architecture, and consists of a centre and wings, and the apartments are both numerous and spacious. A grand staircase of oak with carved

"Wharton, the scorn and wonder of our days,
Whose ruling passion was the lust of praise ;
Born with whate'er could win it from the wise,
Women and fools must like him, or he dies.
Though wondering senates hung on all he spoke,
The club must hail him master of the joke.
Shall parts so various aim at nothing new ?
He'll shine a Tully and a Wilmot too.
Thus, with each gift of nature and of art,
And wanting nothing but an honest heart ;
Grown all to all, from no one vice exempt,
And most contemptible to show contempt ;

THE GARDENS OF ORLEANS HOUSE, 1882.

balustrade, &c., gives access from the hall to the principal chambers in the upper storeys. From the drawing-rooms and library windows open upon a broad terrace walk, which extends the whole length of the river front. The gardens and grounds, about nine acres in extent, are admirably laid out, and include a wilderness, fernery, flower-garden, lawns, &c.

In a house, called The Grove, long since swept away, but which stood in or near what is now King Street, in the western part of the town, lived for some time the witty and clever, but disreputable, Duke of Wharton, whose character is summed up by Pope in one of his "Moral Essays" in the following often quoted lines :—

His passion still to covet general praise,
His life, to forfeit it a thousand ways ;
A constant bounty, which no friend has made ;
An angel tongue, which no man can persuade ;
A fool, with more of wit than half mankind ;
Too rash for thought, for action too refined ;
A tyrant to the wife his heart approves,
A rebel to the very king he loves.
He dies, sad outcast of each church and state,
And, harder still, flagitious, yet not great.
Ask you why Wharton broke through every rule?
'Twas all for fear the knaves should call him fool."

"It is difficult," remarks Horace Walpole, in the "Royal and Noble Authors," "to give an account of the works of so mercurial a man, whose library was a tavern, and women of pleasure his muses. A thousand sallies of his imagination may have been lost, for he wrote for fame no more than he acted for it." Perhaps Horace Walpole on this occasion, as on many others, "hit the right nail on the head." The duke must have been indeed "mercurial." "Like Buckingham and Rochester, Philip Duke of Wharton comforted all the grave and dull," says Horace Walpole, "by throwing away the brightest profusion of parts on witty fooleries, debaucheries, and scrapes, which may mix graces with a great character, but can never make one." Mr. Seward observes that the character of Lovelace in "Clarissa" has always been supposed to be that of this noble-man; and the supposition is rendered the more probable as Richardson printed the *True Briton*, in which the duke wrote constantly.

Well and wittily is it remarked by Bolton, in his "Extinct Peerage," that Philip, Duke of Wharton, "succeeded his father, Thomas, in all his titles and abilities, but in none of his virtues." And it is indeed strange that the man who could give £2,000 as a present to a poet, and administer a witty rebuff to an officious ambassador, could be guilty of such a silly and unmeaning trick as knocking up his guardian in the middle of the night, in order to borrow a pin; or at another time, in France, serenading respectable persons at their country châteaux, one of whom very nearly killed him by a stray shot, mistaking him for a robber.

Some interesting facts about the Duke are to be found in a scarce work, entitled "Memoirs of the Life of his Grace Philip, late Duke of Wharton, by an Impartial Hand." It is prefixed to two octavo volumes, published in 1732, entitled "The Life and Writings of Philip, late Duke of Wharton," but which contain only the seventy-four numbers of the *True Briton*, and the speech on the bill of pains and penalties against Atterbury, the paging of which is a continuation of that of the *True Briton*, although it has a title-page of its own dated 1724. There is another publication, in two volumes octavo, without date, entitled "The Poetical Works of Philip, late Duke of Wharton, and others of the Wharton Family, and of the Duke's Intimate Acquaintance, particularly Lord Boling-broke, Dean Swift, Lady Wharton, Doctor Delany, Lord Dorset, Major Pack, the Hon. Mrs. Wharton, &c." These two volumes, however, appear to have been all printed in 1727 (before the duke's death), with the exception only of this general title-page and a life of the duke, which is substantially the same with that noticed above, and is here stated to be "communicated by a person of quality, and one of his grace's intimate friends." The first volume contains very little that is even attributed to the

duke; but in the second are some letters in prose, addressed to Lady Wharton, his father's first wife, and her poetical paraphrase of the "Lamentations of Jeremiah."

The duke died at Tarragona, in Spain, in 1731, and a vindication of his character is to be found in a volume of scarce broadsides in the British Museum. It bears no printer's name, but only the date 1728; it was probably printed in Dublin.

During Pope's time the Grove was the residence of his friend, the younger James Craggs, who succeeded Addison in the post of Secretary of State in 1718, and who, like his father, was ruined by the South Sea scheme. Craggs was the friend of Steele and Tickell, and the opponent of Sir Robert Walpole in Parliament. The Grove, which was pulled down many years ago, is said to have been originally built by Inigo Jones for the Earl of Rochester. Its site is marked by a solitary cedar, with a pond near it.

At Twickenham the Duke of Wharton was the neighbour and acquaintance of Lady Mary Wortley Montagu, who wrote an epilogue for a tragedy which he began on "Mary Queen of Scots." This poem was never finished, and all of it that remains is a brace of couplets preserved in a "Miscellany," like "flies in amber." They run as follows:—

> "Sure were I free, and Norfolk were a pris'ner,
> I'd fly with more impatience to his arms
> Than the poor Israelite on the serpent gaz'd,
> When life was the reward of every look."

Lady Mary Wortley Montagu lived at Saville House, close by the Grove. She came to reside there mainly through the persuasion of Pope, with whom at one time she lived on terms of great inti-macy and friendship; but they quarrelled, and hated each other cordially for the remainder of their lives. Lady Mary died in 1762, and her successor here was Lady Saville, from whom the house derived its name; she was the mother of Sir George Saville, who, among many others, is said to have been the original of Richardson's "Sir Charles Grandi-son."

Twickenham House, a fine old building, standing on the south side of the main road, near the rail-way bridge, has a little history of its own, as having been the residence of Sir John Hawkins, who enjoyed the distinction, according to the poet, of being buried "in his shoes and stawkings," and who was described by the Earl of Rochford (then one of the Secretaries of State) as "the best magistrate in the kingdom." Sir John was a devoted fisher-man—a pastime in which his residence on the banks of the Thames enabled him freely to indulge.

He brought out, with notes, an edition of "Izaak Walton's Complete Angler," and also "The History of Music" and a "Life of Dr. Johnson." Hawkins was one of the original members of the Literary Club, and in the gardens of Twickenham House, as we learn from Mr. Cobbett's "Memorials," there is a building which was used for the meetings of the club. Attached to the house is a circular room with a domed roof, now used as a drawing-room; this, Mr. Cobbett tells us, was originally Sir John's concert-room. The grounds contain a curious relic, consisting of a garden-fence, curiously wrought with sword-blades brought from the field of Culloden. Twickenham House has been long the residence of Dr. Hugh Diamond.

Nearer the town of Twickenham, on the site of what is now Heath Lane Lodge, stood in former times a house which was the seat of more than one Earl Ferrers. Mr. Cobbett, in his work above mentioned, states that "tradition asserts that Laurence, the 'mad' Earl Ferrers, who shot Mr. Johnson, his steward, was taken from this house to execution." This statement, however, is very doubtful. There was in the original house a portrait of one of Lord Ferrers' daughters—the lovely Lady Frances Shirley, who was one of Pope's personal friends, and who was sung by Chesterfield as "Fanny, blooming fair."

It will not be forgotten that Pope commemorates the residence of Fielding in this place in his "Parish Register of Twickenham":—

"When Feilding met his bunter muse,
And as they quaffed the fiery juice,
Droll Nature stamped each lucky hit
With unimaginable wit."

The aristocratic owner of Strawberry Hill has not failed, as Scott observes in his "Lives of the Novelists," to stigmatise the lowness of Fielding's habits, and of the society which he kept.

Fielding, though sprung from a collateral branch of the Feildings, Earls of Denbigh, did not care to follow the latter mode of spelling his name. On being asked why his father had departed from the accepted orthography, he replied, somewhat cynically, that "he supposed it was because he was the first of his race who knew how to spell."

Another resident here was Paul Whitehead, notorious as a venal politician and a second-rate satirist. Dr. Doran, in his "Habits and Men," speaks of him as "one of the fine gentlemen of his day, who associated only with the finest of that class. At Twickenham he had not only his country house, but a coruscant circle of wits around him, whose brilliancy was not considered as tarnished by the most mouldy blasphemy."

Dr. Donne, the poet, was also an inhabitant of this place. He died in 1631, and has been immortalised by Isaac Walton. Here, too, lived Mrs. Margaret Godolphin, perhaps the only virtuous lady of the vicious Court of Charles II., the story of whose "saintly life" has been told so well by her friend and correspondent, John Evelyn.

Robert Boyle, the celebrated philosopher, at one period of his life lived at Twickenham. His name occurs in the parish register, but the exact locality where he resided is unknown. He was the fifth son of the great Earl of Cork, and died in 1691. Mr. Boyle founded the lectures which bear his name.

Edward Stillingfleet, D.D., Dean of St. Paul's, and afterwards Bishop of Worcester, may also be numbered among the former residents of Twickenham; and so was the Rev. Dr. Waterland, the author of many learned works, and sometime vicar of the parish, who died in 1748. Another celebrated vicar was the Rev. George Costard, who wrote and published several works on astronomy, and contributed to the "Transactions of the Royal Society," of which he was a member.

Andrew Stone, at one time preceptor to George III., lived here in style, occupying a large old-fashioned brick house near the river-side. He was a brother of the founder of the bank of Martin, Stone, and Co., at the sign of the "Grasshopper," Lombard Street. He was a friend of Horace Walpole, who mentions him in one of his works. He is buried in the north aisle of the nave of Westminster Abbey.

Twickenham Common was till recent times an open space, doubtless available as a playground for the children of the poor, and as pasturage for their donkeys and geese.

"But times are altered, trade's unfeeling train
Usurp the land, and dispossess the swain."

Here may be seen the house formerly occupied by General Gunning, brother to those celebrated beauties the Duchesses of Hamilton and Argyll and Lady Coventry. The Marchioness of Tweed-dale resided in it before General Gunning.

In Ailsa Park Villas lived Lord Beaconsfield's sister Sarah. She was betrothed to a Mr. Meredith, a gentleman of wealth, and of literary repute as the patron of Thomas Taylor, the translator of Aristotle. She died in December, 1859, and is buried in the Willesden Cemetery.

Coming down to more recent times, we find that here "Boz," in the first flush of prosperity caused by the success of "Pickwick," took a cottage for part of the summer of 1838. Here Talfourd, Thackeray, Jerrold, Maclise, Landseer, Stanfield, Cattermole, and Harrison Ainsworth, were among his visitors, as narrated by Forster, in his "Life of Dickens ;" and here he indulged to the full in "the grand enjoyment of idleness," abandoning himself to what must at that time have been an inexperienced delight—the luxury of laziness.

Montpelier Row was the last residence of Mr. Augustus Mayhew, one of the "Brothers Mayhew," the author of "Paved with Gold," "The Greatest Plague of Life," &c., who died at the close of 1875.

its builder and first occupant, Sir Godfrey Kneller, who called it in his lifetime "Whitton House." It was built in 1710. The hall and staircase were painted by La Guerre, under the direction and with the occasional assistance of Sir Godfrey. The house was made the artist's summer residence.

Sir Godfrey Kneller lives in the verses of half the poets of his age ; few, however, paid him a higher compliment than Matt Prior :—

KNELLER HALL.　(See p. 94.)

We must not omit to mention amongst the celebrated persons who have resided at Twickenham the Lady Augusta Murray, the unhappy wife of the late Duke of Sussex, and the mother of his two accomplished children.

Mr. W. Andrews, in his "Book of Oddities," records a curious devise of property here as lately as 1862, when Mr. Henry Budd left an estate, called Pepper Park, to his son, on condition of his not wearing a moustache ; in event of his doing so, the property to pass to a brother.

On the north-eastern side of the parish, and just within the boundary of the hamlet of Whitton, stands a building of some interest and importance, namely, Kneller Hall, so called after

"When Kneller's works of various grace
　　Were to fair Venus shown,
　The goddess spied in every face
　　Some features of her own.

"But viewing Myra placed apart,
　　'I fear,' says she, 'I fear,
　Apelles, that Sir Godfrey's art
　　Has far surpassed thine here.'"

Again, Dryden thus sings the praises of Sir Godfrey :—

"At least thy pictures look a voice ; and we
　Imagine sounds, deceiv'd to that degree,
　We think 'tis somewhat more than just to see."

Sir Godfrey Kneller was a native of Lubeck, in

Germany, and was born in 1648. Having evinced at an early age talents of no mean order, he became a pupil of Ferdinand Bol and of Rembrandt. He subsequently visited Italy, studied at Rome under Carlo Maratti, and came to England in 1674. He was shortly after commissioned by the Duke of Monmouth to paint a portrait of the king, and his success as a portrait painter was at once established. Sir Godfrey received the appointment of portrait painter successively to Charles II., James II., William and Mary, Anne, and George I. It was not only royalty, however, that sat to Kneller; indeed, there was hardly a person of note or distinction in his day whom he had not painted. Bishop Burnet, John Evelyn, the "Court beauties" of his day, the Admirals at Hampton Court, and the members of the Kit-Cat Club, are amongst Sir Godfrey's most noted works. He was knighted by King William, and created a baronet by George I.

Among the anecdotes told of Sir Godfrey Kneller is one to the effect that he painted so fine a full-length picture of Lady Kneller, that, leaving the door of his studio open, Lady Kneller's favourite spaniel got access to it, and seeing, as he thought, his beloved mistress, he jumped up at her likeness and injured the picture, which had been taken from the easel and placed against the wall.

Sir Godfrey's vanity displayed itself in his last moments. Pope, who came over to visit him two days before his death, observes that he had never seen in his life such a scene. He was sitting up in bed, and contemplating the plans which he was making for his own monument!

Sir Godfrey died in 1723, and is said, but falsely, to have been buried in the garden of Kneller Hall, but of the place of his interment there is no trace there, for he lies in Twickenham church. There is a monument to his memory, with an inscription by Pope, in Westminster Abbey.

Some time after the death of Sir Godfrey Kneller the mansion became the residence of Sir Samuel Prime; and in 1847 it was purchased by the Committee of the Council of Education, to be used as a normal training school, and Dr. Temple, now Bishop of Exeter, received the appointment of Principal. In 1856 the establishment passed into the hands of the War Department, and in the following year a school of military music was opened here. What with alterations and enlargements at different periods, the house may be said to have been almost entirely rebuilt since Kneller's time.

CHAPTER VIII.

TWICKENHAM (continued).—POPE'S VILLA.

"Pope, to whose reed beneath the beechen shade,
The nymphs of Thames a pleased attention paid."—LORD LYTTELTON, " The Progress of Love."

Parentage and Birth of Alexander Pope—His Education—His Early Admiration for Dryden—His first Essays Poetic Effusions—Is introduced to Sir W. Trumbull and Wycherley—His Friendship with the Misses Blount—Translates the " Iliad "—Takes up his Residence at Chiswick—Publication of the " Odyssey "—Pope's Narrow Escape from Drowning—Publication of the " Miscellanies," "The Essay on Man," and other Poems—Death and Burial of Pope—Pope's Skull—Character and Temperament of Pope—His Personal Appearance—His Popularity—His Visitors—His Fondness for Animals—His Love of Economy—His Rank as a Poet—His Will—An Account of Pope's Villa and Grotto—Sale of the Villa to Sir William Stanhope—Its subsequent History.

APART from the name of Horace Walpole, there is none that is more closely associated with Twickenham than that of Alexander Pope; and it is mainly owing to the memory of these two men that Twickenham has been so long "the favourite retreat of scholars, poets, and statesmen."

Alexander Pope was born in London in the month of May, 1688. His parents were members of the Roman Catholic Church; his father, according to the poet's own account, was "of a noble family;" but according to some of his biographers, he kept a linendraper's shop in the city; others state that he was a mechanic, a hatter, and even a farmer. In a foot-note in his "Moral Essays," it is stated that Mr. Pope's father was of "a gentle man's family in Oxfordshire, the head of which was the Earl of Downe, whose sole heiress married the Earl of Lindsey." His mother was the daughter of William Turner, Esq., of York. She had three brothers, one of whom was killed; another died in the service of King Charles; the eldest, following his fortunes, and becoming a general officer in Spain, left her what estate remained after the sequestrations and forfeitures of her family. Be this, however, true or not, Pope's father left London during the childhood of his son, and retired first to Kensington, and then to Binfield, on the borders of Windsor Forest, and there, in his twelfth year, the youthful poet joined him. Young as he was, Pope here formed his first plans of study, and in the seclusion of the country set himself vigorously to read, and occasionally to write. He had received the rudiments of his education in Latin and Greek from the family priest, and he was for a short time at a Roman Catholic school at Twyford, and also at a school near Hyde Park Corner, in London. His poetic abilities displayed themselves even at that early age, for he is credited with having written a play, based on certain events in the "Iliad," and made up of the speeches in Ogilby's translation, which was acted by the elder boys in the school, the part of Ajax being sustained by the master's gardener. Whilst he was living at Binfield Dryden became the subject of his greatest admiration; and it was to Wills' Coffee-house, in Russell Street, Covent Garden, that Pope, when a mere child, induced his friends to carry him, in order that he might gaze on the great poet whose mantle he was destined in after life so worthily to wear.* "Who does not wish," writes Dr. Johnson, "that Dryden could have known the value of the homage that was paid him, and foreseen the greatness of his young admirer?" In later years Pope became a constant frequenter of "Wills'," though not till after the illustrious Dryden's death. "Pope had now," again writes Dr. Johnson, "declared himself a poet, and thinking himself entitled to poetical conversation, began at seventeen to frequent 'Wills'' . . where the wits of that time used to assemble, and where Dryden had, when he lived, been accustomed to preside."

At the age of twelve Pope wrote his "Ode to Solitude," which was followed soon after by a translation of the first book of the "Thebais" of Statius, and Ovid's "Epistle of Sappho to Phaon." Whilst living at Binfield young Pope formed the acquaintanceship of Sir William Trumbull, by whom he was introduced to Wycherley the dramatist; but his friendship with the latter was but of short duration, owing, it is said, to Pope's somewhat too free strictures on a volume of poems which Wycherley was preparing for publication, and had submitted to Pope for his revision. It was about this time that the intimacy sprang up between Pope and Mr. and the Misses Blount, who were living at Mapledurham, near Reading. Pope was strongly suspected by some of his friends in after life—among others by Lepel, Lady Hervey—of being privately married to his friend and correspondent, Miss Martha Blount, the elder of the two sisters.

"There can be little doubt," observed a writer in the *Gentleman's Magazine*, "that one of the most faithful friendships of Pope's life was that

with the fair-haired Martha Blount. It was an early friendship, with a dash of sentiment about it, that might, under happier circumstances, have ripened into love. And it was a perfectly intelligible friendship. There may be, as Mrs. Oliphant has well said, a love between man and woman which does not point to matrimony, and there seems no ground for the scandal that assailed the life-long intimacy of Martha and the poet. . .

In his early days Pope seems to have felt an equal affection for Teresa, the elder sister; but at a later period, from some doubtful cause, there was a complete estrangement between them. . . Both sisters, by the way, were considered beautiful in their youth, but neither of them married. . . . Martha Blount returned Swift's affection, and was, as Pope told the dean, 'as constant to old friendships as any man'; and in another letter Swift is told that she speaks of him constantly, and 'is one of the most considerate and mindful of women in the world towards others, the least so in regard to herself.'"

At the age of sixteen Pope composed his "Pastorals," but they were not printed till some five years later (1709), when they appeared in "Tonson's Miscellany." He next wrote his "Essay on Criticism," which was followed shortly after by "The Rape of the Lock" and the "Temple of Fame"; "Windsor Forest" and "The Ode on St. Cecilia's Day" were published in 1713. In a letter to Addison, written in this year, Pope speaks of his passion for the art of painting, which he had studied under Jervas, but the pursuit of which he was prevented from following up by the weakness of his eyesight.

The want of money led Pope about this time to issue proposals for a subscription to a translation of the "Iliad." The whole work was completed between his twenty-fifth and thirtieth year. Concerning the writing of this work, an amusing story is told by Pope himself in his correspondence. He writes:—"When I had finished the first two or three books of my translation of the 'Iliad,' Lord Halifax desired to have the pleasure of hearing them read at his house. Addison, Congreve, and Garth, were there at the read. In four or five places his lordship stopped me very civilly, and with a speech each time, much of the same kind. 'I beg your pardon, Mr. Pope; but there is something in that passage that does not quite please me. Be so good as to mark the place, and consider it a little at your leisure. I'm sure you can give it a little turn.' I returned from Lord Halifax's (continues Pope) with Dr. Garth, in his chariot; and as we were going along, was saying to the doctor that my

---

* See "Old and New London," Vol. III., p. 276.

lord had laid me under a good deal of difficulty by such loose and general observations; that I had been thinking over the passages ever since, and could not guess at what it was that offended his lordship in either of them. Garth laughed heartily at my embarrassment, and said I had not been long enough acquainted with Lord Halifax to know his way yet; that I need not puzzle myself about looking those places over and over when I got home. 'All you need do,' says he, 'is to leave them just as they are; call on Lord Halifax two or three months hence, thank him for his kind observations on those passages, and then read them to him *as altered*. I have known him much longer than you have, and will be answerable for the event.' I followed his advice; waited on Lord Halifax some time after; said, I hoped he would find his objections to those passages removed; read them to him *exactly as they were at first*, and his lordship was extremely pleased with them, and cried out, 'Ay, now they are perfectly right; nothing can be better!'"

By the subscription list for his translation of Homer Pope's circumstances were so materially improved that he persuaded his father to remove from Binfield, and take up his residence nearer London; and, accordingly, we soon after find the family settled in Mawson's Buildings, Chiswick.* Here Pope continued the "Iliad," and wrote the "Epistle from Eloisa to Abelard." Pope subsequently took a long lease of a house and five acres of ground at Twickenham, and at once set about the work of improvement, as we shall presently see.

From this time may be dated the most important portion of the poet's career. "He was," writes Mr. Cobbett, in his "Memorials of Twickenham," "one of the very few literary men who in his own or any previous time acquired a competence through their dealings with the booksellers." Happily he escaped from the meshes of the Curlls and Stocks

POPE.   (*From a Contemporary Portrait.*)

of his day. In 1726 Pope published a translation of the "Odyssey," in which he had the assistance of Broome and Fenton. Pope translated twelve books, Broome eight, and Fenton four.

About this time an incident occurred—trifling, perhaps, as it happened, but which might have ended Pope's earthly career. It is recorded by Carruthers, in his "Life of Pope," as follows:—"The poet had been dining with Bolingbroke at Dawley, and late at night the peer sent his friend home in a stately fashion in a coach and six. A small bridge about a mile from Pope's residence was broken down, and the postillion taking the water, the coach came in contact with the trunk of a tree, and was overturned. Before the coachman could get to Pope's assistance the water had reached the knots of his periwig. The glass was broken, and he was rescued, but not until he had received a severe wound in his right hand, which for some time disqualified him from writing. Voltaire, who was on a visit to Dawley, sent his condolences in an *English* epistle, stating that the water into which Pope fell was 'not Hippocrene's water, otherwise it would have respected him.' 'Is it possible,' he added, 'that those fingers which have written the "Rape of the Lock" and the "Criticism," which have dressed Homer so becomingly in an *English coat*, should have been so barbarously treated?'"

The accident here referred to probably occurred either at the north end of the village, near where is the railway station now, or else in the little river Cran, which sweeps round to the east near the Hounslow powder-mills, and runs parallel with the road from Twickenham to Hanworth. In one place on the road to Hanworth it is dammed up so as to form a broad lake.

In 1827 were published two volumes of "Miscellanies" by Pope and Swift, to which Gay and Arbuthnot contributed, and in these "Miscellanies" was printed the piece of satire entitled "Martinus Scriblerus"; this was followed up in 1729 by the publication of the first three books of the "Dunciad,"

---

* See *ante*, p. 5.

in which he took summary vengeance upon certain exasperating scribblers who were, or thought they were, ridiculed in the "Miscellanies." In 1733 Pope published the "Essay on Man," and in the following year appeared his "Characters of Men; or, Moral Essays." These were preceded and followed by imitations of Horace; and in 1742 the list of Pope's poems is concluded with an additional book of the "Dunciad." In the next year Pope's health began to decline, and on the 30th of May, 1744, he died here of asthma and decay of nature.

Pope was buried, as he directed, in Twickenham Church, "in a vault in the middle aisle, under the second pew from the east end." A stone inscribed with the letter "P" marks the spot, which is now hidden by the flooring of the seats.

By some of Pope's biographers it is asserted that the head of the poet was abstracted from his coffin during some repairs of the church. On this subject Mr. Howitt, in his "Homes and Haunts of the British Poets," writes as follows:—"By one of those acts which neither science nor curiosity can excuse, the skull of Pope is now in the private collection of a phrenologist. The manner in which it was obtained is said to have been this:—On some occasion of alteration in the church, or burial of some one in the same spot, the coffin of Pope was disinterred, and opened, to see the state of the remains. By a bribe to the sexton of the time, possession of the skull was obtained for the night, and *another* skull returned instead of it. I have heard that fifty pounds were paid to manage and carry through this transaction. Be that as it may, the undoubted skull of Pope now figures in the phrenological collection of Mr. Holm, of Highgate, and was frequently exhibited by him in his lectures, as demonstrating, by its not large but well-balanced proportions, its affinity to the intellectual character of the poet."

"Such statements," observes Mr. Cobbett, in his work already quoted, "are hard to be disproved, more especially when motives of interest support them. It is fair, however, to the Rev. Charles Proby (the vicar during whose time the alleged theft was committed), and to the then officials of the church, to give, as he communicated it to Mr. Powell, his churchwarden, his unqualified denial of each and every part of the story. Mr. Proby had seen Mr. Howitt's paragraph, and desired, as he was too old to enter into a paper war, that the real facts which gave rise to the report should be published, if a new history of Twickenham were ever written. Mr. Proby's statement is as follows:—
'Upon opening a vault some years ago in the middle aisle of the church, adjoining Pope's, the latter fell in, the coffin was broken, and disclosed the skeleton, which was very short, with a large skull. I was immediately informed of it, when I directed my curate, Mr. Fletcher, to remain in the church, and not to leave until the whole was restored and built up. *A cast of the skull was taken, with my permission*, by the mason employed, who well knew how to accomplish it. I am quite sure that Mr. Fletcher rigidly carried out my instructions. No such abstraction could have been made.'"

Pope throughout his whole life never enjoyed good health. A sickly child, of mild temper, with a sweet voice which earned him the sobriquet of "the little nightingale," his physical weakness determined the bent of his tastes and the nature of his pursuits. In the churchyard at Twickenham there is a stone raised by Pope himself in "gratitude" to his "faithful servant," Mary Beach, who nursed him in his infancy, and constantly attended him for thirty-eight years. It is worthy of remark that the peculiar make and conformation of Pope rendered a faithful servant of inestimable value. Johnson assures us that "he was so weak as to stand in perpetual need of *female* attendance, and was so extremely sensible of cold, that he wore a kind of fur doublet under a shirt of very coarse warm linen, with fine sleeves. When he rose he was invested in stays made of stiff canvas, being scarce able to hold himself erect till they were laced, and he then put on a flannel waistcoat. One side was contracted. His legs were so slender that he enlarged their bulk with three pairs of stockings, which were drawn on and off by the maid: for he was not able to dress or undress himself, and neither went to bed or rose without help. His weakness made it very difficult for him to be clean. His hair had fallen almost all away, and he used to dine with Lord Oxford privately in a velvet cap. His dress of ceremony was black, with a tye wig and a little sword. The indulgence and accommodation which his sickness required had taught him all the unpleasing and unsocial qualities of a valetudinarian. He expected that everything should give way to his ease or humour, as a child, whose parents will not hear it cry, has an unresisted dominion in the nursery.

'C'est que l'enfant toujours est homme
C'est que l'homme est toujours enfant!'

When he wanted to sleep he nodded in company, and once slumbered at his own table while the Prince of Wales was talking of poetry."

'In spite of living so much in the world of fashion and of letters, Pope was, if not averse to society, yet at all events fond of solitude; and this he gained in his garden and grotto at Twickenham. "As much company as I have kept, and much as I like it, I love reading better, and I would rather be employed in reading than in the most agreeable conversation."

Pope became the subject of unnumbered epigrams, odes, references, and allusions, amongst the literary circle of which he was the centre. One complimentary epigram will suffice as an example:—

"On erecting a Monument to Shakespeare, under the direction of Mr. Pope, Lord Burlington, &c.

"To mark her Shakespeare's worth and Britain's love,
Let Pope design, and Burlington approve:
Superfluous care! When distant time shall view
This tomb grown old, his works shall still be new."

Throughout his life his health was bad, and he perhaps imagined it worse than it was. His faults —if such they may be called—were in a great measure consequent on this fact; he was peevish, capricious, and fretful, and demanded incessant attention. His character, indeed, has been very diversely represented by foes and by friends; some, as we have seen, called him "the nightingale," whilst his enemies called him "the wasp" of Twickenham; and Lady Mary Wortley Montagu went so far as to style him "the wicked asp." But every man, it would seem, has his good points; for Lord Bolingbroke, on the contrary, says that he "never knew a man that had so tender a heart for his particular friends, or a more general friendship for mankind." But possibly, Lord Bolingbroke, the "my St. John" of the poet, was not an impartial witness.

Sir Joshua Reynolds thus describes Pope from personal acquaintance:—"He was about four feet six inches high, very hump-backed and deformed. He wore a black coat, and, according to the fashion of the time, had on a little sword. He had a large and very fine eye, and a long handsome nose; his mouth had those peculiar marks which are always found in the mouths of crooked persons; and the muscles which ran across the cheek were so strongly marked that they seemed like small cords."

Pope's diminutive and misshapen person was a standing joke with his enemies, who caricatured him as a monkey in a library or with books. Macaulay, in his "Essays," speaks of him severely as "the little man of Twickenham"—a softened phrase, which means much in the way of disparagement. The following anecdote which has been told respecting his personal appearance will bear repeating:—"A gentleman and his little child were walking with a friend through Twickenham, when Pope met them. The child was alarmed at his

figure, and drew back. The friend told them it was the great Mr. Pope. He wore an old soiled suit of black stained with snuff, cocked hat, and looked poor and mean."

Pope frequently assumed the *nom de plume* of "Martinus Scribblerus" in writing his attacks on those who criticised him adversely. One of his numerous enemies founded on this the title of the "Martiniad," a sort of answer, or counterblast to his "Dunciad," giving the following portrait of Pope's person, cruelly exposing its deformity:—

"At Twickenham, chronicles remark,
There dwelt a little parish clerk,
A peevish wight, full fond of fame,
And 'Martin Scribbler' was his name:
Meagre and wan, and steeple-crown'd,
His visage long and shoulders round;
His crippled corse two spindle-pegs
Support, instead of human legs;
His shrivelled skin's of dusky grain,
A cricket's voice and monkey's brains."

And another lampooner in verse compared the "Dunciad," in terms equally savage and cutting, to the progeny of the fabulous "Pope Joan."

It is stated that Pope seldom or never laughed; that his sole passion was to acquire fame, his most conspicuous weakness "inordinate self-conceit." "He delighted in artifice, and attempted to gain all his ends by indirect methods. 'He hardly drank tea without a stratagem.' Lady Bolingbroke said that 'he played the politician about cabbages and turnips.'" He was somewhat too much inclined to indulge his appetite; fond of highly-seasoned dishes, conserves, and drams. So fond was he of lampreys, that, if we may trust a statement made in the "Life of Nollekens," he would leave off in the midst of writing in order to cook them in a silver saucepan on his own fire.

Like most invalids, even in his own house he was irritable and fussy to a degree, and on account of his temper constantly got into sad trouble with the literary men of his day. For example, not long after the publication of the "Dunciad," in 1728, there appeared in the newspapers a fictitious account—afterwards known to have been written by Lady Mary Wortley Montagu—of a horsewhipping which the poet had received from two gentlemen at Ham. His sensitive nature was so touched that he condescended to insert in the *Daily Post* of June 14th, in that year, the following advertisement:—

"Whereas there has been a scandalous paper cried about the streets, under the title of 'A Popp upon Pope,' insinuating that I was whipped in Ham Walks on Thursday last; this is to give notice that I did not stir out of my house at

Twickenham all that day, and the same is a malicious and ill-grounded remark.—A. POPE."

Pope, as we have already stated, had in former years been on terms of the greatest friendship with Lady Mary Wortley Montagu. So intimate, indeed, was he at one time with her, that it is difficult to distinguish some of her writings from those of Pope, to such an extent were they intermixed. For instance, "Roxana, or the Drawing-Room," and the "Basset Table," though printed among Pope's "Miscellanies," seem really to belong to Lady Mary, and form part of her "Town Eclogues." And yet these once friends lived to become, as we have seen, the bitterest of enemies.

Notwithstanding Pope's fondness for repose and quietude, he had many friends, and probably his vanity was gratified by great people coming and making him an oracle. According to Thackeray, "Pope withdrew in a great measure from this boisterous London company"—that of club-house life—"and being put into an independence by the gallant exertions of Swift and his private friends, and by the enthusiastic admiration which justly rewarded his great achievement of the ' Iliad,' purchased that famous villa at Twickenham which his song and his life celebrated, duteously bringing his old parents to live and die there, entertaining his friends within its walls, and making occasional visits to London in his little chariot, in which Atterbury compared him to ' Homer in a Nutshell.' " In explanation of the above remark, it should be stated that Swift was most active and generous in promoting the subscription for Pope's "Iliad," and that it was he who introduced its author to both Harley and Bolingbroke ; and that it was out of the profits of this literary venture, about £5,000, that he purchased his celebrated villa.

Swift, too, who rarely had a kind word to say of any one, commemorates Pope as one—

"—— whose filial piety excels
Whatever Grecian story tells."

Yet even here, with his garden and his grotto, purchased with the proceeds of his pen though they were, Pope was not happy. He thus comments on his loneliness to Gay, who had congratulated him on finishing his house and gardens :—

" Ah, friend ! 'tis true—this truth you lovers know—
In vain my structures rise, my gardens grow ;
In vain fair Thames reflects the double scenes
Of hanging mountains and of sloping greens :
Joy lives not here,—to happier seats it flies,
And only dwells where Wortley* casts her eyes.
What are the gay parterre, the chequer'd shade,
The morning bower, the evening colonnade,

* Lady Mary Wortley Montagu.

But soft recesses of uneasy minds,
To sigh unheard into the passing winds ?
So the struck deer in some sequester'd part
Lies down to die, the arrow at his heart ;
He, stretch'd unseen in coverts hid from day,
Bleeds drop by drop, and pants his life away."

Though not sweet-tempered, Pope was so witty and well-informed that he enjoyed a sort of popularity, and became the centre of a host of friends ; but to this end, no doubt, his independence largely helped. He has the merit of having been as constant in his friendships as he was bitter in his enmities. And notwithstanding the fact that he had been brought up in the Roman Catholic faith, his three most intimate friends were Bishop Atterbury, a high churchman, Bishop Warburton, a low churchman, and Lord Bolingbroke, an avowed unbeliever.

Pope took under his patronage Gay, who had been one of the household of the celebrated Duchess of Monmouth, and "taught him the art of rhiming." Gay is said to have written at Twickenham his very successful play called "The Beggar's Opera." "Pope," it has been observed by a writer in the *Gentleman's Magazine*, "soon learnt to feel his own superiority to his early patrons, and in the case of Wycherley expressed it too bluntly. His genius, indeed, matured so rapidly that a short time sufficed to place him on a level with men who are still the greatest ornaments of a great literary age—with Addison and Steele, with Swift and Congreve, with Arbuthnot and Bolingbroke. . . It may be doubted, however," he continues, "that Pope was a very genial host, for Swift has a gentle sneer at him for stinginess about wine, and observes that he was a silent, inattentive companion. He said himself that, though he loved company, he loved reading better than talk. Moreever, he never laughed heartily ; and the man who cannot laugh is not likely to enliven conversation."

Swift lived very constantly with Pope at Twickenham ; and here Pope was visited by Voltaire, who, being invited to dine with the poet, talked at table with so much indecency, especially with regard to religion, that the poet's mother was obliged to retire in disgust. Nevertheless, Voltaire was invited to Twickenham more than once subsequently. On one occasion, walking in the garden, Pope confidentially told Voltaire that he was himself the author of a certain "occasional letter," which had really been written by Lord Bolingbroke—such was his vanity.

Pope numbered among his visitors even Frederick, Prince of Wales, who in many ways showed much deference to his taste and judgment. To his visits

Pope alludes with natural pride, when, after enumerating other great and illustrious persons who had honoured him with their regard and friendship, he continued—

> " And if yet higher the proud list should end,
> Still let me add no Follower, but a Friend."

On one occasion, when the Prince of Wales was on a visit here, Pope, after expressing the most dutiful professions of attachment, gave his Royal Highness an opportunity of observing very shrewdly that his (the poet's) love for princes was inconsistent with his dislike of kings, since princes may in time become kings. Said his Royal Highness : " Mr. Pope, I hear you don't like princes." " Sir, I beg your pardon." " Well, then, you do not like kings." " Sir, I must own that I like the lion best before his claws are grown." No reply could well have been happier.

Warburton and Pope met for the first time in Lord Radnor's garden at Twickenham, and Dodsley, the bookseller, who was present, told Dr. Warton that he was astonished at the high compliments paid by Pope to Warburton. The acquaintanceship soon ripened into the most intimate friendship, and not long afterwards we find Warburton writing :—

" I passed about a week at Twickenham in a most agreeable manner. Mr. Pope is as good a companion as a poet, and, what is more, appears to be as good a man." That his friendship with Pope turned out to his own advantage will be easily seen, when it is stated that through Pope's introduction to Mr. Allen of Bath—humble Ralph Allen, who " did good by stealth, and blushed to find it fame "—Warburton gained a wealthy wife, and ultimately the Bishopric of Gloucester. Pope, when he died, left this fortunate prelate the property of his works, which was estimated at four thousand pounds ! Whatever might have been the motive of Warburton in thus officiously advocating a man whom he once so much undervalued, certain it is that he met with an ample reward.

Spence, like Warburton, won the friendship of Pope by praising his poetry ; and his " Anecdotes " of the poet are full of interest for all lovers of literature.

In Pope's translation of Homer beauty of sentiment predominates, and this is particularly the case in his description of the " Dog of Ulysses," taken from the " Odyssey." This is communicated by Pope in a letter to a friend, with an introduction and conclusion which illustrate his happy talent for epistolary composition, and which is quoted here

to show his fondness for animals. " Now I talk of my dog," he writes, " that I may not treat of a worse subject, which my spleen tempts me to. I will give you some account of him (a thing not wholly unprecedented, since Montaigne, to whom I am but a dog in comparison, has done the same thing of his cat). *Dic mihi quid melius desidiosus agam ?* You are to know, then, that as it is likeness that begets affection, so *my favourite dog* is a little one, a lean one, and none of the finest shaped. He is not much of a spaniel in his fawning, but has (what might be worth any man's while to imitate him) a dumb, surly sort of kindness, that rather shows itself when he thinks me ill-used by others than when we walk quietly and peaceably by ourselves. If it be the chief point of friendship to comply with a friend's motions and inclinations, he possesses this in an eminent degree ; he lies down when I sit, and walks when I walk, which is more than many good friends can pretend to : witness our walk a year ago in St. James's Park. Histories are more full of examples of the fidelity of *dogs* than of friends, but I will not insist upon many of them, because it is possible some may be almost as fabulous as those of Pylades and Orestes, &c. Homer's account of Ulysses' dog *Argus* is the most pathetic imaginable, all the circumstances considered, and an excellent proof of the old bard's good-nature. Ulysses had left him at Ithaca when he embarked for Troy, and found him at his return, after twenty years ; you shall have it in verse :—

> " When WISE ULYSSES from his native coast
> Long kept by wars, and long by tempests tost,
> Arrived at last, poor, old, disguis'd, alone,
> To all his friends and e'en his *Queen* unknown ;
> Changed as he was, with age and toils and cares,
> Furrow'd his reverend face and white his hairs,
> In his own palace forc'd to ask his bread,
> Scorn'd by those slaves his former bounty fed,
> Forgot of all his own domestic crew—
> The FAITHFUL DOG alone his rightful master knew !
> Unfed, unhous'd, neglected, on the clay,
> Like an old servant now cashier'd, he lay,
> Touch'd with resentment of ungrateful Man,
> And longing to behold his ancient lord again !
> *Him* when he saw, he rose, and crawl'd to meet
> ('Twas all he could), and fawn'd, and kiss'd his feet,
> Seiz'd with dumb joy—then, falling by his side,
> Own'd his returning lord, look'd up, and DIED !

" Plutarch, relating how the Athenians were obliged to abandon Athens in the time of Themistocles, steps back again out of the way of his history purely to describe the lamentable cries and howlings of the poor dogs they left behind ! He makes mention of one that followed his master across the sea to Salamis, where he died, and was honoured with a tomb by the Athenians, who gave the name of The Dog's Grave to that part of the island where he was buried. This respect to a dog in the most polite people of the world is very observable. A modern instance of gratitude to a dog (though we have but few such) is, that the chief Order of Denmark (now injuriously called the Order of the Elephant) was instituted in memory of the fidelity of a dog, named Wildbrat, to one of their kings, who had been deserted by his subjects. He gave his Order this motto, or to this effect, ' Wildbrat was faithful.'

love of economy, that he wrote most of his verses on scraps of paper, and particularly on the backs of letters.

Swift styles him " paper-sparing Pope ; " but he nevertheless apostrophises his friend in terms of somewhat exaggerated praise :—

> " Hail ! happy Pope ! whose generous mind
> Detesting all the statesmen kind,
> Contemning courts, at courts unseen,
> Refus'd the visits of a queen.
> A soul with every virtue fraught
> By sages, priests, or poets taught,
> Whose filial piety excels

POPE'S HOUSE. (*From a Print dated* 1785.)

" Sir William Trumbull has told me a story, which he heard from one that was present. King Charles the First being with some of his Court during his troubles, a discourse arose what sort of dogs deserved the pre-eminence ; and it being on all hands agreed to belong either to the spaniel or greyhound, the king gave his opinion on the part of the greyhound, because (he said) it has all the good-nature of the other, without fawning ! A good piece of satire upon his courtiers, with which I will conclude my discourse on dogs. Call me a cynic, or what you please, in revenge for all this impertinence, I will be contented, provided you will but believe me when I say a bold word for a Christian, that, of all dogs, you will find none more faithful than,—Yours, &c., A. P."

It has been mentioned, as a proof of the poet's

> Whatever Grecian story tells :
> A genius for all stations fit,
> Whose meanest talent is his wit ;
> His heart too great, though fortune little,
> To lick a rascal statesman's spittle :
> Appealing to the nation's taste
> Above the reach of want is placed ;
> By Homer dead was taught to thrive,—
> Which Homer never could alive ;
> And sits aloft on Pindus' head
> Despising slaves that cringe for bread."

A supplementary volume of the poet s works was published, containing pieces of poetry not inserted in the earlier editions, and also a collection of sentiments, selected from his correspondence, arranged under the title of " Thoughts on Various Subjects," which have often been quoted, showing that Pope was—as a poet should be—

deeply versed in the hidden springs of human nature.

Pope's rank as a poet has been variously estimated, and doubtless there will always be great difference of opinion; in the judgment of some he stands almost without a rival, others would deny him the title of poet altogether, but his popularity has always been great. In contrasting Pope's earlier with his later poems, it has been well remarked that his early gaiety of spirits must have been heightened by the "voluntary vein" of the "Rape of the Lock," which established his reputation, and by the success of his "Homer," which

the first playful effort of satire without ill-nature, at once gay, elegant, and delightful :

'Belinda smiles, and all the world is gay.'

"The man of severer thought now appears in the 'Essay on Man.' The same vein shows itself in the 'Moral Essays,' but the investigation is directed to individual failings, and mingled with spleen and anger. In the later satires we witness the language of acrimony and bitterness. The 'Dunciad' closes the prospect, and we there behold the aged bard among a swarm of enemies, who began his career all innocence, happiness, and smiles."

LADY HOWE'S VILLA AND POPE'S GROTTO.   (*From a Drawing by G. Banet*, 1882.)

rendered him independent in his circumstances. Mr. Bowles has an interesting note, comparing the succession of Pope's original productions with the progress of his mind and character :—"In his earliest effusion—the 'Ode on Solitude'—all is rural quiet, innocence, content, &c. We next see, in his 'Pastorals,' the golden age of happiness, while the—

'Shepherd lad leads forth his flock
Beside the silver Thame.'

"His next step, 'Windsor Forest,' exhibits the same rural turn, but with views more diversified and extended, and approaching more to the real history and concerns of life. The warm passions of youth succeed, and we are interested in the fate of the tender Sappho or the ardent and unfortunate Eloise. As the world opens, local manners are displayed. In the 'Rape of the Lock' we see

Dr. Johnson, in his "Life of Pope," writes as follows with reference to the respective excellences of Pope and his model and predecessor, Dryden. "Dryden," he says, "knew more of man in his general nature, and Pope in his local manners; the notions of Dryden were formed by comprehensive speculation, those of Pope by minute attention. There is more dignity in the knowledge of Dryden, more certainty in that of Pope. Dryden is sometimes vehement, Pope always smooth; Dryden's page is a natural field, Pope's a velvet lawn. If the flights of Dryden are higher, Pope continues longer on the wing. If of Dryden's fire the blaze is brighter, of Pope's the heat is more regular and constant. Dryden often surpasses expectation, and Pope never falls below it. Dryden is read with frequent astonishment, and Pope with perpetual delight."

Thackeray says of the concluding verses of the

"Dunciad" that "no poet's verse ever mounted higher." "In these astonishing lines," he writes, "Pope reaches, I think, to the very greatest height which his sublime art has attained, and shows himself the equal of all poets of all times. It is the brightest ardour, the loftiest assertion of truth, the most generous wisdom, illustrated by the noblest poetic figure, and spoken in words the aptest, grandest, and most harmonious. It is heroic courage speaking : splendid declaration of righteous wrath and war. It is the gage flung down, and the silver trumpet ringing defiance to falsehood, tyranny, deceit, dulness, and superstition. It is Truth, the champion, shining and intrepid, and fronting the great world-tyrant with armies of slaves at his back. It is a wonderful and victorious single combat in that great battle which has always been waging since the world began. . . In considering Pope's admirable career, I am forced into similitudes drawn from other courage and greatness, and into comparing him with those who achieved triumphs in actual war. I think of the works of young Pope as I do of the actions of young Bonaparte or young Nelson. In their common life you will find frailties and meannesses as great as the vices and follies of the meanest men ; but in the presence of the great occasion the great soul flashes out, and conquers transcendent. In thinking of the splendour of Pope's young victories, of his merit, unequalled as his renown, I hail and salute the achieving genius, and do homage to the pen of a hero."*

"Although now regarded as by far the greatest poet of the day," writes the Rev. T. Thomson, in the "Comprehensive History of England," "neither place nor pension rewarded his (Pope's) labours ; for being a Papist in religion and a Tory in politics, every avenue of Court patronage was closed against him. He was thus obliged to depend for recompense upon the patronage of the reading public, as yet not numerous enough for a poet's wishes and wants ; and therefore, at the age of twenty-five, he commenced in earnest to write for money, by undertaking a translation of the works of Homer, which had long been a desideratum in the literary world, and was so successful that he was enabled, when not more than thirty years old, to purchase his classical villa at Twickenham, on the Thames, where he spent the rest of his life in study, combined with gardening. . . In poetry, Pope was a follower of Dryden, who was the founder of what has been called the 'poetry of artificial life. But he polished and perfected what the other had

founded, and thus became the leader of the school, in preference to Dryden. And here the comparison which Johnson has drawn between the pair may be alluded to, as the best estimate which has yet been formed of their respective merits. To Dryden, indeed, belonged a strength, majesty, and fervour, which his successor never attained ; but, on the other hand, Pope exhibited a delicacy and tenderness of feeling, and a sustained, well-balanced dignity of thought and style, of which Dryden was incapable. This distinction can be easily felt by a comparison of 'Alexander's Feast' and the 'Elegy on Mrs. Anne Killigrew,' Dryden's best productions, with Pope's 'Epistle of Eloisa to Abelard,' his 'Elegy on the Death of an Unfortunate Lady,' and the 'Rape of the Lock.' In the same manner, as satirists, both were equally terrible, the one in 'Mac Flecno' and 'Absalom and Achitophel,' the other in the 'Dunciad' and his 'Epistles' ; but if Dryden's satire was an iron mace, that shattered and crushed while it killed, Pope's was the keen-edged scimitar of the Eastern sultan, that with a silent wave bereaved the shoulders of their head or the body of a limb. While both were thus poets of the highest order, the superior polish and epigrammatic point, as well as better sustained and even dignity of the poetry of Pope, have caused it to be more universally quoted, and given it a greater influence than the more energetic, but unequal, productions of the other. Indeed, with the exception of Shakespeare, no writer throughout the whole range of English poetry has ever been the source of such frequent reference as the bard of Twickenham."

In speaking of the illness and death of Pope, Mr. Cobbett, in his "Memorials of Twickenham," says :—"Among his latest acts was one of kindness to the talented and unprincipled poet, Savage. In his illness he was patient and placid, viewing the approach of death with magnanimity and resignation. The infidel Bolingbroke is said to have been disgusted at the firmness of Pope's Christian hope. During a lucid interval in the course of a temporary aberration of reason with which he was attacked, he was found busily engaged early one morning on an essay on the 'Immortality of the Soul.' Shortly before his death he observed, 'I am so certain of the soul's being immortal, that I seem to feel it within me.' On the third day before his death he desired to be brought to the table where his friends were at dinner. All present noticed that he was dying. Miss Anne Arbuthnot exclaimed involuntarily, 'Lord have mercy upon us ! this is quite an Egyptian feast !' Next day he sat for three hours in a sedan-chair in his garden, taking his last look

---

* "English Humourists," pp. 289-90.

at scenes so dear to him, then in their early summer beauty. To this occasion Dr. Johnson's incredible statement about Martha Blount appears to belong. He says that one day, as Pope was sitting in the air with Lord Bolingbroke and Lord Marchmont, he saw his favourite, Martha Blount, at the bottom of the terrace, and asked Lord Bolingbroke to go and hand her up. Bolingbroke, not liking the errand, crossed his legs and sat still; but Lord Marchmont, who was younger and less captious, waited on the lady, who, when he came to her, asked, 'What, is he not dead yet?' She is said, continues the Doctor, 'to have neglected him with shameful unkindness in the latter time of his decay.' The improbability of the question," continues Mr. Cobbett, "is seen on the face of it. Could Martha Blount be possibly ignorant whether Pope were alive or dead? Or, if the question were really put, it need not necessarily be construed harshly—nay, it may have been so uttered as to imply pity and tenderness for the lingering agonies of the sufferer."

In the "Imitations of Horace," Pope has these curious lines respecting himself:—

" Weak tho' I am of limb, and short of sight,
    Far from a lynx, and not a giant quite;
    I'll do what Mead and Cheselden advise,
    To keep these limbs and to preserve these eyes;
    Not to go back is somewhat to advance,
    As those move easiest who have learned to dance."

Speaking of his obligations to these great physicians and to others of the faculty, he says, about a month before his death, in a letter to Mr. Allen, "There is no end to my kind treatment from the faculty; they are in general the most amiable companions and the best friends, as well as the most learned men I know."

If we may believe Mallet, when Pope was in a dying state Mallet went to see him. As he sat by the bedside, the poet, in a delirium, said that he felt his head open and Apollo come out of it, and enter that of Mallet. For this story, however, we have no authority except that of the person whom, if true, it compliments so highly.

The will of Pope is so illustrative of his character and connections, that we may be pardoned for quoting it in part:—

" The last will and testament of Alexander Pope, of Twickenham, Esq., In the name of God, Amen. I, Alexander Pope, of Twickenham, in the county of Middlesex, make this my last will and testament. I resign my soul to its Creator, in all humble hope of its future happiness, as in the disposal of a being infinitely good. As to my body, my will is that it be buried near the monument of my dear parents

at Twickenham, with the addition, after the words *Filius fecit*, of these only—*et sibi*, *qut obiit anno* 17—, *ætatis*——, and that it be carried to the grave by six of the poorest men of the parish, to each of whom I order a suit of grey coarse cloth as mourning. If I happen to die at any inconvenient distance, let the same be done in any other parish, and the inscription be added on the monument at Twickenham. I hereby make and appoint my particular friends, Allen, Lord Bathurst, Hugh, Earl of Marchmont, the Hon. William Murray, his Majesty's Solicitor-General, and George Arbuthnot, of the Court of Exchequer, Esq.—the survivors or survivor of them—executors of this my last will and testament."

He leaves his MSS. to his "noble friend" Lord Bolingbroke, or, in event of his death, to Lord Marchmont. And then, after bequeathing individual books, busts, statues, and pictures, to different friends, as Lord Mansfield, Lord Bathurst, and Mr. G. Arbuthnot, he leaves his library to Ralph Allen and Dr. (Bishop) Warburton; other bequests, in the way of money, to buy mourning-rings and family pictures, he leaves to his sister-in-law and sundry friends; £100 to his servant John Searl, £20 to the poor of Twickenham. He leaves £1,000 and the furniture of his grotto, the urns in his garden, his plate, household goods, chattels, &c., to his friend Martha Blount, with a reversion to his sister-in-law, Mrs. Magdalen Rackett. This will, which is dated December 12th, 1743, is witnessed by his neighbour Lord Radnor, the Rev. S. Hales, minister of Teddington, and Dr. Joseph Spence, Professor of History in the University of Oxford.

From speaking of the man we will now pass on to an account of the house which he made so famous. When Pope took the lease of the premises here, consisting of a cottage and five acres of ground, he at once set about the work of improvement. The house itself, except by its being freed from contiguity with ten still smaller structures, was not much altered.

The author of "Verses occasioned by Warburton's New Edition of Pope's Works" (1751) gives us some information on the localities of Pope's Villa:—

" Close to the grotto of the Twickenham bard,
    Too close, adjoins a tanner's yard.
    So verse and prose are to each other tied,
    So Warburton and Pope allied."

The allusion is thus explained by Mr. J. B. Nichols, in the *Gentleman's Magazine* for 1836:— " Pope's Villa in his time was, we believe, in the neighbourhood of small mean houses; a tallow-chandler's was close to him, and we here find a tanner's yard joining the grotto. The house itself was old and in bad repair; the grounds included about half the present garden that fronts the Thames."

Mrs. Vernon, from whom the poet held his lease for life, died about a year before Pope. He had then some idea of purchasing the property (valued at about £1,000), if any of his "particular friends" wished to have it as a residence. No such arrangement was made, and after the poet's death, the house, as we shall presently see, was bought by Sir William Stanhope. The name of Mrs. Vernon is immortalised by the poet in his "Imitations of Horace ":—

> "Well, if the use be mine, can it concern one
>   Whether the name belong to Pope or Vernon?"

In his "Imitations of Spenser," Pope speaks of the place to which his long residence here had so much attached him as a town "which fairer scenes enrich." And such would seem to have been the case; for these five acres of land, Horace Walpole tells us in one of his letters, Pope twisted, and twirled, and rhymed, and harmonised, till they appeared "two or three sweet little lawns opening and showing beyond one another, and the whole surrounded with thick impenetrable woods."

The house, or "villa"—a "villakin" Swift called it—when it was occupied by Pope, consisted of "a small body with a small hall, paved with stone, and two small parlours on each side, the upper storey being disposed on the same plan." Pope added somewhat to the building; but his chief delight was in laying out the gardens and grounds, and in the formation of the grotto which is so familiar to every reader of Pope's life. The grounds were laid out on the principle of landscape gardening (for he had ridiculed some years before, in a humorous paper in the *Guardian*, the barbarous practice of cutting trees into fantastic shapes, and designing the walks after the stiff and formal rules imported from the Continent), and in adorning his grotto, Pope used his utmost ingenuity in producing a variety.

> "To build, to plant, whatever you intend,
>   To rear the column, or the arch to bend,
>   To swell the terrace, or to sink the grot,
>   In all let Nature never be forgot:
>   Still follow sense, of every art the soul,
>   Parts answering parts shall slide into a whole."

Pope acted on the principles laid down by him in these lines, and in his little grounds steered clear of the Italian and Dutch styles of gardening. In fact, in laying out his garden, Pope carried out the precepts of his pen:—

> "First follow Nature, and your judgment frame
>   By her just standard, which is still the same.
>
> *   *   *   *
>
> Those rules of old discovered, not devised,
>   Are Nature still, but Nature methodised.
>   Nature, like Liberty, is but restrained
>   By the same laws which first herself ordained."

A writer in the *Gentleman's Magazine*, in 1801, observes that "the far-famed willow came from Spain, enclosing a present to the late Lady Suffolk, who came over with George II., and was a favourite of the king. Mr. Pope was in company when the covering was taken off the present. He observed that the pieces of sticks appeared as if there were some vegetation in them, and added, 'Perhaps they may produce something we have not in England.' Under this idea he planted it in his garden, and it produced the willow-tree that has given birth to so many others."

The famous willow died in 1801. Cuttings of it had been sent to St. Petersburg, at the request of the Empress of Russia, in 1789. A correspondent of the *Gentleman's Magazine* writes, under date of July 8, 1801:—"Last month I went with a friend to Twickenham for the amusement of angling. My first care, however, was to visit the sacred willow planted by the hand of Pope; and to my bitter grief, only two or three feet of the trunk remain, the upper part having been cut away." What was left of the trunk, it is said, was converted into "Popeian relics" by an eminent jeweller, who worked it up into trinkets and ornaments of all kinds, which had an extensive sale.

In order that the view from his own garden might not be hindered or obstructed, three walnut-trees were, at Pope's request, cut down in the garden of his neighbour. The fact is mentioned in one of Pope's poems, where it is stated that they belonged to a "lord." Warton says the peer alluded to was Lord Radnor. The Countess of Hertford, in her correspondence with the Countess of Pomfret, says that the trees belonged to Lady Ferrers, "whom he makes a lord."

No sooner was the poet settled in his new abode than, like one of the clients of the Muse, one of that

> "Genus ignavum, somno quod gaudet et umbrâ,"

he set to work upon the erection of the above-mentioned "grotto."

The grotto was (and is) a subterranean passage constructed under the roadway, which separates the two portions of the grounds, which lie on either side of the high road from Twickenham to Strawberry Hill and Teddington. The house stands between this road and the river. The garden beyond the road and the lawn sloping down to the banks of the Thames contain many large trees, under which Pope doubtless used to sit, including some of the finest and earliest planted cedars of Lebanon in the neighbourhood of London. The grotto was formed to obviate the necessity of crossing the high road every time the best part of the gardens had to be reached. On either side of it is a chamber, and these, together with the intervening passage, richly lined with felspar and Devonshire and Cornish marbles, mostly the gifts of the poet's friends, preserve the grotto to us much as it was a century and a half ago, when he described its beauties in his letters. Among the contributors of natural specimens in the formation of this grotto were Sir Hans Sloane, and Dr. Borlase the historian of Cornwall. Some of the letters which Pope addressed the latter gentleman are still preserved at Castle Horneck, near Penzance, the seat of Mr. John Borlase.

Addison suggests in his *Spectator* (No. 632) that the making of grottoes* is a work on which the ladies might well employ their hands. "There is a very particular kind of work which of late several ladies in our kingdom are very fond of, and which seems very well adapted to a poetical genius. It is the making of grottoes. I know a lady who has a very beautiful one, composed by herself, nor is there one shell in it that is not stuck up by her own hands." And he apostrophises the fair designer in the following lines, half in jest, half serious :—

> "To Mrs. ———— on her *Grotto*.
>
> " A *grotto* so compleat, with such design, ·
> What hands, *Calypso*, cou'd have form'd but thine ?
> Each chequer'd pebble, and each shining shell,
> So well proportion'd, and dispos'd so well,
> Surprising lustre from thy thought receive,
> Assuming beauties more than Nature gave.
> To her their various shapes and glossy hue,
> Their curious symmetry they owe to you.
> Not fam'd *Amphion's* lute, whose powerful call
> Made willing stones dance to the *Theban* wall,
> In more harmonious ranks cou'd make them fall.
> Not ev'ning cloud a brighter arch can show,
> Not richer colours paint the heav'nly bow.
>
> " Where can unpolish'd Nature boast a piece
> In all her mossy cells exact as this ?
> At the gay parti-colour'd scene we start,
> For chance too regular, too rude for art.
> Charm'd with the sight, my ravish'd breast is fir'd
> With hints like those which ancient bards inspir'd ;
> All the feign'd tales by superstition told,
> All the bright train of fabled nymphs of old,
> The enthusiastic muse believes are true,
> Thinks the spot sacred, and its genius you."

"A grotto," remarks Dr. Johnson, "is not often the wish or pleasure of an Englishman, who had more frequent need to solicit than exclude the sun, but Pope's excavation was requisite as an entrance to his garden ; and, as some men try to be proud of their defects, he extracted an ornament from an inconvenience, and vanity produced a grotto where necessity enforced a passage."

The best description of Pope's grotto, and of the poet's satisfaction and pleasure in it, is contained in an often-quoted letter of the poet to his friend Edward Blount, dated June 2, 1725 :—

"I have put the last hand to my works of this kind, in happily finishing the subterraneous way and grotto. I there found a spring of the clearest water, which falls in a perpetual rill, that echoes through the cavern day and night. From the river Thames you see through my arch up a walk of the wilderness, to a kind of open temple, wholly composed of shells in the rustic manner ; and from that distance under the temple you look down through a sloping arcade of trees, and see the sails on the river passing suddenly, and vanishing as through a perspective glass. When you shut the doors of this grotto, it becomes on the instant, from a luminous room, a camera-obscura, on the walls of which all objects of the river, hills, woods, and boats are forming a moving picture in their visible radiations ; and when you have a mind to light it up it affords you a very different scene. It is finished with shells, interspersed with pieces of looking-glass in angular forms ; and in the ceiling is a star of the same material, at which, when a lamp (of an orbicular figure of thin alabaster) is hung in the middle, a thousand pointed rays glitter, and are reflected over the place.

"There are connected to this grotto by a narrower passage two porches : one towards the river, of smooth stones, full of light, and open ; the other toward the garden, shadowed with trees, rough with shells, flints, and iron ore. The bottom is paved with simple pebble, as is also the adjoining walk up the wilderness to the temple, in the natural taste agreeing not ill with the little dripping murmur and the aquatic idea of the whole place. It wants nothing to complete it but a good statue, with an inscription, like that beautiful one which you know I am so fond of :—

> " ' Hujus Nympha loci, sacri custodia fontis,
>   Dormio dum blandæ sentio murmur aquæ.
>   Parce meum, quisquis tangis cava marmora, somnum
>   Rumpere ; sive bibas, sive lavere, tace.'
>
> " ' Nymph of the grot, these sacred springs I keep,
>   And to the murmur of these waters sleep ;
>   Ah ! spare my slumbers, gently tread the cave !
>   And drink in silence, or in silence lave.'

---

* A similar grotto, at Amwell, in Hertfordshire, stands recorded as having been visited by Dr. Johnson.

"You'll think I have been very poetical in this description, but it is pretty near the truth. I wish you were here to bear testimony how little it owes to art, either the place itself or the image I give of it."

At the entrance to the grotto was a stone, inscribed with the following line from Horace:—

"Secretum iter et fallentis semita vitæ."

In Pope's "Miscellanies," the following lines are addressed as an apostrophe to the pilgrim visitor:—

"Thou who shalt stop where Thames' translucent wave
　Shines a broad mirror through the shadowy cave,
Where lingering drops from mineral roofs distil,
　And pointed crystals break the sparkling rill,
Unpolish'd gems no ray on pride bestow,
　And latent metals innocently glow:
Approach. Great Nature studiously behold!
　And eye the mine without a wish for gold.
Approach: but awful! lo! the Ægerian grot,
　Where, nobly pensive, St. John* sat and thought;
Where British sighs from dying Wyndham stole,
　And the bright flame was shot through Marchmont's soul.
Let such, such only, tread this sacred floor,
　Who dare to love their country, and be poor!"

On another occasion we find him writing:—

"Know, all the distant din that world can keep
　Rolls o'er my grotto, and but soothes my sleep.
There, my retreat the best companions grace,
Chiefs out of war, and statesmen out of place.
There St. John mingles with my friendly bowl
The feast of reason and the flow of soul:
And he, whose lightning pierced the Iberian lines,
Now forms my quincunx, and now ranks my vines,
Or tames the genius of the stubborn plain
Almost as quickly as he conquer'd Spain."†

Pope's fondness for and pride in his Twickenham villa—my "Tusculum," as he called it—is expressed by him in letters and poems continually. In a letter to his friend Mr. Digby, he writes:—

"No ideas you could form in the winter can

make you imagine what Twickenham is in the summer season. Our river glitters beneath an unclouded sun, at the same time that its banks retain the verdure of showers; our gardens are offering their first nosegays; our trees, like new acquaintances brought happily together, are stretching their arms to meet each other, and growing nearer and nearer every hour; the birds are paying their thanksgiving songs for the new habitations I have made them; my building rises high enough to attract the eye and curiosity of the passenger from the river, when beholding a mixture of beauty and ruin, he inquires what house is falling or what church is rising; so little taste have our common Tritons of Vitruvius, whatever delight the poetical god of the river may take in reflecting on their streams my Tuscan porticos or Ionic pilasters."

In some verses, entitled "The Cave of Pope: a Prophecy," to be seen in the third volume of "Dodsley's Collection of Poems," the curiosity of future visitors and their pilfering of gems as relics is duly prophesied as follows:—

"When dark oblivion in her sable cloak
　Shall wrap the names of heroes and of kings,
And their high deeds, submitting to the stroke
　Of time, shall fall amongst forgotten things.

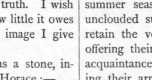

THE OBELISK TO POPE'S MOTHER.

'Then, for the muse that distant day can see,
　On Thames' fair bank the stranger shall arrive
With curious wish thy sacred grot to see;
　Thy sacred grot shall with thy name survive.

"Grateful posterity from age to age
　With pious hand the ruin shall repair;
Some good old man, to each inquiring sage,
　Pointing the place, shall cry, 'The Bard lived there.'

"Whose song was music to the listening ear,
　Yet taught audacious vice and folly shame.
Easy his manners, but his life severe,
　His word alone gave infamy or fame.

"Sequestered from the fool and coxcomb wit
　Beneath this silent roof, the muse he found;
'Twas here he slept inspired, or sat and writ;
　Here with his friends the social glass went round.

---

* Lord Bolingbroke.　　　† Charles Mordaunt, Earl of Peterborough.

" With awful veneration shall they trace
　　The steps which thou so long before hast trod,
　With reverend wonder view the solemn place
　　From whence thy genius soar'd to Nature's God.

" Then some small gem, or moss, or shining ore,
　　Departing each shall pilfer, in fond hope
　To please their friends on ev'ry distant shore,
　　Boasting a relic from the cave of Pope."

It need scarcely be remarked that the above prophetic lines have been amply fulfilled.

It is said that the original mansion, as left by

Horace Walpole, however, viewed the alterations and enlargements made by Sir William Stanhope in a very different light, and criticised them somewhat severely in a letter which he wrote to his friend Sir Horace Mann, in 1760.

On the death of Sir William Stanhope, the property passed to his son-in-law, the Right Hon. Welbore Ellis (afterwards created Lord Mendip), who seems to have had a special veneration for the poet's memory, and to have guarded with reverence

" POPE'S VILLA." (See p. 110.)

Pope, was humble and confined, and that " veneration for his memory enlarged its dimensions." Upon his decease the estate was sold to Sir William Stanhope, brother of the Earl of Chesterfield. By him the house was enlarged by the addition of wings, and the gardens were also extended by the addition of a piece of ground on the opposite side of the lane, connected with the premises by a second subterraneous passage, over the entrance to which were placed the following lines, from the pen of Lord Clare :—

" The humble roof, the garden's scanty line,
　Ill suit the genius of the bard divine ;
　But fancy now displays a fairer scope,
　And Stanhope's plans unfold the soul of Pope."

every memorial, and preserved the house, as far as possible, in its original condition.

Lord Mendip was a worshipper of the muses, and also well known in the political world ; and during his occupancy of Pope's Villa the place became celebrated for its fine statuary, marbles, and Oriental vases.

A view of Pope's house (still so called) is given in the *Gentleman's Magazine* for 1807. It is a tall and spacious mansion, and very different to the humble dwelling of the poet ; and the dwelling represents the building as consisting of a centre and wings, whilst a large double flight of stone steps leads up to the centre of the river front. The willow which was planted by Pope figures in the foreground.

After the death of Lord Mendip the estate was sold to Sir John Briscoe, and on the decease of that gentleman, in 1807, it passed by sale into the hands of the Baroness Howe. Her ladyship's connection with Pope's residence is soon told. She rased the house to the ground, and with complete indifference to its associations, as far as possible, blotted out every memorial of the poet.

Miss Berry, in her "Journal," under the date of November 21st, 1807, writes:—"We went into Pope's back garden, and saw the devastation going on upon his 'quincunx' by its now possessor, Baroness Howe. The anger and ill-humour expressed against her for pulling down his abode and destroying his grounds are much greater than one would have imagined."

Lady Howe built for herself a new mansion, not on the site of Pope's house, but about a hundred yards to the north of it. It was formed partly out of a dwelling which had been erected by Hudson the painter, Sir Joshua Reynolds's master. Lady Howe was the daughter of the celebrated Admiral Lord Howe, the "hero of the glorious 1st of June." She was twice married—firstly to the Hon. Penn Assheton Curzon, by whom she had a son, afterwards created Earl Howe; and secondly to Sir Jonathan Wathen Waller, Bart. The baroness and Sir Jonathan were long remembered in the neighbourhood for their hospitality. The garden parties, which were frequently attended by members of the royal family, were held almost weekly during the summer months, and the "1st of June" was always a red-letter day with them, being celebrated by a rowing-match on the Thames, when a silver cup was competed for. Mr. Brewer, in the "Beauties of England and Wales," suggests that Lady Howe may have been tempted by the chance of selling the building materials of the old house, which were worth, he estimates, about forty or fifty pounds; and adds, "If the baroness had been desirous of constructing a more commodious residence than that inhabited by Lord Mendip, she might, without any great blot to the grounds or injury to the prospect, have suffered the central part of the structure to remain, the portion once inhabited by Pope, and so highly reverenced and carefully preserved by Lord Mendip." But this hint, alas! was given too late. Probably Lady Howe did not want to be the proprietor of a public exhibition; she knew nothing of Pope, and perhaps cared less; and she was, no doubt, annoyed by his admirers coming to view the house and grounds which the poet had rendered famous. Pope's house is stated to have stood exactly over the entrance to the grotto, which formed as it were a part of the basement.

The author of a "Tour of a Foreigner in England," published in 1825, writes as follows with reference to a pilgrimage which he made to Pope's residence:—"I reached Twickenham by an agreeable walk along the banks of the Thames, where at every step the eye is greeted by a succession of varied prospects and elegant structures. So many splendid buildings may perhaps be displeasing to the lovers of the wild or purely rural scenery; but one is soon reminded that among these villas once arose the residence of Pope, the poet of civilisation. There he modernised the sublime muse of Homer, for whose simple dignity he indeed occasionally substitutes the meretricious graces of a coquette. There, too, Pope applied the language of poetry to philosophy, and composed satires and epistles such as Horace would have written had he lived at the Court of Queen Anne. In 1807, Baroness Howe pulled down Pope's Villa, and built in its stead a residence better suited to a lady of rank, and, no doubt, infinitely more comfortable. How many do the English sacrifice for that favourite adjective! The famous grotto, which Pope himself adorned with shells and minerals, has been almost entirely stripped by the 'pilgrims of his genius.' The weeping willow which the poet planted with his own hands is dead, and another bends its branches over the remains of the withered trunk. Farther on, in a more retired part of the grounds, is the obelisk which Pope erected to the memory of his mother. The best work he ever wrote could not have afforded me so much pleasure as the sight of this monument of filial affection. Happy the son who can deposit a wreath of laurel on the grave of the parent whom he has rendered proud and happy by his well-earned fame!"

In January, 1840, "Pope's Villa," as the new structure was wrongly called, was advertised for sale, and the building materials of the same shortly after. In the end, the Baroness Howe's house was partly taken down, its outside wings being demolished, and the central portion cut up into two tenements.

Subsequently a scheme was set on foot for building a new house, "exactly like Pope's," and for restoring, as far as possible, the grotto to its original condition; but this idea was ultimately abandoned. A new house, however, was built shortly after by a Mr. Thomas Young, a tea merchant, who gave to it the name of "Pope's Villa." It does not stand on the site of the original residence of Pope, but is nearer to it than was Lady Howe's. The building is a "combination of an Elizabethan half-timber house and a Stuart renaissance, with the addition of Dutch and Swiss, Italian and Chinese features." Such is the description of it given by the author of "Rambles by Rivers," who adds that it was probably designed when its architect was fresh from a diligent study of the paintings in Lord Kingsborough's work on "Mexican Antiquities." Some people, however, have suggested more simply that its design was, in the main, copied by the tea merchant who built it from one of those elaborate Chinese ornamentations which are to be seen on tea-chests.

In 1876 "Pope's Villa" and the grounds adjoining were again advertised for sale by public auction, and later on it became for a time the residence of Mr. Labouchere, M.P. Whatever may be the ultimate fate of that building is of no national importance. Suffice it to say that, beyond his tomb in Twickenham Church, the only memorials of the poet now visible here are the gardens and the famous grove in which he took such great delight, and also the grotto—or rather, the tunnel, for it has been despoiled of most of its rare marbles, spars, and ores, and is now a mere damp subway.

CHAPTER IX.

TWICKENHAM (continued)—STRAWBERRY HILL.

"Some cry up Gunnersbury,
  For Syon some declare,
And some say that with Chiswick House
  No villa can compare.
But ask the beaux of Middlesex,
  Who know the country well,
If Strawb'ry Hill, if Strawb'ry Hill,
  Don't bear away the bell."

William Pulteney, Earl of Bath.

"Strawberry Hill Shot"—Colley Cibber a Resident there—Other Tenants—Lease of the House by Mrs. Chenevix—The Property purchased by Horace Walpole—His Description of the Place in 1747—Enlargement of the House by Walpole—Description of the Building, and particulars of some of its Principal Contents—The "Chapel" in the Gardens—The Earl of Bath's Panegyric—Biographical Notice of Horace Walpole—Macaulay's Estimate of his Character—Strawberry Hill Bequeathed to Marshal Conway—The Hon. Mrs. Damer—The Waldegrave Family—Sale of the Contents of Strawberry Hill in 1842—Subsequent History of the Building—Little Strawberry Hill and Mrs. Clive—The Misses Berry—Alderman Matthew Wood—"The Bachelors."

NOT far from Pope's Villa, at the corner of the Upper Road, leading to Teddington, is Strawberry Hill, the celebrated villa of Horace Walpole (afterwards Earl of Orford). Everybody has heard of Strawberry Hill, with its brick and mortar turrets, its Gothic windows, and its lath-and-plaster walls. It has been much, and perhaps deservedly, ridiculed; but, although the mansion has been considerably altered and enlarged since Walpole's time, its interior is not only fitted up with much good taste, and even splendour, but contains many articles of great historical interest.

The house stands on a piece of ground called in old documents "Strawberry Hill Shot." It was originally a small tenement, built towards the end of the seventeenth century by the Earl of Bradford's coachman, and let as a lodging-house. This cottage, says Mr. Cobbett, in his "Memorials of Twickenham," was called by the common people Chopped-straw Hall, as "they supposed that by feeding his lord's horses with chopped straw he had saved money enough to build his house."

Colley Cibber, we are told, was one of the first tenants of the above-mentioned cottage, when he was in attendance for acting at Hampton Court, and one at least of his plays was written here, namely, "The Refusal; or, the Lady's Philosophy." In consequence of its pleasant and healthy situation, the cottage became at different times the summer residence of many great personages, among others, of Dr. Talbot, Bishop of Durham, and of Henry Bridges, Marquis of Carnarvon, son of James, Duke of Chandos. It was afterwards hired by Mrs. Chenevix, a noted toy-shop keeper of Regent Street. After her husband's death, this good lady sub-let the house to Lord John Sackville, second son of Lionel, Duke of Dorset, who resided in it for about two years.

In May, 1747, Horace Walpole took over the remainder of Mrs. Chenevix's lease, and in the following year purchased the fee-simple of the property by Act of Parliament, it being then in the hands of three minors of the name of Mortimer. Walpole, in a letter to Field-Marshal Conway, gives the following particulars of the place shortly after first taking possession of it. They have been often quoted, but will bear repetition :—

"TWICKENHAM, June 8, 1747.

"You perceive by my date that I am got into a new camp, and have left my tub at Windsor. It is a little plaything house that I got out of Mrs. Chenevix's shop, and is the prettiest bauble you ever saw. It is set in enamelled meadows, with phillagree hedges.

A small Euphrates through the place is rolled,
And little fishes wave their wings in gold.

Two delightful roads, that you would call dusty, supply me continually with coaches and chaises; barges as solemn as Barons of the Exchequer move under my window. Richmond Hill and Ham Walks bound my prospects; but, thank God, the Thames is between me and the Duchess of Queensberry. Dowagers as plenty as flounders inhabit all around, and Pope's ghost is just now skimming under my window by a most poetical moonlight. The Chenevixes had tricked the cottage up for themselves. Up two pairs of stairs is what they call Mr. Chenevix's library, furnished with three maps, one shelf, a bust of Sir Isaac Newton, and a lunar telescope without any glasses. Lord John Sackville *predecessed* me here, and instituted certain games called *cricketalia*, which have been celebrated this very evening in honour of him in a neighbouring meadow."

At the time it passed into the hands of Walpole the property consisted of the cottage and some five acres only, but this was subsequently extended by the purchase of outlying lands. Walpole soon conceived the idea of enlarging the cottage, and at once determined to adopt the Gothic style of architecture, in order, as he informs us, to prove, if he could, its adaptability to domestic buildings and their decorations. "Walpole's experiments in Gothic architecture" (writes Eliot Warburton), "as exemplified in his various plans and improvements at Strawberry Hill, showed that he was learning the art of building while he was practising it. In the game of putting up and pulling down, which he carried on for so many years, he was like a tyro at chess, who knows only the names of the pieces and their appropriate positions. . . . . He never became a first-rate architect. Nevertheless, he contrived to put together a structure which will outlast in interest buildings erected on more correct principles, and constructed with materials much more durable and solid."

"The Castle," as Walpole chose to call it, "was not entirely built from the ground, but formed at different times, by alterations of and additions to the old small house. The library and refectory, or great parlour, were entirely new built in 1753; the gallery, round tower, great cloister, and cabinet, in 1760 and 1761; the great north bed-chamber in 1770."

In spite of all his social pleasures, in September, 1774, Walpole bitterly complains of want of occupation. "What can I do?" he asks his cousin Conway. "I see nothing, know nothing, do nothing. My castle is finished; I have nothing new to read; I am tired of writing; I have no new or old bits for my printers; I have only backwoods around me." This idleness, however, was partly affected; for in general Walpole complained of having too much, not too little, on his hands. "He had

always," writes Eliot Warburton, "something to do; as a correspondent, as an author, as a connoisseur, as a patron, as a politician, as a fine gentleman, there was always plenty for him to employ his thoughts upon."

That he still went on with the enlargement of his "castle" is clear from the fact that in 1776 the "Beauclerk tower" and "hexagon closet" were added; continual additions, in fact, were made to the building, according as Walpole's stock of articles of *vertu*—"knick-knacks," as they have been vulgarly called—increased. What the results of Walpole's efforts as an architect were has been variously estimated. To some critics the work has appeared as possessing "the genuine appearance of former times, without the decay;" some have approved, together with its possessor, of "the choice selection of the best specimens of what is called Gothic architecture;" whilst others have not hesitated to stigmatise it as "the most trumpery piece of gingerbread Gothic ever constructed: as a whole, monstrous; in detail, incorrect;" or to sum it up as "a rickety, miserable, oyster-grotto-like profanation."

The designs for different parts of the edifice were collected from all quarters—at home and abroad. The embattled wall by the road-side was copied from a print of Aston House, Warwickshire, in Dugdale's history of that county, whilst portions of the ornamentations of tombs of bishops and princes in various cathedrals were made to do duty in the component parts of fire-places, doorways, and windows. Most of the windows were filled with painted glass. The general effect of the whole has been poetically summed up in the following lines by Maurice:—

" At every step we take fresh raptures move,
　Charm in the house and ravish in the grove.
　Within, the richest silks of China glow,
　Without, the flow'rs of both the tropics blow;
　What matchless colours in the solar beam,
　Warm, vivid, varied, thro' the casements stream!
　Here the deep ruby seems to blush in blood,
　There the bright topaz pours a golden flood;
　With Heav'n's blue vault the beaming sapphire vies,
　And emeralds glow with ocean's azure dyes;
　While thro' those casements to th' astonish'd sight,
　O'er hills and valleys ranging with delight,
　A brighter, richer landscape shines display'd
　Than ever Poussin sketch'd or Claude pourtray'd!"

The entrance to the house has been considerably altered. Originally, after entering by the north gate into the grounds, the first noticeable object was an "oratory," wherein were "vessels for holy water, and an enshrined saint." An iron screen, copied from the tomb of Roger Niger, Bishop of London, in Old St. Paul's, parted off the "abbot's garden" on the right. On the left, before the entrance to the house was reached, a small cloister had to be passed, in which were two objects of interest. The first was a bas-relief in marble of the Princess Leonora D'Este—"Dia Helionora"—with whom Tasso was in love. This was sent to Horace Walpole from Italy by Sir William Hamilton, minister at Naples. The second was the blue-and-white china tub in which Walpole's favourite cat was drowned. To the pedestal on which it stood was affixed the first stanza of Gray's well-known ode on the occasion :—

> "'Twas on this lofty vase's side,
> Where China's gayest art has dy'd
> The azure flow'rs that blow ;
> Demurest of the tabby kind,
> The pensive Selima reclin'd,
> Gaz'd on the lake below ! "

The hall, in its original condition, was small and gloomy, being lighted only by two narrow windows of painted glass. It was connected with the staircase, in the well of which depended a Gothic lantern. This latter, and also the balustrade, at each corner of which is an antelope (one of Lord Orford's supporters) holding a shield, were designed by Mr. Richard Bentley, the son of the learned Dr. Bentley, Master of Trinity College, Cambridge.

On the left of the hall, approached through a small passage, over the entrance to which is an ancient carving in wood of the arms of Queen Elizabeth, is the refectory or great parlour, "hung," says Walpole himself in his description of the building, "with paper *in imitation of stucco !*" This apartment contained several portraits of members of the family, most of which are still at Strawberry Hill, although differently placed. Amongst them may be mentioned Sir Robert Walpole, his two wives and three sons; an early production of Sir Joshua Reynolds's, called "A Conversation," representing George Selwyn, Lord Edgcombe, and G. I. Williams, all intimate friends of Walpole's; and the three beauties, the Ladies Laura, Maria, and Horatia Waldegrave, by the same eminent master.

In the waiting-room was a bust of Colley Cibber, formerly the property of Mrs. Clive the celebrated actress, and after her death presented by her brother, Mr. Rastor, to Lord Orford. There was also a bust of Dryden, who was great-uncle to Catharine Shorter, Horace Walpole's mother ; and a curious emblematic picture of a man standing (small whole length), with a bust of Charles II., seemingly previous to his restoration.

The contents of the china-room adjoining were much prized by the owner, and fill no less than thirteen pages of his list. Among them were "two Saxon tankards, the one ornamented with Chinese figures, and the other with European." "These tankards," wrote Horace Walpole, "are extremely remarkable. Sir Robert Walpole drank ale : the Duchess of Kendal, mistress of King George I., gave him the former ; a dozen or more years afterwards, the Countess of Yarmouth, mistress of King George II., without having seen the other, gave him the second ; and they match exactly in form and size." The floor of this apartment has some ancient tiles with armorial bearings from Gloucester cathedral. The upper part of the chimney was copied from the window of an ancient farm-house, formerly called Bradfield Hall, belonging to Lord Grimston, in Essex; and the lower part from a chimney at Hurstmonceaux, in Sussex; it was adorned with the arms of Talbot, Bridges, Sackville, and Walpole, the principal persons who have inhabited Strawberry Hill.

The chimney-piece in the Little Parlour is remarkable as having been taken from the tomb of Thomas Ruthall, Bishop of Durham, in Westminster Abbey. In this room, amongst other things, was the original model in terra-cotta, by Mrs. Damer, of two sleeping dogs, which she afterwards executed in marble for the Duke of Richmond.

On the first landing of the staircase is a boudoir formerly known as the Blue Breakfast Room, which contained several portraits of the Digby family and others. In this room was preserved the watch given to General Fairfax by the Parliament, after the battle of Naseby; also a curious picture of Rose, the royal gardener, presenting to Charles II. the first pine-apple raised in England. This picture was bequeathed by the grandson of Loudon, the nurseryman, to the Rev. Mr. Pennicott, of Ditton, who gave it to Walpole.

On the staircase was a suit of steel armour which had belonged to Francis I. It was purchased in 1772 from the Crozat collection, on the death of the Baron de Thiers, and realised £320 5s. at the Strawberry Hill sale in 1842. Amongst other articles here were an ancient curfew, or cover-fire, and the top of a warming-pan which had belonged to Charles II., with his arms and the motto "Sarve God and live for ever."

The library contained a valuable collection of about 15,000 volumes, chiefly of antiquarian and historical subjects. The book-cases were modelled from the choir of Old St. Paul's, as represented by Dugdale, and the chimney-piece was copied partly from the tomb of John Eltham, Earl of Cornwall, in Westminster Abbey, and partly from that of

Thomas, Duke of Clarence, at Canterbury. The most remarkable objects in the library were an old painting representing the marriage of Edward VI.; a silver-gilt clock, richly chased, presented by Henry VIII. to Anne Boleyn, on their marriage; a screen of the first tapestry made in England, and the osprey eagle modelled life-size in terra-cotta by Mrs. Damer.

In the Star Chamber, so called from the adorn-ment of its ceiling with golden stars in mosaic,

actor, for twenty guineas. Among the treasures of the library are Bentley's set of original designs in illustration of Gray's poems. They are immor-talised by the latter in his "Stanzas to Mr. Bentley" :—

> " In silent gaze the tuneful choir among,
>   Half pleas'd, half blushing, let the Muse admire,
> While Bentley leads the sister art along,
>   And bids the pencil answer to the lyre."

Though Bentley had been very useful to Horace

STRAWBERRY HILL IN WALPOLE'S TIME.
(*From Contemporary Drawings by Paul Sandby.*)

stood the famous bust of Henry VII., designed for his tomb by Torregiano. The chimney-piece in the Holbein Room was designed chiefly from the tomb of Archbishop Warham, at Canterbury. A part of the room is divided off by a screen, the pierced arches of which were copied from the gates of the choir of Rouen cathedral. Two highly interesting relics were preserved in this room, among them being "a very ancient chair of oak, which came out of Glastonbury Abbey;" and "the red hat of Cardinal Wolsey, found in the great wardrobe by Bishop Burnet, when clerk of the closet. From his son, the judge, it came to the Dowager Countess of Albemarle, who gave it to Mr. Walpole." This red hat was bought by Mr. Charles Kean, the

Walpole in putting Strawberry Hill together, yet he did not retain the great man's friendship for long, for, as was the case with Walpole and Lady Mary Wortley Montagu, the Misses Blount, and others, a quarrel arose between him and the lord of Strawberry Hill, which put an end to their friendship.

The gallery, nearly sixty feet in length, was the largest and most attractive apartment in the house. "The ceiling is taken from one of the side aisles in Henry VII.'s Chapel. The great door is copied from the north door at St. Albans, and the two smaller are parts of the same design. The side recesses, which are finished with a gold network over looking-glass, is taken from the tomb of Archbishop Bourchier at Canterbury."

STRAWBERRY HILL, 1882.

Leaving the gallery by its great door, we reach the new boudoir, drawing-room, and other rooms added to the house by its present owner. This new wing was built about 1860, and though erected to harmonise with the general edifice, is, it is almost needless to add, as solid and substantial as the latter is fragile. The drawing-room contains a large number of family portraits of the Waldegraves and Walpoles, and also Magni's celebrated piece of sculpture, "The Reading Girl," exhibited at the London International Exhibition of 1862. In the adjoining boudoir are a Madonna by Sasso Ferrato, and a few other pictures. A wide staircase leads from this room into the garden. The new dining-room is enriched by a large number of pictures, mostly from the old collection.

Returning to the original part of the building, we pass from the further extremity of the gallery into the Round Drawing-room. The design of the chimney-piece of this room was copied from the tomb of Edward the Confessor, and executed in white marble inlaid with scagliola. The ceiling was taken from a round window in Old St. Paul's.

The "Tribune" is "a square room, with a semicircular recess in the middle of each side, with windows and niches, the latter taken from those on the sides of the north door of the great church at St. Albans. The roof, which is copied from the chapter-house at York, is terminated by a square of yellow glass." In this room was formerly preserved the large collection of miniatures by Petitot and other masters, and also a vast number of antiquarian objects. Among the latter was one of the seven mourning rings given at the burial of Charles I.; the dagger of Henry VIII., which was purchased by Mr. Charles Kean for £54 12s.; a pendant golden heart-shaped ornament, richly jewelled and enamelled, made in memory of the Earl of Lennox, Regent of Scotland, who was murdered in 1572. This jewel was purchased by the Queen at the sale in 1842. Here, too, was a curious silver bell, made for Pope Clement VII. by Benvenuto Cellini, "with which to curse the caterpillars." The bell came out of the collection of Leonati at Parma, and was bought by the Marquis of Rockingham. Walpole, who prized it very highly, exchanged for it all his collection of Roman coins. It was purchased by Lord Waldegrave, at the sale in 1842, for the sum of £252.

The fireplace of the "Great North Bedroom" was designed by Walpole from the tomb of Bishop Dudley in Westminster Abbey; the room itself was originally hung with crimson damask, and contained several interesting pictures, the most noticeable of which were those of Henry VIII.

and his children, and the original sketch of "The Beggar's Opera," with portraits of Walker as Macheath, Miss Lavinia Fenton (afterwards Duchess of Bolton) as Polly, Hippesley as Peach'em, and Hall as Lockit. Among the curiosities preserved in this room was the "speculum of cannel coal" used by the famous impostor Dr. Dee in the reign of Queen Elizabeth.

The "Beauclerk Closet," originally hung with blue damask, is an hexagon in shape, and was built in 1776 on purpose to receive seven drawings by Lady Diana Beauclerk, in illustration of Walpole's tragedy of "The Mysterious Mother." A portrait of Lady Diana, by Powell, after Sir Joshua Reynolds, which formerly hung in this room, has been removed to the billiard-room; as also has a portrait of Mrs. Clive, by Davison, which formerly adorned the library over the Round Drawing-room, now a bedroom.

So multifarious was the collection of Strawberry Hill, that no less than 113 quarto pages are devoted to the details of it in the second volume of Walpole's printed works; and in order that no visitor might be deceived as to its precise nature and definite complexion, Walpole remarked, in a letter to a friend :—" The chief boast of my collection is the portraits of eminent and remarkable persons, particularly the miniatures and enamels, which, so far as I can discover, are superior to any other collection whatever. The works I possess of Isaac and Peter Oliver are the best extant; and those I bought in Wales for three hundred guineas, are as well preserved as when they came from the pencil ! "

Walpole never allowed large parties to go over Strawberry Hill; he made an exception, however, in favour of great people, as shown by the following letter to the celebrated actress, Mrs. Abington :—

"MADAM,

"You may certainly always command me and my house. My common custom is to give a ticket for only four persons at a time ; but it would be very insolent in me, when all laws are set at nought, to pretend to prescribe rules. At such times there is a shadow of authority in setting the laws aside by the legislature itself; and though I have no army to supply their place, I declare Mrs. Abington may march through all my dominions at the head of as large a troop as she pleases ;—I do not say, as she can muster and command, for then I am sure my house would not hold them. The day, too, is at her own choice ; and the master is her very obedient humble servant,

"HOR. WALPOLE.

"Strawberry Hill, June 11th, 1780."

In the gardens Walpole in 1771 erected a sham chapel, but this has been demolished and removed. It was built of brick, with a front of Portland stone, copied from the tomb of Bishop Audley in Salisbury Cathedral. Fronting the door stood a " shrine " of mosaic work, three storeys in height, having on one side, in a recess, a figure of an ancient king of France, and on the other side a figure of the Virgin Mary in bronze. On a tablet over the doorway of the chapel the following particulars were given :—

" The shrine in front was brought in the year 1768 from the Church of Santa Maria Maggiore, in Rome, when the new pavement was laid there. The shrine was erected in the year 1256, over the bodies of the holy martyrs, Simplicissa, Faustina, and Beatrix, by John James Capoccio and his wife, and was the work of Peter Cavalini, who made the tomb of Edward the Confessor in Westminster Abbey. The window was brought from the church of Bexhill, in Sussex. The two principal figures are King Henry III. and Eleanor of Provence, his queen, the only portraits of them extant. King Henry died in 1272 ; and we know of no painted glass more ancient than the reign of his father, King John, of Magna Charta memory."

At the end of the winding walk in the garden was placed a large seat in the form of a shell, carved in an oak, which had a very pretty appearance.

That Strawberry Hill and its varied contents—its pictures, and statuary, and curiosities—should have been made the subject of verse by the aspirants for poetic fame at the end of the last century is scarcely to be wondered at. Maurice thus writes :—

" Hail to the Gothic roofs, the classic bow'rs,
  Where, laurell'd Damer ! glide thy tranquil hours ;
  Where the rude block, from Parian quarries brought,
  Bursts into life, and breathes the glow of thought ;
  While all the cherish'd Arts and Muses mourn
  Round polish'd Walpole's venerated urn—
  In one lov'd spot their blended charms combine,
  And in their full meridian glory shine !—
  Of rarities, from many a clime convey'd,
  O'er many an ocean, to this hallow'd shade :
  How bright ! the rich assemblage charms my eyes,
  What prodigies of daring Art surprise !
  In pictures, vases, gems of various hue,
  And bring all Greece and Latium to my view !
  While Albion's chiefs, of more sublime renown,
  And ermin'd senators, in marble, frown,
  Bright polish'd helms heroic times recall,
  And gleaming corslets hang the storied wall ! "

The Earl of Bath's panegyric on his son's residence is well known. The humorous composition was completed by Walpole himself. The first stanza is given as the motto to this chapter ; of the remainder, as here given, Lord Bath wrote only the second stanza :—

" Some love to roll down Greenwich Hill,
  For this thing and for that,
  And some prefer sweet Marble Hill,
  Though sure 'tis somewhat flat ;
  Yet Marble Hill and Greenwich Hill,
  If Kitty Clive* can tell,
  From Strawb'ry Hill, from Strawb'ry Hill,
  Will never bear the bell !

" Though Surrey boasts its Oatlands
  And Clermont kept so jim,
  And some prefer sweet Southcote's,†
  'Tis but a dainty whim ;
  For ask the gallant Bristow,‡
  Who does in taste excel,
  If Strawb'ry Hill, if Strawb'ry Hill,
  Don't bear away the bell ?

" Since Denham sung of Cooper's,
  There 's scarce a hill around
  But what in song or ditty
  Is turn'd to fairy ground—
  Ah, peace be with their mem'ries !
  I wish them wondrous well ;
  But Strawb'ry Hill, but Strawb'ry Hill,
  Must bear away the bell !

" Great William ‖ dwells at Windsor,
  As Edward did of old ;
  And many a Gaul, and many a Scot,
  Have found him full as bold :
  On lofty hills like Windsor
  Such heroes ought to dwell ;
  Yet little folks like Strawb'ry Hill,
  Like Strawb'ry Hill as well ! "

In January 1772 the mansion of Strawberry Hill suffered considerably from the effects of an explosion at the powder-mills at Hounslow. Walpole thus amusingly makes mention of it in a letter to the Hon. H. S. Conway :—" The north side of the castle looks as if it had stood a siege. The two saints in the hall have suffered martyrdom. They have their bodies cut off, and nothing remains but their heads."

The career of Horace Walpole may be briefly summed up thus :—Born in 1717, he was the third son of Sir Robert Walpole, by his marriage with the daughter of a Mr. John Shorter, who had been " appointed Lord Mayor of London by the special favour of King James II." Mr. Walpole was educated at Eton (where he commenced his friendship with Gray), and whence he proceeded to King's College, Cambridge. In 1738 he was appointed to a Government post, which he shortly after exchanged

---

* Mrs. Clive, the celebrated actress, lived near Strawberry Hill, in a house which Walpole bought, and gave to her, and of which we shall have more to say hereafter.
† Woburn Park, near Chertsey, the seat of Mr. Philip Southcote.
‡ William Bristow, Esq., brother of the Countess of Buckingham, friend of Lord Bath, and a great pretender to taste.
‖ William, Duke of Cumberland, who defeated the rebels at Culloden in 1746.

for the sinecure office of Usher of the Exchequer, at a salary of £3,000 per annum. Other posts followed in quick succession, mainly through the influence of his father, which brought the sum total up to about £17,000 per annum. In 1739 he travelled abroad, in company with Gray, visiting Florence, Venice, &c. On their return, Walpole was elected M.P. for Callington, in Cornwall. He afterwards sat for Castle Rising and for King's Lynn in Norfolk. In Parliament he evinced his filial piety by a spirited speech against a motion made by Lord Limerick for an inquiry into his father's conduct. But he was not fond of public life, and in 1767 he communicated to the Mayor of Lynn his intention of abandoning his seat in Parliament. Not long before his death he declared that "he was *once*, forty years ago, at the late Duke of Newcastle's levee, the only minister's levee, except that of his father's, at which he was ever present."

He soon turned his attention to the fine arts and literature. In 1753 he became one of the fashionable contributors to the periodical paper entitled *The World ;* and in 1757 he set up a printing-press at Strawberry Hill ; and between that date and 1784, when he printed his "Description of Strawberry Hill," a large number of works were produced, including Walpole's "Royal and Noble Authors," his "Anecdotes of Painting in England," and "The Castle of Otranto." Walpole, although an author himself, held the profession of an author in contempt ; for in one of his letters to Hume he remarks :—"You know, in England (speaking of writers) we read their works, but seldom or never take any notice of authors. We think them sufficiently paid if their books sell, and of course leave them to their colleges and obscurity, by which means we are not troubled with their vanity and impertinence."

Walpole's fame as an author rests mainly upon his "Letters." "He loved letter-writing," says Lord Macaulay, who ranks his "Letters" above all his other works, "and had evidently studied it as an art. It was, in truth, the very kind of writing for such a man : for a man very ambitious to rank among wits, yet nervously afraid that while obtaining the reputation of a wit he might lose caste as a gentleman."

It cannot be said that Walpole was a patron of men of letters. He has been much blamed in regard to his conduct towards the unfortunate Chatterton, who, having left a provincial attorney's office, came to London to starve, and ultimately to die by his own hand. He appealed in his penury to Walpole, who is said to have turned a deaf ear to his case. Walpole is stated to have gone to

Paris with the young poet's compositions—which had been sent to him with Chatterton's request for help—in his possession, to have neglected his request for their return, and to have repudiated his complaint of such conduct as an insolent piece of presumption. On Walpole's return he found a very resentful letter from Chatterton, peremptorily requiring the papers, and telling Walpole that "he would not have dared to use him so had he not been acquainted with the narrowness of his circumstances." The following are the poor boy Chatterton's verses to Horace Walpole :—

" Walpole ! I thought not I should ever see
  So mean a heart as thine has proved to be :
  Thou, nursed in luxury's lap, behold'st with scorn
  The boy who, friendless, fatherless, forlorn,
  Asks thy high favour. Thou mayst call me cheat—
  Say, Didst thou never practise such deceit ?
  Who wrote Otranto ? But I will not chide ;
  Scorn I'll repay with scorn, and pride with pride.
  Still, Walpole, still, thy prosy chapters write,
  And flimsy letters to some fair indite ;
  Laud all above thee ; fawn and cringe to those
  Who for thy fame were better friends than foes ;
  Still spurn the incautious fool who dares to plead,
  And crave thy service in the hour of need.
                .   .   .   .
  Had I the gifts of wealth and luxury shared,
  Not poor and mean—Walpole ! thou had'st not dared
  Thus to insult. But I shall live, and stand
  By Rowley's side when thou art dead and damned ! "

Of the struggles of poor Chatterton, from the time of his arrival in London until his tragic end by poison in a garret in Brooke Street, Holborn, we have already spoken at some length in the pages of OLD AND NEW LONDON.*

Walpole gathered around him at Twickenham a select social circle, which included Garrick, Mrs. Pritchard, Kitty Clive, Paul Whitehead, the two Misses Berry, General Conway, the Ladies Suffolk and Diana Beauclerk, George Selwyn, Richard Bentley, Gray, Lord Edgecombe and Strafford, and Sir Horace Mann. The friendship of Walpole for Hannah More did not commence till 1784, when he was sixty-seven years of age ; and that with the two Miss Berrys dates only from 1788, when he met them with their father at the house of Lady Herries. At the age of seventy and more his heart warmed towards them as it had never warmed towards any woman before, and he never was happy except when they were with him or when they were corresponding with him. They both outlived him some sixty years ! When they went to Italy, the doting old beau wrote to them regularly once a week ; and when, on their return, they

* See Vol. II., p. 545.

anchored at the neighbouring villa—which, by the way, they called Little Strawberry Hill, in his honour —then and then only does he seem to be contented. His friendship for these two young ladies reminds us in some of its details of that of Pope for Martha and Teresa Blount.

Still, although he steered clear of the meshes of matrimony, there was nothing that Walpole liked better than acting as squire or cicerone to fine ladies, and especially in a pleasant row on the river Thames. But twice at least his gallantry nearly cost him his life: on one occasion, in returning with Lady Browne from Lady Blandford's in the ferry-boat, when the boat was carried down the stream to Isleworth, and forced against the piers of the new bridge; and again, in 1778, when in a boat with his two nieces, Miss Keppel and Lady Bridget Tollemache, to see the Goldsmiths' Company returning in their barges from a dinner *al fresco* close to Pope's Villa, when their boat was run down by some half-drunken cits, and the party were much alarmed, though not actually upset. On this Walpole remarks in one of his letters, that " Neptune never would have had so beautiful a prize as the four girls !"

In 1791, in his seventy-third year, Walpole succeeded to the Earldom of Orford, on the death of his nephew, an event which he himself commemorated in a few lines, called an " Epitaphium vivi Auctoris," as follows :—

" An estate and an earldom at seventy-four !
  Had I sought them or wished them, 'twould add one fear
    more—
  That of making a countess when almost four-score.
  But Fortune, who scatters her gifts out of season,
  Though unkind to my limbs, has still left me my reason ;
  And whether she lowers or lifts me, I'll try
  In the plain simple style I have lived in to die :
  For ambition too humble, for meanness too high."

Carrying out these principles in action, Horace Walpole would never assume the earldom, and seldom even signed his name as " Orford." He amused himself to the last with adding to the treasures and decorations of Strawberry Hill, where he was, in 1795, honoured by a visit from the queen and royal family. He never even took his seat in the House of Peers, but ended his days amidst his books and art treasures, surrounded by his friends. He died at his house in Berkeley Square on the 2nd of March, 1797, and with him died the last survivor of the family of Sir Robert Walpole.

Of Walpole's personal appearance we have the following particulars, written by Miss Hawkins in 1772 :—" His figure was not merely tall, but more properly long, and slender to excess; his complexion, and particularly his hands, of a most unhealthy paleness. . . . His eyes were remarkably bright and penetrating, very dark and lively ; his voice was not strong, but his tones were extremely pleasant, and, if I may say so, highly gentlemanly. I do not remember his common gait, he always entered a room in that style of affected delicacy which fashion had made almost natural : *chapeau bras* between his hands, as if he wished to compress it under his arm, knees bent, and feet on tiptoe, as if afraid of a wet floor ! His dress in visiting was most usually, in summer, when I most saw him, a lavender suit, the waistcoat embroidered with a little silver, or of white silk worked in the tambour, partridge silk stockings and gold buckles, ruffles' and frill, generally lace. I remember when a child thinking him very much undressed if at any time, except in mourning, he wore hemmed cambric. In summer no powder, but his wig combed straight, and showing his very smooth pale forehead, and queued behind ; in winter powder."

" In everything in which Walpole busied himself," writes Lord Macaulay, " in the fine arts, in literature, in public affairs, he was drawn by some strange attraction from the great to the little, and from the useful to the odd. The politics in which he took the keenest interest were politics scarcely deserving of the name. The growlings of George the Second, the flirtations of Princess Emily with the Duke of Grafton, the amours of Prince Frederick and Lady Middlesex, the squabbles between Gold Stick-in-waiting and the Master of the Buckhounds, the disagreements between the tutors of Prince George — these matters engaged almost all the attention which Walpole could spare from matters more important still : from bidding for Zinckes and Petitots, from cheapening fragments of tapestry and handles of old lances, from joining bits of painted glass, and from setting up memorials of departed cats and dogs. While he was fetching and carrying the gossip of Kensington Palace and Carlton House he fancied that he was engaged in politics, and when he recorded that gossip he fancied that he was writing history."

Burke, indeed, was not unjustly severe when he characterised Walpole as an " elegant trifler," and Strawberry Hill as a " Gothic toy." Dr. Aikin has drawn his character in these words :—" Horace Walpole, though forming his plan of life chiefly upon a system of personal enjoyment, possessed kind and social affections, and was capable of very generous actions to his friends. He had seen too much of the world to give easy credit to professions and appearances ; but he respected virtue, and had warm feelings for the rights and interests of mankind. As an author, if he does not merit a place in the higher ranks, he has done enough to preserve his name from oblivion."

Crabbe, in his "Tales of the Hall," sums up Walpole's taste for castle-building, as exemplified in his work at Strawberry Hill, in the following mock-heroic lines :—

> " He built his castles wondrous rich and rare,
> Few castle-builders could with him compare ;
> The hall, the palace, rose at his command,
> And these he filled with objects great and grand."

Walpole bequeathed Strawberry Hill and its contents, in the first instance, to his cousin, Marshal Conway, and to the Countess of Ailesbury during their lives ; then to their daughter, the Hon. Mrs. Damer, the sculptress, for her life ; and after her, to Lord Waldegrave.

Marshal Conway, who was for many years a Member of Parliament, seems to have been one of those many mediocrities who found their way into high official position under the good old patronage system which prevailed through the first twenty years of the reign of George III.

Mrs. Damer made Strawberry Hill her abode for several years, most of her time being occupied in her favourite pursuit of sculpture. At a somewhat early period of her progress Mrs. Damer attained almost to perfection in the art, and acquired a celebrity not only in her own country, but on the Continent of Europe, her title to which will be readily acknowledged when the number and excellence of her works are called to mind. They include the following figures, statues, and designs :—

1. The Dog, for which she was so highly honoured by the Academy of Florence.

2. An Osprey, formerly belonging to Horace Walpole, and exhibited in his collection at Strawberry Hill, but afterwards the property of Sir Alexander Johnston.

3. Charles James Fox, which she presented to the Emperor Napoleon at Paris, on his return from Elba.

4. The colossal bust of Nelson, executed by her in marble, shortly after he returned from the battle of the Nile, and sat to her for it, and which she presented to the City of London, whose officers placed it in the Council Chamber at Guildhall, where it now stands.

5. A bust of Nelson, executed in bronze by her for the King of Tanjore, and presented by her to His Highness.

6. A similar bust, presented by her to King William IV. when Lord High Admiral, which is now at Windsor.

7. Heads of Thames and Isis, for the keystones of the bridge over the Thames at Henley ; presented by her to the Town of Henley, near which stood her father's country-house, called " Park Place."

8. Two Dogs, executed in marble, and presented by her to her sister, the Duchess of Richmond ; now at Goodwood.

9. Several pieces for Boydell's Shakespeare.

10. A bust of herself, presented by her to Payne Knight.

11. Her mother, the Countess of Ailesbury.

12. Miss Farren (the late Lady Derby).

13. Miss Berry, editor of Horace Walpole's works.

14. Prince Labomirthy.

15. Peniston Lamb, the eldest son of the late Lord Melbourne.

16. The second Lord Melbourne, when a child.

17. Sir Humphrey Davy.

18. Queen Caroline, consort of George IV.

HORACE WALPOLE.
(From a Portrait by Sir Joshua Reynolds.)

Finding, however, the situation of Strawberry Hill lonely when her mother died, Mrs. Damer gave up the house and property, together with the £2,000 per annum left to her by its founder for its maintenance, to Lord Waldegrave, in whom the fee was vested under the will, and removed to a mansion of Lady Buckinghamshire, at East Sheen.

Strawberry Hill has since continued in the possession of the Waldegrave family, though they did not care to reside there. In 1842 the contents of the house were sold by public auction. The sale lasted from April 25th to May 21st, and realised the sum of £33,468. It was conducted by Mr. George Robins in a large temporary building erected on the lawn for the purpose.

"The fate of Strawberry Hill," writes Eliot Warburton, " was lamentable. For four-and-twenty days the apartments sacred to Horatian pleasantries echoed with the hammer of the auctioneer. Circumstances that need not be more particularly alluded to rendered this degradation unavoidable, and it was only with difficulty that the most sacred of the family possessions could be preserved from the relentless ordeal of a public sale." The shrine which had been visited with so much interest and veneration was now overrun by a well-dressed mob, who glanced at its treasures, and at the copious catalogue in which they were enumerated, with a like indifference. But doubtless, at the actual sale this indifference changed to the most anxious desire to obtain possession of some relic of the man whose name was invested with so many pleasant associations ; and the more interesting portion of the thousand trifles created a degree of excitement for the library. But above all, I should like to have a little drawing or two by a certain amateur artist, and trust, at all events, that they will not be allowed to go into the hands of mere strangers. Altogether, I suppose, they will bring a good deal of money ; and so passes the glory of this world ! Vanity of vanities ! "

The treasures of Strawberry Hill made their way into royal and private hands, and some found a

LITTLE STRAWBERRY HILL IN 1813. (*From a Contemporary Sketch.*)

which would almost have reconciled their former owner to such a distribution."

Lord Jeffrey, in a letter to Miss Berry, written at the time of the sale, gives his own "private opinion" of the value of the collection in the following words : " I have been amusing myself lately," writes his lordship, "by looking over the catalogue of the 'Strawberry Hill' collections, and, as you may suppose, have had you often enough in my mind as I went through names and little anecdotes which must be pregnant to you with so many touching recollections. I should like, if I were rich enough, to have some twelve or twenty of the pictures and miniatures, but would really give nothing for the china, furniture, and *bijouterie*, and not a great deal refuge in other collections, which they still swell and probably will continue to swell, until some ducal, or at least noble, family is in difficulties, when they will put in an appearance at the rooms of Messrs. Christie and Manson.

The house remained from the above date dismantled and neglected, and in a most forlorn and desolate condition for some time, until it became the property of its late possessor, Frances, Countess of Waldegrave, who, having thoroughly renovated and much improved and enlarged the building, made it, from the sumptuousness of its interior adornment, inferior to few of the mansions of the nobility in the kingdom ; and under her rule Strawberry Hill became famous for its *réunions* and garden-parties, at which royalty was often present.

Lady Waldegrave, the widow of the seventh Earl, carried it in marriage to her second husband, Mr. Chichester Fortescue, now Lord Carlingford. She was the daughter of Braham the singer, and was celebrated as one of the leaders of society in London.

After the death of the countess, Strawberry Hill became once more unoccupied as the residence of the Waldegrave family, and in 1881 it was again offered for sale. The property still (Dec. 1882) remains in the market; it is rumoured that it is about to be turned into an American hotel, but as yet, happily, this is not true.

At the end of a verdant meadow bordering upon the lower road to Teddington, and just on the confines of Twickenham parish, Walpole purchased a comparatively small house, in which the celebrated Kitty Clive, the actress, resided, and which is still known as Little Strawberry Hill. He would constantly trip across that field, accompanied by his pet spaniel, in order to enjoy the society of that fascinating woman.

Born in 1711, Mrs. Clive made her first appearance in boy's clothes, in the character of Ismenes, the page of Ziphores, in the play of "Mithridates," at Drury Lane Theatre. In 1732 she married a gentleman of the law, a brother of Lord Clive; but the union was soon dissolved, being unproductive of happiness to either party. During the year 1769 she quitted the stage, though to the last she was admirable and unrivalled. Retiring to this spot, she lived in ease and independence, and died here, beloved by her friends, and respected by the world. No individual ever took a more extensive walk in comedy—the chambermaid in every varied shape which art or nature could lend her—characters of whim and affectation, from the high-bred Lady Fanciful to the vulgar Mrs. Heidelberg—country girls, romps, hoydens, dowdies, superannuated beauties, viragos, and humourists—engaged her versatile talents with an inimitable felicity. It was a saying that "no man could be grave when Clive was inclined to be merry." At the same time her character throughout life was exemplary. Not only Horace Walpole, but many other persons of rank and eminence, courted her society, attracted by her wit and drollery; besides which, as old Pepys would have said, "a mighty pretty woman she was too." Mrs. Clive retired from the stage to this pleasant retreat very soon after speaking her farewell epilogue, written by Walpole, on her benefit night, April 24th. "Kitty," in spite of all her attractiveness, must have been a formidable person in her way.

The following anecdote rests on Horace Walpole's authority :—"When some persons in the neighbourhood wanted to stop up a foot-road, the opponents were very numerous, but they wanted a leader; some one then suggested that Mrs. Clive should be applied to; and on the morning of the meeting, Kitty—not 'the beautiful and young,' but the old and red-faced—appeared on the scene, with so determined an aspect that the assailants laid down their arms."

The "elegant trifler" wrote the following inscription for an urn to the memory of Mrs. Clive, which is placed in the garden :—

> "Ye smiles and jests still hover round;
> This is mirth's consecrated ground :
> Here liv'd the laughter-loving dame,
> A matchless actress, Clive her name.
> The comic muse with her retired,
> And shed a tear when she expired."

Mrs. Clive died suddenly on the 7th of September, 1785, at the age of seventy-five, and was buried at Twickenham. A marble tablet on the outside of the east end of the church bears an inscription to her memory, by Miss Pope.

Miss Mary and Miss Agnes Berry afterwards occupied the cottage, which was bequeathed to them for life by Walpole. The Misses Berry first took up their residence here after their return from Florence in 1791, and the cottage continued to be their residence for many years. "In the person of these ladies," observes Mr. Cobbett, "the memories of those who well recollect them are united to the older and more celebrated days of Twickenham. The elder of the two, born in the third year after King George the Third's accession, lived to be in her old age privately presented to Queen Victoria."

In 1813 Little Strawberry Hill was taken on lease by Mr. Matthew Wood, M.P., Alderman of London; during his occupancy the cottage enjoyed a fair share of popularity. The author of "Excursions through England," in describing Little Strawberry Hill, says :—"Hither have the citizens of London made delightful aquatic excursions during the summer season of the year. Indeed, it is usual for the members of the Corporation to indulge in these excursions under every mayoralty. These sons of pleasure generally travel by land to Kew, where they embark, and proceed to Hampton, the accustomed spot of destination. Some, indeed, have gone up as far as Oxford; and a few have had courage to penetrate the fountain-head, near Cheltenham, in Gloucestershire! The members of the Corporation are accompanied by their wives, and allowed to take a friend. These excursions in the City barge are not unfrequent, and when the heavens smile, impart no inconsiderable gratification. The entertainment provided is liberal, the company disposed to please and to be pleased; whilst a band of music, whose tones are reverberated from the opposite banks, soothes the senses, delights the imagination, and exhilarates the heart." The City State barge, which was often to be seen during the summer months on the reaches of the river about Twickenham, was named the *Maria Wood* after Alderman Wood's beautiful daughter.

One at least of the Miss Berrys must have been a woman of taste, for she was the designer, and apparently the engraver, of Mrs. Damer's bookplate. Both the Misses Berry died in 1852, Agnes in January, and her elder sister in November, at the age of ninety, and both lie buried in Petersham churchyard, where an epitaph from the pen of the Earl of Carlisle is inscribed to their memory.

However charming and attractive Strawberry Hill may have been in the last century, in consequence of the literary and social circles of which it formed the central point, the neighbourhood was not without its drawbacks. For instance, owing probably to the large extent of open and unenclosed lands about Twickenham, the highwaymen and footpads would try their skill on noble and gentle travellers in their carriages. Horace Walpole, writing in 1782, complains that, "having lived there in tolerable quiet for thirty years, he cannot now stir a mile from his own house after sunset without one or two servants armed with blunderbusses."

Though Strawberry Hill still stands, and though its grounds are as yet intact, yet probably they are both doomed to destruction. "Coming events," they say, "cast their shadows before them;" and therefore it may be worth while to add that on the opposite side of the road a large tract of land, extending up to the Strawberry Hill railway station, has been taken in hand by a firm of London builders, who are rapidly covering the green fields with villas.

In Strawberry Vale, almost opposite to Little Strawberry Hill, on the margin of the river, is a row of suburban villas, the last of which, called "The Bachelors," is a landmark familiar to rowing-men; this, too, is the last house in the parish of Twickenham on the confines of Teddington.

CHAPTER X.

TEDDINGTON AND BUSHEY PARK.

"Hæ latebræ dulces, etiam si credis, amœnæ."— *Horace.*

Situation and General Appearance of Teddington—Rise and Progress of the Village—Upper Teddington—Etymology of Teddington—Early History, and Descent of the Manor—"Queen Elizabeth's Hunting-Box"—The Manor House—The Parish Church—Dr. Stephen Hales—"Peg" Woffington—Extracts from the Parish Register—The Church of St. Peter and St. Paul—Recent Improvements in Teddington—The River Thames—"Swan-upping"—Bushey Park—The Ranger's Lodge—A Village Patriot.

PURSUING our pilgrim way in a south-westerly direction, a road, skirting on the one side the grounds of Strawberry Hill, and on the other the greenest of Thames-side meadows and eyots, conducts us to the lower end of pleasant Teddington, a place familiar to all anglers and boating-men, as marking the first lock and weir upon the Thames, and consequently, the ending of the tidal way—though as a matter of fact the effects of the tide are scarcely felt at all above Richmond and Twickenham. From this point, however, the mud banks which more or less mark every tidal estuary disappear, and we see Father Thames flowing along all the more full and brimming, but not the less picturesque, because of the artificial means by which his course is regulated.

But a few years ago—long since the accession of Queen Victoria—Teddington was a quiet rural village, with its two or three squires, its "Grove," its "Manor," its little waterside church, and its broad expanse of open meadows. Now all is changed: rows of spruce villas and "neat" terraces have sprung up along the roads to Twickenham and to Hampton Wick, and all over the upper end of the village, which now must soon call itself a town, with its grand "hotels" and magnificent "stores," which have fairly driven out the keepers of its hostelries, and threaten to swallow up the "small trader" class. This growth of Teddington is in a great measure owing to the introduction of the railway.

The district which is called Upper Teddington is provided with a church, schools, a large hotel, and shops of a more attractive and showy nature than those in the older part of the village. A large portion of the parish is still cultivated as market-gardens.

Teddington is situated on the left bank of the

Thames, and adjoins the southern end of Twickenham. The main road from Richmond Bridge to Bushey Park and Hampton Court passes through the older part of the village, which possesses a few good shops and public buildings. There is here a station on the Kingston extension line, in connection with the South-Western Railway. The village has long been a favourite spot for the disciples of Izaak Walton, and three of its principal inns—the "King's Head," the "Royal Oak," and "The Anglers"—are largely patronised by the fishing fraternity. The river about Teddington and Twickenham abounds in barbel, roach, and dace, in such quantities as to induce many who delight in angling to fix upon this spot for their summer "outing." Readers of Pope will not have forgotten the following lines, descriptive of fishing in the Thames :—

> " In genial spring, beneath the quiv'ring shade,
> Where cooling vapours breathe along the mead,
> The patient fisher takes his silent stand
> Intent, his angle trembling in his hand—
> With looks unmov'd he marks the scaly breed,
> And eyes the dancing cork and bending reed.
> Our plenteous streams a various race supply—
> The bright ey'd perch, with fins of Tyrian dye,
> The silver eel in shining volumes roll'd,
> The yellow carp in scales bedropp'd with gold,
> Swift trouts diversified with crimson stains,
> And pikes, the tyrants of the wat'ry plains ! "

The Queen's state barge, though no longer used on public occasions, is kept high and dry at Teddington. We have already mentioned this barge in OLD AND NEW LONDON. (See Vol. III. p. 309.) It is of antique shape, with lofty bows, and is said to date from 1600. Its form is familiar to all who remember the engraving of Charles I. feeding the swans on the river at Hampton Court. It has not been used since 1849.

The parish of Teddington extends from the river on the one hand—close by which stands the parish church and the main portion of the mother village—towards Twickenham on the other, and stretches also westward in a very irregular manner to the gates of Bushey Park.

Fortunately, in treating of the early history of this parish, we are largely assisted by a most careful series of papers which appeared in the local "Parish Magazine" in 1875-76, from the pen of the ex-vicar, the Rev. D. Trinder.

Teddington has been thought by casual and superficial scholars to have been so named as being the place at which the Thames ceases to be a tidal river—"Tide-end-town"; but in all probability that mode of spelling its name is not two centuries old : at all events, there is no proof of its use before the year 1700. Previously it was known as "Todyngton," "Tuddington," or "Totyngton."

If it be true, as suggested by Mr. Trinder, that "tot" means a small grove, and "ing" a meadow or pasture, then the name of Totyngton was not inappropriate to the place, but very descriptive of it, being "derived from the beautiful meadow, as older inhabitants remember it, sloping from the manor-house down to the river-side, with 'The Grove' in the background—an attractive and pretty spot, the choice of which does justice to the good taste of our British and Saxon ancestors." But we have our doubts as to the meaning above assigned to the word "tot," which appears in such names as Tothill, Tottenham, Totham, Totteridge, Tooting, &c., and which is generally believed to point to a lofty beacon.*

There is no record as to the founder of Teddington, whether he was a Briton, a Roman, or a Saxon. No Roman remains have been found in situ ; and probably the place grew gradually into existence as a fishing station long before it obtained its Saxon name of "Tuddyngton," or "Todyngton." As far as appears from history and tradition, there was no ford here, nor indeed any need of a ferry, because there was little or no intercourse between the "Mid Saxons" and the men of the "South Rey," or Surrey. "Remote from thoroughfares, and lying in the midst of an extensive forest, to which Bushey and Richmond Parks originally belonged, the place was reached only by the river—that silent highway. But when reached, it presented good fishing ground and fair pasturage, and these were just the advantages that the Briton of old times valued. Accordingly, it is scarcely unhistorical to assume that the forerunner of our water-side population was some ancient Briton, who paddled his cranky canoe on the flood-tide to the first fall of the river, and rejoicing to find there plenty of fish and meadows sloping to the river, built his clay and straw-thatched hut somewhere between the old church and the river, fenced round the meadow for his cows, and set up his idols in the neighbouring grove for the chance of some Druid passing that way."

"Centuries of quiet rolled over this retired fishing station. The lordly Roman doubtless bought the fish, revelling in the costly dish of lampreys ; and perhaps in his hunting expeditions drank a bowl of milk at the poor Briton's river-side hut, but took no further notice of it, and passed on his way."

Teddington was in the Saxon times a "tithing" in the Hundred of Spelthorne. As a tithing, it must even then have been the abode of ten

---

* See "Old and New London," Vol. IV., p. 14.

families of freemen, for it was part and parcel of the Anglo-Saxon constitution that every freeman should belong to a *tithing*, a *hundred*, and a *shire*, the members of each tithing being security for the good behaviour of each other. Thus a mutual dependence of each man upon his neighbour was established, and also along with it the principle of self-government. The chief officer in the county was the sheriff, or shire-reeve, who was assisted in his judicial functions by the alderman (elder), who was the supreme judge of the county court. The court of the Hundred took cognisance of matters too important for the *tithing* to decide; and as an alderman was chosen by each Hundred, so a tithing man was appointed by each Tithing to collect the king's dues and fines, and to preserve the peace. In some places this right would seem to have belonged to the manor court; and it is only within the last few years that the inhabitants of Teddington have ceased to assemble in vestry at Easter to appoint a head-borough or tithing-man, as their Saxon ancestors did before them ten centuries ago.

In the times before the Conquest there was doubtless here the usual complement of slaves and ceorls, or churls, dependent on some Thane or noble Saxon, whose flag they followed, and whose leadership they acknowledged under the king. The Thane would naturally erect near his manor-house a chapel, or "bell-house;" and this was done here. The little "Bell House" probably was dedicated from the first to St. Mary. The monks of the Order of St. Benedict at Staines had the charge of the parochial duties here before the Conquest; but in all probability Teddington was annexed by gift of Edward the Confessor to the more important Abbey of Westminster.

Mr. Trinder writes in the magazine above mentioned :—"It was not until the Saxon pirate, blue-eyed, fair-haired, and keen as his own long sword, swarmed upon the coast, explored the rivers, and gave his name to the land of the South Saxons (Sussex), those of the west (Wessex), those of the east (Essex), and to that which lay below them (Middlesex), that our name was heard. The place took the fancy of the plunderer, and a Saxon village with a Saxon name arose. Hence we have certain wide limits between which the historical origin of Teddington lies; for the Kingdom of Middlesix was founded A.D. 527, and in A.D. 838 a General Council of the United Saxon Kingdom was held by Egbert at the neighbouring town of Kingston-on-Thames—an event which shows the importance of the place, and the unlikelihood that any available places in its neighbourhood, especially on the banks of the river, had remained unoccupied."

Though no mention of the place occurs in Doomsday Book, yet authentic records show that even before the Conquest Teddington was closely connected with Staines, and that the Manor of Teddington was held by the abbot and convent of Westminster, King Edgar having granted to that body "the monastery which is called Staines, and all that belongeth to it, viz., Teddington, Halliford, Feltham, and Ashford." Again, we find that early in the thirteenth century the Manors of Teddington and Sunbury were assigned for the support of one Robert Papillon, who had been deposed from the abbotship of Westminster. In 1223, some disputes having arisen as to the question of patronage, it was agreed that the Abbot of Westminster should nominate and appoint the chaplain of Teddington.

In 1371, and again in 1427, "Todyngton" was taxed at nine marks, equal to about £6, as its rateable value, and was called upon to contribute 6s. 8d. to the service of the king. As the whole Hundred of Spelthorne produced the sum of £21, the population of it would not probably exceed 1,300 adults. What proportion of this belonged to Teddington may be inferred from the fact that in the year of the battle of Agincourt, when Henry V. required large supplies for his glorious, but fruitless, campaign in France, the Hundred of Spelthorne raised a tenth and a fifteenth, amounting to nearly £52, out of which Todyngton supplied 37s. 5½d. Somewhat later—namely, in 1435—this charge of a tenth and a fifteenth was found to be in excess of what this part of the country could bear, owing to its having been " desolated, laid waste, destroyed, or excessively impoverished;" the parish received a remission of 8s., along with Sunbury and Staines, whilst Feltham and Bedfont received each nearly double of that amount.

In 1539, Abbot Boston, of St. Peter's, Westminster, surrendered into the hands of his royal master the manor and advowson of Teddington. The manor then became part of a larger demesne, " the honour of Hampton," which the king formed into a royal hunting chase. Thenceforward the chaplain of Teddington was appointed by the lord of the manor, who was bound to provide a stipend of £6 4s., a charge which has been continued to the present day, though, owing to the change which has taken place in the value of money since then, it ought to be nearly £50.

In 1603, James I. granted the reversion of the manor to John Hill, whose son appears also in connection with it a few years later as Mr. Auditor Hill; he was probably, therefore, a nominee of Lord Buckhurst, formerly Lord Treasurer. It would seem that among the inhabitants of Teddington were several official personages, for the two monuments in the church belonging to the Stuart era commemorate an "Escheator" for the county of Somerset, and a "yeoman in ordinary" to Queen Elizabeth.

About the year 1670 the manor came by purchase into the hands of Sir Orlando Bridgman, who succeeded, on the fall of Clarendon, as Lord Keeper of the Great Seal. On his ceasing to hold this

THE QUEEN'S BARGE.

office, in 1672, he retired to Teddington, where he relieved many of the clergy who had suffered during the reign of the Puritan faction. He was buried here two years later. In 1833, when the church was altered, his coffin was found open, but his remains, having been embalmed, were almost perfect, even to his pointed beard. It was this Lord Keeper, an ancestor of the present Earl of Bradford, who settled on the church the slender endowment which it has enjoyed down to the present time.

It was only about the year 1850 that the "court-leet" of the Manor of Teddington was last held. The bailiff (a Norman official, who displaced the old

Saxon beadle, or rather, bedel) used to summon all the tenants of the manor, whether copyholders or freeholders; but this has now disappeared, the manor having been sold, and the copyholders' lands having been enfranchised.

The manor probably grew out of the first settlement in Saxon times, the proprietorship of the Thane under the later Saxon kings having been little different, save in name, from the seignoralty of the Norman lord, and having gradually been merged in it. It is probable that the residence of the feudal lord stood on or near the site of the present Manor House, but it is not mentioned in "Domesday"—nor, indeed, as already stated, is the "vill" of Teddington itself.

The "Old House" has been from time immemorial styled "Queen Elizabeth's Hunting-box," and there is no doubt that the tradition is genuine; for the royal chase which Henry VIII. had formed stretched in every direction around Hampton Court, and could not have stopped short of the present boundary-wall of Bushey Park, and probably it extended even further. Outside of it lay a large tract of unenclosed waste, the common land of the parish, leaving but a small portion for private domains and farms. On the other side of the river was Richmond Park, running up to and almost touching the old Deer Park, near which stood the palace of Sheene. Now, between these palaces and scenes of royal sport no half-way house could be more conveniently situated for a halting place, where the virgin queen could rest from the labours of the chase; and "the Old House, in strict Elizabethan style, with its simple construction and triple gables, bespeaks the purport of its erection, and justifies the tradition." In all probability it was built early in Elizabeth's reign, when the queen was young and devoted to the pastime of the chase; and Leicester dates a letter from Teddington in 1570.

There was, indeed, in the parish another Elizabethan residence, namely, the Manor House; but there is no proof that this was ever in the hands of the queen or of members of her Court, except that its reversion was granted in 1582 to Sir Amias Paulet; neither is there any proof that he ever lived there, and the fact that the arms of Lord Buckhurst were found carved in one of its apartments would seem to point to the conclusion that the house dates its erection from the early part of the seventeenth century. In the last century the old mansion was for many years the residence of Viscount Dudley rebuilt the house. Queen Elizabeth's hunting-seat was pulled down recently to make room for a new road.

The parish church, dedicated to St. Mary, is a brick-built structure, of little or no architectural pretensions, though prettily situated in the meadows,

The Anglers, Teddington Ferry.

and Ward, who made great alterations in the house and remodelled the grounds. Walpole, in a letter to the Earl of Strafford, dated 28th July, 1787, says that Lord Dudley here constructed "an obelisk below a hedge, a canal at right angles with the Thames, and a sham bridge, no wider than that of a violin." All these things, however, were done away with by a Captain Smith, who came into possession of the property through marrying his lordship's widow, and who also to a great extent near the river. The south aisle doubtless formed part of an earlier building, though patched and coated over, and much altered in outward appearance. In the church still survives the original chapel of the hamlet, but probably more than once renewed and rebuilt.

On the south wall is a brass, asking the prayers of the faithful for John Goodyere and Thomasyne, his wife. The north aisle was built about the middle of the last century, mainly at the expense of the then minister of the parish, Dr. Stephen Hales, who also built the tower in the following year. The chancel is a recent addition, and is constructed of brick in the Decorated style of architecture.

At the east end of the chancel is a mural monument to Henry Flitcroft, the eminent architect patronised by Lord Burlington. The oldest monument is dated 1674, and commemorates Sir Orlando Bridgman, who was commissioner for Charles I. at the treaty of Uxbridge, and after the Restoration held successively the posts of Chief Baron of the Exchequer, Chief Justice of the Common Pleas, and Lord Keeper of the Great Seal : from this last-named office, however, he was dismissed in 1672, for refusing to sign the Declaration of Indulgence.

Paul Whitehead, the poet, who died in Henrietta Street, Covent Garden, was buried in Teddington churchyard in December, 1774; but his heart was deposited in the mausoleum of his patron, Lord Le Despencer, at High Wycombe, whence it was stolen in 1839. Here, too, lies Richard Bentley, the sometime friend of Horace Walpole, and his adviser and draughtsman in the erection and decoration of Strawberry Hill. There is also a tablet here to the memory of Mr. John Walter, the founder and principal proprietor of the *Times*. He had a residence at Teddington, where he died in 1812.

This church contains also the remains of Dr. Stephen Hales, Clerk of the Closet to the Princess of Wales (mother of George III.), and for upwards of half a century incumbent of Teddington. Dr. Hales was one of the most active Fellows of the Royal Society, and a frequent contributor to its " Transactions." He was the author of " Hæmostatics," a treatise on the circulation of the blood, and of a similar treatise on the " Sap in Vegetables." To his practical turn the country was indebted for some improvements in the ventilation of prisons, hospitals, and ships of war, and these very largely reduced the deaths by " gaol fever" in Newgate.

" Plain Parson Hale " (whose name has been deprived of a letter by Pope by the inexorable laws of rhyme) was this same Dr. Stephen Hales, who was also one of the witnesses to Pope's will. Dr. Hales seems to have been a simple, benevolent man, delighting in his quiet village and pastoral duties. He rebuilt the tower of Teddington church, as stated above, and at a ripe old age he was interred beside it, dying in 1761, in his eighty-fourth year. Pope had a sincere regard for his amiable and scientific neighbour ; but, according to Spence, he

looked with horror on some of his experiments. " I shall be very glad to see Dr. Hales, and always love to see him, he is so worthy and good a man. Yes, he is a very good man ; only I'm sorry he has his hands so much imbrued in blood. What! he cuts up rats? Ay, and dogs too ! Indeed, he commits most of those barbarities with the thought of being of use to man ! But how do we know that we have a right to kill creatures that we are so little above as dogs, for our curiosity, or even for some use to us? I used to carry it too far ; I thought they had reason as well as we. So they have, to be sure : all our disputes about that are only disputes about words. Man has reason enough only to know what is necessary for him to know, and dogs have just that too. 'But then they must have souls, too, as unperishable as ours!' And what harm would that be to us?"

Here, in 1760, was buried the once popular and charming actress, Margaret—or, as she was commonly called, " Peg "—Woffington. She is said to have been a native of Dublin, and, according to the inscription on her tomb, was born in 1720. Her histrionic talent appears to have been displayed even in childhood ; as in 1728, being one of Madame Violante's Liliputian company, she obtained great applause by enacting the part of Polly in the *Beggar's Opera*. Her first speaking character on the Dublin stage was Ophelia, which she performed on February 12th, 1737; and on November 6th, 1740, she made her *début* in London, at Covent Garden Theatre, in the part of Sylvia, in Farquhar's comedy of *The Recruiting Officer*. In the following season she performed at Drury Lane Theatre, and was pre-eminently distinguished in the higher walks of comedy ; in some characters, particularly in that of Mrs. Loveit, she surpassed Mrs. Oldfield. In tragedy she had also considerable merit, but had not the power of touching the passions equal to Mrs. Cibber or Mrs. Pritchard. Among her best characters were " Cleopatra," " Roxana," and the " Distressed Mother." Having in her youth been taught by Madame Violante all that a dancer of first-rate reputation could teach her, she had accustomed herself to French society ; and upon a visit to Paris, Dumesnil willingly imparted to her all the manner she professed of the dignified passion of the French drama, and this infected Mrs. Woffington with the prevailing pompous mode of elocution which preceded Garrick's style, and in which she was confirmed by Cibber, who at seventy was delighted to fancy himself her gallant. She maintained a decided preference to male society, and is said to have more than once presided at the meetings of the Beef-Steak Club. Her act ing in male attire, in which she was fond of display-ing herself, was unequalled ; and Sir Harry Wildair was one of her most admired characters. In 1757, being then engaged at Covent Garden, she rendered her last acknowledgments to her friends in the character of Lothario, for her benefit, and took her farewell leave of the public on May 17th as Rosa-lind, one of her most favourite parts, in male attire, in which she at the close resumed the female costume, just to "make curtesy and bid farewell." While speaking the epilogue, she was seized with an indisposition from which she never recovered, though she retained the unrivalled beauties of her face and person to the last. She died March 28th, 1760.

Her monument, on the east wall of the north aisle, near the pulpit, is of marble, and bears the following inscription :—"Near this monument lies the body of Margaret Woffington, spinster, born October 18th, 1720, who departed this life March 28th, 1760, aged thirty-nine years." The arms on the monument are, *Or, three leopards' faces, gules.* On the lower compartment is another inscription, as follows :—" In the same grave lies the body of Master Horace Cholmondely, son of the Honour-able Robert Cholmondely and of Mary Cholmondely, sister of the said Margaret Woffington, aged six months." A reference to Sir Egerton Brydges' "Peerage of England" shows "Master Horace" to have been born February 18th, 1753, and bap-tised March 16th following at St. George's, Hanover Square. The date of this sepulture, therefore, was August, 1753.

The parish registers commence in Elizabeth's reign, the first baptism and burial recorded being dated 1558, and the first marriage three years later.

In 1635, one Matthew Rendall, curate of Ted-dington, as mentioned in Neal's "History of the Puritans," was denounced by an aggrieved par-ishioner, and suspended by the bishop under the High Commission for preaching long sermons ! Possibly many congregations would be glad if such a penalty could be inflicted now for the same offence.

At the Reformation several acres of land which had been left to the church for the maintenance of services then voted superstitious were surrendered to the king, who gave them out among his courtiers or devoted them to the payment of his personal debts. At this time there were seventy-two "housel-ing people," that is, Easter communicants, and "but one priest found to serve the cure": words which would seem to imply that the parish had not gained by the recent changes in religion.

John Cosens, DD., the author of " The Tears of Twickenham," " Œconomics of Beauty," and other poems, was Dr. Hales' successor in the incumbency of Teddington.

The church of St. Peter and St. Paul, in Upper Teddington, was partly erected in 1866, and com-pleted (with the exception of the tower and spire) in 1873, under the incumbency of the Rev. Daniel Trinder. The edifice is constructed of yellow brick, with dressings of red brick ; it is in the Early English style of architecture, and was built from the designs of the late Mr. G. E. Street, R.A. Close by is a commodious school-house, of similar architecture, which was built in 1874. In 1875 a new school chapel was erected at Teddington Wick.

Lewis, in his "Topographical Dictionary" (1835,) mentions here large bleaching-grounds and manu-factories of candles and of spermaceti ; but these no longer exist.

That rapid strides have been made of late years in the growth of Teddington and the number of its inhabitants will be easily seen when it is stated that in 1835 the population was given as 895, whilst between the years 1861 and 1871 it had increased from 1,183 to 4,063. The town—for such it is—has now grown sufficiently large to have its Mutual Instruction Society, which is well supported, and also a working-man's club and horticultural and building societies ; and will shortly have its town hall.

Among the " eminent inhabitants " of Tedding-ton whose names have not already been mentioned above was William Penn, the celebrated Quaker, and founder of the colony of Pennsylvania. The son of Admiral Sir William Penn, he was born in London in 1644, and studied at Christ Church, Oxford, but was expelled from the University in consequence of the enthusiasm which he displayed in the new doctrine of Quakerism, which had its rise about that time. It was from Teddington, in 1688, that Penn dated the letter in which he rebutted the charge of being a Papist which had been brought against him. Francis Manning, the author of a translation from the French of a "Life of Theodosius the Great," lived here for many years ; and, according to an entry in Sir Joshua Reynolds's pocket-book, quoted in Leslie and Taylor's "Life of Reynolds," John Wilkes—of whom we have already spoken at some length in our account of Brentford (see page 38, *ante*)— occupied for a short time " an out-of-the-way lodging in the second turning past Teddington Church" whilst still an outlaw, and during a sur-reptitious visit to England.

In Walpole's time there lived here a gentleman named Prescott, who used to beat his wife so unmercifully that she ran away, aided by a groom, and shortly afterwards "swore the peace" against her husband. The case came before Lord Mansfield, who asked the groom if he had not helped his mistress to escape. "Yes, my lord; and my master has never yet thanked me for it!" was the cool reply. "Why should he thank you, my lad?" asked his lordship. "Because, my lord, if I had not done so, he would have murdered his wife, and then he would have been hanged for it." Lord Mansfield and the Court were so amused that they acquitted the witty lad of all blame for his share in the transaction.

The river Thames at Teddington, as we have already observed, is a familiar friend to the "brethren of the angle," who have long regarded the neighbourhood and the "weir" as among the pleasantest of all their river memories. "These memories," writes Mr. S. Carter Hall, in his "Book of the Thames," "are in truth very pleasant, for, although it has 'fallen from its high estate,' and is by no means as productive of sport as it used to be, there is still plenty to be had in several 'pitches,' where abound all the various denizens of the populous river, while enjoyment is ever enhanced by associations of the past," which are suggested at every spot of ground beside which the punt is pushed or moored. The venerable and picturesque lock of Teddington—the first, by the way, to be met with in the voyage up the river, and one which has often been made the subject of an artist's sketch—has given way before the "march of improvement" to a new and more substantial structure of masonry. In bygone times, before the construction of bridges, locks, and other obstructions, the tide, in all probability, ascended much higher than Teddington. At the present time it flows but feebly some way below this parish, and high water here is nearly an hour and a half later than at London Bridge, a distance of nineteen and a half miles.

It may be interesting to know that the "intake" of all the London Water Companies, as authorised by the Metropolis Water Act of 1852, must be above Teddington Lock. A Government Commission, consisting of Professors Graham, Miller, and Hoffman, in 1852-4, reported that enormous supplies of spring water were to be obtained at a very small cost from the chalk strata surrounding London ; but the companies, evidently led on through a feeling of self-interest, persisted in still having recourse to the Thames, though they were forced to have their "intake" above Teddington

Lock, which still contains many particles of impurity, and therefore seeds of disease, brought down from the towns higher up the river.

In the pages of OLD AND NEW LONDON[*] we have spoken of the interesting ceremony called "Swan-upping" on the Thames, a custom which has been observed for upwards of four centuries. As the duties of the "swan-upper," or marker, however, are confined principally to that portion of the river which lies above Teddington Lock, we may be pardoned for again reverting to the subject. From Teddington to Oxford, over the whole hundred and odd miles of which old Father Thames winds his silvery course, there is perhaps no prettier sight than a herd of swans. The royal bird, "floating double, swan and shadow," sails up and down the long reaches, and in and out among the eyots, a thing of wonderful beauty and grace—a noble ornament to a noble river. Poets of all ages and all countries, from the mythical Orpheus of Thrace down to our own poet laureate, have claimed the creature as their own. Apart altogether from his exquisite beauty and majesty, and the conscious grace with which, "with arched neck between his white wings mantling," he "proudly rows his state with oared feet," tradition claims for the bird of Apollo the divine gift of song, and tells us how, when the swan seeks the waste, to die there unseen and alone, "her awful jubilant voice, with a music strange and manifold, flows forth on a carol free and bold, as when a mighty people rejoice with shawms, and cymbals, and harps of gold." Nor is it poets alone who delight to honour the noble bird, and to claim in him a special property. Ever since the lion-hearted Richard brought back to England from the fair island of Cyprus the first "cobs" and "pens" that ever floated on the Thames, the swan has remained a royal bird, guarded jealously by special statutes, and with a royal swanherd deputed to watch over him. The subject can only keep swans by special licence, along with which he has also granted to him a swan mark, or device, to be cut with a sharp knife in the upper bill. But our swanholders have sadly fallen off since the days of "good Queen Bess," when "close upon a thousand corporations and individuals" were privileged to keep "a game of swans." A swannery is now as rare a sight as even a heronry itself. Our old customs and institutions are dying out, and swans, being fowl, must go the way of all flesh. The Corporation of Oxford has a swannery by prescription, although no swans are now reared, and it is doubtful whether the privilege has not long since abated. The noble Abbotsbury "game" is still kept up by the Earls of Ilchester, in Dorset. And upon the Thames, the Crown, conjointly with the Worshipful Companies of Vintners and Dyers, still sends out on each 1st of August an organised expedition of "swan-uppers" to catch and "nick" the young birds. But even thus, the numbers of our "games" are sadly decreasing. Some century and a half ago the Vintners' Company had no less than 500 cobs between London Bridge and Staines. There are now little more than 500 birds, cobs, pens, cygnets, and grey birds, all told, between London Bridge and Cricklade Weir. Of these, the Queen owns 397, the Vintners' Company 55, and the Dyers' Company 67.

Turning once more inland, we will now make our way towards the historic region of Hampton and Hampton Court.

At the extreme south-western end of Teddington are the entrance-gates and lodge of Bushey Park. The park is upwards of a thousand acres in extent, and with its noble avenue of horse-chestnut trees, more than a mile in length, forms a stately approach to Hampton Court Palace.

Bushey Park, lying as it does on the confines of both Teddington and Hampton, is actually in the former parish, and forms a good connecting link between them and the avenues, which were planted by William III. in true Dutch fashion. The principal avenue has four others on each side of it. The breadth of these nine avenues is upwards of 560 feet, and they cover nearly seventy acres. These avenues are perhaps unequalled for extent and beauty in Europe. At nearly the farther extremity of the avenue is a circular piece of water, called the Diana Water, from a fine bronze fountain of that goddess, seven feet in height, placed in the centre of it. It stands on a block of statuary marble, and is surrounded by small figures, also of bronze.

Immediately to the right of the entrance to Bushey Park stands the house formerly occupied by William IV. He lived here for thirty-six years like a country gentleman, superintending his farm and entertaining his neighbours with great hospitality. His Majesty, whilst residing here, like a true sailor, had a part of the foremast of the *Victory*, against which Nelson was standing when he received his fatal wound, deposited in a small temple in the grounds, from which it was removed to the upper end of the dining-room, where it supported a bust of Nelson. Mr. Jesse tells us in his delightful "Gleanings" that a large shot had

passed completely through this part of the mast, and that while it stood in the temple a pair of robins had built their nest in the shot-hole, and had reared a brood of young robins, to which the king and Queen Adelaide were much attached.

The original lodge was inhabited by Bradshaw the regicide, in the time of Oliver Cromwell. Charles II., it is on record, gave it to a keeper who rejoiced in the name of Podger, and who had shown his loyalty during the troubles of the Commonwealth; and he afterwards partook of an entertainment from him at the lodge. On taking down the old church at Hampton a few years ago, Podger's tomb was discovered under the reading-desk; it is now put up in the new church. The present building is a square, substantial brick edifice; it was erected by Lord Halifax in the reign of George II.

Lord North lived here while premier, and used to gather around his hospitable and jovial table at Bushey Park the distinguished men of all countries; and here he would spend his Saturdays and Sundays among his children, throwing aside all the cares of official life.

The great feature of Bushey Park is its splendid avenue of chestnut-trees, already mentioned, which forms a great attraction to Londoners and others during the early summer months, when their branches are heavily laden with the spiry flowers, and the leaves are of their brightest colour. With the exception of its avenue, Bushey Park is somewhat scantily supplied with trees, though in the open space behind the lodge there are some fine oaks and thorns, survivors of the forest of Middlesex. There are still several hundred head of deer in Bushey Park. Norden, who wrote an account of Hampton Court in the reign of Queen Elizabeth, describes the parks belonging to the palace, and says that they were surrounded with brick walls, except on the north side, which was protected by the river. One park was a place for "deare," and the other for "hares"—a distinction which is worth noticing. Other writers have spoken of the "Old Park," the "New Park," the "Middle" or "North Park," and the "Hare Warren"; at present, however, the royal demesne is known only by the special names of the "Home Park" and "Bushey Park." As there is most wood in the former, it is probable that to it was originally applied the name of the "Deer Park," and that Bushey Park—which, no doubt, took its name from being dotted over with *bushes*, and on that account made a capital retreat for hares and rabbits—was known as the "Hare Warren."

"Among the records preserved by the steward of the manor of Hampton," observes Mr. Jesse, in his "Gleanings in Natural History," "is a strong remonstrance from the inhabitants of that place to Oliver Cromwell, complaining of his having encroached upon their rights by adding a part of their common to Bushey Park. This remonstrance seems to have had its effect, as a grant of some land in the neighbourhood was made over to them in lieu of what had been taken from them. The ancient boundaries of Bushey Park are found in several places."

There is a right-of-way, in the shape of a footpath, through Bushey Park, which had been closed for many years during part of the reign of George II. This right-of-way, however, was re-established by the energy and determination of an inhabitant of the former place, one Timothy Bennet, who carried on the humble avocation of a shoemaker, and who was "unwilling," as was his favourite expression, "to leave the world worse than he found it." Brewer, in his "Account of Middlesex," suspiciously intimates that this "village patriot" must have been backed by some persons of wealth or influence, else he would not have carried his point. The story is that Timothy Bennet consulted an attorney upon the practicability of recovering this road for the public good, and the probable expense of a legal process for that purpose. "I do not mean to cobble the job," said Timothy, "for I have seven hundred pounds, and I should be willing to give the awl, that great folks might not keep the upper-leather wrongfully." The lawyer informed him that no such sum would be necessary to try the right; "then," said the worthy shoe-maker, "as sure as soles are soles, I'll stick to them to the last." And Lord Halifax, the then Ranger of Bushey Park, was immediately served with the regular notice of action; upon which his lordship sent for Timothy, and on his entering the lodge, his lordship said with some warmth, "And who are you, that have the assurance to meddle in this affair?" "My name, my lord, is Timothy Bennet, shoemaker, of Hampton Wick. I remember, an't please your lordship, to have seen, when I was a young man, sitting at work, the people cheerfully pass my shop to Kingston market; but now, my lord, they are forced to go round about, through a hot sandy road, ready to faint beneath their burthens, and I am unwilling to leave the world worse than I found it. This, my lord, I humbly represent, is the reason why I have taken this work in hand." "Begone," replied his lordship, "you are an impertinent fellow." However, upon mature reflection, we are told, his lordship, convinced of the equity of the claim, beginning to compute the shame of a defeat by a shoemaker, desisted from his opposition, notwithstanding the opinion of the Crown lawyers, and re-opened the road, which is enjoyed by the public without molestation to this day. Honest Timothy died about two years after, in the 77th year of his age, and was followed to the grave by all the populace of his native village; and such was the estimation in which he was held that a mezzotint portrait of him was published, bearing an inscription which sets forth that this man succeeded in putting the law of the land into operation, to the furtherance of British liberty, because "he was unwilling to leave the world worse than he found it."

CHAPTER XI.

HAMPTON.

"Whose turf, whose shade, whose flowers among
Wanders the hoary Thames along
His silver-winding way."
GRAY.

Situation and Boundries of the Parish—Early History of the Manor—It passes into the hands of Cardinal Wolsey—The Parish Church—The School of Industry—The Grammar School—Princess Frederica's Convalescent Home—Lady Bourchier's Convalescent Home—Noted Hostelries—Hampton Racecourse—Boxing Matches—Hampton Bridge—Thames Angling—Southwark and Vauxhall, and the Lambeth Water Companies—David Garrick and his Villa—Sir Christopher Wren's Residence at Hampton Court Green—Holland the Actor—Lord Sandwich—Sir Andrew Halliday—Sir Richard Steele—Hampton Wick—Abbs Court.

THE village of Hampton is somewhat irregular in shape, having grown up as a sort of fringe round the edge of Bushey Park. It occupies the outer curve of a long reach of the Thames, and extends from Hampton Wick on the east to Sunbury on the west, including within its bounds the whole of

Hampton Court Palace and a portion of Bushey Park.

The place is mentioned in Domesday Book by the name of Hamntone, and it is stated that the manor in the reign of Edward the Confessor, belonged to Earl Algar; it is added that the sum of "three shillings was payable as dues for fishing and laying nets in the Thames;" and that "the whole value of the manor was but forty shillings." In 1211, Lady Joan Grey, of Hampton, left her manor and manor-house there, with several thousand acres of land, to the Knights Hospitallers of St. John

Innworth, Esher, Oatlands, together with the manors within the limits of Hampton Court Chase, and also the manors of Hampton, Hanworth, Feltham, and Teddington, and even Hounslow Heath.

The parish church, dedicated to St. Mary, at the entrance of the village, is a plain, commonplace edifice, dating its erection from 1830, when it was built in the place of the old church, which had become dilapidated. The old building was constructed chiefly of brick, and, according to the author of the "Beauties of England and Wales," "was evidently composed at various periods." The

HAMPTON, FROM THE RIVER.

of Jerusalem. "In the year 1180 there was at Hampton a 'Preceptory,' in which resided a sister of the Order of St. John. She was removed, with other sisters of the same order, from Preceptories in various places, to a convent at Buckland, in Somerset.*

Of this estate Cardinal Wolsey obtained a lease for ninety-nine years from Sir Thomas Docwra, the last prior. On the suppression of the Order of St. John, the Crown annexed it, and in 1540 the Parliament created Hampton Court a separate "honour." Some idea of the vast extent of the manor may be formed when it is stated that it comprised within its bounds the lesser manors of Walton-upon-Thames, Walton Legh, Byflete, Weybridge, East and West Moulsey, Sandon, Weston,

chancel bore marks of considerable antiquity, and was partly formed of stone and flint. A somewhat rough and coarse picture of the old church, painted about a century ago by a local artist, shows a red brick building of the conventional type, so common along the Middlesex shore of the Thames, with a heavy square tower, but no marks which would help us to assign it to any particular era. In front is a heavy-looking gate, from which stone steps lead down to the river-side. The new church is constructed of white brick, in the Perpendicular style of architecture, and it consists of a nave and aisles, and a square pinnacled tower at the western end. The church contains several interesting monuments, preserved from the old church. At the entrance is one under a canopy, supported by Corinthian columns, to Mrs. Sibel Penn, nurse to Edward VI.: it comprises a tomb, with her effigy, arms, and a

* "Dugdale's Monasticon," vol. ii. p. 554.

long rhyming epitaph. Mrs. Penn died in 1652, and the inscription on her monument, close to the entrance, tells us that—

" To Court she called was to foster up a king
   Whose helping hand long lingering sutes to spedie end did bring."

Here is buried Richard Tickell, a political writer, grandson of Tickell the poet. " He distinguished himself," says Mr. John Fisher, in his "Environs of London," "by publishing a political pamphlet, called 'Anticipation,' in which the debate on the king's speech at the opening of Parliament was so successfully anticipated that some of the members who had not seen the pamphlet are said to have made use of almost the very words put into their mouths." Tickell committed suicide in 1793. According to a letter from Walpole to Miss Berry, he "threw himself from one of the uppermost windows of the palace at Hampton Court, an immense height." Here, too, was buried Edward Podger, whom we have mentioned in our account of Bushey Park.* He was Page of Honour to Charles I., Groom of the Bedchamber to Charles II., and died in 1714, according to Le Neve, " at the age of 96, of the anguish of cutting teeth, he having cut four new teeth, and had several ready to cut, which so inflamed his gums that he died." There is a memorial of David Garrick, nephew to the great actor, with an inscription from the pen of Mrs. Hannah Moore ; and another to the memory of Richard, son of George Cumberland, the cele- brated dramatic writer. John Beard, a famous singer, who died in 1791, lies buried here. He left the stage on his marriage, half a century pre- viously, with Lady Henrietta Herbert, daughter of James, Earl of Waldegrave, and widow of Lord Edward Herbert; some years later, however, he returned to the stage, and acquired great popu- larity. In 1759 he married, as his second wife, a daughter of John Rich, the patentee of Covent Garden Theatre, to the management of which he succeeded on the death of his father-in-law.

The churchyard is old, and is full of most aris- tocratic corpses. Here lie Lord Charles Fitzroy, Lady Emily Ponsonby, Lady Roberts, Lord and Lady Munster, Lady Guillamore, and innumerable Pagets, &c., who died at the palace, and whose bodies were brought hither for interment.

Amongst the celebrities buried here are Thomas Rosoman,† the well-known owner of Sadler's Wells Theatre (1782), and his wife (1776), the latter with a poetical inscription ; the Rev. Dr. Mortimer,

late head master of the City of London School ; Huntington Shaw, the artist (1710), who wrought the fine iron gates at the entrance of Hampton Court palace ; Dr. Smethurst (who was tried for poisoning a lady), and also his first wife ; Thomas Ripley, architect, who designed the Admiralty.

In a nameless grave near the public path, at the north-east corner of the churchyard, lie the remains of a woman who enjoys the unenviable reputation of having stirred up mischief between Lord Byron and his wife, and so having caused their sepa- ration. How she did so must for ever remain a mystery. Her name, be it here recorded, was Mary Anne Clermont. The mischievous old maid is described in the register as " of Hampton Wick." She died May 11th, 1850, at the age of 77. It is said that before living at Hampton Wick she re- sided at Walton-on-Thames. Our readers will remember the scathing lines beginning—

" Born in a garret, in a kitchen bred."

In the street leading away from the river and the church towards New Hampton is a School of Industry, which bears on its front the date 1804. The street consists of private houses in good and large grounds, with here and there a shop between them.

The Grammar School, founded in the middle of the sixteenth century, is well endowed, and has a branch school at Hampton Wick. At one time the village abounded in private schools ; at one of these Lord Dufferin and Sir Frederick Roberts were brought up.

As might be expected from the number of wealthy families who have lived within its borders, Hampton is fairly well off for parochial charities ; one of the most useful of these is the Princess Frederica's Convalescent Home for Married Women after Childbirth. Lady Bourchier has a Convalescent Home here, at Hope Cottage, for four or five cases ; it was established in 1868, and is intended " for female servants, needlewomen, &c., on payment of a small weekly fee." At Tangley Park, in the im- mediate neighbourhood, is a Female Orphan Home, which was instituted in 1855, and has done much good work in the support and education of desti- tute orphan girls.

Hampton is within fifteen miles of London, and has its railway-station on a branch of the London and South-Western Railway, and also a station on the Thames Valley Railway. It can boast of several good inns and places of refreshment for visitors, notably the " Red Lion," the " Greyhound," and the " Bell," the last-mentioned house being much frequented by anglers.

---

* See *ante*, p. 131.
† His name is perpetuated in Rosoman Street, Clerkenwell.

Here is another inn, bearing for its sign "The Widow's Struggle," a sign which, as Mr. Larwood says, in his "History of Signboards," "may possibly be the romance of a life. Who knows?"

Mr. Larwood tells us that the "Toy" Inn, at Hampton—a name probably dating from the frivolous age of the second Charles—used to be a favourite resort with Londoners till 1857, when it was pulled down in order to make room for the erection of private houses. Tokens of this house in the seventeenth century are in existence. Lysons also tells us that "in the survey of 1653, in the Augmentation Office, mention is made of a piece of pasture-ground near the river, called the Toying Place, the site probably of a well-known inn near the bridge now called the Toy." The "Toy" is said to have been built by Oliver Cromwell, as a dormitory for his Roundhead soldiers, of whom he was very fond—but at a distance, for he did not like admitting them into the palace.

What is called the Hampton Racecourse is on the opposite side of the river, on an open common, known as Moulsey Hurst (in Surrey), and is approached by a ferry across the Thames. The summer and autumn races here bring down a large and motley assemblage of low betting-men from London.

This spot in former times was famous—or rather, infamous—for "boxing matches," and at such times was the resort of large numbers of the votaries of "fisticuffs" and patrons of the "noble art of self-defence." That the pugilists themselves thought much of their performance on those occasions may be inferred from the following notice, which was printed in May, 1817 :— "Thomas Oliver begs leave to inform his friends and the public that he regrets the disappointment of his combat with Painter, not only as regards himself, but that the amateurs should be disappointed. Oliver having been taken by the authority of a warrant, he is held in sureties to keep the peace. In justice to himself and regard for his friends, he begs leave to state that he is in good training, and is ready to depart either for Calais or Waterloo, the field of English glory ! ! !"

A bridge over the Thames connects Hampton Court and East Moulsey. The first bridge here was erected in pursuance of an Act of Parliament, passed in 1750, in favour of one James Clarke, the then lessee of the ferry under the Crown. It was a light wooden structure, of eleven arches, or spans; the present structure is an iron girder bridge of five spans, and was built in 1865.

"Many years since," says the "Book of the Court," "a man named Feltham rented Hampton Court Bridge, where he made several alterations. As he was anxious to thrive by his tolls, he kept the gate locked when nothing was passing. One morning the royal hunt came across Hounslow Heath to the bridge, where the stag had taken water and swum across. The hounds passed the gate without ceremony, followed by a large party, crying 'The King!' Feltham opened his gate, which he closed again after they had rushed through without paying ; when a more numerous and showy party came up, vociferating more loudly, 'The King!' He stood with the gate in his hand, though menaced with horsewhips. 'I'll tell you what,' said he, 'hang me if I open my gate again till I see your money. I pay £400 a year for this bridge, and I laid out £1,000 upon it. I've let King George through, God bless him : I know of no other king in England. If you have brought the King of France, hang me if I let him through without the blunt !' Suddenly the king himself appeared among his attendants ; Feltham made his reverence, opened his gate again, and the whole company went over to Moulsey Hurst, where the hounds were at fault. The king, chagrined for the moment, sent back Lord Sandwich to know the reason of the interruption. The man explained the mistake, and added that when royal hunts passed over this bridge a guinea had been always paid, which franked all, and that this was 'his first good turn.' Lord Sandwich returned to the king, but his Majesty hastily desired him to pay for all his attendants, who amounted to less than forty of the whole party. The matter was eventually satisfactorily explained to the king, who, crossing the bridge some time afterwards, on a visit to the Stadtholder, then resident at Hampton Court, pulled down the carriage window, and laughing heartily, said to old Feltham, 'No fear of the King of France coming to-day.'"

Hampton is a favourite place for pleasure-parties on the water, and on fine afternoons in summer quite a fleet of small yachts may be seen with their white sails spread upon its long and open reach. But it is even more famed as the head-quarters of the disciples of Izaak Walton.

"Hampton," writes Mr. Thorne, in his "Handbook of the Environs of London," "may be considered the head-quarters of the Thames Angling Preservation Society ; and here and a little higher up on the Surrey side are the ponds and streamlets made by the Thames Conservancy, and maintained by the Society, for hatching and rearing fish ova— chiefly salmon, grayling, and trout. The young fish are kept in the streams for eight or nine months, when, being considered able to take care of themselves, they are turned into the river. About 50,000 fish are annually sent into the Thames from these ponds; and anglers acknowledge a decided improvement in the fishing. The river here is strictly preserved along what is known as Hampton Deep, which extends from the lawn of Garrick Villa to Tumbling Bay, 960 yards. From 20 lbs. to 30 lbs. of roach or perch are accounted a good day's fishing."

The Southwark and Vauxhall and the Lambeth Water Companies derive their supplies from the Thames above Hampton; but year by year the drainage-ground or watershed of the Thames is being more densely populated, and consequently a larger quantity of pollution finds its way into the river. So bad is the condition of the Thames water, though artificially filtered, that the Commissioners appointed to inquire into the domestic water supply of Great Britain recommended, in their report to her Majesty in 1874, "that the Thames should, as early as possible, be abandoned as a source of water for domestic uses, and that the sanction of the Government should be in future withheld from all schemes involving the expenditure of more capital for the supply of Thames water to London;" and the press and many members of both Houses of Parliament have strongly urged the necessity of acting on this recommendation.

A large male otter, measuring forty-seven inches from snout to tail, was shot in the Thames here in January, 1880.

The western part of Hampton is called Thames Street, because it extends along the river in the direction of Sunbury. Its pleasant rural aspect is much spoiled by the three gigantic reservoirs of as many water companies—the West Middlesex, the Grand Junction, and the Southwark and Vauxhall. It is said that they take from the river upwards of 100,000,000 gallons of water daily; but this can hardly be the case, as they do not supply anything like the whole area of the metropolis. Their tall shafts are anything rather than an ornament. Beyond them is the new Grammar School, a building of the domestic Tudor style.

At the northern extremity of the parish a considerable village, called New Hampton, has sprung into existence within the last few years. The district was made into a separate ecclesiastical parish in 1864. The church, dedicated to St. James, consists of a chancel, nave, and north aisle, and is a red brick building in the Early English style.

When we have said that the present church is built of brick in the Gothic style of George IV., we have really described it. It has no chancel, but spacious galleries, and pointed windows without mullions or bracery. In fact, it is simply an edifice of the churchwarden style of art. The monuments removed from the former structure adorn its walls, but many of these are so "skied" as to be unreadable from the floor. On either side of the communion-table are the Moses and Aaron of the last century, and also two oak chairs elaborately carved by the hands of Dr. Merewether, late Dean of Hereford, a former curate of Hampton.

Among the vicars of Hampton was Dr. Samuel Croxall, Chancellor and Canon of Hereford, and Archdeacon of Salop. This gentleman was the author of an edition of "Æsop's Fables," a dramatic piece called *The Fair Circassian,* and several political pamphlets in the Whig interest, written during the reign of Queen Anne.

Hampton appears to have been classic ground as far back as the reign of Elizabeth; at all events, Ben Jonson, in his "Epigrams," speaks of his own retirement—

" 'Mongst Hampton's shades and Phœbus' grove of bays."

At a short distance eastward from the church, and close by the river-side, is a spot which has long been held sacred by lovers of the Thespian art—namely, " Garrick's Villa." The house, although separated from the river by a lawn and the roadway, forms a prominent feature in the landscape on approaching Hampton by water, its tall central portico and pediment standing out boldly amid the foliage of the surrounding trees.

Garrick purchased the house and grounds in the middle of the last century, and made many alterations and improvements in them. To the house, which was originally distinguished as Hampton House, considerable additions were made from the designs of Adam; and several purchases having been made by Garrick for the purpose of extending his premises, the gardens were laid out with much taste, and under his own direction.

Hampton House was thus described by a local writer of Garrick's time :—" It stands in the town of Hampton, but is quite concealed by a high wall. Nothing can be neater or fitted up with more decent elegance than this little box; every room shows the true taste and genius of the owner; the whole is like a fine miniature picture, perfectly well finished, though exceedingly small. The drawing-room is, however, of a handsome size, and may be called a large room; 'tis hung with canvas painted in all greens in the most beautiful colours imaginable, and decorated with carvings of the same colour. The garden is laid out in the modern taste, with a passage cut under the road to a lawn, where, close by the water-side, stands the Temple of Shakespeare. This is a brick building in the form of a dome, with a handsome porch, supported by fine pillars. Opposite to the entrance, in a niche, stands a statue of the poet by Roubilliac, as large as life, at his desk in the attitude of thought. The figure is bold and striking; the drapery finished in the most elegant manner." The statue of Shakespeare was bequeathed by Garrick to the British Museum, and now stands in the hall of that institution. Walpole proposed to adorn the outside of the Temple with a motto from Horace—

"Quod spiro et placeo, si placeo, tuum est,"

along with the following English version, spun out, as will be seen, into four lines :—

"That I spirit have and nature,
That sense breathes in every feature;
That I please, if please I do,
Shakespeare, all I owe to you."

At Garrick's villa, Henry Angelo, when a boy at Eton, spent one at least of his summer holidays. He describes the house as "standing by the roadside, and having (like Pope's villa at Twickenham) a short tunnel under the road, connecting the grounds with the classic summer-house by the river-side which enshrined the bust of Shakespeare."

"A garden on a flat, it is said, ought to be highly and variously ornamented, in order to occupy the mind, and prevent its regretting the insipidity of an uniform plan. The effect of such a walk is admirably exemplified in Mr. Garrick's polished ground at Hampton; but surely it would have been time enough to have represented Shakespeare there in stone or marble when the very genius of Shakespeare no longer presided."— Cradock's "Memoirs."

Garrick first saw the light of day on the 20th of February, 1716, at the Angel Inn, Hereford, at which city his father, Captain Peter Garrick, of the Old Buffs, was then on a recruiting expedition. His mother, whose maiden name was Arabella Clough, was the daughter of one of the vicars of Lichfield Cathedral. David received his early tuition under the care of Mr. Hunter, master of the Grammar School of Lichfield, and in 1735 he became a pupil of Dr. (then plain Mr.) Samuel Johnson, with whom, in March, 1736, he set out for the metropolis. Shortly after his arrival in London he entered himself on the rolls of the Society of Lincoln's Inn, with the view of following the profession of the law. On the death of his father, however, he commenced business as a wine merchant, in partnership with his elder brother, Peter Garrick. This partnership was soon dissolved, and in 1741 David Garrick finally resolved to adopt the profession of the stage, and, under the assumed name of Lyddal, made his first appearance at Ipswich as Aboan, in the play of *Oroonoko*. So great was his success in that character, that he was induced by the manager of the Ipswich Theatre to make his *début* in London, at the theatre in Goodman's Fields, of which he was also the proprietor. Here, in the character of Richard III., Garrick at once established his reputation as an actor.

His fame, indeed, was such, that Drury Lane and Covent Garden were soon deserted. Quin was jealous of his success, remarking, in his queer way, that "Garrick was a new religion; Whitfield was followed for a time, but they would all come to Church again!" Garrick, who had a happy talent in pointing an epigram, gave this reply :—

"Pope Quin, who damns all churches but his own,
Complains that *Heresy* corrupts the town;
Schism, he cries, has turn'd the nation's brain,
But eyes will open, and to Church again!
Thou great Infallible, forbear to roar,
Thy bulls and errors are rever'd no more;
When doctrines meet with general approbation,
It is not *Heresy*, but—*Reformation!*"

At the close of the season, in May, 1742, Garrick played for three nights at Drury Lane Theatre, and then set off for Dublin, accompanied by Mrs. Woffington. In Ireland he sustained his reputation, and so great was the crowd at the theatre that, in conjunction with the heat of the weather, an epidemic ensued which was called "the Garrick fever." In the following October Garrick returned to London, and commenced an engagement at Drury Lane in Otway's tragedy of *The Orphan*. In 1745 he was for a short time joint manager, with Mr. Sheridan, of a theatre in Dublin, but in 1746 he again returned to London, and was engaged by Mr. Rich, the patentee of Covent Garden Theatre. On the close of that engagement, he purchased, in conjunction with Mr. Lacy, the Theatre Royal Drury Lane, which he opened in September, 1747, with the play of *The Merchant of Venice*, Dr. Johnson writing a prologue for the occasion.

In 1749 Garrick married Eva Maria Violette, the daughter of a respectable citizen of Vienna. She had been educated as a dancer, and had made her first appearance at Drury Lane some three years previously. Her real family name was Veigel, but she assumed the name of Violette by command of the Empress Maria Theresa,

Mrs. Garrick was said to be "the most agreeable woman in England." Sterne, who saw her among the beauties of Paris in the Tuileries Gardens, declared "she could annihilate them all in a single turn." Even Horace Walpole could forsake his cynicism, and say of her that her "behaviour is all sense and all sweetness." "During the twenty-eight years of their married life," observes a writer in *Chambers's Journal*, "David was not so much the husband as the lover; and his affection was rewarded with a love as true and as constant as his own. Mrs. Garrick survived her husband more than forty years, and for at least thirty of these she would not allow the room in which David died to be opened. Buried, at her own request, in her wedding sheets, she occupies the same grave with her husband at the base of Shakespeare's statue, "until the day dawn and the shadows flee away. Doubtless a helpmate so attractive, and so congenial and pure, greatly aided the actor in striving to attain his ideal."

In September, 1769, Garrick put into execution his favourite scheme of the jubilee in honour of Shakespeare, at Stratford-on-Avon, and produced a pageant on the subject at Drury Lane in the following month. In June, 1776, having been manager of Drury Lane Theatre for nearly thirty years, Garrick took his leave of the stage in the character of Don Felix in *The Wonder*.

Garrick died at his house in the Adelphi on the 20th of January, 1779, in the sixty-fifth year of his age, his disorder gradually increasing, and admitting of no remedy. His physicians knew not how to designate his illness. Observing many of them, the day before his death, in his apartment, he asked who they were; being told they were physicians, he shook his head, and repeated these lines of Horatio, in the *Fair Penitent* : —

> "Another and another still succeeds,
> And the last *Fool* is welcome as the former!"

Few men have been the subjects of more epi-grams, repartees, and *bon mots* than David Garrick, and few men living in the society of the witty and the learned have had more poetry addressed to them. Dr. Barnard, Dean of Derry, Johnson's friend, for instance, thus apostrophises him :—

> "The art of pleasing teach me, Garrick,
> Thou who reversest odes Pindaric,
> A second time read o'er;
> Oh, could we read thee backward too,
> Last thirty years thou should'st review
> And charm us thirty more!"

From the *Gentleman's Magazine* for 1761 we cull the following :—

> "Says *Garrick*, amongst other sociable chat,
> What could I without *Shakespeare* do? tell me that."

It was replied—

> "Great connexions you have with each other, 'tis true :
> But, *now* — what can Shakespeare do, sir, without you?"

The following colloquial epigram appeared about the same time :—

> "*Wilmot.*
> "You should call at his house, or should send him a card,
> Can Garrick alone be so cold?

> "*Garrick.*
> "Shall I, a poor player, and still poorer bard,
> Shall folly with Camden make bold?
> What joy can I give him, dear Wilmot, declare :
> Promotion no honours can bring ;
> To him the Great Seals are but labour and care.
> Wish joy to your country and king."

GARRICK.

Wishing Sir Joshua Reynolds to make one of a party to dine with him at Hampton, and finding some difficulty in persuading him to come so far from Leicester Fields, Garrick said to him, "Well, only come, and you shall choose your dinner, though that is a favour I would not grant to everybody with such an insatiable *palette* as yours."

"David would indulge some few friends"—says Charles Dibdin—"but it was very rare—with what he used to call his *rounds*. This he did by standing behind a chair, and converging into his face every possible kind of passion, blending one into the other, and, as it were, shadowing them with a pro-digious number of gradations. At one moment you laughed, at another you cried; now he terrified you, and presently you conceived yourself something horrible, he seemed so terrified *at* you. Afterwards he drew his features into the appearance of such dignified wisdom that Minerva might have been proud of the portrait; and then—degrading, yet admirable, transition—he became a driveller. In short, his face was what he obliged you to fancy it—age, youth, plenty, poverty, everything it assumed."

The following lines were written by Garrick to a

conversation with him said, "Dear sir, I wish you were a little *taller;*" to which he replied, "My dear madam, how happy should I be, did I stand *higher* in your estimation."

"Will your figures be as large as life, Mr. Foote?" asked a titled lady, when he was about to bring out at the Haymarket his comedy of *The Primitive Puppet Show*. "No, my lady," replied Foote, "they will be hardly larger than Garrick."

Garrick having a green-room wrangle with Mrs.

HAMPTON HOUSE.
(*From a Print published in* 1787.)

nobleman who asked him if he did not intend being in Parliament :—

> "More than content with what my labours gain,
> Of *public favour* tho' a little vain,
> Yet not so vain my mind, so madly bent,
> To wish to *play* the *fool* in parliament ;
> In each dramatic unity to err,
> Mistaking *time* and *place*, and *character!*
> Were it my fate to quit the mimic art,
> I'd 'strut and fret' no more in any part ;
> No more in *public scenes* would I engage,
> Or wear the *cap* and *mask* of any stage." *

Garrick's stature was slightly under the middle size, but manliness, elasticity, ease, and grace, characterised his deportment. A lady one day in

Clive, after listening to all she had to say, replied, "I have heard of tartar and brimstone, and know the effects of both ; but you are the *cream* of one and the *flower* of the other."

Garrick once gave at his lodgings a dinner to Harry Fielding, Macklin, Havard, Mrs. Cibber, &c., and fees to servants being then much the fashion, Macklin, and most of the company, gave Garrick's man (David, a Welshman) something at parting—some a shilling, some half-a-crown, &c., whilst Fielding, very formally, slipped a piece of paper in his hand, with something folded in the inside. When the company were all gone, David seeming to be in high glee, Garrick asked him how much he got. "I can't tell you yet, sir," said Davy, "here is half-a-crown from Mrs. Cibber, Got pless

---

* *Gentleman's Magazine*, 1761.

hur—here is a shilling from Mr. Macklin—here is two from Mr. Havard, &c.—and here is something more from the poet, Got pless his merry heart." By this time David had unfolded the paper, when, to his great astonishment, he saw it contained no more than one penny! Garrick felt nettled at this, and next day spoke to Fielding about the impropriety of jesting with a servant. "Jesting!" said Fielding, with a seeming surprise, "so far from it, that I meant to do the fellow a real piece of service; for had I given him a shilling or half-a-crown, I knew you would have taken it from him; but by giving him only a penny, he had a chance of calling it his own."

A gentleman asked a friend who had seen Garrick perform his first and last character if he thought him as good an actor when he took his leave of the stage at old Drury as when he first played at Goodman's Fields, he gave for an answer the following *extempore*:—

> " I saw him rising in the East
>   In all his energetic glows ;
> I saw him setting in the West
>   In greater splendour than he rose."

By the same, on his being told Wilson was thought to be a better actor than Ned Shuter :—

> " I've very often heard it said,
>   Nine tailors make a man ;
> But can nine Wilsons make a Ned?
>   No, bless me if they can."

It is related by a friend of Garrick that, in walking up the stage with him, until the burst of applause which followed one of his displays in *Lear* should subside, the great actor thrust his tongue in his cheek, and said in a chuckle, "Joe, this is stage feeling."

We have seen how that Garrick and Johnson came up to London with the view of starting in the "race for wealth." While the career of the former was one long-continued success, that of Johnson was anything but prosperous, the great lexicographer being at times almost on the verge of starvation. "Sudden prosperity had turned Garrick's head," writes Lord Macaulay; "continued adversity had soured Johnson's temper. Johnson saw with more envy than became so great a man the villa, the plate, the china, the Brussels carpet, which the little mimic had got by repeating what wiser men had written, and the exquisitely sensitive vanity of Garrick was galled by the thought that whilst all the rest of the world was applauding him, he could obtain from one morose cynic, whose opinion it was impossible to despise, scarcely any compliment not acidulated with scorn."

Mr. Cradock writes in his "Literary Memoirs":— " The strongest likenesses of Garrick are best preserved by Sir George Beaumont, who was intimately acquainted with him ; the two drawings of Garrick, in " Richard," and "Abel Drugger," are superior, in point of resemblance, to either of the celebrated pictures, from which they are chiefly taken ; the prints from them are just published by Mr. Colnaghi."

Garrick's widow continued to occupy the villa long after her husband's death, and she entertained her friends here nearly to the last. She died in the Adelphi, in the year 1822, at the age of nearly 100.

Old anglers who have fished in the Thames about here will remember at the bottom of the lawn two willows, rendered sacred by adjoining the temple erected to Shakespeare. They were planted by Garrick's own hand. In the midst of a violent storm, which proved fatal to one of them, Mrs. Garrick was seen running about, like Niobe, all tears, exclaiming, " Oh, my Garrick ! my Garrick !"

A fonder pair never lived than David Garrick and his wife ; when alive they might easily have claimed the Dunmow flitch of bacon.

Garrick's villa is still kept, so far as modern taste will allow, in the same state in which it was when occupied by its illustrious owner. The paintings and the sculptures on the wall are still there ; their colours have been slightly renewed where necessary, and the modern furniture has been dressed in Chinese patterned chintz to correspond. The classical medallions, designed by Bentley or Wedgwood, still run round the walls below the cornices, and the marble mantelpieces, with their slight and slender carvings, remain in *statu quo*. The eastern wing and the central portion of the house are unaltered, or almost unaltered ; but the old dining-room on the west of the entrance-hall is now made to do duty as a billiard-room, a new dining-room of lofty proportions having been added to the western end. In order to add this room to the house, it was found necessary to sacrifice four fine trees, under which Garrick doubtless had often sat. The lower room in the eastern wing is low, the height so gained being thrown into the upper room, which was evidently designed for music, and is still used as the chief drawing-room. Garrick's bed-room, on the first floor, has a northern aspect, and it remains but little changed.

The original statue of Shakespeare in the octagonal temple in the garden was of marble ; a duplicate of it, worked in less ambitious stone, still occupies the same post of honour. The walls of the temple are adorned with stuffed fish, trophies of the rod, caught in the river adjoining. It forms a large and pleasant summer-house. It is overshadowed by a noble group of cedars, Scotch firs, and lime-trees, and the land slopes deliciously down to the river.

The villa was owned by Mrs. Garrick till her death, in the year 1822 (as above stated), when it was bought by a gentleman named Carr. He sold it to a Mr. Philips, from whom it was purchased, about 1864, by Mr. Edward Grove, whose widow still occupies it, and feels a most praiseworthy pride in the preservation of the fabric and all its associations.

The greater part of the village of Hampton forms the margin of an extensive "green," on one side of which is a broad roadway, and also a foot-path overshadowed by trees, known as the "Maids of Honour Walk."

At the end of his long and active career, Sir Christopher Wren retired in peace to his home at Hampton Court Green, his spirit not embittered by the ungrateful treatment which he had received, and simply saying that henceforth he desired to spend his days in tranquil study. Cheerful in his solitude, and as well content to die in the shade as in the blaze of his noontide fame, his son observes of him, in his "Parentalia," that "the vigour of his mind continued with a vivacity rarely found in persons of his age till within a short period of his death, and not till then could he quit the great aim of his life—to be a benefactor to mankind." The five last years of his life were spent here in complete repose, returning to London occasionally to superintend the repairs of Westminster Abbey, his only remaining employment, and filling up his leisure hours with mathematical and astronomical studies. Time, though it enfeebled his limbs, left his faculties unclouded to the last. His great delight, to the very close of life, was to be carried into the heart of the huge city to see his great work, "the beginning and completion of which," says Horace Walpole, "was an event which one cannot wonder left such an impression of content on the mind of the good old man, that it seemed to recall a memory almost deadened to every other use." Wren's death was as calm and tranquil as the tenor of his existence had been. On the 25th of February, 1723, his servant, conceiving that he slept after his dinner longer than usual, entered his room, and found him dead in his chair.

Holland, the actor, who was buried at Chiswick, was the son of a baker in this village. On the stage he was an imitator of Garrick, who so much valued him that he played the Ghost in *Hamlet* to aid his benefit. Foote, who attended his funeral, regarded him in another light, as may be gathered from the fact that, after the interment was over, a friend accosting him with, "So, Foote, you have just come from my dear friend Holland's funeral," he replied, sarcastically and heartlessly, "Yes; we have just put the little baker into his oven."

Lord Sandwich (writes Cradock in his "Memoirs"), as First Lord of the Admiralty, in 1771-2, occupied "a retired mansion belonging to Lord Halifax, on the edge of Hampton Green."

Here, too, lived Sir Andrew Halliday, the eminent physician, to whom we owe the first general movement in favour of the lunatic poor. When a poor and unknown student at the University of Edinburgh, he addressed a pamphlet on the subject to Lord Henry Petty, afterwards Marquis of Lansdowne, then Chancellor of the Exchequer. A Parliamentary inquiry was appointed, which led to the passing of an Act in 1808 for the establishment of county asylums.

Not content with the town house in Bury Street already mentioned,[*] Sir Richard Steele, on his marriage with Mistress Scurlock in 1707, took for his wife a country house here, which he called "The Hovel," and to which he soon added a chariot and pair, enjoying also the luxury of a horse for his own riding, and going abroad like a dandy of the time, in a laced coat and a large black buckled periwig, which, Thackeray reckons, must have cost somebody fifty guineas. He was at this time a well-to-do gentleman, with the proceeds of an estate in Barbadoes, and his twofold office of gentleman-waiter on H.R.H. Prince George and one of the writers of the *Gazette*. "But," adds Thackeray, "it is melancholy to relate that with these houses, and chariots and horses, and income, Captain Steele was constantly in want of money, for which his beloved bride was asking as constantly. In the course of a few pages we find the shoemaker calling for money, and some directions from the captain, who has not thirty pounds to spare. He sends his wife—'the beautifullest object in the world,' as he calls her— . . . now a guinea, then half a guinea, then a couple of guineas, then half a pound of tea; and again no money and no tea at all, but a promise that his 'darling Prue' shall have some in a day or two; with a request, perhaps, that she will send over his nightgown and shaving plate to the temporary lodgings where the nomadic captain is lying hidden from the bailiffs. To think that the pink and pride of chivalry should turn pale before

* See "Old and New London," Vol. IV., p. 202.

a writ! Addison sold the house and furniture at Hampton, and after deducting the sums which his incorrigible friend was indebted to him, handed over the residue of the proceeds of the sale to poor Dick, who was not in the least angry at Addison's summary proceedings, and, I dare say, was very glad of any sale or execution the result of which was to give him a little ready money."

Hampton Wick is that portion of the parish abutting upon the Thames at the foot of Kingston Bridge. It was made into a separate parish for ecclesiastical purposes, and the chapel of St. John the Baptist, which was built in 1830, has become the parish church of the district. It consists almost entirely of detached villas, inhabited by wealthy Londoners. In a map of 1823, a park on the west side of the village of Hampton, away from the river, appears as belonging to the late Sir C. Edmonstone, Bart.

Near Hampton Court was a pleasant seat, "Abbs Court," which belonged in Pope's days to Edward Wortley Montagu, the husband of Lady Mary Wortley Montagu, whose general avarice and habit of selling his game is satirised (under the name of Wordley) by Pope in his "Imitations of Horace":—

"Delightful Abbs Court, if its fields afford
Their fruits to you, confesses you its lord.
All Wordly's hens, nay, partridges, sold to town,
His venison too, a guinea makes your own."

CHAPTER XII.
HAMPTON COURT PALACE.

'Let any wight (if such a wight there be),
To whom thy lofty towers unknown remain,
Direct his steps, fair Hampton Court, to thee,
And view thy splendid halls : then turn again
To visit each proud dome by science praised,
'For kings the rest' (he'd say), 'but thou for gods wert raised.'"
J. P. ANDREWS, *after* GROTIUS.

Wolsey Lord of the Manor—Terms of the Lease—Reconstruction of the House—Biographical Sketch of Wolsey—Hampton Court Presented to Henry VIII.—Grand Doings in Wolsey's Time—Henry's Wives at Hampton—The Fair Geraldine—A Woman's Promise—Queen Elizabeth at Hampton—The Maids of Honour—The Hampton Court Conference—Oliver Cromwell—Dutch William—His Alterations to the Building—The Georges at Hampton Court—Miss Chudleigh—An Application from Dr. Johnson—Later Inmates.

IN the preceding chapter we have seen how, early in the reign of Henry VIII., Cardinal Wolsey acquired a lease of the manor of Hampton from the prior of the Order of St. John of Jerusalem, or Knights Hospitallers. He had been induced to fix upon this spot as the site of his residence by certain physicians, whom he had asked to choose for him the most healthy and pleasant site within an easy distance of London, the springs of Coombe Wood, in the immediate neighbourhood of Hampton, affording water best suited to the requirements of the cardinal, who was at that time suffering from some internal complaint. In the *Gentleman's Magazine* for January, 1834, is printed a copy of the lease of the manor and manor-house, extracted from the Cottonian Manuscripts as follows:—

"This Indenture made between Sir Thomas Docwra, Priour of the Hospitall of Seynt John Jerusalem, in England, and his bredren knights of the same hospitall, upon that oone partie, and the most reverend fader in god Thomas Wulcy, Archebisshop of Yorke and primate of England upon that other partie, Witnessith that the said priour and his bredren with theire hole assent and auctorite of their Chapitur, have graunted and letten to fferme to the said Archebusshop, their manor of Hampton Courte, in the countie of Midd., with all landes and tenements, medowes, leanes, and pastures, rentes, and services, vewe of ffranciplegis, perquesites of courts, ffishing and ffishing weres, and with the waren of conys, and with all manner proufites and commodites, and other things what so ever they be in any manner of wise to the forseid manor belonging or apperteigning. To have and to holde the foreseid manor with the appurtenaunces to the foreseid most Reverend ffader in god Thomas Wulcy, Archebisshop of Yorke, and to his assignes ffro the ffest of the Nativite of Seynt John Baptist last past before the date hereof unto thend and terme of lxxxxix yeres than next following, and fully to be ended, yielding and paying therefor yerely to the seid priour and his successours in the tresoury of there hous of Seynt John's of Clarkenwell beside London, fifty poundes sterling at the ffestes of the purification of our Lady and of Seynt Barnabe thappostle, by even porcions. And also payeing and supporting all manner of charges ordinary and extraordinary due and goying oute of the seid manor, with the appurtenances during the seid terme. And the seid Archebusshop and his assignes yerely during the seid terme shal have allowance of the seid priour and his successors in the paymentes of the rent and ferme of fifty poundes aforesaid iiij^{li.} xiij^{s.} iiij^{d.} sterling, at the ffestes aforeseid, by even porcions, towards and for the exhibition of a preste for to mynister divine service within the Chapell of the seid manor. And the seid priour and his brethren for them and their successors graunten the seid Archebusshop and his assignes yerely during the seid terme shal have and take at their libertie foure loades of woode and tymber able for pyles for the reparacion and sustentacion of the were called Hampton were, the same woodes and tymber to be felled and conveyed at the costes of the seid Archebusshop, and his assignes at their libertie at all tymes during the seid terme shall take down, alter, transpose, chaunge, make, and new byeld at theire propre costes any howses, walles, mootes, diches, warkis, or other things within or aboute the seid manour of hamptoncourte, with the appurtenaunces, without empeche- ment of wast and without any payne or punysshment to be or ensue to the seid Archebusshop and his assignes during the seid terme. And the seid Archebusshop and his assignes shall bere all manner of reparacions of the seid manour with the appurtenaunces during the seid terme, and in thend of the seid terme all the same shall leve to the seid priour and bredren and to theire successours sufficiently re- pared. Ffurthermore, the seid Archebusshop and his assignes shall leve the seid priour and his successours m^{l.} couple of conys in the waren of the seid manour, or elles for every couple that shall want iiij^d And moreover the seid priour and his bredren graunted that the seid Archebusshop and his assignes shall have and occupie during the seid terme all suche parcells as be conteyned upon the bak of this enden- ture, and in thend of the same terme all the same shall leve and delyver to the seid priour and his successours, or the value of the same. And if it happen the seid yerely fferme or rent of v^{li.} during the seid terme of lxxxxix yeres, to be behynde and not pade in part or in the hole after eny terme of payment befor specified which it ought to be paid by the space of two hole yeres, that then it shalbe lawful to the seid priour and his successours to re-enter into the same manour and othre the premisses dismised, and theym to have ayen as in their first and pristinat estate, this endenture or eny therin conteigned notwithstandyng. And the seid priour and his bredren promitte and graunte for theym and theire successours, and theym bynde by thies presentes to the seid Archebisshop, that when so ever the said Archebisshop or his assignes at any oone tyme within the terme of this present leas shall come to the seid priour and his bredren, or to their suc- cessours, and demaunde to have a newe graunte and lesse of the saide manour of hamptoncourte with the appurtenaunces to theym to be graunted under their commen seale of the seid hospitall for the terme of other lxxxxix yeres next ensuying this present terme, that then the seid priour and his bredren nowe being or their successours than for tyme beyng for that oone tyme shall graunte and make a newe leesse of the seid manour of hamptoncourte with the appurtenaunces to the seid Arche- bisshop and to his assignes under the common seale of the seid hospitall for the terme of othre lxxxxix yeres after the forme, tenour, and effecte of the seid covenauntes and agre- mentes conteyned in this present endenture, the substaunce thereof in nowise chaunged nor mynyshed. And at the delyverie of the same new endenture this endenture to be cancelled if it shall than rest and be in the keeping of the seid Archebisshop or his assignes. And if the seid endenture fortune to be lost, and be not in the keping of the seid Archebisshop or his assignes, nor in the kepyng of any per- son or their uses, then the seid Archebisshop or his assignes, before the seid newe graunte or lesse to be made, shall surrendre and so promytte by thies presentes to surrendre

all suche title and interest as they or any of theym have or may have, by reason of this formar lease at all tymes after suche surrendre and newe lesse made utterly to be voide and of no effecte. In witnesse whereof to the oone part of theis presente endenturs towardes the seid Archebusshop re- maynyng, the said priour and his bredren have put their common seale. And to that othre part of the same enden- turs towardes the seid priour and his bredren remaynyng the seid Archebusshop hath put his seale. Yeven in our Chapitur holden in oure house of Seynt John's of Clarkenwell beside London, the xj day of Januarie, in the yere of our lord god a thousand fyve hundreth and fourteene, the sixt yere of the reigne of our soveraigne lord king Henry the Eight.

"*In the Chapel*, First, a chalesse of silver, a pix of copur for the sacrament, ij alter clothes, a corporaxe, ij candle- stikes of laton, a massebook, a porteux, a pewter botil for wyne, a crewet of pewter, a crosse of tynne, a paxbrede of tree, an alter clothe of whyte and blue lyke unto armyn, an ymage of our lord of tree, an ymage of our lady of tree, an ymage of seynt John, an ymage of seynt Nicholas, an ymage of the crosse paynted on a borde, ij alte clothes, ij pewes with a chest of wynscott, an holy waterstok of laton with a stryngel of laton, ij bells in the towre, one of them broken.—Of *bedsteddis* in all xx^{ti.}, ii towrned chyars.— *In the parlour*, a table of Estriche bourde with ij tristells. —*In the haule*, ij tables dormant, and oon long table with ij tristells, a close cupbourde, iiij fourmes, iiij barres of yron about the harthe.—*In the kechen*, a pot of bras cont. v galons, a cadron sett in the fournace cont. xx. galons, a spyt of yron, ij awndyrons, a trevet, ij morters of marbil, a cawdron of iij galons, di. a stomer of laton, a flesshehoke, a frying pan, ij pailes, a barre of yron in the kechen to hange on pottes, a grete salting troughe, a steping fatte, an heire of the kyln of xxiij yerdes, ij grate byunes in the kechen, a byune in the buttry, a knedyng troghe.—*In the stable*, a pitchfork, a dongfork.—A presse in the *towre- chambre*, a great coffar in oon of the towre chambres; a parclose in the towre, a parclose in the parloure."

Wolsey had no sooner taken possession of the manor than he set about rebuilding the manor-house in a style of grandeur that was, perhaps, unsur- passed at that time by few mansions in England, and upon a scale of unparalleled magnificence. Of that building, however, there is now but little or any portion left standing; for after the cardinal's " fall," Henry VIII., with a view, no doubt, to remove from the palace some portion of its founder's *prestige*, demolished the great hall and chapel, and replaced them with erections of his own. The popular belief which attributes to the cardinal the erection of the present hall is therefore incorrect. The present hall was the work of Henry, and was in all probability in no way superior, but rather the contrary, to that of the cardinal, whose taste and architectural skill were notorious. The design of Wolsey's building appears to have comprehended five distinct courts, the whole composed of brick, and highly ornamented; and the interior was so capacious that it is said to have been provided with two hundred and eighty beds for visitors of superior rank. Only two of the courts of Wolsey's palace now remain, so that but little idea can be formed of the extent of the building as he left it. Mr. Jesse, in his work on Hampton Court, observes that Wolsey "had evidently meant to construct at Hampton such a splendid specimen of Grecian correctness as might give a new bias to the architecture of this island. It is probable that he was unable to contend with the still lingering relics of prejudice, and therefore we have to regret that the Gothic and Grecian styles were blended in the cardinal's magnificent building with equal bad taste and impropriety."

These ancient buildings—or, at least, such of them as remain—are extremely interesting. Their

The clerk of the works received 8d. *per diem*, and his writing clerks 6d. each.

In 1838, whilst removing one of the old towers built by Wolsey, the workmen came upon a number of glass bottles which lay among the foundation. They were of a curious shape; and it has been suggested that they were buried to denote the date of the building.

Here Wolsey lived in more than regal splendour; and when it is considered that he had nearly one thousand persons in his suite, we shall be less surprised at the vastness of his palace.

Before proceeding with a more detailed account of the building, it will be best to give a

HAMPTON COURT BRIDGE. (*From an Engraving by J. C. Allen, after P. Debouit*)

structure is of red brick, interlaced with dark-coloured bricks in diagonal lines, the windows, cornices, and dressings being of stone. Wolsey appears to have employed the Warden and certain members of the Freemasons as his architects in building his palace, as he did also at Christ Church, Oxford, originally called Cardinal's College. In an article in the *Edinburgh Review*, by Sir F. Palgrave, on the "Architecture of the Middle Ages," are given some curious accounts of the expenses of the fabric of Hampton Court Palace, extant amongst the public records of London. The following items are extracted from the entries of the works performed between the 26th February, 27 Henry VIII., to March 25th, then next ensuing :—

Freemasons.

Master, at 12d. the day, John Molton, 6s.

Warden, at 5s. the week, William Reynolds, 20s.

Setters, at 3s. 8d. the week, Nicholas Seyworth (and for three others), 13s. 8d.

Lodgemen, at 3s. 4d. the week, Richard Watchet (and twenty-eight others), 13s. 4d.

short biographical sketch of Wolsey, and to deal with the history of the palace since Wolsey's time.

Thomas Wolsey, afterwards "Archbishop of York, Chancellor of England, Cardinal Priest of Cicily, and Legate a latere," was born at Ipswich, in Suffolk, in 1471. He was descended, according to some of our best historians, from poor but honest parents, and of good reputation; the common tradition is that he was the son of a butcher. Feeling a stronger inclination for the disputations of the schools than for the business of his father, he acquired the rudiments of grammar, and received a learned education; and entering the University of Oxford at a very early age, he took the degree of Bachelor of Arts when he was fourteen years old, and in consequence was commonly called the "Boy Bachelor." He was soon after elected a Fellow of Magdalen College. His next step was to have the care of the school adjoining that college committed to him, and to receive as pupils three of the sons of the Marquis of Dorset, who, in reward for the progress which they made under his tuition, presented him to the rectory of Limington, in Somerset, which happened to be vacant at that time, and was in his lordship's patronage. During his residence in that locality a piece of ill-luck appears to have befallen "Mr."

was presented. In the early part of the reign of Henry VIII., Fox, Bishop of Winchester resolved to introduce Wolsey to royal favour, and in a very little time he obtained such a footing in Henry's good graces that he was appointed to the most trusty and confidential posts. Notwithstanding his sacred calling, we are told that Wolsey participated

CARDINAL WOLSEY. (*After Holbein.*)

Wolsey. He was put in the stocks, as some say, on a charge of drunkenness, by Sir Amias Paulet, an affront which he is reported to have resented somewhat unmercifully in after life, when Sir Amias happening to come within his clutches, he sentenced him to keep within the bounds of the Temple for five or six years.

Wolsey was next appointed chaplain to Henry VII., who employed him in a secret negotiation for his proposed marriage with Margaret of Savoy. His reward for the talent he displayed in that business was the Deanery of Lincoln, to which he

in the dissipations of the youthful Henry, which afforded him numerous opportunities "to introduce business and State affairs, to insinuate those political maxims and that line of conduct he wished his monarch to adopt." In due course Wolsey became a member of the Council, and subsequently sole and absolute minister. He was now made almoner to the king, and other honours flowed thick and fast upon him. In 1513 he obtained the Bishopric of Tournay, in Flanders, and before the end of the year succeeded to that of Lincoln.

In 1515 he reached the height of his ambition, being created a cardinal, by the title of "Cardinal of St. Cecilia beyond the Tiber." He was also Chancellor of England.

" And now," writes his biographer, "the splendour of retinue and magnificence of living he so loved began to distinguish his establishment, which might be said to have been almost more than royal ; his train consisted of eight hundred servants, many of whom were knights and gentlemen ; some even of the nobility put their children into his family as a place of education, and, in order to ingratiate them with their patron, allowed them to bear offices as his servants."

Of the pomp and state of the cardinal at this time the following account is given by Mr. G. Howard, in his " Wolsey and his Times " :—" The cardinal rose early, and as soon as he came out of his bedchamber he generally heard two masses, either in his ante-chamber or chapel. Returning to his private apartments, he made various necessary arrangements for the day ; and about eight o'clock left his privy chamber ready dressed, in the red robes of a cardinal, his upper garment being of scarlet, or else of fine crimson taffeta or crimson satin, with a black velvet tippet of sables about his neck, and holding in his hand an orange, deprived of its internal substance, and filled with a piece of sponge, wetted with vinegar 'and other confections against pestilent airs, the which he most commonly held to his nose when he came to the presses, or when he was pestered with many suitors.' This may account for so many of his portraits being painted with an orange in the hand. The Great Seal of England and the cardinal's hat were both borne before him 'by some lord, or some gentleman of worship right solemnly ;' and as soon as he entered the presence-chamber, the two tall priests, with the two tall crosses, were ready to attend upon him, with gentlemen ushers going before him bareheaded, and crying, 'On masters before, and make room for my lord.' The crowd thus called on consisted not only of common suitors, or the individuals of his own family, but often of peers of the realm, who chose, or were perhaps obliged, thus to crouch to an upstart—a character not in very great repute in those days. In this state the proud cardinal proceeded down his hall, with a sergeant-at-arms before him, carrying a large silver mace, and two gentlemen, each bearing a large plate of silver. On his arrival at the gate, or hall door, he found his mule ready, covered with crimson velvet trappings. When mounted, his attendants consisted of his two cross-bearers and his two pillar-bearers, dressed in fine scarlet and mounted on great horses capa-

risoned in like colour, of four men on foot, with each a pole-axe in his hand, and a long train of gentry, who came to swell his triumph as he proceeded to the Court of Chancery, where he generally sat until eleven o'clock to hear suits and to determine causes. With all this state he seems to have affected some degree of familiarity ; for, previous to taking his seat in the court, he generally stopped at a bar made for him below the chancery, conversing with the other judges, and sometimes with individuals of less apparent consequence. As soon as his chancery business was over, he commonly proceeded to the Star-chamber, where, as has been— we hope truly—reported of him, ' hee neither spared high nor low, but did judge every one according to right.' "

Dr. Johnson has drawn the character of the cardinal in the following energetic lines :—

" In full-blown dignity see Wolsey stand,
    Law in his voice and fortune in his hand ;
    To him the church, the realm, their powers consign,
    Through him the rays of regal bounty shine ;
    Turn'd by his nod, the stream of honour flows,
    His smile alone security bestows !
    Still to new heights his restless wishes soar,
    Claim leads to claim, and pow'r advances pow'r ;
    Till conquest unresisted ceas'd to please,
    And right submitted left him none to seize !
    At length his sovereign frowns, the train of state
    Mark the keen glance and watch the sign to hate ;
    Where'er he turns he meets the stranger's eye,
    His suppliants scorn him and his followers fly ;
    Now drops at once the pride of awful state,
    The golden canopy, the glittering plate,
    The regal palace, the luxurious board,
    The livery'd army, and the menial lord !
    With age, with cares, with maladies oppress'd,
    He seeks the refuge of monastic rest ;
    Grief aids disease, remember'd folly stings,
    And his last sighs reproach the *faith* of kings ! "

Among the younger scions of the nobility who were placed under the guidance of Wolsey was the youthful Lord Percy, who, accompanying the cardinal to court, had frequent opportunities of seeing and conversing with the beautiful and unfortunate Anne Boleyn, whose affections he gained, and whom he privately agreed to marry. This coming to the ears of the king, the cardinal was forthwith charged to summon his pupil's father to the presence of his royal master, and the contract was formally broken. The Lady Anne, as readers of English history know, was soon after dismissed the Court, and sent to one of her father's estates in the country, the contract being dissolved by the cardinal, as having been made "without the king's or the young lord's father's knowledge," Earl Percy soon after marrying a daughter of the Earl of Shrewsbury.

"It has been conjectured, not without reason," writes Mr. J. F. Murray, in his "Environs of London," "that upon this apparently unimportant incident depended the future of the cardinal's power, Anne never having forgiven him for depriving her of Percy, though, to augment her rising influence with the king, it was necessary that she should dissemble, and she accordingly, with womanly dissimulation, appeared to treat Wolsey with the greatest external respect.

"The determination of Henry to repudiate Katharine, his queen—the first fatal declension from his position as king and father of his people to that of a brutal and wanton tyrant—and the honest opposition of Wolsey to that iniquitous procedure, hastened the hour of his downfall. Anne Boleyn, now recalled to Court, industriously fostered the dislike to the cardinal which had grown up in the mind of Henry, and the crisis of Wolsey's fate had arrived."

Long before this, however—namely, in 1526—Wolsey had thought it expedient to "present" Hampton Court Palace to the king; but it was a gift not of love, but of despair.

It has been suggested that it was in a vault of this palace that the incident occurred which opened Henry's eyes to the wealth acquired by his favourite cardinal. As the story goes, the king's fool was paying a visit to the cardinal's fool, and the jocose couple went down into the wine vaults. For fun, one of them stuck a dagger or some other pointed instrument into the top of a cask, and, to his surprise, touched something that chinked like metal. The meddlesome pair upon this set to work, and pushed off the head of the cask, discovering that it was full of gold pieces. Other casks, by their sounds, gave indications that they held wine, and not gold. The king's fool stored up this secret, and one day, when Henry VIII. was boasting about his wine, the fool said, satirically, "You have not such wine, sire, as my Lord Cardinal, for he hath casks in his cellar worth a thousand broad pieces each;" and then he told what he had detected. Whether this be true or not, it is certain that Wolsey was so far awake to the fact that he was so suspected by the monarch as to deem it prudent to present him with Hampton Court.

There was one memorable circumstance connected with Wolsey's palace, namely, that it did not present to the beholder a moat, a drawbridge, or loopholes, without which, up to that time, no nobleman thought of erecting a mansion. What Wolsey spent on Hampton Court can only be guessed at. After the great lord cardinal died Henry set himself to the carrying out of various improvements; and in return for the "present" of his palace, Henry VIII. bestowed upon Wolsey the manor-house of Richmond, an old and favourite residence of his predecessor, Henry VII., and also of Henry VIII. himself in the early part of his reign; or, as Stow quaintly puts it, "in recompense thereof, the king licensed him to lie in his manor of Richmond at his pleasure, and so he lay there at certain times."

Although the cardinal thus relinquished the right of possession, he occasionally lived at Hampton Court Palace at a subsequent period. In 1527, in obedience to the desires of King Henry, Wolsey here feasted the ambassadors of the Court of France. An account of this entertainment is given in Cavendish's "Life of Wolsey," which, as it is well calculated to convey an idea of the magnificence with which this palace was furnished on State occasions, and is such an interesting feature in the history of the building, we may be pardoned for quoting it in these pages:—

"Then there was made great preparation of all things for this great assembly at Hampton Court; the Cardinall called before him his principal officers —as steward, treasurer, controller, and clerk of his kitchen—to whom he declared his mind touching the entertainment of the Frenchmen at Hampton Court, commanding them neither to spare for any cost, expense, or travayle, to make such a triumphant banquet, as they might not only wonder at it here, but also make a glorious report of it in their country, to the great honour of the king and his realm. To accomplish his commandment, they sent out caters, purveiors, and divers other persons, my lord's friends, to make preparation; also they sent for all the expert cookes and cunnyng persons in the art of cookerie which were within London or elsewhere, that might be gotten to beautify this noble feast. The purveiors provided, and my lord's friends sent in such provision as one would wonder to have seen. The cookes wrought both day and night with suttleties and many craftie devices, where lacked neither gold, silver, nor other costly thing meet for their purpose; the yeomen and groomes of the wardrobe were busied in hanging of the chambers, and furnishing the same with beds of silk and other furniture in every degree; then my Lord Cardinall sent me (Mr. Cavendish), being his gentleman usher, with two other of my fellows, thither, to foresee all thing touching our rooms to be nobly garnyshed: accordingly our pains were not small nor light, but daily travelling up and down from chamber to chambers. Then wrought the carpenters, joiners, masons, and all other artificers necessary to be had to glorify this noble feast. There was carriage and re-carriage of plate, stuff, and other rich implements, so that there was nothing lacking that could be imagined or devised for the purpose. There was also provided two hundred and eighty beds, furnished with all manner of furniture to them belonging, too long particularly to be rehearsed; but all wise men do sufficiently know what belongeth to the furniture thereof, and that is sufficient at this time to be said.

"The day was come to the Frenchmen assigned, and they ready assembled before the hour of their appointment, whereof the officers caused them to ride to Hanworth, a place and parke of the Kinge's, within three miles, there to hunt and spend the day untill night, at which time they returned againe to Hampton Court, and every one of them was conveyed to their severall chambers, having in them great fires, and wine to their comfort and relief, remaining there untill their supper was ready. The chambers where they supped and banquetted were ordered in this sort: first the great wayting chamber was hanged with rich arras, as all other were, and furnished with tall yeomen to serve. There were set tables round about the chamber, banquetwise covered; a cupboord was there garnished with white plate, having also in the same chamber, to give the more light, four great plates of silver set with great lights, and a great fire of wood and coales. The next chamber, being the chamber of presence, was hanged with very rich arras, and a sumptuous cloth of estate furnished with many goodly gentlemen to serve the tables, ordered in manner as the other chamber was, saving that the high table was removed beneath the cloth of estate toward the middest of the chamber covered. Then there was a cupboord being as long as the chamber was in breadth, with six deskes of height, garnyshed with guilt plate, and the nethermost desk was garnyshed all with gold plate, having with lights one paire of candlestickes of silver and guilt, being curiously wrought, which cost three hundred markes, and standing upon the same, two lights of waxe burning as bigge as torches to set it forth. This cupboord was barred round about, that no man could come nigh it, for there was none of all this plate touched in this banquet, for there was sufficient besides. The plates that did hang on the walls to give light were of silver and guilt, having in them great pearchers of waxe burning, a great fire burning in the chimney, and all other things necessary for the furniture of so noble a feast.

"Now was all things in readiness, and supper tyme at hand; the principal officers caused the

trumpetters to blow to warne to supper; the officers discreetly went and conducted these noblemen from their chambers into the chambers where they should suppe, and caused them there to sit downe, and that done, their service came up in such abundance, both costly and full of suttleties, and with such a pleasant noyse of instruments of musicke, that the Frenchmen (as it seemed) were rapt into a heavenly paradise. You must understand that my Lord Cardinall was not yet comen thither, but they were merry and pleasant with their fare and devised suttleties. Before the second course my lord came in, booted and spurred, all sodainely amongst them, and bade them *preface,*[*] at whose coming there was great joy, with rising every man from his place, whom my lord caused to sit still and keep their roomes, and being in his apparell as he rode, called for a chayre, and sat down in the middest of the high paradise, laughing and being as merry as ever I saw hym in all my lyff. Anone came up the second course, with so many dishes, suttleties, and devices, above a hundred in number, which were of so goodly proportion and so costlie, that I thinke the Frenchmen never saw the like. The wonder was no less than it was worthie indeed. There were castles, with images the same as in St. Paul's Church for the quantity, as well counterfeited as the painter should have painted it on a cloth or wall. There were beasts, birds, and personages, most lively-made and counterfeited, some fighting with swords, some with guns and cross-bowes, some vaulting and leaping, some dauncing with ladies, some on horses in complete harnesse, jousting with long and sharp speares, with many more devices. Among all, one I noted was a chesseboord, made of spiced plate, with men thereof the same; and for the good proportion, and because the Frenchmen be verie cunning and expert in that play, my Lord Cardinall gave the same to a gentleman of France, commanding there should be made a goodlie case for the preservation thereof in all haste, that he might convey the same safe into his country. Then took my lord a boule of gold filled with ippocrass, and putting off his cappe, said, 'I drink to the king, my soveraigne lord, and next unto the king, your master,' and therewith drank a good draught. And when he had done, he desired the *graund maistre* to pledge him, cup and all, the which was well worth 500 markes, and so caused all the boordes to pledge these two Royal Princes; then went the cups so merrily about, that many of the

---

[*] An obsolete French term of salutation, abridged from *Bon pron voux face: i.e.,* "Much good may it do you."

Frenchmen were faine to be led to their beds. Then rose up my lord, and went into his privy chamber to pull off his bootes, and to shift him, and then went he to supper, and making a very short supper, or rather, a repast, returned into the chamber of presence to the Frenchmen, using them so lovingly and familiarly, that they could not commend him too much ; and whilest they were in communication, and other pastimes, all their liveries were served to their chambers ; every chamber had a bason and an ewer of silver, a great liverey pot of silver, and some guilt ; yea, and some chambers had two liverey pots, with wine and beere, a boule, a goblet, and a pot of sylver to drink in, both for their wine and beere ; a silver candlesticke both white and plaine, having in it two sizes, and a staff torche of waxe, a fine manchet, and a cheat loaf. Thus was every chamber furnished through the house ; and yet the cupboords in the two banquetting chambers were not touched. Thus when it was more than time convenient, they were conveyed to their lodgings, where they rested that night. In the morning, after they had heard mass, they dined with the Cardinall, and so departed to Windsor."

Such were the merry and grand doings at Hampton Court Palace in the days of Wolsey's prosperity. " It would have been out of nature, on entering Hampton Court," observes Mr. Howitt, in his " Visits to Remarkable Places," " not to pause and contemplate for a while the singular story and fate of the great man who raised it. These ancient towers and courts are full of the memory of that strange fortune, and will be for many a long generation yet; and now that the great mass of the people is at once admitted to education and to this place, the history of Wolsey—at one time said to be a butcher's son, at another stretching his lordly hand over this realm, making foreign princes tremble at it, and reaching it out even to the papal tiara, and then again a poor and sinking suppliant, exclaiming—

" ' O father abbot,
An old man broken with the storms of state
Is come to lay his weary bones among ye ;
Give him a little earth for charity ! '

—will be more widely known and wondered at. But many have been the sad and singular passages which have occurred to royal and ambitious heads in these chambers since then."

In 1538, Henry, as stated above, made Hampton the scene of his sylvan sports. He extended his chase through fifteen parishes, and enclosed the whole as hunting-grounds, which he kept strictly preserved for his own use. After his death the wooden paling was removed, and his chase thrown open. In 1537 Jane Seymour died here, after giving birth to Edward VI. On this occasion Henry VIII., contrary to his usual habit (for he married that queen within twenty-four hours after the execution of Anne Boleyn), went into mourning, and compelled all his Court to do so. Whether it was that he was really attached to her, or whether he had not had time to get tired of her—she only having been married for seventeen months—historians do not pretend to decide. Suffice it to say he had her body removed to Windsor, and interred there with great pomp, and he remained a widower for some years, when he espoused Anne of Cleves. In 1540 the ill-fated Catharine Howard was openly shown as queen at this palace, with much splendour and many joyous celebrations. Here, too, after Catharine Howard had met her fate upon the scaffold, Henry married his last wife, Lady Catharine Parr, who fortunately survived him. Henry's last festival at Hampton Court occurred in the year 1545.

The palace was chosen by the guardians of Edward VI. as his residence, and he was residing here when the Council rose against the authority of the Protector Somerset, and the young king was removed by him hence to Windsor Castle, lest the Council should obtain possession of his person. Two of his servants having died of the " black death " in 1550, King Edward and his attendants removed from London hither in hot haste, and remained till the alarm had passed away.

About this time the garden of Hampton Court was the frequent scene of interviews between the youthful and accomplished poet the Earl of Surrey, and the " fair-haired, blue-eyed Geraldine," the most interesting particulars of whose personal and family history have been handed down to us compressed within the compass of a sonnet by her gallant lover himself. The " fair Geraldine," who proves to have been the Lady Elizabeth Fitzgerald, afterwards the wife of a certain Earl of Lincoln—of whom little is known, save that he married the woman whom Surrey had loved—was half-sister of " Silken Thomas," and daughter of Gerald, ninth Earl of Kildare, an ancestor of the Duke of Leinster. Her mother was the Lady Elizabeth Grey, her father's second countess, whose grandmother, Elizabeth Woodville, became queen of Edward IV. The Fitzgeralds, as Surrey tells us in the sonnet above alluded to, derive their origin from the Geraldi of Tuscany; hence—

" From Tuscan came my ladye's worthy race,
Fair Florence was sometime their ancient seat."

"Fair Geraldine" was born and nurtured in Ireland. As above stated, her father was Earl of Kildare, her mother allied to the blood royal :

> "Her sire an Earl, her dame of Prince's blood."

fourteen or fifteen, as it appears from contemporary dates ; and Surrey says very clearly,

> "She wanted years to understand
> The grief that I did feel."

HAMPTON COURT, AS FINISHED BY KING HENRY VIII.
(From a Drawing by Hollar, Engraved by J. Pye, and published by the Society of Antiquaries.)

She was brought up (through motives of compassion after the misfortunes of her family) at Hunsdon, in Hertfordshire, with the Princesses Mary and Elizabeth, where Surrey, who frequently

But even then her budding charms made him confess, as he beautifully expresses it,

> "How soon a look may print a thought,
> That never may remove !"

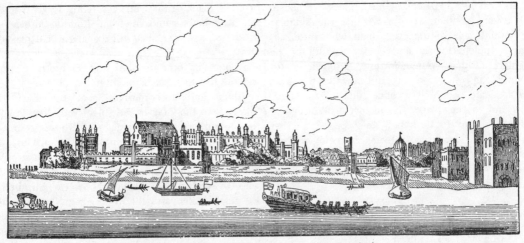

OLD HAMPTON COURT.   *(From an ancient Painting.)*

visited them in company with the young Duke of Richmond,* first beheld her :

> "Hunsdon did first present her to mine eyes."

She was then extremely young, not more than

The garden here has also been generally credited with being the scene of the following story :—
"Henry Carey, cousin to Queen Elizabeth, after having enjoyed her Majesty's favour for many years, lost it in the following manner :—As he was walking one day, lost in thought, in the palace garden, under the queen's window, the latter perceived him, and asked him in a joking way what

---

* Natural brother of the Princesses ; he was the son of Henry VIII., by Lady Talbot.

he was thinking about, and added, 'What does a man think of when he is thinking of nothing?' 'Of a woman's promise,' answered Carey. 'Well done, cousin,' said Elizabeth. She retired, but she did not forget Carey's answer; for some time afterwards he solicited the honour of a peerage, and reminded the queen that she had promised it to him. 'True,' said she; 'but you will remember, cousin, that it was *only a woman's promise!*' Seeing that Carey looked disappointed and vexed, the queen added, 'Well, Sir Henry, I must not confute you: anger makes dull men witty, but it keeps them poor.'"

Here Queen Mary and her husband, Philip of Spain, passed their honeymoon in great retirement;

contemporary chronicle, still preserved in the British Museum, affords several particulars of her entertainment on this occasion. "On Christmas Eve, the great hall of the palace being illuminated with a thousand lamps artificially disposed," writes Lucy Aikin, "the king (Philip) and queen supped in it, and the princess was seated at the same table with them, next to the cloth of estate. After supper she was served with a perfumed napkin and a plate of 'comfects' by Lord Paget, but retired to her ladies before the revels, masking, and disguising began. On St. Stephen's Day she heard matins (? mass) in the queen's closet adjoining the chapel, where she was attired in a robe of white

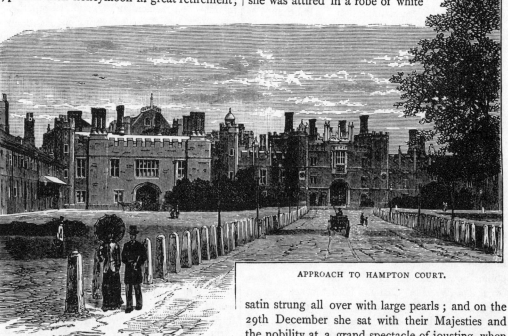

APPROACH TO HAMPTON COURT.

satin strung all over with large pearls; and on the 29th December she sat with their Majesties and the nobility at a grand spectacle of jousting, when two hundred spears were broken by combatants, of whom half were accoutred in the Almaine and half in the Spanish fashion."

and here, after her imprisonment at Woodstock, the queen's sister—the Princess Elizabeth—was invited to spend some time with the royal pair, when she was entertained with "banquets, masqueings, and all sorts of revelries."

Hither again the Princess was sent as a sort of State prisoner on March 15, 1554, on reaching London from Ashridge, in obedience to her sister's commands.

At Christmas following the Princess Elizabeth was once more invited by her sister as a guest, probably on account of the presence of the Duke of Savoy, whose suit the queen thought that her sister would be more likely to accept if she met him personally and saw his attractive qualities. A

About the end of the following April the princess was again admitted to visit her royal sister, who was expecting her confinement; but she was as much a prisoner as a guest, and the intercourse of the two sisters would seem to have been mutually repulsive. At all events, after a few weeks spent at one or two of the seats of royalty in the neighbourhood of London, she was allowed to establish herself permanently at Hatfield House, in Hertfordshire, which thenceforth was her home till she succeeded to the crown.

From Hampton Court, Queen Mary, when stricken with her last and fatal sickness, in the autumn of 1558, was carried to Westminster to die. After her accession to the throne, Elizabeth made Hampton Court one of her favourite residences, and here she continued occasionally to assemble her brilliant Court, and to "keep Christmas" in right royal fashion, as Mary, Edward, and her father had done before.

In the "pleasances" of Hampton Court Palace, as one of the ambassadors to her Court tells us, Queen Elizabeth delighted to "go a walking" with her ladies and a gay train of attendants, especially on cold frosty mornings. Did space permit, much interesting gossip could be related touching those fair attendants upon royalty, called "Maids of Honour," from Queen Elizabeth's time to the present day; but we must be content with a few general remarks concerning them. Pope in describing prudery (to a maid of honour) as

> "A beldam,
> Seen with youth and beauty seldom,"

plainly proves, by adding,

> "'Tis an ugly, envious shrew,
> Who rails at dear Lepel and you,"

that the "dear Lepel"—"youth's youngest daughter"—the fairest of the maids of honour of the time when Lady Suffolk was lady of the bedchamber both to the king and queen—had been made a mark for the ill-nature of the Court. Yet Pope's was an era when there were wars and rumours of wars to occupy the whispers of Kensington and Hampton Court—when there was a king to squabble with his ministers, and afford public news to keep in movement the private echoes of Windsor Castle. Had "sweet Lepel" been railed at during a period of petticoat government, when the back-stairs, instead of being haunted by Herveys, Walpoles, and Chesterfields, had been the resort of mantua-makers and milliners, "black, white, and grey, with all their trumpery," Pope would have known that the "*railing*" was an inevitable concomitant of the "*post*" of—Maid of Honour. He would have rather addressed the future Lady Hervey with "Be thou as chaste as ice, as pure as snow, thou shalt not escape calumny!"

Grammont has recorded the recreations of the high-born maidens of his time, who, disguised as orange-girls, escaped from the purlieus of the palace of Whitehall to frequent those of the theatres; and St. Simon acquaints us on what grounds the Duchess de Noailles, mother of the maids of honour of Anne of Austria and her royal successor, was forced to have double iron bars affixed to their chamber windows. The Queen of Scots had her Maries; and she who recorded in song that

> "There was Mary Seyton, and Mary Betoun,
> And Mary Carmichael, and me,"

hath also bequeathed to posterity the confession of her fault. Queen Elizabeth was forced, by the incontinence of *her* fair attendants, to find them occasional lodgings in the Tower of London, even when so great a man as the gallant Raleigh was the avowed author of the mischief; and Pope and Lady Mary Wortley have told remarkable tales of the honourable maidenhood of Queen Caroline's Court.

"In the furniture of the palaces," writes Bohun, in his "Character of Queen Elizabeth," "her Majesty ever affected magnificence and an extraordinary splendour. She adorned the galleries with pictures by the best artists; the walls she covered with rich tapestries. She was a true lover of jewels, pearls, all sorts of precious stones, gold and silver plate, rich beds, fine coaches and chariots, Persian and Indian carpets, statues, medals, &c., which she would purchase at great prices. Hampton Court was the most richly furnished of all her palaces; and here she caused her naval victories over the Spaniards to be worked in fine tapestries, and laid up among the richest pieces of her wardrobe. . . . When she made here any public feasts, her tables were magnificently served, and many side-tables adorned with rich plate. At these times many of her nobility waited on her at table. She made the greatest displays of her regal magnificence when foreign ambassadors were present. At these times she would also have vocal and instrumental music during dinner, and after dinner, dancing."

The joyful tidings of the defeat of the Spanish Armada arrived on Michaelmas Day, and, as the story goes, was communicated to Queen Elizabeth whilst at dinner here, partaking of a *goose*. Hence the origin of eating that savoury dish on Michaelmas Day.

Here, James I., immediately after his accession, assured his Roman Catholic subjects of his intention to grant them "toleration"—a promise which he never fulfilled. Here, too, a few weeks afterwards, he held a conference between the divines of the Established Church and the Nonconformist body, over which he presided, and which resulted in the victory of the former. It was settled at this conference that there should be certain amendments in the Prayer Book, and that "care should be taken that one uniform translation of the Bible should be provided and read in the Church, and that without notes." The king forthwith appointed a commission of fifty-four, and took exceeding interest in the work, calling it "our translation." The king in 1604 wrote a letter to the Bishop of London, urging that provision should be made for some of the translators by prebendal stalls and livings. The Bishop of London accordingly issued letters. The translation, delayed by the death of one of the translators, came out in 1611. The king's printers printed it, and asserted on the title-page, "Appointed to be read in churches." Notwithstanding that Lord Selborne tells us that a fire at Whitehall destroyed the rolls and patents of the period, a catena of evidence, beginning with 1612 up to 1640, is supplied by the Visitation Articles, showing how this version of 1611 was deemed lawful and authorised, and enforced by episcopal and archidiaconal authority.

In 1606 the king and queen gave here a splendid series of entertainments, extending over a fortnight, to Francis, Prince of Vaudemois, son of the Duke of Lorraine, and to a large company of noblemen and gentlemen. Here, in 1618, died the queen of James, Anne of Denmark.

Charles I. resided at Hampton Court both in his happiest and most melancholy days. Like Philip and Mary, his Majesty and his queen, Henrietta Maria, daughter of Henry IV. of France, came here in 1625 to spend their honeymoon. On summer evenings he and the queen and the rest of the court, would "take barge" on the Thames and amuse their leisure hours by feeding the swans.

Laud was appointed Dean of the Chapel of Hampton Court in 1626, soon after his translation to Bath and Wells; but his memory is associated less with Hampton than with Lambeth Palace.

In 1641 King Charles took refuge at Hampton Court during the troubles in London. It is related that "one day whilst his Majesty was standing at one of the windows of the palace, surrounded by his children, a gipsy or beggar-woman came up to it, and asked for charity. Her appearance excited ridicule and probably threats, which so enraged the gipsy that she took out of her basket a looking-glass, and presented it to the king; he saw in it his own head decollated. Probably with a natural wish to conciliate so prophetical a beggar, or for some other reason, money was given to her. She then said that the death of a dog in a room the king was then in would precede the restoration to his family of the kingdom which the king was then about to lose. It is said that Oliver Cromwell afterwards slept in the room referred to. He was constantly attended by a faithful dog, who guarded his bed-room door. On awakening one morning, he found the dog dead, on which he exclaimed, in allusion to the gipsy's prophecy, which he had previously heard, 'The kingdom is departed from me.' Cromwell died soon after, and the subsequent events are sufficiently known."

In 1647 the ill-fated Charles was brought hither by the army from Holmby, in Northamptonshire. Whilst here he was treated with respect, and even kindness, being allowed also the melancholy satisfaction of often seeing his children, through the favour of the Earl of Northumberland. His Majesty was kept here, not actually in imprisonment, but under restraint, by the Parliament and the army from the 24th of August down to the 11th of November, when he escaped. Great had been the change in his circumstances during those few months—the generals, who had been hopeful that they might come to an arrangement with the king, found that he was only playing with them to gain time, and carry his own schemes. The Scotch Commissioners could do nothing with him; and, alarmed by rumours that in the ranks of the soldiery were men who would not scruple to assassinate him, Charles departed, to put himself in a worse condition in the Isle of Wight.

We find in the "Diary" of John Evelyn, under date of October 10th, 1647, the following entry:—"I came to Hampton Court, where I had the honour to kisse his Majesty's hand, he being now in the power of those execrable villains who not long after murder'd him."

In 1651 the Parliament sold the whole of the estate of Hampton Court to a Mr. John Phelpe, a member of the Lower House, for the sum of £10,765 19s. 6d.; but in 1656, Oliver Cromwell, enriched by the wreck of the State, again acquired possession of the palace, for which he appears to have had a special liking, and made it one of his principal places of residence. The marriage ceremony of his daughter Elizabeth, who espoused Lord Falconberg, was here celebrated in 1657; and in the following year the Lord Protector's favourite daughter, Mrs. Claypole (who is said to have severely remonstrated with him, in her last hours, on the subject of his dangerous ambition), here breathed her last. Hither Oliver Cromwell would repair, when Lord Protector of the Realm, to dine with his officers. Mr. Secretary Thurloe thus records the fact in sundry minutes in his pocket-book, given by John Milton to his nephew, Mr. John Philips:—"Sometimes, as the fit takes him, to divert the melancholy, he dines with the officers of his army at Hampton Court, and shows a hundred antic tricks, as throwing cushions at them, and putting hot coals into their pockets and boots ! At others, before he has half dined, he gives orders for a drum to beat and call in his foot-guards, like a kennel of hounds, to snatch off the meat from his table and tear it in pieces, with many other unaccountable whimsies ; immediately after this, fear and astonishment sit in his countenance, and not a nobleman approaches him but he fells him ! Now he calls for his guards, with whom he rides out, encompassed behind and before, for the preservation of his Highness, and at his return at night, shifts from bed to bed for fear of surprise." Once, we read, he narrowly escaped assassination while riding through the narrow part of Hammersmith, on his way to this pleasant London suburb. George Fox, the Quaker, in his "Chronicles," relates how he went out on a day in 1658 to protest to Cromwell against the severities inflicted on the eccentric members of his persuasion, and meeting the Protector riding in Hampton Park at the head of his life-guard, Fox said what he believed he was inspired to say, and withdrawing, felt a "waft of death" go out against the Protector. Nor was it many days afterwards that, on the advice of his physicians, Cromwell left Hampton Court for Whitehall, the place of his decease on September 3rd, 1658.

In an article in the *Gentleman's Magazine* for 1877, entitled "Oliver Cromwell at Hampton Court," are published some details of an "Inventory of Goods and Servants at Hampton Court," taken by order of the House of Commons, in June, 1659. This interesting document is preserved in the State Paper Office, among the uncalendared papers of that period. The reason for taking the inventory is set forth in a kind of preamble, " so as there be not embezzlement of " the goods. "In looking over the inventory," observes the writer of the article in question, " it is curious to note that only four looking-glasses are mentioned. This could not have arisen from any scarcity of that article at the period, because in the celebrated inventories of the palaces of Henry VIII. there are fourteen mentioned and fully described. The first mentioned in Hampton Court was in the ' rich bed-chamber,' and is thus described : ' one large looking-glass in an ebony frame.' Then ' in the lower wardrobe ' were ' two small looking-glasses, one of them being broke.' The fourth hung in a room which, in the time of Charles I., was occupied by the Bishop of Canterbury, and during Cromwell's Protectorate was used by his daughter, Mrs. Claypole, as a nursery. The description is as follows : ' One large looking-glass in an ebony frame, with a string of silk and gold.' The absence of any

further reference to looking-glasses is rather suggestive. Perhaps Oliver Cromwell objected to them on principle, as leading to vanity ; or possibly such as were in use were regarded as personal property, and the owners carried them away when they left the place. Hampton Court has been greatly altered since Cromwell's time, and there is not one chamber which is now associated with his memory. The Great Hall, of course, remains, in which were two organs—the larger one a gift from Cromwell's friend, Dr. Goodwin, President of Magdalen College, Oxford ; but the hall is more closely associated with the grand entertainments given by Wolsey, and the revels of Henry VIII., than with Cromwell. In like manner the chapel is only in a general way associated with his memory. More interesting reminiscences will occur in the ' Mantegna Gallery,' as it is called, after the painter of a series of pictures now hung in it. In Cromwell's time this was called the ' Long Gallery.' The pictures, nine in number, and of gigantic size, formed at one time part of a collection belonging to the Marquis of Mantua, the whole of which Charles I. purchased, at a cost of £80,000. They represent the triumphs of Julius Cæsar, and were painted by Andrea Mantegna. . . . Cromwell must have looked upon these grand pictures every time he strode along the gallery. They seem now to identify themselves with his spirit, and to depict the ideal triumphs that he would fain have won for England."

After the death of Cromwell it was thought undesirable to allow the palace to be stripped, in anticipation of the arrival of Charles II. Charles, apparently forgetful of his royal parent's misery, often enjoyed the song and dance of revelry in this palace.

At Hampton Court he spent a large part of his time both before and after his marriage with Catharine of Braganza. For a king to aspire to "happiness" is a pretension beyond his condition of life. It suited Lady Castlemaine as little that Charles should be "well acquainted" with his youthful bride as it suited the courtiers that he should think himself happy in wedlock. Before the royal party arrived at Hampton Court for the enjoyment of the honeymoon, mischief had been at work ; and though the month was May (a season that seems expressly created by nature for honeymoons) breezes were blowing more boisterous than the turbulent equinox. Still, strangely enough, Hampton Court, in the hours of her after life, was a spot ever dear to Catharine of Braganza, on account of its memory of the transient dream of happiness connected with her honeymoon.

A small summer drawing-room in the suite of apartments overlooking the river was the favourite chamber selected by the unhappy queen for receiving such persons as she admitted to private audience. Nothing could be simpler than the furniture of this unadorned chamber; the mouldings and wainscotings were of pure white, and the hangings of pale sea-green damask; a chair and footstool, somewhat richer than the rest, alone served to mark the seat of the queen herself, whose pale and sallow complexion was not shown off to advantage thereby. Here, however, "the blazing and audacious beauty of Lady Castlemaine often 'paled' its ineffectual fires before the mild lustre of the queen's girlish and almost saintly meekness."

Here, deserted by the servile tribe of flatterers, an object of pity to some, of contempt perhaps to more, Catharine was obliged to look on tamely, and see the homage of the courtiers paid before her face to other "stars," while she was abandoned and desolate in a foreign country; her only chance of winning even decent courtesy of her profligate husband depended on the degree of patience which she could exhibit.

James II. occasionally visited Hampton Court palace, and at times held his councils there. A good story is told about the poet Waller and King James. His Majesty treated Waller with great familiarity, and one day took him into the royal closet, and asked him how he liked one of the pictures, at the same time pointing to a lady's portrait. "My eyes, sir, are dim," answered Waller, "and I cannot distinguish it." "It is the Princess of Orange," said the king. "She is like the greatest woman in the world, sir," answered Waller; and on the king asking whom he meant, he answered again, "Queen Elizabeth." "I wonder," said his Majesty, "that you should think so; but I must confess she had a wise council." "And, sir," asked Waller in return, "did you ever know a fool choose a wise council?"

William III. and his queen appear to have preferred this palace to all their other residences. Specimens of the beautiful embroidery of her Majesty and her female attendants might at one time be seen here.

Many persons were angry because "Dutch William" tried to improve upon a structure which had been good enough for the many royal personages who had preceded him; but it was not his habit to study public opinion. Sir Christopher Wren pulled down various portions of the old palace, leaving untouched, however, the entrance court, and only so far altering the middle quadrangle as to introduce, with bad taste, an Ionic

colonnade amongst Wolsey's antique turrets. The third quadrangle, or Fountain Court, is almost entirely Wren's work, as are also the grand eastern and southern fronts. It is from the Fountain Court that the State Apartments are reached by a staircase, which was painted by Verrio, a man who regarded William as an usurper, which led Lord Orford to make the satirical remark that this artist painted the staircase as badly as if he had spoilt it out of principle.

Mr. J. T. Smith, in his work above quoted, observes:—"King William III., who took every opportunity of rendering these apartments as pleasing to him as those he had left in 'the house in the Wood,' introduced nothing by way of porcelain, beyond that of delf, and on that ware, in many instances, his Majesty had 'W.R.,' surmounted by the crown of England, painted on the fronts. Of the various specimens of this clumsy blue-and-white delf, displayed in the numerous rooms of this once magnificent palace, the pride of Wolsey and splendour of Henry VIII., the eight large pots for the reception of King William III.'s orange-tree, now standing in her Majesty's gallery, certainly have claims to future protection. As for the old and ragged bed-furniture, it is so disgraceful to a palace, that, antiquarian as I in some degree consider myself, I most heartily wish it in Petticoat Lane."

John Evelyn was again at Hampton Court shortly after William III. ascended the throne, for under date of July 16th, 1689, he writes in his "Diary":—"I went to Hampton Court about buisinesse, the Council being there. A greate apartment and spacious garden with fountaines was beginning in the park, at the head of the canal."

It was in the park that the king met with the accident that caused his death. Macaulay writes:—"On the 20th of February, 1702, William was ambling on a favourite horse, named Sorrel, through the park of Hampton Court. He urged his horse to strike into a gallop just at the spot where a mole had been at work. Sorrel stumbled on the molehill, and went down on his knees. The king fell off and broke his collar-bone. The bone was set, and he returned to Kensington in his coach, but the jolting of the rough roads of that time made it necessary to reduce the fracture again." It is not to be wondered at that William never recovered this double shock to his system, and that fever supervening, he died a few days subsequently.

The sister of Queen Mary, then Princess of Denmark, and afterwards Queen Anne, here gave birth on the 24th of July, 1689, to the Duke of Gloucester, who died at eleven years of age, and thus made room for the house of Brunswick. His royal mother occasionally resided here after her accession to the throne.

It is to this place that Pope alludes when he thus apostrophises Queen Anne, the first English sovereign by whom we know for certain that "Bohea," the new and fashionable beverage of that day, was patronised :—

> Oh ! had I rather unadmired remained
> In some lone isle or distant northern land,
> Where the gilt chariot never marks the way,
> Where none learn Ombre, none e'er taste Bohea !"

The sovereigns of the house of Brunswick have not shown any great partiality for Hampton Court Palace as a royal abode. George I. sometimes visited the palace, as did his successor on the

HAMPTON COURT, FROM THE RIVER.

> "Here thou, great Anna, whom these realms obey,
> Dost sometimes counsel take, and sometimes tea."

Tea, it must be remembered, was a rare article in those days. It had not then been many years introduced into England, for in Pepys's "Diary," under date of September 25th, 1660, we find this entry :—"I did send for a cup of tee (a China drink), of which I had never drank before."

In the "Rape of the Lock" Belinda is made to exclaim :—

> "Happy ! ah, ten times happy had I been,
> If Hampton Court these eyes had never seen !
> Yet am I not the first mistaken maid
> By love of courts to numerous ills betrayed.

throne, who was the last monarch who made it his residence. The two first Georges, however, were devoid of taste, and illiterate, and that may account for the fact. "It is curious that not one solitary epistle in the handwriting of George II. is known to exist. This circumstance is more remarkable if we refer to his gallantries and intrigues, so severely commented upon and recorded by Walpole and others." Such is the statement of a writer in the columns of the *Times*.

Miss Chudleigh may be regarded as the ideal and type of the set of pert, or even malapert, young ladies who acted as maids of honour in the courts of the first two Georges. A good story is told by Charles Knight in his "London," which, whether it be true or false, is at all events characteristic of her transcendent impudence :—Apartments in Hampton Court palace having been allotted to her mother, the king good-naturedly asked Miss Chudleigh one day how the old lady felt in her new abode. "Oh, very well, if the poor woman had only a bed to lie upon !" "That oversight must be repaired," said the king. On this hint, the maid of honour (who continued a maid of honour for twenty years after her clandestine marriage with the Hon. Mr. Hervey, afterwards Earl of Bristol) acted, and in due time there appeared among the royal household accounts, "To a bed and furniture for the apartments of the Hon. Mrs. Chudleigh, £4,000." The king, who, though decidedly fond of money, was a man of his word, paid the bill, but remarked that if Mrs. Chudleigh found the bed as hard as he did, she would never sleep in it.

MISS CHUDLEIGH.

For the last century or more apartments in Hampton Court Palace have generally been bestowed on the poorer female members of noble families, or on widows of distinguished generals and admirals who have died in the service of their country. It is not generally known that once at least in his life Dr. Johnson cast a longing eye upon this privileged place. At all events, the following letter was published a few years ago in the *Athenæum* :— "The following interesting letter of Dr. Samuel Johnson has never been in print :—'My Lord, —Being wholly unknown to your lordship, I have only this apology to make for presuming to trouble you with a request—that a stranger's petition, if it cannot be easily granted, can be easily refused. Some of the apartments are now vacant, in which I am encouraged to hope that, by application to your lordship, I may obtain a residence. Such a grant would be considered by me as a great favour ; and I hope, to a man who has had the honour of vindicating his Majesty's government, a retreat in one of his houses may be not improperly or unworthily allowed. I therefore request that your lordship will be pleased to grant such rooms in Hampton Court as shall seem proper to, my lord, your lordship's most obedient and most humble servant, SAM. JOHNSON, Bolt Court, Fleet Street, April 11, 1776.' Endorsed, 'Mr. Samuel Johnson to the Earl of Hertford, requesting apartments at Hampton Court, 11 May, 1776.'— The answer : 'Lord C. presents his compliments to Mr. Johnson, and is sorry that he cannot obey his commands, having already on his hands many engagements unsatisfied.' "

In 1795, William, Prince of Orange, Hereditary Stadtholder of Holland, driven from Holland by the advanced wave of the French Revolution, found here a hospitable asylum ; "and here," writes gossiping Sir Nathaniel William Wraxall, "the princes of our royal family and the nation at large vied in demonstrations of respect, compassion, and attention towards him." It was his son who was at one time designed to be the husband of our Princess Charlotte, but Providence decreed otherwise.

In 1810, after being deposed from the Swedish throne by the great Napoleon, Gustavus IV. came to England, and occupied a set of apartments here. He died in February, 1837.

The favoured inmates of Hampton Court palace during Her Majesty's reign have consisted largely of members of the following families, all of whom are more or less nearly connected with the Peerage :—Paget, Grey, Byng, Capel, Talbot, Ponsonby, Murray, Cathcart, Ward, Swinburne, Crofton, &c. In many cases these persons have been the widows of distinguished officers of the army and navy who have fallen in battle in the service of their country.

Since the year 1839 those parts of the palace which are not occupied by private residents, and the gardens, have been thrown open to the public, and during the summer months the whole place forms daily a great attraction to hundreds of sightseers, both English and foreign, who come to it by road or rail or river.

CHAPTER XIII.

HAMPTON COURT PALACE (*continued*).

"A place which Nature's choicest gifts adorn,
   Where Thames' kind streams in gentle currents turn,
   The name of Hampton hath for ages borne ;
   Here such a palace shows great Henry's care,
   As Sol ne'er views in his exalted sphere,
   In all his tedious stage !"—CAMDEN.

Early Reminiscences of Hampton Court Palace—Description of the Building—The Principal Entrance—Wolsey's Courts—The Clock Tower Court
   —A Curious Timepiece—The Great Hall—Theatrical Entertainments given here—The Withdrawing Room—The Kitchen Court—The
   Fountain Court—Sir Christopher Wren's Alterations and Additions to the Palace—The Chapel—The State Apartments- The "Beauty"
   Room—The Tapestry Gallery—The Cartoons of Raffaelle—The Gardens—The Wilderness and Maze—The Home Park—The Royal Stud
   House—A Narrow Escape of the Palace.

It is remarked in OLD AND NEW LONDON *
that although Windsor Castle is unequalled as a
royal residence of the type of a mediæval stronghold, yet Hampton Court is, after all, but a poor
substitute for the Château of Versailles. Nevertheless, few places possess more attractions than
Hampton Court. Its interest is not that of old
feudal associations : it was never half-palace, half-
fortress. It was never surrounded by a moat, nor
could it ever boast of a drawbridge or frowning
battlements and watch-towers ; all these things had
been banished by "society" when Hampton Court
palace was founded. The better portion of it, as
we have shown in the preceding chapter, was the
creation of that princely-minded churchman—the
last of that race of English dignitaries who combined in themselves the powers and attributes of
the priest and the noble. Founded by a cardinal,
continued by one king, completed by another, and
since inhabited by many of royal blood and station,
and containing within its walls some of the finest
efforts of the painter, and the most elaborate productions of the obsolete but beautiful skill of the
workers of tapestry, Hampton Court palace is a
building that well repays the visitor. Nor are these
attractions confined to the palace itself : its parks
and gardens, extending to many hundreds of acres,
are equally attractive, and afford plenty of scope
for the most reflective mind to ruminate upon, or
for the most frivolous to carry out the best of his
enjoyment in his own peculiar way.

The Rev. A. C. Cox, in his "Impressions of
England," writes :—" In the grounds of the palace,
and in Bushey Park, I found a formal grandeur, so
entirely becoming a past age, and so unusual in this,
that it impressed me with a feeling of melancholy
the most profound. Those avenues of chestnuts
and thorns, those massive colonnades and dreamy
vistas, wear a desolate and dreary aspect of by-

gone glory, in view of which my spirits could not
rise. They seemed only a fit haunt for airy echoes,
repeating an eternal *Where?* Nothing later than
the days of Queen Anne seems to belong to the
spot. You pass from scenes in which you cannot
but imagine Pope conceiving, for the first time, his
'Rape of the Lock,' into a more trim and formal
spot, where William of Orange seems likely to
appear before you, with Bishop Burnet buzzing
about him, and a Dutch guard following in the
rear. Then, again, James the Second, with the
Pope's nuncio at his elbow, and a coarse mistress
flaunting at his side, might seem to promise an
immediate apparition ; when once more the scene
changes, and the brutal Cromwell is the only
character who can be imagined in the forlorn area,
with a file of musketeers in the background,
descried through a shadowy archway. Here is a
lordly chamber, where the meditative Charles may
be conceived as startled by the echo of their tread ;
and here another, where he embraces for the last
time his beloved children. There, at last, is
Wolsey's hall, and here one seems to behold old
Bluebeard leading forth Anne Boleyn to a dance.
It still retains its ancient appearance, and is hung
with mouldering tapestry and faded banners, although its gilding and colours have been lately
renewed. The ancient devices of the Tudors are
seen here and there in windows and tracery, and
the cardinal's hat of the proud churchman who
projected the splendours of the place still survives
in glass, whose brittle beauty has thus proved less
perishable than his worldly glory.

"Yet let no one suppose the magnificence of
Hampton Court to consist in its architecture. One-
half is the mere copy of St. James's, and the other
is the stupid novelty of Dutch William. The
whole together, with its parks and with its history,
is what one feels and admires. I am not sure but
Royal Jamie, with his bishops and his Puritans on
either side, was as often before me when traversing

* See Vol IV., p. 122.

the pile, as anything else : and for him and his conference the place seems fit enough, having something of Holyrood about it, and something scholastic or collegiate also. Queen Victoria should give it to the Church, as a college for the poor, and so add dignity to her benevolence, which has already turned it into a show for her darling 'lower classes.' I honour the queen for this condescension to the people ; and yet, as I followed troops of John Gilpins through the old apartments, and observed their inanimate stare and booby admiration, it did strike me that a nobler and a larger benefit might be conferred upon them in a less incongruous way. Perhaps the happiest thought would be to make it for the clergy just what Chelsea is to the army and Greenwich to the naval service."

As we pass round the open courts and issue from under the low archways, we almost expect a robed and chained official of " the cardinal's " splendid household admonishing a "clerk of the kitchen," or conversing with a "gentleman of the chamber ;" nor would it startle the ear of fancy to hear the silence broken by the hearty, but coarse, laugh of "bluff King Hal" himself, sauntering familiarly with the cardinal, during one of those visits when the monarch came to Hampton to enjoy the hospitality—and, alas ! to envy the splendour—of his host. We wander into the blooming, though rather formally-disposed gardens ; and as we saunter up a shady avenue we can almost hear the rustle of the silks and brocades of a group of lords and ladies attending the royal Anne.

In imagination it is easy to picture to oneself the Watteau-like group formed by the Belindas and Sir Plumes of the age when Pope wrote his " Rape of the Lock"; when French glitter was spread over Dutch uniformity, as they loiter by the side of the canal, the beaux elaborately complimentary, and the belles condescendingly attentive, yet with a dash of something that keeps familiarity at fan's length. But it is time now to pass from these fanciful themes to a description of the reality.

Skirting the picturesque green, or common, of Hampton, the visitor enters the palace through an archway in the western quadrangle—that portion of the edifice appropriated, for the most part, to families who have obtained small Government pensions, with apartments in the palace. The west front exhibits, to some disadvantage, the monastic style of architecture, with all its stateliness and gloom. The pillars of the principal gateway are surmounted by a large lion and unicorn, as supporters of the royal arms, and each of the side gates by a military trophy. Along the left side of

the area of the outer court are barracks and such-like offices ; the greater part of the right side is open towards the river. In front are two other gateways—that to the left leading to the "kitchen court," the other conducting to the first quadrangle. This chief gateway is in excellent keeping with the older parts of the building. It is flanked with octagon towers, pierced with a fine pointed arch, over which are cut, in high relief, the royal arms, and above them projects a large and handsome bay window, framed of stone.

Through this archway is entered the first of Wolsey's courts remaining. There were originally five courts, the three first of which were pulled down to make way for William III.'s great square mass of brickwork. The writers who saw the palace in its glory describe it in entirety as the most splendid palace in Europe. Grotius says :— " Other palaces are residences of kings ; but this is of the gods." Hentzner, who saw it in Elizabeth's time, speaks of it with astonishment, and says :— " The rooms, being very numerous, are adorned with tapestry of gold, silver, and velvet, in some of which were woven history pieces ; in others Turkish and Armenian dresses, all extremely natural. In one chamber are several excessively rich tapestries, which are hung up when the queen gives audience to foreign ambassadors. All the walls of the palace shine with gold and silver. Here is likewise a certain cabinet, called ' Paradise,' where, besides that everything glitters so with silver, gold, and jewels, as to dazzle one's eyes, there is a musical instrument made all of glass, except the strings."

The two courts which remain are said to have consisted only of offices ; and, indeed, in old views of the palace the first court is represented much lower than the next, which did not itself nearly equal the stateliness of the rest. Mr. Howitt, in his " Visits to Remarkable Places," observes that " the old dark red brick walls, with still darker lines of bricks in diamond shapes running along them—the mixture of Gothic archways and square mullioned windows—the battlemented roofs, turrets, and cupolas, and tall twisted and cross-banded chimneys, all are deeply interesting, as belonging to the unquestionable period of Wolsey—belonging altogether to that Tudor or transition style when castles were fast turning into peaceful mansions, and the beauties of ecclesiastical architecture were called in to aid in giving ornament where before strength had only been required."

Of late years attempts have been made here and there at a restoration in the original style of such portions of the original structure as required repair ; and quite recently the fine oak gates, which had been laid aside as lumber for many years, have been re-hung, after careful repair, at the entrance gateway ; they are of massive dimensions, are ornamented with the usual linen-fold pattern, and are evidently of Wolsey's time. The outer face of the gates is pierced with shot and bullet-holes, which may have been occasioned during skirmishes in the civil wars, when fighting was going on out-side the palace between the Cavaliers and Round-heads ; or, as has been suggested, the holes may have been made through the gates having been set up as targets for the villagers of Hampton.

The work of restoration has included the vault-ing and flanking turrets of the gateway, and also the vaulting to the gateway of the second, or Clock-tower Court, which we now enter. This court, called also the " middle quadrangle," is somewhat smaller than the former, measuring 133 feet from north to south, and about 100 from east to west. It received the name of the Clock Court from an astronomical clock which adorns the gateway on the east side. This curious and antique timepiece was removed some years ago, but in 1880 the dial was replaced, and now, with new works by Messrs. Gillett and Bland, again shows not only the hours of the day and night, but also, among other things, the day of the month, the motion of the sun and moon, the age of the moon, the phases and quarters of the moon, and other interesting matters connected with the lunar movements. The dial is composed of three separate copper discs of different sizes, with a common centre, but revolving at various rates. The smallest of these is 3ft. 3½in. in diameter, and in the middle of this is a slighly projected globe, painted to represent the earth. The quarters marked on the centre disc by thick lines are numbered with large figures, and round the edge this disc is divided into twenty-four parts, a red arrow painted on the second disc pointing to these figures, and showing at once the quarter in which the moon is and the time of " southing." Next to the figure of the earth in this centre disc, a circular hole, 10in. in diameter, allows a smaller disc travelling behind to show the phases of the moon. On the second disc, 4ft. 1½in. in diameter, but of which only the outer rim is seen, are twenty-nine divisions, and a triangular pointer, projecting from behind the central disc, shows the moon's age in days. The largest of the three discs is 7ft. 10in. in diameter. There are many circles painted on so much of the rim of this as is seen, the inner, or—following the order above observed, and proceeding from the centre—the first circle, giving the names of the months, the second the days of the

month (only twenty-eight for February), the third the signs of the zodiac, and on the rim, with 30 degrees for each space filled by a sign, a circle divided into 360 parts. A long pointer, with a gilded figure of the sun attached, projecting from behind the second disc, shows on this third or outermost disc of the dial the day of the month and the position of the sun in the ecliptic. This pointer performs another duty, acting like the hour-hand of an ordinary clock, and showing the time of day or night as it passes the twenty-four figures—two sets of twelve—painted on the stonework within which the dial revolves. The diameter of this outer immovable circle on the stone is 9ft. 8in., and the figures of the hours, Roman numerals, are 9in. in length. About the original clock very little is known, and even the name of the maker is not to be found in any of the works in which information on a matter of so much interest would be looked for. The date of its con-struction is known, and but little more. On a bar of the wrought-iron framework to which the dial is fixed is to be found, deeply cut and distinctly engraved, " N.O., 1540." One other evidence of its antiquity is derived from an entry, men-tioned by Mr. E. J. Wood, in his " Curiosities of Clocks and Watches," of a payment made in 1575 to one George Gaver, " serjeant painter, for paint-ing the great dial at Hampton Court Palace, con-taining hours of the day and night, the course of the sun and moon," and so on, though the author has not given a reference to the record in which he found this fact set down. Since Master Gaver exercised his art in decorating the dial-face, many clockmakers, it seems probable, from time to time repaired and altered the works ; for Dr. Derham, describing the condition of the clock in 1711, when it had been recently repaired by Mr. Lang Bradley, of Fenchurch Street, said it had been found that the original pricked wheel and pinion had been re-moved, by some ignorant workman, as he supposed. Judging from the numbers given by Dr. Derham of the toothing of the wheels, the clock, it appears, even with the changes made by Mr. Bradley, could not have performed its functions accurately. It is not unlikely that the astronomical clock had long been useless, for as early as the year 1649 another clock-face had been placed on the other side of this gate-tower, over the entrance to the Great Hall, and a striking part had been added to the works of the clock.

In 1835 the works of the old clock were removed, but what became of them is not known. On the works of the clock removed in 1880 was found the following inscription :—" This clock, originally made for the Queen's Palace in St. James's Palace, and for many years in use there, was, A.D. 1835, by command of His Majesty King William IV., altered and adapted to suit Hampton Court Palace by B. L. Vulliamy, clock-maker to the King ;" and on another plate on the clock—"Vulliamy, London, No. 352, A.D. 1799." The motive-power of this clock had evidently not been sufficient to drive in addition the astronomical dial, and the useless dial had been taken down and stowed away in a workshop at the palace, the gap left being filled by a painted board. When Mr. Bland, of the firm of Gillett and Bland, who had been commissioned by the Office of Works to make a new clock, examined the wheels by which the dials were to be moved, he found by the number of teeth in some of the wheels that the astronomical clock could not possibly have served its purpose. New wheels were therefore cut. The new works drive both the astronomical dial and the hands of the ordinary clock-face on the opposite or western side of the tower. In the mechanism many ingenious contrivances have been employed, and the clock is guaranteed not to vary more than five seconds a week. The bells are in the little hybrid classical cupola of painted wood which disfigures the nobly-proportioned Tudor tower of Cardinal Wolsey's palace. That on which the hours are struck weighs about 18 cwt., and two smaller bells chime the quarters. The large bell has plainly at some time been hung for ringing, and was probably fixed for striking when the two small bells, which were brought from another tower of the palace, were placed with it. In size, the clock—*i.e.*, the mechanism within the clock-chamber—is, giving over all measurements, 7ft. 6in. long, 3ft. 6in. wide, and 3ft. 6in. deep, the main wheels being 14, 16, and 16 inches respectively in diameter. The clock face, of slate, on the west side of the tower, is 5ft. 8in. in diameter. It may interest the visitor to know that the small circular space, 3ft. in diameter, above the square clock front, now filled with a slab of slate, on which is cut the monogram of William IV., was, as the form of the brickwork behind shows, filled at an earlier period (probably until Vulliamy's clock was put up) by a clock dial, perhaps the one spoken of in a description of the palace in 1649 quoted by Mr. Wood. It is said that in the "clock-case upon the Great Hall there is one large bell and a clock under it, very useful for the whole house, having a fair dial or finger, upon the end of the said Great Hall, facing in the Great Court."

The south side of the Clock Court is partly concealed and disfigured by a colonnade, supported by pillars of the Ionic order, the design of Sir Christopher Wren. The oriel windows above each

of the gateways of this court are adorned with the arms of Henry VIII., whilst on the face of the octagonal turrets on either side of the archway are busts of the Cæsars in terra-cotta. These, with other medallions in the adjoining court, were the gifts of Pope Leo X. to Cardinal Wolsey. Over the archway leading into the Clock Court are the arms of Wolsey, together with his motto— "Dominus mihi adjutor"—"God is my helper."

The south of the Clock Court is occupied by the Great Hall. This splendid apartment was built— or at all events completed—by Henry VIII., whose arms and cognisances enrich the ceiling, after the death of Wolsey. The archway forming the entrance to the hall has a rich fan-traceried roof. This handsome groined ceiling, having become ruinous and in danger of falling, was restored in 1880, the greatest care being taken to preserve and reproduce the exact form and details of the original. The apartment is reached by a short flight of stone steps. The following details of the hall are quoted from Mr. Jesse's able description of the building, in his "Summer's Day at Hampton Court :"— " The dimensions of this very noble room are —in length 106 feet, in breadth 40 feet, and in height 60 feet. The roof is very elaborately timbered, and richly decorated with carvings of several of the royal badges and with pendent ornaments, executed in a style which shows that the Italian taste had already made considerable advances in this country.

"Seven capacious windows on one side, and six on the other side, with a large window at each end, all placed considerably above the floor, throw a fulness of light throughout the apartment. A bay window on the daïs, extending from the upper part of the wall nearly to the floor, contributes very essentially to the cheerfulness of the general effect. This window has been enriched by Mr. Willement with compartments of stained glass, containing the arms, initials, and badges of King Henry VIII., the arms and motto of Queen Jane Seymour, 'Bown'd to obey and serve,' and the full insignia and motto of Wolsey, 'Dominus mihi adjutor.' On the lower part is seen the following inscription—' The lorde Thomas Wulsey, Cardinal, legat de latere, Archbishop of Yorke, and Chancellor of Englande.' The whole of the stained glass in the hall and in the presence-chamber is modern, and of Mr. Willement's fashioning and framing.

"It was, if we may trust tradition, upon one of the panes of glass of this window that Henry Howard, Earl of Surrey, so famous for the tenderness and elegance of his poetry and for his martial nature, wrote some lines with a diamond on the "fair Geraldine"; and it is told, with what certainty we know not, that the first play acted in this hall was that of 'Henry VIII., or the Fall of Wolsey.' Shakespeare is said to have been one of the actors in this play.

"Above the entrance-door, leading into the presence-chamber, or withdrawing-room, has been inserted a richly-carved stone bracket, inscribed 'Seynt George for merrie Englande,' on which, in full panoply, stands our patron saint, surrounded by a halo of ramrods, transfixing with his spear his antagonist, the dragon. On each side of this stands a smaller bracket, bearing figures clothed in bright plate armour. These figures were placed here by permission of the Board of Ordnance from the stores in the Tower. He has also arranged a fine group of armour under the east window.

"Between each of the side windows there is a noble pair of the horns of deer, with finely-carved heads of the animal, and carved wreaths round each of them. These horns, which form a part of a large collection, were probably placed in the hall in the reign of Henry VIII., when it was called the Hall of Horns. They have been preserved in the palace, and the

THE CHAPEL.

tioned. From the under part of the side windows to within a few inches of the pavement, the walls are covered with tapestry of such excellent design, and such costliness of material, that it may be

safely asserted that its parallel does not exist in Europe at this time. Three pieces hang on each side of the hall, and two others at the daïs end.

"'For round about the walls yclothed
    were
      With goodly arras of great
      majesty,
    Woven with gold and silke so close
    and nere,
    That the rich metal lurked privily,
    As feigning to be hidd from envious
    eye ;
Yet here, and there, and everywhere, unwares
It shewed itselfe and shone unwillingly ;
Like a discoloured snake, whose hidden snares
Through the green grass his long bright-burnished back
    declares.'"   SPENSER.

INTERIOR OF THE GREAT HALL.

original colours have been restored as nearly as it was possible to do so. Over the horns are banners, having the devices of Henry VIII. and the arms of Wolsey, and of his several benefices, painted on them. The stringcourse above the tapestries has also been enriched with the rose, portcullis, &c., in colours. The most interesting, however, of the decorations to be seen in this truly regal apartment have yet to be men-

This noble apartment is commonly spoken of as "Wolsey's Hall," but it was probably only designed by him. Mr. Brewer, in the "Beauties of England and Wales," says that "it has been supposed that

as this room is not described in the account by Cavendish of Cardinal Wolsey's entertainment of the French ambassadors, it was entirely a part of the additional buildings raised by King Henry. But it formed so important a feature in the design of the mansion, that we may safely ascribe the exterior walls and embellishments to the magnificent Wolsey, though we shall speedily show that

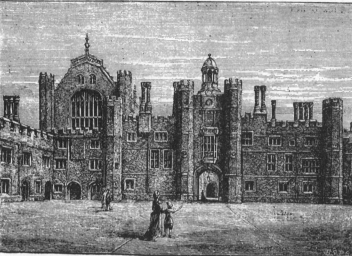

THE FIRST COURT.

the interior was not completed till 1536, or the succeeding year." At a meeting of the British Archæological Association here in 1882, Mr. Hubert Hall stated that from the accounts kept at the Record Office, and the papers in the British Museum, it was clear that " this hall was not finished when Wolsey was compelled to 'give' the palace to Henry VIII., and that it was completed by the king." Till about 1770, when it was restored, it had a large open fireplace in the centre, and the roof above was pierced by a lantern, which added picturesqueness to the external sky-line.

The subjects of the arras tapestry—eight in number—ranged round the hall illustrate the history of Abraham, and are as follows :—(1) God appearing to Abraham, and blessing him. (2) The birth and circumcision of Isaac, and the expulsion of Hagar and Ishmael. (3) Abraham sending his servant to seek a wife for his son Isaac. (4) The Egyptians sending away Abraham and Sarah with gifts. (5) Abraham entertaining three angels. (6) Abraham purchasing the Cave of Machpelah for a

burying-place. (7) Abraham and Lot parting. (8) Abraham offering up Isaac. The tapestries are mentioned by Evelyn in his " Diary." Of them he says :—" I believe the world can show nothing nobler of the kind than the stories of Abraham and Tobit." They are supposed to have been executed by Bernard Van Orlay, a pupil of Raffaelle. They were bought by Oliver Cromwell, and valued in the inventory at £8,260. At the entrance to the hall are some smaller pieces of similar tapestry, but of earlier date.

At the west end of the hall is the "Minstrels' Gallery," above which is arranged a group of armour, halberts, pikes, and banners.

This hall (as stated above) was occasionally used as a theatre for plays and masques in the merry days of Queen Elizabeth. It was again used for a similar purpose as late

FOUNTAIN COURT.

as the reign of George I., when, however, not more than seven plays were performed. It is significant that one of these dramas, acted on the 1st of October, 1718, was *Henry VIII*. Sir R. Steele, being asked by a grave nobleman—after Shakespeare's *Henry VIII*. had been performed here—how it pleased the king, replied—"So terribly well, that I was afraid, my lord, I should have lost all my actors; for I was not sure the king would not keep them to fill the posts about the Court, for that he saw them so fit for the play."

On the 16th of October, 1731, the hall was

again used for a theatrical performance for the entertainment of the Duke of Lorraine, afterwards Emperor of Germany. Not until towards the close of the last century were the disfigurements to this hall removed. In 1829, during the rebuilding of Hampton church, the hall was fitted up for the purposes of divine service, and was used as the parish church for about two years.

After an interval of 150 years, the great hall, in 1880, was once again the scene of a theatrical entertainment. This was an amateur dramatic performance, given by special permission of Her Majesty the Queen, in aid of Princess Frederica's Home at Hampton. A stage was erected above the daïs at the east end of the hall, the large withdrawing-room forming a splendid "green room" for the performers. The plays performed were *Yellow Roses*, a dramatic sketch by Sir Charles Young, which was enacted by the author and Lady Monckton, and *Tears*, an amusing trifle, in which also Sir Charles Young and Lady Monckton assumed the principal characters.

"The circumstances of regal banqueting connected with the hall," writes Mr. Brewer, in the "Beauties of England and Wales," "are equally numerous and interesting. The unfortunate Catharine Howard was here first openly shown as queen, as also was Catharine Parr, her more prosperous successor. Henry VIII. often kept wassail within these walls; and here, during the Christmas of 1543, he entertained Francis Gonzaga, the Viceroy of Sicily. Edward VI. likewise presided, in puerile magnificence, over the table in the high place in the hall. Philip and Mary kept their Christmas at Hampton Court in 1554."

The withdrawing-room is entered by a doorway from the centre of the daïs in the hall, and is a noble apartment, sixty-two feet in length by twenty-nine feet in width, and the same in height. The ceiling is beautifully enriched with pendent ornaments, interspersed with the cognizances of the rose, portcullis, and other badges, and with coats-of-arms. The walls of this chamber are hung with tapestry in seven compartments, supposed to be of an early period of the French school. The subjects are as follows:—"Fame," "The Triumph of Virtue," "The Influence of Destiny," "The Death of Hercules," "Peace and War," &c. Above the tapestry are seven large cartoons, painted by Carlo Cignani, the subjects of which are as follows:— "Cupid riding on an Eagle," "The Triumph of Venus," "Cupid with a Torch," "Apollo and Daphne," "Jupiter and Europa," "The Triumph of Bacchus, Venus, and Ariadne," and "Cupid and a Satyr." These cartoons were designed for frescoes

painted in the ducal palace at Parma, about the year 1660.

A passage on the north side of the great hall leads to Tennis Court Lane, whence a good view is obtained of the older parts of the palace, of which the Kitchen Court, with its curious circular erection, is not the least interesting.

The Fountain Court, or Eastern Quadrangle, as it is now called, was built, as we have already noted, by Sir Christopher Wren, in 1690. It is encircled by a colonnade of the Ionic order, with duplicated columns. Wren was appointed to the office of Surveyor-General of his Majesty's Works in 1668, and was employed by William III. to pull down part of the old palace, and to build in its place the quadrangle now under notice. The alterations and additions made here by Sir Christopher are far from being favourable specimens of his art. The studies made by him from the buildings of Louis XIV. had but too visible an effect on his palaces and private buildings; so that, as Horace Walpole remarks, "it may be considered fortunate that the French built only palaces, and not churches, and therefore St. Paul's escaped, though Hampton Court was sacrificed to the god of false taste." Wren's failure at Hampton Court palace, however, may be largely attributed to his having worked there under the directions of King William, one of whose favourite residences it was, and whose taste in architecture was of the lowest grade; indeed, when the arrangement of the low cloisters was criticised, the king took the whole blame on himself, acknowledging that they had been constructed by his own particular orders.

The Fountain Court is nearly a square, more than a hundred feet each way. In the area is a grass-plat railed in, with a circular basin in the centre, and a small fountain playing. This court occupies the site of the chief or grand court, which was described by Hentzner, in the reign of Elizabeth, as "paved with square stone, and having in its centre a fountain which throws up water, covered with a gilt crown, on the top of which is a statue of Justice, supported by columns of black and white marble."

The chapel is situated on the north side of the Fountain Court. The edifice having undergone alterations in successive reigns, its architecture can scarcely be assigned to any particular period. On the outer wall, on either side of the door, are the arms of Henry VIII. impaling those of Seymour, and the initials "H. J." united by a true lover's knot. From these indications it appears probable that the chapel was a part of the additional buildings constructed by King

Henry, and finished during the short-lived felicity arising from his marriage with Jane Seymour. Mr. Lysons, in his notice of Hampton Court, gives the following particulars concerning the chapel :— " Before the civil war this chapel was ornamented with stained glass and pictures, which were demolished in 1645, as appears by the following paragraph, taken from a weekly paper of that date : 'Sir Robert Harlow gave order (according to the ordinance of Parliament) for the pulling down and demolishing of the Popish and superstitious pictures in Hampton Court, where this day the altar was taken down, and the table brought into the body of the church, the rails pulled down and the steps levelled, and the Popish pictures and superstitious images that were in the glass windows were also demolished, and order given for the new glazing them with plain glass ; and among the rest there was pulled down the picture of "Christ nailed to the Cross," which was placed right over the altar, and the picture of Mary Magdalen and others weeping by the foot of the cross, and some other idolatrous pictures, were pulled down and demolished.' The chapel was fitted up in its present state by Queen Anne ; it is pewed with black and white marble, and fitted with Norway oak. The carving is by Gibbons. The original roof remains—a plain Gothic pattern, with pendent ornaments. Hentzner, who visited England in Queen Elizabeth's reign, speaks of the chapel as most splendid ; and says that the queen's closet was transparent, with windows of crystal."

The State apartments are approached from the Fountain Court by means of the grand staircase, the walls and ceiling of which were painted by Verrio with mythological subjects, supposed to be allusions to the marriage of the Thames and Isis. Upon the ceiling are represented Jupiter and Juno seated upon a rich throne, with Ganymede riding upon Jupiter's eagle, and presenting to him the cup. Juno's peacock is in the front, and one of the fatal sisters is waiting, with her scissors in her hand, ready to cut the thread of life, should Jove give her orders. Verrio—the propriety of whose taste may be estimated by the fact of his having introduced himself and Sir Godfrey Kneller in one of his pictures in long periwigs, as spectators of our Saviour healing the sick—was paid for the whole palaces of Windsor and Hampton Court ceilings, sides, and back stairs at the rate of 8s. a foot, exclusive of gilding, and had wine daily allowed him, and lodgings in the palaces, and, when his eyesight failed, a pension of £200 per annum and an allowance of wine for life. He was devoted, from religious and

political feelings, to the government of James II., and it seems that he was prevailed on with much difficulty even to *paint* for the successor of his former master.

The first room entered is the Guard Chamber, the walls of which are partly covered with arms and military trophies, in the shape of halberts, muskets, swords, &c., fancifully disposed in various ornamental forms. On the lower panels of this apartment are a few pictures, mostly portraits of admirals and military subjects ; and including a spirited battle-piece, by Giulio Romano, and Canaletti's " Ruins of the Colosseum." It will be impossible in the space at our disposal to mention anything near a tithe of the pictures and objects of interest that meet the eye of the visitor whilst passing through the long suite of rooms, nearly thirty in number. Most of the chambers are hung with tapestry, and have painted ceilings. In one he will be attracted by the picture of " St. William," painted by Giorgione ; in another by the portrait of Bandinelli the sculptor, by Correggio, which has always been considered a picture of great delicacy ; nor will the paintings by Velasquez fail to arrest his attention. In the Audience Chamber, pictures by Ricci, Giulio Romano, Rubens, and Sebastian del Piombo, will meet his gaze ; whilst in the King's Drawing-room he may compare the " Agony of our Saviour in the Garden," by Nicholas Poussin, with a military picture by the late Sir William Beechey, in which George III. is represented as reviewing the 10th Hussars. In the bed-room of William III. he may feast his eyes on the counterfeit presentments of the " beauties " of the Court of Charles II. In this chamber is the State bed of Queen Charlotte, the hangings of which were worked for her Majesty by the orphan daughters of clergymen. The ceiling of this room, which is in good preservation, was painted by Verrio, and is intended to represent " Night " and " Morning." The clock in this room was made by Daniel Quare, and requires winding-up only once in twelve months. The portraits round the room are as follows :—Anne, Duchess of York ; Lady Byron ; Princess Mary, as Diana ; Queen Catharine ; Mrs. Knott ; Duchess of Portsmouth ; Duchess of Richmond ; Nell Gwynne ; Countess of Rochester ; Duchess of Somerset ; Mrs. Lawson ; Countess of Northumberland ; Lady Denham ; Countess of Sunderland ; Lady Middleton ; Lady Whitmore ; Countess of Ossory ; Duchess of Cleveland ; and the Countess de Grammont. Of the above portraits, those of the Duchess of Somerset, Mrs. Knott, and Mrs. Lawson, were painted by Verelot, the Duchess of Portsmouth by Gasker, and the remainder by Sir Peter Lely. There are thirteen other portraits of ladies, whose names are unknown.

Another apartment, formerly known as the "Beauty Room," contains the portraits of Queen Mary, consort of William III., and the following eight distinguished ladies of her court:— The Duchess of St. Albans ; Isabella, Duchess of Grafton ; Carey, Countess of Peterborough ; the Countess of Ranelagh ; Mary, Countess of Essex ; Mary, Countess of Dorset ; Lady Middleton ; and Mrs. Scrope. These "beauties" were painted by Sir Godfrey Kneller. "The thought," says Lord Orford, "was the queen's, during one of the king's absences, and contributed much to make her unpopular ; as I have heard from the authority of the old Countess of Carlisle (daughter of Arthur, Earl of Essex), and who died within these few years, and remembered the event. She added that the famous Lady Dorchester advised the queen against it, saying—'Madam, if the king was to ask for the portraits of all the wits in the court, would not the rest think he called them fools ?'"

It is on record that among the visitors one day, in the middle of the last century, were "those goddesses, the Gunnings"—the two fair sisters who turned the heads of half London, and became respectively Lady Coventry and Duchess of Hamilton. As they were going into the "Beauty Room" another batch of visitors arrived. The housekeeper said : "This way, ladies ; here are the beauties." The fair Gunnings flew, or pretended to fly, into a passion, and asked her "what she meant by her words ; for they had come to see the palace, and not to be made a show themselves."

The Queen's Gallery—or, as it is sometimes called, the Tapestry Gallery, from seven pieces of tapestry, taken from the history of Alexander the Great, from paintings by Le Brun—is eighty feet long and twenty-five feet wide. The tapestries have now given place to an interesting and well-arranged collection of pictures, among which the Elizabethan group is well worth the attention of the visitor ; among them are two large pictures, representing the embarkation of Henry VIII. at Dover, and the meeting of that king and Francis I. of France in the field called the Cloth of Gold, near Calais.

"These pictures are not only historically very interesting, but," says Mr. Jesse, "a curious fact is connected with one of them. After the death of Charles I., the Commonwealth were in treaty with a French agent, who had expressed his desire of purchasing these pictures for the King of France. Philip, Earl of Pembroke, who was a great admirer and an excellent judge of painting, and considered these valuable pictures an honour to an English palace, came privately into the royal apartments, cut out that part of the picture where King Henry's head was painted, and, putting it into his pocket-book, retired unnoticed. The French agent, finding the picture mutilated, declined purchasing it. After the Restoration, the then Earl of Pembroke delivered the mutilated piece to Charles II., who ordered it to be replaced. On looking at the picture in a side light, the insertion of the head is very visible. It may fairly be doubted whether Holbein painted these pictures, they are too coarse ; besides, he did not arrive in England till six years after the interview depicted, and therefore could not have taken the many excellent English portraits which are introduced into the pictures at that time. It is, however, immaterial, as their intrinsic merit and historical interest will always demand attention."

Throughout the whole of the State apartments there is much to gratify the taste of those who love to revel in "Pictureland," particularly if their taste or curiosity leads them to penetrate the semblances of those who lived in "the good old times," whether they be by Rembrandt, Titian, the Claudes, the Guidos, Caravaggio, Spagnoletto, Mantegna, or Holbein.

Among the paintings which enrich the principal apartments there now remain but comparatively few of those which were brought together with so judicious a hand by Charles I. The most noble purchase made by that king—the seven great cartoons of Raffaelle, which found here for many years their appropriate home—have been removed to the South Kensington Museum, as more easily accessible to the student as well as the London sight-seer. They had previously been on view at Windsor Castle, and before that occupied an octagonal apartment at Buckingham Palace.* These cartoons were executed by Raffaelle while engaged in the chambers of the Vatican, under the auspices of Popes Julius II. and Leo X. As soon as they were finished they were sent to Flanders to be copied in tapestry, for adorning the Pontifical apartments ; but the tapestries were not conveyed to Rome till after the decease of Raffaelle, and probably not before the dreadful sack of that city in 1527, under the pontificate of Clement VII. ; when Raffaelle's scholars having fled from thence, none were left to inquire after the original cartoons, which lay neglected in the store-rooms of the manufactory, the money for the tapestry having never

---

* See "Old and New London," Vol. IV., p. 64.

been paid. The revolution that happened soon after in the Low Countries prevented their being noticed during a period in which works of art were wholly neglected. They were purchased by Charles I., at the recommendation of Rubens, but had been much injured by the weavers. At the sale of the royal pictures in 1653 these cartoons were purchased for £300 by Oliver Cromwell, against whom no one would presume to bid. The Protector pawned them to the Dutch Court for upwards of £50,000, and after the revolution King William brought them over again to England, and built a gallery for their reception in Hampton Court. Originally there were twelve of these cartoons, but four of them have been destroyed by damps and neglect. The subjects were "The Adoration of the Magi," "The Conversion of St. Paul," "The Martyrdom of St. Stephen," and "St. Paul before Felix and Agrippa." Two of these were in the possession of the King of Sardinia, and two of Louis XIV. of France, who is said to have offered 100,000 louis d'ors for the seven, which are justly represented as "the glory of England, and the envy of all other polite nations." The twelfth, the subject of which was " The Murder of the Innocents," belonged to a private gentleman in England, who pledged it for a sum of money ; but when the person who had taken this valuable deposit found it was to be redeemed, he greatly damaged the drawing, for which the gentleman brought an action against him.

In spite of the additions made to the collection of pictures here by Charles I., Mr. J. T. Smith, in his " Book for a Rainy Day," somewhat sneeringly endeavours to give the chief praise to Henry VIII. as the greatest promoter of the taste for the fine arts in England. " It is curious to observe," remarks Mr. Smith, " how fond Horace Walpole, and indeed all his followers, have been of attributing the earliest encouragement of the fine arts in England to King Charles I. That is not the fact ; nor is that monarch entitled, munificent as he was, to that degree of praise which biographers have thought proper to attribute to him as a liberal patron ; and this I shall immediately prove. King Henry VIII. was the first English sovereign who encouraged painting, in consequence of Erasmus introducing Hans Holbein to Sir Thomas More, who showed his Majesty specimens of that artist's rare productions. Upon this, the king most liberally invited him to Whitehall, where he gave him extensive employment, not only in decorating the panels and walls of that palace with portraits of the Tudors as large as life, but with easel pictures of the various branches of his family and courtiers, to be placed over doors and other spaces of the State chambers. Holbein may be recorded as the earliest painter of portraits in miniature, which were mostly circular, and all those which I have seen were relieved by blue backgrounds. He was also the designer and draughtsman of numerous subjects for the use of the Court jewellers, as may be seen in a most curious volume preserved in the print-room of the British Museum, many of the drawings in which are beautifully coloured."

Mr. William Howitt, in his " Visits to Remarkable Places," thus concludes his notice of the pictures at Hampton Court :—" Here we must quit the presence of these noblest of the conceptions of the divine Raffaelle—rejoicing, however, that they are now free to our contemplation as the very landscape around them, and that we can, at our pleasure, walk into this fine old palace, linger before these sacred creations at our will, and return to them again and again.

" Quitting them, we shall now hastily quit the Palace of Hampton Court ; for though there is a small room adjoining, containing Casanova's drawing of Raffaelle's celebrated picture of 'The Transfiguration,' and several other interesting paintings, and yet another long Portrait Gallery, filled from end to end with the forms and faces of celebrated persons by celebrated artists, we can but gaze and pass on ; and yet, who would not delight to have that one room to himself, to haunt day after day, and to ponder over the features and costumes of Locke, Newton, Sheridan, Boyle, Charles XII. of Sweden, Caroline, the Queen of George II., made interesting to all the world by the author of 'Waverley,' in the interview of Jeanie Deans ? Who would not pause a moment before even the little Geoffrey Hudson, and think of all that diminutive knight's wrath, his duel, and his adventure in the pie ? Lord Falkland's fine and characteristic face is a sight worth a long hour's walk on a winter's morning ; and the Earl of Surrey, flaming in his scarlet dress, scarlet from head to foot—who would not stop and pay homage to the memory of his bravery, his poetry, and his Geraldine ? But there are Rosamond Clifford and Jane Shore. Lely had not brought the Graces into England in their day, and therefore, instead of those wondrous beauties which we expect them, we find them— ghosts.

" Here, too, is another portrait of Queen Elizabeth, a full-length by Zucchero, where 'stout Queen Bess' is not in one of her masculine moods of laconic command—when she looked 'every inch a queen' —but in a most melancholy and romantic one indeed. She is clad in a sort of Armenian dress —a loose figured robe, without shape, without sleeves, and trimmed with fur—a sort of high cap, and Eastern slippers. She is represented in a wood, with a stag near her; and on a tree are cut, one below the other, after the fashion of the old romances, the following sentences:— INJUSTI JUSTA QUERELA. — MEA SIC MIHI. — DOLOR EST MEDICINA DOLORI. And at the foot of the tree, on a scroll, these verses, supposed to be of the royal manufacture :—

" ' The restless swallow fits my restless minde,
In still revivinge, still renewinge wrongs ;
Her just complaints of cruelty unkinde
Are all the musique that my life prolonges
With pensive thoughtes my weepinge stags I crowne,
Whose melancholy teares my cares expresse ;
Hes teares in sylence, and my sighes unknowne,
Are all the physicke that my harmes redresse.
My onely hopes was in this goodly tree,
Which I did plant in love, bringe up in care,
But all in vaine, for now too late I see
The shales be mine, the kernel others are.
My musique may be plaintes, my physique teares,
If this be all the fruite my love-tree beares.'

"We step through the door on which Jane Shore's spectral visage is hung, and lo! we are on the Queen's Staircase, and descend once more to the courts of Wolsey. Long as we have lingered in this old palace, we have had but a glimpse of it. Its antiquities, its pleasantness, and its host of paintings, cannot be comprehended in a visit : they require a volume; and a most delicious volume that would be which should take us leisurely through the whole, giving us the spirit and the history, in a hearty and congenial tone, of its towers and gardens, and all the renowned persons who have figured in its ⌐ rts, or whose limned shapes now figure on its walls."

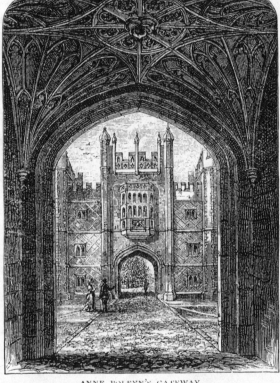

ANNE BOLEYN'S GATEWAY.
(*From Lysons.*)

The gardens of Hampton Court are about forty-four acres in extent. They were originally laid out by Cardinal Wolsey, and greatly improved by Queen Elizabeth and Charles II. It is said that the gardens were closed against the public in the time of George I., who, being unaware of the circumstance, inquired of the gardener one morning why the gates were shut against the people. "Because, your Majesty," replied the man in office, "they *steal* the flowers." "What," returned the good-natured monarch, "are my English subjects so fond of flowers? Plant more, then!" This story, however, is told also of Kensington. George III. also took great pride and pleasure in them, and often drove over from Kew to visit them.

The public gardens are separated by an iron fence from what is called the Home Park. The gardens and park were put into their present form by Messrs. Loudoun and Wise, gardeners to their Majesties William and Mary. The gardens themselves are perfectly flat, and are laid out in the Dutch style—stiff and formal, with long-drawn avenues and opening glades, after the fashion of the Low Countries. The east front of the palace is open to the gardens, and is here seen to the best advantage. It is constructed of bright red brick, with stone dressings, and in the centre four fluted three-quarter columns, of the Corinthian order, sustain an angular pediment, on which are sculptured in bas-relief the triumphs of Hercules over Envy. Along this front of the building there is a broad gravel walk, leading, on the one hand, down to the banks of the Thames, and on the other to a gate, called the Flowerpot Gate, which opens on the Kingston Road. At the southern end of the east front is the entrance to the private garden, which contains a few rare plants, the remains of Queen Mary's botanical garden. Here, too, is a large

HAMPTON COURT.

(*From a Print published about* 1770.)

lean-to house, containing the famous grape-vine. The inside dimensions of this house are seventy-two feet in length by thirty feet in breadth. The vine is planted inside the house, and the roof is almost entirely covered with branches, some of which are over a hundred feet in length. The average yearly produce of this vine is said to amount to about 1,200 pounds, and the grapes are sent to supply her Majesty's table. The tree is believed to have been planted in 1768 by Lancelot Brown, who was once chief gardener here, and who afterwards became so much noted as one of the first practitioners of the English style of landscape gardening. On approaching the vine we pass two large greenhouses, which contain some orange-trees and other plants. Amongst them is an orange-myrtle, said to have been brought to this country by William III.

In the reign of Charles II., the large semicircle on the east side of the palace was planted ; but it was not till the reign of William III. that the grounds were brought to anything like perfection. At this period the art of clipping yew and other trees into regular figures and fantastic shapes reached its highest point, being greatly favoured by the king. Four urns, said to be the first that were used in the gardens, were also planted by William III. in front of the palace. Walpole says that the walls were once covered with rosemary, and that the trees were remarkable specimens of the "topiary" art, as the fashion of clipping trees into stiff unnatural forms was then called.

On the northern side of the palace is a large space of ground, called "the Wilderness," which was planted and laid out by William III. In this part of the grounds is a labyrinth, or maze, which affords much amusement to visitors. Near the labyrinth is an entrance known as the "Lion Gates," which are particularly handsome, being designed in a bold and elegant style. The large stone piers of the gates are richly decorated, their cornices supported by fluted columns, and surmounted by two colossal lions *couchant*.

Hampton Court Palace is supplied with water from some springs in Coombe Wood, whence it is conducted through pipes which were laid down by Cardinal Wolsey at a very great outlay. The distance is about two miles, in the most direct line, and the leaden pipes which convey the water are carried across the bottom of the River Thames. There are two pipes from each conduit, making altogether eight miles of leaden pipes.

Hampton Court (or the Home) Park immediately adjoins the palace gardens, and is about five miles in circumference. It extends from the borders of the gardens to Hampton Wick, and is bounded on the south by the River Thames, and on the north by the high road to Kingston. This park is well stocked with deer. It is watered by a canal about half a mile in length, having a fine avenue of lime-trees on each side of it. Another canal to correspond was partly excavated by William III., and near it the spot is still pointed out where the accident happened which cost him his life. The avenues in this park were planted by William III. Near the upper deer-pen is a fine old oak-tree about forty feet in circumference; and there is also near the stud-house an elm known by the name of "King Charles's Swing," which is peculiarly curious in shape. A building, called the Pavilion, which was erected by Sir Christopher Wren in the reign of William III., was the occasional residence of the late Duke of Kent, in his official capacity as "ranger" of this park.

In the park may still be seen some lines of fortifications, which were originally constructed for the purpose of teaching the art of war to William, Duke of Cumberland, when a boy—the same duke who became so celebrated afterwards in the Scottish rising of 1745.

The Stud-house, in the centre of the Home Park, was founded by the Stuarts; but George IV. was its great supporter and maintainer, for both as prince regent and as king he was devoted to racing, and began breeding race-horses here systematically and on an extensive scale.

The cream-coloured horses used on State occasions by the sovereign are kept here. They are descended from those brought over from Hanover by the princes of the Brunswick line, being a special product of those countries. The breed is kept up here most religiously, and the animals are the last representatives of the Flemish horses, once so fashionable. They are slow and pompous in their action, and many of them are upwards of twenty years old. They look small in comparison with the great lumbering state coach; but most of them are sixteen, or at least fifteen, hands high. The State harness and trappings of each horse do not weigh less than two hundred-weight.

Here are kept the Arabs and other Eastern horses presented to her Majesty. It is not etiquette to give any of them away, much less to sell them ; nor are they put to any use, nor killed when they get old. They have a happy enjoyment of life, till death calls them away.

"Nimrod," writing in *The Turf* in 1834, observes that "great regard has always been paid here to what is known in sporting circles as 'stout blood'—namely, horses of sinew and strength, rather than of speed." He adds a list of the sires and mares kept here, and also states that "from prudential motives the royal stud at Hampton Court was broken up, only one or two sires and mares being kept."

Sir Richard Steele was, for a time, surveyor of the royal stables here; and the Earl of Albemarle, Groom of the Stole, lived for some years at the "Stud-house," which is still the official residence of the Master of the Horse, though not generally occupied as such.

In December, 1882, the entire palace had a narrow escape from being destroyed, a large portion of the upper rooms in the east wing, overlooking the gardens and the fountain court, and which were in the occupation of private families, having been accidentally burnt.

In a leading article, congratulating the country on the fact that the galleries have been spared, the *Times* made the following remarks, which may most appropriately close this chapter :—"Hampton Court is pre-eminently the palace of the ordinary Londoner's predilection.

PLAN OF THE MAZE.

This is not, perhaps, because of its historical interest as a relic of Wolsey's magnificence, or as the home of the Stuarts and the elder Georges, nor even exclusively because of the interest attaching to its gallery of pictures. Its place in the heart of Londoners is largely due to more homely associations. It is easily and quickly reached from London, and its surroundings are rich in everything that the country-going Londoner has learnt to love. Its stately and rich-toned buildings, its well-kept gardens, its spacious parks with their matchless trees, and its unrivalled situation on the banks of the placid Thames, all give it an attraction which for variety of charm can hardly be matched in England. To this must be added the fact that the palace contains the only national collection of pictures which is open to the public on Sundays, and this, perhaps, accounts as much as anything else for the pre-eminent popularity which Hampton Court enjoys. Thousands to whom the historical associations of the place are rather vague, thousands more whose enjoyment of a gallery or pictures is

neither very intelligent nor very keen, find their way throughout the summer to Hampton Court, and return much the better for their outing, even if their knowledge of history remains as vague as ever, and their feeling for art as cold. For this reason alone—because of the simple and wholesome pleasures it affords in one way or another to every visitor—the destruction of Hampton Court would have been regarded as an irreparable calamity. Apart from its surroundings, moreover, which we suspect attract more visitors than its contents, the palace itself is a building which the country could ill afford to spare. It is a record of pomp of Wolsey and of the genius of Wren, and its history includes associations as diverse as the theological lucubrations of James I. and the revels of his scapegrace grandson, the gloomy broodings of Cromwell in his hours of dejection, and the busy statecraft of William III. Of the treasures of its picture gallery it is unnecessary to speak at length. The collection, as a whole, is rather copious than select. Some few pictures are undoubtedly of priceless value; the art of the world would be palpably the poorer for their destruction. Others, again, are interesting as specimens of painters whose works are rare, or as commemorating events of moment in English history. But these are only a small percentage of the whole. The remainder are interesting rather because they have long hung on the walls of Hampton Court, and seem to partake of the character of the place, than because they can claim any very eminent merit of their own. There is some royal furniture also of ancient date in several of the public rooms of the palace, and a portion of this is reported to have been damaged by the floods of water employed to extinguish the fire. Such things have a certain popular interest, no doubt, but if anything was to be destroyed, it is safe to rejoice that a capricious fate has spared the pictures and only taken the upholstery. If by an irreparable stroke of fortune the Holbeins, the Mantegnas, or any other of the real treasures of the gallery had been destroyed, it would have been a poor consolation to learn that Queen Anne's bed had been preserved, or even that her portmanteau was safe."

CHAPTER XIV.

FELTHAM, SUNBURY, AND HALLIFORD.

" Est et honor campis."—Ovid.

Situation, Etymology, and General Appearance of Feltham—Population, &c.—Notice of the Parish in Domesday Book—Descent of the Manor —The Parish Church—Death of Miss Frances Kelly, the Actress—Middlesex Industrial School—The Convalescent Home—Sunbury— Its Etymology—History of the Manor—Col Kenyngton, otherwise Kempton—A Royal Palace—Kempton House—Kempton Park Race-course—Sunbury Common—Sunbury Parish Church—Roman Catholic Chapel—The Village of Sunbury—Sunbury Place—The Pumping Stations of the London Water-works Companies—Thames Angling Preservation Society—The Manor of Charlton—Halliford.

THE parish of Feltham lies to the south-west of Hampton, and is particularly flat and uninteresting. It is bounded on the east by the parish of Hanworth, which we have already dealt with in a previous chapter (see pages 69, 70). The name, according to Mr. Brewer, in the "Beauties of England," is supposed to be a corruption of *Feldham*, signifying the "Field Village, or Village in a Field."

The country all about here, and indeed as far west as Staines, is covered with market gardens, or fields devoted to vegetable produce, which is sent up to market at Covent Garden. The village of Feltham is long and straggling; it is chiefly of a rural and humble character, and contains a few old-fashioned houses and shops; but in the immediate neighbourhood, particularly to the north and west of the village, and at Feltham Hill, about a mile to the south, are several better-class villas and residences of a more ornamental description. There is also here a station on the Windsor branch of the South-Western Railway. In 1871 the number of houses in the parish was 387, whilst the population numbered 2,748 souls, but this estimate included upwards of 900 persons in the Middlesex Industrial School. This number has somewhat decreased since that period, being, according to the returns for 1881, only 2,709.

The manor of Feltham is thus noticed in "Domesday Book":—"Earl Moreton (Mortain in Normandy) holds the manor of Feltham, taxed at twelve hides. The arable land is twelve carucates. There are six hides in demesne, on which is one plough; three more might be employed. The villanes have eight ploughs. There are fourteen villanes, who hold a virgate each; five others have each a virgate each, and two slaves, or bondmen. There is meadow-land equal to ten carucates, and pasture for the cattle of the village. The total value is £6 per annum; when it came into the Earl's possession it was only £4, but in the reign of King Edward it was £8. Two thanes were then seised of this manor: one of them, a vassal of the king, held five hides as a separate manor; the other, a vassal of Earl Harold, had seven hides as

a separate manor also, and could alien to whom he pleased."

From the above extract it will be seen that this parish was devoted to agriculture as far back as eight centuries ago.

The two manors above referred to were united under the Earl of Mortain, and became subsequently the property of Hawise, Countess of Rumaze, who gave the conjoined estate to the Hospital of St. Giles' Without-the-Bars, near Holborn, in whose possession it remained till the dissolution in 1537, when it was surrendered to the king, Henry VIII. Early in the seventeenth century the manor was granted in fee to trustees for Lord Cottington, and it was subsequently sold, together with the advowson, to Sir Thomas Chamber. Since then, the property has changed hands many times. "The manor of Feltham," observes Mr. Brewer, in his "Beauties of England and Wales," "is only nominal, and exercises no manorial rights, the whole of this parish being subject to the jurisdiction of the adjacent manor of Kennington"— now Kempton.

The greater part of this Thames valley would seem to have been anything rather than a haunt to the Muses, who doubtless thought it dull and tame. It has, in fact, no literary history.

The parish church, which stands on the road to Sunbury, is a plain brick-built edifice, dating from the beginning of the present century, when the taste for ecclesiastical architecture was at a very low ebb. It is dedicated to St. Dunstan, and replaced the former parish church, which had become ruinous and dilapidated. The old church is described in Lysons' "Middlesex" as "a small structure, consisting of a chancel, nave, and a north aisle. It is built of flint and stone, chiefly the *lapis compositus*, commonly called the 'plum-pudding' stone. At the west end is a wooden tower and spire, almost covered with ivy, issuing from a single stem, eighteen inches in girth." That building was taken down in 1802, and the present church erected in its place. This latter edifice was enlarged by the addition of aisles in 1856. At the west end is a tower with an embattled parapet, surmounted by a spire. The edifice contains a few monuments preserved from the old church, but none of general interest.

It appears from a survey made by order of Parliament in 1650, that Job Iggleton, the then incumbent, was presented by President Bradshaw, who possessed the estates of Lord Cottington which were confiscated for his attachment to the royal cause.

In the churchyard is the grave of William Wynne Ryland, an eminent line engraver of the last century, who was executed in 1793 for forgery on the East India Company.

Another church of greater pretensions has of late sprung up near the railway station, to meet the wants of an increasing population.

At Feltham, in December, 1882, died " a nonagenarian and something more," Miss Frances Maria Kelly, an actress of some note in her time. Born in the year 1790, she was one of the last survivors of a great school of actors, her first appearance on the stage dating as far back as 1807. In the following year she was a member of Mr. Colman's company at the Haymarket, and she enjoyed a high reputation at Drury Lane, Covent Garden, and the English Opera House. Among her contemporaries were Mrs. Siddons, John Kemble, Edmund Kean, and Mrs. Jordan. In 1840, as recorded in OLD AND NEW LONDON,* Miss Kelly founded a school for acting in Dean Street, Soho, which afterwards blossomed into a theatre, and is now known as the Royalty.

In the fields to the west of the village stands the Middlesex Industrial School or Reformatory for boys convicted of crime. It was opened in 1859, and is under the charge and control of the magistrates for the county of Middlesex. The building, which, since its foundation, has been greatly enlarged, is capable of accommodating about 1,000 boys, who are sentenced to detention here for periods varying from one to three years, the ages of the boys ranging from seven to fourteen years. It is constructed of red brick with stone dressings, and consists of a large principal building, a chapel, infirmary, workshops, farms, sewage works, &c.; in the grounds is the model of a ship, for the purpose of enabling the boys to practise seamanship, or at all events to learn the rudiments of nautical tactics. Nearly 150 acres of land are kept under cultivation by the inmates, so as to supply the wants of the establishment.

At Feltham a convalescent home has been established in connection with Mrs. Hilton's

Crèche, Orphan Home, and Infant Infirmary, at Stepney. There is also a " Nunnery" here, under the superintendence of " Father Ignatius."

Passing southward by Feltham Hill and Meadhurst Park, we now make our way towards Sunbury, a pleasant river-side village a mile and a half above Hampton Court, in the Hundred of Spelthorne, and a spot which has long been a favourite resort of anglers. The name of this place is often written, in ancient records, " Sunnabyri," or " Sunneberie," the derivation of which is from two Saxon words : " sunna," the sun, and " byri," a town. In " Domesday Book " the manor is entered under the name of " Suneberie," and is there described as parcel of " the ancient demesnes of the church of St. Peter," otherwise Westminster Abbey, to which it was given in the time of Edward the Confessor. In 1223 it was assigned to the Bishop of London, and the vicarage to the Dean and Chapter of St. Paul's. The latter arrangement holds good to the present day. James I. conveyed the manor to the Stratfords, and in 1693 it was possessed by Sir John Tyrwhit, son-in-law of Francis Phelips, who had become possessed of the property in 1676. Early in the last century it was sold to John Crosse, and having subsequently changed hands several times, finally passed into the hands of the Mitchisons, by whose family the manor is still possessed. The manor-house, now the seat of Mr. William Anthony Mitchison, is a large red-brick building, on the western side of the parish.

Besides the principal manor of Sunbury, and a manor formerly styled " Cerdentone," but now Charlton, there is a manorial district, mentioned in " Domesday Book " under the name of Chenetone. " This manor," observes Mr. Brewer, in the " Beauties of England," " was afterwards termed *Col Kenyngton*, or *Cold Kennington*, and is now known by the name of Kempton. Robert, Earl of Cornwall and Mortain, was succeeded in his title and estates by his son William, who rebelled against Henry I., and his estates were seized by that king in the year 1104. The manor thus becoming vested in the Crown, the manor-house was constituted a royal dwelling, and it so remained until the reign of King Edward III." Lysons, in his " Middlesex Parishes," makes the following observations respecting this manor :—"It is probable, from the name of this manor, that the manor-house had been a royal palace during the reign of the Saxon kings. It must be observed that where Kennington occurs in the date of royal charters, it has hitherto, I believe, been always understood of Kennington, near Lambeth, where also was a palace ; for I cannot find that even tradition has preserved the memory of the palace which once stood in Kempton Park, but, on the contrary, supposes the traces of ancient buildings which occur there to have been the remains of a religious house, of whose existence there are no proofs either from history or record."

The manor-house, or palace of Col Kenyngton is mentioned in a survey made by order of Edward III. in 1331, for the purpose of inquiring into the state of the palace and park at that time. The original

calculated at 30s. The house called the *Aumerye* is so ruinous that it threatens to fall down. There is wanting in the larder a door with proper fastenings, which may be made for 2 shillings. The repairs of the chamber beyond the gate, with the steps leading to it, are estimated at 100 shillings. The dresser in the great kitchen and hall is quite broken down. The repairs of the farm-house and the gate next to the granary are estimated at 40s. The repair of the park-wall is estimated at 13s. 4d., and that of the walls round the manor at 10s."

HALLIFORD.   (*See page* 176.)

of this document is preserved among the public records, and it describes the palace as having fallen, through neglect, into a state of dangerous dilapidation. A translation of this document is given by Lysons in his account of the parishes of Middlesex, in which the following particulars occur :—" There are dilapidations in the great hall, and in the pantry and buttery at the east end, the expense of repairing which is estimated at £4 6s. 8d. The great chamber, with the chapel and wardrobe adjoining, are much out of repair, as are the Queen's chamber, with the chapel and wardrobe adjoining. The repairs of the cellar under the Queen's chamber are estimated at 13 shillings. The repair of the chamber called the *Aleye*, which must have new beams, are

The custody of the ancient manor of Col Kenyngton was granted by the reigning sovereign to different persons, either for a certain term of years or for life, on condition of their paying yearly a valuable consideration, until 1631, when it was granted in fee to Sir Robert Killigrew. The manor-house is mentioned in the diary of the first Lord Shaftesbury as the seat of his relative, Mr. Carew Raleigh, whom he occasionally visited there. Later on, the manor was inherited by Sir John Chardin Musgrave, who sold it to a Mr. Edward Hill. By this gentleman many noble and venerable forest-trees, by which the park was thickly adorned, were cut down, and the demesne despoiled of much of its picturesque beauty. Kempton Park, however, has still some fine pollard-oaks dotted up and down it. It is about 300 acres in extent, and is bounded on the east and north by a little stream, or rivulet, a tributary of the Thames, which rises near Bedfont and Feltham. The Thames Valley branch of the South Western Railway also skirts the north side of the park. In a map of Middlesex published in 1823, Kempton House figures as the property of F. Manners, Esq., but it has since several times changed hands.

entered by a pointed and embattled gateway. The interior of the mansion is not yet finished, but many of the rooms have an air of comfort, and are of agreeable proportions." The author adds in a foot-note :—"Since the above account of Kempton House was written, the 'Gothic greenhouse,' forcing-houses, &c., have been sold by public auction. At the same time, some painted glass in the windows and doors was exposed to sale in a similar manner. It would thus appear that it is not intended to complete the mansion ; but

SUNBURY CHURCH. *(See page 176.)*

Kempton House, at the beginning of the present century, appears to have been a sort of rival to "Strawberry Hill." Writing in 1816, Mr. Brewer thus describes the mansion in the "Beauties of England" :—"The present mansion of Kempton is an imitation of the Gothic style, different parts of which were executed under the direction of both the last-named gentlemen (Mr. Hill and Mr. Fish). Indeed, it is evident that the whole was constructed in attention to a single design. The building is extensive, but has, on the exterior, all the gloom of the ancient English style, without any of those fascinating graces which were sometimes produced by genius while revelling in entire disdain of rule. Yet ample use is made of what is termed the Gothic; even the stables and greenhouse have embattled parapets, and the garden is

we have suffered our article to remain as previously written, from a consideration that it may be the only descriptive notice extant of a costly building that will probably soon be levelled with the ground."

The present house is a good substantial mansion of the ordinary type. There are no traces visible of the ancient palace. About 400 acres of Kempton Park are enclosed within a ring fence, and set apart as a race-course. It is close by the Sunbury Station, on the Thames Valley Railway, and is much such another place as "Sandown," near Esher, in Surrey. Here steeplechases and coursing races take place, and its spring and autumn meetings are largely patronised.

Sunbury Common is a large tract of not very good or profitable land, occupying the northern part of the parish, towards Ashford. It has been largely enclosed during the past half century.

The parish church of Sunbury, dedicated to St. Mary, was built in the middle of the last century, on the site of an older church which had been taken down. It was erected by Mr. Wright, who was some time Clerk of the Works at Hampton Court, and was long an unsightly brick structure, of little or no architectural pretensions. Its appearance, however, has been immensely improved of late years by the insertion of new windows and the carrying out of other structural arrangements, including a porch at the western end, enriched with arcades at the sides and decorative carvings, and a semi-circular chancel. The church is, in fact, one of the cleverest transformations of a "Church-warden" structure into a Byzantine church to be seen in the kingdom. The tower, which is a conspicuous object as seen from the river, is surmounted by a parapet and· a singular-looking cupola. On the south wall of the church is a monument to Lady Jane, sister of Philip, Duke of Wharton, and the last of her noble family. Her ladyship was the wife of Mr. Robert Coke, of Longford, in Derbyshire, and died in 1761. The churchyard is tolerably crowded with tombstones, but there are none calling for particular mention.

Besides one or two places of worship for Dissenters of different denominations, there is in the village of Sunbury a Roman Catholic chapel of some little architectural pretensions. It was consecrated by Archbishop (now Cardinal) Manning in 1869, and is built of Kentish rag and Bath stone, in the Early English style. The altar, which is enriched with precious stones and mosaic work, was the gift of Mr. Richard Lamb, of River Meades.

The village of Sunbury lies principally along the left bank of the River Thames, and contains several good old-fashioned brick-built dwelling-houses and shops. In Lewis's "Topography" (1835) the population is given as 1,863, a number which had increased in 1871 to 3,368 (when the houses are recorded in the census returns as 663), and ten years later to 3,500.

Sunbury appears to have been formerly a favourite locality for the residence of gentry, its "sunny" situation on the north bank of the Thames, with its pleasantly-situated villas, rendering the spot one of the most attractive in the immediate neighbourhood of London. Among the residents here at the end of the last century was the celebrated Admiral Lord Hawke.

At the eastern end of the village is Sunbury Place, which, at the commencement of the present century, was the occasional residence of the Hon. Percy Wyndham. The mansion is described in the "Beauties of England" at that time as showing four fronts, and as having an ornamental pavilion at each corner.

The opposite, or Surrey, shore is here flat, and of no very interesting character; but the river scenery in the neighbourhood, with its eyots and weirs and swans, is pleasant and attractive to water-parties and fishermen. Both here and on the opposite shore are the pumping-works and filtering reservoirs of two or three London Water-works Companies. At Sunbury are the rearing ponds of the Thames Angling Preservation Society, and the broad reach of the river at this point affords good fishing for jack and barbel, and occasionally trout. Nearly 700 yards of the river, extending from the weir eastward to the break-water, are known as "Sunbury Deeps," and are maintained by the Thames Conservancy.

Passing from the regions of fact to those of fancy, we may remark that through Sunbury passed Oliver Twist, under the charge of Bill Sykes, on his way to commit the burglary at Shepperton. "As they passed Sunbury church," writes Charles Dickens, "the clock struck seven. There was a light in the ferry-house opposite, which streamed across the road, and threw into more sombre shadow a dark yew-tree, with graves beneath it. There was a dull sound of water not far off, and the leaves of the old tree stirred gently in the night wind. It seemed like quiet music for the repose of the dead."

The manor of Charlton mentioned above was given in far-off ages to the Abbey of Merton, in Surrey, by which it was held till the Reformation, after which it passed into the hands of Sir John Mason. Since the beginning of the seventeenth century the manor has been several times alienated. The hamlet of Charlton lies about two miles to the north-west of the village of Sunbury.

Halliford, called in old maps (as late as 1790) Harleyford, extends westward from Sunbury along the river bank. It consists of two divisions, Upper and Lower, the former being a hamlet of Sunbury, and the latter a hamlet in the parish of Shepperton. It is a favourite haunt of anglers, the reaches of the river here abounding in perch and chub. We shall describe it in the next chapter.

CHAPTER XV.

SHEPPERTON, AND THE VALLEY OF THE THAMES.

"While Thames
Among his willows from thy view retires."
AKENSIDE.

Situation and General Appearance of Shepperton—The River Exe—The Village and its Surroundings—Population—Early History and Descent of the Manor—The Manor-house—The Parish Church—The Rectory - Waterside Taverns—Thames Angling—House-boats on the Thames—River Scenery—Shepperton Green and the Railway Station—A Singular Story—Lower Halliford—Discovery of an Ancient Canoe and other Antiquities—The Valley of the Thames—The Wall Closes—Coway Stakes—Littleton.

WHERE the country is a dead flat, and the scenery as unromantic as that of Holland : where the parish churches have been robbed of all antiquity and of more than half their interest : where there are no feudal castles and few old manor-houses : and where the literary associations of the place are a blank—it is scarcely possible to find materials for a chapter which shall satisfy the intelligent reader.

The parish of Shepperton, or Sheperton, is situated to the west of Sunbury, and lies so low that it is often flooded in the winter, and the meadows present the appearance of an inland sea, reaching for miles in either direction, and quite obscuring the banks of the river. There are, too, plenty of pollard-willows, marking the lines of brooks which abound.

The eastern portion of the parish of Shepperton, extending for upwards of a mile down the river towards Sunbury, is known as Lower Halliford, and is so called from a ford over the Thames, a little to the east, by which Julius Cæsar is supposed to have crossed into Middlesex, and of which we shall have more to say presently.

A small river, called the Exe, which rises near Staines, and runs through the park of Littleton, finds its way into the Thames between Upper and Lower Halliford.

Lower Halliford consists for the most part of a small collection of humble, old-fashioned habitations, the gardens of which slope pleasantly down to the water-side. There are, however, one or two dwellings of a better kind, including some pretty villas. The Thames, which here makes an abrupt bend, is crossed at this point by an iron bridge, which connects Lower Halliford with Walton, in Surrey.

Shepperton is a quaint, old-fashioned village, with no one principal street, but built irregularly along several roads, which cross each other. Some of the cottages are very substantial and old-fashioned, their doorways and timbers carrying us back to the days of the Tudors. The village itself is situated on the banks of the Thames, and is of small extent; but there are a few good and substantial dwelling-houses scattered about in the

neighbourhood. In 1871 the number of houses in the parish amounted to only 241, the population numbering 1,126 souls, which has since increased to nearly 1,300.

In the "Domesday Book" the name of this parish is written *Scepertone*, and in other ancient records it is entered as *Scepertune*. *Sceapheardton*, it may be stated, is the Saxon term for the habitation of shepherds. In the " Domesday Record " the manor is said to be held by the Abbot of St. Peter (Westminster Abbey), to whom it was either given or confirmed by Edward the Confessor. The condition of the locality at that distant period may be judged from the fact that "there was land to seven ploughs, and meadow equal to the same. Pasture for the cattle of the village, and one 'wear,' valued at six shillings and eightpence. A priest had fifteen acres."

The manor was alienated, among several others belonging to the Abbey of St. Peter, by Gervase, the abbot, a natural son of King Stephen. It has since passed through various hands, and remained for nearly a century with the Beauchamp family. In the fifteenth century it was possessed by John Tiptoft, Earl of Worcester, who was executed in 1471. At a subsequent period it was vested in the family of Spiller; and at the beginning of the present century it was the property of the Dugdales, of Merevale Hall in Warwickshire.

The manor-house was purchased by the late Mr. William S. Lindsay, M.P., one of the most successful shipowners of our time. He died in 1877, and it is now occupied by his widow. The park lies low, and is frequently flooded. It contains some fine elms.

In most of the parish churches along the Thames Valley the towers alone survive from the pre-Reformation times, the bodies having been pulled down and rebuilt at various dates. But the reverse is the case at Shepperton, where there is a cruciform building, substantially of the Decorated or Edwardian period, though sadly "beautified "—or rather, mutilated—while a most puny and meagre modern brick tower, of the true Churchwarden type, with an embattled parapet, has been added to the west end. The tower, with its parapet, was built in 1710, at the expense of the then rector, the Rev. Lewis Atterbury, a brother of the celebrated Dr. Atterbury, Bishop of Rochester.

From the mention of a priest in the Norman survey, it would appear that there was a church at Shepperton at a very early period, but no marks of such remote antiquity are observable in the present structure.

William Grocyn, who was instituted to this rectory in 1504, is supposed by Newcourt, the author of the "Repertorium," to have been the celebrated friend of Erasmus, and who was largely instrumental in rendering the Greek language a general object of study.

The old rectory, a most substantial red brick building, with projecting beams and a picturesque roof, adjoins the north side of the churchyard. Before it is a small square, now gravelled, but which once, doubtless, was a village green. One side of it is occupied by a hostelry, much frequented by the angling fraternity, "The Anchor." There are other smaller inns, all of them in the same line of business. In fact, the river at Shepperton, and from thence to Chertsey up stream, and to Halliford down, is "piscosissimus." During the summer months the disciples of Izaak Walton flock hither in large numbers, and some good sport is obtained, the river at this point being particularly plentiful in roach, barbel, perch, and jack. "'Tis observed by Gesner," writes honest Izaak Walton, in his "Angler," "that there is none bigger salmon than in England, and none better than in Thames." Salmon have been caught in Shepperton Deep many years back, but they are no longer taken here. Recently much antagonism has existed, respecting the right of fishing in the Thames, between the anglers and the "riparian" owners of land abutting upon the river; and the question has been taken up by a society called the Thames Rights Defence Association.

Of late years a fashion has grown up of spending a part of the summer in a house-boat on the river. These house-boats are much affected by the artist tribe: we see signs of the craft in the easel, the palette, and the paint-box left outside, and on the pictures which adorn the walls of the dwelling-room. These human water-houses, moored to the banks, are simply caravans set on a substantial boat instead of on wheels.

The Thames at this point has many pleasant reaches, and across the river we see Oatlands Park and the fir-woods about Walton and Weybridge. Oatlands was the favourite residence of the Duke and Duchess of York. It is now an hotel for resident families.

In our account of Teddington (see page 130, *ante*) we have spoken at some length of the swans on the Thames. They are to be met with here in plenty during the bright days of summer, and add not a little to the beauty of the river scenery—

> "The gentle swan, with graceful pride,
> Her glossy plumage laves,
> And sailing down the silver tide,
> Divides the whispering waves."

What a charming description of the long reaches about Shepperton, Twickenham, Teddington, and Richmond!

The present Shepperton Green—a long, narrow strip of land, pleasantly fringed with stately elms and chestnut-trees—lies between the village and the railway-station, which is about half a mile distant to the northward, and where is the terminus of the Thames Valley branch of the South-Western Railway.

Shepperton is one of those fortunate places which possesses no "history" worth recording, and, consequently, we may be pardoned for quoting a singular item of information concerning it which appears in "Social Gleanings." The writer remarks:—

"Either the late Mr. Fisher, or Mr. Elwes, of Kempton Park, Sunbury, Middlesex, was in the habit of paying an annual visit to the Rev. Mr. Hubbard, the rector of Shepperton—that well-known rendezvous on the banks of the Thames for the disciples of Izaak Walton. The rector's son, who told me the story, described a peculiarity in regard to this annual visit worth recording. The visitor was stone blind, both his carriage horses were stone blind, and his coachman was a Cyclops, having only one eye."

Here, at the commencement of the present century, lived Mr. Josiah Boydell, a gentleman of some little antiquarian taste. Among the objects which he possessed was a canoe, which would appear to have been constructed in a very remote and rude age. This interesting vestige of antiquity was discovered in September, 1812, and was presented to Mr. Boydell, who furnished the following particulars of it to Mr. Brewer, the author of the "Beauties of England":—"The canoe is obviously hewn out of one solid block of oak, and when perfect the dimensions must have been as follows: the entire length 12 feet, the depth of the sides 20 inches, the width across the top 3 feet 6 inches in the middle. The sides are 1½ inches thick, the keel or bottom is, in the middle, 15 inches wide and 2 inches thick, but grows narrower as it approaches the ends.

Throughout the whole there is not any appearance of a peg or nail having been used. At one end was a piece hewn out of the solid wood, and left across the boat, apparently to hold the sides together ; and it is supposed that there was a similar piece at the other end ; but one end and one side of this curious relic were unfortunately broken before it was inspected by Mr. Boydell. This canoe was found about twenty yards within the brook, in the part nearest to Shepperton town, and was lying in a shelving position, buried in a bed of gravel, within two inches of a layer of peat. Above was a mass of gravel 3 feet 6 inches in depth, and over that were 4 feet of mud. Within a few yards of the canoe, and beneath an equal mass of gravel, mud, &c., was found a stag's horn, the stem and one of the sharp antlers being perfect. . . . Near the above was found a boar's tusk, supposed to be of the wild black breed, and perfect, with the exception of the extreme point, where half an inch appears to have been broken off."

All sorts of antique articles of manufacture, of British, Roman, Saxon, and more recent periods, have been found from time to time in the bed of the Thames. Some idea of their number and variety may be formed if we state that the list of them, including celts, urns, and other pottery, swords, spear-heads, bosses, shields, daggers, seals, pilgrims' tokens, pyxes, axe-heads, coins, &c., occupies a column in the index volume of the Royal Archæological Institute.

The whole valley of the Thames is considered by geologists to be quite "an after-thought" of Nature, having come into being, as shown by Professor Ramsay, after the close of the Miocene age. The vegetation preserved in the London clay is of a tropical and even Indo-Australian character, being composed of palms, cypresses, &c., not unlike those of Tasmania and the Philippine Islands.

"In some small fields, to the north-east of the village, termed the Wall Closes," writes Mr Brewer, in the "Beauties of England" (1816), "are several artificial inequalities of surface, which Gale and Dr. Stukeley conjecture to be the remains of a Roman camp. Mr. Lysons, in his 'Middlesex Parishes,' supposes these to be merely the vestiges of buildings on the site of the old manor-house ; and, according to the tradition of the neighbourhood, an ancient mansion assuredly appears to have occupied a portion of the Wall Closes. But these earthworks, though much levelled within the last twenty years, would still seem more extensive than the probable site of a manorial dwelling, even allowing it to have possessed the ornamental circumstances of terrace walks. The adjacency of remains, confidently supposed to be Roman, induces us to believe that there may be foundation for the conjecture of Dr. Stukeley in regard to these inequalities of surface ; but it certainly appears difficult to pursue them through any traces bearing resemblance to the form of a regular encampment."

At a short distance eastward from Lower Halliford is the site of the celebrated Coway Stakes, which are by tradition said to have been placed across the Thames to oppose the passage of Julius Cæsar over this river, when in pursuit of Cassivelaunus, and many antiquaries have agreed as to the probable connection with fact of such a traditionary assertion.

We read in the account of the second expedition of Julius Cæsar (B.C. 54), that, having landed at Pevensey, he marched further inland, and came upon the Thames at a distance of about eighty miles from the sea. He found the river fordable at only one point ; here the natives were drawn up in array to oppose his passage, and the river was fortified with sharp stakes. He, however, effected his passage, though only with great difficulty, and pursued his way into the territory of Cassivelaunus —probably Hertfordshire, the ancient home of the Cassii. The British chief submitted, and Cæsar returned to Rome, carrying off some of the natives as hostages.

The exact spot where Cæsar crossed the Thames has been for centuries a matter of dispute amongst antiquaries, many of whom have claimed Wallingford, and others Kingston, as the place. But it is recorded, on the most undoubted authority, that stakes sheathed with lead or iron were to be seen at this spot under water down to the seventeenth, and even the eighteenth, century.

Camden and Hearne, two of the very highest authorities on this matter, strongly incline to the belief that Coway Stakes mark the spot, following the testimony of the Venerable Bede, who makes this statement on the authority of a London priest, Nothelin, afterwards Archbishop of Canterbury; and he adds that the remains of the stakes were visible in his own time. Mr. T. Wright, however, in his "Celt, Roman, and Saxon," whilst agreeing in the main in this view, suggests that these stakes, though of Roman workmanship, were of later date, and perhaps connected with the navigation or fishery of the Thames in a way which we cannot now explain.

Camden was the first in recent times to point out Coway Stakes as the ford which the Britons defended. "It is impossible," he observes, "I should be mistaken in the place, because here the river is scarce six feet deep ; and the place at this day, from those stakes, is called Coway Stakes ; to which we may add that Cæsar makes the bounds of Cassivelan, where he fixes this his passage, to be about eight miles distant from that sea which washes the east part of Kent, where he landed ; and that the tide probably ran up as high as this spot.

Of the stakes themselves, Gale, the antiquary, says :—" The wood of these stakes proves its own antiquity, being by its long duration under the water so consolidated as to resemble ebony, and will admit of a polish, and is not in the least rotted.

SHEPPERTON, FROM THE RIVER.

SHEPPERTON RECTORY. (See page 178.)

now this ford we speak of is at the same distance from the sea ; and I am the first, that I know of, who has mentioned and settled it in its proper place." *

The position of these stakes is described in the *Archæologia* by the Hon. Daines Barrington, who inspected the spot in 1740, and it is said that one of them is preserved in the British Museum, having been obtained here in 1777. It must be remembered that in early times there were no weirs or dams so near to the mouth of the river,

It is evident, from the exterior grain of the wood, that the stakes were the entire bodies of young oak-trees, there not being the least appearance of any mark of any tool to be seen upon the whole circumference ; and if we allow in our calculation for the gradual increase of growth towards its end, where fixed in the bed of the river, the stakes, I think, will exactly answer the thickness of a man's thigh, as described by Bede ; but whether they were covered with lead at the ends fixed in the bottom of the river, is a particular I could not learn." None of the stakes remain now, the last having been removed about the year 1840. They are said to have been capped with metal for convenience of driving, but whether it was with brass, iron, or lead, is very uncertain, as the different accounts vary.

Both Daines Barrington and Dr. Owen, it may be observed, doubt whether Cæsar ever did pass the Thames at all. They allege that stakes intended to oppose the landing of an enemy would have been so placed as to line the friendly shore with their armed points inclining to the adverse bank; whereas Coway Stakes range directly *across* the river, and therefore could not have obstructed troops attempting to pass the ford. Those who are thus minded suppose that *the Stakes of Coway were merely intended for a fishing weir!* And yet some still say that the stakes were too massive and armed for a mere fishery. These are the opinions of the learned, and such is the glorious uncertainty of antiquity.

In the *Archæological Journal* for September, 1866, will be found a full account of the campaign of A. Plautius, by the late Dr. E. Guest, with a plan of the fortified ford at Halliford and the Coway Stakes. Dr. Guest thinks that the stakes mentioned as protecting the ford were there many years before the arrival of the Romans.

Mr. Brewer, in his work above quoted, writes :— " We confess that the position of the stakes appears an insuperable objection to believing that they were meant to oppose the landing of an enemy intent on passing from the Surrey to the Middlesex shore; but their massive and armed character would appear to be the result of too much labour and cost to allow of our supposing that they are no more than the remains of a weir for fishing." In the same work it is observed that "Mr. Bray (a writer not likely to be misled by careless and futile assertion) 'was informed by a fisherman who has lived at Walton, and known the river all his life, that at this place he has weighed up several stakes of the size of his thigh, about six feet long, *shod with iron;* the wood very black, and so hard as to turn an axe.' On St. George's Hill, at a short distance from the Thames, on the Surrey shore, is a camp, called Cæsar's Camp, appearing to be Roman, which comprehends in its area more than thirteen acres, and which probably communicated with a much larger castrametation at Oatlands. We have already observed that Stukeley supposed he had discovered the remains of Roman works at Shepperton; on Greenfield Common he also notices an encampment; and on Hounslow Heath, in the parish of

Harmondsworth, nearly in a line with the presumed march of Cæsar when pursuing Cassibelan, were, until lately, the perfect remains of a camp appearing to be formed by the Romans." In a foot-note the above writer remarks :—" We cannot avoid observing that, in a meadow immediately bordering upon Coway Stakes, on the Middlesex side of the river, there are vestiges of a broad raised road, which would appear to have led from a spot near the present bridge of Walton towards Halliford. The road terminates about 100 yards on the Halliford side of the river, but the cessation may be accounted for by observing that a mill, with large enclosures, occupied, within memory, the space now level."

About midway between Sunbury, Shepperton, and Laleham, is Littleton, where formerly stood a magnificent mansion, the seat of the Wood family. It stood in a pleasant but level park, but was burnt down a few years ago, and has not been rebuilt. The house was rather of the Dutch type, reminding one of Kensington Palace. It contained some fine pictures, which perished in the flames, including Hogarth's celebrated painting of " Actors Dressing." It is not intended to rebuild the mansion. The late General Thomas Wood, of Littleton, was for ten years M.P. for Middlesex, and colonel of the 84th Regiment, and his father, Colonel Thomas Wood, was for upwards of half a century M.P. for Brecon, and colonel of the East Middlesex Militia. General Wood died in 1872, when the property passed to his son, Mr. Thomas Wood, the present owner.

Littleton would seem to be one of the smallest parishes in Middlesex; at all events, according to the census of 1881 it had only about twenty inhabited houses, and a population of 126 souls. The church, dedicated to St. Mary Magdalen, is an ancient structure, of Early English architecture, but of no particular interest. The chancel, which contains several brasses and memorials of the Wood family, was restored a few years ago.

CHAPTER XVI.

LALEHAM, ASHFORD, AND STAINES.

"Such tattle often entertains
My lord and me as far as Staines,
As once a week we travel down
To Windsor, and again to town."—POPE's *Satires*.

Situation and General Description of Laleham—Remains of a Roman Castrametation on Greenfield Common—Mention of Laleham in Domesday
Book—Descent of the Manor—The Parish Church—Laleham House—Dr. Thomas Arnold and his Residence here—The Village of Laleham—
Population—The River Thames at Chertsey Bridge—Chertsey Meadows—Laleham Burway—Ashford—Descent of the Manor—The Village
of Ashford—The Common—Population—The Parish Church—The Parish Registers—The Welsh Charity School—The West London
District Schools—The Town of Staines—The Roman Road and Roman Antiquities—The Boundary Stone of the Thames Conservancy—
The Ancient Forest of Middlesex—The Notice of Staines in Domesday Book—A Benedictine Abbey—The Parish Church—An Ancient Guild
—The Town of Staines—Markets and Fairs—Population—Inns and Taverns—The Thames and the Water Supply—The Bridge—Duncroft
House—Staines Moor—Yeoveney—Runnymede—Magna Charta Island—Ankerwyke—Egham—Cooper's Hill and Sir John Denham.

PURSUING our course along the left bank of the Thames, we soon reach the south-western limit of the county of Middlesex, and, at the same time, the most westerly point of the jurisdiction of the Thames Conservancy at Staines. Laleham, the first village through which we pass, possesses nothing attractive in the way of scenery, but is simply a continuation of the dead level which pervades the district which we have just left behind us. The village is situated about midway between the towns of Chertsey on the south and Staines on the north. It has but few historical associations, but it is stated in *The Gentleman's Magazine* that Queen Anne had a fishing-box on the river side here, though no proof of the fact is given, and no allusions to it occur in the diaries and personal biographies of her reign.

Dr. Stukeley notices the remains of a Roman castrametation on Greenfield Common, in the parish of Laleham, which he supposes to have been the camp in which Julius Cæsar halted after passing the Thames. But Stukeley is not always to be trusted. Indeed, the statement is considered by the inhabitants to be altogether a myth; but traces of a camp in the Ferry Field are still very evident, as also are others on the top of St. Ann's Hill, on the opposite side of the Thames.

Mr. Brewer, in the "Beauties of England and Wales," observes that "Dr. Stukeley pursues his supposition to a great extent, and raises several hypotheses on grounds entirely conjectural. If Cæsar crossed the Thames at Coway Stakes, it is quite possible, and perhaps probable, that he might then form an encampment here on his march toward Hertfordshire. But every appropriation of the relics to a particular passage of history must needs proceed from an unsatisfactory ingenuity of surmise." Mr. Lysons, having carefully examined and measured these remains about the year 1800, says:—"There are two camps; the fosses, being very

discernible, as measured with a line, are nearly as follows:—North side of the outward camp, about 400 feet; south side, about 390; east side, about 420; west side, nearly 500. North side of the inner camp, about 245 feet; south side, about 230; east side, about 285; west side, about 290."*

Between Ashford and Bedfont Roman coins and other objects have been dug up, in quantities sufficient to make it probable that these level plains were the site of a camp or station during the occupation of the Imperial Eagles.

Laleham is recorded in "Domesday Book" under the name of *Leleham*, and it is stated that "the Earl of Moreton (Mortain, in Normandy) holds in Leleham two hides, which are held under him by the Abbot of Fescamp in Normandy." Robert Blount is also described as holding eight hides of the king in this parish, which were held under him by "one Estrild, a nun."

In the thirteenth century the manor of Laleham formed part of the possessions of Westminster Abbey, and early in the seventeenth century it was annexed, together with the smaller manor of Billets, in this parish, to the Honour of Hampton Court, and subsequently granted in fee to the trustees of Sir Henry Spiller, by whose daughter it was afterwards conveyed in marriage to Sir Thomas Reynell.

About the middle of the last century, Laleham House, together with the lordship of the manor, was bought by Sir James Lowther, who, having for several years represented the counties of Cumberland and Westmoreland in Parliament, was elevated to the peerage in 1784 by Mr. Pitt as Earl of Lonsdale. His lordship, having no issue, obtained a new patent in 1797, creating him Baron and Viscount Lowther, with remainder to the heirs male of his cousin, the Rev. Sir William Lowther, Bart., of Swillington, in whose favour the

* "Middlesex Parishes," p. 197.

earldom was revived. Laleham, however, in 1803, passed, by purchase, into the hands of the Earl of Lucan.

The quaint old parish church, dedicated to All Saints, stands near the river-side, and consists of a nave with north aisle and chancel, with chancel-aisle. Here Dr. Arnold used frequently to officiate when residing here with his pupils, 1820—28. The edifice is a low, irregular structure, built at different periods, the more modern parts, including the tower at the west end, being constructed of brick. The nave and side-aisle are separated by circular arches with round pillars, which have Norman capitals. The interior of the edifice has lately been restored and renovated, the old-fashioned " pews " giving way to open benches. Over the communion-table is a large picture representing the miracle of Christ walking on the sea, painted by Mr. George Henry Harlow, and presented in 1811 by Mr. George Hartwell of this parish. The monumental inscriptions in this church do not contain anything remarkable. Among them is one to the Rev. Dr. Downes, who died in 1798, and who is there said to have been one of " his *Magestie's* chaplains in ordinary ;" and one, dated 1780, to the memory of Sir George Perrott, Baron of the Exchequer. The chancel-aisle mentioned above belongs to the family of the Earl of Lucan, who is at once a gallant field-officer and a great practical agriculturist. His seat, Laleham House, stands in a park of considerable extent on the southern side of the village. It was the residence of Donna Maria, Queen of Portugal, when in England. Lord Lucan was in command of a division of cavalry in the Crimean War, 1854, and was wounded at Balaclava. His lordship is not forgetful of his duties as a landowner, for in 1864 he erected in the village some schools, with a residence for the masters. Laleham House—or, " the great house," as it is called by the natives— is now the residence of Lord Bingham, the eldest son of the Earl of Lucan.

At the lower end of the village stood the house formerly occupied by Dr. Thomas Arnold, the distinguished scholar and schoolmaster. It was a large and substantial old-fashioned brick building, with a large garden attached. ' Arnold settled," writes Dean Stanley, "in 1819 at Laleham, near Staines, with his mother, aunt, and sister, where he remained for the next nine years, taking seven or eight young men as private pupils for the Universities, for a short time in a joint establishment with his brother-in-law, Mr. Buckland, and afterwards independently by himself." In the following year he married Miss Mary Penrose, youngest daughter of the Rev. J. Penrose, Rector of Fledborough, Nottinghamshire.

Here, it is remarked by Arnold's biographer, a great and decisive change came over his character. "The indolence and restlessness by which his early years had been marked entirely disappeared, and he acquired those settled, serious, earnest views of the nature and purpose of life which actuated him ever after. It was this 'intense earnestness' which gave him so much power over his pupils, and which roused every one who came within the sphere of his influence to the consciousness that they had powers to cultivate, duties to discharge, and a mission to accomplish."

" His situation," writes Dean Stanley, "supplied him exactly with that union of retirement and work which, more than any other condition, suited his natural inclinations. . . . Without undertaking any directly parochial charge, he was in the habit of rendering constant assistance to the Rev. Mr. Hearn, the curate of the place, both in the parish church and workhouse, thus uniting with his ordinary occupation a familiar intercourse with his poorer neighbours. Bound as he was to Laleham by all these ties, he long loved to look upon it as his final home ; and the first reception of the tidings of his election at Rugby was overclouded with deep sorrow at leaving the scene of so much happiness. Years after he had left it he still retained his early affection for it, and till he had purchased his house in Westmoreland, he entertained a lingering hope that he might return to it in his old age, when he should have retired from Rugby. Often he would re-visit it, and he delighted in renewing his acquaintance with the families of the poor whom he had known during his residence ; in showing to his children his former haunts ; in looking once again on his favourite views of the great plain of Middlesex, the lonely gravel walks along the banks of the Thames, the retired garden, with its 'Campus Martius' and its 'wilderness of trees,' which lay behind his house, and which had been the scenes of so many sportive games and serious conversations ; the churchyard of Laleham, then doubly dear to him, as containing the graves of his infant child, and of his mother, aunt, and his sister Susannah, who had long formed part of his domestic circle."

The cedars which graced the garden alone remain to mark the spot. The greater part of the garden, and the "Campus Martius," have been converted into an arable field.

Arnold's life at Laleham was on a smaller scale the precursor of his subsequent life at Rugby. He would keep no pupil whom he could not "sophronise," to use his favourite Oxford term : none whose presence would be likely to infect his companions. One of his pupils, in after life, declared that the most remarkable thing which used to strike him was the wonderful heartiness of tone and feeling which prevailed in the little house at Laleham. He "gave such an earnestness to life;" every pupil was made to feel that there was a work for him to do, and that his happiness as well as his duty lay in doing that work well. This created a respect for the tutor which re-acted on his disciples, and set them to toil in earnest to prepare themselves for their commencing career as a step towards after life.

Whilst at Laleham, Arnold's own studies were chiefly philology and history, and here he commenced, in the shape of a lexicon, his work on Thucydides, which afterwards gave him such credit as a scholar. Here, too, he began to write a short history of Greece, which was never finished ; and contributed to the *Encyclopædia Metropolitana* several important articles on the history of Rome from the times of the Gracchi to that of Trajan. Whilst here, also, he made himself a German scholar, and made practical acquaintance with Niebuhr and Bunsen. The sermons contained in the first volume he published were preached in Laleham church, where also most of his children were baptised. At Laleham, his eldest son, Mr. Matthew Arnold, so well known as poet, essayist, and scholar, was born, in 1822.

Arnold's life at Laleham must be regarded as a preliminary and probational existence, during which he was working out mentally, and testing by partial and limited experiment, those school reforms which he afterwards carried out into practice at Rugby, thereby justifying the prophecy of Dr. Hawkins, the late Provost of Oriel College, Oxford, that "he would change the face of education all through the public schools of England." As the place where this great movement was first conceived, Laleham must always be a place of interest to all persons who take an interest in the progress of English public-school education.

To Laleham, and its pleasant mixture of hard work and fresh and youthful interests, Dr. Arnold constantly recurs in his correspondence with his friends at Rugby and at Fox How ; and he never mentions the place without some tender and touching word, which shows how truly he loved its recollections to the very last. Arnold died suddenly at Rugby in 1842, shortly after having been appointed Professor of Modern History at Oxford. His successor at Rugby was Archbishop Tait. His house at Laleham was pulled down about the year 1864, and the materials were used in the construction of a National School.

The village of Laleham possesses a few old-fashioned houses of a humble kind. Most of the inhabitants belong to the agricultural class, but the village is much frequented during the summer months, like its more popular neighbours, Hampton and Sunbury, by the lovers of the gentle craft of angling. In 1871 the number of inhabited houses in the parish amounted to 110, the population amounting to 567 souls, a number which was somewhat diminished in the course of the next ten years, when the sum-total, as recorded in the census returns, was 544.

The Thames here becomes somewhat contracted in width, and being very shallow, runs with considerable strength south-east in a tolerably straight line for nearly two miles, the view in that direction being closed by Chertsey Bridge, which spans the Thames. It is of stone, and has seven arches, and was built in 1780—85, from the designs of Mr. James Payne, at a cost of about £13,000. Across the river and meadows, and at some little distance from the bridge, we see the tower of Chertsey Church, and further westward is St. Anne's Hill, the seat of Lady Holland, and at one time the favourite residence of Charles James Fox. Many interesting recollections cling to the neighbourhood of Chertsey, for—

"Here the last accents flow'd from Cowley's tongue,"

as may be seen from the inscription inserted in the walls of his house, by his friend and brother angler, Mr. Clark. Shakespeare, too, has given the village of Chertsey immortality in his *Richard III.* In the Chertsey meadow, across the ferry, on the Surrey side, are to be seen the remains of an encampment of undoubted Roman character, probably an outlying portion of the station *Ad Pontes*, which modern antiquarians have usually identified with Staines.

A meadow, called Laleham Burway, belongs to the parish of Laleham, though on the opposite side of the river. There is a tradition that it was given by an abbot of Chertsey to the Laleham fishermen as an acknowledgment of their having supplied the Abbey with fish during a time of pestilence and dearth. The meadow was used as a common ground by the inhabitants of Laleham, and their cattle used to cross the Thames every morning to pasture on it, but Laleham Burway, like so many other commons, is now "enclosed and divided."

But we must not longer linger over the view, and so, turning our steps northward, we will at once make our way to Ashford.

The general surroundings of this village, as of those which we have lately been describing, are a dead flat all away to Feltham in one direction, and to Staines in another; but the country around is nevertheless well-cultivated ground and woodland. It is sufficiently diversified, at all events, to have pleased the eye of Arnold. Scattered about in the fields are plenty of pollard oaks, marking the site of what once was part of the great forest of Middlesex.

This parish is noticed in the "Domesday Survey" by the name of *Exeforde*, and in ancient records of a subsequent period by those of *Echeleford* and *Eckleford*, from the ford over the little river Exe, or Echel, which, however, runs at some little distance west of the village.

King Edgar is said to have granted the manor of Staines, with land at Ecclesford, to the abbey and convent of Westminster. On the surrender of that monastery, this manor (together with Staines) was annexed to the honour of Hampton Court. The manor of Ashford was granted by Queen Elizabeth, in 1601, to Guy Godolphin and John Smythe, and it has since then been held by different families. It is now (January, 1883) the subject of litigation.

Ashford, which is a very scattered parish, was, till recently, a chapelry annexed to Staines, but with regard to its civil jurisdiction it has long been a separate parish. The village is situated nearly a mile to the south of the great western road, and about fourteen miles from London. Twenty years ago the neighbourhood was very aristocratic; and even at the present time there are many wealthy residents. The village consists for the most part of substantial houses occupied by gentry. Ashford Common extended south-east almost as far as Sunbury Common. Here George III. formerly held frequent reviews of cavalry, but the display of military pomp many years ago yielded to the humbler labours of the plough. The Common has long been enclosed. The old village of Ashford lies half a mile east-ward of the station on the Windsor branch of the South-Western Railway; a new village is now rapidly springing up in the direction of Sunbury. In 1871 the number of inhabited houses in the parish was 181, and the population amounted to 1,019 souls, a number which has now swelled up to 2,281; but this is inclusive of the inmates of two public institutions in the parish.

The parish church, which stands near the entrance to the village, is a modern erection, dating back only from the year 1858. It is dedicated to St. Matthew, and is in the Gothic style of architecture. The edifice comprises a chancel, nave, aisles, south transept, and a tower and dwarf spire at the south-west angle. It was built by subscription. Mr. Butterfield was the architect of the present church, which is the third that has stood near the same site within the last century. The previous church was dedicated to St. Michael.

The original church stood in the same church-yard, but further east, near a tall fine yew-tree. It was an ancient building of brick and stone, the south door exhibiting evidences of Norman or Saxon workmanship in its zig-zag mouldings. The edifice which succeeded it, and was erected in 1796, was a plain brick building, with a tower sur-mounted by a tall spire. That church was built chiefly by a voluntary subscription among the inhabitants, but the chancel was rebuilt at the expense of the lord of the manor.

The church of Ashford was formerly served by a curate appointed by the vicar of Staines, and is said by Newcourt, in the "Repertorium," to be endowed with "a house, twenty-eight acres and a half, and two yards of glebe." Among the tombs in the churchyard is one to the memory of the Rev. John Jebb, D.D., Dean of Cashel, father to the celebrated Bishop Jebb. In the floor of the nave, near the font, is inserted a brass, removed from the old church; it has upon it the effigies of Edward Woode and his wife, six sons, and two daughters, and is dated 1525.

The registers of Ashford are very imperfect, none of them going back further than 1699. They are in existence from that date to 1708, afterwards there is a gap down to 1760; and their absence is accounted for by a fire in which they perished along with the original church plate. New plate of a very handsome type was purchased, and this, too, was for some time lost to the parish, having found its way into private hands, from which it has only lately been recovered. The church books contain some curious entries. Amongst others, very many of sums paid for killing "vermin" and sparrows. Among the charitable bequests is one, now producing about £7 yearly, and divided between three old men and three old women; it was left by a Mrs. Anne Webb to her dog, for life, with reversion to the poor as above. She left other charities to poor chimney-sweep boys in London, in the place of a treat which she used to give them in her lifetime; and also a duplicate of her canine legacy to the parish of Merton, in Surrey.

There are several charitable institutions in this parish. Near the railway-station, on the road to Stanwell, is the Welsh Charity School. The institution belongs to the Honourable and Loyal Society of Ancient Britons. It was originally intended for poor Welsh orphans of either sex, but is now a middle-class school for Welsh girls; and it was founded in 1714–15. The present school was erected in 1857, and is a large stone-fronted building of Elizabethan architecture, and holds 200 children.

The West London District Schools are situated to the west of the station, about midway between Ashford and Staines. The inmates are pauper children, mainly from the parishes of Fulham,

caused this town, contrary to what is generally the case, to expand in an easterly direction. It consists mainly of one long street, which runs from east to west, and terminates at Staines Bridge, which joins the town to Egham, in Surrey.

The Roman road from London to Silchester is supposed to have crossed the Thames in this neighbourhood, but the exact spot where it crossed is not known with any certainty, though Egham is generally identified with the Roman Bibracte. As

LALEHAM CHURCH. (See page 188.)

Paddington, and St. George's, Hanover Square. The edifice, which is constructed of brick with stone dressings, covers a large space of ground, and is capable of containing nearly 800 children. It was built in 1872.

The town of Staines, which we have now reached, lies about two miles westward from Ashford, and at the extreme west of the Thames Valley, in Middlesex, being situated at the mouth of the Colne, which, rising in Hertfordshire, and passing by Harefield, Uxbridge, and Colnbrook, debouches here into the Thames in several channels. The meadows along the banks of the Colne being low and flat, whilst its waters are "brimming" both in summer and winter, have

Staines was the Roman station *Ad Pontes*, it is scarcely a matter of wonder that its neighbourhood is rich in Roman remains. For instance, in a pit near Savery's Weir, on the Thames, between Staines and Laleham, a large brass coin of the Emperor Trajan was dug up in 1858. It was found at the depth of six feet from the surface, and was much defaced. The coin is described minutely in the *Journal of the Archæological Institute.**

Within the last few years very many strong confirmations of the Roman origin of Staines have been found in a variety of antique objects that have been dug up in its vicinity—Roman bricks,

* Vol XVI., p. 179

tiles, vases, and swords, one of the last being found by dredging in the Thames. Pins, tweezers, and strigils, from a Roman bath, have also been disinterred. A very fine collection of these has been made by Mr. Ernest Ashby, a resident in the town, who has formed out of them the nucleus of a private museum. Axe-heads made of flint and other rude materials, probably of an earlier period, and stags' horns of very large size, have been unearthed in the vicinity.

tion refers to the boundary-stone by the side of the river, which is said to bear date A.D. 1280, together with the words, " God preserve the City of London." This stone was repaired and raised on a pedestal in 1781, during the mayoralty of Sir Watkin Lewes. The stone—be it Roman, Saxon, or Norman, in its origin—still stands on the north bank, a little above the bridge, near the church, on the Lammas lands. It is adorned with the City arms and motto, and the names of sundry Lord Mayors who have visited

THE CITY BOUNDARY STONE.

STREET IN STAINES.

it officially for the purposes of enforcing their jurisdiction, or on swan-upping expeditions. On its base it bears engraved the words "Conservators of the River Thames," who, it may here be mentioned, regard the river above this point as the Upper Thames ; whilst from here down to Yanlet Creek, at the mouth of the Medway, it is called the Lower Thames.

The Court of Conservancy of the Thames, over which the Lord Mayor presides, holds eight sittings every year, within the counties of Middlesex, Surrey, Kent, and Essex. It is in this capacity that the Lord Mayor of London is comically apostrophised by Tom Hood as—

" Conservator of Thames from mead to mead,
	Great guardian of small sprites that swim the flood,
	Warder of London stone."

Antiquaries are not agreed as to whether this town derives its name from a Roman milestone, or milliarum, placed here, or from the stone on the banks of the Thames which marks the limits of the jurisdiction of the Lord Mayor of London over the western portion of the river. Dr. Stukeley endeavours to support the former theory by asserting that near Staines Bridge there are traces of an old Roman road.

It is generally said, however—and we suppose that the statement may be accepted—the derivation of the name of the town is usually given as from "Stane,"or "Stana,"the Saxon term for stone ; and it is supposed by Camden, and by various subsequent writers, as stated above, that the appella-

When Alderman Venables, as Lord Mayor, went by barge to Oxford, in 1826, it was part of the programme that the City banners should be waved over the stone. It may be added that several attempts were made in former times to extend the Lord Mayor's jurisdiction over the Thames as far as Oxford ; but in this the City did not succeed, and ancient custom has determined the limit as already mentioned.

The citizens of London, we know, had the right of "free warren": that is, they were at liberty to hunt in certain limits around their city; and this circuit included the "warren" of Staines. A forest anciently extended from this place to Hounslow eastwards, but it was disafforested and diswarrened early in the thirteenth century, and the district has since been gradually enclosed.

It is said that the town was once surrounded by a moat or ditch; but if this ever was the case, very scanty traces of it remain, except in what is known as Penton Ditch.

Staines figures only once in pre-Norman history, namely, in A.D. 1009, when the Danes, hearing that an army was marching from London to oppose them, are said to have crossed the river here on their way to their ships from Oxford, which they had burnt.

The next period which furnishes materials for a historical notice of Staines occurs subsequent to the Norman conquest. In the survey made by order of William I., the circumstances of property in this place are described in the following manner:—"The Abbot of St. Peter holds *Stanes* for nineteen hides. There is land to twenty-four ploughs. Eleven hides belong to the demesne, and there are thirteen ploughs therein. The villanes have eleven ploughs. There are three villanes of half a hide each; and four villanes of one hide; and eight villanes of half a virgate each; and thirty-six bordars of three hides; and one villane of one virgate, and four bordars of forty acres; and ten bordars of five acres each; and five cottages of four acres each; and eight bordars of one virgate; and three cottagers of nine acres; and twelve bondmen; and forty-six burgesses, who pay forty shillings a year. There are six mills of sixty-four shillings; and one wear (guort) of six shillings and eight pence, and one wear which pays nothing. Pasture for the cattle of the village. Meadow for twenty-four ploughs, and twenty shillings over and above. Pannage for thirty hogs; and two arpents of vineyards. Four berewicks belong to this manor, and they belonged to it in King Edward's time. Its whole value is thirty-five pounds; the same when received in King Edward's time forty pounds. This manor laid and lies in the demesne of the Church of St. Peter [at Westminster]."

Here, in the Saxon days, is said to have stood a Benedictine abbey, the monks of which would seem to have served the adjoining parishes. Both Speed, in his "Catalogue of Religious Houses," and Weever, in his "Funeral Monuments," confirm this assertion, and add that the abbey, or priory, was founded by Ralph, Lord Stafford; but Newcourt shows that the Priory of Staines alluded to by those writers is really situated at Stone in Staffordshire, which place, like Stone, near Dartford in Kent, was often termed *Stane* in ancient records.

The distance from Staines Bridge to London Bridge is twenty miles by land, and, in consequence of the circuitous course of the Thames, more than double that distance by water. Staines is in Spelthorne Hundred, and in the rural deanery of Hampton. It is a vicarage to which the chapelries of Ashford and Laleham were formerly annexed, but these have been separated, and formed into distinct parishes. The *Penny Cyclopædia* of 1839 speaks of all three as *one*. Sundry disputes having arisen on the subject of patronage between the Bishop of London and the Abbey of Westminster, it was agreed that the vicarage of Staines should be devoted to the use of wayfaring and sick folk at Westminster Abbey, and that the vicar of Staines should appoint chaplains for Laleham and Ashford. The vicar of Staines held under the great abbey by a curious tenure—namely, that of supplying two large wax candles for the altar of St. Peter's church, to be burnt on the eve of Epiphany.

It is certain that the Norman church was not the earliest here. We learn on the authority of Leland,[*] that, in the Saxon times, Ermengildis, daughter of King Wulfhere, before the year 700, built a small chapel in the forest here; and also that its successor, erected by the first Christian King of Mercia, was built "ex lapidibus" and "venustiori modo" than its predecessor.

From this statement it appears probable that the earliest Christian church here was of wood, very small and simple in plan. At all events, we learn that as far back as the ninth century a building of that description was standing here, and that the rude tenements of the Saxon town clustered round "God's Acre." This little oratory, in due course of time, was probably superseded by a church of stone.

The present church, dedicated to St. Mary, is a modern structure, ugly and plain, and stands in the midst of meadows on the banks of an arm of the Colne. Its Norman predecessor having become dilapidated, the nave was rebuilt in the last century; but one corner of it fell down about the year 1828, and the present structure

---

* See Parker's "Glossary of Architecture," iii., 9.

erected on the same site, the lower part of the tower being made to do duty. It was built in the dark ages of church architecture, the reign of George IV., and tells its own tale—an imitation Gothic structure of the poorest type. Its square embattled brick tower is said to have been erected by Inigo Jones in 1631, but it is scarcely one of the best specimens of his artistic design. The church was erected under an Act of Parliament which conferred freehold rights in pews to the contributors of certain sums to the building fund. The architect was a man named Watson, who is said to have been chosen by competition, securing his election to the job by sundry presents of barrels of oysters and cods' heads and shoulders to the sapient committee to whom the choice of an architect was entrusted! In Walpole's "Anecdotes of Painting," it is stated that Inigo Jones lived for some time at Staines; but it does not appear that any notice of his residence here is to be found in the parish books.

In a small apartment under the staircase leading to the gallery at the west end of the old church were for many years preserved two unburied coffins, containing human remains. They were placed beside each other on trestles, and bore respectively the following inscriptions :—" Jessie Aspasia, the most excellent and truly beloved wife of Fred. W. Campbell, Esq., of Barbreck, N.B., and of Woodlands, in Surrey. Died in her 28th year, July 11th, 1812." "Henry E. A. Caulfield, Esq., died Sept. 8th, 1808, aged 29 years." As it was naturally supposed that coffins thus open to inspection would excite much curiosity, a card was preserved at the sexton's house, which stated, in addition to the intelligence conveyed by the above inscriptions, that the deceased lady was the daughter of W. T. Caulfeild, Esq., of Raheenduff, in Ireland, by Jessie, daughter of James, third Lord Ruthven, and that she bore with tranquil and exemplary patience a fatal disorder, produced by grief on the death of her brother. These coffins were buried on the erection of the new church.

The church and churchyard are singularly deficient in interesting tombs and monuments. Dame Letitia Lade, who lies buried between the church and the road, was a cast-off mistress of the Prince Regent, who married her to his coachman, one Mr. John Lade, whom he knighted as a reward for his pliancy in the matter, or for his skill in handling the ribbons. It is said that Sir John Lade also is buried here, but his name is not recorded on the tombstone.

The church has a peal of eight bells, remarkably sweet in their tone, and said to be the finest belonging to any of the churches in the Middlesex valley of the Thames, excepting Fulham.

The church books contain some curious entries : lists of books, plate, and moneys in the hands of the churchwardens, entries of sums paid to " distressed gentlewomen," " poore schollers," " poore ministers " and their wives; to a " poore gentlewoman to ransom her husband " (sixpence) ; and sixpence to a " poore merchant's wife." In 1657 sixpence is paid for an "houre glass." Two years later about £20 is spent on the re-casting, &c., of a bell; and in 1660 £3 for painting the king's arms. There are other disbursements for " prosecuting ye Quakers;" for going to London by water, (sixpence); "given to a poore Mayde, 2s."; for "excommunicating Pritt," 17s. ; for ferrying to church, 1s. ; and sundry collections in answer to briefs.

It is perhaps worth notice that the Rev. Gerald Wellesley, brother of the great Duke of Wellington, was at one time vicar of Staines, and largely improved the vicarage.

A guild, in honour of God and the Virgin Mary, was founded in 1456, by John Lord Berners, Sir John Wenlock, and several other persons, over the chapel of the Holy Cross in the church of Staines. This guild consisted of two wardens and a certain number of brethren and sisters. The lands appertaining to it were valued, in 1548, at £11 17s. 6d. per annum, including 6s. 8d. for a chamber, called the chantry-priests' chamber.

The town consists mainly of one long straggling street, irregularly built. The High Street, towards the west end of the town, forks off, and is continued to the north-west by Church Street, which leads to the parish church. The main street of the town is upwards of a mile in length, and contains a fair sprinkling of commodious shops and good old-fashioned houses ; whilst in the immediate neighbourhood are extensive mills, and linoleum and other manufactories. In Church Street is a large brewery, belonging to the Messrs. Ashby ; another brewery in the town belongs to Mr. Harris. At the west end of the High Street stands a handsome new Town Hall, which has been built in the place of a smaller one in a miserable and low thoroughfare known as Blackboy Lane.

Staines was a great place for the "Society of Friends," whose meeting-house is a specimen of the architecture of years long gone by. There are also chapels for different denominations of Dissenters. A large new town, with a mission chapel destined to blossom into a church, has of late years sprung up about the railway-station, which here forms a junction of the Windsor and the Wokingham lines. The internal polity of the town was formerly regu-

lated by two constables and four " head-boroughs."
The government is now vested in a Local Board;
whilst the welfare of the town is further enhanced
by the advantages gained from a Literary and
Scientific Institute, and also a Mechanics' Institute.

There was a weekly market held on Friday, but
it has long been discontinued; two fairs, however, are
still held annually. One of these fairs was granted
by Henry III., in the year 1228, to the abbot and
convent of Westminster. The fairs are held on the
11th of May for horses and cattle, and on the
19th of September for toys, &c.

The *Penny Cyclopædia* gives the population of
Staines in 1839 as 2,486. From the census
returns in 1871, we learn that the parish contained
722 inhabited houses, and that the population then
numbered 3,659 souls, a number that is by this
time nearly doubled.

Lying as it did, in the good old coaching days, on
the high road to Salisbury and the south-western
counties, just one stage west of Hounslow, Staines
was a large posting-town, and its inns were very
numerous. Many of these since the days of railways have been turned into private houses, and
such hostelries as remain depend mainly for support
on boating parties and on the disciples of Izaak
Walton.

If not literally the " half-way house," Staines was
at all events one of the resting places, and a halt
for changing horses, in the coaching and sporting
days, on the " royal road " to Windsor. Hence
the town was a favourite with good old George III.
and Queen Charlotte and their family ; and hence
probably it came to pass that royalty took part
in the ceremony of opening the new bridge across
the Thames.

The Vine Inn, " at the bridge foot," is often
mentioned by the first Lord Shaftesbury in his
" Diary " as an inn where he slept a night on his
way between Dorsetshire and London. The
tavern, however, has long passed away. Readers of
Swift will not forget how the prude Phillis, having
run off with her father's groom, John, the couple
settle down to lead a cat-and-dog life as landlord
and hostess of the Blue Boar, which still exists
and flourishes :

" They keep at Staines the old Blue Boar."

To one at least of these inns an anecdote
attaches, which may be worth recording here :—

A lady of fashion in the last century is said to
have cut with a diamond on a pane of glass the
following inscription, " Dear Lord D—— has
the softest lips of any man in England." Foote,

coming into the room soon after, scored underneath the following couplet :—

" Then as like as two chips
    Are D——'s head and his lips."

While on the subject of inns and taverns—of
which, by the way, Staines possesses a fair share—it
may not be out of place to note the fact that at
the Staines and Egham races the landlord of the
" Cricketers," near Chelsea Bridge, used to display
a signboard which had been painted by George
Morland, and which travelled about with him.

The water supply of Staines has of late years
been largely augmented by the Sunningdale District Water Company, which has been formed for
the purpose of supplying the several parishes of
Staines, Egham, and Old Windsor.

The river Thames in the neighbourhood of
Staines is highly favourable for boating and fishing
parties, and as a natural result the town is much
frequented by visitors during the summer months.

Staines Bridge was for many a century the only
one above London Bridge leading to the west of
England ; hence the importance of it to the sovereign, especially as it helped to connect both
Windsor and Portsmouth with the metropolis ; and
hence, probably, it happened that the barons
assembled at Runnymede while enforcing King
John to sign the Magna Charta ; and hence, in
1262, we read of three large oak-trees being granted
by the Crown out of Windsor forest for the repair
of this edifice. Numerous grants of *pontage*, or a
temporary toll to defray the charge of repairs, were
made at different times previous to the year
1600.

In 1791 an Act of Parliament was obtained for
the erecting of a new bridge, and under enactment,
certain tolls were allowed to be taken, on which the
sum expended in raising the structure was charged.
In pursuance of this Act a stone bridge of three
arches was begun in August, 1792, and was opened
in March, 1797. But the work had been executed
with so little skill that one of the piers shortly gave
way, and the bridge was necessarily taken down.
A similar fate befel its successor—an iron bridge of
one single arch, which, through some structural
defect, had to be supported and propped up with
wooden piles and framework. This bridge in the
end was considered altogether unsafe, and the
present stone bridge was built in 1832, and opened
by William IV. and Queen Adelaide, the approach
to it, at the same time, being altered and improved.
Some remains of the approaches of the former
bridge may still be seen, especially on the Surrey
side of the river.

Quite close to the vicarage and church is Duncroft House, at one time the property and occasional residence of Lord Cranstoun. It is said that King John slept here the night after signing Magna Charta at Runnymede, but the tradition may be doubted. The house is a late Elizabethan or early Jacobean structure, resembling in its details portions of the Charter House in London. The room said to be King John's has a fine oak chimney-piece, curiously inlaid ; and the timbers of the upper part of the house are massive and strong. An earlier structure may possibly have occupied the spot, but no traces of it exist.

Staines Moor, extending upwards to Stanwell, consists of common-lands, over which the poor of Staines have certain rights of turbary, &c.

Yeoveney, a hamlet consisting of a farm-house and a few cottages, about a mile to the north of the town, was an ancient chapelry attached to the mother-church of Staines. Its chapel has long since disappeared ; and even its site is not known for certain, though an oak door, said to have formed a part of it, is still preserved in the neighbouring farm-house.

Within sight of Staines, though on the other side of the river, is Egham, between which and the riverside is the meadow of Runnymede, on which Egham races are annually held, and on which it is said that Magna Charta was signed. The roadway between Staines Bridge and Egham was built by the monks of Chertsey. Akenside, the author of " The Pleasures of Imagination," wrote the following spirited lines as an inscription for a column to be erected here :—

> " Thou who the verdant plain dost traverse here,
>   While Thames among his willows from thy view
>   Retires ; O stranger, stay thee, and the scene
>   Around contemplate well. This is the place
>   Where England's ancient Barons, clad in arms
>   And strong with conquest, from their tyrant king
>   (Then rendered tame) did challenge and secure
>   The charter of thy freedom. Pass not on
>   Till thou hast blest their memory, and paid
>   Those thanks which God appointed the reward
>   Of public virtue. And if chance thy home
>   Salute thee with a father's honoured name,
>   Go, call thy sons, instruct them what a debt
>   They owe their ancestors, and make them swear
>   To pay it, by transmitting down entire
>   Those sacred rights to which themselves were born."

A small eyot a little higher up the river, opposite Egham and Ankerwyke, still bears the name of Magna Charta Island. In it is kept and shown a table bearing the names of the proud Barons who forced the King to sign the Charter. Here are some of the finest trees in the kingdom, the park having

once been a religious house ; but these are beyond our limits. A walnut tree at Ankerwyke, which still stands and thrives, is said to have been vigorous when it witnessed the signing of Magna Charta.

"A small island opposite Runnymede, now covered with willows, was the temporary fortified residence of the barons, where, in 1215, they retired from the pressure of the surrounding army, personally to receive the signature of the king to the great *palladium* of English liberty."

At Egham resided the great and good Judge Doddridge, who lies buried in Exeter Cathedral ; but the place is chiefly memorable on account of Cooper's Hill, an eminence near the London Road, the beauties of which are celebrated in a poem written in 1640 by Sir John Denham, and which acquired for him from Dr. Johnson the just and merited rank of an "original author." The following four lines of "Cooper's Hill," having reference to the Thames, which is now before us, have been often quoted, but will bear repetition :—

> " Oh ! could I flow like *thee*, and make thy stream
>   My great *example*, as it is my theme ;
>   Though deep, yet clear, tho' gentle, yet not dull,
>   Strong without rage, without o'erflowing full."

A good story is told of Sir John Denham. There was in the Puritan army a poetaster named Withers, some of whose lands at Egham Sir J. Denham had got into his clutches. When Withers was taken prisoner by the Cavaliers, Denham interceded with King Charles for his life, because as long as he lived he (Sir John) would not be reckoned the worst poet in England.

On the west side of Cooper's Hill stands the Indian Civil Engineering College, founded by Government in 1871 for the scientific training of young men as civil engineers for service in India. The college is built upon an estate formerly called Ankerwyke Purnish, which was given to the nuns of Ankerwyke, on the opposite side of the Thames, by Hugh, Abbot of Chertsey, in the reign of King Stephen.

The father of the poet Denham, who was also a Sir John Denham, lived for some time at Egham, in the house now the vicarage. He was for some time Chief Baron of the Exchequer in Ireland. Pope sang his praises in the following lines :—

> " On Cooper's Hill eternal wreaths shall grow
>   While lasts the mountain or while Thames shall flow ;
>   I seem through consecrated walks to rove,
>   I hear *soft music* die along the grove ;
>   Led by the sound, I rove from shade to shade,
>   By godlike poets venerable made.
>   *Here* his first lays majestic Denham sung,
>   *There* the last numbers flow'd from *Cowley's* tongue !"

BEDFONT CHURCH. (*From an old Print. See page* 195.)

CHAPTER XVII.

STANWELL, BEDFONT, AND CRANFORD.

" Ecce horti campique nitent."—OVID.

Situation and General Aspect of Stanwell—Stanwell Heath formerly a rendezvous for Middlesex Elections—The Domesday Book Notice of Stanwell—The Forced Exchange of the Manor, *temp.* Henry VIII.—Subsequent Descent of the Manor—The Village of Stanwell—The Old School-house—Population—The Parish Church—Staines Moor, Stanwell Moor, and Poyle Park—West Bedfont—East Bedfont—The Parish Church—The " Peacocks"—Discoveries of Antiquities—Descent of the Manor of Bedfont—Spelthorne Sanatorium—Middlesex Industrial School for Girls—The " Black Dog"—Population of Bedfont—Cranford—Census Returns—The Village—Descent of the Manor— The Park—Cranford House—Cranford le Mote—The Parish Church—The Vicarage.

THE parish of Stanwell stands high in comparison with the flat country all around it, and its church spire forms a conspicuous landmark. The village lies about two miles nearly due north from Staines. The parish is separated from Buckinghamshire by a branch of the river Colne, and in other directions is bounded by Bedfont, Staines, and Harmondsworth. Down to the end of the last or beginning of the present century, upwards of 500 acres of land in the parish were an open waste, of which some 350 acres formed a portion, or continuation, of Hounslow Heath. This state of things, however, is now all altered, and what was once barren and profitless has been turned into green pastures and smiling cornfields.

It would appear from " Bubb Dodington's Diary " that in the reign of George II. Stanwell Heath was the great rendezvous of the electors of Middlesex, before they rushed off to the poll at Brentford Butts, as already recorded by us.*

In the " Domesday Survey," *Stanwelle* is stated to be held of the king by Walter Fitzother. " There were four mills, yielding seventy shillings, and four hundred eels, save twenty-five ; and three wears, which produced one thousand eels, meadow for twelve ploughs (or each to twelve carucates). Pasture for the cattle of the village ; and pannage for one hundred hogs. Its whole value was fourteen pounds ; when received six pounds."

William, the eldest son of the above-mentioned Walter Fitzother, held the post of Warden of Windsor Castle, and in consequence of this

* See *ante*, p. 38.

appointment he assumed the name of Windsor. His descendants possessed the manor of Stanwell until the year 1541, when it passed from them to the Crown by a very singular and unjustifiable method, if the story generally received be indeed correct.

Sir William Dugdale, who heartily disliked the memory of Henry VIII., on account of his dissolution of the monastic houses, and who had the account from the lips of Thomas, Lord Windsor,

king, with a stern countenance, replied that it *must* be, commanding him, *on his allegiance*, to repair to the Attorney-General, and settle the business without delay. The Attorney-General showed him a conveyance, ready prepared, of Bordesley Abbey, in the county of Worcester, with all its lands and appurtenances, in exchange for the manor of Stanwell. Being constrained, through dread of the king's displeasure, to accept of the exchange, he conveyed this manor to his Majesty,

STANWELL VILLAGE GREEN. (*See page* 194.)

relates in the following manner the story of the forced exchange of this manor by the then lord, in consequence of an "*invitation*" of the king :—

"The manor of Stanwell continued in the Windsor family till the year 1543, when King Henry the Eighth, having been advised to dispose of the monastic lands by gifts or exchange to the principal nobility and gentry, thought fit to make an exchange of this sort with Andrews, Lord Windsor. To this purpose he sent a message that he would dine with him at Stanwell, where a magnificent entertainment was accordingly provided. The king then informed the owner *that he liked his place so well that he was determined to have it*, though not without a beneficial exchange. Lord Windsor made answer that he hoped his Highness was not in earnest, since Stanwell had been the seat of his ancestors for so many generations. The

being commanded to quit Stanwell immediately, though he had laid in his Christmas provision for keeping his wonted hospitality there, saying that they should not find it *bare Stanwell*."

According to the above-mentioned story, Lord Windsor conveyed the manor to the king *before* Christmas; but the deed of exchange, which is preserved in the Public Record Office, bears date the 14th of March, 33rd of Henry VIII. (1543), or more than three months subsequent to that season.

The title of Windsor would seem to have been happily chosen, for the original occupants of the manor-house here could see, across the well-watered meadows of the Colne, the towers of that royal castle and town from which they took their title.

In the year 1603, the manor and the demesne

lands were granted by James I. to Sir Thomas, afterwards Lord, Knyvet. The Princess Mary, daughter of King James, was placed under the care of this nobleman at Stanwell, and died there in 1607. The estate was subsequently vested in the family of the Carys, Lords Falkland, and in 1720 it was sold by John, Earl of Dunmore. A few years later it was purchased by Sir John Gibbons, Bart., K.B., and it is now the property of his descendant, Sir John Gibbons, Bart. The manor-house, called Stanwell Place, is a spacious modern mansion, standing in a small park.

The village of Stanwell is somewhat secluded, lying as it does off the main roads, and the ordinary beaten track of commerce. It is situated on the east side of the park, and the cottages and other buildings are scattered round a small, but picturesque, village green, which has about it sufficient evidences of rural life to render it a charming " bit" for the pencil of an artist. The ancient school-house on the London Road, which was built and endowed for the charitable instruction of poor children, in accordance with the will of Thomas, Lord Knyvet, has remained down to the present time as a monument of his care for the requirements of future generations.

According to the census returns for 1871, the number of inhabited houses in the parish was 364, the population amounting to 1,955 souls; but this number included upwards of 300 in the district of St. Thomas, Colnbrook, and nearly 250 in Staines Union Workhouse, which is situated to the south of the village, and abuts upon the Bedfont Road. In 1881 the population had increased to 2,155, inclusive of the inmates of the workhouse, but exclusive of Colnbrook.

The parish church of Stanwell, dedicated to St. Mary, is an ancient building, composed of stone interspersed with flint, and is a mixture of the Early English, Decorated, and Perpendicular styles of architecture. Unlike most of the churches of the Thames Valley, it consists of a nave, with clerestory, a double chancel, aisles, a picturesque wooden porch with tiled roof on the north side, and a low square tower at the western end. The church was thoroughly restored in 1863, at which time the north aisle was rebuilt and the porch added. The tower is constructed of flint and stone, in chequer work, and from it rises a lofty octagonal shingled spire, somewhat out of the perpendicular. The interior is spacious, well lighted, and much superior to the generality of the village churches in this county. Its nave and aisles are divided by Pointed arches, which spring from massive pillars, some being octagonal, and others

circular. Some of the windows are filled with stained glass. On the south wall of the chancel are two stone stalls and the remains of a piscina, beyond which, towards the nave, extends an arcade of eight niches, or seats, probably intended for the accommodation of the brethren of Chertsey Abbey, to whom the rectory of Stanwell was appropriated by Richard de Windsor about the year 1415.

There was in this church an " Easter Sepulchre," formed, as will be seen, out of one of the tombs.* " On the north side of the chancel," writes Mr. Bloxam, in his " Gothic Architecture," " is a high tomb, over which is a canopy with an obtuse arch, ornamented with quatrefoils. Beneath this arch were placed upright in the wall brass plates, with the effigies of the deceased and his wife, all long ago removed. This is the monument of Thomas Windsor, who died A.D. 1486. By his will, made in 1479, after directing that his body should be buried on the north side of the ' quier ' of the church of our Lady of Stanwell, " afor the ymage of our Lady wher the sepulture [sic] of our Lord stondith;" he adds, ' I will that there be made a playne tombe of marble, of a competent hyght, to th' entent that yt may ber [bear] the blessed body of our Lord, and the sepulture at the tyme of Estre to stand upon the same.' "

The above Thomas Windsor was the father of Andrews, first Lord Windsor, the nobleman who, as stated above, was " despoiled" by the king of the manor of Stanwell.

On the same wall as the above tomb is one of a more stately character to the memory of Thomas, Lord Knyvet, and Elizabeth, his wife, which rises nearly to the roof of the chancel. This monument is of veined marble, with columns of the Corinthian order, and, as stated in " Walpole's Anecdotes of Paintings," was the work of Nicholas Stone, who received for executing it the sum of £215. The effigies of Lord and Lady Knyvet are represented life-size, in a kneeling attitude. On a tablet is an inscription in Latin, setting forth at considerable length the descent and virtues of the deceased, both of whom appear, from an inscription on the floor, to have died in the year 1622.

This church appears in former times to have been particularly rich in monumental brasses, but these have mostly disappeared, either by theft, or in that most dangerous of processes, " restoration."

The rectory of Stanwell was formerly a sinecure in the patronage of the Windsor family. In 1415

---

* The same is the case with Harlington Church, as will be seen presently.

Richard de Windsor exchanged the rectory and advowson for the manor of West Bedfont, with the Abbot and Convent of Chertsey. At about the same time a vicarage was endowed, to which the Abbots of Chertsey presented until the Dissolution, since which period the patronage of the vicarage has remained with the Crown, through the Lord Chancellor.

The celebrated Dr. Bruno Ryves, author of the "Mercurius Rusticus, or an Account of the Sufferings of the Royalists," was vicar of this parish. He was deprived during the Civil War, but recovered his preferment on .the Restoration. We have already had occasion to mention him in our account of Acton.*

To the west of the village are Staines Moor and Stanwell Moor, broad expanses of land bordering upon the River Colne, the latter being partly covered with houses; and also Poyle Park, a small seat in the neighbourhood of Colnbrook, a part of which village, as shown above, belongs to the parish of Stanwell.

West Bedfont, a hamlet about half a mile east of Stanwell, on the road to East Bedfont, was in former times an independent manor, but it now forms part and parcel of the manor of Stanwell.

The roadway by which we now make our way to Bedfont follows the course of the "Queen's River," which ripples merrily along through the meadows on our left; whilst at a short distance further northward flows the "Duke of Northumberland's River," on its way to unite its waters with the River Crane, in the neighbourhood of Hounslow.

Bedfont, formerly called East Bedfont, in order to distinguish it from West Bedfont, lies on the high road, about equidistant from Hounslow and Staines. With its long village green and pond, both fringed with fine elms and other trees, and its irregular string of houses and cottages retreating so gracefully behind their gardens on either side of the road, it has a quaint and primitive air, which would hardly lead one to believe that he is within thirteen miles of the great metropolis. The quaintness of its appearance is increased by its little Norman church, with its wooden tower and dwarf steeple, and its pair of trim and formal yew-trees, cut out into the shapes of peacocks, with the date 1704, and the initials of the churchwardens of that time, still legible in the cropped foliage. The local tradition is that they represent satirically two sisters who lived at Bedfont, and who were so very haughty that they both refused the hand of

some local magnate, who thus immortalised them, being "as proud as peacocks." This, however, is a legend only. These are some of the grotesque shapes with which a stiff, formal, and unnatural age loved to decorate its gardens, lawns, and alleys; and they are only a "survival" of what once was a common fashion.

If the peacocks have rendered the two maiden ladies above mentioned immortal, they have in their turn been immortalised by Thomas Hood, who makes them the subject of one of the most serious of his early "serious" poems :—

"Where erst two haughty maidens used to be,
    In pride of plume, where plumy Death hath trod,
Trailing their gorgeous velvet wantonly,
    Most unmeet pall, over the holy sod :
There, gentle stranger, thou may'st only see
    Two sombre peacocks. Age, with sapient nod
Marking the spot, still tarries to declare
How once they lived and wherefore they are there.

"Alas! that breathing vanity should go
    Where pride is buried; like its very ghost
Unrisen from the naked bones below,
    In novel flesh, clad in the silent boast
Of gaudy silk, that flutters to and fro,
    Shedding its chilling superstition most
On young and ignorant natures—as is wont
To haunt the peaceful churchyard of Bedfont."

Pope, who must often have seen these quaint artificial ornaments, satirised them in No. 173 of the *Guardian* :—"How contrary to simplicity is the modern practice of gardening! We seem to make it our study to recede from nature not only in the various tonsure of greens into the most regular and formal shapes, but even into monstrous attempts beyond the reach of the art itself; we run into sculpture, and are yet better pleased to have our trees in the most awkward figures of men and animals than in the most regular of their own. . . . A citizen is no sooner proprietor of a couple of yews, but he entertains thoughts of erecting them into giants, like those of Guildhall. I know an eminent cook who beautified his country seat with the coronation-dinner in greens (evergreens), where you see the champion flourishing on horseback at one end of the table, and the queen in perpetual youth at the other." And he adds a list of some fifteen or sixteen subjects cut in evergreens, from Adam and Eve and Noah's Ark down to Queen Elizabeth, which are to be disposed of by an "eminent town gardner," of his acquaintance. In spite of all Pope's quiet satire, those at Bedfont still hold their place; but at Harlington, as we shall presently see, the yew-tree has been allowed of late to grow at its own sweet will.

The church itself is Norman, as shown by its

* See ante, p. 15.

ornamental and round-headed south doorway and a similar chancel arch, and a small round-headed window in the north wall of the chancel. At the north-east angle of the nave, near the chancel arch, is a double recess, which looks as if it had once formed an aumbry or the reredos of an altar. On the plaster being recently stripped off the wall, two fresco paintings were revealed, the one representing the Crucifixion, and the other the Last Judgment. The great Judge is seated, in His human nature, with the five wounds conspicuous, and over His right eye is a daub of dark paint, as if pointing to a passage in the Book of Ecclesiastes, where God is said to "wink at the sins of men." Both paintings, it may be added, though they can still be deciphered, have suffered severely from iconoclasts or friendly plasterers. On the wall of the chancel is a small brass of Jacobean date, as shown by the ruff and frill. In the south wall of the nave, close to the chancel arch, is a recess with a small window, which may have contained the steps to a rood-loft, or possibly have been a place for lepers, &c., to hear mass. The frescoes are of the twelfth or thirteenth century, and have been attributed to the reign of Stephen.

Behind the church on the north is an ugly excrescence, forming a huge transept, of modern date, and of the "Churchwarden" style. This church was restored "upon the old lines" in the year 1866.

It is probable that Bedfont was at one time a Roman station, for in a field between the village and Feltham have been dug up considerable quantities of Roman coins, mixed with urns, bones, &c., and the vestiges of some barrows of uncertain date.

The name of this parish is Bedefunt and Bedefunde, in the "Domesday Record," and the principal manor is there said to be held by Richard of Walter, the son of *Other*. Another manor at Bedfont, noticed in the same record, is described as lying within the manor of Feltham, and was held by the Earl of Moreton, half-brother of the Conqueror. The principal manor of Bedfont and the manor of Hatton, included within the same parochial district, are described in the "Beauties of England and Wales" as the property of the Duke of Northumberland. On the Sion House stream, at the eastern extremity of the parish, are some powder-mills.

In 1878 an institution known as the Spelthorne Sanitorium was opened here, as a refuge for women "who have fallen into habits of intemperance." It affords accommodation for about twenty "patients," who are employed in laundry and needlework.

Adjoining, and under the same management, is the Middlesex Industrial School for Girls.

The village of Bedfont, beyond the church and its famous yews, and the institutions just referred to, contains nothing of interest to detain the visitor, excepting, perhaps, he may feel inclined to make a call at the "Black Dog," whose former landlord is commemorated in Colman's "Random Recollections" in the following lines :—

"Harvey, whose inn commands a view
 Of Bedfont's church and churchyard too,
 Where yew-trees into peacocks shorn,
 In vegetable torture mourn."

The inhabitants of the village, as may be inferred from its surroundings, are almost wholly employed in agriculture. In the year 1871 the population, including that of the hamlet of Hatton, amounted to only 1,288 souls, whilst the inhabited houses were set down in the census returns at 279. In the year 1881 the population had increased to 1,452.

Making our way in a north-easterly direction, and passing through the hamlet of Hatton, we soon arrive at Cranford, a spot which, from the sylvan beauty of its park, forms quite an "oasis in the desert," the greater part of the country around being level and uninviting arable land, or in parts cultivated as wheat-fields and orchards. Cranford Bridge, which has taken the place of the *Ford* over the Crane, or *Cran*, from which the parish took its name, lies two miles west of Hounslow, along the old Bath road. That part of it which was open heath half a century ago is now enclosed, and covered with houses and market-gardens.

It is a straggling village, with a population of some 500 souls, which is a diminution of about 50 from the number recorded in the census returns for 1871. The place possesses no regular "street," and seems to have grown up at haphazard round the outside circuit of Cranford Park, for the last two centuries and a half one of the residences of the Earls of Berkeley, and now belonging to Lord Fitzhardinge. There is nothing to remark about it, except that at the lower end of the village there is, as above stated, a bridge of three arches over the River Crane. The park is small, containing about 140 acres, and is very strictly preserved. The manor-house, which stands near the centre of it, is a dull, heavy-looking structure of any and every age, not built upon any regular plan. The stabling is fine and good, and evidently in former days formed a most important part of the mansion. It is rarely inhabited by the family, owing to the superior attractions of Berkeley Castle as a residence.

About the time of the Conquest the manor of Cranford, or Craneforde, as it is termed in "Domesday Book," was divided, and the separate manorial districts were distinguished by the names of Cranford St. John and Cranford le Mote. The first of these was for some time possessed by the Knights Templars, and after the abolition of that order, was vested in the Knights Hospitallers of St. John of Jerusalem. The manor of Cranford le Mote was long the property of the Abbot and Convent of Thame, in Oxfordshire. On the dissolution of the religious houses, both these manors were granted by Henry VIII. to Henry, Lord Windsor, and after several intermediate transfers, were purchased, in the year 1618, of the co-heirs of Sir Roger Aston, gentleman of the bedchamber to James I., by Elizabeth, Lady Berkeley, for the sum of £7,000.

Inside the park, the Crane is artificially dammed up so as to form a lake; but it is as straight as an arrow, thus showing that it was planned in the old artificial days of gardening—not unlike the straight "canal"* in St. James's Park. It abounds with fish and wild fowl, and the game all over the property is very strictly preserved.

For a long time Cranford House has been for most of the year untenanted, except by a caretaker, and it has somehow gained the reputation of being haunted. The Hon. Grantley Berkeley, in his "Life and Recollections," has given a detailed account of these nocturnal visitants. The house contains, besides a few family portraits, others of Dr. Harvey, Dean Swift, Fuller the historian, Sir William Temple, &c. The residence of the Berkeley family here is thus celebrated by Mr. W. Wilkes, in his ambitious and rather prosaic poem of "Hounslow Heath":—

> "Two miles from Hounslow towards the west is plac'd,
> With all the beauties of retirement grac'd,
> A grand and rural seat in Berkeley fam'd,
> Gay Crantford's castle by the Muses nam'd;
> Where health's preserved in unpolluted air,
> Where smiling peace extirpates every care;
> Where Amalthea holds her golden horn,
> And brisk diversions wake with every morn."

The Hon. Thomas Moreton Fitzhardinge-Berkeley, son of the fifth Earl of Berkeley, lived for many years at Cranford Cottage, in the immediate outskirts of the park. He died in August, 1882, never having assumed the title, although by a decision of the House of Lords, in 1811, he was virtually declared entitled to it.

The manor-house of Cranford le Mote occupied a moated site, at a short distance from the church on the north-east. The ancient building on this spot, which was the residence of Sir William Fleetwood, Receiver of the Court of Wards about the commencement of the seventeenth century, was taken down about the year 1780.

The church, dedicated to St. Dunstan, adjoins the manor-house, and having no aisles, remains in its original tiny proportions. As is so frequently the case along the Middlesex valley of the Thames, the tower is the only original part of the building which still stands. The nave and chancel have been modernised, the latter with heavy, but substantial, mahogany and oak.

On the walls are some fine Jacobean and more recent monuments to members of the Berkeley family, but these are not in a good state of repair. In the chancel there is a fine Jacobean monument to Sir Roger Aston, whose kneeling figure and those of his two wives and daughters, exhibit the fanciful ruffs, frills, &c., of the period. At his foot is a small bambino, representing a son who died in infancy. The marriages of the daughters are recorded, with some pride, upon the panel below, whilst the armorial bearings of Aston, with several impalements, are introduced in several parts of the monument together with a narrative inscription of considerable length. Close by the above is a mural tablet of black marble set in a frame of alabaster, to the memory of the celebrated Dr. Thomas Fuller, author of the "Church History of Britain," the "Worthies of England," and many other learned works. Dr. Fuller was warmly patronised by George, Lord Berkeley, in whose family he was chaplain, and by whom he was presented to the rectory of Cranford in 1658. Fuller died at his lodgings in Covent Garden in August, 1661, his body was brought from London and buried in the chancel of Cranford church, 200 clergy following him to the grave, and his funeral was conducted under the immediate direction of Lord Berkeley, who defrayed all the expenses incident to the solemnity. The successor of Dr. Fuller as rector of Cranford was the eminent divine John Wilkins, afterwards Bishop of Chester.

Under the chancel repose several members of the Berkeley family. Mr. Henry Berkeley, formerly for many years M.P. for Bristol, and the great advocate of the ballot, lies under a plain tomb-stone beneath the east window of the chancel. In the churchyard are some fine yews and other evergreens, which, if the truth must be told, make the edifice dark and damp. The rectory, an old structure modernised, stands just within the park gates.

---

* See "Old and New London," Vol. IV., p. 54.

HARLINGTON CHURCH.　(*See page* 199.)
(*From an Engraving dated* 1803.)

CHAPTER XVIII.

HARLINGTON AND HARMONDSWORTH.

Situation of Harlington—The Village and Population—The Manor—The Parish Church—Dr. Trapp—The Yew Tree in the Churchyard—The
Local Charities—The Earldom of Arlington—Dawley Court—Lord Bolingbroke—Harmondsworth, Situation, and Nature of the Soil—Its
Etymology—Harmondsworth Priory—The Manor—An Ancient Barn—The Parish Church—The Village—Census Returns, &c.—Heath
Row—A Roman Encampment—Sipson—Longford—Colnbrook.

HARLINGTON is a small straggling village, about a mile and a half north-west of Cranford, and nearer to Southall and Hayes, and also some three miles south of Uxbridge. It is in the Hundred of Elthorne and Union of Staines. The village contains several very old cottages, probably of the sixteenth century; much of the parish is still devoted to market gardens, and especially to cherry orchards, which impart to the lanes in the locality a green and shady aspect.

Good brick earth is obtained on the surface, especially in the northern part, though gravel predominates below, and the result is that much brick-making is carried on in the neighbourhood. In 1871 this parish contained inhabited houses to the number of 254, whilst the population amounted to 1,296 souls. According to the census returns for 1881 the number of the inhabitants had increased to 1,538. The acreage of the parish is set down at 1,464, and the rateable value at £11,433.

The name of Harlington appears to have been originally spelt Herdington, or Herdyngton. Under the former name it is mentioned in "Domesday Book" as a manor answering for ten hides, and having "land for six ploughs," and held under Earl Roger by Alured and Olaf. It speaks of a priest as owning half a hide of land there, and of twelve *villani*, holding half a virgate each; mention is made also of eight cottagers and one bondsman. Its whole value is given as one hundred shillings. "It is taxed," writes the author of the *Antiquarian Cabinet*, "in the ancient valors at nine marks yearly. In the

King's Books it is valued at £24. The Inquisition taken in 1650, by order of the Parliament, states the parsonage to be worth £140 a year, exclusive of 36 acres of glebe. Some of these acres, however, are now lost to the living, though its money value is largely increased."

The chief manor appears to have been divided at an early period into two, both of which now belong to the Berkeley family. The manor of Hardington, Harlington, or "Lovells," having been in the hands of the Harpendens, the Lovells, and the great Lord Bolingbroke, passed to the Earl of Uxbridge, who sold it to the late Earl of Berkeley. The other manor of Harlington-cum-Sheperton came to the same family by the marriage of George, Lord Berkeley, with a daughter of Sir Michael Stanhope.

There is in this parish a third reputed manor, of small extent, which is noticed in the "Norman Survey" under the name of "Dalleger." It answered in "Doomsday" for three hides. It was afterwards called Dalley, or Danley; and under the more recent name of Dawley it belonged to Lord Bolingbroke, and now to Count Fane de Salis.

The church, dedicated to St. Peter and St. Paul, stands near the north end of the village, and consists of nave, chancel, and a square embattled tower. A north aisle was added at the restoration of the building in 1881. The edifice is chiefly built of flint, with stone facings, and the chancel is higher than the nave. There is a fine Norman font, and also a Norman south doorway, with zig-zag mouldings. One singular and interesting feature in the ornamentation of this doorway is that the outer member of the arch comprises a series of cats' heads, the tongues being fancifully

carved, and turned over a moulding corded and beaded. The pillars which support the arch are of modern brick, but the capitals are Norman, and are dissimilar and much embellished.

The Easter Sepulchre.

The Norman Door. Harlington.

"BITS" FROM HARLINGTON CHURCH.

The mouldings have been formerly cut away to admit the addition of a wooden porch of much more recent date, finely carved. This, however, has been raised, and the defects of the noble doorway have been repaired. This doorway is altogether a very handsome specimen of late and elaborate Norman work, its ornamentation being equal to the well-known examples of Iffley, Barfreston, and Patrixbourne, near Canterbury.

This church, which has been carefully restored upon the old lines, affords examples of nearly every style of architecture. There are two early Norman, or possibly Saxon, windows north and south of the nave; the Decorated windows on the sides of the chancel are very fine in their tracery;

and the east window, of post-Reformation Gothic, cannot fail to remind visitors of Oriel and Wadham Colleges at Oxford. The church altogether is, perhaps, the best specimen of a mediæval country church in all the Middlesex valley of the Thames. It is rendered all the more picturesque by a fine yew-tree—said to be 700 years old—on the south side of the churchyard, and a noble cedar in the vicarage garden adjoining it on the north.

In the church are brasses to members of the Lovell family, and one, half-length, to John Yarmouth, a former rector, who is duly robed in the Eucharistic vestments. On the north wall of the chancel is the monument of Dr. Joseph Trapp, rector of this parish in 1732—47, and some time Professor of Poetry in the University of Oxford. He died in 1747. His monument bears the following lines :—

" Death, judgment, heaven, and hell ! think, Christian, think,
    You stand on vast eternity's dread brink ;
    Faith and repentance, piety and prayer,
    Despise this world, the next be all your care.
    Thus, while my tomb the solemn silence breaks,
    And to the eye this cold dumb marble speaks,
    Tho' dead I preach : if e'er with ill success,
    Living, I strove th' important truth to press,
    Your precious, your immortal souls to save ;
    Hear me, at least, oh, hear me from my grave."

Dr. Trapp's want of poetical ability, as exemplified in his attempts to translate Virgil and Milton, is recorded in some severe epigrams. There is a portrait of him in the Bodleian Library.

The Bennets, Lords Tankerville, are still buried here, though the family have long lived in Northumberland. On the floor is a memorial to Charles, Earl of Tankerville, who died in 1767 ; and the last earl, who died in 1859, has also a memorial here. There are also monuments to various members of the family of Lord De Tabley, his first wife having been a De Salis.

There are some fine modern tombs and two painted windows erected in memory of members of the family of De Salis of Dawley Court, whose fortunes were founded in this country by one Peter de Salis, sent hither as envoy in 1709 from the Emperor Joseph I.

A fresco painting on the south wall of the nave was discovered on removing the monument of Sir John Bennet, Lord Ossulston, who died in the year 1695. The monument, which has been replaced, has upon it busts of Lord Ossulston and his two wives.

Affixed to the south wall of the nave is a carved hour-glass of oak, thought by some to be of the thirteenth or fourteenth century. The Easter sepulchre—a handsome piece of stone carving on the north side of the chancel—is thought by some antiquarians to be the reredos of an altar. The registers, which commence in 1540, are in fairly good condition ; they are curious as containing the names of many " travellers"—one result of the parish being situated just one day's tramp on the great road to the west from London.

Among former rectors was a John of Tewkesbury, who was the author of some learned books ; and also John Kyte, who resigned the living in 1510 ; he was probably the same person who was sent as ambassador to Spain, and died in 1537 Bishop of Carlisle. He was a native of London, and is buried at Stepney.

The magnificent old yew-tree in the churchyard above referred to grows now in a healthy and natural fashion; but, as shown in our illustration taken early in the present century, it used to be clipped and cut into artificial shape. From some verses by the parish clerk, John Saxy, affixed to a large copper-plate engraving, it would seem that in 1729 this yew-tree was upwards of fifty feet high. It was surrounded at the base by a circular seat, over which hung a large canopy, formed by the dark boughs of the tree, in the words of this rural poet—

" So thick, so fine, so full, so wide,
    A troop of Guards might under 't ride."

Some ten feet higher up again was another smaller canopy, above which the tree towered up solid, till its topmost leaves formed a sort of nest in the shape of a globe, with a cock or hen seated above it.

" A weather-cock, who gapes to crow it,
    ' The globe is mine and all below it,' "

writes the rhymer, who adds his deliberate opinion of the tree, that—

" It yields to Harlington a fame
    Much louder than its Earldom's name."

Without going quite so far as the worthy clerk, we may state that the tree, until it ceased to be clipped, some half century ago, was the great curiosity of the place, and was visited by scores of persons. It is thought to be as old as the Conquest, and it is still one of the largest yew-trees in the home counties : its branches formerly reached to the church porch, and are said to have covered a space of 150 feet. The clipping and clearing of the tree was a village holiday, as important in its way and in its place as the scouring of the White Horse on the Berkshire Downs. The last occasion on which it was clipped was in 1825.

In our view of the church the old yew does not appear to be so high as when sung of by the parish clerk. It figures also in Loudon's "Arboretum Britannicum," but in that work its dimensions are exaggerated.

The fantastic idea of thus clipping the yew-tree was a survival of the old formal style of gardening which prevailed under our Tudor and Stuart sovereigns.

The charities in this parish are considerable. One rector, named Cooper, left an annual sum to the clerk for repairing his tomb; but this reverend gentleman's body has been removed from his grave to another part of the churchyard; the benefaction, however, remains. Some land was left to the bell-ringers to provide them a leg of pork for dinner on Guy Fawkes' Day, and this is called the Pork Half-Acre. The land has since been sold for £100, and the proceeds invested for their benefit; and about fourteen acres were set apart for the poor at the last enclosure, in lieu of their ancient right to cut turf.

Dawley Court, in this parish, once the residence of the great Lord Bolingbroke, is no longer standing, except the steward's apartments, or what is said to have been the laundry, consisting of two fine rooms. This for many years has been the only building on the estate, the remainder of the land having been cut up into prosaic brick-fields.

The mansion itself was pulled down about the year 1776.

The manor-house at Dawley must have been a spacious structure; it was the residence of the Lovells and of the Bennets before it came into the hands of Lord Bolingbroke. Its succeeding owner, Lord Uxbridge, is said to have built round it a wall nearly a mile long, to keep out the small-pox.

Dawley became the property of the Bennets early in the sixteenth century. Sir John Bennet, who appears to have been the first of that name residing here, was a distinguished member of Parliament in the reign of Queen Elizabeth, and was judge of the Prerogative Court of Canterbury in the reign of James I. In 1617 he was sent as ambassador to Brussels, to interrogate the archduke on behalf of his royal master, the King of Great Britain, concerning a libel written and published, as it was supposed, by Erycius Puteanus, in his Imperial Highness's dominions. His eldest son and successor, Sir John Bennet, of Dawley, ancestor of the Earls of Tankerville, received the honour of knighthood in the lifetime of his father at Theobalds, in 1616. He was the father of Henry Bennet, who

will be remembered as a member of the "Cabal Ministry," and who was raised to the peerage in 1663 as Viscount Thetford and Earl of Arlington. His lordship meant to choose this place as that from which he should derive his title; but the scribes of the Herald's College, or some other officials, were not as attentive to their "H's" as they should have been, and so, when the patent reached his hands, or when he read his new dignity in the *Gazette*, he found that he had been created Earl, not of Harlington, but of "Arlington." It was too late for any alteration to have been made, for "the proof had been worked off," so Arlington he remained; and the street which runs out of Piccadilly towards St. James's Palace is Arlington also.

The Arlington coronet is now merged in the ducal title of Grafton, through the marriage of the first duke with Lady Isabella Bennet, only daughter of the above-mentioned earl; consequently, the Duke of Grafton reckons among his inferior titles the barony of "Arlington, of Harlington, county of Middlesex."

From the Bennets Dawley Court passed to the celebrated Lord Bolingbroke, and became his favourite country house, or, as he liked to style it, his "farm." He lived here during a memorable period of his eventful life, the time of his estrangement from public affairs, and from the gay world as well. To use his own figurative language, he was now "in a hermitage, where no man came but for the sake of the hermit; for here he found that the insects which used to hum and buzz about him in the sunshine fled to men of more prosperous fortune, and forsook him when in the shade." Here he was often visited by "Glorious John Dryden."

Lord Bolingbroke adorned his house with paintings of rustic subjects, "trophies of rakes, spades, prongs," &c. (as Pope tells us in a letter addressed by him from hence to Swift), and over the door he placed an inscription, slightly altered from Horace :—

" Satis beatus ruris honoribus."

Living as he did within some six or seven miles of Dawley, Pope was a constant visitor here; and so was Voltaire occasionally, whilst staying in London.

It is said that some of the same wild oxen which are now to be seen at Lord Tankerville's park in Northumberland were kept here in the time of the Bennets; but this is probably an error.

A poem, entitled "Dawley's Farm," in the first

volume of the *Gentleman's Magazine*, gives us some glimpses of the place as it appeared in 1731 :—

" See, emblem of himself, his villa stand,
　Politely finish'd, elegantly grand !
　Frugal of ornament, but that the best,
　And with all curious negligence express'd.
　No gaudy colours deck the rural hall,
　Blank light and shade discriminate the wall ;
　Where through the whole we see his lov'd design,
　To please with mildness, without glaring shine,
　Himself neglects what must all others charm,
　And what he built a palace calls a farm.

　Here the proud trophies and the spoils of war
　Yield to the scythe, the harrow, and the car,
　To whate'er implement the rustic wields,
　Whate'er manures the gardens or the fields.

　*　　*　　*　　*　　*　　*

　Here noble St. John, in his sweet recess,
　Sees on the figured wall the stacks of corn
　With beauty more than theirs the room adorn ;
　Young winged Cupids smiling guide the plow,
　And peasants elegantly reap and sow.

　*　　*　　*　　*　　*　　*

　O, Britain ! but 'tis past.　O lost to fame,
　The wondrous man, thy glory and thy shame,
　Conversing with the mighty minds of old—
　Names like his own in time's bright lists enroll'd,
　Here splendidly obscure, delighted lives,
　And only for his wretched country grieves."

Lady Luxborough, Lord Bolingbroke's sister, mentions the place in one of her letters in terms which fully justify these not very poetical lines. She writes :—" When my brother Bolingbroke built Dawley, which he chose to call a ' Farm,' he had his hall painted in stone colour, with all the implements of husbandry placed in the manner one sees, or might see, arms and trophies in some general's hall ; and it had an effect that pleased everybody."

Voltaire occasionally came here whilst staying in London ; and Pope, who lived within some six or seven miles of Dawley, was a constant visitor.　In a letter written from hence by Pope to Dean Swift, we find the following :—" I now hold the pen of my Lord Bolingbroke, who is reading your letter between two hay-cocks ; but his attention is somewhat diverted by casting his eyes on the clouds—not in admiration of what you say, but for fear of a shower.　He is pleased with your placing him in the triumvirate between yourself and me ; though he says that he doubts he shall fare like Lepidus, while one of us runs away with all the power, like Augustus, and another with all the pleasures, like Anthony.　It is upon a foresight of this that he has fitted up his farm.　Now his lordship is run after his cart, I

have a moment left to myself to tell you that I overheard him yesterday agree with a painter for £200 to paint his country hall with trophies of rakes, spades, prongs, &c., and other ornaments, merely to countenance his calling his place a farm."

His lordship, we are told, was happy in possessing " a mind formed for the world at large, and not dependent on the contingencies of court favour " ; though it is to be regretted that the poetical warmth of his imagination often led him, in his retired as well as in his busy hours, to flights of dangerous mental indulgence.　A temper so ardent could never find a semblance of repose but in extremes.

" In the earlier days of his character," writes Mr. Disraeli, " Lord Bolingbroke meditated over the formation of a new party—that dream of youthful ambition in a perplexed and discordant age, but destined in English politics to be never more substantial than a vision.　More experienced in political life," he continues, " Lord Bolingbroke became aware that he had only to choose between the Whigs and the Tories, and his sagacious intellect, not satisfied with the ¨superficial character of these . . . divisions, penetrated their interior and essential qualities, and discovered, in spite of all the affectation of popular sympathy on the one side, and of admiration of arbitrary power on the other, that his choice was, in fact, a choice between oligarchy and democracy.　From the moment that Lord Bolingbroke, in becoming a Tory, embraced the national cause, he devoted himself absolutely to his party ; all the energies of his Protean mind were lavished in their service ; and although . . . restrained from advocating the cause of the nation in the Senate, his inspiring pen made Walpole tremble in the recesses of the Treasury ; and in a series of writings, unequalled in our literature for their spirited patriotism, their just and profound views, and the golden eloquence in which they are expressed, eradicated from Toryism all those absurd and odious doctrines which Toryism had adventitiously adopted, clearly developed its essential and permanent character, discarded the *jus divinum*, demolished passive obedience, threw to the winds the doctrine of non-resistance, placed the abdication of James and the accession of George on their right basis, and in the complete reorganisation of the public mind laid the foundation for the future accession of the Tory party to power."　But a man of fashion, and fond of society and of politics, Lord Bolingbroke soon found that the country was wearisome, and resolved to part with his beloved Dawley.　He sold it in 1739, when the house was nearly all pulled down again. One wing alone was left, and this was made into a steward's residence. The lands were bought by the Pagets, then Earls of Uxbridge, and living at Harmondsworth, from whom again they passed into the hands of the family of De Salis. The once beautiful grounds where Bolingbroke read Pope's letter as he reclined on a haycock are now turned into brick-fields, through which pass a canal and the Great Western Railway—a mournful commentary on the short-lived pleasures of great men.

It is said that on grand occasions in Lord Bolingbroke's or Lord Uxbridge's days the road from Dawley to West Drayton used to be hung with artificial lamps, to guide his aristocratic visitors on their way home at night; and one of the fields which it crosses is still called "The Lanterns."

It might be said of "Dawley Farm" as truly as of Canons itself (of which we shall speak hereafter):—

"Another age shall see the golden ear,
Imbrown the slope and nod on the parterre;
Deep harvests bury all his pride has plann'd,
And laughing Ceres re-assume the land."

But here the transformation is almost more complete, for Ceres herself has had to give way in her turn to the goddess, if there be one, who presides over brick-fields and brick-makers.

Opposite the Dawley Manor Farm, and near the church, are to be traced the remains of a moated grange, in a meadow still known as "The Moats"; but nothing is known of its history.

The parish of Harmondsworth adjoins Harlington on the west, and is separated from Buckinghamshire by a branch of the River Colne. The whole district is flat and uninteresting, but the soil is fertile, and productive of good crops of corn and vegetables, whilst much fruit finds its way from this locality to the London markets. The land hereabouts is intersected by several small rivulets, or streams, which creep in dull obscurity, without imparting to any portion of the parish the elements of the picturesque.

The name of the parish is familiarly pronounced "Harmsworth" by the "natives." In the "Domesday Book" it is written *Hermondesworde*, and it is stated in that record that the Abbot of the Holy Trinity at Rouen held the principal manor of the king. Tanner says that there was here a priory of the Benedictine order, which was a cell to the above-mentioned abbey of the Holy Trinity, but no traces of such a priory have been discovered in recent times.

Cobbett mentions, in his list of religious houses confiscated by Henry VIII., an alien priory here, which was granted in the first year of Edward VI. to one of the Tudor courtiers, Sir William Paget. He gives, however, no particulars as to its name, its site, or its value. Perhaps it was the same as the above.

"This manor," observes the author of "The Beauties of England and Wales," "shared the fate of many other possessions of the alien priories, and was seized by King Edward III. in the year 1340. The arable land belonging to the demesne was then valued at 4d. an acre, the meadow at 8d., and the pasture at 2d. There were two watermills: one for corn, let at 18s. per annum; the other for malt, at 8s. The manor was afterwards conveyed to William of Wykeham, who settled it upon the collegiate establishment of his foundation; but it was again obtained by the Crown, in exchange for other possessions, in the reign of Henry VIII. By Edward VI. it was granted to Sir William Paget, from whom it descended to the present noble possessor, the Marquis of Anglesey. As a manorial custom, of a character not very frequent, it may be observed that tenants have a right of fishery in all the rivers and common waters within the manor on Wednesdays, Fridays, and Saturdays. It is probable that the ancient manor-house occupied the site of a farm-dwelling near the church, which claims notice, as there is in the attached yard a barn of remarkably large dimensions, it being 191 feet in length and 38 feet in breadth."

The fine old barn above mentioned is perhaps the most interesting object of antiquity in this neighbourhood. The walls are built of conglomerate, commonly called "pudding-stone," and found in this locality. The body of the barn is divided into a nave and aisles by two rows of massive pillars. There are three floors, and the roof is of open timber-work, in good preservation. In former times the building was much larger, having an angular projecting wing, or transept, at the north end, which was pulled down about the year 1775, at the same time as the old manor-house, near which it stood. This portion of the old barn was re-built—or rather, the roof of it was re-erected on walls of modern brick-work and supported by the original oak columns—at Heath Row, about a mile and a half distant. The building, of which we have given an engraving on the next page, is commonly called "the Gothic barn," because its interior is so like the nave of a cathedral.

The manor was sold by the Pagets, and is now

the property of Mr. George Harmond. Although the mansion has disappeared, the gardens and stables still remain. Some subordinate manors in the parish, lying in the hamlets of Longford, Sipson, and other parts, formerly belonging to the Pagets, have passed into the the hands of the Earl of Strafford and other owners.

The parish church, dedicated to the Virgin Mary, notwithstanding that it was restored in 1863, bears the marks of considerable antiquity, portions of it dating as far back as the Norman times. It is a tolerably fine building, rather like those of West Drayton and Harlington.

The village of Harmondsworth consists chiefly of scattered rural dwellings, many of which are in that ancient and simple mode of construction—half timber and plaster, projecting upper storeys, and thatched roofs—so favourable to the picturesque. There are also one or two old mansions, with cedars in the grounds. But to the parish, as a whole, no historical interest whatever is attached. According to the census returns for the year 1871 the parish contained 326 inhabited houses, the number of the population being 1,584, which had increased to 1,800 in the course of the next ten years.

THE OLD BARN AT HARMONDSWORTH.   (See page 203.)

The body of the structure is composed of stone and flint, and is of the Perpendicular style of architecture. It consists of a nave with aisles, chancel with north aisle, and a square brick tower of modern erection at the south-west corner. The tower, however, is poor, and cased with plaster. The south doorway is of Norman workmanship, but not a richly-worked specimen of that style of architecture; the chief feature of it, however, is a range of birds' heads, the beaks being thrown over a torus-band moulding. In the south side of the chancel are three stalls, or seats, together with a piscina and credence table. In digging a grave of unusual depth in the churchyard in the year 1870, some silver coins, twenty-five in number, belonging to the Tudor and Stuart periods, were discovered.

Heath Row, mentioned above, lies in the eastern part of the parish, to the south of the great western road, and it takes its name from its situation on the margin of Hounslow Heath. Close by this spot are slight traces of the Roman encampment which Stukeley, as already stated in our account of Coway Stakes, believed to have been formed by Cæsar after he had crossed the Thames, and during his progress towards Hertfordshire. This camp, of which a view is given in the "Itinerarium Curiosum," is considered to have measured about 300 feet square, and to have been defended by a single ditch. The hamlet of Sipson—or Shepiston, as it was sometimes called—is situated in this neighbourhood.

Longford is a hamlet in this parish, on the road to Slough. It takes its name from its situation on a branch of the River Colne, which supplies Hampton Court with water, and which is crossed by a bridge, erected in 1834, called the Queen's Bridge. The district hereabout lies low, and is subject to inundation from the overflowing of the stream above mentioned.

Colnbrook, which lies about two miles west of Longford, is the utmost limit of our perambulation in this direction, being just on the borders of the jurisdiction of the Metropolitan Police. The town is located on four channels of the River Colne, over each of which there is a bridge. The greater part of the town, Colnbrook proper, is in Buckinghamshire; but the eastern part, forming part of the parish of Stanwell, is in the county of Middlesex. The town contains many old houses and hostelries, in one of which Queen Elizabeth is said to have been in the habit of resting for the night on her way to Windsor Castle. It is a long straggling town, and stands in two counties and in four parishes, and, like Uxbridge and Maidenhead, it has only lately been made parochial.

THE GATEHOUSE, WEST DRAYTON. (*See page 207.*)

CHAPTER XIX.

WEST DRAYTON AND HAYES.

Satis beatus ruris honoribus.' —Paraphrased from Horace by Lord Bolingbroke.

Situation and Boundaries of West Drayton—Its Vegetable Products, Fishing, &c.—Its Etymology—Descent of the Manor—The Old Manor-house—Burroughs, formerly the Seat of General Arabin—The Parish Church—The Burial-ground—The Village of West Drayton—Population—The Catholic Church of St. Catharine—Thorney Broad—The Race-course—Yiewsley—Hayes—The Grand Junction Canal—Census Returns—Boundaries of the Parish—Its Nomenclature—Condition of the Parish in Tudor Times—Acreage of the Parish—Descent of the Manor—The Village of Hayes—Yeading Manor—Botwell—Cotman's Town—Wood End Green—The Parish Church—The Rectory - Distinguished Rectors—Schools and Charities—Extracts from the Parish Registers.

TAKING a fresh start north from Harmondsworth, a journey of a couple of miles brings us to Drayton—or, as it is commonly called, West Drayton, probably to distinguish it from Drayton Green, close by Castle Hill, Ealing, some four miles eastward. Drayton is a large, irregular village, on the western border of Middlesex. The parish is separated on its western side from Buckinghamshire by the river Colne, which meanders peacefully along through meadows and corn-fields, and having here and there upon its banks a mill or a farmyard, which imparts a certain amount of life and animation to a landscape which might otherwise, perhaps, be considered dull and monotonous. It is bounded in other directions by the parishes of Hillingdon, Harlington, and Harmondsworth. A considerable quantity of fruit is grown in this neighbourhood, which in due course mostly finds its way into the London markets. The Grand Junction Canal passes by the village, a little to the north of the railway station. The name points to its sylvan and rural origin. It is the town or village of "dreys," as the squirrels' nests are still termed in the rural districts of Hampshire and Berkshire.

Beyond describing the descent of the manor, there is almost nothing historical to record in connection with the parish of Drayton. Out of the way of turmoil and strife, the place has apparently enjoyed from the earliest period of its existence one of peaceful retirement and seclusion. We find in the "Domesday Book" the name of the parish written *Draitone*, and it is there stated that it belonged to the canons of St. Paul's, to whom it had been given by King Athelstan. It is also recorded in the above-mentioned survey that "it answered for ten hides, that there was a mill rented at thirteen shillings and fivepence, pasture for the cattle of the village, and a stream rented at thirty-two pence." According to Bawdwen's "Translation of Domesday for Middlesex," "its whole annual value is said to be six pounds; the same when received; in King Edward's time eight pounds." In a survey, bearing date 1181, it is stated that "the manor of Drayton was taxed in the time of Henry I. and William the Dean at ten hides, as it still is. It paid then 5 shillings to the sheriff, but since the war, 10 shillings, besides which, it pays 11 shillings for the right of frank-pledge."

The manor of Drayton remained in the possession of the Dean and Chapter of St. Paul's until about the middle of the sixteenth century, when Henry VIII. obtained it in exchange for other lands, and shortly afterwards granted it to Sir William Paget, who, during the latter years of Henry's reign, had been actively and confidentially employed, often as a diplomatist upon secret and important missions, and who at one time filled the office of Secretary of State. Besides the manor of Drayton, Sir William Paget received a legacy of £300 from the king, who constituted him one of his executors, and of the council to Edward VI. Sir William Paget subsequently formed a close alliance with the Protector Somerset, and was thus retained to do good service for the State. In 1552 he was summoned to Parliament as Baron Paget of Beaudesert, in the county of Stafford; but

having taken a prominent part in the Government of the Protector, and shared in the downfall of his patron, he was committed to the Tower, fined £6,000 by the Star Chamber, and divested of the insignia of the Garter. Within a short time, however, he obtained his liberty, with a general pardon for all offences, and a remission of the debt due to the Crown. On the death of Edward, he espoused the cause of Mary, and after her accession to the throne was sworn a member of the Privy Council. He had also a restoration of the Garter, and obtained several important grants from her Majesty. On the accession of Elizabeth, in 1558, Lord Paget retired from public life, at his own request; and Camden informs us that her Majesty "retained an affection and value for him, though he was a strict zealot of the Romish Church."

On the attainder of Thomas, third Lord Paget, in 1587, on suspicion of favouring Mary, Queen of Scots, his property was confiscated to the Crown, the manor of Drayton being afterwards granted to Sir Christopher Hatton for life. It was subsequently leased to George Carey, afterwards Lord Hunsdon; but after the death of Lord Paget the reversion was granted (in 1597) to William, the son of that nobleman, who was restored by Act of Parliament, at the commencement of the reign of James I., to his rank and honours, and to a grant also of the remainder of his father's estate. From William, Lord Paget, the manor of Drayton descended to the grandson of Henry, seventh lord—Henry, Earl of Uxbridge—who had been advanced to that earldom in 1714. On the death of the earl without issue, in 1769, this manor devolved, in conjunction with the barony of Paget, to Henry Bailey, Esq., his heir-at-law, who assumed the name of Paget, and was created Earl of Uxbridge in 1784. The second earl is better known to history as Field-Marshal the Marquis of Anglesey, one of the Duke of Wellington's companions-in-arms in the Peninsula and at Waterloo. Lord Uxbridge sold this manor in 1786 to Mr. Fyshe De Burgh, and it has since continued in the possession of his descendants.

The Manor House, which was erected by the Paget family, has long since been demolished, having been pulled down by the Earl of Uxbridge about the middle of the last century. It was a spacious red brick mansion, standing to the south of the church, and was approached by stately avenues of trees. Its gardens surrounded the churchyard. Some of the walls which enclosed the gardens are still standing, together with a large part of the out-offices and stables, the upper chambers of which were formerly occupied by the servants and retainers, and the principal entrance to the courtyard. This gate-house is of red brick, not unlike some of the details of Hampton Court, and commands a view down the street to the entrance of the Hall. Though low, it is massive, and a fine specimen of the Tudor style. It consists of a Pointed arch, flanked on either side by large octangular turrets; it is in very good preservation, and still inhabited as a separate dwelling-house. The original oak doors remain. The site of the old mansion is now occupied, with some attached ground, by a market gardener. The manor-house and the church here stood close together, in accordance with the old Christian theory of the sacred edifice being built originally as the chapel or oratory for the dwellers in "the great house" and their dependents. The present residence of the De Burghs, lords of the manor, called Drayton Hall, is a commodious dwelling, at a short distance from the church, and was formerly the property of Lord Boston.

An old and spacious mansion in this village was formerly the residence of General Arabin, and was sometimes called Burroughs, or Buroughs, from the circumstance of a house on this spot having in bygone times belonged to Sir Thomas Burgh, who was esquire of the body to King Edward IV. "This," observes the author of the "Beauties of England and Wales," "is the site of a small manor belonging to the Bishop of London, which was granted in the year 1462 to the above-mentioned Thomas Burgh, by whom it was aliened in 1476. This manor was given by King Edward VI. to the Bishop of Westminster; and on being surrendered again to the Crown in 1550, was granted to the see of London. This small manorial district is now united with the manor of Colham Garden, in the parish of Hillingdon, which is also the property of the Bishop of London." The mansion was bought, on a sale of the property in lots, by Robert, sixth Earl Ferrers, of whose family it was purchased by the above-mentioned General Arabin. The writer of the notice in the "Beauties of England" concludes as follows:—"This is a residence of the dull, secluded character, favourable to traditional story. Many a marvellous tale is accordingly told respecting its hall, its chambers, and the pensive shaded walks of the grounds. Among these stories, it may be mentioned as the most remarkable that not a few rustic neighbours believe the mansion of Burroughs to have been an occasional residence of Oliver Cromwell, and that the body of the Protector was privately conveyed to this place when threatened with disgraceful exposure, and was re-buried beneath the paving of the hall."

The parish church of Drayton, which lies at the east end of the village, bears a "strong family likeness" to those of the neighbouring parishes of Harlington and Harmondsworth, being a handsome Gothic structure of the Perpendicular style. It is built of stone and flint. It is dedicated to St. Martin, and comprises a chancel, a clerestoried nave, side aisle, with an open porch, formed of wood, projecting a considerable distance from the south wall, and a massive western tower profusely overgrown with ivy, and surmounted by a small wooden turret. Some of the windows are filled with stained glass, and the church is in good repair, having been thoroughly restored in 1850, at which time the old-fashioned pews were superseded by open benches. The font is octangular and very curious, being elaborately ornamented. In the upper part, which is divided into panels, are represented the "Crucifixion of Our Lord," a sculptor at work on some foliage, and "Our Lady of Pity;" the remaining panels being filled with angels holding shields. The chancel contains several monuments, chiefly to the families of the De Burghs and Pagets. The helmets and banners which adorned them are gone. In the floor are brasses to the memory of Richard Roos, citizen of London (1406); Robert Machell, gentleman, a retainer to the Lord Paget (1557); and John Goode, an eminent physician (1581).

Besides the churchyard, there is here another burial-ground, at some distance from the church, and not far from the present hall. This singular arrangement was brought about by the wish of Sir William Paget, who, in the year 1550, procured an Act of Parliament enabling him to give an acre of ground, forming the present parochial cemetery, in exchange for the ancient place of burial, which he enclosed within his garden wall. This ground is now laid out as a flower-garden.

The village of West Drayton is about fourteen miles from London, and there is a station about half a mile to the north, on the Great Western Railway.

West Drayton proper has a population of a little over a thousand. This is a slight increase over the number recorded in the census of 1871, when there were 984 souls, the inhabited houses at that time being given as 192. In the centre of the village, and facing a broad open green, is the Roman Catholic Church of St. Catharine, the first stone of which was laid by Archbishop (now Cardinal) Manning in 1868. In the district of West Drayton there is a large straggling population of Roman Catholics of very humble means, and previous to the establishment of the mission their religious welfare was much neglected, those who had the inclination to attend Divine service having to travel a distance of six miles to the church at North Hyde. Services were first introduced in a barn at West Drayton, and it was in that humble sanctuary that the Archbishop first administered the rite of confirmation to the hitherto poor, neglected children.

Thorney Broad, about three-quarters of a mile south of the railway station, is a favourite spot for trout-fishing. Indeed, the disciples of Izaak Walton find much to occupy their attention during the fishing season, in the rivers and streams hereabouts. Trout have been turned into the Colne, but not yet with great success. A race-course was established at West Drayton about the year 1865, in a large river-side meadow, on the south of the railway. The periodical gatherings which take place there were a great nuisance to the neighbourhod, the sports being among the most frequented of those suburban races which are patronised by the lowest classes of sporting "roughs."

Near the station is a small cluster of houses, with the "Railway Inn." This spot is known as Yiewsley—the lee or meadow adorned with yews, which form so marked a feature in the villages of West Middlesex; but it is a hamlet actually belonging to the parish of Hillingdon. St. Matthew's Church, in this district, was built from the designs of Sir Gilbert Scott in 1869.

The first stone of the new schools at Yiewsley was laid by Bishop Claughton in August, 1871. The schools will hold about 300 children.

From the hamlet of Yiewsley we turn our steps once more eastward, following, for the most part, the courses of the Grand Junction Canal and the Great Western Railway, and leaving Cowley, Uxbridge, and Hillingdon, away on our left, to be dealt with on our return journey.

After our long perambulations through the flat and level districts which are called the Valley of the Thames, but which scarcely form a valley—for the lack of hills, at all events on the Middlesex side—it is pleasant to find ourselves once more on a slight "upland," at the ancient village of Hayes, crowned with its historic church. It stands about a mile to the north of the Great Western Railway, which has a small station near the meeting of the parishes of Hayes and Harlington, and named after the former. The district all round the railway station in every direction is covered with brick-fields, which sadly mar its appearance; but these are rather decreasing in number, the supply of clay being not inexhaustible. The Grand Junction Canal—which conveys goods, and once conveyed

passengers also, below Uxbridge and London —runs here almost parallel with the railway; and the cottages are all inhabited by an industrial population, who find their occupation in either brick-making or barge-driving. In 1871 the number of inhabited houses in the parish amounted to 524, with a population of 2,654 souls. This latter number was gradually increased during the ten following years, for, according to the census returns for 1882, Hayes numbered a population of 2,891.

The village of Hayes is very extensive, and, unlike its neighbours, it has a history. It is bounded on the south by Heston, Harlington, and Cranford, and on the west by Hillingdon; and northwards it extends to Northolt and Ickenham, while eastwards it originally stretched as far as Hanwell, for Southall and Norwood were once portions of it. The fact is that Hayes was, in Anglo-Saxon times, a country residence of the Archbishop of Canterbury, who held the manor and the rectory of Hayes. Consequently, though most of the parochial duties were discharged by a vicar, who held the "cure of souls," the rector of Hayes was always a great Church dignitary, whose ecclesiastical rank invested the place with an honour and a sanctity peculiar to itself.

It is very remarkable that whilst in some counties nearly every name mentioned in "Doomsday Book" has disappeared, in Middlesex the names of well-nigh every parish and hundred remain almost unchanged, after the lapse of eight centuries. Thus, in that ancient record this place figures as *Hesa*—probably then pronounced as Haisa—in the Hundred of Osulvestane, or Ossulston.* After a description of the king's land, the book tells us that "Archbishop Lanfranc holds Hesa for forty-nine hides; there is land for forty ploughs. To the demesne pertain twelve hides; and there are two ploughs there. Among the freemen and the villanes there are twenty-six ploughs, and there could be twelve more."

Lysons tells us that the name is probably derived from the Saxon word "Haeg," a hedge (in French "Haye"), which comes very near to its present appellation. From Hesa it became Hease, Heyse, Hays, Heesse, Hesse, and Hese, at different times.

The old road from London to Oxford passes though the whole length of the parish, nearly bisecting it. In the days of the Tudors the western part of the parish was an open heath, adjoining that of Hillingdon; and it would seem,

---

* It is now in the Hundred of Elthorne.

from the map of John Norden (about 1625), that the road ran in a somewhat different direction, turning to the north, along what is now called Mellow Lane, the fine old trees of which point backwards to the distant past, and look like the features of an ancient highway; and this is confirmed by local tradition. The course of the road was doubtless altered as enclosures were gradually made.

The manor and parish of Hayes apparently have differed greatly in extent at different times. In the Saxon era it is said to have comprised thirty-two hides, or about 3,840 acres. In "Doomsday," the hides in the hands of Lanfranc are given as fifty-nine, which would give about 7,080 acres, if we reckon 120 acres to the hide. According to the Ordnance Survey of the year 1865, the exact acreage is 5,772, of which nearly 1,520 acres are arable, nearly 1,250 pasture-land, while 300 are occupied as brick-fields, woods, osier-beds, orchards, &c., &c. (This includes the "precinct" of Norwood.) "Little care, however," writes Mr. Mills, in an unpublished "History of Hayes," "has been taken of the boundaries of the parish. The custom of 'beating the bounds' has not been performed for a great number of years, and few boundary stones or other marks exist, and such as are in existence have been mostly defaced." The fact is, that a divided rule never answers. The rector left the vicar, and the vicar left the rector, to see to this duty on "Rogation Days," and between the two, that useful ceremony was neglected.

The earliest mention of Hayes is in A.D. 830, when a priest—Warherdus, or Walherdus—bequeathed the manor of Hayes, which he styles his own patrimony, to the church of Canterbury. And if it be true that manors were so called from *manere*, it is probable that he lived here, and exercised the "cure of souls" as well as the rights of a "squire" over his tenants. The next owner of the manor who is mentioned by name is Stigand, the last Saxon archbishop, who crowned King Harold. Lanfranc we have already mentioned. He died in 1089, and was succeeded, after a four years' interval, by the saintly Anselm, who was not only the owner of the manor, but occasionally resident here, as well as at Harrow and Mortlake. One Whitsuntide, we are told, the king summoned Anselm to his neighbourhood at Windsor. On this occasion he stayed at Hayes, where he was visited by nearly all his suffragan bishops, who in vain persuaded him to make up his quarrel with William. In the long run the worthy ecclesiastics prevailed, and here or at Windsor the king handed to him the pall which had been sent from Rome by Pope Urban, as the sign of his metropolitan jurisdiction. It is pleasant to think that so sweet and pious a character as Anselm must have walked along the roads and trod the fields about Hayes. As a writer, a philosopher, and a leader of men, he was one of the foremost characters of his own age, and is regarded by all parties as one of the brightest ornaments of the English Church.

The early history and patronage of this church and of the manor are coincident down to the reign of Henry VIII. Hayes was a "Peculiar" of Canterbury—that is, although situate in Middlesex, which is in the diocese of London, it was directly under the spiritual control of the Archbishop of Canterbury—like Harrow-on-the-Hill. This arrangement lasted into the present century; but through the abolition of all such "peculiar" jurisdictions by Act of Parliament, it is now subject to the see of London, and the present rector attends the visitations of the Bishop of London and the Archdeacon of Middlesex.

To mention the several owners of this manor and rectory from Anselm to the Reformation would be to give a list of the Archbishops of Canterbury. But amongst them should be mentioned the names of Thomas à Becket, Langton, Islip, Langham, Simon de Sudbury, Fitz-Alan, Morton, and Warham, all of whom must have been occasional visitors at least at the Rectory House, which still has something quite palatial about it.

Archbishop Cranmer is said to have presented in 1543 the manor, with the advowsons of both the rectory and the vicarage, to Henry VIII., in exchange for other preferments. Five years later we find the king bestowing them on Sir Edward North, afterwards Lord North, one of the greatest possessors of Church lands. In the year 1613 Lord North sold both the manor and the advowsons, which have passed into the hands of several private families in succession—as Millet, Franklyn, Jenyns, Cooke, Ayscough, Blencowe, and Villiers, many of whom lie buried in the church. The manor now belongs to Sir Charles Mills, of Hillingdon; and the rector's family hold the consolidated advowson of both rectory and vicarage.

There were formerly several handsome mansions in this parish, and a few still remain, but none are worthy of individual description, or to which literary and other recollections are attached. The aspect of the village, in spite of brick-fields, railways, and canals, is still rural and peaceful. Mr. Mills writes, in his "History of Hayes":—"In a perambulation of the village for the purpose of discovering and describing antiquities, I was charmed to find within twelve miles of the bustle, din, and smoke of London the real country, with its wide, rich pastures and waving corn, its trees, hedge-rows, wild flowers, and gardens; and, to complete the picture, I should have been happy to have added, interspersed with timber-built houses with overhanging storeys, gables, and dormers; but truth compels me to admit that such is no longer the case. Here and there may still be seen the thatched one-storey cottage, with low bulged walls and other details, which would delight the painter and the poet. Some chimney-stacks at Yeading,

family, and now by Mr. Thomas Salt, of Weeping Cross, Staffordshire. "Yealding" is really Saxon for "Eald," or old, and "ing," a meadow; the property belonged five centuries ago to the Bishops of Lichfield and Coventry, who had a charter of free-warren within its limits. A little more than a century ago the Court Rolls of the manor mention that John Turner, a copyholder, was permitted to plant a grove of elm-trees across "the waste of Yealding Green;" the trees that Mr. Turner planted can still be identified, but the "waste"

WEST DRAYTON.

FONT IN WEST DRAYTON CHURCH.

built with thin kiln - burnt bricks, and affording the large chimney-corners of a former age, a gable next the churchyard, and some cottages near Botwell Cross, are all the objects that can claim the attention of the antiquary, and these only in a very moderate degree."

Within the parish there would appear to have been several manors: not only those of Norwood and Southall, now erected into separate and distinct parochial districts, but also those of Yealding, or Yeading, Botwell, and Hayes-with-Park-Hall. The last two, however, have long disappeared as manors proper, though they exist as hamlets; Yeading remains: it was owned by the Petit

and the "green" they were to adorn are both gone. So true are Goldsmith's lines—

> "Trade's unfeeling train
> Usurp the land and dispossess the swain."

Lysons tells us, in his "History of Middlesex," that the principal hamlets in Hayes are Botwell, Yeading, Hayes End, and Wood End; to these he might have added Cotman's Town, all of which still retain their ancient names. Botwell and Yeading are distinct places, and form the centres of two localities devoted to brick-making. Cotman's Town is the cluster of houses to the east of the church, beyond which lies a district called Cold Harbour. Wood End Green lies between the west end of the church and Hillingdon.

The parish church is dedicated to St. Mary the Virgin, to whom Mr. Mills thinks that it was dedicated by Anselm himself. If so, however, nothing of that structure remains, except a stone in the north face of the tower, some ten feet square, and carved with triangles arranged in the form of crosses. The font is a fine specimen of the transitional

Norman style, of English marble, and has a solid base, supporting a central pillar, with detached shafts, carrying a massive bowl, which is externally sculptured with foliage. Doubtless, however, there remain at the west end of the church, where they fence off the lower part of the tower from the nave.

The axes of the nave and chancel have not the same orientation—as is the case at St. Mary's,

1. HAYES CHURCH.
2. HAYES VILLAGE, through the Lych Gate.

HAYES.

was a smaller and plainer church here in the old Saxon times, one which was probably constructed of wood, as at Staines and elsewhere.

The chancel, which is of the Early English style, was probably erected about the year 1220. The nave is mostly of the Decorated, or Edwardian period; and the north and south side aisles followed as necessity arose. At the east end of each aisle was a chantry chapel, with an altar, and a separate endowment for a chantry priest. These chapels were marked off by screens, parts of which still

Oxford, and other well-known instances. The chancel deflects considerably to the north-east. It is thought by some persons that in such cases the true east point had not been chosen by the builders of the earlier portion, whether nave or chancel, and that the builders of the latter portion intended to correct their blunder; while another theory has been maintained which attaches to it a symbolical meaning—namely, that it was intended to represent the Saviour on the cross, whose sacred head inclined at a slight angle to the right or the left. It is more probable that it was an ingenious device of the architect to give an appearance of greater length to the interior.

The walls of the church are mostly of flint and chalk, the latter probably imported from the Buckinghamshire or Hertfordshire hills; the facing, for the most part, is of rough-hammered flint. The walls are solid and substantial, and have worked into them several fragments of wrought stone, portions of an earlier structure. The external buttresses are simple; those at the angles of the chancel have niches for the statues of saints—probably the patron saints of the church. The windows are of various dates, ranging from 1220 down to 1600, examples of almost every style being shown—and their details are well worth study. The great east window is of Elizabethan date and workmanship, and has recently been filled with painted glass, commemorating an event in the life of a son of the present rector.

The north and south doorways are under Pointed arches, the latter having in front of it a handsome wooden porch. At the west end is a fine specimen of Perpendicular architecture, the door and window being under one main arch, a sill-window separating the door from the three-light window above. The tower is of three storeys, but looks bare and unadorned, being devoid of buttresses. It contains a peal of six bells.

The nave has a lofty pitch, and a plain waggon-headed roof, divided into compartments, and lit by some very late and ugly-shaped dormer windows. The carved crosses at the intersections of the panels are curious, and the seamless cóat, the nails, the spear-head, and the wounded hands and feet, and the other emblems of the Passion, appear on nearly all of them. Mixed with them are fleur-de-lys and Tudor roses, marking the late period of its construction. Fine roofs of oak, and of a more artistic style, cover the chancel and side aisles. In the chancel are an ancient aumbry, a piscina in a very perfect state, and sedilia—all of elegant proportions. In the flooring are some good old encaustic tiles. The walls, previous to the recent restoration of the church, were covered with hatchments, and several flags, coats of armour, and helmets hung on them; but these were all decayed, and, as too often is the case, disappeared on that occasion. Over the communion-table there formerly hung a painting of the "Adoration of the Magi," given by the lord of the manor, Mr. Jenyns, in 1726; but it now stands on the ground near the vestry, at the east end of the south aisle. On the wall of the north aisle, near the door, is a roughly-executed life-sized fresco of St. Christopher, representing that saint as carrying on his shoulder the Divine Child as he strides through the water. Below can be seen the crab, the eel, the flat-fish, and a mermaid with her comb in her hand. Above is a figure fishing. Such an ornament is frequent on the walls of churches in Norfolk and Suffolk, but very rare in Middlesex.

The pulpit, of deal, was made to stride across the entrance to the chancel, with a desk on either side for the curate and parish clerk, thus blocking up the view of the east end altogether Happily this monstrosity—the production of some tasteless churchwarden or lord of the manor—is a thing of the past, and a decent, and even handsome, pulpit has been set up elsewhere in its stead.

In the church is a parish muniment chest of curious structure, more than three centuries old; it is of oak, and the top is made out of one solid block of timber. It is bound with iron, and has very substantial bands, hinges, and locks. At the entrance of the churchyard is an old and picturesque lych gate, in a very fair state of preservation.

In the chancel is a fine monument to Sir E. Fenner, a judge of the King's Bench, who died in 1611; and there is another Jacobean monument, the inscription on which has been long stolen. Sir Edward Fenner's monument is of alabaster and choice marbles, and represents the worthy judge in a recumbent position. In the north aisle is a Purbeck marble slab, with brass, commemorating Walter Grene, who died in the fifteenth century, but the exact date is lost. At the east end of the south aisle is an altar-tomb to Thomas Higate, part of the brass on which has disappeared. Here, cut in brass, in the attitude of prayer, may be seen the worthy squire and his dame, with their nine children, with inscriptions in Latin and English verse—neither very good. Of the remaining monuments little need be said, except that they seem to imply that the dead are uniformly virtuous, and to suggest, therefore, that we must look among the living for the vicious and wicked. The inscription over one of the rectors of the parish, the Rev. Mr. Samuel Spence, 1730, should not be omitted here, as suggestive of the happy *via media* between Romanism and Dissent, of which we have heard so much:—

" Just underneath there lays (lies) a priest interred,
  Not led by error into faction's herd ;
  No Sectaries encouraging at home :
  Proof against those as well as those of Rome,"

Under the east window of the chancel, on the outside, is a monument to William Walker, lecturer on astronomy, 1816, inventor of the Eidouranion, &c. Four persons are recorded in the churchyard as having died upwards of ninety years old, and the parish has produced at least one centenarian.

The registers do not commence till the first year of Elizabeth. In them are some quaint manuscript notes and apothegms from Cicero, &c. They note the usual number of "burials in woollen"—burials of foreign women; and in 1748-9 they record the fact that both John and Charles Wesley preached in the church. The registers from 1762-68 have been stolen.

No doubt the rectory, a little to the east of the church, stands on the site of the archbishop's former country-house, and possibly on the manse of the priest Warherdus. The rectory is perhaps the largest and best in the entire county, and probably there are few better rectory-houses in England. It is large, lofty, solid, and substantial, built very largely of solid oak; and its possession has always been sold along with the advowson. Two rooms in the house are still pointed out as having been occupied by Cranmer: one on the ground floor formed part of the great dining-hall, but is now divided into two storeys; the other, on the first floor, at the back of the house, now cut up into bed-rooms, is traditionally said to have been his library. In the former is a lofty carved oak chimney-piece, thought by some to be as old as the Reformation, and the panelling of the walls is probably coeval with it. On the ground floor there is a set of wainscot oaken architraves, finely moulded. The remainder of the house was largely altered and modernised in 1862.

The rectory garden is extensive, and its paths must have been often trodden by the archbishops of the Norman and Plantagenet eras. In one part there are a few traces of an ancient moat, in which, as the local tradition runs, was once found a flagon, which was deposited in the British Museum. No record, however, of such an article is to be found, either at Hayes or at Bloomsbury. Beyond the garden to the east is a fine avenue of shapely lime-trees. Here, again, local radition connects the trees with Eugene Aram, who is said to have frequently walked beneath their shade : but there is not a shadow of proof for the story. Equally shadowy is another tradition that Queen Elizabeth once attended service in the parish church, whilst staying at "Pinkwell." No such place is known to exist or to have existed near Hayes, and there is no record of the queen's visit in the books of the parish.

The rectory is a valuable one, and was once even more so than it is now. In 1793 it is given as worth £1,038 a year, with a small deduction for the payment of the "curates" of Norwood and Southall. It is now stated officially as worth £700 a year and a house.

Two or three of the rectors and vicars of Hayes have some interest attaching to their names. Henry Gold, who became vicar in 1520, was implicated in the doings of Elizabeth Barton, "the Holy Maid of Kent." The maid was a servant at Allington, in Kent, where, having been subject to hysterical fits, her mind became disordered, and she pretended that she saw visions which God had revealed to her from heaven, to the effect that in case the king should divorce his lawful wife, Catharine of Arragon, and take another spouse, his royalty would not last a month. The "Maid" and her accomplices, or dupes, were examined by the Star Chamber, conveyed to the Tower of London, convicted of high treason, attainted, and executed at Tyburn, April 20, 1534. On this occasion Gold was one of the number. The "Maid" at the last confessed her imposture. Amongst her lying wonders, one has been thus set forth by a writer of the period :—

> "That candles were alighted without fire:
> The candle ment is even hir tender hart,
> Which Edward Bocking set on flaming fire,
> For he must play the ghostly father's part,
> And shrift was such as they did both desire.
> The place was apt, they toke their times by night ;
> I think I have resolved this riddle right."

In the beginning of the seventeenth century the rectory was held by the Rev. Robert Wright, who was nominated first Warden of Wadham College, Oxford, but resigned that post because the foundress, Dorothy Wadham, would not suffer her Warden to marry. He afterwards became Bishop of Lichfield and Coventry, and was one of the twelve bishops accused of high treason, and committed to the Tower in 1642, "for preferring a petition, and making a protestation to the subverting of the fundamental laws of Parliament." He escaped, however, from the scaffold.

Another rector, Patrick Young, ejected in 1640, is worthy of note, as being a man who, "though he sided with the Presbyterians, could not be loved by them, as he had too much learning to comply with their eclesiastical mould, and too much honesty to digest their politicks." He was stripped of his preferments by either the Presbyterians or Independents—it is not certain by which—and retired to Broomfield, in Essex, where he died in retirement and melancholy.

The parish is educationally better off than most. There are national schools at Wood End Green, which were opened in 1836. In 1860–3 were built some larger schools, out of the benefaction of a Dr. Triplett, who left a large sum for that purpose at his death, in 1670, for the benefit of Hayes, Petersham, and Richmond. The learned doctor was a Prebendary of Westminster and York, and he lies in Poets' Corner. The poor parishioners of Hayes also benefit by Lady Dacre's charity of Emmanuel Hospital at Westminster. Among the other benefactors to the parish is Robert Cromwell, whose family are mentioned in the registers in 1596–8, and who gave some lands, the proceeds of which were to be laid down in " six gowns of strong blue cloth for as many poor widows, or other women, of Hayes." These benefactions are all administered by a board of trustees of the amalgamated charities.

The Tithes Commutation Act, passed in 1836, put an end to the annual payment of tithes throughout the kingdom; but this measure was anticipated, so far as Hayes was concerned, in 1809, when the Act was obtained for enclosing the common and extinguishing the tithes.

We will conclude this chapter with the following remarks of Mr. Mills on the Hayes Registers :— " Here we may read of the baptisms of children bearing their fathers', and of children bearing only their mothers' names, and many of children marked as bastards and baseborn ; of marriages completed, and of one begun, and not completed ; of burials of rich and poor, lords of the manor, esquires, knights, ladies, coachmen, &c., and of that of Elias Dupree, said to have been hunted to death in the parish, and to whose memory a slab is said to be affixed in Gloucester Cathedral; and of many ' strange women.' Also many singular entries arising out of and illustrating the laws relating to burial in woollen : how John Hart, a farmer, to escape a certain part of the due on a baptism (20s.), declares that he is not worth £50 per annum in real estate, or £600 personal ; then of Roger Jenyns, ' Esquire,' in haste, possibly finding himself excluded from or not sufficiently appreciated in John Jenyns' will, hurries off to James Clitherow, the magistrate, gives sworn information that John Jenyns had

been that day buried in a coffin fitted with velvet —in which case there would be a fine, and Roger, as the informant, would be entitled to one-half. Again, Rachel Lee (honest London woman) desires to be buried in linen ; she pays the £50 fine, and has her desire. Again, we read of taxes and fines, or penalties, on births, deaths, and marriages ; there are payments under the two first heads, but I find no mention of single men or of widowers remaining unmarried, and paying the fines or penalties. We read of ' Plague Years,' of a time when the year ended in March instead of in December, and of numerous instances of longevity. We find these registers signed by vicars, and sometimes—when they could write—by churchwardens, and when they could not, then marked by them with a cross. We read of two of the Wesleys preaching here. We read of an early attempt at a popular week-day service, which met with great success at its introduction.

" As to education, we may gather from the marriage register that, whereas in 1763, out of every 100 persons married only 37 could write their names, in 1872 the percentage of those who could do so had risen to 69. Finally, we may read in these registers that peace has not always been the rule. The clergy have turned their backs on each other in the church ; some parishioners have smoked their pipes, drank their beer, made noises, and rung the church bells during service, while others have not refrained from cock-fighting and digging graves in the churchyard, in defiance of authority.

" There is much, then, in these old registers that we must regret to lose. These books allowed the man of taste and education to make his remarks, and to enter them in the language that he liked best. Did he wish to quote Cicero, or to protect a book by a malediction, to state where he dined on Sunday, to express his opinion on taxes and other matters, he did so freely in these registers. But now that the hard and fast forms prevail, printed in columns, with certain ink to be used, and certain exact particulars only to be stated, no room is left for taste ; and while science and statistics may be advanced, the individuality of man and the interest of the ancient record must alike disappear."

CHAPTER XX.

NORWOOD, SOUTHALL, ETC.

"Pagos et compita circum."—VIRG. *Georg.*, ii. 328.

The "Precinct" of Norwood—Situation and Boundaries of the Parish—Census Returns—Early History of the Manor—The Village—The Parish Church—Schools, &c.—Southall—The Church and Vicarage—The Manor House—The Grand Junction Canal and the Paddington Canal—The Metropolitan Workhouse School—Dorman's Well—Southall Park—Southall Market—Northolt, or Northall—General Description of the Locality—The Parish Church—Greenford—Its Etymology—The Soil, and Census Returns—The Parish Church—The Rectory and Advowson—Distinguished Rectors—Chemical Works at Greenford Green—Horsington Hill and Wood—Perivale—Extent and Population—Descent of the Manor—The Parish Church—West Twyford—Descent of the Manor—Twyford Abbey—The Chapel—Willesden Junction Station—Boundaries and Extent of the Parish of Willesden—Railway Communication—The River Brent—Sub-division of the Manor of Willesden—The Parish Church—Church End—Willesden Green—The "White Hart" and "Spotted Dog" Taverns—Brondesbury—The Jewish Cemetery—Warwick Dairy Farm—Harlesden—Cricklewood—Neasdon—The Metropolitan Railway Carriage Depôt—Sherrick Green and Dollis Hill—Stonebridge Park.

THE village of Norwood is officially and legally described as a "precinct" in the civil parish of Hayes. The "precinct" is a term which savours of a cathedral city, and no doubt it was given to this hamlet on account of the connection of Hayes with the see of Canterbury in ancient times.

Norwood—the "north wood"—doubtless was so called with reference to the Thames and its "riparian" dwellers, just as Norwood, in Surrey, derived its name from its relative situation to the great town of Croydon. The village lies on the edge of Osterley Park, between Heston and Southall, and the country around, although somewhat level, is nevertheless well-wooded and pleasant. The Grand Junction Canal skirts the village on its northern side. Like the district which we have just left, much of the land hereabouts is well adapted for brick-making, a branch of industry which is still largely carried on here, though somewhat on the decline; whilst in the immediate outskirts of the village are market gardens and orchards, with an occasional farm. Many of the inhabitants are engaged as bargemen on the canal.

No literary interest attaches to the parish, which is very small, and shows but little signs of increasing in population, lying in a retired spot, far away from a railway station. In 1871 the population of the entire "precinct," which includes the inmates of Hanwell Lunatic Asylum, and also those of Marylebone Workhouse Schools on Southall Green, was given in the census returns as 5,882, and in 1881 the number was returned as 6,688.

The first mention of Norwood as a manor occurs in the will of Warherdus, A.D. 830, who left it to the church of Canterbury. It then contained 120 acres. No mention of it is made in "Domesday," when it probably was joined to that of Hayes. At the time of the Reformation it belonged to the Cheesemans, who held it under the archbishop, to whom a knight's fee (£5) was payable at every death or alienation. It afterwards was in the hands of Fynes, Lord Dacre, and his

widow, the worthy founder of sundry almshouses in Westminster,* on whose death, in 1595, the manor was sold. It was afterwards in the hands of the Childs, of Osterley Park, and later on it belonged to the Earls of Jersey, from whom it passed to Sir Charles Mills, Bart. The Earl of Jersey is, however, the chief landowner.

Norwood consists of several handsome and substantial houses, surrounding a triangular village-green of some twenty acres, adorned with fine elms. The cedars, yews, and evergreens in the various gentlemen's gardens help to give the village a leafy and well-wooded appearance, even in the winter.

At the north corner of the green, nearly opposite to the vicarage, stands the church, which modern restoration, by the importation of colour both inside and outside, has rather succeeded in disguising, so that it looks like a new erection of the Cambridge Camden, or the Oxford Architectural Society. It is small, with a dwarf wooden tower and spire, and a fine wooded porch on the south side. One of the arches dividing the nave from the north aisle is Norman.

The restoration of the church was carried out in 1864, down to which period there were several helmets and coats of armour hanging upon the walls; but these have all disappeared, except one helmet, which is kept loose on a canopied altar-tomb on the north side of the chancel, within the altar rails; and even from this some stray visitor, with light fingers, but without a conscience, has managed to carry away part of the vizor.

Some of the windows contain fragments of old painted glass; but the east window is filled with modern coloured glass, which was inserted on the restoration of the church. In the chancel is a brass to the memory of Francis Awsiter, dated 1624, and in the nave one to Matthew Huntley, dated 1628. There are a few interest-

---

* See "Old and New London," Vol. IV., p. 23.

ing monuments and tablets, notably the altar-tomb mentioned above, which is to the memory of Edward Cheeseman, who was Cofferer to Henry VII., and who died in 1547. Another monument, consisting of a sarcophagus bearing upon it a life-sized semi-recumbent effigy of the deceased, commemorates John Merick, Esq., of Norcut, who died in 1749. The font, which is large, and designed for entire immersion, is of an octangular form, and ornamented with quatrefoils. A fine yew-tree stands in the churchyard, as in most of the Middlesex parishes.

forced into a separate district. In 1838 a small chapel was erected on a waste spot of land then called Southall Green; but it is of no interest whatever, and serves only as a specimen of the very worst and poorest attempts at modern Gothic art before its revival by the elder Pugin and Sir Gilbert Scott.

Opposite the church is a small and modest vicarage, with a good garden in the rear. Adjoining it is Elmfield Lodge, a handsome villa of the suburban type, with a magnificent cedar-tree on its lawn. Here was born Mrs. Challice, the

SOUTHALL MANOR HOUSE.

In the early part of the last century a small portion of land and some cottages were bequeathed by one Francis Courtney for the purpose of charitably educating poor children in the parish "till the world's end." In 1772 Elisha Biscoe bequeathed a large sum of money for the purpose of educating and clothing thirty boys and ten girls belonging to the parishes of Norwood, Heston, and Hayes. The school-house of Norwood was erected in 1767.

Southall is quite a new parish, having really been called into existence by the construction of the Great Western Railway. It is the centre of a very flat and dreary district. As Norwood was cut off from the mother church of Hayes, so has Southall in its turn been cut off from Norwood and

accomplished authoress of "Memories of French Palaces," "Distinguished Women of France," and of several novels, a lady whose premature death was deeply regretted.

Between the green and the railway-station stands a fine old manor house, of the Jacobean type, with plain mullioned windows. In its hall is a finely-carved oak mantel-piece, not unlike those which we have seen in the Charter House, London,* and at Duncroft House, Staines.† The entrance-hall is fine, and retains its Elizabethan windows and Jacobean fire-place, and many of the other rooms still remain in their original state. It was formerly

---

* See "Old and New London," Vol. II., p. 393.
† See page 191, ante.

the seat of a family named Awsiter, who left their mark on history, having been merchants, aldermen, or lawyers in the City of London.

The grounds in the rear are laid out in the trim fashion of the reign of William III., so prevalent family of Shoredyke, and afterwards by those of Cheeseman, and of Fynes, Lord Dacre. It has since passed, along with that of Norwood, to the Childs and Villierses.

The Grand Junction Canal, which, as we have

INTERIOR OF PERIVALE CHURCH.　(*See page* 221.)
(*From an Etching by W. L. Wilkins*, 1848.)

about this neighbourhood, the yews being carefully clipped and rounded off into artificial shapes.

Northall and Northolt are but variations of the same name, as we shall presently see; so it is probable that Southall is only another form of Southolt—the Southern Holt, or wood. The manor of Southall was held in the Plantagenet times under the Archbishop of Canterbury by the already stated, separates the two villages of Norwood and Southall, receives the waters of the Paddington Canal at Bull Bridge, a short distance westward from the green, where there is commodious wharfage. Close by the railway-station stands the Metropolitan Workhouse School, a large building, which will hold between 500 and 600 children, who are here lodged, educated, and taught various branches of industry. Dorman's or Domer's Well, a farm-house about half a mile north-east of Southall Street, was formerly the seat of Lord Dacre whilst he held the lordship of the manor. Southall Park, a large red-brick mansion facing the Great Western Railway, formerly the seat of Sir William Ellis, stands in some pleasant grounds, and is now a private lunatic asylum.

The village of Southall doubtless once derived great benefits from its weekly market, the charter for which was granted in 1698 by William III. "A lease of this charter," we are told in the "Beauties of England," "was purchased by Mr. William Welch in the year 1805, at which time there were weekly markets of some consequence for the show of cattle at Beaconsfield, Hayes, Hounslow, and Knightsbridge. Mr. Welch, immediately on acquiring possession of his lease, constructed a market-place at Southall peculiarly well-adapted for showing cattle and accommodating the dealers. He has also, in other respects, acted with so much spirit and judgment that the neighbouring markets are now almost discontinued, while this at Southall is become inferior only to Smithfield in regard to the sale of fat cattle in Middlesex."

From Southall Station, a walk of about three miles brings us to Northolt, or, as it is sometimes written, Northall, which, as stated above, is simply another form of this word. The name of the village is generally spelt Northall in ancient documents ; but Norden terms the place Northolt, and derives the latter syllable from the "German *holt*, signifying a wood." The mode of spelling used by Norden has been followed to this day.

The route thither, after crossing the great western road, lies along narrow lanes and cross-roads, and for the most part over what in summer-time would be green and smiling meadows, but which in winter, or during a prevalence of wet weather, are little better than a huge morass. The village of Northolt—the name of which in the "Domesday" Survey appears as *Northala*—is quiet and retiring, the few humble dwellings which it contains being mostly inhabited by farm labourers and brick-makers, the land in the neighbourhood being chiefly under grass, dotted over here and there with a busy homestead, its barns and hay-ricks affording an agreeable relief to the surrounding trees.   At the brick-fields hereabouts large quantities of bricks are made, and carried up to London by the barges on the Paddington Canal, which skirts the eastern side of the parish. The village green is intersected by the roadway running north-east to Sudbury and Harrow-on-the-Hill; and the church, dedicated to St. Mary, stands on the

summit of a small hillock, on the east side of the green.   The architecture is a mixture of the Decorated and Perpendicular. It is built chiefly of flint and rubble, almost hidden by a thick coating of cement, and whitewashed over ; it consists of a nave and narrow chancel, with a wooden belfry turret, surmounted by a short octagonal spire, which rises from the western end of the tiled roof. The windows of the chancel are filled with stained glass, that over the communion-table being a modern imitation of the Decorated period ; the window at the south-east corner of the nave is also of painted glass, the work of Mr. George Harris, F.S.A., of Islip Manor, the "squire" of the parish, and was inserted in 1871. The font is octagonal, of the Perpendicular style, but the lid bears date 1624. A gravestone in the floor of the chancel, within the altar rails, commemorates Samuel Lisle, Bishop of St. Asaph, who died in 1749 ; there is also a similar memorial to Thomas Arundell, dated 1697 ; brasses to Henry Rowdell (1452), Susan, wife of John Gyfforde (1560), and to Isaiah Bures, vicar of this parish (1610). On the south wall of the chancel is a tablet to the memory of Lancelot Shadwell, Esq., who died in 1861, son of the Vice-Chancellor Sir Lancelot Shadwell, who was lord of the manor of Northolt, and with whose family it has still continued. In the church-yard is buried Dr. Stephen Demainbray, who died in 1782, having been some time Astronomer to the Royal Observatory at Richmond.

The extensive valley to the north-west of this parish was the scene of several skirmishes during both the Wars of the Roses and the Civil War in the time of Charles I.

From Northolt the road winds somewhat circuitously in a south-easterly direction to Greenford, a small and retired village, situate on the road towards Sudbury and Harrow, and about nine miles from Hyde Park Corner. There is, in summer-time, a pleasant walk thither from the churchyard of Northolt, across the meadows, stretching away eastward, through which the Paddington Canal winds its course, and which are also watered by numerous streams and bournes. The village of Greenford consists of about twenty or thirty cottages and small shops, together with a commodious school-house, and other buildings. `

In legal documents the name of this parish is usually written Greenford Magna, or Great Greenford, to distinguish it from Greenford Parva, or Perivale, which lies about two miles eastward, on the road towards Twyford Abbey. Greenford probably took its name from a ford over the River Brent, which meanders pleasantly through the meadows on the south-east. The parish is said by Northcourt, in his "Repertorium," to have been called in ancient documents *Grenefeld*, and also Gernford; in the confirmation of Edward I., and also in "Domesday Book," however, it is written *Greneforde*, so that the name may be said to have undergone but little or no alteration since the time of the Conquest.

The soil hereabouts is a fertile clay, and the parish is almost wholly agricultural. In 1871 the this day. A modern brick-built mansion near the church is termed the manse house.

The parish church, dedicated to the Holy Cross, on the west side of the village street, is a small building, apparently of the fourteenth century, being of the Early Perpendicular style. The edifice is peculiar in having no constructional west end, the space being occupied by a timbered turret, carrying a low shingle spire, painted white. With the exception of this turret and spire, which are devoid of all

PERIVALE CHURCH, EXTERIOR. (*See p.* 221.)

number of houses in the entire parish was 116, with a population of 578, a number which had somewhat diminished in the next decennial period.

The manor of Greenford Magna was given to Westminster Abbey by King Etheldred. In the "Norman Survey" it is said that "the Abbot of St. Peter holds Greneforde for eleven hides and a half." There was "pannage for three hundred hogs, and pasture for the cattle of the village." Upon the dissolution of religious houses, this property was made part of the revenues of the short-lived Bishopric of Westminster; but was surrendered to the Crown in 1550 by Thomas Thirlby, the only bishop of that see. The manor, however, was in the same year granted to the Bishop of London and his successors, with whom it has continued to dignity, the church consists of a nave and a narrow chancel, which are separated by a Pointed arch. The original chancel-arch, of rude Early English work, was re-constructed upon a larger scale in 1871, since which time the whole fabric has been restored in a most thorough manner, the work consisting of a new nave roof of open timber and a fresh seating of varnished pitch-pine; the floor of the chancel being raised, fresh windows opened, and the walls of the chancel, which were rough-cast, being re-faced with flint-work and stone dressings. The windows of the chancel contain many fragments of stained glass, chiefly dating from the middle of the fifteenth century, collected and re-arranged by the Rev. Edward Betham, a former rector. They include a number of examples of the arms of King's College, Cambridge, the patrons of the living, some heads of angels, foliage, and crowns, and some curious quarries, probably Flemish, representing windmills. There are also several brasses—notably, a half-length figure of a priest in eucharistic vestments, that of Richard Thornton, who died in 1544; close by is a second priest's brass, that of Thomas Symons, dated 1508; a third brass is an effigy of a lady wearing a butter-fly head-dress. At the south-east end of the nave is a mural monument to Bridget, wife of Simon Caston, dated 1637. The effigy of the deceased is kneeling before a desk, on which is an open book; before her kneel her five children, whilst in a niche in the upper compartment is the three-quarter effigy of a man in mourning attitude and garb. On the north wall of the chancel is a mural tablet, with two kneeling figures, commemorating Michael Gardner, a former rector of this parish, who died in 1630, and Margaret, his wife. There are also several inscriptions to the Castell family. The pedestal of the font bears the name of Francis Coston, and the date 1638.

The rectory and advowson of Greenford, in con-junction with the manor, were possessed at an early period by the Abbey of St. Peter, West-minster. John de Feckenham, the last abbot of Westminster, held the rectory of Greenford in the middle of the sixteenth century. On the subsequent grant of the manor to the see of London, the advowson became the property of Sir Thomas Wroth, of Durance. On the last alienation of the rectory and advowson, they were purchased, in 1725, by the Provost and Scholars of King's College, Cambridge.

Edward Terry, who was appointed to the rectory of Greenford in 1629, was a man of some note in his day. He had a few years previously accom-panied some merchants to the East Indies. On his arrival there, he was sent for by Sir Thomas Roe, then ambassador to the Great Mogul, with whom he resided as chaplain for more than two years at the court of that emperor. He is said by Anthony Wood to have been "an ingenious and polite man, of a pious and exemplary conversation, and much respected in the neighbourhood where he lived." During his residence at Greenford—the benefice of which parish he enjoyed for more than thirty years—he published several works, among which was "A Character of King Charles II.," printed in 1660. He died in that same year, and was buried in the chancel of his church.

The Rev. Edward Betham, whose name is mentioned above, and who was rector towards the close of the last century, built at his own cost a school-house, and provided an endowment for the salary of a master and mistress, and for gifts to the poor of the parish.

The hamlet of Greenford Green, which lies away about a mile to the north of the village, is chiefly noticeable for the chemical works of Messrs. Perkin and Sons, which give employment to a large number of hands. The building covers a large space of ground, and its tall chimney-shafts are a landmark all around.

Between this place and Harrow are Horsington Hill and Wood, which command a fine view across the meadows to Harrow and Pinner, the church-spire of Harrow crowning the hill, and forming a pleasing object in the landscape.

Perivale, formerly known as Greenford Parva, lies about two miles eastward from Greenford Magna, and about the same distance to the north of Ealing Station, on the Great Western Railway. It has borne its present name, which Lysons regards as a corruption of Parva, only since the sixteenth century. Norden supposes that the term Perivale has reference to the salubrity of the vale in which the village is situated, and calls it "Pery-vale, more truly Purevale." The village is located in the valley of the Brent; and what with its old-fashioned look and its extreme seclusion—which is almost as perfect as if it were a hundred miles from London—it is not to be wondered that its growth is very slow; indeed, but little progress appears to have been made during the last century, for in 1816 Mr. Brewer described it, in the "Beauties of England," as containing five dwellings only, whilst according to the census returns for 1881 the number of inhabited houses is seven, whilst the population is set down as 34 souls. The Rev. C. J. Hughes, the rector of Perivale, in a letter to the Times (1882), writes :—"A parish in Wales with only 21 inhabitants and 620 acres in extent . . . . is hardly so peculiar as a parish seven miles from the Marble Arch, with only 34 inhabitants and 626 acres in extent. The parish of Perivale, adjoining Ealing parish, and less than two miles from Ealing Station, fulfils these con-ditions (there are in all five houses), being the smallest parish in the diocese of London, and one of the smallest in England."

It need scarcely be stated that such a retired spot as Perivale should be devoid of "historic interest." In "Domesday Book," however, it is recorded that "Gulbert held in Greneford three hides of Geoffry (de Mandeville). There was land to one plough and a half; but land for one plough only was used. Pannage for forty hogs. The value of the land was stated at twenty shillings;

when received, ten shillings; in King Edward's time, forty shillings. Two Sokemen held this land; one was a canon of St. Paul's, the other was a vassal of Asgar's, the master of the horse. In the same village Ansgot held half a hide of Geoffry de Mandeville; and Ælveve, the wife of Wateman, held half a hide of the king." The subsequent history of this little district, until the reign of the second Edward, appears to be a blank. At that time the manor of Greenford Parva—then called Cornhull, or Cornhill—together with the advowson of the church, was surrendered to the Crown, in exchange for the churches of Cestreton and Wors-field, in Warwickshire, by Walter de Langton, Bishop of Coventry and Lichfield. The king granted it shortly afterwards to Henry de Beau-mont, by whose descendants it was alienated, in 1387, to Thomas Charleton. After this period it successively became the property of various families, and was purchased about the middle of the last century by Richard Lateward, Esq. On the death of Mr. Lateward, the manor passed by bequest to John Schreiber, Esq., who afterwards took the name of Lateward.

The parish church, as may be imagined for so small a district, is very diminutive. The building bears marks of age, apparently of the fourteenth century, and on its north side stands the vicarage, an interesting half-timbered building, of semi-Gothic architecture. Like most of the parish churches which we have lately described, that of Perivale is constructed chiefly of flint and stone, and consists of a nave and narrow chancel, with a square wooden tower and a short spire at the western end, and a south porch. The interior was restored, and the east wall rebuilt, in 1875. The nave is separated from the chancel by a dwarf screen, apparently of seventeenth century workmanship, and in some of the windows are fragments of stained glass, among them being representations of St. John the Baptist and St. Matthew. In the south-west corner is a small hagioscope. The font-cover bears the date 1665, though the font itself is undoubtedly much earlier. On the floor of the chancel is a brass to the memory of Henry Myllet, who is represented in effigy, together with his two wives and fifteen children; it is dated 1500. There are a few monuments to former lords of the manor of Green-ford Parva—including the families of Lane, Harri-son, Myllet, and Lateward—but none of them are of sufficient public interest to merit description. Here, in 1765, was buried Philip Fletcher, Dean of Kildare, brother of Dr. Fletcher, Bishop of Kildare, and author of a poem in Dodsley's collec-tion called "Nature and Fortune," and of another entitled "Truth at Court," which acquired some little popularity at the time of its publication, but which is now well-nigh forgotten.

Passing in an easterly direction for about a mile, we come to another parish almost as small as Perivale—namely, Twyford, or West Twyford, so called to distinguish it from the hamlet of East Twyford, in the adjoining parish of Willesden. This parish—if it may be called one—comprises only about 200 acres, and but eight houses, with a population of seventy-five. Twyford is described by Lewis, in his "Topographical Dictionary," in 1835 as being "in the Kensington division of the Hundred of Ossulston," and as containing a population of forty-three souls.

It is not a little singular that within a mile and a half of the great railway junction at Willesden, and within six or seven miles of Hyde Park Corner, there should have been, down to a com-paratively recent date, an extra-parochial liberty, whose inhabitants own no ecclesiastical allegiance to the Bishop of London. But so it is. The land, having belonged to one of the smaller religious houses, Twyford Abbey was forgotten to be in-cluded in the general survey.

The whole " parish" of Twyford contains less than 300 acres, and but one important house—Twyford Abbey and its dependent farm-buildings. It does not appear that this district ever possessed a resident population. Mr. Brewer, in the " Beau-ties of England," states, on the authority of the records of St. Paul's, that " there were six tene-ments in Twyford in the earlier part of the fifteenth century, one of which formed the residence of the minister, and the rents of the others assisted in supporting him. These tenements were situated near the church." In the year 1251, according to Lysons' "Environs of London," there were ten inhabited houses in the parish, in addition to the manorial seat. Only one of these, the manor-house, was remaining in the reign of Queen Eliza-beth, and the parish continued in the same de-populated state until the beginning of the present century.

In the "Domesday Survey" the manor of Twyford is dealt with under the name of "Tveverde," and it is there stated that Gueri, a canon of St. Paul's, holds two hides of land; the record proceeding:— "There is land to one plough and a half. There is a plough in the demesne, and a half may be made. There are two villanes of one virgate, and one bordar of six acres, and three cottagers. Pannage for fifty hogs," &c.

Early in the twelfth century the manor was

leased to Walter de Cranford and his wife, "with all the tithes of corn, sheep, and goats," by the Dean and Chapter of St. Paul's. It afterwards passed through various changes of ownership, and towards the end of the fifteenth century it was procured by a citizen of London, one John Philpot, with whose family it remained through many generations. In the last century it was conveyed, by the marriage of an heiress, to the Cholmeley family, of whom it was purchased in 1806 by "Thomas Willan, Esq., of Marybone Park." This is probable that the place took its name of Twyford.

On the lawn, close to the house, is a small chapel. It is built of plain brick, covered with stucco, and an attempt was made early in this century to give it a Gothic character by the addition of a porch and some other minor details. The chapel is much improved in appearance by a luxuriant growth of ivy, the effect of which is heightened by the various elms and cedars that stud the lawn. The building contains a few monuments of interest.

TWYFORD ABBEY.

gentleman pulled down the old manor-house, which was at that time occupied as a farm. The building was surrounded by a moat, and approached by a drawbridge. The building having been demolished, the moat was filled up. Mr. Willan shortly after commenced the erection of a new manor-house on a fresh site hard by, from the designs of Mr. Atkinson. It is a handsome residence in the "Strawberry Hill" Gothic style of architecture; the principal front is advanced and embattled, with octagonal turrets at either end. The surrounding grounds are pleasantly wooded, and of an ornamental character. The River Brent, which forms the northern margin of the parish, winds through the grounds. Besides this, another brook runs near it. Both these streams are, or were, fordable at a certain point, and from this circumstance it One of these is to Robert Moyle, Esq., Prothonotary of the Common Pleas, who died in 1638, and who is represented by a bust habited in a black cap and gown. Another monument, with a bust, commemorates Walter Moyle, Esq., who died at Twyford in 1660. On the north wall is a tablet to the memory of Henry Bold, the author of some humorous poems, who died in 1683.

About two miles due east from Twyford Abbey lies what was once the village of Willesden, or Wilsdon, but which is now a rapidly-increasing suburb of London. The western side of the parish is skirted by the London and North-Western Railway, which has a station at Harlesden, about a mile from Willesden proper, called the Willesden Junction Station, which serves also for the North London line. There is here almost as great a network of railways as at Clapham Junction,* the lines radiating hence to almost all parts of London, both north and south of the Thames; and the arrangement of the station is, if possible, more consummately bewildering to the unhappy traveller who has to "change."

The parish of Willesden is bounded on the east by the Edgware Road, and stretches away north to Wembly and Neasdon, west to Twyford, and southward to Acton and Shepherd's Bush. It comprises in all between 4,000 and 5,000 acres, the greater part of which was meadow and pasture-land, intersected by pleasant lanes and hedge-rows. At the beginning of this century the houses were comparatively few and widely scattered. Even as

London Line; Harrow Road, on the Midland; at Neasdon, on the Metropolitan Extension, and also on the Midland Railway; and at Willesden Green, on the Metropolitan. All the above stations are situated within the boundaries of the parish. There is also a station at Dudding Hill, on the Midland Railway, a short distance north-eastward of Willesden Church; that at Harrow Road meeting the requirements of the new district called Stonebridge Park.

The River Brent waters the north and west sides of the parish, but this stream is subject to floods, which are very injurious to the land on its immediate borders.

The name of this place is written "Wellesdone"

WILLESDEN CHURCH.   (*See p. 224.*)
(*From a Print in the "Gentleman's Magazine," xci.*)

recently as 1861 the population did not amount to 4,000; but in the course of the next ten years, so rapid had been the increase of buildings in the neighbourhood, the number amounted to almost 16,000. According to the census returns for 1881, the population has now swelled up to over 27,000. Such has been the rapidity with which the builder has invested this once rural and retired district, that the green fields are now fast disappearing in all directions, to give place to streets and rows of villa residences. One great cause for all this rapid extension of the metropolis is undoubtedly the facility which is afforded by the railways for communication with the City and other parts of London; for, apart from Willesden Junction, mentioned above, there are stations at Brondesbury, on the North-Western, North-London, and Metropolitan Railways; at Kensal Green, on the North

in the "Norman Survey," and the manor is there stated to belong to the Canons of St. Paul's, to whom it had either been given or confirmed by King Athelstan. The manorial district was afterwards sub-divided, so that there are now in Willesden eight distinct manors, "seven of which," says Mr. Brewer, in his "Beauties of England," "are held by the same number of prebends (prebendaries) in St. Paul's Cathedral, or by their lessees." The manor of Twyford is in lay hands.

The parish church, dedicated to St. Mary, dates probably from the early part of the fourteenth century, a few fragments being of even an earlier period. Most of the marks of its antiquity were removed on the restoration of the building, about 1850, down to which time the church consisted of a nave and chancel, a south aisle and porch, and a square embattled tower at the western end of the aisle. The exterior at that time appeared rugged with age, and an interesting air of antiquity prevailed over the whole structure, except that the large east window had been contracted, and a mean framework of wood substituted for the stone mullions. The walls were partly covered with stucco; but the church had a picturesque appearance, and was often a subject for the artist's pencil. In 1851 it was carefully repaired and enlarged; and again, in 1872, a further and more complete restoration was made, a north aisle, porch, and transept being added, the interior of the tower being at the same time opened out to the body of the church. During these restorations, fragments of Norman work, in the shape of the round arches of two narrow windows, were discovered on removing the north wall. In the north wall of the chancel is an Easter sepulchre; and another is in the south wall of a chantry which is formed of the eastern bay of the south aisle, and which opens into the aisle and chancel by arches. The font is probably late Norman. The old-fashioned pews were replaced by open benches, and new sedilia, reredos, and pavement of encaustic tiles, were placed in the chancel in 1872. Most of the windows are filled with painted glass, the subject of that over the altar being the crucifixion of Our Lord. The pulpit, of carved oak, was erected in 1877, in memory of members of the Wood family.

Scattered about are four or five ancient brasses, the earliest of which, dated 1492, commemorates Bartholomew de Willesden; and there are also several ancient monuments, one of which, with kneeling figures, is in memory of Richard Paine, who was "gentleman pensioner to five princes," and who died in 1606. Sir John Franklyn, who died in 1647, is also commemorated here; as also is General Charles Otway, "an officer of great bravery in the reigns of Anne and George I."

In the description of this edifice in the "Beauties of England" (1816), it is stated that "the whole furniture of the church is of a rustic and humble description; yet devotees from various parts were formerly attracted to this spot by an image of Our Lady, renowned for dispensing benefits among those who visited it in pilgrimage." An inventory of the goods and ornaments belonging to this church, taken about the middle of the thirteenth century, makes mention of "a scarlet banner, with the figures of the Virgin Mary of cloth of gold," the gift of the vicar, and "also two large images of the Virgin;" and in another inventory, taken about 1547, mention is made of two "Masers" that were "appointed to remayne in the church, for to drink yn at brideales," but these have long since disappeared, along with the jovial custom referred to. With

reference to this entry, Mr. Brewer, in the "Beauties of England," remarks:—"It will be recollected that wine, in which sops, or pieces of cake, or wafer, were immersed, was first blessed by the priest at marriages, and then drunk by the bride, the bridegroom, and their company. The allusions to this custom are numerous in our old dramatists."

It is doubtful whether "pilgrimages to Our Lady of Wilsdon" ever became so popular with Londoners as those to the holy martyr of Canterbury and to "Our Lady of Walsingham," both of which were suppressed, and the images destroyed, about the same time, in 1548.

Francis Close, some time Dean of Carlisle, who died in 1882, was in early life a curate here. Having held for a short time the curacy of Church-Lawford, near Rugby, he was transferred hither in 1822. Two years later, however, he was appointed to a curacy at Cheltenham, of which parish he became rector in 1856. He held that appointment, exercising an almost absolute sway over the Evangelical circles of that fashionable watering-place, till 1856, when he was nominated to the Deanery of Carlisle, a post which he resigned about a twelvemonth before his death. He was almost the last of the followers of Simeon, Venn, Thomson, and Wilberforce, and the rest of the "Clapham sect."

In the *Gentleman's Magazine* is given a spirited little engraving of Willesden church as it appeared a little more than half a century ago. It shows the western end of the building, with its tall tower backed by trees. In the churchyard, and to the right of the view, several cottages are represented. The churchyard in former times was encumbered with some old buildings; but these have all been pulled down, and the grave-yard extended, laid out with ornamental walks, and planted.

Mr. Harrison Ainsworth selected Willesden as the scene of some of the exploits of the romantic Jack Sheppard, whom he declares to have been buried in Willesden churchyard; but the interment does not appear to be recorded in the parish register, which, it may be added, dates from the middle of the sixteenth century. Mr. Harrison Ainsworth himself lived for some time at Kensal House, in this parish; and hence, probably, his association of this locality with the name of Jack Sheppard.

Church End is the name given to the cluster of houses in the immediate neighbourhood of the parish church. A short distance to the north is Queen's Town, a district which, although quite of modern growth, can boast of its Working Men's Institute, its Workman's Hall, &c. About half a mile further northward is Willesden Green. In

1880 a new ecclesiastical district, St. Andrew's, was formed here. A school for the new district, constructed of red brick, with stone dressings, and which also serves the purposes of a church, stands at the junction of Villiers and Chaplin Roads.

Willesden Green was formerly one of the most rustic spots in the neighbourhood of London, and the tea-gardens of its roadside tavern, the "Spotted Dog," used to be a favourite resort for Londoners. Its rural character, however, is now altogether changed, for in the place of picturesque old cottages, long rows of streets are fast springing up in all directions, and the humble and cosy tavern just mentioned has blossomed into a large "hotel," fitted up after the modern style. The "White Hart Inn" and pleasure-grounds at Church End, and the "Old Spotted Dog" at Neasdon, are also favourite summer haunts for Londoners.

The outlying hamlets of Willesden are Brondesbury, Harlesden, Neasdon, Dollis Hill, Sherrick Green, and Stonebridge Park.

Brondesbury is of great antiquity, and gives its name to a prebendal stall in St. Paul's Cathedral, the lands comprised in the hamlet having been for many centuries attached to that office. It lies in the eastern part of the parish, near the Edgware Road and Kilburn Wells, and is now being rapidly covered with houses. It was formed into a separate ecclesiastical district in 1866. Christ Church, which stands at the corner of Willesden Lane, is a large building in the Early English style, cruciform in plan, with a lofty tower and spire. Several of the windows are filled with stained glass.

The Jewish Cemetery, in Willesden Lane, comprising about twelve acres, was consecrated in 1863, and is prettily laid out and planted with shrubs and evergreens, and has a rabbi's house and mortuary chapel, built of Kentish rag-stone. Here, in 1874, was buried Baron Meyer de Rothschild, of Mentmore, Bucks, M.P. for Hythe; and in 1876 Baron Anthony de Rothschild was interred here.

A short distance southward of Brondesbury, near the Elgin Road, Maida Vale, is a large establishment known as the Warwick Farm Dairy, recently erected for Messrs. Welford and Sons, at a cost of upwards of £20,000. The buildings cover about two acres of ground.

Harlesden is another rapidly-increasing district, about one mile south-west from Willesden church. Willesden Junction station, as mentioned above, is in this neighbourhood. The ecclesiastical dis-

trict of All Souls was formed here in 1875. The church, of Early English design, was consecrated in 1879. The Presbyterian church, built in 1876, is a Gothic structure, of cruciform shape; and the Wesleyan chapel, erected in 1882, is a large red brick building, also of Gothic design, with a tall spire. Harlesden House is a large mansion here, the grounds of which have become famous for their floricultural displays. Much of the land in Harlesden, comprising portions of the Manor Park Estate, has been sold of late years for building purposes.

Cricklewood, a hamlet of Willesden, lying on the Edgware Road, to the north-west of Brondesbury, and closely bordering upon Hampstead, still retains much of its rural character, notwithstanding that it contains a railway-station on the Midland line.

Neasdon, a short distance further westward, is also intersected by the Midland and South-Western Junction Railways, which have a station here at Dudding Hill. The reservoir of the Regent's Park Canal, which extends to this hamlet, covers upwards of 360 acres of ground. There are also extensive works here in connection with the Metropolitan Railway, as a depôt for the carriages, engines, and rolling stock generally, belonging to that company, and for the repair of the same. The works have been constructed upon a plan similar to those belonging to the Great Eastern Railway Company at Stratford,[*] and gives employment to about 500 hands.

Sherrick Green and Dollis Hill are both pretty little hamlets. The former lies in a secluded valley, watered by one of the feeders of the river Brent; and the latter in an upland, well-wooded district. Dollis Hill House, which occupies a commanding site here, is the residence of the Earl of Aberdeen.

Stonebridge Park, about a mile to the south-west of Willesden church, on the main road to Harrow, comprises a large number of villas, occupied chiefly by City men, who prefer the quiet retirement of the country to the noise and bustle of the town. It has a large hotel and a station on the Midland Railway.

We must now beg the reader to accompany us, in imagination, on a railway trip as far as West Drayton, which we have already visited and described,[†] in order to start afresh in our explorations in that neighbourhood.

---

* See "Old and New London," Vol V., p. 573.
† See *ante*, pp. 205-8.

CHAPTER XXI.

COWLEY AND HILLINGDON.

"Ruris amatorem . . . . . . salvere jubemus."—HORACE.

Situation and Boundaries of Cowley—Cowley Peachey—Cowley Church—Graves of Dr. Dodd and the Rev. John Lightfoot—Barton Booth, the Actor—Census Returns—Cowley House—Cowley Grove—Hillingdon—The Cedar House—Etymology of Hillingdon—Hillingdon Heath—Dawley Court—The Manor of Colham—The Church of St. John the Baptist—Tomb of John Rich, the Actor—The Church Library—The Parish Registers—An Old Engraving—Charities—The Village of Hillingdon—The Cemetery—Census Returns—The "Red Lion" Inn—Flight of Charles I. from Oxford.

A WALK of a mile and a half northwards from West Drayton, through Yiewsley, we arrive at Cowley, a singularly scattered parish geographically, consisting of isolated patches of land, mixed up with Hillingdon in such a way as defies description, and must puzzle the authorities when they come to "beat the bounds." It is bounded on the west by the Colne, more than one of whose branches run through it; and it is also intersected by another rivulet, the Blackwater, or Cowley Brook, which runs from Hillingdon, and finds its way into the Colne. It is a small parish of between 300 and 400 acres, scattered about on the cross-road between West Drayton and Uxbridge. Its name is said by Lysons to be derived from the Anglo-Saxon *Co'l leag*, the cold meadow. Mr. Thorne, however, inclines to a simpler derivation—that of "Cow" and "ley," or lea, the Cow's Meadow; but in the "Domesday Book" it figures as "Cove lei." The manor, formerly in the hands of the Abbey of Westminster, passed many centuries ago into the hands of the Peacheys, whence a part of the parish is still called "Cowley Peachey."

The chief part of the population is gathered into Cowley Street, along the road to Uxbridge, from which town Cowley is about a mile distant. The neighbourhood is mostly agricultural, and the meadows and lanes are pleasant and open.

The quaint little church, dedicated to St. Lawrence, stands adjoining the rectory, a little to the east of the village, on the Hillingdon Road. It consists of a small nave and chancel, but the latter is not cut off, as usual, by a chancel-arch, and it has a roof of red tiles, which, being of lofty pitch, while the tower is low, gives a high-shouldered appearance to the structure. The tower and spire belong to the last century.

The church, in spite of some partial restorations, remains very much in the same state as in the last century, the royal arms being there, and tiers of galleries towering to the ceiling at the west end. Where the chancel-arch would naturally be looked for is a solid beam of oak, which supports the Creed, the Lord's Prayer, and the Ten Commandments. Before the Reformation it probably was the rood-beam. The east window consists of an Early English triplet of lancets; and there are one or two other good windows of the Decorated period, some of them filled with modern painted glass. The monuments in the church are numerous, but of no general interest; the most ancient is one to the memory of Walter Pope, yeoman, who died in 1502. In the churchyard, in an angle formed by the western tower, lies in a nameless grave the body of the unfortunate Dr. Dodd, who was executed for forgery in the year 1777.* Here, too, lies the body of the Rev. John Lightfoot, the learned botanist and naturalist, and some time Lecturer of Uxbridge, where we shall meet him again, who died in 1788.

The parish, small and remote as it is, has its dramatic associations. Barton Booth, the actor, of Drury Lane celebrity, and also his widow, lie buried here. The latter, who died in 1773, erected a monument to the memory of her husband in Westminster Abbey, which is ornamented with his bust in medallion, and bears a somewhat fulsome inscription.† Booth, it appears from Davies's "Life of Garrick," was the owner of a small estate in this parish.

Altogether, this parish is almost the least changed of any in Western Middlesex, for whilst it figures in the census of 1871 as having only ninety-two inhabited houses, with a population of 491 souls, the number had not amounted to 500 when the returns for 1881 were taken. Still, it contains several good houses, the largest and most important being Cowley House, the seat of Mr. William Hilliard, who is lord of the manor and patron of the rectory. This mansion contains a fine collection of family pictures, including two by Gainsborough, which were exhibited at South Kensington in 1862.

Cowley Grove, the residence of General Van Cortlandt, C.B., is a conspicuous house at the entrance of the village on the Uxbridge side, and is memorable as having been, as it is believed, the residence of Booth the actor above-mentioned. Booth became famous as a tragedian; he was the

---

* See "Old and New London," Vol. V., p. 190.
† See "Old and New London," Vol. III., p. 223.

great hero of the stage between the reigns of Betterton and Quin, and was the first representative of the part of Cato in Addison's fine tragic poem. The house was afterwards occupied for many years by John Rich the actor and some time patentee of Covent Garden Theatre.

It is quite pleasant, after our long tour amongst the flattest of meadows and arable lands, to find oneself again on breezy uplands, and few parishes in Middlesex can exhibit a more delightful variation of scenery than Hillingdon, which we enter from Cowley. It is diversified by, at all events, two large parks—belonging respectively to Sir Charles Mills and Mr. Cox—and by several smaller houses, standing in extensive grounds. Among them is the "Cedar House," a fine red brick Elizabethan mansion, to the north of the church; and a still larger house some little distance to the south, the successor of an earlier mansion given or sold by the Bishop of London, in the seventeenth century, to the Bishop of Worcester, who needed a resting or halting place in his progresses to and from London. The latter building was used as the rectory previous to the erection of a new house on the opposite side of the road. The reason assigned, in the endowment of the vicarage of Hillingdon, for the appropriation of that church to the see of Worcester was, "that the Bishop of Worcester, being often sent for by the Archbishop and by the king to London, had not, in his way, any inn in this neighbourhood where, upon unavoidable and pressing occasions, he might sleep and lodge as he ought."

Lysons says that the Cedar House was so called from a fine cedar on the front lawn, which tradition assigns to Mr. Samuel Reynardson as its planter. He lived here from 1678 to 1721, but the house was known by its present name some years previously. Gilpin, in his "Forest Trees," published in 1791, mentions this tree as the finest cedar that he had seen, and considers that it was between 130 and 140 years old. Loudon, however, shows that Mr. Gilpin's estimate is an exaggeration, and mentions especially the cedars at Wilton House, near Salisbury, as far larger and finer.

Mr. Reynardson, of Cedar House, was a man of great learning, especially in botany. His garden was full of rarities. Like Solomon, he "spoke of trees, from the cedar that is in Lebanon, unto the hyssop which springeth out of the wall." It was, therefore, natural for the next generation, who knew him only at second-hand, to credit him with having planted the cedar which gave its name to his house. After the death of Mr. Richardson, the house was occupied by General Richard Russell.

Norden, in the MS. additions to his "Speculum Britanniæ," supposes that Hillingdon derives its name from "its situation on a hill, or downe." "Hillingdon Heath, a considerable tract of land to the south-east of the village," observes Mr. Brewer, in the "Beauties of England," "affords a sanction to this mode of derivation, as its comparative eminence is sufficiently proved by the extent of prospect which it commands at many points." To the south of the heath is Dawley Court, the property of the Count de Salis, which we have already noticed.* The house, which is in the parish of Hillingdon, stands on an estate formerly called Coomes, *alias* Little London, and was sometimes called Hillingdon Place.

It would appear that in the Saxon times the parish of Hillingdon comprised concurrently two manors, named respectively Colham and Uxbridge, or Woxbridge; but how far they were identical or independent is not quite certain. In "Domesday" the only mention is that of the Manor of Colham, which was taxed at eight hides, and was held by the Earl of Arundel. "The land is seven carucates; there are six hides in demesne, on which are three ploughs; and the villains have three ploughs. There are six villains, who hold a virgate each, and four others who hold two virgates jointly. The priest had one hide. There are ten bordars, each of whom has five acres; there are four cottars and eight slaves. There are two mills, meadow pasture for the cattle of the manor, pannage for 400 hogs, and one acre of vineyard." It appears from the same document that it was then valued at £8 yearly, having stood at only £6 when it came into the earl's possession, though under Edward the Confessor it was held from the king at £10 rent. In very early times the Manor of Colham formed part of the Honour of Wallingford, and belonged in part to the Abbot of Evesham before it was seized by the Conqueror. In Henry II.'s time it was in the hands of the Bassets, and in 1246 it belonged to William de Lang Espée, Earl of Salisbury. It then devolved on the Earls of Leicester, and from them on the Le Stranges, from whom it came by marriage into the hands of the Stanleys; and Thomas Earl of Derby died at his manorhouse of Colham in 1521. After the death of Ferdinand Earl of Derby in 1594, it passed to his widow, Alice, of whom we shall hear more presently, when we reach Harefield. We will only mention here the fact that when the burgesses of Uxbridge disputed her ladyship's claim, in right of her manor, to a toll on the markets and fairs of the

---

* See *ante*, p. 201.

town, she maintained her right at law, and by threatening them with a prosecution before the Star Chamber, forced the good people within it to recognise her rights and to sue for her pardon. This done, she forgave them, and even sent them some venison for a civic feast. The lordship of the manor passed from her to the Lords Chandos, and from them to the Pitts; and having passed through two or three intermediate families, was purchased in 1782 by the De Burghs of West Drayton.

According to Leland, the manor-house of Colham

were part of the original structure. The embattled tower at the western end, which was built early in the seventeenth century, remains nearly in its original condition. The roofing of the church is new throughout, and some of the windows, the tracery of which has been renewed, are filled with painted glass. The Perpendicular font is curious, and there are on the walls of the church many monuments and inscriptions to local worthies.

On the north wall of the chancel is a costly monument of marble to the memory of Henry

HILLINGDON CHURCH ABOUT 1740.
(*From an old print at the Vicarage*).

was an ancient building, situate about a mile above Uxbridge, between Longford and Colnbrook. It was taken down many years ago. Colham Green, about a mile to the south, is a hamlet of Hillingdon.

The old church, dedicated to St. John the Baptist, stands between the village green and the common. The former is a quaint and irregular open space of about an acre and a half, adorned with two or three elm-trees many centuries old, and reminds one of the Green at Stanwell.

The church stands on a slight elevation. It is of the Decorated or Edwardian period, and consists of spacious nave, chancel, side aisles, and transepts. The latter were added by Sir Gilbert Scott when he restored the church, in 1848, but look as if they

Paget, Earl of Uxbridge, who died at the family seat at Drayton in 1743. The deceased is represented by a semi-recumbent effigy, habited in Roman costume. On the monument is a lengthy inscription, commemorating his social qualities, &c. His lordship had been created Baron Burton in 1712, during his father's lifetime, and he was advanced to the Earldom of Uxbridge in 1714. The title, however, became extinct on the death of the grandson of that nobleman, in 1769, but was revived in 1784 in the person of Henry Bailey, ninth Lord Paget, whose son and successor was created Marquis of Anglesey, in consequence of his gallant military achievements on the Continent. On the opposite side of the chancel is the monument of Sir Edward Carr, who died in 1635. The effigies of the deceased and of his lady (Jane, daughter of Sir Edward Onslow) are represented kneeling before books. Sir Edward is attired in rich armour; and at the foot of the monument, on a projecting pedestal, are the effigies of his two daughters. In the floor of the chancel is the brass of two figures, under a double Gothic canopy. They represent a knight and his lady: the former in armour and bare-headed, and the latter habited in a mantle and kirtle, with a veiled head-dress. The inscription is gone, but the brass is supposed to cover the tomb of John, Lord le Strange, and Jane, his wife, who was the daughter of Richard Woodville, Earl Rivers, and sister of Elizabeth, queen of Edward IV. This Lord Strange died in 1476. Mr. Brewer, in his work already quoted, says that "it is known that a tomb was placed for Lord le Strange and his lady in this church, and the Latin inscription to their memory is preserved in Weever, and has been reprinted in Gough's 'Sepulchral Monuments,' in the 'Environs of London,' and in 'Ecclesiastical Antiquities.'"

The most important tomb in the churchyard is that containing the remains of John Rich the actor, mentioned above. Rich was the first and most famous of English harlequins, a character which he performed under the assumed name of "Lun." His "matchless art and whim" in the representation of this mute hero are recorded by Garrick. He died in the year 1761, having been for many years the lessee of Covent Garden Theatre.* Among other tombs in the churchyard is that of Major-General Richard Russell, son of Sir John Russell, and grandson of Oliver Cromwell. He died in 1793, having been for many years a resident of the Cedar House, in this village.

In the vestry at the west end of the south aisle is a church library. It was left by Mr. Reynardson, of the Cedar House, in 1721. It contains a large number of works on divinity, natural history, and medicine, together with some voyages and travels, and numerous historical and poetical publications, and a first edition of the "Eikon Basilike." The books are, on the whole, in a fair condition.

The registers commence in the year 1559, the second year of Elizabeth. As usual, the records are absent during the troubled years of Parliamentarian rule, 1644-49; from this latter date to 1653 they are confused and imperfect.

With the restoration of Charles II. came a new vicar, one Thomas Boston, who seems to have been both a scholar and a wag. At all events, his

entries are comical, and full of sarcastic allusions to the "sectaries," whose sway was just over. He calls base-born children "terræ filii," and he records all sorts of incidents, including the murder of one of his parishioners: but newspapers, it must be remembered, were then in their first infancy. He chronicles the fact of children baptised at home, though not in weak health, and of the contempt of the law by their parents in omitting to bring them afterwards to the church. He notes also, in terms of harsh censure, the invasion of his rights by the neighbouring clergy, who dared to baptise and to bury those whom he claimed as his parishioners. It is probable, judging from the entries in the register, that the population of Hillingdon under Charles II. could scarcely have been a third of what it is now. Among the burials are recorded those of many Londoners, showing that even two centuries ago the neighbourhood was attractive to strangers on account of its healthiness. In spite of the two towns—for so they are called—of Hillingdon and Uxbridge having been a stronghold of Nonconformity, there are many proofs in the register that Hillingdon was greatly used as a halting-place between London and the quarters of the Court at Oxford in the reign of Charles I.

In 1665 the burial list is increased by several entries of deaths, probably of strangers and wayfarers, who died of the plague.

In 1663, the hearse of the Archbishop of Canterbury, Dr. Juxon, on its way from London to Oxford, appears to have been met at the church gate by the vicar in surplice and hood, "the great bell solemnly tolling all the while"—probably as a loyal mark of respect to the prelate who had stood by the side of King Charles on the scaffold at Whitehall.

Mr. Boston died in 1677, and the registers of succeeding vicars scarcely call for remark.

In the vicarage is a copy of a curious engraving of the church in its former condition, probably about 1740 or a little later. The tower is much the same as now, but the southern aisle is a monstrous high-shouldered erection, with "churchwarden" windows. To the south of the churchyard stands a lofty yew, clipped, as at Bedfont, into a fantastic shape; and there is a row of four smaller yew-trees along the west front, by the side of a lych-gate, below which again are the parish stocks, the terror of small boys. There is still living an old parishioner who can remember as a boy climbing these yew-trees. The engraving is very scarce, and the vicar's copy has been made by him a heir-loom for his successors.

---

* See "Old and New London," Vol. III., p. 228.

Up to 1871 a considerable amount of bread was given away in doles for several charities ; but owing to abuses and scandals, these gifts, with the sanction of the Charity Commissioners, were commuted for a money payment towards providing clothing for poor school children and help for necessitous parishioners.

The village of Hillingdon is situated on the main road between London and Oxford, and is fourteen miles from Hyde Park Corner, and rather more than a mile from Uxbridge Station, on a branch of the Great Western Railway. The Grand Junction Canal passes through the parish ; and at the western end of the village, fronting the Uxbridge Road, is the cemetery, which was consecrated in 1867. It comprises an area of about six acres, and contains two mortuary chapels. These buildings, which are constructed of Kentish rag-stone with Bath stone dressings, and have tiled roofs, are in the Decorated style of architecture, from the designs of the late Mr. Benjamin Ferrey, F.S.A.

Hillingdon, in 1871, appears by the census to have had 1,615 inhabited houses, with a population of 8,237, a number which was increased by upwards of fifteen hundred in the course of the next ten years.

One of the principal hostelries in the village, the " Red Lion," directly opposite the church, has been a noted house in its day. Here Charles I. rested after his escape from Oxford, with his chaplain, Dr. Hudson, and Ashburnham, his groom of the chamber, when besieged by Fairfax, in April, 1646, and hence he made his way by cross roads towards Hertfordshire.

The following extract from the evidence of " Dr. Michael Hudson's Examination before the Committee of Parliament touching the King's Escape from Oxford to the Scots at Southwell," as printed in Peck's " Desiderata Curiosa," is of interest :— " After we had passed Uxbridge, at one Mr. Teasdale's house a taverne in Hillingdon, we alighted and stayed to refresh ourselves, betwixt 10 and 11 of the clocke [Monday morning, April 27], and there stayed two or three hours, where the king was much perplexed what course to resolve upon, London or Northward. The consideration of the former vote, and the apparent danger of being discovered at London, moved him to resolve at last to go Northward and through Norfolke, where he was least knowne. . . . About 2 of the clocke we took a guide towards Barnet."

In order to meet the requirements of the increasing population of this parish, a new church was erected in 1865 at Hillingdon End, near to Uxbridge, but of this we shall have more to say presently.

CHAPTER XXII.

UXBRIDGE.

THE town of Uxbridge, to which we next come, though spoken of in legal documents as a " borough and manor," is really neither the one nor the other, in the full acceptation of those terms. It is, in its origin, a hamlet of the parish of Hillingdon, and probably grew up gradually and naturally at the ford over the Colne. Its origin, no doubt, is to be sought in the Saxon times; and Messrs. Redford and Riches, in their " History of Uxbridge," state that " there are reasons which render it probable that it was one of the regular, though possibly smaller, boroughs established by King Alfred, or by some of his immediate successors." Its name does not occur in " Domesday," but as early as the year 1139 it is mentioned in a curious deed by one Brian Fitz-Count, under the name of Oxebridge ; and it is constantly mentioned in later times under this name, and as Woxbridge. Skinner, half as much in jest as in earnest, says in his " Lexicon " that its right name is Waxbridge, and defends the name as appropriate, on account of the waxy and tenacious nature of the clay which composes its surface soil.

That Uxbridge was reckoned a borough is clear from an ancient (Henry II.) grant from Gilbert Basset, in which its inhabitants are spoken of as burgesses, and from several manuscripts and legal records, in which the " borough ditch " is mentioned.

Though we now generally restrict the term borough to towns which return members to Parliament, we are not justified in doing so, for a borough is originally nothing but a burgh, or town, with a certain amount of local government and local privileges.

It is supposed by some that, like Oxford, the town derived its name from the number of oxen* continually passing through it from Buckinghamshire and the western counties on their way up to London; but probably the last syllable of the name is a variation of Bruge, an equivalent to Burgh, for the Colne appears to

town of Uxbridge is of a date long subsequent to the Plantagenet or even the Tudor era. It was just before the beginning of the war between King Charles and his Parliament, in 1644, that Uxbridge was chosen as the place where certain royal commissioners should meet those of the

THE TREATY HOUSE, UXBRIDGE. (*See page* 232.)
(*From the "History of Uxbridge,"* 1818.)

have been crossed here by a ford, and not by a bridge, down to a comparatively recent era. The ditch by which the town was surrounded in old times enclosed about eighty-five acres, and a portion of the ditch was visible in 1818, when the "History of Uxbridge" was published.

The chief historic event connected with the

rebel party, in the vain hope of bringing the differences between them to an amicable issue. The hope was vain, for religion and politics were both engaged in the conflict, the king being resolved to stand by Episcopacy, while the Roundheads were equally anxious to get rid of everything that looked in the Popish direction. On the king's part, the commission was headed by the Duke of Richmond, the Earls of Southampton, Hertford, Kingston, and Chichester, and Sir Edward Hyde, afterwards Lord Clarendon. The Presbyterians

* A writer in the *Cornhill Magazine* (1882) argues that the first syllable in Oxford and Uxbridge is the same; but has nothing to do with "oxen." It is simply the Celtic *uisg*=water, as in Usk. The suggestion is well worthy of consideration.

were represented by the Duke of Northumberland, Lords Pembroke, Denbigh, and Salisbury, Sir Harry Vane, and Bulstrode Whitelock; whilst the Scotch sent Lord Loudoun, then Lord Chancellor, Lord Argyll, and other great persons from the north of the Tweed, as their spokesmen.

Lord Clarendon gives, in an often-quoted passage of his "History of the Great Rebellion," an interesting account of their session, from which it appears that one side of the town was assigned to the king's commissioners, and the other to those of the opposite party. "There was a good house at the end of the town, which was provided for the treaty, where was a fair room in the middle of the house, handsomely dressed up, for the commissioners to sit in, a large square table being placed in the middle, with seats for the commissioners, one side being sufficient for those of either party, and a rail for others who should be thought necessary to be present, which went round. There were many other rooms on either side of this great room, for the commissioners on either side to retire to when they thought fit to consult by themselves, and to return again to the public debate; and there being good stairs at either end of the house, they never went through each other's quarters, nor met but in the great room."

And then Clarendon goes on to record the ceremonious civilities practised on either side, and the professions of intense wishes for peace from those who had bitter war in their hearts all the while. He tells us also how the king's commissioners would gladly have attended the services in the parish church, but that the Book of Common Prayer had been superseded by the Parliament, so that they were obliged to have the Church prayers read in the great room of the inn.

The debates at the conference lasted about three weeks, when the commissioners on either side agreed to separate and return to their masters. The king was resolute in his demands for the establishment of Episcopacy; the Parliamentarians were equally resolved to have none of it. The king's friends went back to Oxford, and the others to London, leaving the state of matters, if anything, rather worse than they had found it.

The conference gave rise to no little dissension and bitterness throughout the country; and one famous Presbyterian, Christopher Lover, preached against the intended treaty, saying that "no good could come of it, for that the king's emissaries had come from Oxford with blood-stained hands." This warlike gentleman afterwards lost his head under Cromwell.

The mansion which was the scene of the con-

ference is described in the "Perfect Occurrences," a journal of the time, as "a very fair house at the farther end of the town, in which house were [was] appointed to them a very spacious room, well-hanged, and fitted with seats for the commissioners."

The great room, mentioned by Clarendon, is still standing in its original state, as is also the presence chamber, so called, adjoining. It is a fine large apartment, wainscoted with dark oak.

The house was then much larger than now, and it stood in a large garden, with an ornamental "Lodge" entrance; the high road now passes through a part of its grounds. It had been previously the seat of the Bennets, who afterwards became Earls of Arlington and of Tankerville; and at the time of the treaty it was called "Mr. Carr's house."

The Earl of Northumberland was the only commissioner on the opposite side who was accommodated here; Lord Pembroke lodged in another "fair house," now a brew-house or beer-house.

Each party had its place of rendezvous, and the best houses of the inhabitants were put into requisition for the accommodation of the commissioners and their attendants. Each party took a principal inn for its head-quarters, like the Oxford and Cambridge crews at Putney before the annual boat-race. It may be interesting to note that the king's commissioners chose the "Crown," and the Parliamentarians the "George"—both near the market-place, and on opposite sides of the way. In the year 1818 the "Crown" stood opposite to the "White Horse," and its grounds reached from the High Street down to the Colne. The name has long since been transferred to the "Treaty House" itself, which is now an inn, and bears the name of the "Crown and Treaty," or, as it is locally styled, "The Crown and treat ye." At the above date the "George Inn" remained, though partly converted into a private dwelling-house.

The Treaty House was visited more than once by Edmund Burke on his way between Beaconsfield and London, while his horses were feeding, and was found by him to be "most amusing and interesting."

In the rear of the Treaty House is an octagonal building, said to have been formerly used as a "round-house"; and the garden front is enriched by excellent brick-work, especially in fine hexagonal stacks of chimneys.

The town of Uxbridge lies at the foot of one of the ranges of small hills which occupy the north-western corner of Middlesex, by which flow the clear waters of the twin rivers, formed by the union of the Colne, Gade, Verum, Chess, and Misbourne. The larger of these streams, the Colne, is crossed by a substantial bridge of five arches. The smaller of the two, the Frayswater, flows through the lower part of the town, and turns the town mills, after which it separates the borough and the suburb of Chiltern View from the more populous district of St. John's.

The Grand Junction Canal also runs through Uxbridge, connecting the chief towns of the midland counties with the Thames at Brentford, and with London at Paddington. At one time the canal boats carried passengers between Uxbridge and London; but the business did not answer, and has long since been abandoned.

The bridge across the Colne, at the west end of the town, is still called the High Bridge: it consists of two parts, the central portion standing on an island. A bridge is mentioned as existing here as early as the reign of Richard II., when it was in a very ruinous condition; but it would seem that it was adapted only for horses, not for carts or waggons. This improvement dates only from the time of Henry VIII., when Lord Loughborough and Sir Edward Peckham, the one resident in Buckinghamshire and the other in Middlesex, enlarged and widened it, "out of charitie." It is probable that in this case charity began "at home." It was repaired in 1600, at the cost of Lady Derby, the lady of the manor, being then of wood. The present bridge is of brick, and dates from about 1770, the high road being slightly diverted at the time. At the foot of the bridge, on the Buckinghamshire side, is a river-side inn, with the quaint sign of the "Swan and Bottle." It is a favourite haunt of anglers. Leland, in his "Itinerary," mentions two wooden bridges here. That which he describes as the more western is the High Bridge, mentioned above; and he tells us that it crosses "the great arme of Colne river," while "the lesser arme goeth under the other bridge, and each of them serve a great mill." We have a proof of Leland's accuracy in the fact that the two mills and the two bridges are still there, though the latter are now built of more solid materials than wood.

From its position on the great western highway and on the Colne, there is no doubt that Uxbridge was fortified at a very early date; indeed, we already know that it had its town ditch. From documents in existence, it is clear, however, that it had also—at all events at times—a garrison. At the outbreak of the great rebellion it was under the command of a Captain Lampton, or Lambton, and the troops under him are styled "the garrison," and the register of burials records the deaths of more than one soldier "from the garrison." In 1647, when the western parts of Middlesex were held by the Parliamentarians, their head-quarters were fixed for some time at Uxbridge; and Lysons tells us in whose houses Cromwell, Fairfax, Ireton, Fleetwood, &c., were quartered. Even as late as 1688-9, the accounts of the chapel-wardens and overseers contain entries for the repairs of the "guard-house;" but under the tranquil reigns of our Brunswick line, the need of garrisons and guard-houses here has ceased to exist.

It is said that a Roman road ran from High Wycombe towards Beaconsfield and Uxbridge, but if so, its course cannot now be traced. To the north of the town, near Breakspears and Harefield, sufficient remains of Roman burials have been found to justify the supposition that the road to Verulam or to London passed not far from Uxbridge.

The chief streets of Uxbridge are the High Street, extending the whole length of the town from south-east to north-west; Windsor Street, formerly called the Lynch, running south-west from the market-house and church; and Vine Street, bounding it on the south-east, and probably marking the site of an ancient vineyard. The eastern part of High Street is legally styled Hillingdon End, and, in fact, is situated in Hillingdon parish.

Uxbridge disputes with Brentford the claim to being the chief or county town of Middlesex. In 1871 the parish contained 659 houses, and a population of 3,364 souls—a number which has somewhat diminished since that time, seeing that according to the census returns for 1881 the sum total of the inhabitants was only 3,346.

The "Chequers" is the oldest inn in the place, and may date back to the sixteenth, or even as remote as the fifteenth, century. It has some fine and substantial timbers in its roof and staircases, but much of the inside, as well as of the outside, is modernised. In former times the inns and taverns were numerous, compared with the size of the town, being nearly three times as many as there are at present.

The corn and flour trade is the staple business of Uxbridge, but there are also a few manufactories, breweries, an iron foundry, and saw and planing mills; whilst in the neighbourhood, on the south and south-west, are extensive brickfields.

The fairs at Uxbridge are now four in number. They are principally cattle fairs, and are held on Lady Day, on July 31st, on September 29th, and October 11th. The two last are used as statute fairs. In olden days the town must have worn a gay and festive appearance on these annual gatherings, when the steward of the Countess of Derby and the bailiffs of the town clothed in her ladyship's livery, and preceded by bands of music, used to march in solemn state to open the proceedings.

The market-house was built in 1788. It stands partly on the site of an older and smaller structure, which projected into the High Street. The present building, however, might well be removed, as it sadly obstructs the view of the parish church. It

reminding one of the description which Macaulay gives us of the leading high roads of the kingdom in the days of the Stuarts.

It is only since 1856 that Uxbridge has reached the honour of a separate ecclesiastical parish, having previously, since 1842, ranked only as a "district chapelry." It was originally a mere hamlet of Hillingdon; and though the parish church was built as far back as the reign of Henry VI., yet until the present reign it was only a chapel-of-ease,

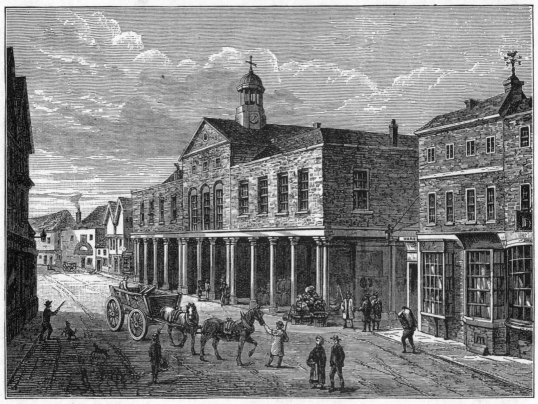

MARKET HOUSE, UXBRIDGE.
(*From the "History of Uxbridge," 1818.*)

is open below. On the upper floor are spacious rooms, used for educational and other purposes, and also a large granary for storing corn from one week to another. Weekly markets are held on Thursdays and Saturdays; at the former a good deal of corn is sold, whilst the latter is for cattle, pigs, and articles of domestic use. The market on Thursdays is the result of a charter, or grant, from Gilbert Basset, who probably held this manor and the Honour of Wallingford, as a reward for his fidelity to King Henry II. and his mother, Matilda, in their struggle against Stephen.

Though the great Oxford road passes through Uxbridge, yet even as late as 1797–8 the highways about here were almost impassable from mud,

or curacy, annexed to that rectory. In 1869, by an Order in Council, Uxbridge was made a Vicarage; it was, however, called a Vicarage as far back as 1548.

The church is dedicated to St. Margaret. It is supposed that an older chapel stood on this site as far back as 1281; and that it had attached to it a religious house, which was suppressed by Henry VIII. No particulars, however, of its existence are known for certain.

The present church was terribly "beautified" by amateur architects during the last century. In 1872 the fabric was restored to something like its normal condition by the removal of galleries and a thorough renovation of its walls, under the superintendence of Sir Gilbert Scott. It consists of a nave and one side aisle, with a short chancel, and a tower at the north-west corner, in which is a peal of six bells. There is a very fine oak roof to the south aisle. The font is of Perpendicular workmanship, and handsome of its kind. On the north side of the chancel is a handsome monument, in the Jacobean style, to Leonora, Lady Bennet, who is represented in a reclining posture, in her every-day dress, a charnel-house being seen beneath her.

Among the burials in 1755 is that of a widow aged 104. During the Great Rebellion the banns of marriage appear to have been published not in the church, but in the open market-place, and the ceremony was performed by a civil magistrate.

The Rev. John Lightfoot, F.R.S., one of the chief founders of the Linnæan Society, was " Lecturer" of Uxbridge in the middle of the last century. He died in 1788, and lies buried at Cowley, as mentioned above.

THE FONT.   ST. MARGARET'S, UXBRIDGE.
(*From the " History of Uxbridge," 1818.*)

The curfew was rung regularly here during the winter months at eight p.m. until thirty or forty years back, when it was discontinued owing to the economy of the local authorities.

The registers of Uxbridge are in fair condition. They commence in 1538; but the marriage registers cease with 1694, from which date all weddings were ordered to be solemnised only in the mother church of Hillingdon. They contain the usual amount of curious entries. One young woman brings her illegitimate child to be christened, but she has to purchase the baptismal rite dearly, for she is forced to do public penance in the church on the same day. On another page are recorded the baptisms of four children, all born at one birth.

The lecturership and the vicarage are now accidentally held by one and the same person. His parsonage, which adjoins the railway-station, is the house built for the lecturer on land purchased for that minister, and is not, therefore, correctly termed the vicarage.

The lecturer's house is of the Queen Anne type and old-fashioned, oak-panelled within, and with a lofty roof. It is built of red brick; and a handsome modern drawing-room was added early in this century. The story runs that one day the Duchess of Portland, being at Bulstrode Park, said to the then lecturer that she hoped soon to call on him and his wife. "Madam," he replied, "I am sorry to say that I have no room fit to receive your Grace in." "Then," said the duchess, "I will build you one;" and in a few weeks she was as good as her word.

We have already stated that all the eastern part of the town of Uxbridge lies in the parish of Hillingdon. The church being small, it was accordingly felt that the accommodation for the increase in the population was inadequate, and so about the year 1860 a subscription was commenced for building a new church at the entrance of the town, on the Hillingdon Road. In the event, Sir Gilbert Scott was engaged as the architect; and the result was that in 1865 a handsome and spacious Gothic church, of the Decorated style, was completed and dedicated to St. Andrew. It consists of a lofty nave, chancel, and side aisles, and its tower is surmounted by a shingled spire, 170 feet high. A vicarage house close by was purchased, and good schools were built. A considerable part of the northern suburbs of Uxbridge lies in St. Andrew's district. Though officially styled St. Andrew's, Hillingdon, it so thoroughly belongs to the town of Uxbridge that it is better to deal with it here.

A small church, St. John's, of very unpretending character, was built about 1835 to the west of the town, on Uxbridge Moor, to meet the wants of a large population at the west end of the town, including the families of many boatmen.

Uxbridge has always been a stronghold of Nonconformity. The Quakers (who have been largely engaged in trade) have a meeting-house, which dates from 1693; and a letter from George Fox, one of the founders of that sect, addressed to the townsfolk of Uxbridge in no measured terms of reproach, is printed *in extenso* in the "History of Uxbridge," already referred to. The annals of the Presbyterian chapel here go back at least as far, and the Independent chapel was built in 1796. There are also meeting-houses for the various denominations of Wesleyans, Congregationalists, &c.

The various sects of Nonconformists made a sad display of their variations when they met at the Treaty of Uxbridge. As Butler says, in his "Hudibras," Part I., cant. ii. :—

"For when we sware to carry on
The present reformation,
According to the present mode
Of churches best reformed abroad,
What did we else but make a vow
To do we know not what, nor how?
For no three of us will agree
Where or what churches these should be."

Uxbridge is well off for literary societies and for educational and charitable endowments.

On the north-east of the town the ground rises gradually, and on its breezy heights is a public recreation-ground—all that remains of an extensive common, which was enclosed early in the present century. From this spot an extensive view is gained of the Thames Valley and of the level country reaching eastwards to Harrow and Hampstead. It is, perhaps, worthy of note that the old common contained a large rabbit-warren—said to be the only one in Middlesex.

There is also a race-course in the neighbourhood, but the races have taken place only occasionally since 1865, the meetings, like those at Acton and other metropolitan suburbs, having been voted a great nuisance by the majority of the inhabitants.

At a short distance from the town, on the London road, stands Hillingdon House, a large mansion, which was built in 1717 by the last Duke of Schomberg, who had lived for several years in an ancient house on the estate. The property afterwards passed into the hands of the noble family of Chetwynd, and towards the end of the last century it was purchased by the Marchioness of Rockingham. It has since changed hands on several occasions, its owner at the beginning of the present century being Mr. Richard Henry Cox, the well-known army agent. A rivulet, a tributary of the Colne, passes through the grounds, where it has been expanded into a lake. Beyond it, to the north, is Hillingdon Court, the seat of Sir Charles Mills, Bart.

On the edge of what was once Uxbridge Common, and in the immediate vicinity of the town, Mr. Thomas Harris, the joint patentee of Covent Garden Theatre, had a residence at the beginning of the present century. The house, a large brick building, was probably built about a century earlier. The gardens were originally laid out in straight lines and formal parterres, after the fashion of those times. Mr. Harris added considerably to the adornment of the grounds, of which the following description is quoted from the "Beauties of England:"—"A mimic hermitage, fancifully bedecked with vestiges of marble sculpture, spars, stained glass, and with apposite mottoes, opens to an apartment of handsome proportions, hung throughout with pictures, which the admirers of the histrionic art cannot fail to hold in very precious esteem. Here is preserved a large and valuable collection of original portraits of the principal theatrical performers from the date of Garrick, when all the stage was nature, to the present period, at which a monotonous, half-singing style of recitation is so often employed as a substitute for simplicity and truth. In addition to this interesting series of portraits, there are, in the same garden-saloon, pictures representing Melpomene and Thalia, and two fine paintings by Northcote from scenes in Shakespeare's tragedy of 'Richard III.' The house is still standing, but has been somewhat modernised, and in the gardens are some fine cedars."

In the troublous times of the Reformation, Uxbridge witnessed the horrors of seeing several persons who ventured to reject the dominant creed burnt at the stake. Fox has recorded their names; they appear to have been three at the least. Tradition says that the scene of their suffering was the Lynch Green, near Windsor Street, a little to the west of the burial-ground. This was in August, 1555.

A singular story, which refers to this town, is told by Mr. H. Fynes Clinton respecting his great-great-grandfather, one Norreys Fynes, alias Clinton. He was in the Royalist army under Charles I., and was taken prisoner at Northampton; but Prince Rupert having captured a man of importance, a Mr. Wright, of Uxbridge, an exchange of prisoners was arranged, and the trumpeter announcing this exchange arrived in the market-place at Uxbridge just as the rope had been put round and the last psalm or hymn was being sung, at the end of which he was to be turned off. Thus the existence of a large collateral branch of the ducal family of Newcastle for some minutes depended on the length to which a psalm was drawled out.

We may perhaps be pardoned for here introducing an amusing anecdote concerning a former Lord Mayor of London, whose early life was connected with this town, namely, Sir William Staines, who was London's chief magistrate in 1801. He started in life as a bricklayer's labourer, and at City banquets, with great glee, he used to introduce the following anecdote:—When he was a youngster, he was employed in repairing the parsonage house at Uxbridge. One day, going up the ladder with his hod of mortar, he was accosted by the parson's wife, who told him that she had had a very extraordinary dream. She told him that she had dreamed he would one day become Lord Mayor of London. Astonished at such a prophecy, Staines could only scratch his head, and thank her for such a vast promotion. He said he had neither money nor friends. The parson's wife, however, was not so easily to be turned from her prognostication, and this dream had evidently left a great impression. Her mind was bent on young Staines, and Lord Mayor he should be. The same dream occurred again, and the same communication was repeated to him that he was to be Lord Mayor. The matter passed off, and young Staines left the parsonage house at Uxbridge with no other impression than the kindness which had been shown

and the notice that had been taken of him. It was not until he became sheriff that this dream came to be talked about, though there is little doubt that the dream made a lasting impression upon his own mind, and was an incentive to laudable industry through life. The Uxbridge parson had by this time become old, but he lived long enough to be chaplain to Staines when sheriff, and he died during his shrievalty.

On the north and west sides of the town, the Colne (or, as it was formerly called, Colney) pursues its course in two branches, each "brimming and very fishful," through the meadows and on either side of Uxbridge Moor, the principal arm going on to Colnbrook, and dividing the counties of Middlesex and Buckinghamshire. The clearness and purity of its stream have long been celebrated. Milton, who must often have walked by its banks when living at Horton, on his way to Harefield, in his "Epitaphium Damonis," also has immortalised its waters in Latin verse, thus translated by Cowper:—

"What ho! my friend—come, lay thy task aside;
Haste, let us forth together, and beguile
The heat beneath yon whisp'ring shades a while,
Or on the margin stray of Colne's clear flood,
Or where Cassibelan's grey turrets stood.
There shalt thou cull me simples, and shalt teach
Thy friend the name and healing powers of each,
From the tall bluebell to the dwarfish weed,
What the dry land and what the marshes breed;
For all their kinds alike to thee are known,
And the whole art of Galen is thine own."

The Colne has its sources among the chalk hills of Hertfordshire. The rights of fishing in the river still belong to the town-folk of Uxbridge, and form, indeed, almost the only rights left to them since the enclosure of their common.

Just above Uxbridge, on the opposite side of the river, at the junction of the roads leading to the Chalfonts and to Rickmansworth, is the pretty and retired village of Denham, a place haunted by the followers of Izaak Walton and the gentle craft. Sir Humphry Davy, the genius of angling in the nineteenth century, who often used to invite his London friends to join him for a day at the Fishery, writes:—"A light carriage, with good horses, will carry us to the ground. . . . The river is most strictly preserved; not a fish has been killed here since last August."

Denham was, under the Stuarts, one of the resorts of the proscribed Roman Catholics; and frequent mention is made in "Troubles of our Catholic Forefathers" of Sir George Peckham's house in this parish, as having sheltered priests from the bloodhounds of the law.

CHAPTER XXIII.

ICKENHAM, RUISLIP, AND HAREFIELD.

"The Chestnuts"—Ickenham—Census Returns—The Village Green and Pump—The Parish Church—Descent of the Manor—Swakeleys—Visit of Samuel Pepys—A Curious Baptismal Register—Crab, the English Hermit—Ruislip—Boundaries and Population—Outlying Hamlets—Agricultural Produce, &c.—Extract from the Domesday Survey—Ruislip Priory—The Manor Farm—The Vicarage—The Parish Church—Charities, &c.—The Parish Records—Primitive Condition of the Inhabitants of Ruislip—Schools—The Grand Junction Canal Company's Reservoir—Ruislip Park—Eastcott—Northwood—How Theodore Hook obtained a Dinner without paying for it—Harefield, its Situation and Extent—Its early History—Descent of the Manor—Visit of Queen Elizabeth to Harefield—Lord Keeper Egerton, and the Countess of Derby—The Newdigate Family—The Parish Church—Moor Hall—Breakspears.

CONTINUING our pilgrimage northward from Uxbridge, by way of the Recreation Grounds, we pass "The Chestnuts," a small mansion built under the Stuarts, on the road towards Ickenham, and now the residence of Sir William Stephenson. It is interesting as having once been occupied by William Wilberforce the philanthropist, and before him by Bishop Horne, the commentator on the Psalms.

Turning eastward, shortly after passing the "Warren House," a walk of between two and three miles brings us to the village of Ickenham, the houses of which place, few in number, are located round the village green, or scattered about in picturesque confusion in the surrounding lanes. The entire area of the parish is under 1,500 acres, and the population in 1881 numbered only 376 souls, being a slight diminution upon the census returns in 1871.

The main roads running north and south from Hillingdon to Ruislip, and that from the eastern side of Ickenham to Harefield in the north-west, cross on the Green, in the centre of which stands the village pump. This structure was erected about 1860. It has a tall conical roof, and is surrounded with seats. On the north side of the Green, in an angle formed by the two cross-roads, stands the village church. This building, almost hidden from sight by tall trees, is small and ancient, apparently dating as far back as the fourteenth century, the architecture showing examples of the Decorated and Early Perpendicular styles. It consists of a nave, north aisle—or rather, a double transept—and chancel, with a wooden belfry surmounted by a dwarf spire—similar to that of Norwood, Northolt, and other places which we have visited—rising from the western end of the nave. The bells, three in number, bear the date of 1582. The walls of the body of the church are composed of flint and stone, mostly encased with plaster. On the south side of the nave is a wooden porch, and the red tiles form a pleasant contrast. The chancel arch is modern, having been added when the church was restored a few years ago. In the chancel there is a brass commemorating William Say,

gent., who died in 1582, "registrar to the Queen's Majesty in causes ecclesiastical," with effigies of himself, his wife, and sixteen children; also one with figures of the deceased and his wife, to the memory of Henry Edmund, who died in 1584. There are also several other monuments to the family of Shordiche, formerly lords of the manor; and also to the Turners, Clarkes, and Dixons, families which have been at one time or another connected with this parish, either as landowners or as residents. A mural tablet on the west wall, executed by Banks, to the memory of Mr. John George Clarke, a barrister-at-law, who died in 1800, is curious: it bears upon it a figure typical of Religion, which is represented with a book in one hand, the other resting on a coffin partially hidden by a pall.

In the churchyard there is a very fine yew-tree; and at the west end of the church there is an unsightly charnel-house belonging to the family of the Clarkes, of Swakeleys.

This parish—which figures in ancient documents, under the respective names of Ticheham and Tykenham—is noticed in the Domesday survey, where it is recorded that "three knights and one Englishman held the manor, under Earl Roger. It answered for nine hides and a half. Land for six ploughs; pasture for the cattle of the village; pannage for two hundred hogs;" &c.

"The manor of Ickenham," observes Mr. Brewer in the "Beauties of England," "has been the subject of less frequent family alienations than is usual with property near the metropolis. It was conveyed in 1348 to John de Charlton, citizen and mercer, for life, with remainder to Nicholas Shordiche, Ivetta his wife, and their heirs." The manor remained in the hands of the Shordiche family for many generations, down to the end of the last century, when it passed to the present family of Clarke, of Swakeleys.

The most interesting feature of this parish is Swakeleys, a fine old substantial square red-brick mansion of Tudor architecture, standing in an extensive park, just outside the village, on the Hillingdon Road, and surrounded on all sides by broad green meadows and pasture-lands. The mansion consists of a centre with two slightly projecting wings, the latter terminating in large bay windows, and in the upper storey is a range of scroll-work pediments and gables, above which rise clusters of ornamented chimney stacks. The entrance is through a porch in a central turret, which opens into a hall paved with black and white stone. At the lower end of the hall is a handsome carved oak screen, painted white, and adorned with busts of Charles I. and others. This screen was probably designed for a loftier room, as it reaches nearly to the ceiling. The entrance hall is likewise remarkable for its fine massive Jacobean chimneypiece, on which are busts of Milton and Harrington.

The staircase, also of oak, has the walls and ceiling painted with several classical subjects, the principal one being the "Death of Dido," from Virgil's "Æneid." The long gallery is now cut up into three apartments, the centre forming a ballroom or drawing-room.

The grounds belonging to the house are somewhat flat, but well wooded, and are intersected by a little rivulet, which is dammed up into a miniature lake. The estate is strictly preserved, and the rabbits and pheasants walk and run about almost tame by the road-side, as we drive through the park.

Though very much smaller than either the one or the other, Swakeleys has about it many points of resemblance to Knole and Holland House; indeed, next to Holland House, this is the most interesting Jacobean mansion in the whole county of Middlesex. The gardens are quaint and trim, laid out in something of the old-fashioned style, and a long avenue of elms adorns the front of the house to the south.

This estate probably derives its name from Robert Swalclyve, who owned it four centuries ago. About the middle of the fourteenth century the estate passed to John de Charlton, who, as above stated, was the owner of the manor of Ickenham. On the attainder of Sir Richard de Charlton, in 1486, his property was forfeited to the Crown, but was shortly afterwards granted to Sir Thomas Bourchier, whose descendant, Henry Bourchier, Marquis of Exeter, sold Swakeleys, about 1550, to one Robert Pexall. The property later on was divided, one portion falling into the hands of Oliver Becket, and the other passing to the family of Brocas. Norden, writing of Swakeleys in 1596, in his "Speculum Britanniæ," mentions it as "some time a house of the Brockeyes, now of Sir Thomas Sherleye's." In 1629 the manor became the property of Edmund Wright, afterwards Sir Edmund Wright,

an alderman of London, by whom the present mansion was erected about ten years later, as appears from the date, 1638, with the initials E.W., to be seen in different parts of the building. Sir Edmund was chosen Lord Mayor of London in 1641, after the removal from that office, by Act of Parliament, of Sir William Acton. The mansion subsequently became the property and residence of Sir William Harrington, one of the judges who sat on the trial of King Charles I., and who, on the Restoration, escaped the fate of his associates by flight. It afterwards passed to Sir Robert Vyner, Lord Mayor of London, whose familiar and facetious conduct on the entertainment of Charles II. at Guildhall * were long remembered. Pepys, in his Diary under date of September 7, 1665, gives us the following insight into Sir Robert Vyner's mansion of Swakeleys shortly after he purchased it :—"To Branford [Brentford]. . . There a coach of Mr. Povy's stood ready for me, and he at his house ready to come in, and so we together merrily to Swakeley, to R. Vyner's ; a very pleasant place, bought by him of Sir James Harrington's lady. He took us up and down with great respect, and showed us all his house and grounds, and it is a place not very moderne in the garden nor house, but the most uniforme in all that ever I saw ; and some things to excess. Pretty to see over the screene of the hall, put up by Sir J. Harrington, a Long Parliament man, the King's head and my Lord of Essex on one side, and Fairfax on the other ; and upon the other side of the screene, the parson of the parish and the lord of the manor and his sisters. The window-cases, door-cases, and chimneys of all the house, are marble. He showed us a black boy that he had, that died of a consumption ; and, being dead, he caused him to be dried in an oven, and lies there entire in a box. By and by to dinner, where his lady I find yet handsome, but hath been a very handsome woman ; now is old. Hath brought him over £100,000, and now he lives, no man in England in greater plenty, and commands both king and council with his credit he gives them. After dinner Sir Robert led us up to his long gallery, very fine, above stairs ; and better, or such, furniture I never did see."

After one or two changes of ownership, Swakeleys passed by sale in 1750 to the family of the Clarkes, and is now the seat of Mr. Thomas Truesdale Clarke. The patronage of the rectory of Ickenham had been annexed to the manor time out of mind, until it was purchased by Mr. Thomas Clarke, in 1743.

---

* See " Old and New London," Vol. I., p. 405.

"A branch of the noble family of Hastings," observes the author of the "Beauties of England," "formerly resided in this parish, and it appears that here 'Katharine, the dowgter of the Lord Hastyngs and the Lady his wyff, was borne, the Saterday before our Lady-day the Assumption, being the 11 day of August, and was christened the 20 of August, the Godmother Quene Kateryn, by her *debite*, beyng her syster, one Mr. Harberd's wiff; the other Godmother the Lady Margaret Dugles, the Kyng's nece, and the Godfather the

of Ickenham, we again find ourselves in a remote and straggling village, four miles from every railway station, and therefore most primitive. Out of its entire population of some fifteen hundred souls, only a hundred or so live round the original village green, now an open roadway, on the eastern side of which stands the finest and handsomest village church in all Middlesex, Harrow only excepted. The churchyard has been raised in its level by the burials of the inhabitants for centuries, and at its south-west and north-west

SWAKELEYS.

angles are some picturesque church-houses, which show by their projecting timbers that they have stood there for centuries.

Ruislip, which is always pronounced as Ricelip, has had its name spelt in an almost endless variety of ways, as Riselepe, Rouslip, Rueslyppe, Ruslip, and Rislepe. It is bordered on the north by the hills of Hertfordshire; whilst Northolt and Ickenham touch it on the south. On the west and north-west it is bounded by Harefield. It is said to be the largest parish in Middlesex, with the single exception of Edmonton; its area being about 6,350 acres, with a population in 1871 of 1,482. Of these, however, no less than 500 belong to Eastcot, while 500 live on Ruislip Common; about 250 also live in the ecclesiastical district of Northwood. In 1881, as in many rural parishes, the number of the inhabitants had somewhat diminished.

Lord Russell, beyng the Lorde Prive Seale, by hys *debite*, Master Francis Russell, hys son and heyre, 1542.' This daughter of Francis Lord Hastings, afterwards Earl of Huntingdon, whose baptism is thus curiously recorded, was married to Henry Clinton, Earl of Lincoln. Anne Parr, daughter of the Marquis of Northampton, and wife of William Herbert, afterwards Earl of Pembroke, is the personage described as 'one Mr. Harberd's wiff.'"

Roger Crab, a singular fanatic, of whom a very curious account was published in a pamphlet entitled "The English Hermit, or the Wonder of the Age; 1655," resided for many years in this parish. We shall have more to say regarding this worthy when we visit his tomb at Stepney.

At Ruislip, about a mile and a half to the north

It comprises several hamlets, which were doubtless manors in former times, and East-cote,

Southcote, and West-cote, still remain as local names. A moated manor-house at Southcote has been pulled down only within the memory of the present generation.

Owing to its remote situation Ruislip has undergone but little change for many generations. At the end of the last century more than half the land in the parish was open and unenclosed, or "common fields." The north-west side of Ruislip is described in 1810 as consisting chiefly of woodland copses.

The demand for hay in the metropolis has slowly but surely brought about the extinction of arable which is taxed at 30 hides. The land is 20 carucates; there are 11 hides in demesne, on which are 3 ploughs. The freeman and villans have 12 ploughs between them, and five more might be employed. The priest has half a hide. Two villans hold a hide jointly. There are 17 villans who have a virgate each, 10 who have half a virgate each, and 7 bordars who have each 4 acres. There are 8 cottars and 4 slaves. Four foreigners hold 3 hides and a virgate. There is pasture for the cattle of the manor, and a park for beasts of the forest. Pannage there is for 1,500 hogs,

RUISLIP.

land in this locality, and so only a few acres remain under cultivation. This would have been a sad misfortune to the poorer inhabitants, but it is compensated by a new industry which has sprung up, that of sorting and cutting up firewood, of which the supply is inexhaustible. This occupies the women and children as well as the cottars.

The poor, in compensation of their ancient common lands, have the right of turning their cattle out to graze on certain meadows at Ruislip and Eastcote.

In "Domesday Book" the manor and rectory were held by the same person, the lord of the former receiving both the rents and the tithes, and paying the clergy. The following is an extract :— "Ernulph de Hesding holds the manor of Rislepe, and twenty pence rents. The total value is £20 per annum. When entered on by its present owner it was £12; in King Edward's time it was £30. It was then the property of Wilward the King's Thane."

The Ernulf here mentioned gave the manor to a monastery in France, and it is uncertain whether the monks built a priory here or found one in existence, at the time of the transfer; but in 1259 it appears that there was at Ruislip a religious house with a prior, dependent on the abbey of Bec in Normandy. Before the end of the same century, it would seem to have been annexed to the priory of Okeburn, or Ogborne, in Wiltshire. The latter, however, was confiscated by Henry IV., and soon afterwards we find the manor of Ruislip in the hands of John, Duke of Bedford (the king's third son), who bestowed the manor on the Dean and Canons of Windsor, who still are its owners and patrons. According to Cobbett's "History of the Reformation" the annual value of the abovementioned priory at the Dissolution, was £18. On the death of the Duke the manor was given (1442) to the University of Cambridge, but subsequently to the Provost and Fellows of King's College, Cambridge, who still own the manor farm— a moated house a little north-west of the church, and probably standing on the site of the former priory.

Little is known of the other manors in Ruislip, except that in the year 1378 that of Southcote was held by Alice Perrers, under the priors of Harmondsworth and Okeburn. It now belongs to the Sheppard family.

In 1650 the vicarage of Ruislip was valued at £60, including 29 acres of glebe; but this value has been largely augmented by the enclosure of the common fields.

The prior of Okeburn would seem to have first appointed a vicar to discharge the spiritual duties of the parish; and the list of vicars is pretty complete from 1300 to the present time.

The parish church is dedicated to St. Martin: its details are described at length in "Church Walks in Middlesex" (1845). At that time the beauty of the fabric was spoiled by a huge west gallery, and other monstrosities of the "Churchwarden" era. It consists of a nave, chancel, and side aisles, separated from the nave by circular and octagonal pillars placed alternately, with Pointed arches. The south aisle is four feet higher than the north, and has at its western extremity a lofty tower. It is probably the oldest part of the church, and may have been, indeed, the original edifice.

The ancient font is square, supported by four circular pillars rising out of a stone base. It is probably Late Norman or Early English. The nave is separated from the chancel by two low and ancient carved doors, and a Pointed arch, beneath which in former times was the rood-loft.

The roofs of the side-aisles are very handsome, and are in their original condition; the corbels that support the roof timbers are still uncarved. The latter are of oak or walnut, and the carvings of the bosses are fine.

As might be expected in a church belonging to a religious house, there are traces of several altars having formerly existed here; and most of the walls, even those above the arches of the nave, were covered with frescoes, which have been gradually brought to light by the removal of the plaster with which the interior was long disfigured. Those in the nave are said to illustrate the parables of the New Testament; at the east end of the north aisle is a fine fresco of an angel weighing a soul in a balance, the Virgin Mary standing by and lightening the scale by the touch of her finger.

In the chancel is a long series of memorials of the Hawtrey family, whose seat was at Eastcote in this parish. The most ancient of these is to John Hawtrey, Esq., who died in 1593, and contains the effigies, in brass, of the deceased and his wife. Another stone commemorates John Hawtrey, "who made the royal oratory at Cambridge his grave and monument;" he died in 1674. On the south side of the chancel is a marble monument to another of the Hawtreys, Mary, Lady Bankes, who so gallantly defended Corfe Castle, Dorsetshire, against the Parliamentary forces in the Civil War, as did Lady Blanche Arundell at Wardour, and Lady Derby at Lathom House. She was the widow of the Hon. Sir John Bankes, Lord Chief Justice of the Court of Common Pleas, and died within a year of the day on which she saw the restoration of the monarchy.

In the north-west corner of the church is a memorial to the Rev. Thomas Bright, vicar, who left, in 1697, a weekly dole of bread to be distributed to the poor of this parish. The shelves on which the bread is put out are kept bright and clean under the tower.

Ruislip is well off for charities; some were founded by the Hawtreys, and Lady Franklin in 1737 left £100 to be distributed in clothing to poor widows; there are also other charities of later date.

The church has a fair share of new painted windows, but none are deserving of any special notice. The building was well restored about the year 1870 by Mr. Christian and Sir Gilbert Scott, the former undertaking the chancel, and the latter the nave, aisles, and tower. Many of the old open benches remain, and the rest of the church is "free and open" also. There was once here a fine peal of ten bells, but these sadly need renewal.

The registers are fairly kept. They date from the last decade of the 17th century, but contain nothing of special interest, except the record of the deaths of six centenarians between the years 1700 and 1838, a fact which speaks well for the healthiness of the parish.

In the vestry are two fine large oak chests, with ancient bands and locks of iron. In one of these is kept a copy of Jewell's "Apology," with other tracts and sermons by the same prelate; it is in its original covering of board, and has part of the chain by which it was once fastened to a desk in the nave; but it is much torn and defaced.

As a proof of the primitive condition of the inhabitants of this village, it used to be said that "one half of the population of Ruislip would be found to answer to one of four surnames." Remote from other places, the inhabitants never went abroad for their wives.

School-houses were built by King's College, Cambridge, about 1870. Mr. Thomas Clarke, of Swakeleys, established some schools here at the beginning of the present century for the gratuitous education of fifty poor children ; and with the aid of subscriptions from other wealthy individuals, the children of the poorer inhabitants are partly clothed.

The reservoir on Ruislip Common extends from Cannon's Bridge for nearly a mile towards Rickmansworth. It covers an area of 80 acres, and belongs to the Grand Junction Canal Company, who use it to supply the deficiency caused by the waste of water in working their canal. The reservoir is much frequented by anglers.

Ruislip Park, which bounds the village on the east, is the seat of Frederick Tompson-Delmar, Esq. It covers upwards of forty acres of land, and is charmingly laid out with picturesque drives, and ornamented by rare old timber. It is a famous fox-hunting meet.

The hamlet of Eastcote, often called Ascot, lies about a mile eastward from the village of Ruislip, on the road towards Pinner, in the midst of a rich agricultural country. Eastcote House, the residence of Sir Samuel Morton Peto, was formerly the seat of the Hawtrey family, who were once of great note in this parish, and for many years lessees of the rectory, and of whom, as stated above, Ruislip church contains so many memorials. The mansion belongs to Mr. Francis H. Deane. On coming into the possession of his family it was considerably altered and modernised.

High Grove, another mansion in this locality, is the seat of Sir Hugh H. Campbell, Bart. The house stands on a commanding site, and the grounds, about fifty acres in extent, are prettily laid out.

Sir Thomas Franklyn resided at Eastcote in the early part of the last century. His house, which occupies a low site, was afterwards the seat of the Woodroffe family.

Northwood, a long straggling hamlet in the parish of Ruislip, on the road towards Rickmansworth, was in 1854 formed into an ecclesiastical district, which includes within its bounds portions of the parishes of Watford and Rickmansworth, in Hertfordshire. The church, dedicated to the Holy Trinity, is a handsome structure of flint and stone, in the Early English style, and many of the windows are filled with painted glass.

Northwood Hall, the seat of Mr. Daniel Norton, is the principal residence in this locality, most of the poorer inhabitants of which are occupied in agricultural pursuits or employed in the preparation of firewood.

Before we quit Ruislip it may not be out of place to mention a story having reference to the place, which has been related by the Rev. Mr. Barham, and which has Theodore Hook for its hero. Hook and a friend having borrowed a horse and gig, took a drive in the country, and had reached this village when they bethought them of dining. "Of course, you have money with you ? " said Hook. "Not a sixpence ; not a *sou*," was the reply. Theodore was in the same predicament— the last turnpike having exhausted his supply. "Stay," said Hook, reining up ; "do you see that pretty little villa ? Suppose we dine there." The suggestion was capital. "You know the owner, then ? " inquired he. "Not the least in the world," was the reply. "I never saw him in all my life ; but that's of no consequence. I know his name : it's E——w, the celebrated chronometer-maker ; the man who got the £10,000 premium from Government, and then wound up his affairs and his watches, and retired from business. He will be delighted to see us." So saying, up he drove to the door. "Is Mr. E——w at home ? " Answer : "Yes." In they went. The old gentleman appeared, and after a little staring at each other, Hook began : "Mr. E——w, happening to pass through your neighbourhood, I could not deny myself the pleasure and honour of paying my respects to you. I am conscious that it may seem impertinent, but your ability overcame me in regard for the common forms of society, and I and my friend here were resolved, come what might, to have it in our power to say that we had seen you, and enjoyed, for a few minutes, the company of an individual famous throughout the civilised world."

The old gentleman was caught. Shaking of hands and a few more compliments followed, and presently the remark, "But, gentlemen, you are far from town ; it's getting late ; pray do me the honour of staying and dining, quite, as we say, in the family way—now, pray, gentlemen, do stay."

The two visitors consulted gravely. It was impossible. They must return to town, Hook adding a little more compliment, which elicited a still more pressing invitation from the chronometer-maker. At length they agreed to stay and dine, and join in a bottle of "Barnes's best." The dinner despatched, the bottle was multiplied by six. The host was as happy as a king, and would not allow his new friends to depart without a pledge to repeat their visit.

Harefield, to which place we now direct our steps, adjoins Uxbridge on the north, and occupies a wide extent of country lying to the north-west of Ruislip. It is a long and scattered village, and, like Ruislip, extends to the extreme north of the county, where it is bordered by the parish of Rickmansworth. It consists mostly of pleasant upland scenery, from which a good view of the long broad meadows on either side of the river Colne is obtained.

The Colne and the Grand Junction Canal, which unites the Thames at Brentford with Staffordshire and the North, serve as a boundary on the left as you walk from Uxbridge to Harefield, and cut off the wayfarer from the pleasant groves and fisheries of Denham. In fact, the Colne bounds the parish on the west for nearly five miles. This river and its surroundings are evidently alluded to by Milton in the following lines in " L'Allegro " :—

> " Meadows trim, with daisies pied,
> Shallow brooks and rivers wide."

Harefield is more rich in historical associations perhaps than any rural village within the county of Middlesex. When Milton was resident at Horton the old manor house was the residence of Lord Keeper Egerton and his wife, the Countess Dowager of Derby, whom Queen Elizabeth had once honoured by a visit of three days in one of her royal progresses. The courtly knight and his lady survived the costly visit. But we are anticipating the order of events.

Of the early history of Harefield Lysons tells us that in the time of Edward the Confessor the place belonged to the Countess Goda, and that at the Domesday survey it was held by Richard, the son of Gilbert, Earl of Briou. It afterwards passed into the hands of the Bacheworths, and from them by marriage to the Swanlands, and from them in the same manner to the Newdigates ; but was alienated by them to the Andersons, by whom the property was sold at the commencement of the 17th century to the Egertons, from whom it passed in marriage to Grey, Lord Chandos. In 1655 Lord Chandos bequeathed Harefield to his widow, who re-married, first with Sir William Sedley, Bart., and secondly, on the decease of Sir William, with Mr. George Pitt. By this latter husband (in whom and his heirs she had vested all her estates) the manors of Harefield and More Hall—of which latter we shall speak presently— were sold to Sir Richard Newdigate, Bart., Serjeant-at-law, and grandson of Mr. John Newdigate, who had exchanged the estate with Sir Edmund Anderson, and so came back to a squire whose ancestors have held it, with only a temporary interval, for

nearly 600 years—a fact without parallel in Middlesex.

But the greatest event in the history of Harefield was the three days' visit of Queen Elizabeth to Sir Thomas Egerton, to which we have already alluded. It took place in July—August, 1602, and is fully described, from the Newdigate MSS., in J. G. Nichols's " Progresses of Queen Elizabeth," vol. iii., pp. 586—93, and also in the " Pictorial Shakespeare," from which we quote the following particulars :—" The Queen came to Harefield on the 31st of July, and remained there during the 1st and 2nd of August. In those days Harefield Place was a 'fair house, standing on the edge of the hill, the river Coln passing near the same through the pleasant meadows and sweet pastures, yielding both delight and profit. . . .' The weather, we learn from a copy of verses presented to the Queen on the occasion, was unpropitious :—

> " ' Only poor St. Swithin now
> Doth hear you blame his cloudy brow.'

Some great poet was certainly at work on this occasion, but not Shakespeare. It was enough for them to present the sad story of

> " ' The gentle lady married to the Moor.'

Another was to come within some thirty years, who should sing of Harefield with the power of rare fancy working upon classical models, and who thus makes the genius of the wood address a noble audience in that sylvan scene :—

> " ' Yet know, by lot from Jove, I am the power
> Of this fair wood, and like in oaken bower
> To nurse the sapling tall, and curl the grove
> With ringlets quaint, and wanton windings weave ;
> And all my plants I save from nightly ill
> Of noisome winds and blasting vapours chill ;
> And from the boughs brush off the evil dew,
> And heal the harms of thwarting thunder blue ;
> Or what the cross dire-looking planet smites,
> Or hurtful worm with canker'd venom bites.
> When evening grey doth rise, I fetch my round
> Over the mount and all this hallowed ground ;
> And early, ere the odorous breath of morn
> Awake the slumbering leaves, or tassel'd horn
> Shakes the highth thicket, haste I all about,
> Number my ranks, and visit every sprout
> With puissant words, and murmurs made to bless.'

Doubly-honoured Harefield ! Though the mansion has perished, yet are thy groves still beautiful. Still thy summit looks out upon a fertile valley, where the gentle river wanders in silent beauty. But thy woods and lawns have a charm which are wholly their own. Here possibly the *Othello* of Will Shakespeare was acted by his own company ; here is the scene of the ' Arcades ' of John Milton."

The visit of the virgin queen to Harefield was

within a year or two of her death, and when she was upwards of seventy. In the Newdigate MSS. above referred to the curious reader will find how her Majesty was met near the dairy-house by a dairy-maid and a bailiff, who celebrated her praises in alternate verse, whilst the royal personage herself sat on her horse beneath a tree on account of the rain. In another part of the grounds her Majesty was entertained by a "dialogue of welcome" between some fanciful characters, called "Place" and "Time;" and again on the next morning she was serenaded as—

> "Beauty's rose and virtue's book,
> Angel's mind and angel's look."

It should be added that the queen was addressed in the same style of fanciful and fulsome flattery at her departure.

"It has been said," observes Mr. Thorne, in his Handbook of the Environs of London, "that the Lord Chamberlain's company was brought down to Harefield to play *Othello* before her, Shakespeare himself being present probably to direct the performance." But this statement he sees reason to distrust, both on other grounds and on account of the silence of the Newdigate MSS. on the subject. Still, the Egerton Papers, published by the Camden Society, under date August 6th, 1602, give us the following entry among the steward's expenses during Elizabeth's visit to Harefield : "Rewards to the Vaulters, Players, and Dancers, £64 18s. 10d.;" and it is known that Shakespeare was one of the company so indicated. One would like to be certain, however, that the eyes of Shakespeare as well as those of Milton, once looked on these scenes.

We gather from the Life of Milton that during the five years of his early manhood, which he spent mainly at his father's house at Horton, he was a frequent visitor at Harefield ; and the heading of his "Arcades" tells us that it formed "part of an entertainment presented to the Countess Dowager of Derby at that place by some noble persons of her family." As her ladyship was then advanced in years, it is more than probable that these "noble persons of her family" were her little youthful grandchildren, the issue of the Earl of Bridgewater (son of the Lord Keeper Egerton), who had married Lady Frances Stanley, the second daughter of the Countess. One would like to have been there to witness their graceful appearance on the scene "in pastoral habit, and moving toward the seat of state," whereon sat the Countess as a "Rural Queen," as they sang the first stanza of "Arcades," probably alluding to Queen Elizabeth's previous visit—

> "Look, nymphs and shepherds, look,
> What sudden blaze of Majesty
> Is that which we from hence descry?
> Too divine to be mistook.
>   This, this is she
> To whom our vows and wishes bend
> Here our solemn search hath end."

Another stanza sung by the youthful band ran as follows :—

> "Mark, what radiant state she spreads,
>   In circle round her shining throne,
> Shooting her beams like silver threads ;
>   This, this is she alone,
>   Sitting like a goddess bright,
>   In the centre of her light."

It is probable that Milton was thinking of the festivities at Harefield when he wrote in "L'Allegro " :—

> "There let Hymen oft appear
> In saffron robe with taper clear,
> And pomp, and feast, and revelry,
> With masque and antique pageantry ;
> Such sights as youthful poets dream
> On summer eve by haunted stream."

Harefield Place was burnt to the ground in 1660, the fire being traditionally referred to the carelessness of the witty and accomplished Sir Charles Sedley, the profligate companion of Charles II., who is said to have been reading in bed.

"This tradition," observes the author of "The Beauties of England," "is not altogether destitute of an air of probability, for although Sir William Sedley died in 1656, and his widow had in the meantime taken a third husband, George Pitt, Esq., yet it is by no means unlikely that the gay and careless Sir Charles might, in 1660, be at Harefield, on a visit to his sister-in-law."

The mansion was rebuilt by Sir Richard Newdigate, who had re-purchased the property of Mr. Pitt, in 1675, but not quite on the same site as the old house.

Sir Roger Newdigate was residing at Harefield Place, in 1743, when he was elected M.P. for Middlesex. Sir Roger was the founder of the prize for English Verse which bears his name at Oxford, and causes him to be commemorated among the benefactors of the University. Having fixed his principal residence at Arbury, in Warwickshire, Sir Roger sold Harefield Place, disjoined from the manor, to John Truesdale, Esq., from whose executors it was purchased, in 1780, by William Baynes, Esq., whose son, Christopher, was created a baronet, by the title of Sir Christopher Baynes, of Harefield Place.

Mr. Charles Newdigate Newdegate, who inherited the Middlesex estates of Sir Roger, re-purchased

Harefield Place from Sir Christopher Baynes, and having chosen for his residence a seat near at hand, called Harefield Lodge, he pulled down Harefield Place towards the end of the last century.

The avenue of elms through which Queen Eliza-

in the last century may be seen in the *Gentleman's Magazine* for January, 1815. The old manor-house must have been well off for the accessories of shady trees in Milton's time, if he wrote of it, as doubtless he did, without exaggeration—

HAREFIELD PLACE. (*From a Print in the Gentleman's Magazine, 1815.*)

beth rode from Dew's Farm to the house is gone, though several of the trees were still standing in the time when Lysons wrote, and one or two even as late as 1814-15, if we may believe "Sylvanus Urban ;" but, alas ! they are now no more, though vigorous successors have taken their place. The house, too, as above stated, is gone, but its site can still be plainly seen in the rear of the church, where the old garden walls and fine level terraces still attest its former grandeur. A view of it as it was

"O'er the smooth enamell'd green,
　Where no print of step hath been,
　　Follow me, as I sing,
　　And touch the warbled string,
Under the shady roof
Of branching elm star proof,
　　Follow me ;
I will bring you where she sits,
Clad in splendour, as befits
　　　Her deity.
Such a rural queen
All Arcadia hath not seen. "

And the whole demesne must have had beauties and charms, which have disappeared with the old mansion, if he could write with truth—

> Nymphs and shepherds, dance no more
> By sandy Ladon's lilied banks ;
> On old Lycæus, or Cyllene hoar,
> Trip no more in twilight ranks ;
> Though Erymanth your loss deplore,
> A better soil shall give ye thanks.
> From the stony Mænalus
> Bring your flocks and live with us ;
> Here ye shall have greater grace,
> To serve the lady of this place."

The "Arcades" was performed here, as we learn from Milton's Life, in 1635, and the worthy "lady of this place" did not long survive. Her fine marble monument in the chancel of the church bears the date of her death, 1637.

What would one not have given to have seen with his own eyes the poet brushing the morning dew, as he sauntered through the meadows along the bank of his favourite river, the Colne, with its " brimming waves," or quietly trudging along the road through Uxbridge, on his way from Horton to Harefield Place, which doubtless then was, in his own words—

> "Bosom'd high in tufted trees."

The elms and beeches and evergreens behind the site of the house are still fine, but few, except one stately cedar, would seem to be able to recall the look of the poet.

About a furlong south-west of the site of the old manor-house, abutting on the edge of the meadows of the Colne, opposite the " Fishery" at Denham, and standing a little from the road, is an old farm-house, some parts of the interior of which retain the ancient panelling and large fire-places, suggesting that in the olden time large logs were burnt here in the winter, and profuse hospitality was exercised. The house is now cut up into three labourers' cottages. It is still called the Moor Hall, and is the most ancient manor-house in the parish. The greater part of the old hall was pulled down towards the end of the last century.

Lysons tells us that the manor of Moor Hall was the property of the Knights Hospitallers, to whom it was given by Alice, daughter of Baldwin de Clare. Close by it, indeed almost adjoining it, is an Early English chapel, with lancet windows, externally almost perfect, though quite "gutted" in its interior of every vestige of its once sacred uses. The timber roof stands sound and good, just as it did in the days of the Tudors and Plantagenets. This chapel was probably a cell subject to the Priory of St. John at Clerkenwell. Some persons

consider that the building was not a chapel, but a refectory, but for this there are no grounds. The building and cottages are rich in red and grey tints, and they have been often sketched by artists.

A short walk across some upland grass fields leads from Moor Hall to the church, which is situated, as was so often the case, in the middle of the squire's park, some three or four hundred yards from the road.

The church, so far as can be ascertained through the veil thrown over it by a poor modern " restora-

LADY DERBY'S TOMB. (*See page* 248.)

tion," seems to be of the " Decorated" period, but perhaps a somewhat late specimen. It consists of nave and chancel, with aisles on either side. Probably no country church is so rich in mural monuments, mostly of the Tudor and Jacobean eras. The Egertons, Ashbys, and Newdigates innumerable here mix their aristocratic dust with that of their poorer brethren. A really fine collection of helmets, casques, gloves, and other funeral armour, once belonging to the Bacheworths and Swanlands and Egertons, but now taken down from the walls, lies heaped together, dusty and uncared for, on the sedilia to the south of the communion-table. The Brackenbury chapel, which forms the south aisle, is constructed of alternate dice-work, or diversified compartments of flint and stone. The chancel is elevated above the nave, and is reached by an ascent of six steps. On the east wall of the Brackenbury chapel is a monument, bearing a long Latin inscription, to the memory of Sir Richard Newdigate, Bart., who died in 1678. Sir Roger Newdigate, the last baronet of his family, who died in 1806, is also commemorated by a tablet, as also are many other members of that ancient house. The monument of Milton's friend above mentioned, Alice, Countess Dowager of Derby, who died in 1637, occupies the south-east corner of the chancel. It is an elaborate work of art, after the fashion of the above period, being gorgeously decorated with drapery and heraldic ornaments. The effigy of the countess, in her state dress, reposes beneath a lofty canopy, while the lower compartment, which is level with the floor of the chancel, contains the kneeling effigies of her three daughters, Lady Chandos and the Countesses of Bridgewater and Huntingdon. The countess, as stated above, became the wife of Lord Keeper Egerton, who, as the inscription on this monument states, had, by his first wife, an only daughter, who was mother of Juliana, Lady Newdigate. The monuments of various members of the Newdigate family might be said to "adorn" the walls of the church, if it were not that such cumbrous and costly structures sadly detract from the beauty of the sacred edifice itself, and tell rather of human pride and vain-glory than of humility and repent-ance. Among others is a kneeling effigy of Lady Newdigate, formerly one of the maids of honour to Queen Elizabeth. When Mr. Newdigate, as lord of the manor and squire, "restored" the church, he ordered the monuments to be repaired, and their inscriptions and heraldic bearings re-painted.

On the north side of the chancel is a parclose, screening off the chantry and burial-place of the family of Ashby of Brakespeare. A mural tablet on the north wall, bearing the effigy of a man in armour, kneeling at a faldstool beneath a canopy, commemorates Sir Robert Ashby, who died in 1617; and close by is another mural tablet, to the memory of Sir Francis Ashby, who died in 1623. Between this aisle and the nave is a monu-ment to the memory of John Pritchett, Bishop of Gloucester, who died in 1680. He was promoted to the see of Gloucester in 1672, after having been curate of this parish for nearly thirty years.

On the outside of the north wall of the chancel is a most curious monument and epitaph. It con-sists of a medallion, with a portrait, in rather slight relief, of a gamekeeper with his dog and gun, passing through a background of trees. Beneath it is the following inscription, which I believe has never been printed in any collection of epitaphs, though its quaintness well merits such an honour:

"William Ashby of Brakespeare, Esquire, erected this to the memory of his faithful servant, Robert Mossenden, who departed this life Feby. 5th, 1744, aged 60 years.

"In frost and snow, through hail and rain,
    He scour'd the woods and trudg'd the plain;
    The steady pointer leads the way,
    Stands at the scent, then springs the prey;
    The timorous birds from stubble rise,
    With pinions stretch'd divide the skys;
    The scatter'd lead pursues the sight,
    And death in thunder stops their flight.
    This spaniel, of true English kind,
    Who's gratitude inflam'd his mind:
    This servant in an honest way,
    In all his actions copy'd Tray."

The village of Harefield stretches away along the roadside for a considerable distance through a quiet valley, having on the north and east well-wooded uplands, dotted over with lordly domains, and on the south-west broad green meadows, bordering the canal and River Colne. Harefield numbered altogether in 1881 between 300 and 400 houses, with a population of 1,500, being a slight diminution upon the census returns for 1871. The village, with its Lecture Hall and Working Men's Club, possesses a quiet and flourishing ap-pearance, and the name of one of its principal local worthies of bygone times is perpetuated in the "Brakespeare Arms," the sign given to a quiet roadside hostelry.

It may be added, that, lying as it does so far out of the beaten tracks, this parish is perhaps richer than any other within Middlesex in country seats. Towards the northern end are Harefield Park, the seat of Colonel Vernon, and Harefield House, of Sir John Byles. Brakespeare, formerly the seat of the Ashbys, now the seat of Mrs. Drake, is nearer to the church, and towards the centre of the parish. It is said to have got its name from having once belonged to the family which gave Pope Adrian IV. to the Western Church. The house is old-fashioned, and stands on high ground in a pleasantly-wooded park.

Nearer to Uxbridge stands the modern Harefield Place, lately sold by Mr. Newdegate, and now the property and residence of Colonel Cox. All the game hereabouts is strictly preserved; and in con-sequence, as you walk along the shady lanes leading to the "Brakespeare Arms" from the church, you may see partridges and pheasants strutting about to their heart's content, and secure from harm.

CHAPTER XXIV.

PINNER AND HARROW.

"Again I behold where for hours I have ponder'd,
As reclining at eve on yon tombstone I lay;
Or round the steep brow of the churchyard I wander'd,
To catch the last gleam of the sun's setting ray."
BYRON.

Situation of Harrow, and Nature of the Soil—The Village of Pinner—Population—The River Pin—Miss Howard's Charity—Market and Fairs—The Parish Church—Centenarians—A Curious Custom—Schools and Cemetery—Pinner Hill House—Pinner Wood—Pinner Place—Pinner Grove—Pinner Park—Pinner Green, and Wood Hall—Woodrisings—Death of Mrs. Horatia Ward—The School of the Commercial Travellers' Society—Headstone, or Manor Farm—Etymology of Harrow—Domesday Book Record of the Parish—The Manor—Flambards—A Loyal Lady—Extent and Boundaries of Harrow—The Parish Church—Prior Bolton takes Refuge at Harrow—"Byron's Tomb"—The View from Harrow Hill—The Town and Public Institutions of Harrow.

IT is refreshing, after the many miles of dead level river-side scenery through which we have travelled, to " break ground " afresh, and to come at once upon new country. We have left the grassy vale which stretches across the west of the county from Uxbridge and Hayes, and find ourselves, after some four or five miles' walk, at the foot of the only steep ascent which Middlesex can produce, except the "northern heights" of Hampstead and Highgate. The soil is a deep stiff clay; and we shall find that Harrow differs from those other links of the hilly chain of which it once formed part in having no deposit of gravel and sand on its summit.

The broad vale of Harrow, which stretches from the foot of the hill to Edgware and Stanmore in the north-east, and to Uxbridge and Hayes in the south-west, has really no history, and is quite a modern Bœotia. The roads are muddy and miry in winter, and till the beginning of the present century it took a waggoner and his team the best part of a day to carry a load of hay up to London; and even then he often had to lay down a faggot of sticks in the ruts in order to enable him to get along at all. The district, however, smiles sweetly in early June, and has its attractions for the hunter in the depth of winter.

Norden, writing in the reign of Elizabeth, gives the following account of this parish:—"It may be noted how nature hath exalted that high *Harrow-on-the-Hill*, as it were in the way of ostentation to shew it selfe to all passengers to and from London, who beholding the same may saye it is the centre (as it were) of the pure vale; for Harrow standeth invironed with a great contrye of moste pure grounds, from which hill, towardes the time of harveste, a man maye beholde the feyldes rounde about, so sweetly to address themselves to the sicle and syth, with such comfortable haboundance of all kinde of grayne, that it maketh the inhabitants to clappe theyre handes for joye to see theyr

valleys so to laugh and singe. Yet this fruiteful and pleasante country yeldeth little comforte unto the wayfaringe man in the winter season, by reason of the clayish nature of the soyle, which after it hath tasteth the autombe showers it beginneth to mix deep and tirtye, yeldinge unsavory passage to horse and man. Yet the countrye swayne holdeth it a sweet and pleasant garden, and with his whippe and whysell, can make himself melodye, and dance knee deepe in dirte, the whole daye not holdinge it any disgrace únto his person, Such is the force of hope of future proffitt.

The deepe and dirdiest lothsome soyle
Yeldes golden grayne to carefull toyle.

And that is the cause that the industrious and painful husbandman will refuse a pallace, to droyle in theys golden puddles."

Pinner, through which we must pass before reaching Harrow, is situated on the main road running north-westward to Rickmansworth and Amersham, about equi-distant from Ruislip and Harrow-on-the-Hill, being about three miles from each of those places, a mile and a half south-west from Pinner Station on the North-Western Railway, and about thirteen miles from London. It is a busy and thriving village, the main street being broad, well paved, and lighted with gas, and containing several respectable shops and private houses of modern growth, interspersed with many of a more picturesque and antiquated appearance, of the lath-and-plaster style of building, with projecting storeys and gabled roofs. Not the least interesting among these houses is the "Queen's Head," an old-fashioned roadside tavern on the north side of the street, dating its erection from early in the last century, as the date 1705, painted upon its front, bears witness.

In 1871 the number of inhabited houses in Pinner was set down in the census returns as 396, the population amounting to 2,332, of whom about 250 were inmates of the Commercial Travellers'

Schools, of which we shall speak presently. The number of the inhabitants had increased during the succeeding ten years to a little over 2,500.

The village is pleasantly located on the rising ground which forms the north-western side of the vale of Harrow, and from this elevated spot flows one of the feeders of the River Colne, a little rivulet, called the Pin, which is crossed at the bottom of the main street by an antiquated bridge of one arch. Near the bridge stand three dwellings for widows of officers, founded by Miss Maria Charlotte Howard, of York Place, about half a century ago. Miss Howard, it appears, left the sum of £45,000 in money and land to found a charity, to erect twenty-one houses on her property here. They were to have been built in the form of a crescent : the centre house for the trustees, and the remainder to be appropriated to twenty widows, who were to live in them rent and tax free, and to receive each a stipend of £50 a year. The widows of naval men were to have the preference, after them the widows of military men, and afterwards the widows of clergymen. This munificent bequest, however, was never fully carried out, for, owing to some family feud, the estate got into Chancery, with the result that only three of the houses have as yet been built. They are good, substantial brick-built residences, and, in accordance with the stipulation of the bequest, are in the occupation of the widows of officers.

Pinner was simply a hamlet and chapelry of Harrow, and part of the same demesne, but was made into a separate parish about a quarter of a century ago. The village, nevertheless, formerly possessed a weekly market, which was granted by Edward III. in 1336 to the Archbishop of Canterbury, who was at that time lord of the manor. Two yearly fairs were also granted at the same time, of which, however, only one survives. This has degenerated into an insignificant pleasure-fair, which is held annually on Whit Monday.

At the eastern or upper end of the main street stands the parish church, the picturesque effect of which, as seen on approaching it, is heightened by the almost leafless trunk of an aged elm-tree. The church, dedicated to St. John the Baptist, is of ample dimensions, consisting of chancel, with a side aisle or chapel, appropriated to the use of the children of the Commercial Travellers' Schools, transepts, a clerestoried nave of five bays, aisles, south porch, and an embattled tower at the west end. The tower has a pyramidal tiled roof, surmounted by a tall wooden cross, and at the north-west corner a bold turret rises high above the battlements. The interior of the tower is open to the nave, and the bells bear the date of 1772. The building is constructed mainly of flint and stone; and although its erection was completed in 1321, the lancet-shaped windows of the transepts and south aisle would appear to have belonged to a building of much earlier date. The church has been considerably altered and enlarged at various periods, the chancel aisle having been added as recently as 1879, at which time the edifice was thoroughly restored. The nave is separated from the aisles by Pointed arches, springing from octangular pillars. In the south transept are the remains of a piscina of the Perpendicular period. The font is large and of about the same above-mentioned date; the exterior of the basin forms an octagon, the different compartments of which are ornamented with devices of roses, &c., in quatrefoils, the basin itself resting upon an octangular pillar. Several of the windows contain painted glass, that of one of the lancets being of ancient date. The east window, of Perpendicular design, is modern, a reproduction of its predecessor, but is now filled with stained glass. It is of five lights, and was inserted in memory of the Rev. Edward Thomas Burrow, incumbent, who died in 1861. The reredos, which is very handsome, was erected in 1871 by Mr. John Weall, of this parish, in memory of his wife and two daughters. This church contains but few monuments, and even those are but of little interest. Among them is a mural tablet, of black marble, to the memory of John Day, minister of Pinner, who died in 1662. On this tablet is represented the effigy of the deceased in profile, kneeling before a desk; and it has also upon it an inscription, commencing—

" This portraiture presents him to thy sight
Who was a burning and a shining light."

The families of Clitherow, Page, and Hastings, are also commemorated by monumental inscriptions in the church. In the vestry is preserved a small brass, originally in the chancel, to the memory of a "chrysom child," the daughter of Eustace Bedingfeld, dated 1580.

In the churchyard, close by the south porch, is the gravestone of Sir Bartholomew Shower, of Pinner Hill, who died in 1701, and who, if an entry in the parish register is to be believed, was "buried in sheep's wool only." If we may judge from the ages recorded on many of the head-stones here, Pinner would appear to be a healthy place to live in, or at all events one favourable to longevity. Several may be noticed buried here whose ages have exceeded the allotted "three score years and ten." In 1851, Ann, widow of James Winfield, died at the age of 100; in 1553, Betty, the widow of William Evans, passed away at the age of 102; and William Skenelsby, who died in 1775, appears to have reached the extraordinary age of 118.

It is recorded that the barbarous custom of throwing at cocks as a Shrovetide festivity was formerly practised at Pinner with much public ardour, and the money collected at this disagreeable celebration was applied to the aid of the poor's rates. The custom was discontinued about the year 1680.

National schools, capable of holding 300 children, were established in this village in 1866. A new cemetery has been laid out on the east side of the village, it comprises about two acres, and contains two mortuary chapels.

In the neighbourhood of Pinner are several good seats and family residences. Pinner Hill, which lies away on the high ground to the northwest, is the seat of Mr. William Arthur Tooke, at whose cost the church has been principally restored. The house stands in ornamental park grounds, and commands extensive views. It was formerly the residence of Sir Christopher Clitherow, and afterwards of Sir Bartholomew Shower, whose name we have mentioned above. Sir Bartholomew was an eminent lawyer in his day, and was the author of some legal works and political pamphlets. Sir Albert Pell, some time a Judge of the Court of Bankruptcy, lived here half a century ago.

Pinner Wood House, near the above, the residence of Mr. R. H. Silversides, was for some time in the occupation of Lord Lytton, who here wrote his "Eugene Aram."

Pinner Place, the seat of Mr. James Garrard, was formerly the residence of Mr. John Zephaniah Holwell, some time Governor of Bengal, and author of a narrative of the sufferings of himself and fellow-prisoners in the "Black Hole" of Calcutta. Mr. Holwell was also the author of an historical work relating to Hindostan.

Pinner Grove, northward of the village, is approached through a fine avenue of elms, and stands in ornamental park-like grounds. It was formerly the residence of Sir Michael Foster, one of the Justices of the King's Bench in the last century, and afterwards of Sir Francis Milman, Bart., M.D.

Pinner Park appears to have been formerly a district of some importance, as Nicholas, Abbot of Westminster, was appointed its keeper in 1383. The estate, however, has long been broken up and converted to agricultural puposes. In the reign of Henry VIII. it was granted, together with the manor of Harrow, to Sir Edward (afterwards Lord)

North; and in 1630 the property was alienated by Dudley, Lord North, to the Hutchinson family. The estate ultimately passed into the possession of St. Thomas's Hospital, having been purchased in the year 1731 by the governors of that institution, by whom it is now held.

About half a mile north of the village is Pinner Green, and near at hand is an estate, known as Wood Hall. Woodriding is a hamlet further to the north-east; it boasts of some good villa residences and a chapel-of-ease. Here, in March of the year 1881, died, at the age of eighty, Mrs. Horatia Nelson Ward, widow of the Rev. Philip Ward, Vicar of Tenterden, Kent. She was the "little Horatia," the adopted daughter of Emma, Lady Hamilton, whom her father, Lord Nelson, with his dying breath, commended to the care of his ungrateful country.

Close by the Pinner railway station stand the schools belonging to the Commercial Travellers' Society, which were founded in 1845. The building, a large and roomy structure of red brick, with stone dressings, of Gothic design, was opened in 1855, the ceremony being presided over by the Prince Consort. The plan of the building consists mainly of a large central hall, the upper floor of which forms the principal school-room, having beneath it the dining-hall. At each end of the hall are the dormitories, and the residences of the masters and mistresses. In 1868 wings were added to the original building, rendering it capable of holding between 300 and 400 children. A cloister-like arcade, extending along the principal front, on either side of the hall, serves as a covered playground for the children. In 1876–77 the building was extended by means of a subscription amounting to £17,000, raised in a single year by Mr. James Hughes; and in 1878 an infirmary and baths were added, through the bequest of Mr. George Moore, the philanthropist.

The design of this institution is "the clothing, maintenance, and education of the destitute orphans of deceased and the children of necessitous commercial travellers." The institution is carried on by means of donations and subscriptions given for that purpose, and the government of the affairs of the schools is vested in a general court and a board of management. On the walls of the entrance-lobby are several ornamental tablets commemorative of munificent bequests to the institution, and in the board-room are several full-length portraits of governors and others connected with the schools. The institution, it may be added, seems admirably conducted. The boys receive a superior education, and leave the schools at the age of fifteen.

At a short distance from Pinner, towards the south-east, is a farm, termed "Headstone," or, more generally, the "Manor Farm." The dwelling-house is large and of some antiquity, and is surrounded by a moat. The name was formerly written Heggeton, or Hegeston; and a mansion on the site was the occasional residence of the Archbishops of Canterbury in times long gone by. This manor is mentioned in records of the fourteenth century, at which time it was held by the see of Canterbury. When an inquisition was taken of the estates of Archbishop Arundel, who was banished

ages, as stated above, one of the residences of the Archbishops of Canterbury. The most memorable event relating to the visits of these powerful manorial lords occurs in the year 1170. The famous Thomas à Becket, then Archbishop, while travelling towards Woodstock for the professed purpose of paying respect to Prince Henry, who had been recently allowed to participate in the government of the kingdom, was denied access to the Court, and commanded to repair immediately to his own diocese. It is recorded that he passed some days, on his return, at his manor of Harrow,

PINNER, IN 1828. (*From an Etching by Cook.*)

for high treason in the year 1398, it was found that he was possessed, together with other property, "of the manor of Southbury [now Sudbury], in Harrow, consisting principally of 500 acres of land, then valued at 3d. per acre! The manor of Woodhall (a member of the former) chiefly consisted of 120 acres of land, valued at 6d. an acre! The manor of 'Heggeton' (likewise a member of Southbury), comprising a well-built house and 201 acres of land, valued at 6d. an acre, besides meadow."

Mr. Brewer, in the "Beauties of England," says it is to be regretted that the site of the ancient manor-house of Harrow is not known, as the spot would acquire a fair share of interest from its connection with long past scenes of sacerdotal splendour. But this manor-house is most probably the place in question, as it was for many

in the exercise of much dignified hospitality, and during his stay exchanged many acts of kindness with the Abbot of St. Albans. This was only a short time previous to the assassination of Becket, and the spirit of animosity which prevailed very generally in regard to this high-minded Churchman was evinced in a conspicuous manner by the resident clergy of the place. Nigellus de Sackville, rector of Harrow, and Robert de Broc, the vicar, treated him with boisterous disrespect, and are said to have maimed with their own hands one of the horses bearing his provisions, for which offence they were both excommunicated at Canterbury on the ensuing Christmas. It is a tradition in this neighbourhood that it was in the building that occupied the site of the present farm-house of Headstone that Becket sojourned at the period above mentioned; and some even go as far as to assert that he slept here on the night before his assassination. But this tradition has little to support it.

Archbishop Boniface held a visitation at Harrow in 1250, and Archbishop Winchelsye dates from Harrow in the year 1300. It may be added that Cardinal Wolsey, who, among his other preferments, held the rectory of Harrow, is said to have occasionally resided at the old manor-house. King Charles, in his flight from Oxford, came to Harrow;

usually written Herges,* the derivation of which, observes Mr. Brewer, in the "Beauties of England," probably is "from the Saxon *Hearge*, *Hergh*, or *Herige*, which is usually supposed to signify a concourse of armed men, but which is also translated a *church*. If," he continues, "we accept the latter reading, we may suppose that a sacred structure on the lofty hill of Harrow formed a conspicuous feature in this part of the county as early as the beginning of the ninth century, at which

PINNER CHURCH IN 1800.   (*From an old Print. See page* 250.)

and had he not half-heartedly turned aside towards Newark, it is more than probable that there might never have been fought a battle of Worcester.

The present manor-house of "Heggeton," or Headstone, is a good, substantial, modern-looking residence, containing in its structural arrangements portions of an older house. The moat, square in form, and partaking somewhat of the character of those so well known at Ightham and Hever, in Kent, is crossed by a brick bridge, and encloses the house and gardens, &c., the farm buildings, including a barn of great length, being situated in front of the bridge. Some of the outbuildings are ancient and picturesque.

In ancient records the name of Harrow is

time a notice of the place first occurs on record." Lysons supposes the derivation of the name to be from the Anglo-Saxon *Hearge*, which, he says, is "sometimes translated a troop of soldiers, and sometimes a church," and adds his inclination to adopt the latter derivation, which is the same as that given above. Mr. Thorne, in his "Environs of London," observes that "*Herige* was a legion or division of an army; and as, from its commanding position, Harrow would certainly be made a military station by the Romans, it is probable that the name was given to it as the camp or station of a

* Hence Harrow School is often spoken of as Schola *Hergensis*, as well as *Harroviensis*.

legion." The syllable *Har*, it may be added, signified in the olden times *high*, or the high ground.

As we have already observed, Harrow was a place of some consideration for two or three centuries immediately succeeding the Norman Conquest, from its being the occasional residence of the Archbishops of Canterbury. Newcourt, in his "Repertorium," states, on the authority of Somner's "Antiquities of Canterbury," &c., that in the year 822 "Wilfred, Archbishop of Canterbury, recovered this place of *Herges*, together with several other lands which had been taken from the Church of Canterbury by Kenulf, King of the Mercians." If this be true, the connection of Harrow with the Church was of very early date.

"Among the MSS. formerly belonging to Bishop Tanner, now deposited in the Bodleian Library, is a bond executed by Margetta, Prioress of Kilburn, in which the name is written *Hareways*." *

In the "Domesday Survey" it is stated that the manor of *Herges* was held by Archbishop Lanfranc. "It answered (as in the time of King Edward the Confessor) for one hundred hides. There was land for seventy ploughs. Thirty hides belonged to the demesne, on which were four ploughs, and a fifth might be added. A priest had one hide, and three knights held six hides. There was pasture for the cattle of the village, and pannage for two thousand hogs," &c.

This manor of Harrow was given by Archbishop Cranmer, in exchange for other estates, to Henry VIII., and shortly after, it was granted to Sir Edward North, subsequently created Lord North. Concerning this grant, a story to the following effect is related in Collins's "Peerage." The king having taken offence at some part of Sir Edward's conduct, ordered him to his presence, and, after regarding him a while with every indication of anger, said, "We are informed you have cheated us of certain lands in Middlesex!" To this unexpected accusation the knight answered with a humble negative. "How was it, then," resumed Henry, "did we *give* those lands to you?" "Your Majesty was indeed pleased so to do," replied Sir Edward.

It appears that the question was not urged further, and the estates remained in the possession of the North family until the year 1630, when they passed by sale to the families of Philips and Pytts. By the marriage of Alice, daughter of Edmund Pytts, the manor passed to James Rushout, who in 1661 was created a baronet, and the manorial rights have ever since continued in the family.

This Sir James Rushout purchased an estate at Northwick, in Worcestershire, and he was for many years M.P. for Evesham. His son, Sir John, took an active part in public affairs, and was a distinguished opponent of the administration of Sir Robert Walpole. He married Lady Anne Crompton, daughter of the fourth Earl of Northampton, and was succeeded by his son—likewise Sir John—who, after having represented Evesham in several Parliaments, was created Lord Northwick in 1797.

The manor-house of Flambards, formerly the seat of Lord Northwick, and one of the principal residences in the town, derived its name from a former possessor, Sir John Flambard, who lived in the reign of Edward III. The property was subsequently vested in the family of Gerard, from whom, after an intermediate transmission, it passed to that of Page. The last of that name, Mr. Richard Page, commenced re-building the house, which, on his death, was sold to and completed by Lord Northwick. Harrow Park covers part of old Flambards. The name is perpetuated in that of a modern house on the site, occupied by Mr. William Winkley, F.S.A., who owns the picture of Elizabeth the heiress of Sir Charles Gerard and grandmother of the first Lord Lake, a descendant of Henry VII. and Elizabeth of York.

Another manor-house in Harrow parish, called Uxendon, or Oxinden, was the house of a widow named Bellamy, a pious lady, who secreted there several missionary priests—including Anthony Babington, and Father Southwell the poet—when they were being hunted down by Walsingham, under Queen Elizabeth. Mrs. Bellamy perished in the Tower of London.

The old parish of Harrow is not less than forty-five miles in circumference. It meets Hertfordshire on the north, in the neighbourhood of Watford and Bushey; westward it is bounded by Ickenham and Ruislip; southward by Perivale, Twyford, and Willesden; and eastward by Kingsbury and Hendon. At the beginning of the present century, when the whole parish was enclosed under the operation of an Act of Parliament, it contained about 13,600 acres of land, and comprised within its bounds the hamlets of Pinner, Roxey (or Roxeth), Wembley, Harrow Weald, Apperton, Kenton, and Preston, where part of John Lyon's buildings are still standing. Pinner, as we have already seen, is now made into a separate parish for civil purposes.

Harrow was one of the pleasant suburbs occasionally visited by Charles Lamb, and is frequently mentioned in his charming correspondence; but

---

* Park's "History of Hampstead," p. 187.

apart from such occasional visits, and the fact that Byron passed some of his school-boy days within its bounds, there are but few or no literary or artistic reminiscences to be gleaned here, such as we find along the banks of the Thames, and as we have already dwelt upon in dealing with the sister hills of Hampstead and Highgate.*

The parish church of Harrow, from its situation on the summit of a hill, some 300 ft. above the surrounding "plain," and insulated, as it were, in the midst of a country by no means remarkable for the boldness of its hillocks, is an object unusually conspicuous, and cannot fail to attract the notice of all who travel along the North Western Railway. It is recorded that when some divines were disputing with King Charles II. about the *visible Church*, his Majesty said that he "knew not where it was to be found, except, indeed, at Harrow." The church is large and spacious, comprising a chancel, with chancel chapel, a clerestoried nave, aisles and transept, and a square embattled tower at the west end, surmounted by a lofty spire. It appears to have been originally built by Archbishop Lanfranc, in the time of the Conqueror, though not to have been consecrated till the time of Archbishop Anselm, his successor in the see of Canterbury.

Mr. Rule writes, in his "Life and Times of St. Anselm":—"The venerable western doorway of the parish church of Harrow recalls to the historian the last grief-stricken days of Archbishop Lanfranc, who, though he outlived the completion of the sacred fabric, died ere he could cause it to be consecrated. It also recalls the pensive opening of Anselm's primacy and his first *dedicatio ecclesiæ*; for it was beneath the curiously-carved and boldly-sculptured lintel of that venerable western doorway that, on a cold January morning in A.D. 1094, the new Archbishop, arrayed in his pontifical insignia, stood, and making the sacred sign, sang aloud—

'Ecce Crucis signum, fugiant phantasmata cuncta.'

Whereupon the doors unfolded, and entering, he proceeded to perform the more solemn rites of consecration."

But Anselm was not allowed to perform this solemn act without interruption, for it appears that the Bishop of London sent two of his canons to beg him to desist, and to confer with the bishop about their mutual rights. Mr. Rule tells us that, by way of enforcing the bishop's claim, the cathedral dignitaries stole, or ran off with, the holy oil, and so broke off the ceremony. Eadmer, the

historian, tells us that the dispute respecting the consecration of this church was referred to Wulstan, Bishop of Worcester, "the only one of the Saxon prelates then remaining," and that his decision, as most consonant to the customs of the Church, was in favour of the Archbishop; and down to the present day the Archbishop of Canterbury has special rights in Harrow, and is *ex-officio* Visitor of the school; but the patronage of the living has long since passed into private hands.

Lysons, writing in 1795, asserted that "some parts of Lanfranc's building still remain—namely, the circular columns which divide the aisles from the nave, and part of the tower at the west end, where is a Saxon arch of singular form." In a paper read by Mr. Hartshorne at a meeting of the St. Paul's Ecclesiological Society, in 1882, it was stated that the circular columns were of a period long after that of Lanfranc, and that the western arch was evidently not Saxon. It was the fashion in Lysons' time to call all Norman work "Saxon," but it was probable that not one stone of Lanfranc's work now remained. "In all likelihood," continued Mr. Hartshorne, "his work consisted of buildings at the east end only, the church being carried on gradually towards the west, the tower being finally undertaken about the middle of the twelfth century. The date of 1150 would agree very well with the character of the western doorway. It was probable that this tower did not originally come much above the nave, and that it was capped with a pyramidal roof. From inside it could still be seen that the tower was once lighted by windows on the north and south, of which the inner arches remained." The most striking features of the tower are its gigantic buttresses, which are of several types. It is surmised that originally the northern tower had shallow buttresses, but that when the church was rebuilt in the early part of the fourteenth century the tower was raised from what was now the first break in the clasping buttresses. As time went on, the tower failed under the additional weight. "It was the old story of works in the Middle Ages," observed Mr. Hartshorne—"bad foundations and want of cohesion in the walls. The ruptures were remedied by casting the Late Norman pilasters—a work resulting in the formation of the ponderous clasping buttresses, probably in the early part of the fifteenth century. Fully half a century later the men of Harrow, undeterred by the failures of their forefathers, added the present wooden and leaden spire. It was a bold stroke, but it made Harrow Church, in the words of Charles the Second, 'The Visible Church.' . . . The isolated spire of Harrow had, perhaps, left a more vivid impression upon a multitude of cultivated minds than any other erection of the same sort throughout the kingdom. Its unique and commanding position had contributed much to this renown ; but, probably, few had realised upon what a bolstered-up sub-structure this spire was raised. Strictly speaking, it was but a wooden skeleton, craftily enough put together, but exhibiting no lines of beauty, such as might be seen in the delicate entasis of the stone spire at Leighton Buzzard, that fitting crown of a noble cross church. Harrow spire was, in short, a surprising, and not really artistic, result of the vaulting ambition of eager, but unpractical, builders. But what boldness, what belief in their powers to surpass their predecessors, did it not show ! Untrammelled by the exigencies of Revivals, the Harrow men were no mere vulgar copyists : they honestly did their work in the church which they delighted to honour, and we might truly rejoice to-day that the spire still lives to tell the story of their faith."

On a fine clear day, it is said that you can see no less than thirteen counties from the top of the church-tower, almost at the foot of which, a little to the south-west, is " Byron's tomb"—not his grave, but the tombstone on which, when a boy at the school, he would lie at full length on summer afternoons and evenings, and watch the setting sun.

This tomb is an altar-shaped monument, near the south-west corner of the church. It is mentioned in the lines quoted as the motto of this chapter, from the poet's verses " On a Distant View of the Village and School of Harrow-on-the-Hill ;" and it is also thus referred to by Lord Byron in a letter to Mr. Murray, dated May 26, 1822 :—"There is a spot in the churchyard, near the footpath, on the brow of the hill, looking towards Windsor, and a tomb under a large tree (bearing the name of Peachie, or Peachey), where I used to sit for hours and hours when a boy. This was my favourite spot." The tomb was repaired by Mr. John Murray and other admirers of the poet a few years ago.

The whole body of the church, from the tower eastward, was apparently rebuilt in the first quarter of the fourteenth century, and the circular columns mentioned above belonged rather to that period than to Lanfranc's time, as Lysons supposed.

The walls of the church as they now stand are almost wholly modern, externally at least, the building having been "thoroughly restored" by Sir Gilbert Scott in 1840. "Forty years ago," remarked Mr. Hartshorne, in his lecture above quoted, "the stones of this building were alive to tell their own story, for each successive generation of builders had left its mark upon the church in its own style. The story was, perhaps, not always a pleasing one : for instance, the works of the Georgian period did not always commend themselves to our judgment ; but where was any part of that story now? One would have liked to have found on the outside as well as inside some original evidence of the genius of the workmen of the fourteenth and fifteenth centuries—some fragment at least of the ancient Perpendicular, some vestige of old flint work. Not a scrap of any of those things remained. The human interest of an old building was not comprised solely in its date, its early or incidental work or repairs ; we could not choose the one period and reject the other any more than we could pin our historic faith upon the strifes of the Roses and ignore the nobler struggles of the Civil Wars. The whole fabric of an old church was a sermon in stone, easily read, and showing in its successive changes the poverty, wealth, earnestness, and faith of the community in which it was set down ; it was a chapter in the history of a country ; it was in one sense the story of a district. But it was cheering to believe that a restoration of the kind which this church underwent would be nearly impossible at the present day. We had learned much in the last forty years, but the teaching had involved the loss of much that was very precious— much that, properly understood, was of the deepest historical interest, for it was impossible in the case of an old church to divorce history from architecture."

At the time of the restoration of the church in 1840, the chancel was lengthened, and a north aisle added to it ; and the noble open timber roof, of the Perpendicular period, with upright figures of angels playing on musical instruments on the corbels, was exposed. The east window is filled with painted glass, in memory of the Rev. John W. Cunningham, who died in 1861, having been for half a century vicar of this parish. Apart from the tower, the roofing, and the very fine chancel arch, there is now but little of antiquarian interest in the walls of this church, excepting the north and south doorways, both of which are of the Decorated period, that on the south side having a priest's chamber, or parvise, over it. The font, a large circular marble basin, rudely carved, and resting upon a thick cable pedestal, is probably a remnant of Lanfranc's church ; or, at all events, the bowl would appear to date back to the eleventh century ; the rim and base, however, are modern. This font had for about half a century done duty as a water-trough in the vicarage garden, but was restored to the church a few years ago, and now stands near the south entrance.

The tombs and monumental inscriptions in the church are both numerous and interesting. A brass, now fixed on the chancel arch, commemorates John Lyon, the founder of Harrow School. The inscription runs as follows :—" Heare lyeth buried the bodye of John Lyon, late of Preston, in this parish, yeoman, died the 11th day of Octr., in the yeare of our Lord 1592, who hath founded a free grammer schoole in this p'she, to have continuance for ever ; and for maintenance thereof, and for releyffe of the poore, and of some poore schollers in the universityes, repairinge of highwayes, and other good and charitable uses, hath made conveyance of lands of good value to a corporation granted for that purpose. Prayers be to the Author of all goodness, Who make us myndful to follow his good example."

Another brass, representing a knight in armour beneath a canopy, has an inscription in memory of Sir John Flambard, who, in the reign of Edward III., held one of the manors in Harrow. The inscription which Weever records for John Byrkhed, rector of Harrow, who died in 1480, is gone, although the headless figure, canopy, and arms, in brass, are still remaining. There is also the headless brass of another priest, Simon Marchford, who died in 1442.

Among the monuments is one to Dr. Sumner, Head Master of Harrow School, who died in 1771 ; it bears a Latin inscription from the pen of Dr. Parr. Dr. Samuel Garth, an eminent physician in his day and author of "The Dispensary," was buried in the chancel in 1719. In Hay's "Religio Philosophi" it is stated that Garth ordered a vault to be made for himself and his lady in this church, in consequence of an "accidental whim."

Lysons, in his "Environs of London" (1795), says that this church "is in the peculiar jurisdiction of the Archbishop of Canterbury, being reckoned among the parishes belonging to the Deanery of Croydon in Surrey." Peculiars, however, are now abolished, and Harrow is included in the diocese of London.

"Formerly," says Newcourt in the "Repertorium," "there was at Harrow both a rectory and a vicarage ; the rectory was a sinecure, to which the Archbishop collated a rector, who thereupon became patron of the vicarage."

A chantry appears to have been founded in this church by William de Bosco, one of the rectors, in the year 1524.

Among the old rectors, Cuthbert Tunstall, Bishop of Durham from the year 1511 to 1522, was the most remarkable. He was succeeded by William Bolton, the last prior but one of St. Bartholomew's,

in Smithfield. Concerning this last-mentioned worthy a singular story is told. He is reported to have made Harrow-on-the-Hill a "city of refuge" to which he and his brethren retreated at the end of January, 1524, on account of a prophecy which a credulous public had believed, that London would be washed away by a rising of the waters of the Thames, on the 1st of February. Camden says that Prior Bolton "built a house here, for fear of an inundation after a great conjunction of planets in the watery triplicity." He is said to have remained here for two months. Dr. Mackay, in his "Memoirs of Popular Delusions," after telling us how most of the upper classes withdrew on this occasion to Hampstead, Highgate, and the Surrey Hills, adds the following narrative, which does not raise the prior in our estimation :—

"Bolton, the Prior of St. Bartholomew's, was so alarmed, that he erected, at very great expense, a sort of fortress at Harrow-on-the-Hill, which he stocked with provisions for two months. On the 24th of January, a week before the awful day which was to see the destruction of London, he removed thither, with the brethren and officers of the Priory and all his household. A number of boats were conveyed in waggons to his fortress, furnished abundantly with expert rowers, in case the flood, reaching so high as Harrow should force them to go further for a resting-place. Many wealthy citizens prayed to share his retreat ; but the Prior, with a prudent forethought, admitted only his personal friends, and those who brought stores of eatables for the blockade.

"At last the morn, big with the fate of London, appeared in the east. The wondering crowds were astir at an early hour to watch the rising of the waters. The inundation, it was predicted, would be gradual, not sudden ; so that they expected to have plenty of time to escape, as soon as they saw the bosom of old Thames heave beyond the usual mark. But the majority were too much alarmed to trust to this, and thought themselves safer ten or twenty miles off. The Thames, unmindful of the foolish crowds upon its banks, flowed on quietly as of yore. The tide ebbed at its usual hour, flowed to its usual height, and then ebbed again, just as if twenty astrologers had not pledged their words to the contrary. Blank were their faces as evening approached, and as blank grew the faces of the citizens to think that they had made such fools of themselves. At last night set in, and the obstinate river would not lift its waters to sweep away even one house out of the ten thousand. Still, however, the people were afraid to go to sleep. Many hundreds remained up till dawn of the next day, lest the deluge should come upon them like a thief in the night.

"On the morrow it was seriously discussed whether it would not be advisable to duck the false prophets in the river. Luckily for them, they thought of an expedient which allayed the popular fury. They asserted that, by an error (a very slight one) of a little figure, they had fixed the date of this awful inundation a whole century too early. The stars were right, after all, and they,

privileges were obtained for the inhabitants through the intercession of the Archbishops of Canterbury. The market, which was granted in 1262, appears to have fallen into disuse before the reign of Elizabeth. Norden, writing at that period, observes that "Harrow-on-the-Hill was a market-towne in the time of Doct. Borde's peregrination, as appeareth by a little Treatise of his in writing." Although no longer possessed of the benefits arising from a regular mart, Harrow is still but

HARROW CHURCH, INTERIOR. (*See page* 256.)

erring mortals, were wrong. The present generation of cockneys were safe, and London would be washed away, not in 1524, but in 1624. At this announcement Bolton, the Prior, dismantled his fortress, and the weary emigrants came back."

Great doubts, however, it is only fair to add, hang over this entire story.

Outside the churchyard, on the western slope of the hill, a terrace has been formed, with seats for visitors. The view from this spot is very extensive, embracing as it does the green and level expanse of western Middlesex, and commanding a view of Windsor Castle and the Oxfordshire hills.

The town of Harrow could once boast of its weekly market and its annual fair, both of which

little inferior in size and population to some market-towns; what it lacks in that respect being, in all probability, made up to it by its famous school. In 1871 the number of inhabited houses was 1,503, the population numbering some 8,500 souls; but such has been the additional advantage offered of late years by railway communication with the metropolis—for there are now two railway-stations here, one on the North-Western and the other on the Metropolitan line—that nearly 5,000 more have been since added to the number of the inhabitants. The town, too, possesses its Fire Brigade, its Literary Institution and Young Men's Society, and a Workman's Hall. The Public Hall is a large building of "Elizabethan" design, capable of holding upwards of 600 persons ; it was erected in 1877 by a limited liability company. There is also a Cottage Hospital, which was erected in 1872, in the Roxeth Road, on land given by Mr. Charles Leaf, who also bore the principal part of the expense of the building ; the institution is supported by voluntary contributions. Harrow has also its Local Board of Health, its gas and water works, and its weekly *Gazette*. Some races were held here between the years 1864 and 1869, but they have since been abandoned.

In 1873 a Catholic chapel was erected in the Roxborough Road. It is dedicated to Our Lady and St. Thomas of Canterbury, being named after Thomas à Becket, who, as stated above, spent

the hill, and possesses altogether an air of quiet respectability, its shops, most small and unassuming, being largely mixed up with private houses and schools, most of which in the architecture are in keeping with the larger institution to which Harrow at this day owes its fame, and of which we shall speak in the following chapter.

As we have already intimated, Harrow cannot boast of having numbered among its inhabitants, apart from the school, any men whose names have become famous in history ; but it may be worth stating that early in the present century, at the foot of the hill, lived Mr. Benjamin Rotch, some time M.P. for Knaresborough. Though a magistrate for Middlesex and Chairman of the

HARROW. (*From a Pencil Sketch taken in* 1817.)

much of his time at Harrow and Pinner. There are also meeting-houses for different denominations of Dissenters, and many schools for children.

The principal street of the town is at the top of

Commissioners of the Peace, he sent a challenge to the Lord Mayor of London, Alderman Winchester ; but the latter retaliated by a criminal information.

CHAPTER XXV.

HARROW (*continued*).—THE SCHOOL, ETC.

" Again I re-visit the hills where we sported,
    The streams where we swam and the fields where we fought,
    The school where, loud warn'd by the bell, we resorted,
    To pore o'er the precepts by pedagogues taught."—BYRON.

The Distinction between Harrow and Eton as a Public School—The Foundation of Harrow School—" Orders, Statutes, and Rules of the Government of the School "—Extract from the Founder's Will—Directions as to Children to be Educated—Terms of Admission—Government of the School—Forms and Divisions—Number of Scholars—Cost of Board and Education—Prizes and Scholarships—Description of the School Buildings—Athletic Sports and Recreations—Lines in Honour of John Lyon, the Founder—The Practice of Archery—Shooting for the Silver Arrow—Head Masters and Eminent Harrovians.

THE chief interest of Harrow in the present day is centred in its school, which, in spite of the absence of a regular collegiate foundation, stands second

only to Eton among those nurseries of great and distinguished men—the " public schools " of the kingdom. Though resembling it in its aristocratic connection, and in some of its other features, Harrow differs radically and distinctly from Eton. It never was an ecclesiastical foundation, nor even an adjunct to one. At Harrow, therefore, there is no venerable Provost or body of Fellows to act as a check upon the head-master.

The founder of Harrow, as shown in the preceding chapter, was a plain yeoman, John Lyon, who lived in the hamlet of Preston, within the bounds of the parish to which he proved himself so great a benefactor. Even in his middle life he set apart "twenty marks" yearly for the instruction of poor children; and in the thirteenth year of Elizabeth's reign (1571) he obtained letters patent and a charter from the queen, empowering him to found a "Free Grammar School" at Harrow, and to draw up statutes for its regulation and government.

It was nearly twenty years after the issue of the above-mentioned charter, and only two years before his death, which took place in October, 1592, that John Lyon drew up and promulgated the document, entitled his "Orders, Statutes, and Rules for the Government of the School," containing full instructions for the disposal of the property which he intended to devote to that purpose. The sum of £300 was to be expended on the building of a school, with houses for the master and usher, who were to be elected by the governors : the former "to be on no account below the degree of Master of Arts," nor the latter "under that of Bachelor of Arts."

The founder expressly particularises the estates with which, after the death of himself and his wife, Johan, he intends to endow his establishment. At this period a house for the reception of the scholars had not been provided, and the founder thus expresses his intentions on that head :—"And I, the said John Lyon, doe purpose, by y⁰ Grace of God, to build. wᵗʰ some pᵗᵉ of my lands lying within the towne of Harrow uppon yᵉ Hill meete and convenient Roomes for the said Schoole Master and Usher to inhabite and dwell in ; as alsoe a large and convenient Schoole house, with a chimney in it. And, alsoe, a celler under the said Roomes or Schoole house, to lay in wood and coales, which said Celler shall be divided into three several Roomes, yᵉ one for yᵉ Mʳ, the second for the Usher, and yᵉ third for yᵉ schollers."

The property left by John Lyon for the support of his school, and for the repairing of the road between London and Harrow, consists of lands which now bring in, it is said, an income of £4,000 a year ; but it so happens that the lands in Marylebone and Paddington, which now are by far the most valuable, were assigned to the latter of these two purposes, so that the school, though it seems to have been the principal object of Lyon's charity, reaps comparatively but little benefit therefrom.

The founder directs that a competent number of scholars, children of "inhabitants within the parish," shall be educated freely ; but he allows the schoolmaster to "receive over and above . . so many '*foreigners*' as that the whole number may be well taught, and as the place can conveniently contain, at the judgment and discretion of the governors. And of the 'foreigners' he may take such stipends and wages as he can get, except they be of the kindred of John Lyon, the founder, so that he take pains with all indifferently, as well of the parish as 'foreigners,' as well of poor as of rich ; but the discretion of the governors shall be looked to that he do."

No boy can be admitted into the school without passing an entrance examination, sufficient to show that he has mastered the chief difficulties of his Latin Grammar, and has made some progress in his Greek Grammar, and also in Arithmetic. No boy can be admitted after completing his fifteenth year, or in any case without a certificate of good conduct from his master or tutor ; nor can he remain in the school (without special permission) after sixteen, unless he has reached the Shell at least ; after seventeen, unless he has reached the "Upper Remove ; " or after eighteen, unless he is in the Sixth Form.

Every boy at Harrow, however high or low, be he a boarder or a day-boy (home-boarder), is expected to have a private tutor ; and some portion of the work taken up by the lower boys to the school must be previously gone over by him with his tutor in "Pupil-room." In this respect, the system of Harrow agrees in principle with Eton, though in the practice of the two schools there are many points of difference, which we have not space to explain here.

The school is under the control of a governing body, and is subject to the Archbishop of Canterbury and the Bishop of London as Visitors.

The school consists of fifteen "monitors ; " a Sixth Form, divided into two "Removes ; " a Fifth Form, divided into four "Removes : " "the Remove," in two "divisions ; " the "Upper Shell," in two "divisions ; " followed by a third and a fourth "Remove" of the same ; a Fourth Form in three "Removes ; " and, lastly, a Third Form, which contains only a few boys. The Second and First Forms no longer exist.

The numbers of the school, which in the last

century rarely rose above 100, have fluctuated during the present century from 300, under the late Dr. G. Butler and Dr. Longley, to between 70 and 80 under Dr. Wordsworth. Under Dr. Vaughan the numbers steadily rose to between 480 and 500 ; and under his successor, the present Dr. H. Montagu Butler, they have reached 580, which the Governors have now fixed as the limit beyond which it is not desirable that the school should increase.

Every boy at Harrow is obliged to learn French, as part of the system ; but after reaching a certain place in the school he learns either French or German. Of late years much greater prominence has been given to the teaching of modern languages than was the case in former times.

The cost for school-fees, board, and tuition, at Harrow, is about £135 in the larger houses, and in the smaller houses £180 a year. This represents the total of *necessary* expenses, exclusive of "extras" and tradesmen's accounts.

At Harrow there are plenty of motives for exertion, in the shape of prizes and scholarships, which are awarded by public competition. First and foremost stand the "Lyon," or "entrance scholarships" (six or seven in number), of an annual value of from £30 to £80, besides which there are annually given eleven other scholarships, called, after their founders, the Sayer, Spencer, Neeld, Gregory, Botfield, Leaf, Anderson, Baring, Roundell, Clayton Memorial, and Ponsonby, varying from £30 to £100 a year. There are also annual prizes of books, and of gold and silver medals, founded by Mr. A. Beresford-Hope, by the late Sir R. Peel, Isabella Gregory, the late Mr. Beriah Botfield, Lord Charles Russell, Viscount Ebrington, Mr. Oxenham, and Mr. Cyril Flower, for compositions in English, Latin, and Greek prose and verse, modern languages, &c. ; and the successful compositions are publicly recited on "Speech Day," the first Thursday in July. The late Mr. Joseph Neeld also founded an annual prize for mathematics—a gold medal, of the value of ten guineas ; the head master gives prizes for natural science and for English and Latin composition. There are also annual prizes for the knowledge of the Holy Scriptures, Shakespeare, modern history, reading, and English literature.

It is almost needless to add that the monitorial and fagging systems—both, if rightly understood and properly applied, the best guarantees against tyranny and bullying—are in full operation at Harrow.

The school is situated immediately to the south of the church, whilst the houses of the masters are scattered about the town. The school buildings form, as it were, the centre of attraction. These are mostly of red brick ; they stand between the head-master's house and the churchyard. The most interesting part of these buildings is the "Fourth Form Room ;" it is also the largest of all the school-rooms, though small in comparison of the Upper School at Eton. This was the original school-room of Lyon's foundation. It is a small, plain apartment, still containing the original fittings—a canopied master's seat at the further end, a lesser arm-chair and desk for the usher near the centre, and tiers of low benches and backless forms placed on either side of the room. It has an interest peculiar to itself; for on the dingy oak panelling which surrounds it are rudely carved the names and initials of some of the most illustrious sons of Harrow, cut by their own hands when boys : among the number are "Byron," "Robert Peel," "Robinson" (afterwards Earl of Ripon), "Aberdeen," "Temple" (afterwards Lord Palmerston), "Sir William Jones," "R. B. Sheridan," and "Normanby." The names of Harrovians of recent date are carved by a hired and experienced hand, and in a more regular way, so as to prove a record of most who leave the school. The opposite wing of the school buildings contains the old "Speech Room," erected about sixty years ago by subscription, under the auspices of the late Dr. Butler, then head-master, afterwards Dean of Peterborough. It is said to have cost £10,000. In it, as may be inferred from its name, the annual "speeches" were formerly held every summer. It was furnished with seats capable of accommodating about 500, and on "Speech Day" it was filled with all the rank and beauty of the land, even royalty itself not unfrequently being present. The room is now used for the purposes of school examinations. In stained glass in the windows are the armorial bearings of Queen Elizabeth and George III., and of sundry governors, head-masters, and benefactors. The "Fourth Form Room" is used for school prayers for some of the scholars, and on wet holidays and half-holidays instead of the school-yard, for calling over the "bill" of names, as the roll-call, or "absence" of Eton, is here termed.

In 1871, at a meeting of "Old Harrovians," it was decided to celebrate the tercentenary of the foundation of the school by the erection of a new "speech-room" and other buildings connected with different branches of education, including school-rooms, a museum, laboratory, gymnasium, lecture-rooms, &c. In order to carry out these various objects, a subscription was immediately set on foot; and the first stone of the new buildings was laid by the Duke of Abercorn on Speech-day, July 2nd, 1874. The new speech-room stands on the opposite side of the road to the old college chapel, and it was built from the designs of the late Mr. William Burges, at a cost, including the site, of nearly £20,000. It is a semi-circular building, the chord being occupied by a large platform stage, while the tiers of seats rise in rows against the opposite wall. In the floor of the orchestra, below the desk of the head-master, is the keyboard of an organ, trackers being carried under the platform to the pipes against the outer wall. The roof is vaulted in pitch-pine, carried on slender iron columns, and the entire effect is quite dissimilar from any other building of the kind.

The boys of Harrow School attended Divine service in the parish church down to about the year 1840, when, under the head-mastership of Dr. Wordsworth, a chapel was built for them at the north end of the High Street, which they attended for afternoon services. It was a brick building, erected in a style to harmonise with the other portions of the school, from the designs of Mr. C. R. Cockerell, R.A. In 1854 that chapel was pulled down, and a new and larger chapel built on its site. The new school chapel was designed by Sir G. Gilbert Scott, and built under Dr. Vaughan's head-mastership. It is a handsome Gothic structure, consisting of nave, chancel, and side aisles, one of which was erected in memory of the Harrovians who fell in the Crimean war. A few yards beyond the chapel is the Vaughan Library, erected in 1860 in memory of Dr. Vaughan, who was head-master from 1845 to that date. It was built from the designs of Sir Gilbert Scott, and is in the Decorated Gothic style. It is a large and spacious room, and contains not only a good and serviceable library for the use of the boys in the Upper School, together with cabinets of minerals, coins, bronzes, and china, but also some interesting relics of Harrow in the olden days, and a series of portraits of the head-masters from Thackeray downwards, and of sundry illustrious old Harrovians, among whom Lord Palmerston, the Marquis of Dalhousie, Lord Herbert, Lord Byron, and the late Earls of Aberdeen and Ripon, stand conspicuous.

Almost adjoining to the library is the house of the head-master; it is a plain substantial edifice of red brick, with mullioned windows, and, including a wing recently erected, can contain about sixty boys.

In 1864 a sanatorium, which bears the reputation of being well arranged and organised, was erected at a little distance from the school; and in 1874—5 further additions were made in the shape of a gymnasium, and laboratories, and Natural Science schools. All these new buildings have been erected out of the Lyon Memorial Fund of 1871.

There is a covered and other racket-courts just below the school buildings, on the slope of the hill, leading down towards the cricket-field. This is far inferior in beauty to the exquisite " playing fields " of Eton; but the Harrow boys have frequently shown at Lord's that they can produce far better " elevens " than their great rivals. The game of the winter months is football. Not only in cricket and football do the Harrow boys bear away the palm, but also in rifle practice they may be said to hold their ground among the public schools, having carried off the Ashburton Challenge Shield no less than nine times.

By his will John Lyon settled the salaries of the masters, and specified the numbers of the " forms " in the school; their books and their exercises; their school hours, recreations, and vacations; and he recognised as lawful and appropriate games " driving a top," " tossing a hand-ball," and " running and shooting." The latter diversion was even insisted on : for the parents were required to furnish their children with " bow-strings, shafts, and bracers, to exercise *shooting.*"

With such solicitude for the well-being of the scholars, not only during the school hours, but also in play-time, it is not to be wondered that the name of the founder of the school is held in high veneration by Harrovians. As it is written in " The Carthusian "—

" A Harrow man vows that there's οὐδὲν βέλτιον
	To be met with on earth than his founder, John Lyon."

The following lines on "Lyon of Preston, Founder," were sung at the Tercentenary Festival of Harrow in 1871:—

" Lyon, of Preston, yeoman John,
	Full many a year ago,
Built, on the hill that I live on
	A school that you all may know ;
Into the form, first day, 'tis said,
	Two boys came for to see :
One with a red ribbon, red, red, red,
	And one with a blue—like me !

" Lyon, of Preston, yeoman John,
	Lessons he bade them do ;
Homer, and multiplica-ti-on,
	And spelling, and Cicero ;
' Red Ribbon' never his letters knew,
	Stuck at the five times three ;
But Blue Ribbon learnt the table through,
	And said it all off—like me !

" Lyon, of Preston, yeoman John,
    Said to them both 'Go play.'
Up slunk 'Red Ribbon' all alone,
    Limped from the field away ;
'Blue Ribbon' played like a hero's son,
    All by himself played he :
Five score runs did he quickly run,
    And was still Not Out—like me

' Lyon, of Preston, yeoman John,
    All in his anger sore,
Flogged the boy with the Red ribbon,
    Set him the Georgics four ;
But the boy with the Blue Ribbon got, each week,
    Holidays two and three,
And a prize for sums, and a prize for Greek,
    And an Alphabet prize—like me !

" Lyon, of Preston, yeoman John,
    Died many years ago,
All that is mortal of him is gone,
    But he lives in a school I know.
All of them work at their cricket there,
    And work at their five times three ;
And all of them, ever since that day, wear
    A ribbon of blue—like me ! "

It is quite clear that the worthy Master Lyon considered archery a most necessary part of what the old Greek philosophers styled the "gymnastic" part of education. At Harrow, at all events, the practice of archery was coeval with the school ; and here the "gentle art" would seem to have been kept alive down to a comparatively recent date by the observance of an annual custom.

To encourage archery Lyon instituted a prize of a "silver arrow," to be shot for annually on the 4th of August ; but the day was subsequently changed to the first Thursday in July. "In my time," says Bishop Latimer, writing in 1509, "my poor father was as diligent to teach me to shoot as to learn me any other thing, and so I think other men did their children ; he taught me how to draw, how to lay my body to the bow, and not to draw with strength of arms, as divers other nations do, but with strength of body. I had my bow bought me according to my age and strength ; as I increased in them, so my bows were made bigger and bigger ; for men shall never shoot well except they be brought up in it. It is a worthy game, a wholesome kind of exercise, and much commended in physic."

There were six, and in later times twelve, competitors for John Lyon's silver arrow ; and he who first shot twelve times nearest to the central mark was proclaimed the victor, and carried off the prize, a triumphal procession of boys attending him. The competitors were attired in fancy dresses of spangled satin, generally of white and green, with green silk sashes and silken caps.

The Butts were at the entrance, on the left of the London road, entering the village. They were backed by a lofty knoll, crowned with trees ; on the slope of this eminence were cut rows of grassy seats, gradually descending, and worthy, according to Dr. Parr, of a Roman amphitheatre.

We hear from the Harrow "School Lists" that the last contest for the silver arrow took place in July, 1771. In the following September, Dr. Sumner, the head-master, died, and was succeeded by Dr. Heath. The arrow prepared for the next year's contest (being the last ever made for this purpose, and, as the arrow-shooting was abolished in 1772, never shot for) became the property of the Rev. B. H. Drury, one of the assistant-masters, son of the Rev. Henry Drury (himself for many years an assistant, and for some time before his death under-master), to whom it had descended from his uncle, Dr. Heath. Mr. Drury presented it a few years since to the school library, where it is still religiously kept.

The abolition of the practice of arrow-shooting will ever be a source of deep regret to all Harrovians. Nevertheless, Dr. Heath, the head-master who suppressed it, must not on this account be too severely blamed. The reasons which induced him to abandon this ancient custom are stated to have been a serious accident which befel one of the competitors, the frequent exemptions from the regular business of the school which the shooters claimed *as a privilege not to be infringed upon !* as well as the band of disorderly persons whom this exhibition brought down to the village, in consequence of its vicinity to the metropolis. These encroachments and annoyances had at length become so injurious to discipline, as, after some vain attempts at the correction of the evil, to call for the total abolition of the usage.

About the year 1810, the charming spot called The Butts, where the shooting for the silver arrow took place, were denuded of wood, and the knoll itself has at length disappeared, its site being now entirely occupied by private dwelling-houses. The prefatory introduction to the School Lists says that " in the school there may now be seen a humble representation of 'The Butts' on the day of the annual contest." " In that frontispiece " (according to the testimony of the late Rev. H. Drury, in a letter of the 20th July, 1838) " the village barber is seen walking off like one of Homer's heroes, with an arrow in his eye, stooping forward, and evidently in great pain, with his hand applied to the wound. It is perfectly true that this Tom of Coventry was so punished ; and I have somewhere a ludicrous account of it in Dr.

Parr's all but illegible autograph." This testimony is confirmed by that of the late Lord Arden, an old Harrovian, in a letter of the 17th July, 1838:— "I remember a print representing the circumstance of one of the boys having shot so wide of the mark that his arrow struck a man, or boy, in the eye, that the stooping individual in the print represented Goding, the barber, "who," she said, "was shot *in the mouth*, and lost two or three of his teeth thereby." This is evidently another version of the above story, substituting only the gaping mouth as a various reading for the peeping eye.

THE FOURTH FORM ROOM. (*See page* 261.)

which, I believe, was the occasion of the shooting for a silver arrow being discontinued." Whether Lord Arden's conjecture as to the cause of the suppression of the arrow-shooting be correct or not, his lordship's testimony, it has been well observed, is of considerable value, as showing the traditional opinion held in his day about the interpretation of the point. Moreover, a few years ago, a Mrs. Arnold, an octogenarian inhabitant of Harrow, with a clear memory of bygone times, fully believed

The names of many of the successful competitors for the "silver arrow" may be found in the earlier volumes of the *Gentleman's Magazine*, from which we take the following:—

Vol. I. "Thursday, 5 August, 1731.—According to an ancient custom, a silver arrow, value £3, was shot for at 'The Butts,' at Harrow-on-the-Hill, by six youths of that free school, in archery habits, and won by Master Brown, son of Captain Brown, commander of an East-Indiaman." Vol. XXVII.,

p. 381. "Thursday, 4, August 1757.—The silver arrow shot for by the young gentlemen of Harrow School was won by Master Earle." Vol. XXXI., p. 329. "Thursday, 2 July, 1761.—The silver arrow was shot for (as usual) by twelve young gentlemen at Harrow-on-the-Hill, and was won by the Earl of Barrymore." Vol. XXXIV., p. 346. "Thursday, 5, July 1764.—The silver arrow annually shot for at Harrow was won by Master Mee."* Vol. XXXV., p. 344. "Thursday, 4

and bears this inscription (for which, it may be charitably presumed, the learned head-master did not hold himself responsible) : ' Pretium Victoriæ a Carolo Wager Allix potitum tertia Mensis Julii, 1766.' Several of the old people (Mother Bernard, Dick Martin, &c.) told me they remembered well my father's winning it, and that it was very warmly contested, one of the shooters being peculiarly desirous to gain it, inasmuch as three of his brothers in succession had previously been the

SHOOTING FOR THE ARROW.
(*From an Old Print*, 1769.)

July, 1765.—The silver arrow was shot for by twelve youths of Harrow School, and won by Master Davies. Some Indian warriors, at that time in England, were present to witness the exhibition." From a private letter :—"Thursday, 3 July, 1766.— The silver arrow was shot for as usual, and won by Master Charles Wager Allix." Respecting this last-mentioned arrow, Dr. Butler, the head-master, received from Mr. Charles Allix, of Willoughby Hall, Lincolnshire, son of the prizeman, a communication to the following effect :—" It is nearly," he writes, " of the size and shape of a real arrow,

victors. On this occasion, therefore, the boy's father and family were present, and most intense was their anxiety for his success. ' For ' (as Mother B. expressed it) ' the father had stuck up the *three* arrows already in the *three* corners of his drawing-room, and so especially wanted the *fourth* to fill up the other corner.' I have now the bow with which it was won ; and my father has told me that only a week before the day of shooting he discovered that by some one it had been maliciously broken. This discovery plunged him into the deepest despair ; however, he sent the bow immediately to London, for the chance of its being repaired. It was repaired, but considerably shortened. Still, to his inconceivable delight, he

---

* It would be interesting to know if this "Master Mee" was the grandfather of Lord Palmerston, who was an Harrovian, and whose mother, according to the Peerages, was the daughter of one Benjamin Mee, Esq.

found, upon trying it, that he could shoot with it even better than ever, and HE WON THE PRIZE."

With reference to the shooting in 1769, the following interesting anecdote was communicated to the Dean of Peterborough (Dr. Butler) upon the authority of the late Hon. Archibald Macdonald. On the day of the competition, two boys, Merry and Love, were equal, or nearly so, and both of them decidedly superior to the rest, when Love, having shot his last arrow into the bull's eye, was greeted by his school-fellows with a shout, " Omnia vincit Amor ! " " Not so," said Merry, in an under voice ; " Nos non cedamus Amori ; " and carefully adjusting his shaft, shot it into the bull's eye a full inch nearer to the centre than his exulting competitor. So he gained the day. As the name of " Love " does not occur in the list of shooters for that year, it is clear that it must have been a nickname by which one of them was familiarly known.

The " arrow " still forms part of the armorial bear-

ARMS OF HARROW SCHOOL.

ings of the school ; and in the Monitors' Library at Harrow is still to be seen one of the embroidered silk dresses which the boys wore at their annual archery festival. The " silver arrow," however, has not been shot for since the year 1771.

On the abolition of the archery contests, public " speeches " were adopted in their place on the first Thursdays in May, June, and July, and were numerously attended by old Harrovians and friends of the boys. The ten monitors used to speak on each of the three days, together with six of the Sixth Form, according to their seniority, of whom each six so chosen spoke on *one* of the three days only during that year. This custom continued till 1829, when the number of speech-days was reduced by Dr. Longley (then head-master) to two ; and that number was subsequently reduced by his successor, Dr. Wordsworth, in his last year, 1844, to one. The subjects of the speeches used to be passages in prose and verse, selected from the best authors, Greek, Latin, and English. With these, in process of time, were combined original prize compositions, commencing with the year 1820, and increasing in number and variety of style as the kindness of the governors and the bounty of

sundry old Harrovians and others successively added to the list of prizes.

Since the foundation of the school the post of head-master has been held by clergymen of the highest eminence as scholars, and of the most distinguished ability and talents. In 1660 the Rev. W. Howe, Fellow of King's College, Cambridge, was elected to the office. Dr. Thackeray, chaplain to the Prince of Wales, who was head-master at the middle of the last century, was succeeded in 1760 by the Rev. Dr. Sumner, under whose superintendence the number of pupils in the school rose to 250. It is difficult to discover the proximate cause of the sudden rise in the numbers of the school during the head-masterships of Dr. Thackeray and Dr. Sumner (1740–71), except it is to be found in the fact that the former was a personal friend of the Prince of Wales, and a supporter of the side of Bishop Hoadley in the Bangorian controversy, and that possibly Eton was thought too " High Church " for those times, when everything that looked in the direction of the nonjuring communion was at a discount among the aristocracy. It is more than probable, though not at present provable, that such was the case.

On the death of Dr. Sumner, in 1771, Dr. Heath was elected to the office. Mr. (afterwards Dr.) Parr, the defeated candidate on that occasion, had been an assistant-master at Harrow under Dr. Sumner, and he seemed to be generally pointed out, by his learning and abilities, as the successor of the late head-master ; indeed, his popularity with the boys was so great that when the election fell on Mr. Heath they endeavoured to avenge the cause of their favourite by overt acts of rebellion, the " senior form " considering it " an indignity to have an Eton assistant put over them, when they had in their own school a person of superior learning." Among the boys who took part in this rebellion was one Richard Wesley, or Wellesley, afterwards Marquis Wellesley, and elder brother of another Arthur Wesley, afterwards better known as Sir Arthur Wellesley. He was removed by his guardian, Archbishop Cornwallis, to Eton, whither he was soon afterwards followed by his younger brother, who was sent there "under his wing." Had this not been the case, possibly "the battle of Waterloo " would not have been "won on the playing fields at Eton," but on the slope of a hill-side in Middlesex.

But to return from this digression. Such was Dr. Parr's mortification at his failure that he threw up his situation as assistant-master, and retired to Stanmore, where he founded a school, and where we shall meet with him again presently.

That establishment, however, failed in the end, and Mr. Parr was appointed to the living of Hatton, in Warwickshire, and afterwards to a prebendal stall in St. Paul's. Dr. Heath's popularity was by no means enhanced by one of his earliest measures — the abolition of the time-honoured custom of shooting for the silver arrow, as already mentioned.* On Dr. Heath's resignation, Dr. Drury succeeded to the head-master's chair. Under his auspices the school attained a greater eminence than it had ever previously known. At one period the number of scholars exceeded 350, and the whole establishment was, in consequence, much enlarged. Among the pupils under Dr. Heath were two whose names will ever be regarded with the deepest veneration by Harrovians : namely, Lord Byron and Sir Robert Peel. On the retirement of Dr. Drury in 1805, Dr. Butler, afterwards Dean of Peterborough, was elected. The most flourishing condition of the school during Dr. Butler's head-mastership was in 1816, when the numbers amounted to 295. In 1829 Dr. Butler resigned, and was succeeded by Dr. Longley, whose period of office extended over the short space of only seven years, for he resigned in 1836, on being appointed to the bishopric of Ripon. Dr. Longley was translated to Durham in 1856, became Archbishop of York in 1860, was translated to the see of Canterbury in 1862, and died in 1868.

Dr. Longley's successor at Harrow was the Rev. Christopher Wordsworth. He was a Fellow of Trinity College, Cambridge, where his father, a man of eminent learning, was Master. He passed a brilliant career at the University, having won the Chancellor's English medal, and been Porson's prizeman, Browne's medallist, and Craven scholar. On leaving Harrow in 1844 he was appointed successively Canon and Archdeacon of Westminster, and in 1869 he was consecrated Bishop of Lincoln. Dr. Wordsworth's contributions to literature have been numerous and of great value. An edition of "Theocritus," "Athens and Attica," "Greece," a "Tour in Italy," a "Diary of France," the Greek Testament and other portions of the Holy Bible annotated, "Theophilus Anglicanus," and "Memoirs of William Wordsworth," are the best known among his works, which include several volumes of sermons on the passing topics of the day.

Dr. Charles John Vaughan held the head mastership from 1844 till 1859. He was Craven University Scholar and Porson's prizeman at Trinity

College, Cambridge, in 1836 and 1837, and Chancellor's medallist in 1838. He was afterwards elected to a Fellowship of his college. He held the vicarage of St. Martin's, Leicester, from 1841 to his appointment to Harrow. From 1851 to 1879 he was Chaplain in Ordinary to the Queen. He was appointed Vicar of Doncaster in 1860, Master of the Temple in 1869, and Dean of Llandaff in 1879, and he has more than once refused a bishopric.

Dr. Henry Montagu Butler, the present headmaster, is the youngest son of a former head-master, the Rev. George Butler, D.D., who died in 1853. Dr. Butler was born in 1833, and was educated at Harrow School, whence he proceeded to Trinity College, Cambridge, where he closed a brilliant undergraduate career by graduating B.A. in 1855 as Senior Classic. In the same year he was elected Fellow of his college. In 1859, on the retirement of Dr. Vaughan, he was elected to the head-mastership of his old school, over which, as before shown, his father had so long presided.

Of the large number of "eminent men" which Harrow has contributed to the political and literary world, it will be impossible, in the limited space at our command, to do more than briefly notice a few of the most important. As the school was then only of local importance, few names of great note appear in the annals of Harrow previous to the commencement of the last century.

William Baxter, the author of several classical and antiquarian works, entered the school about the year 1668. He was a nephew of the celebrated Richard Baxter, the Nonconformist divine, and a native of Wales. Baxter will be best remembered by his well-known edition of Horace, and his "Glossarium Antiquitatum Britannicarum." He died in 1723.

James Bruce, the celebrated Scotch traveller, was here between 1742 and 1746. After traversing the greater part of Asia Minor, he set off in June, 1768, to discover the source of the Nile. An account of this journey was published in 1790. It is stated in the "Harrow Calendar" that Bruce's long residence abroad "produced no abatement in his attachment to the place of his education." He died in 1794.

Sir William Jones, the distinguished linguist and orientalist, entered the school in his seventh year, under Dr. Thackeray, and was so diligent in his studies that he became known as the "great scholar." In 1766 he became tutor to Lord Althorp, and he afterwards travelled in the East. He published a "Persian Grammar," the "Laws of Menu," &c. In 1783 he was appointed a Judge at Calcutta, where he founded an Asiatic Society.

Dr. Samuel Parr, whose scholarship was the pride of Harrow School, was the son of a tradesman in the town, and was entered on the foundation in 1752. While a boy at the school he fought with Lord Mountstuart. He made such rapid progress with his learning that at the age of fourteen he was at the head of the school. Dr. Parr was a great scholar, but little more. The two dreams of his life were a four-in-hand, attained late in years, and a bishopric. In 1792 he published a "Letter from Irenopolis to the Inhabitants of Eleutheropolis" upon the Priestley controversy. As a schoolmaster, he belonged to the order of the "Flagellants," only his flogging was vicarious; he flogged others, not himself. As a critic, his want of acumen was shown by his signing a confession of faith as a guarantor of the Ireland Shakespeare forgeries. Dr. Parr died in 1825.

The gallant Admiral Lord Rodney, the hero of the 12th of April, 1782, was at school here before he went to sea.

In the present century Harrow can boast that four Prime Ministers of England, all living at the same time, had been its *alumni*—Lord Ripon, Lord Aberdeen, Sir R. Peel, and Lord Palmerston.

Richard Brinsley Sheridan,* the distinguished dramatist, wit, and politician, was a Harrovian. He died in 1816.

Theodore Hook, the eminent dramatist and novelist, whose feats of practical joking have often been mentioned in these pages, displayed his characteristic love for that particular species of wit in the early days of his schoolboy life. "The first night of his arrival here was signalised by a feat of throwing a stone at a window where an elderly lady was undressing. The window was broken, but the lady escaped unhurt. The act was perpetrated at the instigation of Byron." Hook's powers as an improvisatore gained for him a passport into "society." He was patronised by the Prince Regent, and in 1812 was appointed to a Government post in the Mauritius, but was recalled in 1818 in consequence of deficiencies and irregularities in his accounts. He afterwards devoted himself to journalism and literature, and his name will be long remembered in connection

with the publication of that witty Tory organ, *John Bull.*

Sir Robert Peel, Bart., the Conservative statesman, who conceded the Repeal of the Corn Laws, and was instrumental in bringing about the Catholic Emancipation, was a contemporary of Byron at Harrow. The story is told that one day when Peel was being severely thrashed, another little boy ran up to his tormentor, and coolly asked him how many blows he was going to give him. "What's that to you, you little rascal?" was the reply; "be off." "Because," answered the little fellow, "I would take half myself." That brave and generous little boy was Lord Byron. Peel was first elected to Parliament in 1809. In 1817 he was chosen representative of Oxford University, and in 1829 he was elected for Tamworth. Sir Robert Peel was successively Under Secretary for the Colonies, Chief Secretary for Ireland, Home Secretary, Chancellor of the Exchequer, and twice First Lord of the Treasury. He was accidentally killed by a fall from his horse in 1850.

Lord Byron was entered at Harrow, under Dr. Drury, in 1801, and left in 1805. "During his stay there," as we learn from the 'Harrow Calendar,' "he showed symptoms of that morbid melancholy which so unhappily distinguished him in after-life. He himself says that he was 'a most unpopular boy, but led lately.' He was particularly distinguished for the opposition he made to Dr. Butler's appointment after the retirement of Dr. Drury, to whom he had been singularly attached. A reconciliation, however, took place between him and the Doctor before his departure for Greece. He says in his Diary, 'I have retained many of my school friendships and all my dislikes—except to Dr. Butler, whom I treated rebelliously, and have been sorry ever since.'" The poems in which Byron refers to Harrow are the following:— "On a Change of Masters at a Great Public School," "To the Duke of Dorset," "On a Distant View of the Village and School of Harrow," "Lines to Edward Noel Long, Esq." (whom the poet elsewhere addresses as "Cleon"), "Lines written beneath an Elm in Harrow Churchyard," "Lines on Revisiting Harrow." Among his principal friends here were Curzon, Hunter, Long, and

BYRON'S NAME, FROM THE FOURTH FORM ROOM.
(See page 261).

Tattersall, whom he addresses as "Davus" in his "Hours of Idleness," and who is said to have saved the poet's life by arresting a blow made at him by a farmer, in a feud on the subject of the cricket-ground.

The Right Hon. Spencer Perceval, born in 1762, entered Parliament in 1801 as member for Northampton, and was successively Attorney-General, Chancellor of the Exchequer, and Chancellor of the Duchy of Lancaster, and, subsequently, in 1809, First Lord of the Treasury. He was shot by Bellingham in the lobby of the House of Commons in 1812.

Lord Elgin, the ambassador, and the celebrated collector of the Elgin marbles; the third Earl Spencer, better known as the Lord Althorp of the Reform Bill era; Lord Cottenham, some time Lord Chancellor; Lord Moira, afterwards Marquis of Hastings and Governor-General of India; Lord Clare, Governor of Bombay in 1832, addressed as "Lycus" in Byron's "Hours of Idleness;" Earl de la Warr, some time Lord Chamberlain, addressed as "Euryalus" in the same poem; the Marquis Wellesley (before he was sent to Eton); Lords Dalhousie and Herbert; Sir Henry L. Bulwer; the Earl of Shaftesbury; Mr. A. Beresford-Hope; Sir John B. Karslake; the late Viscount Strangford; Bishop Charles Wordsworth; Mr. Herman Merivale; Cardinal Manning; Archbishop Trench; Mr. William Spottiswoode, F.R.S.; the first Lord Rendlesham, author of the famous Thellusson will, which gave so much business to the lawyers; Dr. Douglas, master of Benett (Corpus Christi) College, Cambridge; and the poet Sotheby.

CHAPTER XXVI.

Rura per et valles. — Ovid.

HARROW WEALD, KINGSBURY, ETC.

Rural Aspect of the Locality—The Hamlet of Greenhill—Harrow Weald—Remnants of the Great Forest of Middlesex—Grime's Dyke—All Saints' Church—Weald Park—Daniel Dancer, the Miser—Roxeth—Sudbury—St. John's Church—The Girl's Home, &c.—Wembley—Descent of the Manor—The "Green Man," Wembley Hill—Kingsbury: its Rural Character, Boundaries, &c.—Kingsbury Reservoir—The "Welsh Harp"—Kingsbury Races—The Parish Church—A Supposed Roman Encampment—Fryern Farm and Kingsbury Green—Oliver Goldsmith's Residence—The Hamlet of the Hyde—Kenton.

NOTWITHSTANDING the gradual extension of London, and the speed with which most of the outlying villages and hamlets are being connected one with another in all directions, there are still left a few fields and hedgerows to which the cockney holiday-makers can betake themselves. Here, in the neighbourhood of Harrow and Kingsbury, the fields are still green, the hedgerows fresh, the forest trees put on their summer garb as of yore, and even the smaller streams, which here and there expand into broad lakes and ponds, are not yet forced to burrow underground. It has been observed that the inhabitants of our mighty metropolis are marvellously neglectful of their privileges. With the exception, perhaps, of Vienna, there is no capital in Europe with scenery so beautiful, and so easily accessible. Yet we see innumerable Londoners, even of intelligence and refinement, going on flying trips across the Channel in the briefest holiday-time, or gathering into some overcrowded watering-place, where the charges are outrageous and the accommodation is indifferent. It is certain, however, that if they did otherwise we should have no such sequestered and peaceful scenery anywhere within the borders of the metropolitan counties as is to be met with in the "green lanes" hereabout.

As we have shown in the preceding chapters, Harrow Hill rises abrupt and isolated. Seen from this the elevating country for miles around has the appearance of an almost level plain. This surrounding land is mostly under cultivation either for corn or grass; indeed, the land between Harrow and Heston, which lies away some six miles to the south, still bears an excellent reputation for its corn, as it did in the time of "good Queen Bess." *

In the immediate neighbourhood of Harrow, nestling, as it were, under the sheltering wing of the hill, lie several suburban ecclesiastical districts, some of them at one time being reckoned as hamlets of the mother parish. Between the town and the railway-station, at the foot of the hill to the north, is Greenhill, a small cluster of villas and houses of modern growth. A church for the district, dedicated to St John the Baptist, was built in 1866. It is a cruciform, brick-built edifice, small and unpretending.

* See *ante* p. 44.

Stretching away northward as far as the rising ground about Stanmore and Watford, and bounded on the west by Pinner and on the east by Hendon, is the broad level tract of country known as Harrow Weald, a district which retains in its name an allusion to its former umbrageous and rude character, the term *weald* signifying in the Saxon a wood. It was, in fact, a vast wild woodland, part of the great forest of Middlesex ; and, although it has long been "enclosed" and cultivated, there is still much timber growing here. Britton tells us that much of the timber used for the construction

favoured with due antiquarian observation. This is locally termed Grime's Dyke, and consists of a ditch, or hollow way, lying to the west of the road leading from Harrow to Watford. This dyke is in some places nearly twenty feet wide, but is chiefly overgrown by furze or screened by aquatic weeds." The heights of the Weald, on the common, present some extensive and beautiful landscape scenery.

The hamlet of Harrow Weald lies about two miles north-east of Harrow Station on the North-Western Railway, and consists of a few farm resi-

DISTANT VIEW OF HARROW.

of the roof of Henry VII.'s Chapel at Westminster Abbey was obtained from the forest about Harrow.

"Near the northern extremity of this Weald," observes the author of the "Beauties of England," "is a spot of ground supposed to be the most lofty elevation in the parish of Harrow, and which is said to form a landmark to mariners approaching England from the German Ocean. The attention of the person examining this elevated neighbourhood may be directed to some contiguous trees, so ancient, yet so sturdy under the wear of centuries, that, with a moderate license of conjecture, they may be supposed to present memorials of the great Forest of Middlesex. He will likewise find, near at hand, a curious, but obscure, vestige of some very remote age, which has hitherto not been

dences and private houses. It was formed into an ecclesiastical district in 1845, at which time a church was erected. This is a small building in the Decorated style, and is dedicated to All Saints. A lych-gate at the entrance to the churchyard was erected to the memory of the Rev. Edward Monro, the author of "Sacred Allegories," and who was for upwards of twenty years vicar of this parish, and who founded and conducted here a school for training Church schoolmasters.

Weald Park and Bentley Priory are the principal seats in this neighbourhood ; but, as the greater part of the latter estate lies in the parish of Stanmore, it will be best noticed in the chapter devoted to that place. The former, the seat of Mr. Alexander Sim, is a large castellated mansion on the left of the roadway leading to Bushey, and it stands on high ground, commanding a pleasant view for miles over the surrounding country. In the park is a mineral spring.

Harrow Weald, if it has produced no great and

century, the celebrated John Elwes, a member of Parliament, who possessed property in Marylebone* worth nearly half a million, was accustomed to push his horse across ploughed fields and dine upon hard eggs, to escape the ruinous

THE WELSH HARP AND RESERVOIR. (*See page* 275.)

distinguished men whose names have been handed down to us in the pages of history, has, at all events, contributed one individual whose eccentricities made him famous in his day: namely, Daniel Dancer, commonly known as "the miser of Harrow Weald Common." Probably no class of men has ever exhibited such painful and ludicrous eccentricities as those unhappy people who have devoted themselves to the amassing of money as an end in itself. Towards the end of the last

expense incidental to turnpikes and taverns; and this same legislator, who would play a rubber at whist for a couple of hundred guineas, walked home on foot every night from the gaming house, to save a shilling for a hackney coach! Again, Scheven, a rich banker of Hamburgh, who lived also in the last century, is said to have denied himself not only the comforts, but even the neces-

* See "Old and New London," Vol. IV., p. 242.

saries, of life; and, among other instances of penuriousness, it is recorded that after a faithful service of seventeen years he called in the aid of a German tailor for the purpose of attempting to *turn his coat!*

Daniel Dancer, who was born in 1716, was descended from a respectable yeoman's family in the county of Hertford, and his grandfather appears to have been settled at Bushey, near Watford, where he followed the occupations of mealman and maltster. His father, who resided at Stone Causeway, on Harrow Weald Common, possessed considerable property in land, which he farmed himself; he had four children, and on his death, in 1736, his eldest son, Daniel, succeeded to the estate.

It was in the paternal mansion at Astmiss, at Causeway-gate, that Daniel was doomed by the fates to spend the whole of his life, which seems to have been one uninterrupted dreary blank. His wretched habitation was surrounded by about eighty acres of his own rich meadow land, with some of the finest oak timber in the kingdom upon it; and he possessed an adjoining farm, called Waldos, the whole of the annual value of about £250 per annum, if properly cultivated. But *cultivation* was expensive, and so Daniel permitted grass only to grow there; indeed, in so neglected a state was the place for many years, that the house was entirely surrounded by trees, the fields were choked with underwood, and the hedges of such an amazing height as wholly to exclude the prospect of mankind, and create a dreary gloom all around. A tree had actually pushed its top through the roof of his house, which he entered by means of a ladder, dragged in after him; for he had fastened the rotten door on the inside, for fear of burglars, and determined never to enter the house again through that aperture. Dancer appears to have led the life of a hermit during more than half a century, and to have been as much unacquainted with, and unknown to, the world, although residing within ten or eleven miles of the capital, as if he had been the inhabitant of a desert. His only dealing with mankind arose from the sale of his hay; and he was seldom accosted by anybody, except when he wandered about the common to pick up a stray lock of wool, collect the dung of sheep under the hedges, or trudged along the road in search of paper, old iron, or cast horse-shoes.

His wealth thus brought him no happiness, but, on the contrary, it seemed to carry a curse along with it to its wretched possessor, for he is reported to have been robbed frequently to a large amount. In order the more effectually to secure his wealth and riches, he actually dug a hole, or what military men term a

trou de loup, before the entrance, which he covered over with loose straw, in such a manner as to secure the *principal approach* towards his castle, and entrap any incautious assailant who might have the temerity to invade his darling property. After exhibiting this specimen of his talents as an engineer, the modern Midas seems to have slept in safety amidst his gold.

His sister, who lived along with him for many years, at length died, and left a considerable sum of money behind her, which went towards the increase of his wealth, and served rather to stimulate than diminish his avarice. About this time he commenced an acquaintance with the Tempest family, which, while it soothed his pride, alleviated the sufferings and sorrows of his declining age. The following particulars concerning the death and burial of Miss Dancer are gleaned from a biographical sketch of the miser published shortly after his death:—

"Lady Tempest, who happened to live in his neighbourhood, compassionating the situation of Miss Dancer, took her into her house during her last illness, and treated her with uncommon kindness. But the disease, which, dreadful to relate, is supposed to have proceeded originally from inanition, proved mortal, and rendered all the good old lady's care ineffectual.

"Although Daniel never evinced any affection for his sister, he determined to bury her in such a manner as should not *disgrace the family.* He accordingly contracted with an undertaker, who agreed to take timber in return for a coffin, as Mr. Dancer had no idea of using the precious metals as a vehicle of exchange; he, however, could not be prevailed upon to purchase proper mourning for himself; yet, in consequence of the entreaty of his neighbours, he unbound the haybands with which his legs were usually covered, and drew on a second-hand pair of black worsted stockings. His coat was of a whitish-brown colour; his waistcoat had been black about the middle of the last century, and the immediate covering to his head, which seemed to have been taken from Mr. Elwes' wiggery, and to have descended to Daniel as an heirloom, gave a grotesque appearance to the person of a chief mourner but too well calculated to provoke mirth. This, indeed, was increased by the slipping of his horse's girth at the place of burial, in consequence of which the rider—to the great diversion of some of the Harrow boys who attended—was precipitated into the grave!"

The old miser at length died, in September, 1794, at the age of 78, and was buried in Harrow churchyard.

"Notwithstanding the miserable aspect of the house and its inhabitants—both brother and sister (the former especially, who was nearly naked)—yet on Daniel's death, not only plate, table-linen, and twenty-four pairs of good sheets, but clothes of every description, were found locked up in chests. The female attire, of which there was a correct inventory in the brother's own handwriting, was valued at seventeen pounds. He also, among other apparel, had some excellent boots; but he preferred to encase his legs with the still warmer covering of hay-bands.

"Although he possessed two ancient but tolerably good bedsteads, with the proper furniture, originally belonging, as well as the house, to the Edlins, a family of some property, yet they were carefully secluded from the light of heaven, and both he and his sister slept on sacks stuffed with hay, and covered with a horse rug.

"During the last twenty years Daniel's house is said to have been entered at least fourteen times by thieves, and the amount of his losses is calculated at two thousand five hundred pounds. As the lower part was in such a ruinous state as to admit a person with ease, it was recommended to him to get it repaired; but he replied, 'that this would be only throwing away more money, for then they would get in at the windows.' In order to employ the attention of the marauders, until he should escape to his hiding-place, he was accustomed to strew the ground floor with farthings and sixpences wrapped up in paper.

"The whole of Dancer's property, on his decease, amounted to about ten thousand pounds —a sum which, by proper management, he might have doubled, and at the same time allowed himself all the comforts of life.

"In his miserable habitation were found some hundred-weight of waste-paper, the collection of half a century, and two or three tons of old iron, consisting of nails, horse-shoes, &c., which he had picked up. On the ground floor several pieces of foreign gold and silver were dug up, and some coins, among which were a crown and a shilling of the English Commonwealth."

Roxeth, which unites itself with Harrow on the south-west side, was formerly an outlying hamlet, but since 1863 has been a distinct ecclesiastical district, separated from the parish church. It is, however, a separate manor from that of Harrow, having been granted by the Archbishop of Canterbury in the fourteenth century to Sir William Brembre and his heirs. Prior to that time it appears to have been merely an estate within the manor of Harrow, belonging to William Roxeth,

who was outlawed for felony. Christ Church, which was built in 1862, to meet the requirements of this rapidly-increasing district, is built in the Early English style, of flint, with stone and brick dressings.

Winding round the base of the hill in an easterly direction, we come next to Sudbury, another hamlet of Harrow. "Originally," as we learn from Kelly's "Directory of Middlesex," "it was a large tract of land, extending from the spot on which now stands the railway-station to the foot of Harrow Hill, known as Sudbury Common: it was enclosed shortly after the passing of an Act of Parliament in 1803; for civil purposes it forms a part of the parish of Harrow, but for ecclesiastical purposes part of it is attached to, and forms part of, the ecclesiastical parish of St. John's, Wembley." Sudbury, as a hamlet, is evidently a place of quite recent growth, for it is not described, or even mentioned, by Lewis in his "Topographical Dictionary." The manor of Sudbury—or, as it was formerly called, Southbury (the South Bury)—however, dates from a very remote period, having at the end of the fourteenth century formed, as above stated, part of the possessions of Archbishop Arundel, who was banished for high treason, when an inquisition was taken of his estates.

The church of the united district of Sudbury, Wembley, Appleton, and Preston, dedicated to St. John the Baptist, is situated near the Sudbury railway-station. It was built in 1846, from designs by Sir Gilbert Scott, and is in the Decorated style. In the neighbourhood of the church rows of cottages and a large number of villas have sprung up; and to meet the wants of the inhabitants there have been erected a district school, a Cottage Hospital, Workman's Hall, and a Young Men's Institute. Here, too, is the Girls' Home, a branch refuge for homeless girls of the National Refuges Institution, whose training ship for homeless boys has long been a familiar object off Greenhithe to passengers up or down the Thames. The building, known as Sudbury Hall, will accommodate 100 destitute girls, who are trained for domestic service.

From Sudbury we pass by a pleasant pathway to Wembley, about half a mile to the north-east.

The manor of Wembley in old times belonged to the Priory at Kilburn, in whose possession it continued down to the time of the Dissolution. It was afterwards granted by Henry VIII. to certain persons, who in the same year (1543) conveyed it to one Richard Page. The family of Page long possessed very considerable property in the county of Middlesex; and this property remained vested in their hands until the beginning of the present century, when it was sold by another Richard Page to the family of the Grays, the present owners. The manor-house was rebuilt by Mr. Gray about the year 1810, and is now the seat of the Rev. John Edward Gray. Wembley Park, some 250 acres in extent, is agreeably undulated, abundantly wooded, and watered by a branch of the river Brent.

From Wembley Hill, a local eminence, good views are obtained of the surrounding country. The top of the hill is occupied by the "Green Man" tavern, with its adjacent "tea-gardens," which are largely patronised during the summer months by holiday folks and Londoners.

The seats in this neighbourhood are Wembley House (Mr. John Turton Woolley), Hill House (Mr. Thomas Nicoll), and Oakington Park (Colonel the Hon. Wellington Talbot).

Continuing our course, by a somewhat circuitous path in a north-easterly direction, by Wembley Green, and skirting the park, we arrive at length at Kingsbury, a spot which happily still retains its rural character, and which is also one of the most charming resorts in the whole county for wild fowl and other aquatic birds. The Brent meanders pleasantly through the parish, whilst the meadows on either hand are intersected with field-paths, lanes, and flowery hedgerows, all combining to render it one of the most attractive in the vicinity of the metropolis for the lovers of country scenery. Dotting the lanes leading to the village, a picturesque antiquated cottage may here and there be met with, adding not a little to the rustic beauty of the scene. Altogether it is a curious old-fashioned, out-of-the-way place, with a population numbering about 600. Although most of the houses and farms are of modern growth, there is still, at all events, one cottage, mostly of wood, which dates from the thirteenth, or, at latest, from the fourteenth century.

A writer in the *Hampstead Express* recently, in drawing attention to the closing of some of the field-paths about Kingsbury, observes :—" Ruin seems unnoticed here, as it adds to ' the beautiful and wild.' Our noble old Brent river is a flowery stream ; Cæsar's mansion is gone, also another near it, and two deep recesses in the well-known ' Church-path' field adjoining the church mark the spots where, doubtless, the two old buildings tumbled down when they could stand no longer. Well, it is the same with Kingsbury Bridge in Neasdon Lane, which has fallen into the Brent stream on fragrant herbs and flowers, including wild rue, which is fragrance indeed. This adds to ruined grandeur here, and pilgrims come from all quarters. As history mentions Oliver Cromwell here, so we may imagine his friend Milton the poet, was, for Milton wrote his ' Paradise Regained ' a few miles 'farther west.' Then Lord Byron, when at Harrow School, loved the 'beautiful and wild' around it, so let us imagine him here also."

Kingsbury is bounded on the north by Whitchurch or Little Stanmore, on the east by Hendon, and on the south by Willesden. Westward, as shown above, lies the parish of Harrow, with its adjacent hamlets of Wembley, Sudbury, and Kenton. This parish is mentioned in the Domesday Book under the name of *Chingesberie*, from which circumstance it is conjectured by Mr. Brewer in his "Beauties of England," "it would appear to have formerly contained a royal residence. King Edward the Confessor," he adds, "gave to Westminster Abbey, at the time that he confirmed to that foundation the manor of Chelsea, a third of the fruit growing ' in his woods of Kyngesbyrig ;' and it is probable that a palace in this neighbourhood had appertained to some of the preceding Saxon monarchs." It may, however, be assumed that Kingsbury was merely a royal hunting-box in the weald of Middlesex when the kings of the Middle Saxons reigned at their traditional capital of Brentford. .

At the time of the Domesday survey this district doubtless formed part of the Great Forest of Middlesex ; at all events, it appears to have been thickly wooded, as it afforded "pannage for 1,200 hogs." At the beginning of the present century the whole parish was in the hands of the farmer ; it comprised about 1,500 acres of land, of which about thirty were woodland, sixty were arable, and the remainder were under cultivation as grass land. A large portion of the parish at the present time is covered by the Kingsbury reservoir, a sheet of water some 350 acres in extent. This reservoir, which is sometimes called "Kingsbury Lake," is about two miles in length, and, in one part, about a half a mile in width, the margin of the entire reservoir extending to about eight miles. It was formed in 1838, on that part of the Brent running from near Kingsbury church eastward, beyond the Brent bridge on the Edgware Road and the Welsh Harp station on the Midland Railway ; a branch of the reservoir extends northward on the Silk stream towards The Hyde and Hendon, crossing the Edgware Road at Silk Bridge. The reservoir was constructed for the purpose of supplying the locks of the Regent's Canal. It is well stocked with fish, and at different periods of the year it is still visited by almost all the known species of water-birds. A complete list of the various species of "waders" and of wild fowl that have been observed or shot here since the formation of the reservoir will be found in

"The Birds of Middlesex," by Mr. J. V. Harting, who lived for many years in this parish, and who has preserved a large number of specimens; as also have Mr. Mitford, of Hampstead, Captain Bond, of the Zoological Society's Gardens, and Mr. Warner, of the "Old Welsh Harp," at Kingsbury; these include all the known species of tern, whimbrels (or curlews), the several varieties of snipe, plovers, gulls, widgeons, and spoon-bills, and even such rare birds as the heron, the turnstone, the avocet, and the bar-tailed godwit. During the winter the wild duck and teal are frequent visitants. The fishing in the reservoir, which is rented by the worthy host of the "Welsh Harp," is strictly preserved. From the "Rules and Conditions of the Fishery," it appears that the period for jack and perch fishing extends from the 1st of June to the end of February, and that "bottom fishing" lasts all the year round; that the annual subscription is one guinea, and the charge for "daily fishing with live bait" is 2s. 6d., and for "daily bottom fishing," 1s. To many lovers of the rod and line these waters are comparatively unknown; most of its frequenters are members of recognised clubs, so that the "takes" are jealously weighed, and each finny specimen closely scrutinised. The kinds of fish taken here are jack, bream, perch, and carp, and the weights compare favourably with those of other spots where knights of the rod do mostly love to congregate.

In the rear of the "Welsh Harp," and abutting upon the lake, are some pleasantly-laid-out tea-gardens, which are much frequented during the summer, the boating on the lake serving as a special attraction.

In this parish, close to the "Welsh Harp," a race-course was laid out about twenty years ago, which enjoyed, not without good cause, the reputation of being a nuisance and a disgrace to the whole of our north-west suburbs. The race-meetings were low, vulgar, and commonplace to a degree, and were utterly ignored by the committees who arrange the details of Epsom and Ascot. Their name was unknown to the Jockey Club, and so they were under no sort of regulation which might operate as a guarantee of their being conducted honestly and respectably. They were started and maintained as a mere money speculation by the owners of neighbouring taverns, who netted large sums as "gate-money" as often as these occasions recurred. The bookmakers here were obliged in self-defence to take with them a body of prize-fighters, and the scenes which followed can be better imagined than described. So bad was their order, indeed, and so ineffectual proved all appeals to the law to put them down,

that in the end, about the year 1878, a Bill was introduced into Parliament to suppress all horse-races within ten or twelve miles of the metropolis; and this having been passed, Kingsbury races were abolished, and the racecourse has since been converted into the more creditable uses of a farm. That Kingsbury races were quite modern is proved by the fact that in Ruff's "Guide to the Turf" for 1863 not a single horse-race is mentioned as being run within twelve miles of London; whereas the names of the Alexandra Park, Brentwood, Bromley, Croydon, Ealing, Edgware, Eltham, Enfield, Finchley, Harrow, Hendon, Kingsbury, Lillie Bridge, Streatham, Uxbridge, and West Drayton, figure, in 1873, amongst others, in the list of "Suburban Meetings." At Kingsbury these meetings were held on an average four times a year.

Kingsbury Church stands away by itself at some little distance from the village. It is dedicated to St. Andrew, and is a small building, consisting of nave and chancel, and a wooden tower surmounted by a short spire. The stonework of the windows is of the Perpendicular style, and there was once a wooden porch here of the Decorated period, its barge-boards cut into a handsome ogee arch, but it has been removed. The church, however, is thought by Mr. M. H. Bloxam to be of Anglo-Saxon date, though its rude walls are covered over with coats of plaster and rough-cast, concealing the peculiar features of the structure. The building was restored about the year 1870, at which time the steeple was rebuilt. The churchyard is planted with evergreen shrubs which conceal and dampen the fabric itself.

Dr. Stukeley imagines that this church stands within the area of a Roman encampment, which was Cæsar's second station after his presumed passage of the Thames at Coway Stakes. * Gale, the antiquary, in reference to this opinion, observes that it certainly lies near the great Roman road which led from London to Sulloniacæ and thence to Verulamium (St. Albans). This church was visited by Gale in the summer of 1750, and is described by him as being built chiefly of Roman bricks, which Stukeley thought might have been taken from the ruins of Verulam, but which the former supposed to have "come from the *Kingsbury*, or *Villa Regia*, whence the parish appears to derive its name." "The alleged existence of a Roman castrametation on this spot," observes Mr. Brewer in the "Beauties of England," "may, possibly, be one of those chimerical speculations in which Dr. Stukeley was accustomed to indulge;

---

* See *ante*, p. 179.

but," he adds, "perhaps it may be worthy of notice that a field adjoining the churchyard exhibits evident marks of an artificial inequality of surface."

The church is old and weather-worn, and contains a few monuments of interest, notably one in the chancel, and enclosed by the altar-rails, to the memory of John Bul, who died in 1621. He was "Gentleman of the Poultry to Queen Elizabeth and King James;" and another dated 1626, to Thomas Scudamore, who was also a servant to those sovereigns for a period of 47 years. There is also

his "History of Animated Nature." Here Goldsmith was visited by Boswell, and Mickle, the translator of "The Lusiad." Boswell has inserted a notice of this visit in his "Life of Dr. Johnson." It appears that Goldsmith was not "at home;" "but having a curiosity," writes Boswell, "to see his apartments, we went in, and found curious scraps of descriptions of animals scrawled upon the walls with a black-lead pencil." It appears to have been in or about the year 1773 that Goldsmith joined a fellow-countryman and took up his

HIGH HOUSE FARM.

abode here, giving to the house the name of the "Shoemaker's Paradise," it having been built in a whimsical style by a knight of St. Crispin. Here, besides the works above named, he wrote his popular, but superficial, "History of England," which, on its first appearance, anonymously, passed for the production of Lord Lyttelton.

a brass to the memory of John Shephard and Ann and Matilda, his wives, with their eighteen children, and bears the date of 1520. William, third Earl of Mansfield, who died in 1840, is buried in a vault in the churchyard.

A pathway across the meadows northward of the churchyard leads to Fryern Farm and Kingsbury Green, a collection of cottages and villas somewhat larger than the village itself. From the Green a lane passes eastward to the Edgware Road, near the sixth milestone from London, and at a place called The Hyde. On the left of this lane is a farmhouse, called High House, or Hyde House, Farm, where Oliver Goldsmith was living when he wrote some portions of the "Vicar of Wakefield" and *She Stoops to Conquer*. He engaged this lodging chiefly "for the purpose of deep retirement," while preparing

The house is said to be between 200 and 300 years old, and is of brick, and of two floors. The front portion of the building, with the exception of some of the windows having been renewed and that the heavy beams of the ceiling have given place to flat stucco work, remains in much the same condition as when it was occupied by Goldsmith more than a century ago. The rooms at the back, however, were rebuilt only a few years ago, at which time a small chamber, which had been used by Goldsmith as his study, was unfortunately demolished. This room, we understand, contained a small cupboard, which might have been used by him as a book-case, and bore unmistakable signs of having been occupied by the author of "Animated Nature."

The hamlet of The Hyde is a row of houses and small shops bordering the high road ; but, beyond a Congregational chapel of Gothic design, possesses nothing to attract the notice of the passing stranger. Here the Passionists, under Father Spencer, were located before they settled at Highgate.*

John Lyon, the founder of Harrow School, possessed property not only at Harrow, but in Kingsbury. In the statutes which he made for the regulation of his school he directs that the governor "shall see and provide that tenn loads of wood, that is to say, six good loads of lath bavines, and fower good loads of tall wood, shall be yearely brought into ye schoolehouse from his lands att Kingsbury, to and for ye comon use of ye schollers of ye said schoole."

Kenton is a small hamlet belonging to Harrow, about midway between that town and the Hyde. The district is extremely rural, comprising, as it does, besides the "great house," called Kenton Lodge, and another mansion known as Kenton Grange, merely two or three farmhouses, with their attendant farm-buildings and cottages.

HENDON.

CHAPTER XXVII.

HENDON.

"Flumina amem sylvasque inglorius."—LUCRÆTIUS

Extent and Boundaries of the Parish—The Brent River and Silk Stream—The Old Watling Street—Etymology of Hendon—Mention of the Parish in "Domesday Book"—Descent of the Manor—A Singular Immunity from Tolls—The Manor House—Hendon Place—The Parish Church—Almshouses—Brent Street, Golder's Green—Mill Hill—The Grammar School—Roman Catholic Missionary College—St. Mary's Franciscan Nunnery—St. Margaret's Industrial School—Littleberries—Highwood House—Sir Stamford Raffles—Visit of Baron Bunsen—William Wilberforce the Philanthropist.

CROSSING the Edgware Road, and making our way in a north-easterly direction past the Hendon station on the Midland Railway, after a walk of about a mile up a somewhat steep lane, we find ourselves at the village of Hendon. This is an extensive parish, being about seven miles from north to south, and from two to four miles in width. It is bounded on the east and south-east by Finchley and Highgate, on the south by Hampstead, and on the north by Edgware and Barnet.

* See "Old and New London," Vol. V., p. 393.

The whole parish is pleasingly diversified by hills and valleys, the former commanding extensive and varied prospects, and the latter falling in gentle slopes, agreeably sprinkled with ornamental timber. The land is mostly laid out in meadows and pastures, intersected by pleasant field-paths and shady lanes and hedgerows ; and it is also well wooded, the trees yielding an abundance of timber. In the northern part of the parish the principal elevations are Highwood Hill, Mill Hill, and the rising ground occupied by Hendon village. In the south the little river Brent wanders through the meadows, its bulk being augmented by the numerous head-streams which take their rise in this parish. The Silk stream also flows through the valley westward of the village, and as stated in the preceding chapter, unites its waters with those of the Brent in the Kingsbury Reservoir.

According to Camden and Norden, a Roman road, supposed to be the Watling Street, passed along this neighbourhood, but no traces of it now remain, though the present Edgware Road is presumed to occupy its track. Norden was a resident at Hendon, and must therefore have possessed an accurate knowledge of the existing state of this parish in the time of James I. In his "Speculum Britanniæ" he describes this presumed Roman road as "an auncient high waie, leading to Edgeworth through an olde lane, called Hendon-wante.' The dedication to Norden's "Surveyor's Dialogue" (1607) is dated from his "poore house at Hendon." A lane leading through Colin Deep from Hendon to the Edgware Road is called in old surveys "Ancient Street."

The name of this parish is said to have been originally written *Heandune*, and is derived from two Saxon words which signify *High-down*, and which therefore apply very correctly to its elevated circumstances of situation. In "Domesday Book" the name of the place is written *Handone*, which Norden derives from *Highendune*, "which signifyeth Highwood, of the plenty of wood there growing on the hills." Taylor, in his "Words and Places," asserts that Hendon comes "from the Anglo-Saxon *hean*, poor." But to this Mr. James Thorne takes objection in his "Environs of London," where he says, "the soil is fertile rather than sterile, and it is to *héan*, high, rather than *hean*, poor, that we may look for the probable derivation."

At the time of the Domesday survey—and indeed for some time previously—the manor of Hendon belonged to the Abbots of Westminster. "There was land for sixteen ploughs," and "a priest had one virgate," which would of course imply that there was a church here at that early period. The survey adds that "there was meadow sufficient for two oxen, and pannage for 1,000 hogs," so that it would appear that the greater part of the land formed part of the forest of Middlesex.

The principal manor was alienated by Gervais de Blois, Abbot of Westminster, in the reign of King Stephen, and it continued in lay hands till early in the fourteenth century. During a part of this time it was held by the Le Rous family, who, according to Lysons, probably had a residence here, for, in the 50th year of Henry III., Geoffrey le Rous, Sheriff of the counties of Bedford and Bucks, "petitioned for a remuneration for the burning of his houses and corn, and for the loss of horses, arms, clothes, and other goods, of which he had been despoiled at his manor of Hendon, by John de Egville and other turbulent chiefs of that period, to whom he might officially have made himself obnoxious." In 1312 the manor was restored to the Abbey of Westminster, having been exchanged by the then holder, Richard le Rous, for that of Hodford, also in this parish, and it was afterwards made part of the endowment of the newly-created bishopric of Westminster. The name of Hodford is still given to some of the lands belonging to the Dean and Chapter of Westminster, at North End, bordering on Hampstead Heath. On the dissolution of the see of Westminster in 1550, this manor was granted by the Crown to Sir William Herbert, with whose descendants, the Earls of Powis, it remained till the middle of the last century, when it was purchased by the celebrated David Garrick. A nephew of his, the Rev. George Garrick, was vicar of Hendon for some time. In 1790, after Garrick's death, the manor was sold to a Mr. John Bond, and it has since changed hands several times.

This parish, observes Mr. Brewer, in his work already quoted, possesses a singular *immunity*, which was granted as early as the year 1066, and was confirmed by various subsequent charters. Divers lands in this parish had been granted by King Edward the Confessor to the church of St. Peter at Westminster, that monarch at the same time freeing the inhabitants from all *tolls*, both by land and water. Henry III. and Richard II., by charters, the former dated at Woodstock in the ninth year, and the latter at Westminster, in the seventeenth year, of their respective reigns, confirmed these immunities, which were further conceded and confirmed by the several charters of Henry VIII., Edward VI., and James I. Lastly, William and Mary, by letters patent dated at Westminster in the fifth year of their reign, granted and confirmed to Sir William Rawlinson, Serjeant-at-law, the charters of their predecessors, with all their privileges; and thereby "freed the inhabitants of Hendon from all tolls in all fairs and markets, and from all street tolls, and every other toll whatever, in every fair and every market, and every bridge, and every way and water, and also by sea, for themselves and their wares, for ever."

The manor-house stood near Church End, which is the name given to a cluster of houses built in the neighbourhood of the church, and on or near the site now occupied by Hendon Place. The original mansion was used, in the early part of the sixteenth century, as a country residence by the abbot of Westminster. It was here that Wolsey first rested, when travelling, in a state of disgrace, towards York. Stow, in his "Annals," says that the Cardinal "having sent to London for livery clothes for his servants that should ride with him, in the beginning of Passion week, before Easter, set forward and rode from Richmond to a place of the Abbot of Westminster at Hendon." Norden, writing in the time of Elizabeth, describes the manor-house as the property of Sir Edward Herbert, and the residence of Sir John Fortescue. The family of Nicoll appear to have resided here during the greater part of the seventeenth century. The house was purchased towards the middle of the last century by a Mr. Thomas Snow, who took down the ancient building, which is described as having contained "a spacious gallery," and erected the present house. Among the later occupants of the house have been the Earl of Northampton and Lord Chief Justice Tenterden.

Hendon Place is a well-proportioned and handsome mansion, comprising a body and two wings, and the grounds are rendered attractive by various picturesque undulations. The river Brent, which skirts the eastern side of the grounds, has been artificially widened so as to form a moderate lake, which, with the bridge by which it is crossed, adds not a little to the beauty of the landscape. There are several fine trees on this estate, and among them one or two flourishing cedars. In the *Gentleman's Magazine* for 1779 is a communication from Sir John Cullum, giving the dimensions of a large cedar which formerly stood on the north side of Hendon Place, but which was blown down by a high wind on the 1st of January in that year.

The parish church of Hendon occupies an elevated position on the brow of a hill immediately to the north of the main street. It is a plain-looking edifice, the walls, with the exception of the tower, being covered with plaster. It comprises a nave with clerestory and aisles, a chancel with side chapels, and a square stone tower, with embattled parapets, at the west end; this latter is evidently the most ancient part of the fabric. The greater portion of the church was probably erected late in the fifteenth century, but the windows are mostly modern: those of the clerestory and at the east end of the chancel are filled with painted glass. The font is Norman, square in form, and ornamented on each of the four sides with an arcade of round-headed interlaced arches. The arches of the nave spring from octagonal columns; the whole body and aisles of the church are encumbered with unsightly pews and deep galleries.

In the north chapel of the chancel is the tomb of Sir William Rawlinson, one of the Commissioners of the Great Seal, who died in 1703: the effigy of the deceased, by Rysbach, is represented in a semi-recumbent attitude, attired in legal robes and insignia. Close by is an elaborate monument of veined marble to Edward Fowler, Bishop of Gloucester, who died in 1714. At the west end of the north aisle is the burial-place of Sir Francis Whichcote and his family, over which is an apartment fitted up and used as a vestry-room, by permission of Sir Francis. On the south side of the chancel is a mural tablet to several of the family of Colmore, of Warwickshire. This monument is the work of Flaxman, and bears upon it the emblems of Faith and Hope. There is also a handsome monument to the memory of several branches of the Herbert family, many of whom are buried in this church; Sir Coutts Trotter, Bart., who died in 1838, is also commemorated by an elaborate mural monument. A brass in this church bears date 1564; there is another, very ancient, without date, embedded in a stone slab in front of the vestry door.

In the churchyard, among other tombs and monuments, are those of Sir Joseph Ayloffe, Bart., a distinguished antiquary, and Keeper of the State Papers, who died in 1781; Nathaniel Hone, R.A., who died in 1784; Abraham Raimbach, engraver, who died in 1843, and whose name will be remembered for his numerous works after Wilkie. James Parsons, M.D., "eminent as a physician, man of science, and antiquary," who died in 1770, is commemorated by a monument; and there are also the family vaults of the Earls of Mansfield, and many other local worthies, including Charles Johnson, a dramatist, dated 1748; Edward Longmore, the "Herefordshire Colossus," seven feet six inches high, who died in 1777; and Sarah Gundry, who died in 1807, and whose grave-stone is noticeable on account of its epitaph, which runs as follows :—

" Reader ! she wander'd all the desert through
In search of happiness, nor found repose
Till she had reach'd the borders of this waste.
Full many a flower that blossom'd in her path
She stoop'd to gather, and the fruit she pluck'd
That hung from many a tempting bough—all but
The rose of Sharon and the tree of life.
This flung its fragrance to the gale, and spread
Its blushing beauties : that its healing leaves
Displayed, and fruit immortal, all in vain.
She neither tasted nor admired—and found
All that she chose and trusted fair, but false !
The flowers no sooner gather'd than they faded ;
The fruits enchanting, dust and bitterness ;
And all the world a wilderness of care.
Wearied, dispirited, and near the close
Of this eventful course, she sought the plant
That long her heedless haste o'erlook'd, and proved
Its sovereign virtues ; underneath its shade
Outstretch'd, drew from her wounded feet the thorns,
Shed the last tear, breathed the last sigh, and here
The aged pilgrim rests in trembling hope ! "

The churchyard is kept in very good condition, and from the entrance-gate to the south door of the church runs an avenue of clipped lime-trees, which has a very pretty effect, and there are also several yew-trees of moderate size ; whilst the view from the north side of the old churchyard embraces a large extent of country, including Stanmore, Edgware, Harrow, and the distant hills of Buckinghamshire and Hertfordshire, together with the hamlets of Highwood and Mill Hill, to which latter place a pleasant footpath leads across the intervening valley.

Hendon is a vicarage, but was anciently a rectory also, the latter being a sinecure. The rectors presented the vicars until late in the fifteenth century, when the church was appropriated to the abbot and convent of Westminster, with whom the right of presentation remained until the dissolution of monastic houses. Later on, the advowson was granted, with the manor, to the Herbert family, and it descended in conjunction with the manorial property until the year 1794, when it passed into separate hands.

At a short distance from the church, at the entrance to the main street, are almshouses for six poor men and four women, erected in 1729. They were founded in 1681 by Robert Daniel, who bequeathed the sum of £2,000 for the purpose of building " an almshouse within twelve miles of London." The almshouses, which are of red brick, were repaired in 1853.

At Burrows, a hamlet lying on the road between the village and the railway-station, is the Metro-

politan Convalescent Institution, which affords a comfortable home for forty little girls.

Races have taken place here yearly since 1864, but they have proved to be a great nuisance to the inhabitants.

Brent Street is the name given to a hamlet of Finchley ; one of the houses here was formerly the seat of the Whichcotes, and afterwards of Sir William Rawlinson, whose monument has been already noticed in the church. Although it has been modernised, some parts of the house appear to be of considerable antiquity. A new chapel-of-ease, Christ Church, was built here in the year 1881, the "foundation stone" being laid by Lady Burdett-Coutts. The building is in the Early English style, and was erected from the designs of Mr. Salter. A spacious Congregational church, of Gothic design, has been erected in this locality ; and at the lower end of the street a bridge over the river Brent leads to Golder's Green, another hamlet of Hendon, which is pleasantly situated on the road to Hampstead.

Golder's Green consists of a few decent cottages and villa residences fringing the roadside, the larger part of the "green" proper being now enclosed. The "White Swan" tavern, with its tea-gardens, is a favourite resort of London holiday-makers in the summer-time, the various walks by rural lanes and field-paths in the immediate neighbourhood adding much to the charm of the locality. Of Golder's Hill, at North End, which was once the residence of Jeremiah Dyson, clerk to the House of Commons, and the friend of Mark Akenside the author of the "Pleasures of Imagination," an account will be found in OLD AND NEW LONDON, in the chapter on Hampstead.* Akenside was a frequent guest at his friend's house here, and often made it his home. In one of his poems, " An Ode on Recovery from a Fit of Sickness in the Country," written in 1758, Akenside thus apostrophises this lovely spot :—

" Thy verdant scenes, O Golder's Hill,
    Once more I seek, a languid guest ;
With throbbing temples and with burden'd breast
Once more I climb thy steep aërial way.
O faithful cure of oft returning ill,
    Now call thy sprightly breezes round,
    Dissolve this rigid cough profound,
And bid the springs of life with gentler movement play."

Page Street is the name of a small hamlet which lies in the valley between Hendon Church and Mill Hill. The most conspicuous object here is Copt Hall, the residence of the Nicoll family. The

---

* See Vol. V., p. 448.

house was built early in the seventeenth century by Randall Nicoll, Esq., and is a fair example of the domestic architecture of that age.

Mill Hill surmounts a fine swell of ground, which rises by an easy progress to a considerable height, and the views afforded at different stages of the ascent are both extensive and varied, including, it is said, on clear days, the distant towers of Windsor Castle. Mill Hill has numbered among its inhabitants one or two individuals whose names have become famous. Peter Collinson, the naturalist, had a house here, and formed a curious botanical garden. Linnæus commemorated a visit to this garden by planting several trees. The premises were afterwards purchased by means of a subscription among the Independents for the purpose of a foundation grammar-school, and is now known as Mill Hill College. The school was till lately the only public school for Protestant Nonconformists. It is stated in the *Mirror* (August 8th, 1835) that the original school-house here could boast of having been once the "dwelling of Linnæus, and the occasional residence of architects."

The Nonconformists' Grammar School was established on the basis of a sectional, if not sectarian, limitation only, because all the old foundations were exclusive and sectarian in the opposite direction. Even as a Nonconformist's school, Mill Hill has had a history. It had not only educated many men well known to Evangelical Nonconformity, but some men of larger reputation had been among its alumni. The late Justice Talfourd, Mr. Challis (the astronomer), and Dr. Jacobson (the present Bishop of Chester) were all educated at Mill Hill in the old days. "As the more national foundations became less sectarian," observes a writer in the *Daily News*, "so the Dissenting schools have become less Dissenting. The old Nonconformists always declared that Dissent was forced upon them as an unwelcome necessity, and in the matter of education their descendants are giving proof of the statement. As a sign of the times, we note this change with unmixed satisfaction. It is one of the good results of rendering our middle-class education as far as possible unsectarian. A like policy applied to the highest education in the universities and to the lowest education in the primary schools will have a similar result."

The present building was erected by Sir William Tite in 1825. It is simple and bold, rather than grand, and forms a long Italian villa on a terrace. Its chief front looks away from the road, and commands a fine view of Harrow. It has a noble portico supported by six Italian pillars, and surmounted by a pediment. The dining-hall is near the centre; the chapel at the north end is a poor, mean structure. The cost of the building was above £25,000.

The opening of the universities to Dissenters has helped to fill the school, as, happily, it is now worth the while of Nonconformists, with a view to the advantages held out by the older universities, to be at the expense of a classical education for their sons.

Mill Hill was once the residence of John Wilkes, the politician, and of the late Alderman Sir Charles Flower.

In the "Beauties of England" we read:—"There still remains (1816) on Mill Hill, though in an almost ruinous state, one of the ancient domestic structures of the neighbourhood. This building is in the best taste of the reign of Charles I. The walls of one of the apartments are curiously painted with the story of the Prodigal Son, and over the chimney are the initials of the Nicoll family. The house is now divided, and tenanted by the poor." This building, however, appears to be long since clean swept away; at all events, nothing is now known of its existence at Mill Hill.

Hendon seems to have long been in high favour with Roman Catholics. The "Dames de Nazareth," founded in France by the Duchesse de la Rochefoucauld for the higher education of young ladies, have an establishment here, which is under the special patronage of the Cardinal Archbishop of Westminster; and here they receive, in addition to their French pupils, a limited number of English young ladies.

St. Joseph's College of the Sacred Heart, for Foreign Missions, founded by Bishop Vaughan of Salford, is at Mill Hill. The first stone of this institution was laid by Archbishop (Cardinal) Manning in 1869, and a portion was completed and opened in 1871. The grounds of the college are about forty acres in extent, and the buildings, which are somewhat heavy and in the monastic style, were erected from the designs of Mr. G. Goldie. The architecture of the college is "Lombardo-Venetian," and it is built in the form of a quadrangle surrounded by cloisters, one side of which is occupied by the chapel, which has a lofty campanile tower, surmounted by a gilded statue of St. Joseph, which is seen for miles around. Students of every nationality are admitted, and bind themselves by solemn vows to leave Europe for life upon missionary labours.

Two other Roman Catholic institutions are located at Mill Hill: namely, the Franciscan convent of St. Mary and the St. Margaret's Industrial School.

The church for the ecclesiastical district of Mill Hill was built in 1832, by William Wilberforce. It is dedicated to St. Paul, and is in the Early English style. It is a poor structure. Six alms-houses near the church were erected in 1696, at the charge of Thomas Nicoll, of this parish, for the use of the poor.

Among the seats and mansions in this neigh-

Mr. Scharf gives the following interesting particulars concerning this old house, which stands on a slope near the public road :—

"The mansion is an ordinary square building of red brick, with irregular corners, that has been much added to at various times. The entrance door leads directly into the hall, which has a low flat ceiling, the floor being on a level with the carriage-drive in front. The rooms are irregular, but they enclose a central apartment, which appears

LITTLEBERRIES.

bourhood is Littleberries, a good old substantial residence of brick, which tradition says was built by Charles II. It is often said also that Nell Gwyn lived here; but the assertion rests only on tradition. The house probably does date back to the days of Charles II., and in one room are medallion portraits, which tradition has assumed to be of that king and some of his mistresses, but which, in the opinion of Mr. George Scharf, the Secretary of the National Portrait Gallery, are representations of sovereigns of much more recent date. It has also been stated that the house was at one time tenanted by Louise de Quérouaille, Duchess of Portsmouth; but this is very doubtful.

In *Notes and Queries* for January 21st, 1882,

to have belonged to a former and much more important residence. This central apartment is not large, but lofty; it is floored with wood, and has only one actual door, opening into the staircase hall. It contains an amount of rich wood-carving and mural decoration; it is known as the Gilt Room. Broken pediments, Greek frets, guilloches, egg-and-tongue mouldings, shell patterns, festoons, female masks, and lions' heads are to be seen everywhere. The tone of this elaborate ornamentation is of the period of Queen Anne or the two first Georges."

The panels of the "Gilt Room" are painted with copies, full size, of pictures by Rubens, Van Dyck, and other artists, and of such subjects as "Venus and Cupid," "Hesperides Gathering Fruit," &c. One picture, however, is of a totally different character to the rest : it represents the full-length figure of a young lad, standing, and wearing the robes of the Garter. It is inscribed : "Charles Lennox, Duke of Richmond and Lennox, Born 29 July, 1672, Dyed 27 May, 1723." This picture, in the opinion of Mr. Scharf, seems to have been inserted in the panel in the place of something else. In the coved cornice of this apartment, over the centre of each wall, is a large circular medallion in white plaster of a crowned sovereign, the size of life, in alto-relievo. That above the fire-place, observes Mr. Scharf, in the article above quoted, contains a portrait of Caroline of Anspach, queen consort of George II., of whom there is a portrait on the opposite wall. On the side facing the door, and over the windows, the medallion exhibits a portrait of George I., whilst the remaining medallion, over the door, contains a portrait of William III. The chimney-piece of this room is elaborately carved in wood, the principal figures in the ornamentation being emblematic of "Justice" and "Peace."

SIR STAMFORD RAFFLES.
(*From the bust by Chantrey.*)

"Throughout the whole buildings," observes Mr. Scharf, in the article from which we have quoted above, "there is no indication, either by coronet, garter, or heraldic cognizance, that the place ever belonged to any person of rank or distinction. The only exception where heraldry appears is in the pediment of the summer-house at the end of the grounds. There the arms of the Pawsons of Shawdon, in Northumberland, are carved on a plain shield, and may be referred to a period when the front of the building was altered, and the spaces between the columns filled in with windows of coloured glass. The walls and domed ceiling of the summer-house are decorated with figures and ornaments in white plaster. They include portrait medallions of females, supported by sphinxes, mermaids, and tritons. These faces are all in profile, full of individuality, and probably

represented members of the family who then occupied the house. On the east wall is a curious circular medallion, containing a view in white plaster alto-relievo of the mansion as it formerly appeared from this spot, showing the different levels of ground, and reproducing the building in its original state, including the Gilt Room and steps leading up to it. We see by this that the central façade was flanked on each side by massive walls, large windows, and an elevated roof. In the sloping plane in front of the house there are no basins of water ; nor is any figure introduced so as to give indication by the costume of the exact period when the view was taken."

At Highwood Hill, at the distance of about a mile from Mill Hill, at one time—namely, from 1826 to 1831—lived the great philanthropist, William Wilberforce ; and here, too, dwelt Lord William Russell, previous to his arrest. Highwood House, early in the present century, was the residence of Sir Stamford Raffles, Governor of Java, and founder and first President of the Zoological Society. Wilberforce became Sir Stamford Raffles's "next-door neighbour" in June, 1826, only about a month before the death of the latter. Lady Raffles continued to reside here after the death of her husband, and was here visited on more than one occasion by Baron Bunsen. In the Baroness Bunsen's "Memoirs of Baron Bunsen" appears the following reference to the house and grounds, under the date of 1839 :—

"A visit to Highwood gave an opportunity for commenting upon the dignity, the order, the quiet activity, the calm cheerfulness with which Lady Raffles rules the house, the day, the conversation ; and the place and its neighbourhood were full of those memorials of the honoured dead which served to enhance the natural beauty of the prospect and the interest attaching itself to the residence of Sir Stamford Raffles. The ground of Highwood must have been trodden by the footsteps and hallowed by the life and sorrows of Rachel,

Lady Russell, even though no family recollection exists to mark the spot which she inhabited, when she dated some of her letters from Totteridge, a village lying near. But the beautiful portion of wood in which Lady Raffles' friends have enjoyed walking with her contains within its precincts a chalybeate spring, walled round, and marked by an inscription as having been enclosed by Mistress Rachel Russell, at a date when the eldest daughter of Lord and Lady Russell must have been under twelve years old ; yet is there nothing unreasonable in the supposition that the mother should have caused the work to be performed as a public benefit (the healing quality of the spring being in repute among the poor), and assigned to it the name of her daughter instead of her own. Moreover, in that wood there is a spot, evidently cleared of trees in a regular circle, from the centre of which it was remembered by the lower class of

inhabitants, at the time when Sir Stamford Raffles made the purchase of the ground, that a previous proprietor, about the middle of the last century, had caused the loose stones to be removed, which formed a 'monument to the memory of the gentleman who was beheaded.' This piece of forest might have been a portion of Lady Russell's own large Southampton inheritance ; as an original Russell property it is gone out of remembrance."

Here, at Moat Mount, lived for some time the late Mr. Serjeant Cox, Recorder of Portsmouth, and latterly an assistant judge at the Middlesex Sessions. His name is well known as a man of science and a philanthropist, and as the establisher of the *Field*, *Queen*, and *Law Times* newspapers. He died suddenly in 1880. Mrs. Porter, an actress of some note in the last or beginning of the present century, was also a resident here for many years.

CHAPTER XXVIII.

EDGWARE AND LITTLE STANMORE.

"Lives of great men all remind us
We can make our lives sublime ;
And, departing, leave behind us
Footprints on the sands of time."—LONGFELLOW

Situation and Boundaries of Edgware—General Appearance of the Town—The "Chandos Arms" Inn—The "Harmonious Blacksmith"—Etymology of Edgware—The Descent of the Manor—The Manor of Edgware Bois—Edgware Market—Curious Local Customs—Death of Cosway the Artist—The Parish Church—Almshouses—Population, &c.—Edgware Races—Little Stanmore or Whitchurch—Acreage and Population—Early History of the Manor—Canons—The Family of the Lakes—James Brydges, afterwards Duke of Chandos—He Rebuilds the Mansion of Canons in a magnificent and costly manner—The Parish Church—Handel as Organist here—The "Harmonious Blacksmith."

THE town of Edgware, which we now reach by a cross-road westward from Mill Hill, Hendon, from which it is distant about two miles, together with the neighbouring estate of Canons, has been for the last century and a half associated with no less a name than that of Handel. On this account alone the spot would be worthy of a pilgrimage, notwithstanding that "princely Canons" is a thing of the past.

Edgware is eight miles from Hyde Park Corner, and extends for about a mile along the great high road to St. Albans (*Verulamium*), a thoroughfare which, as we have stated in the preceding chapter, is supposed by Camden, Norden, and other antiquaries, to occupy the track of the ancient Watling Street. The parish is bounded on the east and west by Hendon and Little Stanmore, and on the north and south by Elstree and Kingsbury. The town consists mainly of one wide and long street, made up of the usual class of buildings to be met

with in a small country town, namely, shops mostly small and antiquated, humble cottages, mixed up with a few dwelling-houses of a better kind. There are also a few respectable taverns and hostelries, which, doubtless, in the "good old coaching days" were houses of some consequence. One of these, "The Chandos Arms," keeps in remembrance the associations of the neighbouring palace of Canons. In one of the rooms of this inn is an antiquated fireplace, which was brought from Canons, on the demolition of that mansion. The west side of the street belongs in reality to the parish of Little Stanmore, or Whitchurch. The visitor to Edgware will now look in vain for the blacksmith's shop, in which, according to tradition, Handel took shelter during a shower, and in which worked William Powell, the Edgware blacksmith—or, as he is commonly called, the "Harmonious Blacksmith"—whose performance on the anvil is said to have suggested to Handel the well-known melody named after him.

Of this worthy we shall have more to say on reaching Whitchurch, where he was buried, and where Handel was for many years organist.

Norden conjectures that the name of this parish was originally Edgworth, " signifying a fruitful place upon the edge, or utter part, of the shire ; " but such a mode of etymology, Mr. Brewer contends, in the " Beauties of England," appears to rest entirely on surmise. The Irish Edgworths, of Edgworthtown, whose name has been made so widely known by the writings of Miss Edgworth, came originally from this place, if we may believe their pedigree as set forth by Sir Bernard Burke. Lysons observes that in the most ancient record in which he has seen the name mentioned (dated in the reign of Henry II.) it is written "Eggeswere;" and that the same form of orthography prevailed until the age of Henry VIII., when the present mode of spelling was adopted, and has since been uniformly used in legal and in ordinary writings.

The name of Edgware, or even Eggeswere, does not appear in " Domesday Book." In the latter part of the twelfth century, according to Lysons, the principal manor belonged to Ella, Countess of Salisbury, wife of William Longespee, "who granted it to her son Nicholas and his espoused wife, to be held of her by the render of a sparrow-hawk." Towards the close of the succeeding century, Henry de Lacy, Earl of Lincoln, was the owner of this manor, in right of his wife, Margaret, Countess of Salisbury. The property was afterwards conveyed in marriage by the daughter and heiress of the last Earl of Lincoln, of the De Lacy family, to the Le Stranges, with whom it continued down to the year 1431, when it passed to the Darells, by whom again it was sold shortly after to Thomas Chichele and other persons, as trustees for All Souls' College, Oxford. With that college the property still continues. An inferior manor within this parish, called Bois, or Edgware Bois, was formerly owned by the Priory of St. John of Jerusalem, and afterwards by the Dean and Chapter of Windsor. In the Chartulary of the Priory of St. John this manor is styled *Egelware Bois*, or *Eggesware*. Towards the end of the fifteenth century, this manor having passed by exchange or otherwise to the Dean and Chapter of Westminster, was surrendered by that body to the king. Henry VIII. granted it, in the year 1544, to Sir John Williams and Anthony Stringer, from whom it passed by sale to the Pages. It was afterwards owned by the Earl of Coventry, and subsequently sold to the Lees, by whose representative it is still held. A hamlet, now called Edgware-Bury, lies about a mile and a half northward from the town.

About two miles beyond the town, on the borders of the county, is an eminence called Brockley Hill, which by Camden and other antiquaries is supposed to be the site of the Roman station Sulloniacæ. Of the numerous Roman remains which have been discovered at different times both here and at places in the immediate neighbourhood, we shall have more to say in the next chapter.

Edgware had in former times a weekly market on Thursdays, but that had been " for some time discontinued " when Lysons wrote his "Environs of London" in 1795. Indeed, it is on record that as far back as 1668 the site of the market was conveyed by Sir Lancelot Lake, of Canons, to certain trustees upon trust for a public school. In the year 1867 the Privy Council licensed the holding of a cattle market here on the last Thursday in every month.

The parish records contain some curious items, referring to customs which have long since become obsolete. From some of these, quoted by Lysons, it appears that in 1328 one hundred acres of land were held under the manor of Edgware by the render of a pair of gilt spurs, and fifty acres by the rent of a pound of "cummin." At the court held in 1551, two men were fined here for playing at " cards and tables." In the next year the inhabitants were " presented " for not having a " tumbrel and cucking-stool "—the latter, of course, as a terror to " scolds." In 1558 a man was fined for selling ale at an " exorbitant price," namely, one pint and a half for a penny !

Sir William Blackstone mentions a curious custom appertaining to the manor of Edgware, namely, that it was usual for the lord to provide a minstrel, or piper, for the amusement of the tenants while they were employed in his service— a custom which has been kept in remembrance by the name given to a small tract of land in this parish, called " Piper's Green."

It was on the road to Edgware that the artist Cosway, the favourite of the Prince of Wales, suddenly breathed his last, at the age of eighty, in 1821, whilst being taken out for an airing in the carriage of a friend.

The parish church of Edgware, dedicated to St. Margaret, stands about the middle of the town, on the east side of the roadway, and, with the exception of the tower, is modern and uninteresting. It consists of a chancel, nave, and transepts, and is built of brick, in imitation of the Perpendicular style. The tower, which is constructed of flint and stone, and has an embattled parapet and an octagonal angle turret, is part of a former church, which is supposed to have belonged to a religious house, or monastery, dedicated to St. John of Jerusalem. Kelly tells us, in his "Directory of Middlesex," that "amongst the Augmentation Records is preserved a certificate of the goods and plate of the church and monastery of Edgware at the time of the dissolution of religious houses." The body of the original church having become dilapidated, was rebuilt about the middle of the last century, and this again was renewed or rebuilt in 1845. The east window, of three lights, is filled with stained glass, as also are those of the transepts. The only monument in the church worthy of notice is one to Randulph Nicoll, who died in 1658. He was a native of this parish, and, if the Latin inscription on his monument may be trusted, a man of great learning and accomplishments. In the chancel is a brass representing an infant in swaddling clothes, inscribed "Anthonie, son of John Childe, goldsmith;" the said infant died in 1599, aged three weeks.

The Rev. Francis Coventry, the author of the romance entitled "The Life of Pompey the Little," and of the fifteenth number of the *World*, containing strictures on modern gardening, &c., held the incumbency of this church in the last century. The Rev. Thomas Martyn, Professor of Botany at Cambridge, also held the living for some years.

Close by the church was, in pre-Reformation times, a call, or station, belonging to the abbey of St. Albans, which served as a halting-place for the monks in their journeys to and from London.

In 1680, Samuel Atkinson, a native of Edgware, built and endowed almshouses here for four poor women. There are also in the town almshouses for twelve poor persons, endowed by the late Mr. Charles Day.

Edgware is one of the polling-places for the county of Middlesex, and at the present time the terminus of a branch line of the Great Northern Railway from their main line at Finsbury Park. The town is also within a mile and a half of the Mill Hill Station, on the Midland Railway. At the end of the last century the number of houses in the town, exclusive of almshouses, was 76. In 1871 they had increased to 137, or nearly doubled. The population at the last-mentioned date was 655, to which nearly two hundred more have since been added.

Races were held at Edgware in 1869 and 1873, but they did not acquire the popularity of those at Hampton, Sandown, and other suburban racecourses. They have now died a natural death.

Little Stanmore—or Whitchurch, as the village is more popularly called—lies about half a mile to the west of Edgware. The parish, with the exception of that portion forming one side of the main street of Edgware, is almost wholly agricultural. The entire area of the parish is rather over 1,500 acres, and the number of the inhabitants in 1881 amounted to 818. Much of the land in the parish bordering the main road northward of Edgware is taken up by the demesne of Canons, whilst the remainder is occupied by broad undulating meadows, intersected by shady lanes and avenues of stately trees.

The parishes of Little Stanmore and Edgware run parallel northward as far as Elstree, in Hertfordshire, the boundary of the two being in the middle of the road, in a similar manner to that in which Hendon and Kingsbury are separated. It is probable that at the time of the Domesday Survey both the parishes of Stanmore Magna (Great Stanmore) and Stanmore Parva (Little Stanmore) were united. In that record it is stated that " Roger de Rames held in Stanmere nine hides and a half;" and it is further set forth that "there was land for seven ploughs, pannage for eight hundred hogs, pasture for the cattle of the village," &c. The land held by Roger de Rames—or Reymes, as the name is sometimes written—had been, previous to the Conquest, in the hands of Algar, "a servant of Earl Harold." It was possibly a subordinate manor, and it continued for several generations in the possession of the family of Rames, who owned also much landed estate in the neighbouring county of Essex, which was constituted a barony. Lysons observes that this manor was "in Stanmore Parva, and appears to have been of equal extent with the Earl of Cornwall's manor in Great Stanmore." At the marriage of Isabel, sister of Henry III., with Frederick, Emperor of Germany, " half a knight's fee was paid by Henry Bocoynte for his lands in the parish of Stanmore Parva, held of the Barony of William de Raymes." The estate next passed into the hands of the Prior of St. Bartholomew, in Smithfield, from which circumstance it is conjectured that the property received the ecclesiastical name of "Canons;" for on the dissolution of religious houses, the estate was granted, under the name of the "manors of Canons and Wimborough, in Whitchurch," to Hugh Losse. The old house now known as the "Chandos Arms," on the Whitchurch side of Edgware Street, is supposed by Lysons to have been the mansion formerly occupied by the Losse family. Over the chimney-piece in one of the rooms were formerly to be seen the arms of Losse, with the initials R. L. (Robert Losse), and the date 1557. The next occupiers of Canons were the family of Franklyn, who were living there in the reign of

Elizabeth. John Franklyn, who died in 1596, was buried in the parish church. Early in the seventeenth century the estate was sold by Sir Hugh Losse to Sir Thomas Lake, who had been in early life the amanuensis of Sir Francis Walsingham, and who held the office of Clerk of the Signet to Queen Elizabeth, and also occupied the post of principal Secretary of State under James I.

In this latter capacity Sir Thomas appears to have conducted himself with equal integrity and talent. Fuller, in his "Worthies," says that his "dexterity of dispatch and his secrecy were incredible." But he had unhappily become involved by his wife in a quarrel with the Countess of Essex, and was in consequence dismissed from his office, and sent as a prisoner to the Tower, and fined in the sum of £15,000. In the "Sidney Papers" it is stated that the king advised him to "give up" his wife and daughter, who had been the chief instruments in the quarrel, on which he observed that he could bear ill-fortune with patience, but that he could "not cease to be a husband and a father." Sir Thomas Lake died at Canons in 1630, and was succeeded in the estates by his son, Sir Lancelot Lake, who appears to have taken great interest in the welfare of the parishioners, for he not only founded a boys' school, endowing it with land producing £58 per annum, but "restored to the church those great tythes which had been wrested from her, and of which he was the lay impropriator." The church, therefore (which before this restitution had a donative of only £40 a year), became re-possessed of the rectorial tithe, and from that time, says Lysons, "the incumbents have been styled rectors in the parish register." General Lake, who distinguished himself by his military services in India at the close of the last century, was a descendant of Sir Thomas Lake. The general was raised to the peerage in 1804 by the title of Baron Lake, and three years later was advanced to a viscountcy.

The manor of Canons continued to be held by the family of the Lakes down to about the year 1710, when it was conveyed in marriage by Mary, daughter and heiress of Sir Thomas Lake, and great-granddaughter of the above Sir Thomas Lake, to James Brydges, Esq., afterwards Duke of Chandos.

It would seem from Swift's poems that James Brydges had been one of his friends until he was raised to a dukedom. At all events, he is thus referred to in one of the Dean's bitterest epigrams:—

"James Brydges was the dean's familiar friend,
James grows a duke : their friendship here must end.
Surely the dean deserves a sore rebuke
For knowing James, to say he knows a duke."

This nobleman was Paymaster of the Forces during the war in Queen Anne's reign, under Godolphin's administration, and amassed an immense fortune ; or, in other words, "appropriated" to his own use very large sums of the public money. The House of Commons, in 1711, instituted a committee of inquiry into the public expenditure, when it was found that a deficit existed in the accounts to the extent of thirty-five millions, or that a sum to that amount remained unaccounted for, and, further, that about one-half of that sum was connected with the accounts of Brydges. His answer to the charge was that the accounts had been regularly presented, but that "the mode of scrutinizing and passing them was tedious and complex, owing to a system pursued by the Duke of Newcastle." Great carelessness with regard to the public accounts is said to have existed at that period, and such was the low state of political morality that almost every public man in office was charged with peculation. Johnson, in his pamphlet on the Falkland Islands, sarcastically alludes to the compensation which the nation received at the close of a ten years' war, for the death of multitudes, and the expense of millions, by contemplating the sudden glories of paymasters, and agents, contractors, and commissaries, "whose equipages shine like meteors, and whose palaces rise like exhalations." Chandos gave rise for scandal by the large sums which he spent in building, and by the style of magnificence in which he lived. He had, it appears, determined on building two magnificent houses. He fixed the site of his London residence in Cavendish Square, and the building was commenced with much grandeur of preparation, but was never completed.* His country palace, however, was the favourite object of his attention, and the spot he first selected for its erection was a little to the north of the town of Brentford, on the spot afterwards occupied by the seat of the Earl of Holderness ;† but he shortly relinquished his idea of building his mansion in the neighbourhood of the stately and commanding Syon House, and accordingly removed his workmen to Canons, where he set about the erection of an edifice which was to be the wonder of the age for its splendour. In this great work the Duke is said to have spent no less a sum than £200,000. Its splendour, however, was but short-lived, for in an equal degree the edifice became the wonder of the succeeding age by its abrupt declension and premature ruin.

---

* See "Old and New London," Vol. IV., p. 443.
† See ante, p. 60.

Although the grandeur and magnificence of the mansion became the theme of poetic inspiration, and evoked the satirical remarks of a poetical writer whose verse is calculated to survive the finest building of stone, very little as to detail occurs concerning it in the prosaic pages of topography. Three architects appear to have been employed on the building, namely: Gibbs, James of Greenwich, and Sheppard, who designed the theatres in Goodman's Fields and Covent Garden; and Dr. Alexander Blackwell, the author of a "Treatise on Agriculture," superintended the laying out of the grounds and pleasure-grounds.

The house was commenced in 1715, when the

expense of the building and furniture is said to have amounted to £200,000. Gough, in his "Additions to Camden," sets down the cost at a quarter of a million sterling.

It is somewhat strange that no painting of Canons, as it was in its glory, is known to exist; nor is there any engraving of it in the print-room of the British Museum, though there are two elevations of its principal front in the King's Library, dated in 1721 and 1730, engraved by Hulsberg. These display its chief features: eleven windows in three tiers above one another, divided by lofty columns, the cornice at the top being crowned with six or seven classical and symbolical statues, not unlike those to be seen in old

VILLAGE OF EDGWARE. (*From a Sketch made in* 1858.)

north front was built by Strong, the mason who was employed on the building of St. Paul's Cathedral. "It stood," writes Lysons, in his "Environs of London," "at the end of a spacious avenue, being placed diagonally, so as to show two sides of the building, which at a distance gave the appearance of a front of prodigious extent. Vertue describes it as 'a noble square pile, all of stone; the four sides almost alike, with statues on the front; within was a small square of brick, not handsome; the outhouses of brick and stone, very convenient and well-disposed; the hall richly adorned with marble statues, busts, &c.; the ceiling of the staircase by Thornhill; the grand apartments finely adorned with paintings, sculpture, and furniture' (Strawberry Hill MSS.). The columns which supported the building were all of marble, as was the great staircase, each step of which was made of an entire block, above twenty feet in length. The whole

drawings of the "Queen's House," the predecessor of Buckingham Palace. The building also bore a strong family likeness to Wanstead House, Essex, of which we shall give a description later on in this volume.

In the "Gentleman's Tour through Great Britain," Canons is said to have been "one of the most magnificent palaces in England, built with a profusion of expense, and so well furnished within, that it had hardly its equal. The plastering and gilding were the work of the famous Pargotti, an Italian. The great *salon*, or hall, was painted by Paolucci. . . . The avenue was spacious and majestic; and as it gave you the view of two fronts joined, as it were, in one, the distance not admitting you to see the angle which was in the centre, so you were agreeably drawn in to think the front of the house almost twice as large as it was. And yet when you came nearer you were again surprised by seeing the winding passage opening, as it were, a new front to the eye of near one hundred and twenty feet wide, which you had not seen before; so that you were lost awhile in looking near at hand for what you so plainly saw a great way off."

The building, which was in the Classical or Palladian style, appears to have been designed with the view of standing for ages, seeing that the walls were "twelve feet thick below, and nine feet above." The north front of the mansion was adorned with pilasters and columns of stone; and above every window in each front was an antique head carved in stone, and at the top of each front were ranged statues as large as life. The locks and hinges to the doors of the state rooms were of gold or silver, and the fitting-up of the apartments matched this costliness. Altogether, Canons must have been exceedingly magnificent.

The park, several miles in extent, swarmed with deer, and avenues of elms led to each corner of the house from the surrounding roads. The principal avenue, nearly a mile long, was on the side towards Edgware, and the entrance to it was gained by iron gates enriched with the arms of Chandos, the stone pillars being crowned with the supporters. This avenue was broad enough to admit of three coaches going abreast, and had a large round basin of water in the middle. In an account of Canons, written before its demolition, are the following particulars concerning the adjacent grounds:—"The gardens are well designed in a vast variety, and the canals very large and noble. There is a spacious terrace that descends to a parterre, which has a row of gilded vases on each side down to the great canal; and in the middle, fronting the canal, is a gilt gladiator. The gardens, being divided by iron balustrades, and not by walls, are seen all at one view from any part of them. In the kitchen-garden are curious bee-hives of glass; and at the end of each of the chief avenues there are neat lodgings for eight old

THE DUKE OF CHANDOS.

sergeants of the army, whom the duke took out of Chelsea College to guard the whole, and perform the same duty at night as the watchmen do in London, and to attend his Grace to chapel on Sundays."

Few families have played a more conspicuous part in the history of England than that of Brydges, Lords Chandos of Sudeley, and afterwards Dukes of Chandos. Sir Bernard Burke traces them up to one Sir Simon de Bruge, or Brugge, a knight of large possessions in the county of Hereford in the reign of Henry III., whose immediate descendants for several generations represented both that county and also Gloucestershire in Parliament, whilst one of them fell fighting at Agincourt, and several married the heiresses of illustrious houses. One of their descendants, Sir John Bruges, held Boulogne as governor against the French king in the reign of Henry VIII., who afterwards constituted him Governor of the Tower, and gave him a grant of the manor and honour of Sudeley Castle, which his grandson gallantly held for King Charles against the Parliamentary Roundheads. Henry also created him Lord Chandos of Sudeley, in consideration not only of his nobility and loyalty, but of his quality, valour, and other virtues. Whilst his elder son continued the line of the Lords Chandos, his younger son became the father of a line of baronets, who adopted the orthography of Brydges, and were seated for some generations at Wilton Castle, in Herefordshire, a pleasant seat on the Wye. Sir James Brydges, the third baronet, by the failure and extinction of the elder line about 200 years ago, succeeded to the Barony of Chandos, and was summoned as such to the House of Peers, and sent as ambassador to Constantinople. He married the daughter and heiress of a rich Turkey merchant, who proved herself a "fruitful vine," as she brought him no less than twenty-two children, fifteen of whom lived to be christened, and seven grew up to manhood and womanhood.

James Brydges, the builder of Canons, was born

in 1673, and, in the lifetime of his father, was elected knight of the shire for Herefordshire in several successive Parliaments. In 1707 he was called to the Council of Prince George of Denmark in the affairs of the Admiralty, and was afterwards, as stated above, appointed Pay-master-General of the Forces on active service. With reference to the large sums of money which he secured to himself out of the above offices, Smollett, in his continuation of Hume's "History," writes:—"Mr. Brydges accounted for all the moneys that had passed through his hands excepting three millions;" and he adds that "all means had proved ineffectual to deter and punish those indi-viduals who shamefully pillaged their country; the villany was so complicated, the vice so general, and the delinquents so powerfully screened by artifice and interest, as to elude all inquiry."

At the time of his marriage with the daughter and heiress of Sir Thomas Lake of Canons, he appears to have had a town house in Albemarle Street, for Dean Swift writes, March 3, 1711:—"Mr. Brydges' house in Albemarle Street was much damaged by a fire at Sir William Wyndham's, next door." Lord Chandos died in 1714, and was buried in the parish church of Whitchurch. On the accession of George I., his son and successor was created Viscount Wilton and Earl of Carnarvon, and in 1719 he was advanced to the Marquisate of Carnarvon and Dukedom of Chandos.

About this time a curious event is said to have happened to the duke. When travelling to or from Herefordshire, his Grace stopped at the "Castle Inn" at Marlborough, when, as he drove into the court-yard, his ears were deafened by piercing screams. The duke hastily alighted, and beheld a very lovely young woman, scarcely beyond girlhood, in the grasp of a powerful fellow, the ostler of the inn, who was striking her in a most ferocious manner with a heavy horse-whip. Blood was streaming from her face, neck, and arms; and a crowd stood round, filled with compassion, yet afraid to interfere between the ferocious brute and his victim. But the duke pressed through the group, and sternly ordered the ruffian to desist. The man, daunted by the look and manner of the nobleman, let his whip and victim both fall to the ground, and replied to his questions that the young woman was his wife, and that he had a right to do what he liked to her, offering, however, at the same time, to sell this right to his Grace for a sum of money. Really touched by the sufferings of the beautiful girl, the duke unhesitatingly closed with the offer: a sum of £20 was gleefully accepted by the brute of a husband, and the stricken young

wife became, according to an old English custom, the purchaser's own, to do with as he would. But the duke was a noble-minded gentleman; the cast-off wife was treated by him as his ward, and placed where she would be educated and moulded into a lady. The result of his care gave him com-plete satisfaction; and, some years later, when his second duchess died childless, in 1735, his Grace raised the whilom ostler's cast-off spouse to be his third wife. It is certain that the duke never repented of his bargain, for he says in his will:—"I owe the greatest comfort I have enjoyed in this life (since I have been blessed with her) to my duchess, Lydia Catherine;" and he orders that she shall be buried in the same depository as his own corpse, and that a marble figure of her should be set up in the monument room, but it was not to cost more than £200. A curious book in the British Museum, bound in some crimson velvet that remained over and above the quantity required for covering the coffin of this duchess, tells this story, and much more also, about Canons and its master.

On April 22, 1736, Mrs. Pendarves writes to her friend, Dean Swift:—"The Duke of Chandos's marriage has made a great noise, and the poor duchess is often reproached with her being bred up in Burr Street, Wapping." To this a note is attached, to the effect that "she was a Lady Davall, widow of Sir Thomas Davall, and had a fortune of £40,000." This is borne out by the inscription on her tomb; so that it would appear that the beautiful victim who had been rescued by the duke was married in the interval to a city knight as her second husband, and that she became a third time a wife herself when she married his Grace.

It would be scarcely possible to exaggerate the pomp and grandeur which marked even the every-day life of the owner of "Princely Canons." The author of "A Journey through England" says of the duke:—"When his Grace goes to church he is attended by his Swiss Guards, ranged as the Yeomen of the Guards at St. James's Palace; his music also plays when he is at table; he is served by gentlemen in the best order; and I must say that very few sovereign princes live with the same magnificence, grandeur, and good order."

Though most liberal, his Grace never was im-provident or lavishly profuse. When he first arranged the plan of Canons, one of the ablest accountants in England was employed by him to make out a table of yearly, monthly, weekly, and even daily, expenditure. This scheme was engraved on a large copper-plate, and was an extraordinary specimen of economical wisdom. The duke sold all the garden fruit which was not required for his own table, and would say, "It is as much my property as the corn and hay and the produce of my fields." An aged man, who had been the duke's servant, and who appeared

"The sad historian of the pensive scene,"

informed the writer of an article on Canons, published some forty years ago in the *Chimney-Corner Companion*, that in his occasional bounties to his labourers the duke would never exceed sixpence each. "This," he would say, "may do you good; more may make you idle and drunk."

"Epistle on False Taste," in the "Moral Essays," addressed by Pope to the Earl of Burlington, have been often quoted, and speak for themselves :—

At Timon's villa let us pass a day,
Where all cry out, 'What sums are thrown away!'
So proud, so grand, of that stupendous air,
Soft and agreeable come never there.
Greatness, with Timon, dwells in such a drought
As brings all Brobdignag before your thought.
To compass this, his building is a town,
His pond an ocean, his parterre a down;
Who but must laugh, the master when he sees,
A puny insect, shivering at a breeze!
Lo! what huge heaps of littleness around,

CANONS, ELEVATION OF THE ORIGINAL SOUTH FRONT.

In spite of great losses by his concerns in the African company, and by the Mississippi and South Sea speculations, the duke was ever a liberal patron of learning and merit, as the following story will show :—A clergyman whom he much esteemed was one day looking over the library at Canons, and was bidden by its noble owner to fix upon any book he liked, and it should be his. The gentleman very politely chose one of no great price, but afterwards found a bank bill of considerable value between its leaves. Greatly surprised, he brought the bill and the book back to Canons. The duke took back the bill, but only to exchange it for one of double the value, saying, "Accept that, sir, for your honesty."

It was always said that the Duke of Chandos was abused by Pope under the name of Timon, and probably because his Grace had passed by and forgotten the spiteful little poet in his liberalities to men of letters. The following lines, from the

The whole a labour'd quarry above ground;
Two Cupids squirt before, a lake behind
Improves the keenness of the northern wind.
His gardens next your admiration call,
On every side you look, behold the wall!
No pleasing intricacies intervene,
No artful wildness to perplex the scene;
Grove nods at grove, each alley has a brother,
And half the platform just reflects the other.
The suffering eye inverted Nature sees,
Trees cut to statues, statues thick as trees,
With here a fountain, never to be play'd,
And there a summer-house that knows no shade;
Here Amphitrite sails through myrtle bowers,
There gladiators fight, or die in flowers;
Unwater'd, see the drooping sea-horse mourn,
And swallows roost in Nilu's dusty urn.
My lord advances with majestic mien,
Smit with the mighty pleasure to be seen.
But soft, by regular approach—not yet—
First through the length of that hot terrace sweat;
And when up ten steep slopes you've dragg'd your thighs,
Just at his study door he'll bless your eyes."

In his library the duke could boast of having a valuable collection of MS. records of Ireland before, during, and after the troubles of the Civil War, originally collected by Sir James Ware. When Lord Clarendon was Lord Lieutenant of Ireland (1686), he obtained these MSS. from the heir of Sir James, and brought them to England, and after his death they were bought by the Duke of Chandos. Dean Swift was very anxious that his Grace should present them to the public library at Dublin, but did not see his way to asking the favour. The following lines from the "Essay on Taste" are supposed to refer to the duke's library here :—

> " His study ! with what authors is it stor'd ?
> In books, not authors, curious is my lord.
> To all their dated backs he turns you round :
> These Aldus printed, those Du Sneil has bound.
> Lo ! some are vellum, and the rest as good
> For all his lordship knows, but they are wood.
> For Locke or Milton 'tis in vain to look,
> These shelves admit not any modern book."

The duke's style of living was on a par with the splendour of his house. He dined in public, with flourishes of trumpets announcing each change of dishes. De Foe, in his "Tour through England" (1725), writes :—"Here are continually maintained, and that in the dearest part of England as to house expenses, not less than one hundred and twenty in family, and yet a face of plenty appears in every part of it ; nothing needful is withheld, nothing pleasant is restrained ; every servant in the house is made easy, and his life comfortable." Pope thus deals with the duke's style of living :—

> " But hark ! the chiming clocks to dinner call :
> A hundred footsteps scrape the marble hall ;
> The rich buffet the well-colour'd serpents grace,
> And gaping Tritons spew to wash your face.
> Is this a dinner ? This a genial room ?
> No ; 'tis a temple and a hecatomb.
> A solemn sacrifice, perform'd in state,
> You drink to measure, and to minutes eat.
> So quick retires each flying course, you'd swear
> Sancho's dread doctor and his wand were there.
> Between each act the trembling salvers ring,
> From soup to sweet wine, and ' God bless the king!'
> In plenty starving, tantalised in state,
> And complaisantly help'd to all I hate,
> Treated, caress'd, and sir'd, I take my leave,
> Sick of his civil pride from morn to eve ;
> I curse such lavish cost and little skill,
> And swear no day was ever passed so ill.
> Yet hence the poor are cloth'd, the hungry fed ;
> Health to himself, and to his infants bread
> The labourer bears. What his hard heart denies
> His charitable vanity supplies."

The garden and terraces, the hall, the library, and even the chapel (which was no other than the parish church of Whitchurch), come under the lash of the poet :—

> " And now the chapel's silver bell you hear,
> That summons you to all the pride of prayer ;
> Light quirks of music, broken and uneven,
> Make the soul dance upon a jig to Heaven.
> On painted ceilings you devoutly stare,
> Where sprawl the saints of Verrio or Laguerre,
> Or gilded clouds in fair expansion lie,
> And bring all Paradise before your eye.
> To rest the cushion and soft dean invite,
> Who never mentions Hell to ears polite."

"The graceless saints with which Laguerre disfigured the chapel walls of Canons," observes the author of the "Beauties of England," "probably identify the satire of Pope more unequivocally than any other circumstance of allusion in his essay ; but assuredly the poet should have omitted to censure the Duke of Chandos for a want of correct taste as to music." In Hawkins's "History of Music" it is remarked that "his Grace determined on having Divine service performed in his chapel with all the aid that could be derived from vocal and instrumental music. To this end he retained some of the most celebrated performers of both kinds, and engaged the greatest masters of the time to compose anthems and services with instrumental accompaniments, after the manner of those performed in the churches of Italy." It appears that Handel composed not less than twenty of his finest anthems for the use of this chapel.

Hogarth found a patron in the duke ; and when Pope disgraced his muse by unjust and sarcastic wit levelled at the owner of Canons, the painter punished the bard of Twickenham by representing him as standing on a scaffold whitewashing Burlington House, and bespattering the Duke of Chandos's carriage as it passes along Piccadilly.*

Pope, in a letter written by him to Aaron Hill, denied that there was any truth in the supposition that the character of "Timon ' in the essay above quoted was ever intended to apply to the Duke of Chandos ; and in the Prologue to the Satires he poetically mentions, as the most severe enemy of an honest muse, that fop—

> " Who has the vanity to call you friend,
> Yet wants the honour, injur'd, to defend ;
> Who tells whate'er you think, whate'er you say,
> And, if he lie not, must at least betray ;
> Who to the dean and silver bell can swear,
> And sees at Canons what was never there."

The public, however, would not give credit to

---

* See "Old and New London," Vol. IV., p. 263.

either the prose or the poetry of Pope when his satire exceeded the bounds of fact; and as the duke was highly respected for genuine worth of heart, and was said to have presented the poet with the sum of one thousand pounds as a tribute to his literary merits, much indignation was excited by the presumed libel. In one of the many brochures published against Pope occur the lines—

"Great Chandos' stream of bounty flow'd too high; Chandos' high soul forgets as he bestows."

Whether Pope's lines were or were not really intended to be applied to the Duke of Chandos, the glory of Canons was but of short duration; hence the concluding lines of the essay were, at all events, in a certain sense fulfilled. In a truly prophetic spirit Pope foretells the transformation of the proud and formal domain into pasture and farm-land :—

"Another age shall see the golden ear Imbrown the slope and nod on the parterre; Deep harvest bury all his pride has plann'd, And laughing Ceres re-assume the land."

These lines were sadly verified in the very next generation, as we shall see. The duke's eldest surviving son, John, Marquis of Carnarvon, died in the lifetime of his father, leaving—by his marriage with Lady Catherine Tollemache, a daughter of the Earl of Dysart—one only daughter, also named Catherine. The duke himself died in 1744, and his widow followed him to the grave some six years later. Owing to disputes with the duke's younger son and successor, Henry, second Duke of Chandos, the duchess-dowager ordered that the provisions of her lord's will with regard to her interment should not be carried out, and she was accordingly buried elsewhere; but in the following year her remains were disinterred, and laid in the Chandos vault; no monument, however, representing the duke's best beloved wife was ever placed in the mortuary chapel. His Grace had experienced great losses from several public speculations in which he had embarked, the most important of which was the South Sea scheme, which had been productive of such a wide-spread ruin in the year 1720. He continued, however, to reside at Canons, though, as it would appear, with diminished splendour, till his death.

Under the second duke the estate became more sadly encumbered than ever; and on his death, his executors found it necessary to put Canons up for sale, a special Act of Parliament having been passed to enable them to do so. No purchaser, however, could be found for the mansion and estate as a whole; so at last the house was pulled to pieces,

and the materials sold by auction in 1747, in separate lots, that which had cost half a million to build producing only £11,000. The costly furniture was also sold, crowds flocking to the scene—as a hundred years later crowds flocked to the Stowe and Strawberry Hill sales. The marble staircase was bought by Lord Chesterfield for his house in Mayfair; some of the pillars, too, at Chesterfield House originally belonged to Canons, and were termed by the witty earl "the *canonical* pillars of his house." The fine columns became a portico for Wanstead House, mentioned above, and which has since been also demolished. The equestrian statue of George I. (one of the many sculptures which adorned the grounds at Canons) was transferred to Leicester Square, where it was allowed to perish. The statue of George II. in Golden Square, too, was part of the Canons spoil. One of the marble fireplaces found a settlement at the "Chandos Arms" inn at Edgware; and a grand carving in wood, by Grinling Gibbons, which, as we find in Evelyn's "Diary," was purchased by the duke, was transferred to the great hall of Bush Hill Park, near Enfield.

The immediate cause, or, at all events, one cause, of the break-up and forced sale of Canons was the attempt of the second duke to buy up—at all sorts of fancy prices of course—the whole of the land which lay between his country seat and his town house near Cavendish Square—a house still immortalised by the name of Chandos Street. This he wished to do in order that he might drive his coach and six from the one place to the other without passing the bounds of his estate. Two of the large houses * standing on the north side of Cavendish Square were erected as residences for the duke's porters and other members of his household. In order to carry his idea into effect, the duke would have had to buy up half Marylebone, St. John's Wood, Hendon, and Kingsbury—purchases for which no ducal coffers could have sufficed.

The tourist who wishes to make a pilgrimage to Canons at the present time will find it very much like the play of "Hamlet," with the part of Hamlet left out. The park is still there; but, though for the most part under grass, it is cut up by hedges and railings into separate fields. A few of the fine elms which once formed the avenues still stand like solitary sentinels; the carp and tench still swim lazily about in the two large fishponds on either side of the carriage road which leads up to the present mansion from the town

of Edgware; the shrubberies are still green with
magnificent bays, laurels, cypresses, and other
ornamental trees, interspersed with oaks, hazels,
and chestnuts; and beyond the west end of Whitchurch churchyard may be distinctly traced, though
now grown over with turf—not with corn, as
prophesied by Pope—the splendid road down which
the duke and his duchess used to drive in their
coach and six, and with their tall guards in front,
on Sundays, to hear Handel's music in their velvet-

sion itself may be formed from the fact that the two
porters' lodges, each having six rooms on the ground
floor, being raised a storey higher by the new owner
of Canons, were let to private gentlemen, one of
them being a baronet, Sir Hugh Dalrymple.

Mr. Hallet's villa, built of stone, was a somewhat
modest, but capacious, residence, and has been
enlarged in recent times. The house stands on a
gentle elevation, in the midst of a moderate-sized
and well-timbered park. The property was sold by

CANONS. (*From a Print published in* 1782.)

lined gallery, or tribune, at the west end of the
sacred edifice. But the old mansion itself is clean
gone, though the vistas which it once commanded
may be seen. The iron gates which once closed
the southern entrance now span the centre of the
gardens of New College, Oxford; and it is said
that the golden lamps which lighted the chief
avenue to the house were for many years to be
seen at Day and Martin's shop in Holborn. *Sic
transit gloria.*

Mr. Hallet, a cabinet-maker in Long Acre,
bought the greater part of the estate and a large
quantity of building materials, with which he
erected a villa on part of the site of the original
house. Some idea of the magnificence of the man-

Mr. Hallet's grandson to Captain Dennis O'Kelly,
whose name was well-known in the sporting world
as the owner of a famous race-horse, "Eclipse,"
which in its old age is said to have been brought
hither all the way from Epsom on a carriage made
specially for him. This wonderful horse was bred
by the Duke of Cumberland, and being foaled
during the *great eclipse*, was so named by the duke
in consequence. His royal owner did not survive
to witness the very great performances he himself
had predicted. When a yearling only, the horse
was disposed of by auction, with the rest of his
stud. At four or five years old Captain O'Kelly
purchased half of him for 250 guineas, and in a
short time after gave 750 for the remainder. The

following curious mock epistle in a book of sporting anecdotes, printed at the end of last century, may be of interest to sporting readers even in the present day :—

"AN EPISTLE FROM ECLIPSE TO KING FERGUS.

"DEAR SON,—I set out last week from Epsom, and am safe arrived in my new stables at this place. My situation may serve as a lesson to man : I was once the fleetest horse in the world,

the rest of my progeny, will do honour to the name of their grandsire,　　　ECLIPSE.

"*Canons, Middlesex.*

"P.S. Myself, Dungannon, Volunteer, and Vertumnus, are all here.—Compliments to the Yorkshire horses."

This noble animal, who performed the feat of galloping a mile in a minute, is said to have been stuffed and kept in the hall. One of his hoofs, set in

WHITCHURCH CHURCH : THE EAST END.

but old age has come upon me, and wonder not, King Fergus, when I tell thee I was drawn in a carriage from Epsom to Canons, being unable to walk even so short a journey. Every horse, as well as every dog, has his day; and I have had mine. I have outlived two worthy masters : the late Duke of Cumberland, that bred me, and the Colonel with whom I have spent my best days, but I must not repine ; I am now caressed, not so much for what I can do, but for what I have done, and with the satisfaction of knowing that my present master will never abandon me to the fate of the *high-mettled racer !*

"I am glad to hear, my grandson, Honest Tom, performs so well in Ireland, and trust that he, and

gold, is the property of the Jockey Club, and constitutes a prize annually contended for at Ascot Races, the owner of the winning horse retaining the relic in his possession for a year. The remains of the above famous racehorse are interred in the park of Canons.

The estate was subsequently sold by the nephew of Captain O'Kelly to Sir Thomas Plumer, who was some time Vice-Chancellor of England, and afterwards Master of the Rolls ; and the property, after the death of Sir Thomas, remained in the possession of Lady Plumer till her decease. It was next held by Mr. Thomas Hall Plumer, the eldest son of Sir Thomas, and more recently by Mr. David Begg, M.D., since whose death, in 1868, Canons has been owned by his widow.

The parish church of Whitchurch, close by the southern entrance to the park of Canons, and almost hidden from sight by the trees which surround it, is a small building, dedicated to St. Lawrence, and, with the exception of the tower, which is ancient, was built about the year 1715, at the expense of the Duke of Chandos, as the "chapel" of Canons. The internal decorations, which are in a style very rarely to be seen in country churches, were not completed till five years later. In the words of Pope, quoted above—

"Here sprawl the saints of Verrio and Laguerre."

At all events, the latter artist is said to have painted the ceiling and the walls. On each side of the Communion Table is "The Nativity" and "The Dead Christ," by Bellucci ; behind it, instead of a reredos, is a recess for the organ supported by Corinthian columns. The organ was rebuilt and enlarged in 1878. In the background are paintings of "Moses Receiving the Tables of the Law" and of "The Saviour Preaching." Handel, who resided at Canons for three years as chapel-master to the duke, is said to have composed his sacred drama of *Esther* for the consecration of this church. During his stay here he produced also the two "Chandos" *Te Deums*, the twelve "Chandos" Anthems, and *Acis and Galatea*.

In September, 1790, some thirty years after his death, a grand miscellaneous concert of sacred music, selected from the works of Handel, was performed in his honour and memory in this church.

The large chamber, or mortuary chapel, on the north side of the chancel, built by the Duke of Chandos, and containing one or two monuments to members of his family, reminds the visitor in some degree of the tombs of the Russells at Chenies, in Buckinghamshire. The chamber, which is constructed over the family vault, is reached by a flight of steps. The ceiling and sides are painted, and the floor is paved with black and white marble. Within is a statue of the duke, in Roman costume, as large as life, standing between the statues of Mary, his first wife, and his first duchess, Cassandra, sister of Thomas Willoughby, Lord Middleton, whom the duke married in 1713, just one year after the death of the heiress of Canons. The two last-named effigies kneel on either side of that of the duke, in mourning attitudes. The inscription records the interment of the duke's third wife, "Lydia Catherine, daughter of John Vanhattem, Esq., and widow of Sir Thomas Davall, M.P., who died in the year 1714." This monument was restored by the Duke of Buckingham and Chandos in 1865. At the western end of the church is the "Chandos gallery," containing a spacious semicircular recess, with seats for the owner of Canons. The ceiling of this gallery is painted with a copy of Raphael's "Ascension," by Bellucci.

At the south-eastern corner of the churchyard is a grave-stone to the memory of William Powell, the "harmonious blacksmith." The stone, which bears, in a sunk medallion, a hammer, anvil, laurel wreath, and a bar of music, records his name, and date of death, "February 27th, 1780, aged 78," and adds that "he was parish clerk during the time the immortal Handel was organist of this church." The stone was raised by subscription in 1868, in place of a wooden rail, which formerly bore a similar inscription. This is the blacksmith in whose forge, one afternoon in 1721, Handel is said to have taken refuge during a storm, when he found Powell standing at his work, and singing a beautiful melody, that chimed in exactly with the tone emitted by his anvil, as blow after blow fell upon it. Powell informed his delighted visitor that he had heard the tune, and caught it up, but did not know the name of the composer. So Handel, as the story goes, carried the melody in his head back to Canons, and elaborated the theme into the well-known "Harmonious Blacksmith." The original MS. air, in the treble only, may be still seen in an old book in the British Museum. A lady who endowed some almshouses at Whitchurch has left it on record that Powell was a fine-looking man, nearly six feet high, and that he always wore a clean shirt, with the collar thrown back on his shoulders, and a red cap on his head, and she adds that he sang constantly as he worked. His anvil still exists, and its tone, when struck, is really in the same key as the "Harmonious Blacksmith." Both the anvil and hammer, having been long kept as sacred relics, were sold among the Snoxell collection of curiosities by Messrs. Puttick and Simpson, in June, 1879.

On the north side of the churchyard are some heavy-looking and substantial almshouses, which were founded about 1640 by Lady Lake, the widow of Sir Thomas Lake of Canons, for seven poor persons. The recipients of this charity were to be appointed by Sir Thomas Lake's descendants, as long as they should be possessed of Canons, and afterwards by the minister and churchwardens. The endowment at the present time supports only four persons. The charity had an income of £44 per annum, which has been recently augmented by a bequest of £1,000 by Miss Hurst. The almshouses are built of red brick, of one floor, and form three sides of a quadrangle.